Learning Java with Games

Chong-wei Xu

Learning Java with Games

Springer

Chong-wei Xu
Kennesaw State University
Kennesaw, GA, USA

Additional material to this book can be downloaded from http://extras.springer.com.

ISBN 978-3-319-72885-8   ISBN 978-3-319-72886-5 (eBook)
https://doi.org/10.1007/978-3-319-72886-5

Library of Congress Control Number: 2018933068

© Springer Nature Switzerland AG 2018

This work is subject to copyright. All rights are reserved by the Publisher, whether the whole or part of the material is concerned, specifically the rights of translation, reprinting, reuse of illustrations, recitation, broadcasting, reproduction on microfilms or in any other physical way, and transmission or information storage and retrieval, electronic adaptation, computer software, or by similar or dissimilar methodology now known or hereafter developed.

The use of general descriptive names, registered names, trademarks, service marks, etc. in this publication does not imply, even in the absence of a specific statement, that such names are exempt from the relevant protective laws and regulations and therefore free for general use.

The publisher, the authors, and the editors are safe to assume that the advice and information in this book are believed to be true and accurate at the date of publication. Neither the publisher nor the authors or the editors give a warranty, express or implied, with respect to the material contained herein or for any errors or omissions that may have been made. The publisher remains neutral with regard to jurisdictional claims in published maps and institutional affiliations.

Printed on acid-free paper

This Springer imprint is published by the registered company Springer Nature Switzerland AG
The registered company address is: Gewerbestrasse 11, 6330 Cham, Switzerland

Preface

Developing innovative teaching approaches have been one of the important topics in developing computer science curriculum. An innovative teaching approach has two important aspects. One is that the teaching method should be able to let students see the effects of their programming efforts immediately so that programming will engage students and attract their attention; the other is that the contents of materials would have a connection with the real world, especially with the industry setting.

In order for students to easily see the effects of their programming efforts, many different approaches have been developed, such as the robot approach, the multimedia approach, the gaming approach, the virtual reality approach, and the like. For connecting with the real world, the more industry-oriented materials have emerged. In order to support these new teaching approaches, we would like to develop teaching materials that emphasize on visualization and animation with practical flavor. Hence, video game development is our choice.

A video game is an integration of humanity, mathematics, physics, arts, artificial intelligence, graphics, visualization, animation, sounds, images, programming, and so on. Therefore, discussing all these fields in the video game context will further encourage students to have a passion for sciences, especially for mathematics and physics. In addition, game industry is developing rapidly. Video game development connects with industry setting ever more so than before. The size and complexity of a video game can be tailored for students to handle and a video game can be further extended by imagination without boundaries. For implementing a video game, all features of object-oriented programming (OOP) and component-oriented programming (COP) can be applied. Consequently, video game development is not only for creating games with fun but also a well pedagogical method for teaching OOP and COP.

Video game development is a vast topic covering many areas. We would like to focus ourselves to the 2D video games with the purpose of teaching OOP programming technologies. Video game development is challenging because it is really a problem solving process. It really is a great topic for training brainstorming and logic thinking. Meanwhile, learning programming is by doing. Consequently, the key approach for solving problems is practice. As people say, "Practices make perfect." Fortunately, video games have a special key feature: interactivity. Interactively talking with a video game and interactively developing and ultimately playing the developed video game will engage students' imagination and keep their attention fully.

Specifically, this book intends to teach Java programming through the developments of video games. That is, learning Java programming is the goal and video games are the topic. In addition, the book tries to build up software architecture for video games so that after students finish this book, they will be able (1) to familiarize themselves with the Java language for programming; (2) to develop a general architecture for video games; (3) to increase the ability forward analyzing problems and solving problems. Usually games are decorated with many beautiful images. In order to reduce the complexity, the book is not going to use many images, but concentrates on the technical aspects of programming.

Organization of the Book

The book has 24 chapters that are divided into four parts.

Part I Foundation with Games In-Text: Chaps. 1–4

Java is an object-oriented programming language. That is, the language takes objects as its building units and through the interactions among objects to perform a certain function. A video game is a program in general, which consists of multiple objects. A video game always has an interesting story in particular, which is full of dynamic interactions among objects. Therefore, Java language features are very suitable for realizing video games and video games will fully demonstrate the features of Java language. This part introduces the concepts and essential programming elements of Java language through examples of games-in-text.

Chapter 1 Java Programming and Game Development: A project HelloWorld

Video games are programs. The interesting and engagement of game programming would release "tedious" feeling of the program writing. Games fulfill objects and interactions among objects that fit with the Java object-oriented features. Furthermore, game promotes experiential learning, inquiry-based learning, self-efficacy, goal setting, and cooperation. All of these encourage us to study Java through the construction of games.

Chapter 2 Basics of Java Programming: A Project PrintXmasCard

The simplest program HelloWorld is developed to introduce the fundamental concepts and practices of variables, methods, and classes. And then, the project PrintXmasCard demonstrates user input mechanism, file accesses, and exception handling. Further, primitive data types are summarized and the built-in class String is taken as an example of reference data type. These essentials support the basics of Java programming.

Chapter 3 OO Programming Principle: A Game In-Text GuessInt

Games in-text are simple games since they deal with Strings only. A game GuessInt is played by two players. An initializer thinks of an integer in mind; a player guesses what it is. Java operators are employed to form assignment, if-then-else, and loop statements to support the actions of the initializer and the player in the format of methods. Meanwhile, the reactions among methods accomplish the communications between them.

Chapter 4 UML and Its Usage: A Game WheelFortune In-Text

Multiple objects are reflected in a program as multiple classes. The relationships among multiple classes play a "glue" role for constructing a system. They should be clearly illustrated through a UML class diagram. A game WheelForture-in-text deals with seven classes. A UML class diagram illustrates its structure; a pseudo code describes "what" should be done; finally a source code is implemented.

Part II Games Based on Event-Driven: Chaps. 5–10

Games-in-text explore the special features of games through the employments of simple programming techniques. Due to the fact that GUI is one of the "must have" units of video games, this part starts introducing graphical painting and applies it for making GUIs of games. A GUI mainly consists of two portions. One portion is for displaying games' output; the other is for accepting players' input. The former deals with graphical painting and the latter relates with software components and their semantic events.

Chapter 5 GUI Programming with Graphical Drawing: A Project PaintXmasCard

The project PaintXmasCard demonstrates the graphical painting techniques. Two Java built-in classes JFrame and JPanel construct the basis for painting. The built-in graphic context Graphics provides a rich set of painting methods. In order to arrange components on a GUI, a variety of computations are needed. In addition, one of the most important OOP concepts "inheritance" is brought into the programming practice.

Chapter 6 Java Software Components and Event Handling: Projects CalculatorApp and ImageSlider

Dynamic behaviors are of the spirit of games. The software components and action-event chains provide a strategy that allows the game player to act on software components for generating events, which in turn trigger event handlers to perform embedded dynamic activities. A project CalculatorApp demonstrates an action-event chain and a project ImageSlider illustrates an action-event-update-repaint chain.

Chapter 7 Event-Driven: Adding a GUI for the Game Anagram In-Text

Applying the event-driven technique for the game Anagram enriches a game-in-text with a GUI. The GUI provides a board for displaying dynamically changed output in text and equips the game with software components in order to allow the player inputs data and actions for triggering events to update the state of the game and repaint the GUI after updating. This kind of games is event-driven instead of a continuous "while" loop driven.

Chapter 8 Event-Driven with an Update-Repaint Chain: A Game Blackjack

The game Blackjack further illustrates the event-driven strategy. Its output board not only displays text but also more complicated graphics and images. All of activities of the game follow the input controls issued by the player on software components. In addition, the game clearly exhibits the abstract game model that sets apart the game GUI from the game logic but links them together through event listeners and event handlers.

Chapter 9 Key Control: A Game Sudoku

The events of Java are broadly divided into two categories. The events generated by software components are termed as semantic events. The events generated by hardware mouse or keys are termed as low-level events. The game Sudoku is a famous numerical game played by a single player. It is taken as an example for exposing the event listeners of keys. The player uses keys to browse and fulfill required digits onto the board of GUI.

Chapter 10 Mouse Control: A Card Game Agnes

The other low-level events generated by mouse are adopted for controlling a card game Agnes. In general, mouse is the best device for navigating a two-dimensional space and mouse event listeners provide a rich set of event handlers. The Agnes is a card game played by a single player. The cards in the GUI not only for echoing the dynamic behaviors of the game but also play the role of input mechanism.

Part III Games Based on Animation: Chaps. 11–21

Event-driven produces discrete action-event-update-repaint chains. When these chains become continuous, the consequent update-repaints form an illusion of animation, which drives some components of a video game continuous independently animated. These animated components are termed as sprites. The interactions of these animated sprites cause collisions, which in turn trigger new events that dynamically changing the scenes of the game. The game players are trying to guide or avoid collisions for reaching the goal of the game. These games are animation-driven. This part starts the animation mechanism and builds up a three-layer software structure for games, which is then adopted as a template for developing video games.

Chapter 11 Animation Programming: A Digital Clock and an Analog Clock

All of video games consist of sprites that are independently animated objects. The animation needs a thread. Java provides a built-in class Thread that can be constructed as a game loop to animate sprites. The game loop consists of three steps: updating attributes of sprites, repainting the updated sprites, and pausing for a while. Through a digital clock and an analog clock, the game loop and the animation programming are introduced.

Chapter 12 Merging Visualization, Event Driven, and Animation: A Game WheelVideo

Applying the Thread and the game loop, the game WheelForture-in-text (Chap. 4) is enriched with animation. The GUI has three pieces: a board, a player panel, and an animated wheel. The three pieces cover the three general techniques of visualization, event-driven, and animation. They are needed for almost all of video games. The synchronization of the three pieces is illustrated through a UML sequence diagram.

Chapter 13 Animated Sprites and Collisions: A Game Pong

The animated sprits cause collisions with each other or with static objects. The collisions introduce a new concept and new technique of collision detection and collision handling. The player of a game just follows the game rule to control the sprites in order to prevent collisions or to engage collisions for dynamically changing the game states and scenes. The simple game Pong just starts the introduction of sprites and their animations.

Chapter 14 Multiple Screens: An Extension of the Game Pong

Besides the main screen GUI, usually a game requires multiple screens, such as, splash screen, setting screen, and the like. For organizing multiple screens, the Card layout manager in Java is applied. Then, the game Pong is extended through adding a splash screen and more features, such as, increasing the number of bouncing balls with different animation speed even changing the objective of the game from bouncing to catching balls.

Chapter 15 A Three-Layer Software Structure for Games: A Game PongStruTwo

The extensions of the game Pong explore a fact that the number of sprites and their behaviors, as well as the complexity of the game could be dynamically changed. We need not only new technologies but also a stable software structure for accommodating these changes. Based on the OOP techniques of inheritance, abstract class, and polymorphism, a three-layer software structure is constructed as a template for developing video games.

Chapter 16 Usage of the Three-Layer Structure for Games: A Project SymBall and a Project Tornado

A project SymBall is developed for demonstrating the power of the three-layer software structure for games. The framework has a well-formed structure. Its higher layer allows adding more levels of threads. Its lower layer has a sprite inheritance hierarchy for easily inserting different kinds of sprites and increasing any number of sprites. In addition, another project Tornado further illustrates the stability and flexibility of the framework.

Chapter 17 Image Sprite and UML State Machine: A Game Breakout

Since then, the three-layer software structure for games becomes a software template for developing new video games. We can simply copy the framework to be the basis of a new video game; and then insert the required sprites. The rudimental game Breakout is just based on this strategy. The game also replaces all of sprites with images and introduces the UML state machine to analyze and synthesize game's dynamic activities.

Chapter 18 Sound Effect and Composite Class: Enriching the Game Breakout
To enrich the rudimental game Breakout (Chap. 17), more functions, such as, the score, the counter for the ball-lost, the composite class, and the like are added. Among them, the sound effect is an important piece for all of video games. By adding the sound routines, the template of the three-layer structure for games, GameStruTemplate, is accomplished. It can be the basis for all of video games.

Chapter 19 Changing the Structure of Sprites Dynamically: A Game Worm
The number of sprites and their moving directions are dynamically changed when the game Worm is in execution. It requires a dynamically changeable data structure during the run time. The special "cyclic array" with a linked list feature is applied for supporting the needs. Furthermore, an auto-worm is added to compete with the player-controlled worm and several extensions are proposed for raising the complexity of the game.

Chapter 20 Chess-Like Games: A Game Othello
A chess-like game Othello is introduced to illustrate games played by two players. The game deals with new techniques, such as, to control the take-turn actions between two players, to browse the board, to flip the pieces, etc. The more crucial issue is to physically separate the GUI unit from the logic unit but logically link them together as a complete game. It realizes loosely coupled software following the abstract model of games.

Chapter 21 An Introduction of Artificial Intelligence: Extensions of the Game Othello
The further improvements of the game Othello bring up new ideas. For example, replacing the drawing pieces with the image pieces brings image transparency and frame based animation; switching two players version to single player version introduces artificial intelligence concepts and practices. New developed artificial intelligence algorithms include "first", "random", "best", and "edge".

Part IV Serious Games: Chaps. 22–24

Games are not only for entertainments. A category of games is termed as "serious games" that are simulations of real-world events or processes designed for the purpose of solving a problem. Their main purposes are to train or educate users, though they may have other purposes, such as marketing or advertisement. Serious game will sometimes deliberately sacrifice fun and entertainment in order to achieve a desired progress by the player. We take two examples in CS courses for illustrating the ideas about serious games. These examples also further approve the usefulness of three-layer software structure for games.

Chapter 22 Visualizing Sorting Array Algorithms
Video game techniques are welcomed in many different fields. An effective approach for teaching data structures is to illustrate algorithms with dynamical actions in a multimedia format. Multiple algorithms, such as inserting data, deleting data, and sorting data in one-dimensional array are dynamically visualized through gaming techniques based on the three-layer software structure for games.

Chapter 23 Animating Conversions Between Binary and Decimal
Binary number computations sometimes are a tough topic in oral description and tedious illustration in using black board. Treating numbers as sprites with animation, we can repeatedly

demonstrate binary computation processes. It not only reduces teacher's burden but also enhances students' learning. This chapter covers the conversions of binary integers to decimal, decimal integers to binary, as well as floating numbers.

Chapter 24 Animating Binary Arithmetic Computations

The binary number notation was evolved from signed-magnitude notation to one's complement notation, and finally to two's complement notation. The reason of such an evolvement lies on the disadvantages of one notation and the advantages of the other. Projects that dynamically demonstrate the three notations with their corresponding arithmetic summation processes supply a visual tool for a better learning.

Appendix: The Source Codes of the Three-Layer Structure for Games—GameStruTemplate

For easier studying and accessing the three-layer software structure for games, the source code of the GameStruTemplate is duplicated under the source codes "Appendix". This source code is the same as the source codes in Chap. 18.

Special Features of This Book

This book is a textbook for learning Java programming. The book intends to teach Java programming with the target of video games. Due to the fact that the video games emphasize on problem solving, the book goes through video games' logic analysis, state chart illustration, algorithm design, and loosely coupled software construction for introducing the Java language as well as programming knowledge and skills in such a way to practice "learning by doing".

In addition, multiple topics, such as, mathematics, graphics, artificial intelligence, and programming are merged. Game programming always promotes students with curiosity to analyze, to imagine, and to solve new challenges. Hopefully, the interesting of video games will engage and attract students to learn more effectively and more thoroughly in the process of finding solutions for solving problems.

Who Should Read This Book?

The book is written for the beginner of Computer Science students in mind. It could be used for CS1 or CS2 courses. In considering the complexity of video games, the book is also suitable to be reference book or further-reading book for CS1 and CS2 courses. It could also be textbook for junior or senior gaming courses or for graduate students in learning Java as the second programming language. The book also has practical values in learning either Java programming or game programming for different levels of readers.

The IDEs That Reader May Select

Manually editing, compiling, and executing a Java program is a tedious work. Using an IDE will make our work easier. The better IDEs for writing Java programs includes Eclipse, NetBeans, or others.

We used NetBeans for developing example projects in this book because NetBeans provides a utility "Print to HTML…" under the menu "File", which can print the source code with line numbers on a browser and the printed source code with line numbers are easy to be copied and pasted for writing the book. For programming, any IDEs for Java are good.

In using NetBeans, readers can directly load all of book's example projects onto the IDE with the menu item "Open Project…", and then compile it and run it. If using other IDEs, the source codes in the folder src can be copied. However, due to different settings, the source codes could probably be required certain modifications in order to satisfy the requirements of the IDE in using.

Author sincerely appreciates any feedbacks.

Chong-wei Xu, August 10, 2017
Kennesaw, GA, USA

Acknowledgements

I would like to thank all of the reviewers for their careful evaluation of my book proposal and thoughtful written comments.

I would also like to special thank the individuals at Springer who worked closely with me to make the book possible. I am very grateful to Senior Editor Paul Drougas, Assistant Editor Caroline Flanagan, Project Coordinator Tony Dunlap, and all of team members for their professionalism, commitment, and hard work, as well as to their warmly care and encouragement.

I would personally like to thank my wife, Lili Hu, for her continued patience, accompany, and care; to thank my daughter, Leslie Xu, for her concern and several chapter's editing; and to thank my son, Daniel Xu, for his encouragement and entertaining.

I have used the following books as the textbook or reference book for my video game courses. The authors of these books are my teachers in this field.

- Joel Fan, Eric Ries, and Calin Tenitchi, "Black Art of Java Game Programming", Waite Group Press, 1996.
- Andrew Davison, "Killer Game Programming", O'Reilly, 2005.
- Martin J. Wells, "J2ME Game Programming", Course Technology, 2004.
- Michael Morrison, "Game Programming in 24 Hours", Sams, 2003.

I have referenced to the following video games submitted as course term projects for designing and implementing my corresponding projects in this book.

- Video game Breakout submitted by student Eric Haynes for the course 2005 Spring CSIS4991 Game Programming in Java. I used images and sounds from the project.
- Video game BlackJack submitted by students Ryan Baker and Michael Gayler for the course 2005 Spring CSIS4991 Game Programming in Java. I used images from the project.
- Video game Sudoku submitted by students Brett Davies and Bryan Wiltgen for the course 2007 Summer CSIS4491 Games on Handheld Devices written in J2ME.
- Video game Othello submitted by graduate student Eric Angeli for the course 2006 Fall CS8680 Digital Game Design. I used images and sounds from the project.

Contents

Part I Foundation with Games In-Text: Chaps. 1–4

1 Java Programming and Game Development: A Project HelloWorld 3
  1.1 What is Programming? 3
  1.2 A Computer is Required for Carrying out Programming 4
  1.3 The Essential Architecture of a Computer............................ 4
  1.4 A Memory Hierarchy... 4
  1.5 Programming Languages Are Needed for Communicating
      with Computers 5
  1.6 Java Programming Language and Object-Oriented Programming 6
  1.7 Learning a Programming Language.................................... 7
  1.8 Programming in General 7
  1.9 A Programming Flow in Java 8
  1.10 A Programming Pattern 9
  1.11 We Selected Video Games as our Programming Target................. 9
  1.12 Why Are We Interested in Video Games? 10
  1.13 Game Programming Emphasizes Problem Solving..................... 11
  1.14 A Simplest Program HelloWorld.................................... 11
  1.15 Compile and Execute the Project HelloWorld....................... 12
  1.16 Using the IDE NetBeans 12
  1.17 Learning Some Aspects of Java through the Project HelloWorld 13
  1.18 Summary 14
  1.19 Exercises 14

2 Basics of Java Programming: A Project PrintXmasCard.................... 17
  2.1 Basic Syntax, Semantics, and Conventions in Java:
      Revisit HelloWorld... 17
  2.2 Variables: The Project HelloWorld2 19
  2.3 Variable Type.. 20
  2.4 Variable Scope 21
  2.5 Constructor Method of a Class 21
  2.6 Reprogramming HelloWorld2 with Methods: The Project HelloWorld3 22
  2.7 The First User-Defined Class: The Project ShowMessage 23
  2.8 The Problem of "Hard Coded" 24
  2.9 Adding an Input Portion: The Project ShowMessage2 25
  2.10 Designing and Implementing a New Project:
       The Project PrintXmasCard... 26
  2.11 A New User-Defined Class: The Class XmasCard.java................. 27
  2.12 Using a Permanent Storage File: The Project PrintXmasCard2 28
  2.13 Absolute File Path and Relative File Path 29
  2.14 Setting Up the Channel from the Source File to the Destination File 30
  2.15 Method and Its Parameter 32

xv

2.16	Return Value of a Method	33
2.17	Try-Catch Blocks	33
2.18	Reference Data Type	33
2.19	Primitive Data Type	34
2.20	Type Casting	35
2.21	Summary	35
2.22	Exercises	35

3 OO Programming Principle: A Game In-Text GuessInt 39
- 3.1 The Story of a Game In-Text: The Project GuessInt1 39
- 3.2 Object-Oriented Programming Is Based on Objects: The Project GuessInt2 40
- 3.3 Getting a Random Integer Using a Random Number Generator 44
- 3.4 The Control Statement "if-then-else" 44
- 3.5 The Control Statement "while" 45
- 3.6 Passing Data by Using Function Invocations 46
- 3.7 Verifying Input Data: The Project GuessInt3 46
- 3.8 Catching Exceptions for Possible Errors When Inputting Data 46
- 3.9 Developing Our Own Error Detection Methods 47
- 3.10 Advantages of Try-Catch Approach 50
- 3.11 A Principal Strategy for Designing and Implementing an OOP Program 50
- 3.12 Java Operators 51
  - 3.12.1 Arithmetic Operator 51
  - 3.12.2 Relational Operator 51
  - 3.12.3 Logical Operator 52
  - 3.12.4 "and" and "or" Symbols in Java 52
- 3.13 More Control Statements in Java 53
  - 3.13.1 The Control Statement "switch" 53
  - 3.13.2 The Control Statement "for" 53
- 3.14 The Modifier "Static" (Why main() Method Is a Static Method?) 54
- 3.15 Summary 55
- 3.16 Exercises 55

4 UML and Its Usage: A Game WheelFortune In-Text 59
- 4.1 The Unified Modeling Language (UML) 59
- 4.2 A Game WheelFortune In-Text 59
- 4.3 A Linear Data Structure: Array 60
- 4.4 A Linear Data Structure ArrayList Comes Handy 62
- 4.5 Initializing the Game: The Project WheelFortune1 62
- 4.6 The Game Has Three Players: The Project WheelFortune2 64
- 4.7 Initializing Three Players 64
- 4.8 Assigning the Current-Player 67
- 4.9 The Output of the Project WheelFortune2 67
- 4.10 Initializing the Board and the Wheel: The Project WheelFortune3 67
- 4.11 Mimicking the Wheel Turning 70
- 4.12 The Board Displays the Matched Characters 71
- 4.13 Initializing the Given Sentence Through Reading a Text File 72
- 4.14 Considering Special Cases and Error Cases: The Project WheelFortune4 75
- 4.15 The Driving Force of the Game 79
- 4.16 Terminating the Game 79
- 4.17 An Important Notice 80
- 4.18 Summary 80
- 4.19 Exercises 80

Part II Games Based on Event-Driven: Chaps. 5–10

5 GUI Programming with Graphical Drawing: A Project PaintXmasCard 85
- 5.1 Java Provides a Rich Capacity for GUI Programming 85
- 5.2 Constructing a Basis for GUIs.. 86
- 5.3 Building Up a GUI Foundation: The Project PaintXmasCard1............. 88
- 5.4 A Built-In Graphics Context 89
- 5.5 Computations Involved: The Project PaintXmasCard2................... 90
- 5.6 Arranging the Output Nicely 91
- 5.7 Aligning Substrings Along the Center: The Project PaintXmasCard3 95
- 5.8 Adding an Image into the Christmas Card: The Project PaintXmasCard4 96
- 5.9 Decorating the Christmas Card: The Project PaintXmasCard5............. 98
- 5.10 Superclass and Subclass..100
  - 5.10.1 Access Modifiers: Private, Public, and Protected 100
  - 5.10.2 Constructor super() and Keywords "Super" and "This" 103
  - 5.10.3 Override Method 103
  - 5.10.4 Overload Method 103
- 5.11 Mastering Built-In Classes Used in the Project PaintXmasCard..........104
- 5.12 Summary 104
- 5.13 Exercises 104

6 Java Software Components and Event Handling: Projects CalculatorApp and ImageSlider 107
- 6.1 A GUI Consists of Java Software Components: A Software Calculator 107
- 6.2 The Design of the GUI... 107
- 6.3 Arranging Components Using Layout Managers 108
- 6.4 More Layout Managers 111
- 6.5 A UML Sequence Diagram Illustrates an Action-Event Chain............. 111
- 6.6 Making the Software Calculator Work 112
- 6.7 The Register-Trigger-Execute for Making an Action-Event Chain 115
- 6.8 Controlling the Sequence of Actions for Making a Computation 116
- 6.9 Major Semantic Events and Their Event Listeners 116
- 6.10 Alternative Approaches for Implementing Event Listeners................ 117
- 6.11 Flexibility of Event Handling: A Project ImageSlider..................... 118
- 6.12 Showing a Static Scene: The Project ImageSlider1...................... 118
- 6.13 Adding Dynamic Behaviors: The Project ImageSlider2 119
- 6.14 Interface and Event Listener 124
- 6.15 Abstract Method and Abstract Class 125
- 6.16 More Software Components: JRadioButton and JCheckBox 125
- 6.17 Summary 127
- 6.18 Exercises 128

7 Event-Driven: Adding a GUI for the Game Anagram In-Text. 131
- 7.1 The Story of the Game Anagram..................................... 131
- 7.2 A Text Version of the Game Anagram: The Project AnagramText 131
- 7.3 A UML Sequence Diagram of the Project AnagramText 132
- 7.4 Adding a GUI to the Game Anagram: The Project AnagramGUI........... 137
- 7.5 The Class PlayerPanel.java Implements the Sequence of Actions 138
- 7.6 The Class Board.java Displays the Scrambled Word and the Guessed Word 142
- 7.7 The Class GameCanvas.java Sets Up Communication Paths Among Classes... 147
- 7.8 Graphics and Graphics2D; paint() and paintComponent() 149
- 7.9 Dynamic Activities of the Game AnagramGUI......................... 149

		7.10	Replacing the JRadioButton with a JComboBox. 149
		7.11	Modifying the Class ReadFile.java 152
		7.12	Summary 153
		7.13	Exercises 154

8 Event-Driven with an Update-Repaint Chain: A Game Blackjack 155

	8.1	A Game Blackjack. 155
	8.2	A Brainstorm on the Design 156
	8.3	Preparing a Deck of Cards: The Project Blackjack1 156
	8.4	The Relationship "has" Between the Class Deck.java and the Class Card.java 156
	8.5	Adding Players and Applying Game Rules: The Project Blackjack2 159
	8.6	The Class Player.java Determines the Current Status of Each Player 159
	8.7	The Class PlayerPanel.java Implements the "core" of the Program 163
	8.8	Adding Chips for Gamblers to Bet: The Project Blackjack3. 167
	8.9	The GUI and the Event-Driven in the Project Blackjack3. 167
	8.10	Determining "when to show what" by Using Truth Tables 175
	8.11	The Class GameCanvas.java Sets Up Communication Paths 178
	8.12	Summary 179
	8.13	Exercise 179

9 Key Control: A Game Sudoku. 181

	9.1	The Story of the Game Sudoku 181
	9.2	Two-Dimensional Array. 182
	9.3	A Composite Class Board.java: The Project Sudoku1. 183
	9.4	Applying the Brute-Force Algorithm for Populating the Board: The Project Sudoku2 186

		9.4.1	A Project TestPopulate1 for Validating Every Row. 186
		9.4.2	A Project TestPopulate2 for Validating Both of Rows and Columns 187
		9.4.3	A New Approach for Treating "Dead Case" in the Project TestPopulate3. 190
		9.4.4	A Project TestPopulate4 for Validating All Requirements. 192

	9.5	Key Event and Key Event Listener 194
	9.6	Setting Up Focus for Accepting a Key Event 195
	9.7	Implementing the Key-Event-Update-Repaint Chain: The Project Sudoku3 195

		9.7.1	Adding a New Class NotePanel.java for Specifying All of Key Commands 196
		9.7.2	Developing an Inner Class MyKeyAdapter Inside the Class GameCanvas.java 197
		9.7.3	Creating a New Class CursorMark.java to Implement a cursorMark 200
		9.7.4	Adding Three Attributes into the Class Cell.java. 201
		9.7.5	Adding a Method paintTerminate() in the Class NotePanel.java. 203

	9.8	Summary 203
	9.9	Exercises 203

10 Mouse Control: A Card Game Agnes 205

	10.1	A Card Game Agnes 205
	10.2	Preparing Cards for the Game: The Project Agnes1 206
	10.3	Cards on the GUI Form a "Layout" and a "Foundation": The Project Agnes2 209
	10.4	Mouse Event and Mouse Event Listener 212

Contents

10.5	Dragging a Card to Anywhere: The Project TestDrag	213
	10.5.1 A Project TestDrag1 for Adding a Mouse Listener as an Inner Class	213
	10.5.2 A Project TestDrag2 for Implementing the Event Handler mouseDragged()	214
	10.5.3 A Project TestDrag3 for Eliminating the "Shaking"	216
	10.5.4 A Project TestDrag4 for Implementing the Event Handler mouseReleased()	217
10.6	Dragging and Releasing a Set of Cards: The Project Agnes3	219
10.7	Implementing the Game Rules: The Projects Agnes4 and Agnes5	219
10.8	Adding a Class PlayerPanel.java: The Project Agnes5	226
10.9	Always Showing the Dragged Cards on Top: The Project Agnes6	227
10.10	Summary	229
10.11	Exercises	229

Part III Games Based on Animation: Chaps. 11–21

11 Animation Programming: A Digital Clock and an Analog Clock 233

11.1	Programming Continuous Dynamic Behaviors	234
11.2	How to Tick: The Projects ADigitClock1 and ADigitClock2	234
11.3	Process and Mini-Process	236
11.4	The Java Built-In Class Thread	237
11.5	How to Use the Class Thread?	238
11.6	Applying Thread for Ticking the Digital Clock: The Project ADigitClock3	239
11.7	Trail and Flicker Problems: The Projects ADigitClock4 and ADigitClock5	240
11.8	Animation Technique	243
11.9	A Better Illustration of the Animation Technique	243
11.10	A GUI of an Analog Clock: The Project AnalogClock1	243
11.11	Constructing a Superclass for Two Subclasses: The Project AnalogClock2	248
11.12	Applying Animation to Tick the Analog Clock: The Project AnalogClock3	250
11.13	Setting Clock Time Automatically: The Project AnalogClock4	253
11.14	Summary	255
11.15	Exercises	256

12 Merging Visualization, Event Driven, and Animation: A Game WheelVideo 257

12.1	Adding a GUI to the Game WheelFortune In-Text: The Project WheelVideo1	257
12.2	The Class WheelGUI.java Constructs the Wheel with a Special Painting	258
	12.2.1 Painting a String Along the Radius Direction Around the Center of a Circle	258
	12.2.2 Painting the Wheel in the Project WheelVideo1: The Class WheelGUI.java	259
12.3	The Class Board.java Constructs a Displaying Board	261
12.4	The Class PlayerPanel.java Provides a Control Panel for Players	265
12.5	The Project TestWheel Rotates the Wheel with the Animation Technique	269

		12.5.1	The Project TestWheel1 Turns a Radius Line Circulating Around a Circle 269
		12.5.2	The Project TestWheel2 Turns the Wheel Circulating Around a Circle 273
	12.6	The Collaborations of Classes in the Project WheelVideo2 273	
		12.6.1	The Class PlayerPanel.java Plays the Role of a Control Center. 274
		12.6.2	The Class WheelGUI.java Turns the Wheel in Using the Animation Technique 276
		12.6.3	The Class Board.java Handles Guessed Character and Displays Guesses 280
		12.6.4	The Class GameCanvas.java Sets Up All of Communication Paths 283
	12.7	Summary 283	
	12.8	Exercises 283	
13	**Animated Sprites and Collisions: A Game Pong** 285		
	13.1	The Story of the Game Pong 285	
	13.2	Constructing the GUI: The Project Pong1 286	
	13.3	A Brief Introduction on JavaBeans Model 287	
	13.4	The Class Ball.java Defines the Bouncing Ball in the Project Pong1 288	
	13.5	The Class FieldWall.java Defines the Field-Wall in the Project Pong1 289	
	13.6	The Class Paddle.java Defines the Paddle in the Project Pong1 292	
	13.7	Animating the Ball Sprite: The Project Pong2 293	
	13.8	Applying the Collision Detection Technique: The Project Pong2 293	
	13.9	Allowing the Player to Move the Paddle with Keys: The Project Pong3 297	
	13.10	Adding a Score Counting Mechanism: The Project Pong3 300	
	13.11	Increasing the Degree of Playing Difficulty: The Project Pong4 301	
	13.12	Summary 304	
	13.13	Exercises 304	
14	**Multiple Screens: An Extension of the Game Pong** 305		
	14.1	A Game Usually Has Multiple Screens 305	
	14.2	Applying the CardLayout for Structuring Multiple Screens 305	
		14.2.1	Organizing Screens with an Extra "Container": TestCardLayout1 306
		14.2.2	Using One of the Existing Screens as the "Container": TestCardLayout2 309
	14.3	Adding a Splash Screen: The Project Pong5 312	
	14.4	Formatting the Texts on the Splash Screen: The Project Pong6 316	
	14.5	Extending the Game Pong 320	
	14.6	Increasing the Number of Ball Sprites: The Project Pong7 320	
	14.7	Modifying the Game Story for Catching the Ball Sprites: The Project Pong8 325	
	14.8	Summary 329	
	14.9	Exercises 329	
15	**A Three-Layer Software Structure for Games: A Game PongStruTwo** 331		
	15.1	A Ball Sprite 331	
	15.2	Adding Another Kind of Animated Sprite 332	
	15.3	What If More Types of Sprites? 332	
	15.4	Inheritance Converts Different Types of Sprites to Be the Same Type 333	
	15.5	It Is Necessary to Specify the Type When Getting Out of a Sprite from a Group 333	
	15.6	Replacing Concrete Classes by Abstract Classes with Abstract Methods 334	

Contents

- 15.7 Applying Abstract Classes for Constructing a Sprite Inheritance Hierarchy ... 335
- 15.8 Constructing a Three-Layer Software Structure Framework for Games ... 335
- 15.9 Deriving the Abstract Classes AbsSprite.java and AbsSprite2D.java ... 336
- 15.10 Deriving the Abstract Class AbsGameCanvas.java ... 337
- 15.11 Applying the Three-Layer Game Structure: The Project PongStruTwo ... 338
  - 15.11.1 The Sprite Layer Defines an Inheritance Hierarchy ... 338
  - 15.11.2 The Canvas Layer Defines All of Controlling Functions ... 346
  - 15.11.3 The Frame Layer Defines Multiple Screens Structure ... 351
- 15.12 Why the Three-Layer Game Structure? ... 351
- 15.13 Summary ... 351
- 15.14 Exercises ... 352

16 Usage of the Three-Layer Structure for Games: A Project SymBall and a Project Tornado ... 353
- 16.1 The Outline of the Project SymBall ... 353
- 16.2 Applying the Three-Layer Game Structure for a New Project: SymBall1Init ... 354
- 16.3 One Thread Supports Two Different Animation Tasks: SymBall2ToRight ... 355
- 16.4 The Sprite Inheritance Hierarchy Eases Adding New Sprites: SymBall3ToRL ... 359
- 16.5 Every Sprite Has a Thread to Change Its Color Randomly: SymBall4Twinkle ... 364
- 16.6 A New Project Tornado ... 366
  - 16.6.1 Making a Ball Sprite Circulating Along an Oval: The Project Tornado1 ... 366
  - 16.6.2 Dividing the y-Axis into 13 Sections: The Project Tornado2 ... 368
  - 16.6.3 Assigning Different Colors to Sprites ... 373
- 16.7 Summary ... 373
- 16.8 Exercises ... 373

17 Image Sprite and UML State Machine: A Game Breakout ... 375
- 17.1 The Game Breakout Could Be Understood as an Extension of the Game Pong ... 375
- 17.2 A New Image Branch in the Sprite Inheritance Hierarchy ... 375
- 17.3 Imaging in Java ... 376
- 17.4 Arranging All Bricks in a 2D Format on the GUI: The Project Breakout1 ... 377
  - 17.4.1 Defining the Classes AbsSpriteImage.java and BrickSprite.java ... 378
  - 17.4.2 The Class GameCanvas.java Initializes All of the bricks ... 379
  - 17.4.3 Deriving the Algorithm for Converting a 1D Array to a 2D Array ... 380
  - 17.4.4 The Implementation of the Class GameCanvas.java ... 380
- 17.5 Detecting Collisions by Using PropertyChangeEvent: The Project Breakout2 ... 382
- 17.6 Using Mouse to Control the Paddle Sprite: The Project Breakout3 ... 387
- 17.7 Applying the UML State Machine to Describe Game States [Samek, M., 2008] ... 388
- 17.8 Summary ... 395
- 17.9 Exercises ... 395

18 Sound Effect and Composite Class: Enriching the Game Breakout ... 397
- 18.1 More Steps for Completing the Game Breakout ... 397
- 18.2 Adding the Current Score Counting and the Ball Lost Counting: Breakout4 ... 397
- 18.3 Adding New Abstract Methods in the Class AbsGameCanvas.java: Breakout4 ... 400
- 18.4 Adding Sound Effect with the Game Breakout: Breakout4 ... 403
- 18.5 Constructing a Composite Sprite: Breakout5 ... 409
- 18.6 Modifying the Communication Path: Breakout5 ... 412
- 18.7 Improving the Control of the Ball Sprite: Breakout5 ... 413
- 18.8 A GameStruTemplate Model ... 414
- 18.9 More Extensions of the Game Breakout5 ... 414
- 18.10 Games that Could Be Understood as an Extension of the Game Pong ... 415
- 18.11 Summary ... 415
- 18.12 Exercises ... 416

19 Changing the Structure of Sprites Dynamically: A Game Worm ... 417
- 19.1 The Story of a Game Worm ... 417
- 19.2 Constructing the Class Worm.java as a Composite Class ... 417
- 19.3 Painting a Worm and a Treat Statically on the GUI: The Project Worm1 ... 418
- 19.4 Animating the Worm Along the X-Axis: The Project Worm2 ... 422
- 19.5 The Player Controls the Game Through Keys: The Project Worm3 ... 425
  - 19.5.1 Controlling the Animation Direction of the Worm in Using Keys ... 425
  - 19.5.2 The Worm Eats the Treat ... 427
  - 19.5.3 Terminating the Game If the Worm Hits on Any Edge of the Playing Field ... 430
- 19.6 Adding Another Worm for Extending the Game: The Project Worm4 ... 430
- 19.7 Adding Sound Effects to the Game: The Project Worm4 ... 434
- 19.8 Some Extensions of the Game Worm ... 434
- 19.9 Summary ... 435
- 19.10 Exercises ... 435

20 Chess-Like Games: A Game Othello ... 437
- 20.1 Revisiting the Abstract Model of Games ... 437
- 20.2 The Story and Its UML State Machine of the Game Othello ... 438
- 20.3 Initializing the Game with a Board and Four Pieces: The Project Othello1 ... 439
- 20.4 Building up a Mouse Control Mechanism for Players: The Project Othello2 ... 445
- 20.5 Implementing the Playing Rules: The Project Othello3 ... 450
- 20.6 Linking the Rules with the Sprites on the GUI: The Project Othello3 ... 455
- 20.7 Summary ... 460
- 20.8 Exercises ... 460

21 An Introduction of Artificial Intelligence: Extensions of the Game Othello ... 463
- 21.1 Changing Pieces to Be Images: The Project Othello4 ... 463
- 21.2 Making Background Color of Images Transparent: The Project TestFlip1 ... 463
- 21.3 Animating Image Pieces: The Project TestFlip2 ... 466
- 21.4 Inserting the Image Pieces: The Project Othello4 ... 468

		21.4.1	Replacing the Graphical Drawing Pieces with the Image Pieces..468
		21.4.2	Applying Frame-Based Animation for Animating the Image Pieces..468
		21.4.3	Adding the "import rule.RuleBase" into the Class GameCanvas.java......................................469
		21.4.4	Modifying All of Rule Classes from Drawing Pieces to Animating Image Pieces.......................469
	21.5	Constructing a Single-Player Version of Othello...................470
	21.6	The "First" Algorithm: The Project Othello5First..................470
	21.7	The "Random" Algorithm: The Project Othello6Ran............473
	21.8	The "Best" Algorithm: The Project Othello7Best..................475
	21.9	The "Edge" Algorithm: The Project Othello8Edge................478
	21.10	The Looking Ahead Algorithm: A Discussion......................482
	21.11	Summary...482
	21.12	Exercises..483

Part IV Serious Games: Chaps. 22–24

22 Visualizing Sorting Array Algorithms.................................487
    22.1 A Definition of Serious Games..487
    22.2 A Teaching Tool for Showing Linear Data Structure..............487
    22.3 Preparing the GUI: The Project BubbleSort1......................488
        22.3.1 The Class GameCanvas.java Instantiates Three Objects..........489
        22.3.2 The Class ControlPanel.java Builds Up a "Preferred" arrayList.....490
        22.3.3 The Composite Class BarComposite.java "Has" a Set of Bars......494
        22.3.4 Both the Classes BarSprite.java and ArrowSprite.java Are Simple Classes..496
    22.4 Animating Bubble Sort Algorithm: The Project BubbleSort2....497
        22.4.1 The Bubble Sorting Algorithm..........................497
        22.4.2 A Crucial and Difficult Issue............................497
        22.4.3 Applying a New Thread for Solving the Difficulty..............497
        22.4.4 Setting Attributes for Animating the Bar Sprites.................501
        22.4.5 A Trivial Extra Feature of the Project BubbleSort2..............503
    22.5 Switching the Sorting Algorithm to Be Quick Sort: The Project QuickSort...503
    22.6 Supporting Multiple Sorting Algorithms: The Project MultiSort.......507
    22.7 Summary..510
    22.8 Exercises...510

23 Animating Conversions Between Binary and Decimal...............511
    23.1 Converting an Integer in Any Base to Decimal: The Project AnyToDecimal..511
    23.2 Building Up the Control Panel: The Class ControlPanel.java...512
    23.3 Rendering the Computation Process: The Class RenderSprite.java.........518
    23.4 Converting an Integer in Decimal to Any Base: The Project DecimalToAny..522
    23.5 Converting a Float in Decimal to Any Base: The Project DeciToAnyFloat..523
    23.6 Summary..533
    23.7 Exercises...533

24 Animating Binary Arithmetic Computations ... 535

- 24.1 Summation of Binary Integers in Signed-Magnitude: The Project SumSigned ... 535
  - 24.1.1 The Inner Class SummationListener Performs Summation Computation ... 536
  - 24.1.2 The Class SumSprite.java Renders the Summation Process ... 540
  - 24.1.3 Drawbacks of the Signed-Magnitude Notation ... 546
- 24.2 Summation of Binary Integers in 1's Complement: The Project SumOnesComp ... 546
  - 24.2.1 The 1's Complement Notation Eliminates Subtraction ... 547
  - 24.2.2 The Project SumOnesComp Renders Three Scenes ... 547
  - 24.2.3 Drawbacks of the 1's Complement Notation ... 553
- 24.3 Summation of Binary Integers in 2's Complement: The Project SumTwos ... 553
  - 24.3.1 The 2's Complement Is the Best Notation ... 553
  - 24.3.2 The Three Scenes and Three Special Details ... 553
- 24.4 Reusable Logics and Unshared Differences for the Six Projects ... 560
- 24.5 Summary ... 561
- 24.6 Exercises ... 561

Appendix: The Source Codes of the Three-Layer Structure for Games—GameStruTemplate ... 563

Part I

Foundation with Games In-Text: Chaps. 1–4

Java Programming and Game Development: A Project HelloWorld

Chapter 1 introduces the goal of this book, which is to introduce programming with the Java language, through the mechanism of video game construction. Games are an effective and engaging learning paradigm that heightens student interest. The design and implementation of video games are immersive, innovative, and engaging experiences, which relieve the "tedious" feeling of the program writing process and inject excitement for extending and polishing every design. Video games emphasize inter-object interactions, which fit the Java object-oriented framework. As a starting point, this chapter briefly discusses game programming flow based on the working principles of a computer.

The objectives of this chapter include:
1. The purpose of this book.
2. What is programming?
3. Writing programs requires a computer and a language.
4. Computer structure and working principle.
5. Programming language and Java.
6. Java and Object-Oriented Programming (OOP).
7. Programming in general.
8. A programming flow in Java.
9. A programming pattern.
10. We selected video game as programming target.
11. Why are we interested in video games?
12. Video game programming emphasizes problem solving.
13. The simplest program HelloWorld and the IDE NetBeans.

The purpose of this book is to learn the Java programming through the topic of video game construction. That is, the book merges two topics: Java programming and game development together.

Whenever studying a new topic, we would like to ask three questions: What is it? Why is it? How to make it? This chapter intends to conceptually answer the following questions first: What is programming? Why is programming? And How to programming? And then, we are going to discuss the other three questions: What are video games? Why are we interested in video games? And How to construct video games? Definitely, the rest of the book will be devote to detail the "how to" question by designing video games and develop video games with Java programming in such a way to practice "learning by doing".

1.1 What is Programming?

Starting from elementary school we used pencil and paper to deal with calculations. For example, we can write down the calculation $1 + 2 = 3$. The pencil and paper are tools for helping us to visualize the input of "1" and "2" as well as the output of "3". The summation symbol "+" asks our brain to do the summation computation because our teachers educated us to know the mathematical language. By applying the knowledge, we understand all of these symbols and meanings. All of the digits, the summation symbol, the notation, and the entire computation process are under the control of our brain.

Instead of pencil and paper, today we are using a computer to perform these computations. The word "computer" actually includes two things: "hardware" and "software". The "hardware" is the computer itself, which is the tool like pencil and paper for visualizing input data, output data, and computation symbol. The "software" plays the role of our brain, which is so-called "program". We transfer our knowledge from our brain to be "program", just like we educate computer to perform our brain functions for controlling the "hardware" in order to accomplish the computation. The entire process for making "software" is termed as "programming".

For making a more detail understanding, we need to further understand the technical questions: What is the "hardware" called computer? How to transfer our knowledge from our brain to be "software"? And how can software controls hardware? The scope of this book mainly discusses the second question. A human who knows how to transfer knowledge from human brain to be a program is termed as programmer. Thus, this book intends to educate programmers for designing and implementing software or programs.

© Springer Nature Switzerland AG 2018
C.-w. Xu, *Learning Java with Games*, https://doi.org/10.1007/978-3-319-72886-5_1

1.2 A Computer is Required for Carrying out Programming

A program is implemented on a computer and is executed by a computer. Definitely, a computer is one of the necessary tools for programmers. Today computers are so popular that almost everyone knows and uses a computer. Many people know how to browse the web, how to download applications, and how to play video games using a computer. However, a programmer should know much more than that. He/she should know some fundamental architecture and working principles of computer hardware and system software that controls the computer, such as operating system of the computer, as well the software components that supports the programming efforts, such as compiler, tester of programs, and the like.

From a programmer point of view - what is a computer? An essential answer is that a computer is an electronic device manipulating human being's symbols. This statement gives us several technical implications.

The term "electronic" means that a computer is very fast and accurate. An electron is a tiny particle in an atom. When it flows along a wire, it forms electricity. Its speed has the same degree as the light. As we know, light has the highest speed of 3×10^8 m/s in the world. An electron flow has a speed of 2×10^8 m/s. This speed makes computers very fast. As a very tiny particle, electron also makes computers very accurate.

The term "human being's symbols" includes digits, letters, punctuation marks, music notes, graphical signs, videos, and so on. A computer can manipulate these symbols to assist human being for memorizing, computing, editing documents, composing music, creating video games, etc. Because these human symbols and their manipulations are the functions of human's brain, sometimes people call a computer as a "mind machine" or "electronic brain".

One more important term in the above statement is the "device", which indicates that any computer is just a device. We use different kinds of devices for different purposes in our life. For example, we can drive cars for travel; we can use rice cookers for cooking. No matter which device, it must be under human control and do what human want it to do. Even though a computer looks like very "smart" and "powerful", it is only a device. Human being has ability to control it. We are going to write programs just want to control the computer to do what we would like it to do. And we believe that we are always able to let computers do what we tell them to do. This statement is important for programmers, especially for beginners, who must be with confidence that "I can control my computer to do what I want it to do".

1.3 The Essential Architecture of a Computer

As a device, a computer has its special architecture, which can be very briefly illustrated as Fig. 1.1. That is, a computer consists of three major units: CPU (Central Processing Unit), main memory, and I/O (input/output) unit. The CPU mainly consists of three smaller units: ALU (Arithmetic Logic Unit), CU (Control Unit), and Registers. The ALU is hardware that performs arithmetical and logical computations for the current instruction issued by the program. The Control Unit synchronizes and controls the computations and data flows. The registers are very fast and high quality memories, which are used for fetching current instruction and related data from the program in main memory in order to feed them into the ALU for executing arithmetical or logical computations. The registers are also used to store the computational results of the ALU and transmit them back to the program in the main memory.

The memory is also called main memory or primary memory, which is used to load executable codes with data and provides a supporting environment for executing the program. The I/O unit connects with external devices, such as, keyboard, monitor, secondary memory (hard disk), and so on, as well as provides ports for connecting all of other peripheral devices, such as, mouse, USB, game controller, and the like. The three units are connected through buses, which are the communication channels among the three units. Because of these hardware units, a computer can store human being's symbols, do computations to manipulate these symbols, and communicate with the external world for accepting input and displaying output.

1.4 A Memory Hierarchy

As discussed in the previous section, every hardware unit of a computer has its own memory. The CPU has registers; the main memory itself is a memory; and the I/O unit has so-called secondary memory. The registers and the main

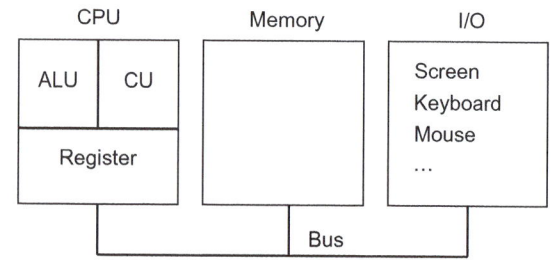

Fig. 1.1 A symbolic architecture of a computer hardware system

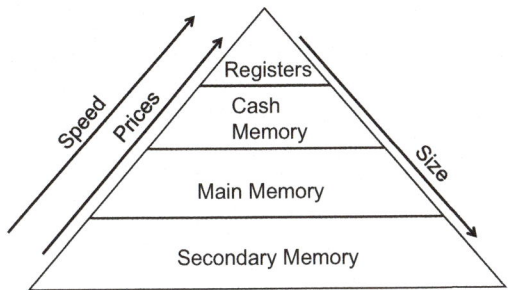

Fig. 1.2 A hierarchy of memories

memory are temporarily storage. It means that the contents of those memories will be lost once the power failure. However, the secondary memory is a kind of permanent storage. That is, the contents of the secondary memory won't be erased even during power failure. Contemporary computers may have some special cash memories. They could be inside the CPU or as part of main memory. Put all of these memories together, a memory hierarchy is formed as shown in Fig. 1.2.

No matter which kind of memory, it looks like a building with a set of rooms. Every room has a room number (memory address) and every room has a certain size. The smallest room is called one Bit. Eight bits are called one Byte. The units for measuring memory size, such as, KB, MB, GB, and the like means Kilobyte, Megabyte, and Gigabyte. However, the units for measuring transmission speed over networks, such as KB and so on means Kilobit.

It is that memory makes computers different from other devices. Due to these memories, computers can "remember" and "accumulate" knowledge, which appear as software that resides in those permanent memories and are executed with the assistants of temporary memories.

Software can be categorized as system software and application software. The former, such as operating systems, graphical packages, programming language compilers, and so on, controls hardware units and the entire computer system. The latter is specially designed software, such as Microsoft Office, Eclipse, video games, and the like, for assisting users doing their jobs or for entertainment. Both of them are programs, which are written in different programming languages and perform a variety of functions. These programs accumulate the human being's best knowledge for making a computer appear so smart and powerful.

1.5 Programming Languages Are Needed for Communicating with Computers

Intuitively, the keyboard mirrors to a pencil and the monitor just like the paper. We can directly use the keyboard to type in "1 + 2 = 3" and they then appear on the monitor. However, if we would like the computer to do the computation for us, that is, we only type in "1 + 2 =" and let the computer calculate the result of "3", then we need a program to control the computer for doing it. We design and implement a program to embed our human being's knowledge about digits and summation symbol and let the program control the computer for carrying out related computation in using its memory and CPU.

In other words, a programmer writes a program, which is used for telling a computer device what to do and how to do it. Obviously, the program should be written in the native language of the computer so that computer can understand it. Actually, using a computer is just like driving a car. When we drive a car, we are speaking "car's native language" by turning the driving wheel to tell the car going to right or left direction or pressing the gas pedal to ask the car to go faster or slower.

As a device, the native language of a computer is called binary language that corresponds to the hardware memory. As mentioned above, the smallest unit of a memory is a Bit, which can only store two values: 0 or 1 just like a switch that has only two situations "off" or "on". If we define 0 as "no" and 1 as "yes", then a computer with one bit can only understand "yes" and "no". In this way, a computer with one bit of memory can be built to memorize and execute two commands. If we would like a computer to execute four commands of addition, subtraction, multiplication, and division, a computer with two bits is needed because two bits can have four combinations: 00, 01, 10, and 11. Thus, we could define 00 as addition, 01 as subtraction, 10 as multiplication, and 11 as division. Following this derivation, three bits can implement eight commands (2^3); 4 bits can carry 16 commands (2^4). In general, the number of commands y is equal to 2 to the power of the number of bits. That is, we can build an x-bit computer to memorize and execute the number of $y = 2^x$ commands.

Similarly, all of human's symbols could be coded as binary-based notations and stored into computer's memory. In fact, all of keys in the keyboard of a computer are coded by using the ASCII (American Standard Code for Information Interchange) code, which has 7-bit. If applying the formula $y = 2^x$ derived above, we can see that 7-bit can represent $y = 2^7 = 128$ different symbols. That is, human's symbols can be represented with a sequence of 0s or 1s in 7 bits. These are called binary codes. Not only commands or data can be represented by binary codes, the addresses of memory locations can also be represented by binary codes. Consequently, humans can communicate with computers in using computer's binary language.

However, such a native language of a computer is hard for human programmers to recognize and remember. When every binary command is assigned a mnemonic name and every binary address of a location in memory is assigned a mnemonic address, it is easier for human programmers to apply mnemonic representations for writing programs than binary codes. This second generation language is called "assembly language", which is formed by replacing the binary coded commands and memory addresses with mnemonic commands and mnemonic addresses. For example, if we define that mnemonic command ADD refers to binary code of 00; SUB to 01; MUL to 10; and DIV to 11, human programmers are able to write a program in using the mnemonic command ADD instead of 00, SUB instead of 01, and the like. And then, software so-called "assembler" is hired to interpret the assembly program back to binary codes for a computer, and then the human programmer can communicate with a computer in an easier way.

Unfortunately, both the first-generation language (binary language) and the second-generation languages (assembly language) have a common problem. The problem is so-called "portable problem" because binary codes are locked with a specific hardware and cannot be ported to another different hardware. The mnemonic symbols of the assembly language are one-to-one corresponding to binary codes. That is, a program written in assembly language is also locked to specific computer hardware. Hence, both binary codes and corresponding assembly language programs can only be understood and executed by the specific computer hardware such that they cannot be ported and executed in another specific hardware.

In order to make programs portable to any kind of computer hardware, a third-generation programming language or so-called "high-level" programming language was designed. The "high-level" means that the language is closer to human's natural language and it is not locked with certain hardware so that it solved the portable problem. A program written in a high-level language is called a source code. A program with source code in high-level programming language cannot be directly understood and executed in computer hardware. It has to be converted to the native language of the computer before execution. For that purpose, a special software layer is added to perform the required conversions.

The conversion process could be either "interpretation" or "compilation". In case of "interpretation", the added software, named as "interpreter", reads one statement from the high-level source code and converts it to the corresponding native language code and then executes it in the hardware. In case of "compilation", the added software, is called "compiler", completely converts the entire high-level source code to the corresponding computer native language code before going to be executed. Different hardware installed different interpreter or compiler to convert the same high-level source code into different low-level executable codes in the native language of the particular hardware. Therefore, a program written in a third generation high-level programming language can be understood and executed by any particular computer. Certainly, the third-generation programming language not only allows programmers to enjoy programming in natural-like language but also guarantees the portability of the program.

1.6 Java Programming Language and Object-Oriented Programming

The third generation programming language includes Fortran, Pascal, C, C++, and Java, just to name a few. All of the third generation programming languages roughly classified into three categories: procedural, functional, and object-oriented programming languages according to programming paradigms. Since the dawn of time, computers are mainly used for computations; the third-generation programming language is mainly procedural. Along the programming targets were getting more and more complicated and closer to mimic the real world, object-oriented programming (OOP) languages emerged.

Due to the fact that this book intends to learn Java programming language and Java is one of the OOP programming languages, here, we are going to very briefly introduce the essential concepts and terminologies of the OOP.

A program is to mimic the real world. Our real world is full of objects, such as the computer you are using, the table under your computer, the textbooks on the bookshelves, and so on. Thus, OOP programs written in Java should describe objects and the interactions among the objects. Java uses a "class" in its code to define a corresponding object in the real world. The correspondence between the real world and the mimicking programs could be briefly depicted as in Fig. 1.3.

Figure 1.3 illustrates the real world on the left column and the corresponding Java programming paradigm on the right column. The two words "abstraction" and "instantiation" in the middle column indicates that a class in a Java program comes from an abstraction of an object in the real world and an object in the real world can be instantiated from a class in a Java program. In the real world, every

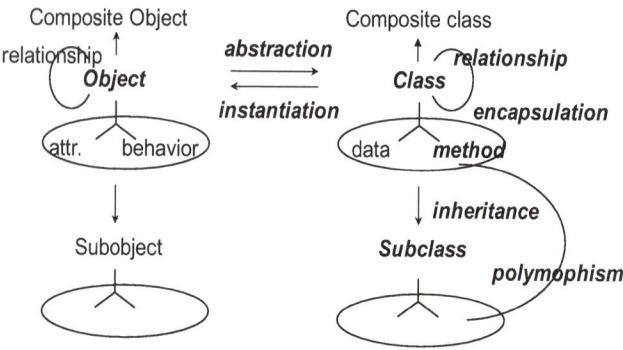

Fig. 1.3 A brief depiction of OOP terminologies

"Object" has a set of attributes and behaviors. For example, a computer is specified by its attributes, such as its maker, kind of processor, memory size, and so on; and its behaviors include storing data, doing computations, displaying results, playing video games, etc. Multiple objects may be constructed as a "Composite Object" through relationships. For instance, multiple computers may form a networked group to perform the functions as a parallel computer, which is a composite object. Meanwhile, an "Object" may be a parent of a set of "Sub-objects". For example, a super object "vehicle" has a set of sub-objects of "cars", "airplanes", "boats", and the like.

An object in the real world is abstracted as a corresponding "Class" in Java programs. A class defines a set of corresponding attributes that can be assigned with different values to distinguish individual instance of an object. At the same time, a class also defines a set of methods for implementing corresponding behaviors. A class is a self-contained unit for encapsulating the set of data. All of the data inside a class are mainly private. All of data must be accessed through corresponding public methods. This is termed as data "encapsulation". Similar with objects, multiple classes may form a "Composite class" based on relationships; and a class may be a parent of a set of sub-classes through "inheritance". Due to the fact that a sub-class "is-a" parent class, often a parent type may have multiple representations of sub-types and thus controlling one parent may realize the control to multiple sub-classes. This is meant by the term "polymorphism". All of these terms will be explored in detail when encountered.

Consequently, the most fundamental Java programming technique is to define a class. For example, a class "Car" may define a set of attributes, such as carMake, carModel, carColor, numberOfDoors, and so on. This Car class can be used to describe different instances of real cars when we assign different values to the corresponding attributes. A real car is an instance of the Car class. When we apply the "new" operator on the Car class in a Java program, we say we instantiate a car object (or instance) as follows.

```
myCar = new Car("Honda", "Odyssey", golden, 4);
hisCar = new Car("Toyota", "Camry", gray, 4);
```

After getting two objects myCar and hisCar, we can apply methods defined in the class to manipulate the object via a dot notation, such as, myCar.wash(), hisCar.sale(), etc.

Java was launched since 1995. It consists of three editions: JavaEE (Java Enterprise Edition), JavaSE (Java Standard Edition), and JavaME (Java Micro Edition). This book is using JavaSE platform. Java is a pure object-oriented programming language by the means that all Java programs only consist of classes. This feature enforces pure and easy object-oriented thinking.

1.7 Learning a Programming Language

Learning a programming language actually includes two aspects. One is the language itself; the other is programming, that is, how to apply the language for writing a program. Any language has syntax and semantics. For example, in using English, we should follow its syntax, such as "I am …", "You are …", "He is …" No one is allowed to say, "I is …" The syntax of a language is defined. Everyone should follow the syntax in using a language. The semantics refer to the meaning of the language. A sentence "I am a person." presents a correct syntax and meaning. A sentence "I am a dog." has a correct syntax, but it has the wrong meaning. Similarly, as a language, Java has its syntax and its semantics. Learning Java means we must master both of them.

Programming is to apply the language for writing a program. Besides the language, it also requires programming knowledge and programming skills. Programming is an art and also is engineering. We are not only to follow books or teachers but more important are own practices and experiences.

1.8 Programming in General

So far we understand that in order to practice programming, we need to have a computer with system software (operating system, graphical package, etc.), a programming language with related supporting software (source code editor, interpreter or compiler, etc.), and programming knowledge and skills. The most important is that we need to be very clear about "what" we are going to pursue and need to obtain ability about "how" to make the "what". "What" is the target that a program should realize. "How" to realize the target is the programmers' ability that correctly applies the programming language and programming knowledge and skills for writing a program.

In daily life, our mind is expressed through natural language. In the programming paradigm, the mind is expressed as algorithms. As people say, an algorithm is like a recipe for cooking, which lists out all of the required raw materials and processes for making a dish. A recipe is written in natural language. A chef follows the processes described in the recipe and adds all of the raw materials for cooking the predefined dish. When customers taste the dish, they may send feedback to the chef or to the recipe writer and then the recipe will be improved.

Similarly, algorithms are written in natural language, in a symbolic language, or in a mathematical format. A programmer needs to implement the algorithms as a program in a selected programming language. When a computer executes the program and generates a result, the programmer and users can further improve the algorithms to make the result of the program better and better.

For writing a less complicated program, usually the algorithm writer, the program implementer, and the application user is one person. Thus, a programmer, especially a beginner, should be educated to be an algorithm writer, an implementer, and an user. As an algorithm writer, he/she should know how to structure a suitable type of algorithms for defining a programming goal. As an implementer, he/she should know a programming language and the program testing technique, as well as knowing the usage of a computer. As a user, he/she should know the goal of the program and possesses the ability to judge problems associated with the result of the program. All of these topics are the subjects of this book.

1.9 A Programming Flow in Java

As we have discussed above, developing a program is a process in which we need to create the source code, and then, the source code should be converted into executable code in computer's native language by a compiler or an interpreter. Due to the Java language adds a JVM (Java Virtual Machine) layer, the source code written in Java will be converted into the so-called "byte code" first. When a run command is issued, the byte code will be loaded into the JVM. Then, the interpreter or compiler in the JVM layer will interpret or compile the byte code as executable code for controlling the underlying hardware when executing the program. This infrastructure makes the Java programs to be "write once, run everywhere". In other words, it is platform independent.

The entire programming process could be depicted as in Fig. 1.4, which divides the process into three time periods.

During the "writing time", the main tasks are designing and implementing the source code of a program. The designers use a text editor for writing an algorithm or pseudo code in natural language, which emphasizes "what" should be done by the program. The programmers use a source code editor to implement the algorithm as source code in Java, which requires the knowledge of the Java programming language, the programming knowledge and skills. In cases, the designers and programmers found out any improper design or implementation, the process loops back to redo.

After making the source code, the programmers may issue a compilation command and enter a "compile time", where a compiler compiles the Java source code as byte code, at the same time the syntax of the source code is verified. And then, a linker is involved to link existing byte codes in APIs or any external libraries with the source byte code. Any syntax or linkage failure will ask programmers for applying their Java programming language proficiency to debug and fix problems by enforcing the process looping back. In this sense, the compiler actually is a very good teacher for checking errors made by programmers and help programmers to better learn the Java language.

The success of the second step will allow programmers or testers to issue a run command for starting the third step "run time". The byte code is then sent to the JVM and to be further interpreted or compiled as executable code. A loader then loads the executable code into main memory to be a process, which is a program in execution. At this time period, the semantics of the program is verified. The execution could be aborted or completed. The programmer compares the output of the program with the predefined "what" the program should perform to see any deficits or failures. If yes, the process has to be looped back for checking the definition of the semantics of the program and the proficiency of the

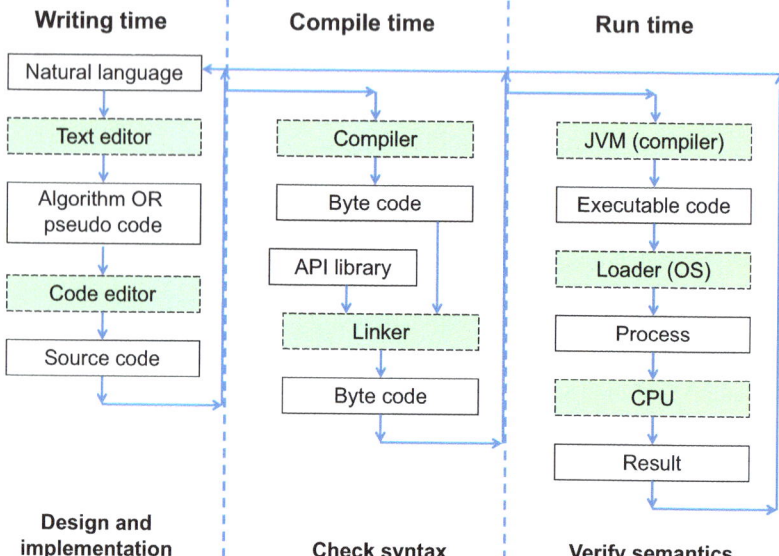

Fig. 1.4 The entire programming process flow in Java (The dashed rectangles refer to required tools; the solid rectangles are results)

```
iterative {
    input part, computation part, output part
}
```

Fig. 1.5 A programming pattern

implementation. Until everything is fine, the program could be a final product to be deployed.

In a commercial environment, the users of a program can only enjoy the execution of the program in run time without authority to interact with the source code as in "writing time" and re-compile the program as in "compile time".

1.10 A Programming Pattern

Clearly, Fig. 1.4 illustrates that a programming process definitely is an iterative process. It follows what we have discussed before. An algorithm looks like a recipe for cooking and recipe writers, chef, and customers should improve the recipe repeatedly and continuously. So does a program, which could also be improved better and better in an iterative process by algorithm writers, programmers, and users.

But, what are the contents involved in a programming process? Indeed, the answer can also be found from recipes. A recipe involves raw materials, cooking process, and a resulting dish. So does a program, which involves input data, computations, and output results. A recipe is written in natural language; but a program relates with a programming language, a compiler, a loader, and a computer.

In short, in order to learn programming in Java, we should learn how to employ the Java programming language for accepting input data and user's controls, for constructing required computations, and for producing and displaying results as output. Combining these two parts together, the entire process of programming could be described as a pattern shown in Fig. 1.5.

Of course, the word "computation" here does not only mean number crunching. The computation could be numerical calculation, event handling, simulation, animation, and any piece of code in execution; correspondingly, the "input" could be data, actions, body gestures, etc.; the "output" could be values, printing, painting, image, music, and so on. Actually, output may also trigger new input and drive a program to another level even another direction.

1.11 We Selected Video Games as our Programming Target

Educating a human to be a programmer not only relies on learning syntax and semantics of the programming language, the more important is to apply the language for programming "what" we would like to be realized. It just likes learning English, we cannot only memorize vocabularies and grammar rules, but we must apply these language elements for writing articles. In turn, from the writing practices, we will learn more and more about the language. The topic of the article could be anything. Similarly, the target for practicing our programming could be anything, such as short examples, image processing projects, video games, and so on. We selected video games as our programming target.

Therefore, firstly we need to have a very brief idea about what video games are. Almost all people have played video games. Video games are designed and implemented mainly for entertainment. People enjoy video games mainly for relaxation, for spending spare time, for fun, or for communicating with friends; except those so-called "serious game" that is usually designed for a special purpose. Games' feedback also might train players' quick response and fast thinking.

There are a variety of video games. Action games are one of genres. Figure 1.6 shows a simplest version of video games called Pong. The figure shows a game title, a playing field, a red ball and a brown paddle, as well as a score label. The game interface seems to represent a single tennis player using a racket to hit a tennis ball against a wall or more like a top 2D projection of a single racquetball player who uses a racket to hit a racquetball and the ball bounces around the surrounding walls in the playing room. Of course, here the function of the paddle is simpler than the actions of a real racket since it can only be moved along the y direction for bouncing the ball.

Every game has a story. The story about the simplest version of the Pong game says, "A bouncing ball is bounced by the up, left, and bottom edges of the playing field and is also bounced by the paddle on the right side. The game player moves the paddle up and down to bounce the ball and

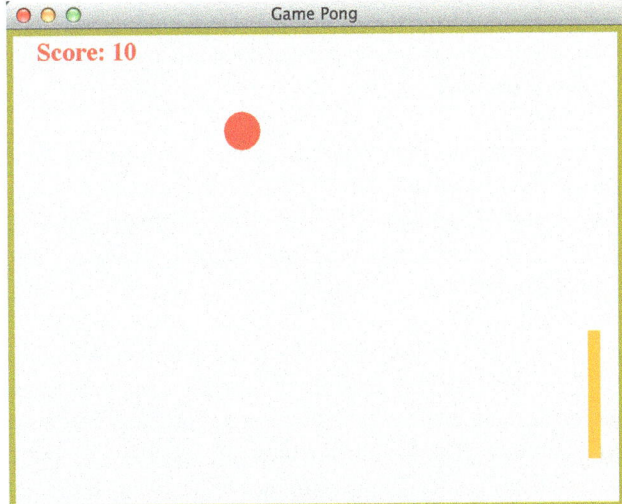

Fig. 1.6 A simplest version of the video game Pong

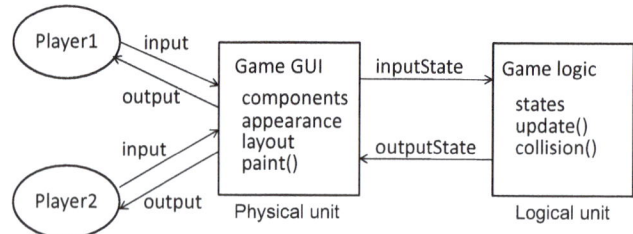

Fig. 1.7 An abstract model of video games with two players

prevents the ball from hitting the right edge of the playing field. Whenever the game player hits the ball, he/she gains some scores; but if he/she loses the ball and allows the ball hitting on the right edge of the playing field, the player loses the game." The more complicated version of the game will be discussed in later chapters.

From this simple game, we can see that a typical video game contains the following major components in general:

1. A story that defines the game, which is the guideline for the design and implementation of the game.
2. A game scene that is a visual interface for displaying the game components and their actions. Here, such as the playing filed, the bouncing ball, and the paddle.
3. A set of game controlling rules and their driving force behind scenes. For game Pong, the controlling rules include the ball movements, the collisions between the ball and the edges of the playing field as well as between the ball and the paddle. The driving force is the animation mechanism. For other individual game, the driving force could be others, such as, a simple while loop, an event, and the like.
4. A mechanism for players to control the game, which usually includes mouse, keys on the keyboard, or even special game controllers. The players' inputs cause events that trigger related event handlers. The event handling functions form an invisible portion behind the scenes to manage the behaviors or moving routes of the game components in order to create or avoid collisions for making new scenarios.

Besides the story, the major components of a typical video game could be modeled as Fig. 1.7. It consists of two portions mainly. One is its GUI; the other is its logic. The GUI is the visible portion for outputting the game scenes and also for the players to input their controls. The logic is the unseen portion that embeds all of the logic of the game as a set of possible built-in rules. When the game player watches the GUI and inputs his/her controls, the control actions are transmitted as input data to the logic for triggering and executing built-in rules. These built-in rules are specially designed potential key points in time and space for changing the states of the game and output data to change the scene on the GUI for the player.

This model is an abstraction for almost all video games and will be a blueprint for constructing video games' structures in a loosely coupled fashion.

1.12 Why Are We Interested in Video Games?

As a practical matter, when game players are immersed in playing games, they are engaged through the quickly changed GUI scenes that are in response to the actions of the players themselves. When game designers and programmers design and implement a game, they are also engaged by the scenes and the logic of the game. Varieties of GUI scenes in a game promote and enforce designers and programmers fulfilling the story with curiosities and imaginations. Interesting game logic provides a wide and deep space for game designers and implementers to open their mind and to fill their creations. When game development is adopted in the education process, the special and rich features of video games described above would relieve the "tedious" feeling of the program writing process.

Video games can play a unique role in education. Games "do all of the things that the learning scientists told us worked well." [Schollmeyer, J.].[1] Games support the following effective learning paradigms identified by learning science [Mayo, M., 2007][2]:

- Experiential learning: "If you do it, you learn it";
- Inquiry-based learning: "What happens when I do this?";
- Self-efficacy: "If you believe you can do it, you will try longer/harder, and you will succeed more often than you would otherwise";
- Goal setting: "You learn more if you are working toward a well-defined goal";
- Cooperation: team learning.

In addition, games are the integration of Humanity, Mathematics, Physics, Art, Artificial Intelligence, Graphics, visualization, animation, sounds, images, programming, and so on. Gaming itself is becoming a Science [Zyda, M., 2007].[3] Consequently, learning and practicing game development will promote the deep understanding and further study of all sciences, especially mathematics, physics, programming skills, and problem solving abilities. In particular,

---

[1] [Schollmeyer, J.] Josh Schollmeyer, "Games get serious," Bulletin of the Atomic Scientists, http://www.thebulletin.org/article.php?art_ofn=ja06schollmeyer_100

[2] [Mayo, M., 2007] Merrilea Mayo, "Games for science and engineering education", CACM, Vol.50, No.7, July, 2007.

[3] [Zyda, M., 2007] Michael Zyda, "Creating a Science of Games", CACM, Vol.50, No.7, July 2007.

games bring industry settings and industry practices into the educational paradigm.

1.13 Game Programming Emphasizes Problem Solving

This book intends to take video games as programming targets for learning Java language. Every game has its own story and own features such that every game challenges us to solve different problems one after the other. In the process for solving problems, we look for the suitable Java language elements and learn the meaning of the Java language elements with the practice. In other words, the Java language elements are arranged following the problems solving practices. This special feature results in a different style for arranging the learning materials of Java programming language. For example,

- The GUI elements and scenes of games are from texts to graphical drawings, and then to images with sounds.
- The driving force of games is from "while" loop to discreet event driven, and then to continuous animation.
- The event handlings of games are from "if-then" statements to event listeners, and then to collisions.
- The player control mechanisms for games are from direct data inputs to semantic events (software components), and then to low-level events (keys and mouse).
- The design tool of games is from UML (Uniform Modeling Language) class diagram to UML sequence diagram, and then to UML state machine.
- The structure of games is from one class to multiple classes, and then to three-layer structure for games.

This problem solving process really realizes the "learning by doing" and at the same time it raises our ability for analyzing and synthesizing problems. The related Java language elements will be understood deeply through their practical applications. Go through a video game construction, we will learn lots of programing knowledge and skills. Hence, a process for constructing a video game is an effective process for learning programming language and problem solving.

1.14 A Simplest Program HelloWorld

Following the programming pattern discussed in section 1.10, every program consists of three parts: input, computation, and output. Thus, a simplest program could be one that only has the output part. Indeed, the output itself could be in different styles. The simplest output style is in plain text. Therefore, the typical simplest example program is the famous program HelloWorld that prints a "Hello World!" in plain text on the screen. That is why it is everyone's first program.

Java language abstracts the output device, the monitor object, as "System.out". Therefore, a Java statement for printing a plain text, which is called String in Java, as a line on the screen is "System.out.println()". What would be printed out should be placed inside the parentheses of the method println(). A string is quoted inside a double quotation mark. Thus, the complete Java statement for displaying the string "Hello World!" on the screen is:

```
System.out.println("Hello, World!");
```

Here, "println()" means "print the string inside the parentheses in one line" and then the cursor is moved to the next line. Due to the fact that Java language is an OOP language, it is class based. The syntax of Java requires that the above statement should be placed inside a method and the method itself should be included inside a class. Any Java program has a main() method, which is the starting point when the program in execution. Since the program has only one statement, it should be placed in the main() method. The main() method in turn should be inside a class. Consequently, a complete source code for the project HelloWorld is as in Listing 1.1.

Listing 1.1 The Project HelloWorld

```
1  /*
2   * HelloWorld.java -- To display a text string
     "Hello World!" on the screen.
3   */
4
5  package helloworld;
6
11 public class HelloWorld {
12
16     public static void main(String[] args) {
17         System.out.println("Hello World!");
18     }
19 }
```

The class that contains the method main() could be thought of as "main class" of the project. That is, as a project, there must be a class that defines the main() method. Here, the class "public class HelloWorld" is the main class since it contains the main() method. The title of the class "HelloWorld" is not fixed but designed by the programmer. The semantics of the method main() is that it is the entry point when the project is put into execution. That is, every project starts its execution from the main() method. It is that every Java program must have one and only one method with the name of main(). As the source code above shows, the main() method has a special title:

```
public static void main(String[] args)
```

Where, the "main" is the name of the method defined in Java. The parentheses and the string inside it "(String[] args)" is called the parameter of the method. The words "public" and "static" are modifiers and the word "void" is the return type of the method. These words "public", "static", "void", and "main" are called "reserved words". Every reserved word has its special meaning and can only be used in certain places in Java programs. The special meaning of these words will be explained and learned later. Here, we may temporarily understand them as syntax for defining a main() method.

1.15 Compile and Execute the Project HelloWorld

Suppose that we used a text editor to edit the source code of the project HelloWorld shown in Listing 1.1 and saved it in a file HelloWorld.java under a folder helloWorld. As mentioned before, we need to compile a Java source code as an executable code and then run the executable code for getting the result. We can navigate to the folder helloWorld and issue the command "javac HelloWorld.java" to invoke the Java compiler for creating a file HelloWorld.class and then type the command "java HelloWorld" to invoke the file HelloWorld.class (the extension "class" can be omitted) for executing the program as follows.

```
// creating a file HelloWorld.class
javac HelloWorld.java <Enter>
// loading the HelloWorld.class into JVM
// and executing
java HelloWorld <Enter>
```

1.16 Using the IDE NetBeans

Clearly, Fig. 1.4 indicates that the entire programming process not only requires editor and compiler but also asks for many other tools, which are shown in the rectangles with dashed lines. A special software tool is known as IDE (Integrated Development Environment) merges intelligent source code editor, compiler, loader, and many more software tools in one application for supporting programming works. Many popular IDEs support Java programming, such as, Eclipse, NetBeans, etc. We selected NetBeans for developing Java projects in this book. The main reason for selecting NetBeans is that its menu "File > Print to HTML" can easily print a source code with line numbers, which eases the citation of source codes for making this book.

Due to the fact that the IDE NetBeans is evolving quickly, here we only feather touch its surface. The home web page of the IDE NetBeans contains many tutorials and articles that provide rich information for learning the IDE in details.

We are going to use the NetBeans for developing Java programs, we need to install Java compiler with the NetBeans. Therefore, we have to download and install JDK (Java Development Kit) first from the following web page:

http://www.oracle.com/technetwork/java/javase/downloads/index.html

And then download and install NetBeans package from its home web page:

http:/netbeans.org/

Currently, computers have either 32 bits or 64 bits architecture and their operating systems mainly have Windows or Mac OS. We should download and install the corresponding version of JDK and NetBeans for matching hardware and system software settings.

It is also possible to download and install one package that combines NetBeans with JDK together, which can be found from the web page:

http://www.oracle.com/technetwork/java/javase/downloads/index.html

After installing both JDK and NetBeans, we need to link them together. For Windows, we can look at the directory "c:\Program Files\Java" to find out the version of the JDK. Then we need to open the Control Panel > System and Security > System > Advanced System Settings. When click and open the "Environment Variables" panel, we can create a new environment variable "JAVA_HOME" and assign the Java version number to it. Furthermore, edit the environment variable "Path" by appending the string "%JAVA_HOME%\bin" on it. After all of these, click several "OK" for saving the settings. These settings allow the IDE NetBeans going through the environment variable "Path" to find the JDK. For Mac OS, we simply install newest version of JDK. The NetBeans will link with it.

The GUI of the NetBeans IDE is split into several areas indicated by the big font letters shown in Fig. 1.8. We may select the menu Files > New Project… or in the Menu bar on the left top portion of the GUI, click the second button symbol (a square with a yellow color), the panel "New Project" will pop up. On the panel, we can click on "Java", then "Java Application", and then the button Next, we will reach the panel "New Java Application". We then type in the Project Name "HelloWorld" and provide the Project Location by clicking the Browse button for selecting a suitable folder as the project saving folder. After we click the Finish button, the NetBeans creates the Java application project folder HelloWorld inside the selected project saving folder and the file HelloWorld.java is automatically opened on the source editor window. We then type in the source code as listed in

1.17 Learning Some Aspects of Java through the Project HelloWorld

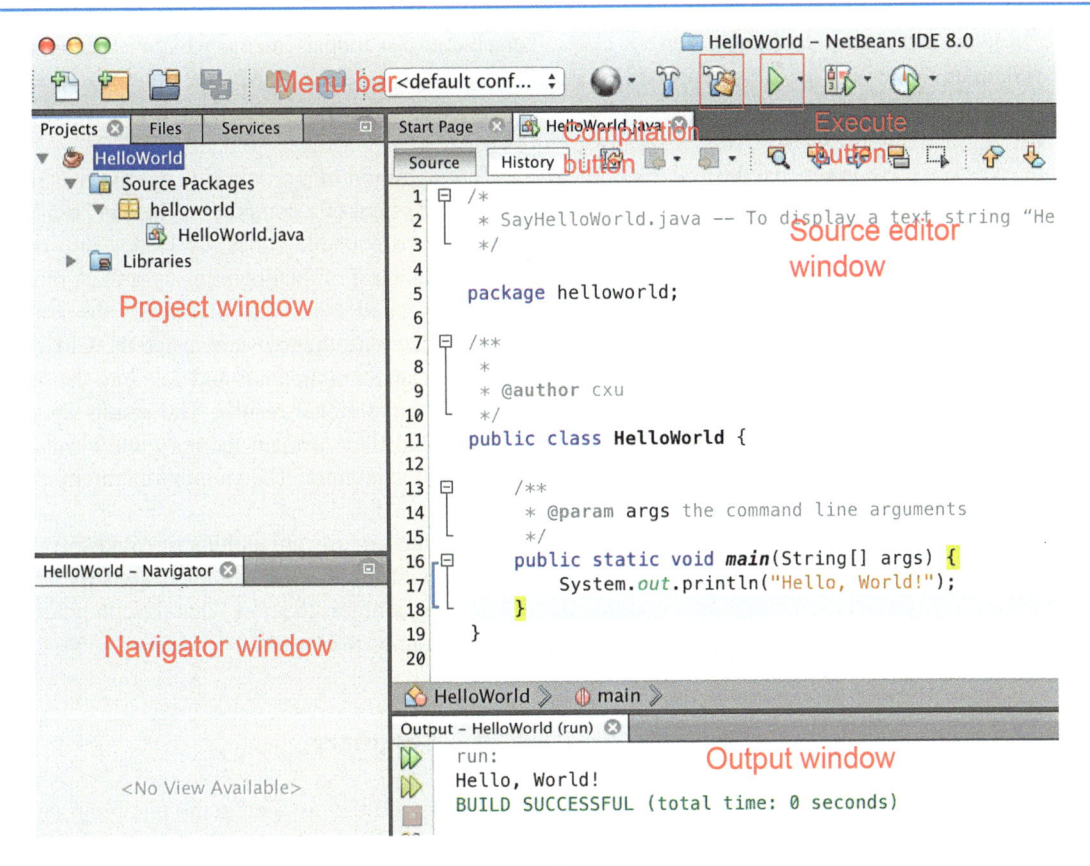

Fig. 1.8 The graphical user interface of the NetBeans IDE

Listing 1.1 in the editor window. After finishing typing, we either select the menu Run > Clean and Build Project or click the compilation symbol button on the menu bar for compiling the project. If there is no error messages for the compilation, we can continue to either select Run > Run Project or click the execution symbol button on the menu bar for executing the project. If everything is fine, the string "Hello World!" will be displayed on the right-bottom "Output" window on the IDE. The output window is also called "console", which is used for displaying compilation information and execution results.

1.17 Learning Some Aspects of Java through the Project HelloWorld

The simplest project HelloWorld not only demonstrates what a Java program looks like but also illustrates some Java language aspects. Writing a program just like writing a paper. In our daily life, a paper consists of sections; a section consists of paragraphs; a paragraph consists of sentences; a sentence consists of words or vocabularies. The words are organized according to the language's syntax requirement. If we think of a project as a paper, then the class HelloWorld.java is equivalent to a section, the method main() is just like a paragraph. The method main() provides a pair of curly brackets for containing a block of statements. Here, it only contains one statement System.out.println() that looks like a sentence, which is a smallest unit carrying a meaning. The statement invokes a method println() (print-line) defined in another class System.out. The class System.out and its methods are called "built-in" class and "built-in" method, which are programmed by experts and included in Java APIs (Application Programming Interfaces), which is also referred as Java libraries. Programmers can directly invoke these built-in classes and methods in their programs. Thus, these built-in classes and methods dramatically reduce programmers' burden. They are one of the important learning aspects we should pursue.

In other words, we may learn from the structure hierarchy of papers and apply the idea for writing programs. We may start from defining variables (words), then structure variables with operators according to the programming language's syntax to a statement (sentence), and then group a set of statements to be a method (paragraph), then organize multiple methods to be a class (section), then involve multiple classes to form a project (paper). This is so-called "bottom up" approach. That is building up a program from the elements to the components to the units. The other approach is called "top down" that means that we design a set of steps for outlining the project, and then refine each step as class, method, and statement. In reality, these two approaches are mixed in the iterative process for making the program better and better.

From Listing 1.1, we also can see that the first three lines have a special pair of symbols "/*" and "*/" at the beginning and the end. This pair of symbols is called "comment", which indicates that everything between them is nothing but a note in English. Comments usually are remarks of some important points or explanations of some special meanings of a piece of code for helping readers to easily understand the program or as a reminder to programmers themselves.

All comments won't be compiled into the executable code by the compiler and won't be executed when the program is in running. In other words, comments are for human readers not for computers so that comments are in natural language and enclosed by special comment symbols. Good comments are required for good programming practices. Good comments increase the readability and maintainability of the program; thus, comments should be helpful and concise. Don't add "unnecessary" comments.

There are two kinds of comment symbols. (1) A pair of "/*" and "*/" is used for making a comment that crosses multiple lines. (2) A double of slashes "//" is used for making a comment at the same line as follows.

```
// print a line of string
System.out.println("Hello World!");
```

Look at the statement System.out.println("Hello World!") further, it displays the string on the monitor. As mentioned above, the program is executed in the primary memory; but the monitor is a peripheral device. The string needs to be sent out from primary memory to external device. It is so-called an I/O operation. This I/O operation is very important, especially for games. Fortunately, the external devices monitor and keyboard must always exist and fairly connected with the I/O unit as part of a computer, we don't need to worry about whether they exist or functioning because these questions are taking care of by system managers not by programmers.

Human programmers uses the input device, such as keyboard, to embed their ideas and thinking into program source codes. These source codes are saved as files on permanent memories, such as, a hard disk, a USB, and the like. A file is a piece of permanent memory in a hard disk or a USB. When the programmer issues a "compile" command, the Java compiler reads the source codes from the source code file and compiles them into executable codes, and then the computer system writes the executable codes into other files, which also still resides in secondary memory. When a user copies a file from the computer to a USB, the file is transferred from one piece of secondary memory to the other. In addition, files can be copied, edited, and can also be organized as directories, which makes a convenient file hierarchy for human users.

The execution of a program is tightly associated with the hardware system of a computer. When an "run" command is issued, the executable codes are loaded into main memory under the control of the operating system. A program in execution is called a process that feeds the commands and required data into the registers inside the CPU, and then the registers transfer commands and data into the ALU for making the computational results. The results are sent back to registers and then to main memory and eventually are displayed on the monitor. The memory hierarchy exists for supporting these operations.

All of these hardware architecture and software concepts are important for programmers because they would be helpful for programmers to know what the computer is doing and how programs are constructed.

1.18 Summary

We understand that a video game is a program written in a programming language. Due to the advantages of games in education, we selected the games as a topic for learning programming. Because a video game is full of objects with visualization, event handling, and animation, the object-oriented Java programming language is suitable to be selected for developing video games. This suitability will be further illustrated clearly as the video games are developed deeper and deeper.

Learning Java programming actually includes two aspects. One is the syntax and the semantics of Java language; the other is about programming knowledge and skills. This chapter introduced some fundamental programming knowledge, such as, hardware of a computer, the process of programming, the pattern of a program, and the like.

However, due to the complexity of video games, usually game development is offered for junior or senior Computer Science majors. Is it possible to migrate video game development to the freshman level in order to make the "tedious" programming more interesting and more challenging? This is the attempt of this book.

1.19 Exercises

Self-reviewing questions

1. What is a computer? What major hardware units does a computer have?
2. What is the functionality of the unit ALU?

1.19 Exercises

3. Why do we need three layers of memory: register, main memory, and secondary memory?
4. Why do we need programming languages?
5. How many different generations in the programming language evolution history?
6. What problem is associated with the first and the second generation programming languages?
7. What is an object-oriented programming (OOP) language? Why do we say that Java is a pure OOP language?
8. What are the major concepts and terms in the OOP paradigm?
9. Why do we need to compile a source code of a program and then execute the program?
10. What is a video game? What are the major units of a video game? Selecting a video game as an example for answering this question.
11. Why do we interest in game development?
12. Why Java language is suitable for game development?
13. Write down the source code for the simplest program HelloWorld without looking at the existing source code.
14. What is a comment? Why do we need comments?

Projects

1. Download and install JDK and NetBeans (or Eclipse).
2. Write a Java program for printing a string "Hello Java!"
3. Write two Java programs. First one is for printing a person's first name and last name in one line. Second program prints the first name in one line and prints the last name in the second line (Hint: explore the difference between System.out.println() and System.out.print()).
4. Write a Java program for displaying the computation "1 + 2 = 3" on the monitor.
5. Write a Java program for printing the pattern shown as follows.

```
-----    =====
---      ===
```

6. Write a Java program for printing the pattern shown as follows.

```
   *
 *****
  ***
   *
```

7. Write a Java program for printing the following pattern.

```
+-----+-----+-----+-----+-----+
|  H  |  E  |  L  |  L  |  O  |
+-----+-----+-----+-----+-----+
```

Basics of Java Programming: A Project PrintXmasCard

Chapter 2 starts Java programming. When we write a paper, we start from words, to sentences, to paragraphs, to sections, and to the complete paper by following the syntax and semantics of our natural language. Writing a program is just like that. We start from variables, to statements, to methods, to classes, and to a complete project by following the syntax and semantics of the Java programming language. We are going to introduce the programming concepts and practices through the designing and constructing of a project PrintXmasCard, which illustrates that a program consists of three parts in general: input, computation, and output.

The objectives of this chapter include:
1. Basic syntax and semantics of the Java programming language.
2. Class-level and member-level access modifiers.
3. Variable, variable type, and variable scope.
4. Constructor method of a class.
5. Constructing a user-defined class.
6. Adding an input part into a class in using JOptionPane.
7. Designing and implementing a new project PrintXmasCard.
8. Accessing a text file through File I/O.
9. Method, parameter, and return value.
10. Primitive data type and reference data type.

The previous chapter sets up our goal to learn the Java programming through the development of video games. It is not only because a process for constructing a video game is just a process for writing a program but also because video games have specific significance in education.

The previous chapter also started our Java programming journey from implementing the simplest project HelloWorld. However, we need more fundamental concepts about programming in general and more essential knowledge about Java programming in particular before involving video games. This chapter is devoted to that purpose.

2.1 Basic Syntax, Semantics, and Conventions in Java: Revisit HelloWorld

Every language has its syntax and its semantics. Our natural language English has its syntax like "I am …," "You are …," and "He is …," which is a set of rules for arranging words or phrases to create well-formed sentences. Any violation of the syntax will be marked as "syntax error." Furthermore, the following two sentences "I am a student" and "I am a car" have correct syntax, but "I am a car" has a wrong semantics since it represents a wrong logical meaning.

As one of OOP languages, Java has its own special syntax and semantics. Java requires that any project should be based on classes and every project must have one class that contains a main() method. The project HelloWorld in the previous chapter just gives us a simple but perfect example for illustrating the syntax for defining a main() function and related class. For emphasizing it, we duplicated the program in Listing 2.1.

Listing 2.1 The project HelloWorld

```
1  /*
2   * HelloWorld.java -- To display a text string "Hello World!" on the screen.
3   */
4
5  package helloworld;
6
11 public class HelloWorld {
12
16     public static void main(String[] args) {
17         System.out.println("Hello World!");
18     }
19 }
```

The title of the main class of this program is:

```
public class HelloWorld{}
```

The word "public" appears in front of "class" is called class-level access modifier. It could be "public" or without an explicit modifier. The semantics of the "public" means that this class can be accessed from anywhere. A class without an explicit modifier means that the class can only be accessed from the same package, which is called "package-private." A package is a group of classes. For example, the "package helloworld" that appears on line 5 of Listing 2.1 indicates that the class HelloWorld belongs to the package helloworld. Currently, the package helloworld has only one class. If multiple classes are defined for a project, then all of the classes in the same project form a package. The codes of one public class are contained in one "independent" file with the same name as the class title and a file extension of ".java." In other words, the class HelloWorld has its own file HelloWorld.java.

The string "HelloWorld" is the name of the class. Programmers define the name string of the class "HelloWorld." Such a string defined by programmers is termed as "identifier." Any identifier can be formed in using letters, digits, and underscore character with the restriction of first character that must be a letter. Of course, for our benefits, any identifier is better to be meaningful. It means that when anyone reads the identifier, the reader may understand what the identifier intends to mean.

The class HelloWorld carries a pair of curly brackets. The contents inside the curly brackets are called "body of the class." The HelloWorld class body contains a main() method, which has the syntax as follows:

```
public static void main(String[] args) {}
```

The main() method also has a "public" in front of its title, which is called member-level access modifier because a method is a member of a class. Besides methods, a class may also have a set of attributes or variables as its members. The member-level access modifiers for methods may be "public," "private," "protected," or without explicit modifier. The meaning of the member-level "public" or without explicit modifier is the same as the class-level "public" or without explicit modifier. A member-level "private" access modifier indicates that only those members that are inside the same class can access the "private" method. The member-level access modifiers for the attributes may be "public," "private," and "protected." The "protected" access modifier means that the member can be accessed by other members inside the same package and all of its subclasses in any package. Its meaning will be explained in detail later.

The sequence of words "void main(String[] argc)" in the title of the main() method represents a typical syntax for defining a method. Since a class is an abstraction of an object, a method inside a class is used for coding a behavior of that corresponding object. A method may perform computations and return the result of the computations. Or a method may only perform some actions without returning any value result. The word "void" here indicates that the main() method performs actions and won't return any value. For those methods that will return a value, the word "void" should be replaced with a data type that matches the data type of the returning value. We will explain this "return type" later after we discussed "data type." Following the return type, a method name should be defined. That is, the position of the "main" should be replaced by a user-defined method name if the method is not a "main" method. After the method name, a pair of parenthesis encloses a "formal parameter" like the "(String[] argc)" here. The "parameter" will also be explained later. Similarly, a pair of curly brackets is needed to enclose the body of the method.

The second word "static" in the title of the main() method has a special meaning. We will explain it in detail later. At this moment, we just simply copy the title of the main() method as listed for defining any main() method in any project.

Java has a convention. Names of classes start with a uppercase letter, like the capital letter "H" in the class title "HelloWorld"; but names of methods are starting with a lowercase letter, like the letter "m" in the title of "main()". In addition, a pair of "()" is used after a method name for indicating it is a method. If an identifier consists of several words, then starting from the second word, each word begins with an uppercase letter, such as the letter "W" in the class name "HelloWorld" and the letter "V" in the method name "setValue()." The words, such as "public," "class," "static," "void," and so on, are called "Java key words" or "Java reserved words" because they are reserved words for Java language itself. That is, in any Java programs, the key words are only used for defining a component and/or a unit dedicated to the Java language, and they cannot be used as an identifier for other purposes. Hence, when a programmer has chances to select any words for defining identifiers, all of the key words are prohibited.

The functions performed by methods and codes demonstrate the semantics of the program. For example, the function of the project HelloWorld is to show "Hello World!" on the screen. For performing this function, we need to invoke "System.out.println()" statement. As mentioned in the previous chapter, "System.out" is the abstraction of the hardware "monitor" in Java. The "println()" is a built-in method defined in the class "System.out." For calling a method defined inside a class, Java uses the dot notation ".println()." The function of the method println() is to print a string inside the parentheses of the method on the monitor as a line and then the cursor will be moved to the next line. By using this statement, the project acts correctly for realizing the function of the project HelloWorld. That is, it has a correct semantics. By contrast, if we replace the "System.out" with "System.in," which is the abstraction of the input device keyboard, the project won't be able to display anything on the screen. That is, the semantics of the project is wrong. The another method "System.out.print()" without "ln" is to print the string inside the parentheses of the method on the monitor and then place the cursor at the next position of the last letter of the printed string without moving to the next line. If we replace the println() method with the print() method, the semantics of the project should be changed as "print the string on the monitor" without "as a line."

By the way, the statements "System.out.print()" and "System.out.println()" can be used to display any type of values, not only strings, on the screen. Therefore, they are used very often to show the values stored in variables and thus often to be employed as a simple debugging tool in writing programs.

2.2 Variables: The Project HelloWorld2

We are happy to see the project HelloWorld works fine. However, the program can only display a "fixed" plain text of "Hello World!" What if we would like to display other strings, such as "Hello, Java!"? The program HelloWorld cannot do it since the string value "Hello World!" is fixed inside the parentheses of the System.out.println(). This is termed as "hard coded." If we would like to display different strings by using the project HelloWorld, we have to edit the program by replacing the string "Hello World!" inside the statement System.out.println() with another string "Hello, Java!". And then, recompile and rerun the project HelloWorld.

However, only programmers are able to complete the process of edit-compile-run since users don't have the source code and users have no authority to touch the source code. In other words, in order to allow the users to display different strings when they run the program, the program needs to be modified with new codes. The new program must have (1) an input part that can accept the user's new input data and (2) a variable that can temporarily store and transfer the inputted data to join computations for generating the output. These two requirements could be conceptually depicted as in Fig. 2.1.

Figure 2.1 shows that a piece of memory is allocated for temporarily storing the data inputted through the keyboard. When the inputted data would join a computation, it will be sent to the CPU, and the computation result will be sent back and to be displayed on the screen. Due to the fact that the piece of memory can be used to store different values over

Fig. 2.1 Variables temporarily store data (the markers 1–9 indicate the sequence of operations)

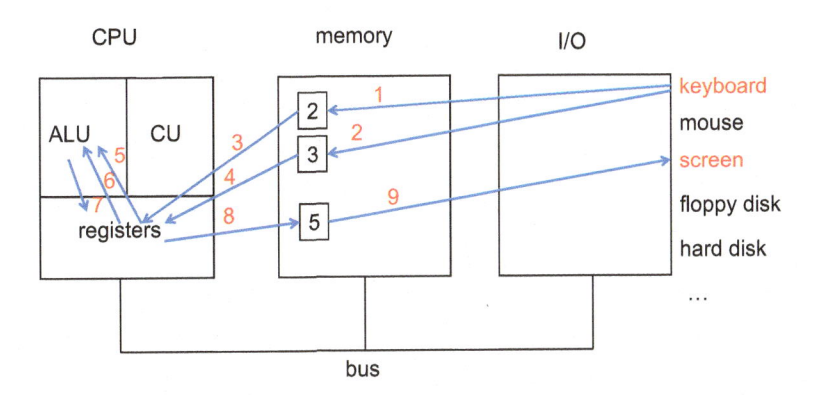

various times, it is termed as "variable." That is, whenever a program needs to store data, a variable is required to be allocated in the memory.

Consequently, the new version HelloWorld2 cited in Listing 2.2 appears different from the old version HelloWorld even though they perform the same function.

Listing 2.2 A new version HelloWorld2

```
 1 /*
 2  * HelloWorld2.java - the main class of the version HelloWorld2
 3  */
 4
 5 package helloworld2;
 6
11 public class HelloWorld2 {
12
13     private String message;
14
15     public HelloWorld2() {
16         message = "Hello World!";
17         System.out.println(message);
18     }
19
23     public static void main(String[] args) {
24         new HelloWorld2();
25     }
26 }
```

The new version HelloWorld2 adds a variable "message" on line 13 as follows:

```
private String message;
```

This is termed as "declare a variable message." The declaration consists of three words. The word "message" is the identifier of the variable, which is created by the programmer. The variable has a type of "String"; and it is a "private" variable that belongs to the class HelloWorld2.java only, and it cannot be directly accessed from anywhere outside the class.

2.3 Variable Type

A variable of a program looks like a "vocabulary" in a paper as mentioned before. The "vocabulary" is an identifier declared by the programmer. In fact, a variable is a mnemonic address of a piece of memory, which can be used to carry data for attending a computation. The statement "message = 'Hello World!'" on line 16 is a "sentence," which is called "statement" in programming domain. A statement is formed by a command and data. The command is the sign "=" that means assigning the value on its right side to the variable "message" on its left side. This statement is called an "assignment statement." Therefore, every variable has two values associated with it. When the variable appears on the left side of the sign "=," it means the address of the memory location; when the variable appears on the right side of the sign "=," it represents the data value stored in the memory location. Considering the fact that different data requires different size of a memory location, every variable thus must have a data type associated with. Consequently, if we would like to have a variable that is used to store a value of "weight," we may declare it with a data type of int (integer) or double as follows:

```
private int weight;
weight = 123;

or

private double weight;
weight = 123.45;
```

Different data type allocates different size of memory location for storing different size of values. Of course, the data type also supports the type checking, which means only same data type is allowed to appear on the two sides of an assignment statement.

2.5 Constructor Method of a Class

Java globally classifies two kinds of data types. One is called "primitive" data type referring to real data, such as int, double, char, and the like. The other kind is termed as "reference" data type that is used to store an address of another memory location that carries an object. When an executable code of a program is loaded into the main memory and to be executed, the program becomes a "process." A process occupies an address space in the main memory. The address space consists of three sections of code, data, and heap. The data with the primitive data types are allocated in the data section, and the data with the reference data types are allocated in the heap section.

For example, the variable "message" in the project HelloWorld2 has a type of String. Here, "String" refers to the built-in class String defined in the APIs of the Java language. Because "String" is a class, the string value "Hello World!" is an object, which is stored in the "heap" area. Thus, the variable "message" does not store the real string but stores the address of the object. In short, variables of primitive data types store real data; but variables of reference data type carry an address that refers to another location in the heap section that stores an object. These two kinds of variables are depicted in Fig. 2.2.

Furthermore, the following two assignment statements mean that the first statement assigns the address of the string "Hello World!" to the variable message. And then, the second statement assigns the address to the other variable anotherString so that both variables hold the same address and refer to the same string.

```
String message = "Hello World!";
String anotherString = message;
```

Because the variable "message" refers to the String data "Hello World!," the statement "System.out. println(message);" performs the save function to display the data "Hello World!" on the screen. That is, the new version HelloWorld2 performs the same function as the first version HelloWorld, even though the new version uses a variable "message."

2.4 Variable Scope

Variables not only have different data types but also have different living times. The different living times are called "variable scope." The scope of a variable means the life span of the variable, which is based on the access modifier and the context of the code. For example, the variable "message" is declared inside the class HelloWorld2.java and its access modifier is "private." That means the life span of the variable "message" starts from the declaration and ends when the class HelloWorld2.java is finished. As mentioned before, a variable is a "piece of memory." Actually a class or a method is also a piece of sealed memory. When the execution of the class is finished, the entire memory location allocated to the class is closed and is returned back to the memory including the memory locations allocated to the variables inside the class. And later, the garbage collection will "erase" the class block from the memory. Similarly, if a local variable is declared inside a method, then its scope is that method. That is the life span of the local variable starts from the method starting its execution and ends when the method ending its execution. This kind of variables is also called "dynamic" variables in contrast with so-called "static" variables (that will be explained later). An easy way for recognizing the scope of "dynamic" variables is to look for the pair of curly brackets. The scope of a "dynamic" variable is the closest curly brackets that enclose the variable. Consequently, a "dynamic" variable can only be accessed in its scope. Or saying, a variable cannot be accessed outside its scope because a "dynamic" variable will be returned to the system before the execution exceeds its scope.

2.5 Constructor Method of a Class

Comparing the new version HelloWorld2 with the first version HelloWorld, we can also discover that the new version adds a new method "public HelloWorld2()" inside the class HelloWorld2.java. This method is different from the method main() with three special features. (1) Its name HelloWorld2 is exactly the same as the class name HelloWorld2. (2) It is a method; but its name starts with a capital letter, which "violates" the convention for declaring a method name. (3) It has the access modifier "public," but it doesn't have a return type indicator or "void."

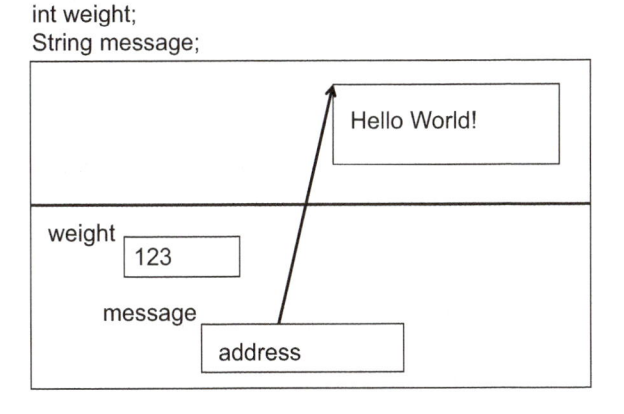

Fig. 2.2 The primitive data type and the reference data type

This kind of special method has a special term as "constructor" of the class that defines it. The goal of a constructor method is to construct an instance object of the class through initializing the attributes of the class. The method main() in the new version has a statement (line 24 in Listing 2.2):

```
new HelloWorld2();
```

The "new" is called "new operator" that is used to instantiate an object of the class that follows it; here it is the class "HelloWorld2". Actually, the "HelloWorld2()" after the "new" operator just refers to the constructor of the class.

Because the constructor is the first method that will be invoked when instantiating an object of the corresponding class, the constructor method is the place for initializing the attributes declared in the class with initial values so that the instantiated objects can be identified. That is, whenever a new object of the class is needed, a "new" operator involves the constructor to instantiate an object just like the first statement in the main() method "new HelloWorld2()" does. This statement instantiates an object of the class and executes the statements inside the constructor method, which initializes the variable "message" with the value of "Hello World!," and then it invokes the print-line statement System.out.println(message) to display the data stored in the variable "message" on the screen as the output of the program. Under this case, the method HelloWorld2() consists of two statements and can be understood as a "paragraph" in a "paper." (Note: the code of this constructor HelloWorld2() is not perfect. Please see the explanation of the next section.)

2.6 Reprogramming HelloWorld2 with Methods: The Project HelloWorld3

We may say that the coding of the project HelloWorld2 is not perfect since the constructor of the class HelloWorld2.java not only initializes the variable "message" but also invokes println() method, which digresses from the subject "constructor is for initializing the attributes defined in the class.

The programming pattern discussed in Chap. 1 indicates that a program should be improved better and better. Clearly, it is better to add a new method printMessage() to cover the printing action in order to move the printing action out of the constructor and make the constructor only for initializing attributes of the class.

The new version HelloWorld3.java class is shown in Listing 2.3. It cleans the function of the constructor and wraps the function of printing into a new method printMessage(). This rewriting makes the code more appearing toward our intension for implementing a Java program defined in the object-oriented paradigm.

Listing 2.3 The new version HelloWorld3

```
 1 /*
 2  * HelloWorld3.java -- To display a text string "Hello World!" on the screen.
 3  */
 4 package helloworld;
 5
10 public class HelloWorld3 {
11
12     private String message;
13
14     public HelloWorld3() {
15         message = "Hello, World!";
16     }
17
18     public void printMessage() {
19         System.out.println(message);
20     }
21
22     public static void main(String[] args) {
23         (new HelloWorld3()).printMessage();
24     }
25 }
```

A tiny attention should be paid to the code in the method main(). Regularly, the main() method instantiates an object of the class HelloWorld3.java by invoking the constructor for initializing the variable "message"; and then the object invokes the printMessage() method to display the String "Hello World!" on the screen as follows:

```
helloWorld3 = new HelloWorld3();
helloWorld3.printMessage();
```

Readers may try the above codes. But, it will raise a new requirement on defining "static" method. In order to postpone the explanation of the new requirement, we simply merge the two statements into one as follows:

```
(new HelloWorld3()).printMessage();
```

The (new HelloWorld3()) is the instantiated object, and it uses the dot notation to invoke the method printMessage().

2.7 The First User-Defined Class: The Project ShowMessage

Now we know that a Java program consists of classes. A class contains a set of attributes and a set of methods. The set of attributes is a set of variables declared inside the class. The set of attributes hold a set of values. When we instantiate an instance of the class, the constructor of the class initializes a set of attributes defined in the class. Different instances would have different set of values assigned to the set of attributes so that one instance can be identified and distinguished from others. That is, different instances have a same set of attributes but with different set of values. However, all of the instances have the same behaviors since the set of methods defined in the class is the same.

To better understand the description above, we take students as an example. In order to represent five "real" students, we can construct a class Student.java, which declares one attribute "name" and one method studyJava(). When we instantiate an instance student1 of the class Student.java and assign the attribute name with a value of "Smith," we mimic the "real" student Smith. Then we can instantiate another instance student2 with a name of "Brown" to mimic another "real" student Brown. Because two objects have different values assigned to the attribute "name," they are distinguishable, and they represent two "real" student objects in the real world. At the same time, both of them have the same behavior studyJava().

Keeping the concept of a class in mind, we can easily figure out that the new version project HelloWorld3 has a variable "message," a constructor, and an action method printMessage(). Putting the variable "message" and the two methods together, it mimics a real object called message in our real life. Consequently, we can group the attribute "message" and the related methods to form a new class, which is the class Message.java illustrated in the project ShowMessage as cited in Listing 2.4. In other words, the project ShowMessage now has two classes: the main class ShowMessage.java and the new class Message.java.

Listing 2.4 The complete code of the project ShowMessage

```
1  /*
2   * ShowMessage.java - A main class for the project ShowMessage.
3   */
4  package showmessage;
5
10 public class ShowMessage {
11
12     public static void main(String[] args) {
13         (new Message()).printMessage();
14     }
15 }
```

```
1  /*
2   * Messsage.java - A class for defining messages.
3   */
4  package showmessage;
5
10 public class Message {
11
```

```
12      private String message;
13
14      public Message() {
15          message = "Hello World!";
16      }
17
18      public void printMessage() {
19          System.out.println(message);
20      }
21  }
```

The function performed by the project ShowMessage is still to "print a message on the monitor." That is, we may design it as a project that has only one class like the project HelloWorld3, or we may also design it as a project that has two classes like the project ShowMessage. The reason for using two classes lies on that the class Message.java could be a reusable component whenever a project needs to print a message on the monitor. For that purpose, the main class ShowMessage.java might go through the statement "messageObj = new Message()" to instantiate an object messageObj from the class Message.java. As mentioned before, the "new" operator invokes the constructor of the class Message.java, which initializes the variable "message" through the assignment statement "message = 'Hello World!'" And then the main class calls the method printMessage() defined inside the class Message.java for printing the message on the monitor with the method invocation statement "messageObj.printMessage()."

After understanding these concepts and practices, we can write down the steps above in using our natural language as follows:

1. Create two classes ShowMessage.java and Message.java. The ShowMessage.java class instantiates an object messageObj of the class Message.java. The constructor of the class Message.java initializes the variable "message" with a String.
2. The ShowMessage.java class then invokes the method messageObj.printMessage() to print the String on the monitor.

This is called a pseudo code, which outlines "what" we are going to do for realizing our goal. It is written in our natural language English. And then, we can follow the pseudo code to map the idea into piece of code in Java as shown in Listing 2.4. The list of the steps in natural language is also formally termed as an "algorithm."

Based on this example, we can see that usually we divide the process for writing a program into two stages. The first stage is called design stage: we design a pseudo code using the natural language to clearly define "what" should be done. The pseudo code could be posted to a team for a discussion, and then the pseudo code could be refined and refined as a "perfect" pseudo code. And then, the "perfect" pseudo code is further mapped onto Java language code in the second stage called implementation stage. It is so-called "top-down" approach. For more complicated projects, we have to make our mind very clear "what should be done" before paying our efforts for the implementation.

This example assures us that building a class and implementing a class is not difficult whenever we know what we are intend to do. In this example, we would like to "print a message on the monitor." The noun "message" could be modeled as an object, which corresponds to a class. In the class we need an attribute "message" for holding a String and a method for realizing the verb "print."

Apparently, the class Message.java is the first class that defined by ourselves in addition to the first class HelloWorld.java. This kind of classes is called "user-defined" class since developers defined it. Every class is a module that mimics a corresponding object in our real world, which makes the object-oriented language further closer to the programming purpose of simulating our life.

One of the programming goals is to design and implement reusable modules so that they can be reused for increasing the reusability and maintainability of our software components and systems. Therefore, more and more modules were prebuilt and optimized as components included in the Java language libraries to reduce the developers' burdens. Java APIs is such a library that provides rich sets of reusable classes and components. These predefined classes in APIs are called as "built-in" classes. The class String is just such a built-in class. Every program can use the built-in class String for its own purpose. The built-in classes dramatically save programmers' efforts since they were perfectly coded by experts and have been debugged and optimized. They can be reused without "reinventing the wheel."

2.8 The Problem of "Hard Coded"

The four projects, HelloWorld, HelloWorld2, HelloWorld3, and ShowMessage, actually perform the same function, "print a string 'Hello World!' on the screen." They either directly place the string inside the println() method or assign the string to a variable in the coding. No matter which way, the value of the string is unchangeable. This is so-called hard coded, which means that the output string cannot be changed when the program is in running time. This kind of programs is useless since the output of the program is fixed.

For allowing a program to change its output, we must allow the program to initialize its input with different values. As mentioned above, the purpose of the constructor of a class is to initialize the value of the attributes defined in the class; thus, one approach for solving the "hard-coded" problem is to modify the constructor "public Message()" defined for the class Message.java as follows:

```
public Message(String inStr) {
    message = inStr;
}
```

And then, when invoking the "new" operator, we can pass in a new message to initialize the variable "message" as follows:

```
new Message("Hello, Java!")
```

This statement can be used to assign any string to the variable "message" when instantiating a new object of the class Message.java such that the program can print different strings on the monitor.

This modification gives the new constructor "Message(String inStr)," a variable "inStr" inside the parentheses, which is termed as the "formal parameter" of the method. As we known that a method is a piece of "sealed" memory. A method usually performs a computation or an action so that it requires input data sometimes. The "formal parameter" of a method opens a "window" for passing in an input data from outside of the method. As a variable, the formal parameter has its own data type. When the method is invoked, the formal parameter accepts an input data that is called an "actual parameter." The formal parameter carries the value of the actual parameter into the method to join the computation or the action defined in the body of the method.

In this case, the formal parameter "inStr" carries the actual parameter of "Hello, Java!" and assigns the value to the variable "message," and then the new value is printed on the monitor.

Clearly, by defining a formal parameter for the constructor "Message(String inStr)," the contents of the variable "message" can be assigned as any other strings. It seems that the "hard-coded" problem is solved. Unfortunately, the statement "new Message('Hello, Java!');" is still predefined inside the codes. Only the programmer can change the value of the actual parameter when he/she codes the statement "new Message('a new string')." In other words, this new input happens in the "compile time"; the user of the program is still unable to assign a new value to the project during the "run time." The only way to really solve the "hard-coded" problem is to provide an input part for the project in order to accept the user's input from outside of the project during "run time."

2.9 Adding an Input Portion: The Project ShowMessage2

Consequently, we further improve the project ShowMessage into a new version ShowMessage2 by adding an input portion for allowing the user to input any string as they like during the "run time."

Where to add and how to adding an input portion into a project? The purpose of the input part is to allow the users inputting a string to be printed on the monitor screen. Thus, we should add the input portion into the class Message.java so that the user-inputted string could be assigned to the variable "message." No doubt, the input part requires an input mechanism to accept the new string issued by the user from the external of the project on the "run time." Java provides different techniques for doing it. Here, we introduce an intuitive one and include it in the new project ShowMessage2. The input mechanism is adopted in the class Message.java as shown in Listing 2.5.

Listing 2.5 The class Message.java in the project ShowMessage2

```
1  /*
2   * Messsage.java - A class for defining messages.
3   */
4
5  package showmessage;
6
7  import javax.swing.JOptionPane;
8
13 public class Message {
14
15     private String message;
```

```
16
17      public Message() {
18      }
19
20      public void initMessage() {
21          message = JOptionPane.showInputDialog("Enter a String: ");
22      }
23
24      public void printMessage() {
25          System.out.println(message);
26      }
27  }
```

Java language provides a built-in class JOptionPane as an input mechanism. In order to access the built-in class, our source code Message.java class must import the built-in class. Thus, the class Message.java needs to add an "import javax.swing.JOptionPane;" statement at the beginning of the class (line 7). The intelligent source code editor in the IDE NetBeans can help us to add the statement into the source code. When we edit a piece of code, if the source code deals with a built-in class, such as the class JOptionPane, we can move the cursor to any empty spot in the source-editing window and right click the mouse for popping up a context menu. Select the menu item "Fix Imports"; the related import statement will be added into the source code. These predefined classes are grouped into packages. The "import" statement should indicate both the package name (e.g., javax.swing) and the class name (e.g., JOptionPane).

In order to add the input mechanism, in the class Message.java, we add a new method initMessage(), where the statement "message = JOptionPane.showInputDialog('Enter a string')" will pop-up a small window for allowing the user to enter input data as shown in Fig. 2.3. The user of the project can enter any String, say "Hello, Java!" into the text field, and click the OK button. The input dialog then assigns the user's input data to the variable "message." And then the content of the variable "message" will be displayed on the monitor through the invocation of the method printMessage() defined in the class Message.java.

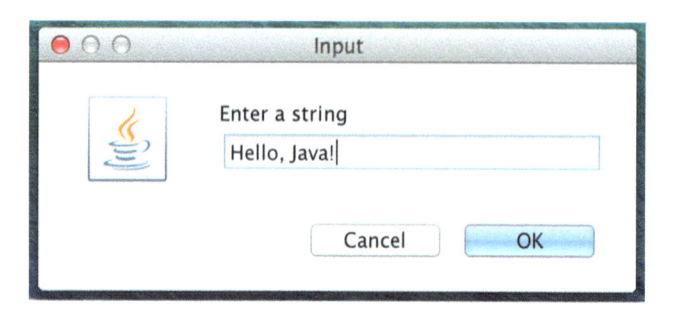

Fig. 2.3 A screenshot of the input mechanism JOptionPane.showInputDialog()

Reaching this point, we can say that the program has no "hard coded." In addition, the program now has two portions: input and output. However, all of the data should be String type because the return value of the input mechanism JOptionPane is a String. In case the user would like to input other data types, for example, int or double, extra codes should be added to convert the inputted String type into int or double type. These conversions will be discussed after we learned other data types.

2.10 Designing and Implementing a New Project: The Project PrintXmasCard

Based on the concepts and experiences gained from the project ShowMessage, we may apply them to more projects. Let us try to design and implement a project PrintXmasCard for making a Christmas card. Every year, we probably send out many Christmas cards for parents and friends. Christmas cards have so many different styles. Assume that we would like to have a box of 12 cards with the same style. In our daily life, for making 12 same style cards, the printing shop should design and produce a mold and then use the mold to print 12 times for producing 12 card objects with the same style.

Following the concept of the object-oriented programming, we can design and implement a class XmasCard.java that plays the role of the printing mold. And then, apply the "new" operator 12 times for instantiating 12 instances of the class XmasCard.java in order to make 12 card objects with the same style. If we would like to have another new style, we can design and implement another class, say XmasCard2.java, to produce the number of instances in the new style as wished. It is the relationship between an object and its corresponding class.

From the two projects HelloWorld and ShowMessage above, we can tell that the output of the programs is the target we are pursuing. Therefore, the output of a program not only determines the code of the output part but also affects the design and implementation of the input part and the computation part. Consequently, when we start writing a program, we

Mom and Dad

Merry Christmas and Happy New Year!

Julie

Fig. 2.4 A Christmas card designed for the project PrintXmasCard

should have a clear mind about what output of the program should be. Now suppose that we would like to have a simple Christmas card as shown in Fig. 2.4.

This Christmas card displays three lines, which refer to the recipient's name, the season greeting string, and the card sender's name, respectively. Obviously, the recipient's name and the card sender's name should be changeable for different receivers and senders. The season greeting is temporally kept as a "hard-coded" string like "Merry Christmas and Happy New Year!" Based on this design, we can start coding the class XmasCard.java.

2.11 A New User-Defined Class: The Class XmasCard.java

The class XmasCard.java is not a prebuilt class in the APIs of the Java language but is defined by us as a programmer. That is, it is a "user-defined class." Besides the class XmasCard.java, the project needs a main class, too. The main class only instantiates an object of the class XmaxCard.java and invokes the methods possessed by the object to make a card.

In order to design and implement the class XmasCard.java, we would be better to work it out in two steps as discussed above. The first step is the design stage in that we draft an outline or a blueprint for making the card. As we mentioned before, the outline is called "pseudo code" or "use case." This step gives us a chance to have a brainstorm and a team work for analyzing and synthesizing different ideas and different styles. And then, in the second step, we turn to implement the pseudo code by using the Java language such that we map the outline in the natural language into the real programming language code.

The class XmasCard.java can be described in a pseudo code as follows:

1. The user inputs the recipient's name (input part).
2. The season greeting string hard coded as "Merry Christmas and Happy New Year!!!" (hard-coded input).
3. The user inputs the sender's name (input part).
4. Print the three strings on a card (output part).

Following this outline, the code of the class XmasCard.java and the main class are as in Listing 2.6.

Listing 2.6 The classes PrintXmasCard.java and XmasCard.java in the PrintXmasCard project

```
 1  /*
 2   * PrintXmasCard -- The main class for printing a Christmas card
 3   */
 4  package printxmascard;
 5
10  public class PrintXmasCard {
11
12      private static XmasCard aCard;
13
17      public static void main(String[] args) {
18          aCard = new XmasCard();
19          aCard.printCard();
20      }
21  }
```

```
 1  /*
 2   * XmasCard.java -- A class for defining a Christmas card
 3   */
 4  package printxmascard;
 5
 6  import javax.swing.JOptionPane;
 7
```

```java
12 public class XmasCard {
13
14     private String recName;
15     private String merryXmas;
16     private String signature;
17
18     public XmasCard() {
19         initCard();
20     }
21
22     private void initCard() {
23         recName = JOptionPane.showInputDialog("Enter recipient's name: ");
24         merryXmas = "    Merry Christmas and Happy New Year!!!";
25         signature = JOptionPane.showInputDialog("Enter sender's name: ");
26     }
27
28     public void printCard() {
29         System.out.println(recName);
30         System.out.println();
31         System.out.println(merryXmas);
32         System.out.println();
33         System.out.println(signature);
34     }
35 }
```

Referring to the output of the Christmas card shown in Fig. 2.4 and the pseudo code above, the XmasCard.java class needs three attributes corresponding to the three lines in the card: the recipient's name, the season greeting, and the sender's name. A method initCard() is implemented to initialize the three attributes. Among them, the recipient's name and the sender's signature are input data provided by the user through the input mechanism JOptionPane. The season greeting is a hard-coded string. The constructor of the class XmasCard.java invokes the method initCard() for getting the three Strings. The other method printCard() produces the output through five invocations of the method println(), which prints out the resulting card.

We could also link the three short strings into a long string and use only one println() to print the long string on the card. Linking shorter strings together as a long string is called string concatenation, which could be made as follows:

```
 System.out.println(recName + "\n\n" + merryXmas + "\n\n" + signature);
```

The string concatenation can be done by using the "+" sign. Two "\n\n" signs are used to make blank lines in the output. A single "\n" represents a new line for making a "new line." Hence, the first "\n" in one "\n\n" moves the cursor to the next line, and the second "\n" further moves the cursor to another line. Thus, one "\n\n" creates a blank line between two printing lines for producing the output exactly as the designed output shown in Fig. 2.4. Definitely, we may alternatively create a new method concatenateStrings() to explicitly concatenate the three short strings.

As long as the class XmasCard.java is available, the main class PrintXmasCard.java uses its main() method to instantiate an object aCard from the class XmasCard.java with the invocation of the method initCard() to initialize three attributes and goes through the "dot notation" aCard.printCard() to invoke the method printCard() possessed by the object aCard for making the required output.

2.12 Using a Permanent Storage File: The Project PrintXmasCard2

For keeping the simplicity, in the project PrintXmasCard, the season greeting string is "hard coded." Definitely, it would be better to have different greeting strings for different cards. The JOptionPane is still a convenient input mechanism to allow users for inputting a different greeting string for making a new card.

However, usually the season greeting string could be a long string, and users do not create it but find it from existing resources; inputting season greeting string by interactively typing is not an enjoyable approach in this case. A more convenient approach for inputting long existing strings is to use text files. As mentioned before, text files are a piece of permanent storage in a secondary memory, such as a hard disk, a USB, and the like, where texts can be stored permanently.

2.13 Absolute File Path and Relative File Path

Using text files has at least two advantages. Firstly, it saves repeated typing efforts and avoids typos during the run time. Secondly, we may pre-implement a library that has a rich set of greeting strings stored in different files. The user simply selects a suitable file and inputs a suitable season greeting from the file to the program.

For using this approach, clearly, we need to complete the following steps:

1. Locate a text file and get the object of the text file.
2. Set up a channel for reading the stored greeting strings from the text file.
3. Input the read-in data to the program.

The first step above is not detailed enough to be mapped into a piece of Java codes. We need to further refine it as follows: (1) specifying the file path and the file name, (2) allocating the URL (universal resource locator) corresponding to the file name, and (3) getting an object of the file. All of these terms and practices will be explained in the following sections.

2.13 Absolute File Path and Relative File Path

For realizing the task (1) above, we need to provide a specification for a file. All of files in a computer are organized as a file system, which is a directory hierarchy plus file names. For example, when we created a file with the name of "toXmas1.txt" under the directory "02_basic," where the project PrintXmasCard2 resides, the file path and the file name of both the project and the text file in Mac OS are as follows:

```
/Users/cxu/Documents/xuJavaGame170512/02_basic/PrintXmasCard2
/Users/cxu/Documents/xuJavaGame170512/02_basic/toXmas1.txt
```

Where "/Users" is the root directory of the entire file system. The group of directories starting from the root directory until the directory "02_basic" is termed as the absolute file path. Thus, for locating a file, we need both the file path and the file name. For allowing the project to access the text file "toXmas1.txt," we need to provide the absolute file path and the file name of the text file for the program. However, once we move the text file to another directory, the program won't be able to get in touch with the text file since the absolute file path of the text file is no longer the same. Even we keep the program and the text file in the same directory, when we move the program and the text file to another computer (assume that a student submitted his program to his teacher), the absolute file path of the text file will also be modified under the new computer.

In order to prevent the disadvantages of using the absolute file path, the other file path is termed as relative file path that is often used for programming. For that, we can place the text file inside the project PrintXmasCard2. For example, we create a new directory txt inside the project as shown in Fig. 2.5.

Clearly, the destination class ReadFile.java and the source text file "toXmas1.txt" have the following file path and the file name, respectively.

```
PrintXmasCard2/Source Packages/printxmas-card/ReadFile.java
PrintXmasCard2/Source Packages/txt/toXmas1.txt
```

That is, when the class "printxmascard/ReadFile.java" would like to access the text file "txt/toXmas1.txt," it should go up to the directory "Source Packages," then go down to the directory "txt," and then reaches the text file "toXmas1.txt." It is called the "relative file path" from "ReadFile.java" to "toXmas1.txt." Actually it is a route that starts from the "ReadFile.java" and ends on the text file "toXmas1.txt." This route is realized by the following code: "../txt/toXmas1.txt," where ".." means climbing up one layer along the directory

Fig. 2.5 (Left) The project structure. (Right) The file structure of the project PrintXmasCard2

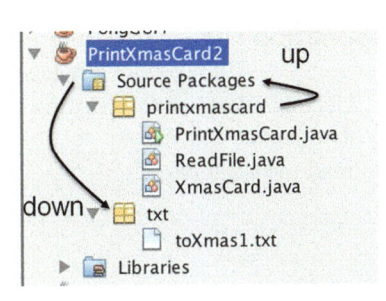

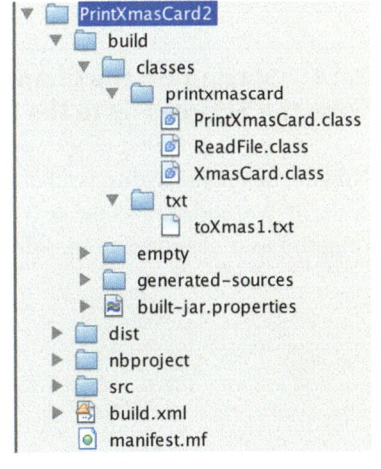

branch and reaching the shared directory "Source Packages" and "/txt" means going down to the directory "txt" and finally reaching "/toXmas1.txt."

Java provides a built-in method this.getClass() that can be used inside a class to return the position of the current class. When we invoke getClass() method inside the class ReadFile.java, it will return the string "printxmascard.ReadFile" (readers may verify it with the statement "System.out.println(getClass().toString());"). And then, the following complete statement will return the absolute file path and the file name for locating the text file toXmas1.txt.

```
getClass().getResource(
    "../txt/toXmas1.txt");
```

In other words, by indicating the relative file path, the code above can find the absolute file path. Due to the fact that the relative file path is a "fixed" string (because the relative positions of the ReadFile.java and the toXmas1.txt is "fixed"), no matter where the project is, the statement above will always guide the class ReadFile.java to get the text file toXmas1.txt correctly. (Readers my verify it with the System.out.println() to show the string returned by the statement "getClass().getResource("../txt/toXmas1.txt")".

The returned absolute file path is the URL of the text file. Thus, the following statement is used to hold the url:

```
URL url = getClass().getResource(
    "../txt/toXmas1.txt");
```

Continuously, the object of the file is instantiated with the following statement:

```
aFile = new File(url.getPath());
```

All of these ideas are implemented in the method initFile() of the ReadFile.java class, which also include the exception checking for "FileNotFound" possibly caused by a mistake in the specification of file path or file name.

2.14 Setting Up the Channel from the Source File to the Destination File

Now we can move to discuss the step 2 listed in the pseudo code. If we understand the text file as a source and the program as a destination, in order to read the contents of the text file and send it to the program, we need to facilitate it with a channel. Java provides many different kinds of channels for different input/output (I/O) cases. It would be a rather complicated topic. Since we talk about the channel between two files (the text file and the program file), we narrow down our attention to File I/O. In addition, we deal with the situation that the program searches for a text file and opens the file for reading; we only need an input part without the concern on the output part. The formats of the data flow from the source to the destination could be bytes (for 8 bits Byte) or characters (in Unicode conversion). Here we only interest in the character format since the data are strings. Therefore, we only discuss the channel called FileReader that is suitable for reading from a text file and transfer character by character along the channel.

The functionality of the FileReader is demonstrated in the project TestFileReader. The "core" code for reading is cited as follows:

```
inputFile = new FileReader(aFile);

int aCh;
String greeting = "";
while ((aCh = inputFile.read()) != -1) {
    greeting += (char) aCh;
}
```

The code indicates that the FileReader can only read in an integer aCh at a time, and we have to use "greeting += (char) aCh;" to convert an integer to a character and then concatenate the characters into a string.

Due to the fact that the program needs a season greeting that is a complete sentence and the contents of the file toXmas.txt contains a season greeting as a complete line, a more suitable flow is line by line. For that, we further adopt the stream BufferedReader to wrap the FileReader for transferring a complete line of words from the text file to the program. These ideas are implemented in the method readGreeting(). Clearly, the method readGreeting() is implemented based on the situation that the text file contains only one complete season greeting string as one line. More complicated situations will be dealt with in later projects. The complete class ReadFile.java is shown in Listing 2.7.

Listing 2.7 The class ReadFile.java in the project PrintXmasCard3

```
1  /*
2   * ReadFile.java -- To read a string from a file.
3   */
4  package printxmascard;
5
6  import java.io.BufferedReader;
7  import java.io.File;
8  import java.io.FileNotFoundException;
9  import java.io.FileReader;
10 import java.io.IOException;
11 import java.net.URL;
12
17 public class ReadFile {
18
19     private FileReader inputFile;
20
21     public ReadFile() {
22         initFile();
23     }
24
25     private void initFile() {
26         File aFile;
27         URL url = getClass().getResource("../txt/toXmas1.txt");
28         aFile = new File(url.getPath());
29         try {
30             inputFile = new FileReader(aFile);
31         } catch (FileNotFoundException ex) {
32         }
33     }
34
35     public String readGreeting() {
36         String line = null;
37         BufferedReader bufferedReader = new BufferedReader(inputFile);
38
39         try {
40             line = bufferedReader.readLine();
41             bufferedReader.close();
42         } catch (IOException ioex) {
43         }
44         return line;
45     }
46 }
```

When the class ReadFile.java is ready, the method readMerryXmas() defined in the class XmasCard.java can easily invoke readFile.readGreeting() to get a greeting string from the text file toXmas1.txt. The implementation of the class XmasCard.java is cited in Listing 2.8.

Listing 2.8 The class XmasCard.java in the project PrintXmasCard3

```
1  /*
2   * XmasCard.java -- A class for defining a Christmas card
3   */
4  package printxmascard;
5
6  import javax.swing.JOptionPane;
7
12 public class XmasCard {
13
14     private String recName;
15     private String merryXmas;
16     private String signature;
17
18     public XmasCard() {
19         initCard();
20     }
21
22     private void initCard() {
23         recName = JOptionPane.showInputDialog("Enter recipient's name: ");
24         merryXmas = readMerryXmas();
25         signature = JOptionPane.showInputDialog("Enter sender's name: ");
26     }
27
28     private String readMerryXmas() {
29         ReadFile rFile;
30         rFile = new ReadFile();
31         return "    " + rFile.readGreeting();
32     }
33
34     public String concatenateStrings() {
35         return (recName + "\n\n" + merryXmas + "\n\n" + signature);
36     }
37
38     public void printCard() {
39         String cardInfo;
40         cardInfo = concatenateStrings();
41         System.out.println(cardInfo);
42     }
43 }
```

2.15 Method and Its Parameter

The method initFile() defined in the class ReadFile.java contains three method calls:

```
URL url = getClass().getResource(
    "../txt/toXmas1.txt");
aFile = new File(url.getPath());
inputFile = new FileReader(aFile);
```

Where, every method receives a value or a variable as its actual parameter. We mentioned before, a method is a sealed location in the memory. The body of the method usually performs a computation or an action, which often requires input data. The parameter of the method just opens a window for accepting the input data from external. Thus, the body code of the method won't be modified, but different input data will produce different results. For example, the same method getResource(String fileName) will return different resource when the value of "fileName" is changed. In this way, a method can be easily reused. The other two statements involve two new operators for instantiating two objects of the corresponding classes. Following different actual parameters, they will instantiate different objects. Therefore, methods and their parameters are very powerful equipment for implementing reusable software units.

How do we know what parameters are required by a built-in method? The intelligent source code editor of the IDE NetBeans is much helpful. Whenever we have an object of a built-in class, we can type a "dot" after the object and wait for a millisecond; the source editor will pop-up a panel that shows all of the methods defined in the class with their parameters.

2.16 Return Value of a Method

The class XmasCard.java has two methods "public String readMerryXmas()" and "public String concantenateStrings()" which use "String" instead of "void" in their method title. At the same time, both methods have a "return" statement to return a String. Similarly, the class also has a method "public String readGreeting()" with the same feature. Each of this kind of methods generates and returns an output, and the output can be assigned to a variable on the left side of an assignment statement. The data type of the returned value must match with the data type defined with the method. At the same time, the returned value must also match with the data type of the variable on the left side of the assignment statement.

Thus, we can say that the parameter of a method plays the role of the input and the return statement of the method performs the output function. Certainly, many methods have both parameter and return statement. They are just like the mathematical notation y = f(x). Consequently, every method in a class may also consist of "input, computation, and output" three portions as depicted in Fig. 2.6.

2.17 Try-Catch Blocks

The method initFile() contains a special try-catch block, which enclosed the statement "inputFile = new FileReader(aFile);." This statement is to open the file aFile.

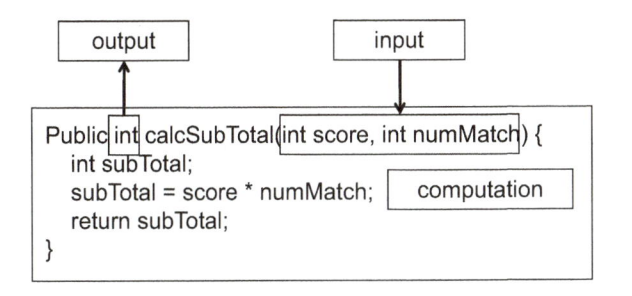

Fig. 2.6 A method may also consist of three portions "input, computation, output"

The open action may be failed due to certain reasons, for example, if the parameter aFile does not exist. In general, under the failure cases, the program has to be aborted because it cannot continue its execution. In contrast, the Java language provides special try-catch block to prevent the execution from abortion. Thus, a try-catch block acts as a special "exception handling." Exception means some predictable errors. The exception handling provides a "try" block to enclose the statement that might have failed. In case of failure, it will throw an exception, and then the "catch" block catches the exception and invokes an exception handler to handle the exception. In this case, the "catch" block intends to catch the exception of "FileNotFoundException." Very often, a "catch" block only prints a message or a trace of the calling stack to announce users what happened or advise users to make some decisions in order to prevent the program from abortion without reasons. In other words, a try-catch block is a kind of predefined error handling mechanism for making the error detection and error handling. We will learn more about the try-catch block along the way as more projects come in.

2.18 Reference Data Type

We learned that the smallest element of a Java program is a variable. The important properties of a variable are its data type and its scope. Java classifies all of data types into two big categories: reference data type and primitive data type.

The data type String is a typical example of reference data type. A statement "private String message" declares a variable "message" that has the data type of String that means the variable message refers to an object of the class String. It implies that a variable with reference data type is always associated with a class. Because a class defines a set of methods that implement the behaviors or abilities of the object, the variable of reference type thus also possesses the set of methods no matter the class is a built-in class or a user-defined class.

The built-in class String has the following defined methods just to name a few. When we have a statement "String helloW = 'Hello World!';," the variable helloW, thus, also has these methods.

1. charAt(int index): It can be used to access every individual character in a String. For example, helloW.charAt(0) will return the character 'H,' and helloW.charAt(4) will give the character 'o' (a character is denoted with a single quotation mark).
2. indexOf(int ch): helloW.indexOf('o'); returns the index of the first occurrence of the specified character 'o' within this string, which should be 4.
3. length(): helloW.length(); returns the length of integer 12 including a blank character and a character '!'.

4. compareTo(String anotherStr): helloW.compareTo("hello world!"); returns −32 since the method compareTo() returns the difference between the two ASCII number of the first different character in the two Strings. The first different character of the two strings "Hello, world" and "hello world!" is the first character of 'H' and 'h'; the method compareTo() returns (the ASCII code value of 'H' minus the ASCII code value of 'h'). If two strings have a different length but the shorter string is part of the longer string, then the method cannot find an index where two characters are different; the method compareTo() returns the length difference of the two strings (thisStr.length() − anotherStr.length()). The result of the comparison could be equal (if zero), less than (if negative), or larger than (if positive).
5. compareToIgnoreCase(String anotherStr): the method ignores the case difference in a comparison. Then, the statement helloW.compareToIgnoreCase("hello World!") returns 0. Because of "IgnoreCase," the character 'H' is equivalent to 'h', the two Strings contain exactly same sequence of characters and have the same length, and the result of the comparison is 0. Otherwise, the result will give the length difference between the two strings.
6. concat(String aStr): helloW.concat(" Ho, Ho."); returns "Hello World! Ho, Ho." The new string is the concatenation of the two strings and is stored in another location.
7. substring(int beginIndex, int endIndex): helloW.substring(6, 8); returns "Wo." The substring starts with the character at the index of 6 inclusively and ends with the character at the index of 8 exclusively. The length of the substring is (8 − 6).
8. contains(String aStr): helloW.contains("ell"); returns true.

We very often use "+" sign to concatenate short Strings into a long one. We have seen the example in the project PrintXmasCard. Here, we demonstrate it again.

```
String longStr = "He" + "llo," + "Java";
System.out.println(longStr);
// It prints "Hello, Java"
```

The concatenation is also very often directly performed inside the println() method.

A "short cut" for converting other data type to be a String type is to concatenate a String with the other data type because any String, even an empty String, concatenates "other type" ends up a String as follows:

```
// an empty String concatenates a double value
String aDoubleStr = "" + 12.34;
```

Consequently, when we study Java, one of the important tasks is to learn every built-in class and the methods defined in that class.

2.19 Primitive Data Type

Another big category of data types is called primitive data type, which includes the following definitions.

1. Integer. An integer is a numerical value without decimal point. Its value could be positive or negative. Java defines four kinds of integers.
   (a) Byte. 1 byte = 8 bits, which expresses the value of [−128, 127].
   (b) Short. 1 short = 2 bytes = 16 bits, which expresses the value of [−32768, 32767].
   (c) Int. 1 int = 4 bytes = 32 bits, which expresses the value of [−2147483648, 2147483647].
   (d) Long. 1 long = 8 bytes = 64 bits, which expresses the range of values [−9223372036854775808, 9223372036854775807]. A value with long data type is distinguished by appending an "L" letter behind the value. For example, long k = 622L;
2. Char. 1 char = 2 bytes (Unicode). A special attention must be noticed: a char requires a single quotation mark. For example,

```
char x = 'a'; // it is the character a
```

We must be clear that 'a' is different from "a." The 'a' (with single quotation mark) is a character (a primitive data type); the "a" (with double quotation mark) is a String (a reference data type).
3. Float and double. Both are numerical values with decimal point.
   (a) 1 float = 4 bytes. The maximum number of digits, including both integer part and decimal part, is 7. A 'f' or 'F' is attached to the end of a value such as:
      float x = 12.33f;
   (b) 1 double = 8 bytes. The maximum number of digits is 15. A 'd' or 'D' might be attached at the end of a value. If a numerical value with a decimal point does not have any letter attached, it will be recognized as a double type. Only those that have an 'f' or 'F' attached are a float type.
4. Boolean. It has only two values of "true" or "false." The value can be explicitly assigned and also can be implicitly assigned. For example,

```
boolean x  = true;

int a = 5;
int b = 10;
boolean x = a < b;
System.out.println(x);
// a "true" is shown on the screen
```

2.22 Exercises

Table 2.1 Summarizes all of the primitive data types in Java

Type	Size (bits)	Range	Example
boolean	1		True, false
char	16	\u0000 … \uFFFF	' ', 'a', 'A'
byte	8	Max = 127	−1, 0, 1, 127, …
short	16	Max = 32767	−1, 0, 1, 32767, …
int	32	Max = 2147483647	−1, 0, 1, …
long	64	Max = 9223372036854775807	−1L, 0L, 1L, …
float	32	+− 10^−38 … +− 10^38	−1.0f, 3.8f, …
double	64	+− 10^−308 … +− 10^308	−1.0, 3.899, …

2.20 Type Casting

The declaration of a variable with a primitive data type contains three parts as follows:

```
private int x;
public double y;
```

The first part is the modifier, the second is the data type, and the third part is the variable identifier. The data type defines the size of the memory location of the variable. Only those variables with the same data type can be assigned to each other. If two variables have different data types as declared above, they have to apply "cast" operation when one of them assigns its value to the other as follows:

```
x = (int)y;
```

The sign "(int)" means the value of variable y is casted from a double to an int. However, a double has 64 bits, and an int has only 32 bits. If the value of y is less than the maximum value of int (e.g., 999.99 < 2147483647), the cast will assign the integer part 999 of y to the variable x. When the value of y is larger than the maximum value of int (e.g., 2147483649.99 > 2147483647), the cast will assign the maximum int value of 2147483647 to the variable x. Under that case, the value assigned to the variable x differs from the original integer portion of y. That implies that "cast" may end with a wrong value. Reference data type is also can be casted. We will see examples later.

2.21 Summary

This chapter introduced a few fundamental programming concepts and statements of Java language. As an OOP language, Java programs are class based. The process for building up a project consists of two stages: the design stage and the implementation stage. In the design stage, a pseudo code is drafted and refined. The implementation stage maps the pseudo code to the source code in Java language.

Any project consists of three parts: input, computation, and output. Every project has a main class with a method main(). A class may use other classes to pursue certain goals. A class consists of a set of attributes and a set of methods. The attributes are variables. Every variable is a piece of memory location for temporarily storing data value. All of the variables have data types associated. The values of attributes distinguish object instances of a class. The methods realize the behaviors or abilities of the object. A method is a sealed memory location, which also possibly consists of input, computation, and output portions. The input, if any, appears as the parameter of the method; the output is the return value or an action. The method body accepts input and produces output through a set of statements that implement a computation or an action.

Every variable has a data type and a scope. Java classifies data types into "primitive" and "reference." A primitive data type stores an assigned value. A reference data type stores an address that refers to an object.

Due to the fact that our real world is made of objects, many corresponding classes are predefined as built-in classes in the Java APIs. We must familiarize ourselves with those built-in classes and their methods. Programmers can create "user-defined" classes to fit own needs. The example projects in this chapter explained and demonstrated these concepts and practices.

2.22 Exercises

Self-Reviewing Questions

1. Why do we need to define classes for writing a Java program?
2. What are the major components of a class?
3. Make an example to explain what an attribute is.
4. What is a variable?
5. What data types are included in the category of primitive data type?
6. What data types are called reference data type?
7. What is the scope of a variable?
8. When do we need the "cast" operation? Do we need to apply the cast operation when we assign an int value to a double variable? Why do you say so?
9. Make an example to explain why do we need to define methods in a class.
10. What method is called constructor of a class? What major function does a constructor method perform?

11. What is the special function of the method main()?
12. What are three major portions of a Java program? Which portion does the simplest program HelloWorld have?
13. A method possibly also has three portions. What is its input portion? What is its output portion? What is its computation portion? Make an example method that has three portions.
14. What are changed from the example project HelloWorld to the project ShowMessage?
15. What are changed from the project ShowMessage to the project PrintXmasCard?

Projects

1. The source code of a small project TryString is cited as follows. Starting from the method main(), following every method call and write down what will be shown corresponding to every println() statement. Finally, compile and run the project included in the directory to verify your answers.

```java
 1 /*
 2  * TryString.java - The main class of the project TryString.
 3  */
 4 package trystring;
 5
10 public class TryString {
11
12     private String sentence;
13     private String subStr;
14
15     public TryString() {
16         sentence = "Hello";
17     }
18
19     public void completeSentence() {
20         sentence = sentence.concat(", World");
21         System.out.println("Complete sentence = " + sentence);
22     }
23
24     public void strLength() {
25         System.out.println(sentence.length());
26     }
27
28     public void getSubStr() {
29         subStr = sentence.substring(7, 9); // (beginIndex, endIndex)
30         System.out.println("Sub-string = " + subStr);
31     }
32
33     public void compareStr() {
34         System.out.println(sentence.compareTo("hello, world"));
35         System.out.println(sentence.compareToIgnoreCase("hello, world"));
36     }
37
38     public void containStr() {
39         System.out.println(sentence.contains(subStr));
40     }
41
42     public void charIndex() {
43         System.out.println(sentence.indexOf('l'));
44     }
45
46     public void convertToString() {
47         String theValue = "" + 123;
```

```
48             int aInt = Integer.parseInt(theValue);
49             System.out.println("aInt = " + aInt);
50
51         }
52
53         public void convertValue() {
54             String aStr = "123";
55             System.out.println("Value is " + String.valueOf(aStr));
56         }
57
58         public void convertType() {
59             String aStr = "" + 12.34;
60             String bStr = String.valueOf(12.34);
61             System.out.println("aStr " + aStr + " bStr = " + bStr);
62         }
63
64         /**
65          * @param args the command line arguments
66          */
67         public static void main(String[] args) {
68             TryString tryString = new TryString();
69             tryString.completeSentence();
70             tryString.strLength();
71             tryString.getSubStr();
72             tryString.compareStr(); // returns -1, 0, +1
73             tryString.containStr();
74             tryString.charIndex();
75             tryString.convertToString();
76             tryString.convertValue();
77             tryString.convertType();
78         }
79 }
```

2. Write a Java program to test the following "cast" operations: assigning a double value to an int variable and vice versa and assigning a double value to a String variable and vice versa.

3. We discussed the concept of variable scope in this chapter. The following class code defines two global variables a and b as well as one local variable c. Will any statement in the code cause a compilation error? Why do you say so? Implement the code as a program, and correct all of errors, and then run it for catching the meaning of "scope."

```
12 public class TryScope {
13
14     private int a;
15     private int b;
16
17     public TryScope() {
18         a = 30;
19         b = 50;
20     }
21
22     public void printGlobal() {
23         System.out.println("a = " + a);
24         System.out.println("c = " + printLocal());
25     }
```

```
26
27      public void printLocal() {
28          int c = 100;
29          System.out.println("c = " + c);
30          System.out.println("b = " + b);
31          return c;
32      }
33
37      public static void main(String[] args) {
38          TryScope scope = new TryScope();
39          scope.printGlobal();
40          scope.printLocal();
41          System.out.println("The global variable a = " + scope.a);
42          System.out.println("The local variable c = " + scope.printLocal().c);
43      }
44 }
```

4. Design and implement a Java program for printing a Birthday Card.

5. Browse Internet for reading more articles about try-catch block in Java.

OO Programming Principle: A Game In-Text GuessInt

This chapter starts learning Java with games. Some simple games deal with Strings only. We call them as games in-text. We selected one of such game as our starting point. The game is called GuessInt that is a two persons' verbal guessing game. One person thinks of an integer between 1 and 100. The other person guesses what the integer would be. From the story of the game to a pseudo code and finally to an implementation, the entire process demonstrates the object-oriented programming principle, discusses several important Java control statements, and touches the try-catch block for exception handling.

The objectives of this chapter include:
1. A game in-text: the project GuessInt.
2. Java programming is based on objects.
3. From story to pseudo code to source code.
4. Random number generators.
5. A formula for getting a random integer in a range.
6. Control statements: if-then-else and while.
7. Checking possible errors when inputting data.
8. Try-catch block and own error checking.
9. A principle strategy for OOP programming.
10. Java operators and the modifier "static."

Even we only have a very limit of Java programming knowledge and skills, we are still able to start applying the fundamental concepts of Java programming for making games. Due to the fact that we only learned writing programs in using String (text) so far, we are going to develop a game in-text first. At the same time, definitely, we will enrich our knowledge and experiences along the way.

3.1 The Story of a Game In-Text: The Project GuessInt1

Some oral games, which are those games that can be played by two persons orally, only deal with text symbols. The first example is "Guess an integer." The game story is simple; person A thinks of an integer between 1 and 100. He/she asks his partner person B to guess what the value in his/her mind is. For making it as a program, we let the computer mimic person A and let the user playing the role of person B.

As the first step, we are going to draft a pseudo code according to the game story. As mentioned that any program consists of three portions: input, computation, and output. Definitely, output comes from computations, and the computations need input. That is, we have to follow the order of input, computation, and then output. In other words, any program has a sequential nature. No matter a program is a procedural, an object-oriented, or even a parallel, the sequential nature must be preserved. Consequently, when we think of a pseudo code, we actually are discovering and organizing the sequence of actions of the program.

For the first version of the program GuessInt1, we draft a simplified pseudo code as follows.

(Input)
1. The program makes an integer givenInt between 1 and 100 and prompts the player "start guessing."
2. The player inputs an integer guessedInt.

(Computation and output)
3. A counter numGuess is increased by one.
4. If (guessedInt > givenInt), the program prompts "too large" and goes to step 2.

© Springer Nature Switzerland AG 2018
C.-w. Xu, *Learning Java with Games*, https://doi.org/10.1007/978-3-319-72886-5_3

5. Else if (guessedInt < givenInt), the program prompts "too small" and goes to step 2.
6. Else if (guessedInt == givenInt), the program prompts "guess correct" and terminates the game, as well as displays the value of the counter numGuess.

The pseudo code above expresses the ideas and the sequence of actions of the game. We exactly follow it to implement the game as the project GuessInt1, which is included in the chapter's folder as reader's reference. The reason we are not going to study the code is that this source code of the project GuessInt1 is procedural not an object-oriented program in nature, which is not our target. What should an object-oriented program look like?

3.2 Object-Oriented Programming Is Based on Objects: The Project GuessInt2

The project GuessInt1 directly follows the pseudo code shown in the previous section. However, the implementation violates the essential principle of OOP programming, even though the code is inside a main class, which only satisfies the format of Java program. So, what does a real object-oriented program look like? From the story of the game GuessInt described in the previous section, we know that two persons, person A and person B, play the game. They interactively communicate to each other for performing the sequence of actions expressed in the pseudo code. Correspondingly, in the OOP paradigm, the project requires two objects to carry out the required actions and meanwhile preserve the actions in the sequence. Two objects are reflected as two classes in an object-oriented program, and actions are dispatched as behaviors into different classes.

Now be careful, the story describes person A and person B. Even though they both refer to persons, they are two persons with different behaviors. We must create two different classes to carry out different behaviors. One class refers to person A who plays a role of game initializer, and the other class refers to person B who plays a role of game player.

Intuitively, a class Initializer.java initializes the game with an integer givenInt in his/her mind and then signals the player to play the game. That means that another class Player.java receives the signal and provides a guessedInt. After the initializer receives the guessedInt, it compares the two integers givenInt against guessedInt. If the two integers are not equal, the player is signaled to guess one more time until the two integers are equal and the game is terminated. In other words, the game should be briefly expressed as follows.

Initializer	Player
1. Makes a givenInt	2. Inputs a qualified guessedInt
3. Match of givenInt and guessedInt?	4. Not match, go to step 2; match, terminate

Clearly, the initializer and the player have different behaviors, and they should be able to communicate to each other for signaling and passing data. How can we make the two classes communicate? There are two approaches. One is making the two classes directly sending data to each other. Actually, we have seen this kind of communication in the project PrintXmasCard, where the class XmasCard.java uses the class ReadFile.java to read a season greeting from the text file toXmas1.txt. And then, the class ReadFile.java returns the data to the class XmasCard.java. We may apply this approach to let the class Initializer.java use the class Player.java for getting the guessedInt. But, this approach makes one class controlling the other class. The other approach is to make a third class to be a "meeting place" for them to exchange data to each other. The second approach is preferred in this game. Thus, we create a third class to take care of communications between the two classes. This third object actually plays the role of a controller that instantiates the two objects and invokes behaviors of the two objects to perform their actions and their interactive activities. This third class could be the main class. However, we would like to make the main class as simple as possible. For all of these considerations, we construct the program with three classes besides the main class.

We name the third class as GamePanel.java, which is created as a "meeting place" that allows all of objects meet and communicate to each other. It is the class that instantiates both objects of the two classes and coordinates the two objects to perform corresponding actions according to the global sequence explored by the pseudo code. According to this design, the program could be depicted as Fig. 3.1. One important point that is worth to be emphasized again is that two partners' communications should strictly follow the global sequence of actions. This is the rule of all sequential programs. The sequence of actions is thus dispatched into two classes as their behaviors in following the sequential order as indicated with the number markers on Fig. 3.1.

Based on the communications among three classes GamePanel.java, Initializer.java, and Player.java, we can write down a new pseudo code for the second version of the game GuessInt2, which satisfies the principle of object-oriented programming.

The pseudo code for the second version GuessInt2 is as follows. (The numbers in parentheses correspond to the markers on Fig. 3.1):

Fig. 3.1 The conversations between the object initializer and the object player

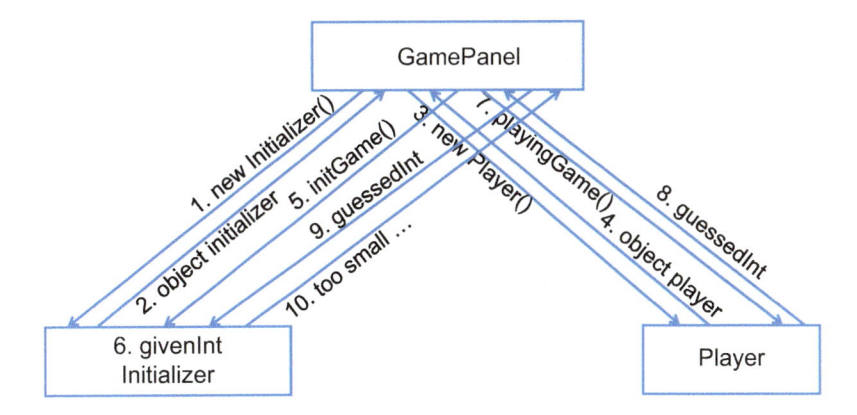

1. GamePanel.java instantiates an object of initializer (1 and 2).
2. GamePanel.java instantiates an object of player (3 and 4).
3. GamePanel.java invokes the method initializer.initGame() (5), which generates an integer givenInt between 1 and 100 (6).
4. GamePanel.java invokes the method player.playingGame() (7), which allows the player to input a guessedInt and return the value to GamePanel.java (8).
5. GamePanel.java feeds the value of guessedInt submitted by the player to the method initializer.receiveGuess() (9), which invokes initializer.isGuessCorrect() method for sending the judgment "too small," "too large," or "correct" to GamePanel.java (10).
6. If "correct," terminateGame() is invoked to display "Totally, you guessed xx times" and the game is terminated; else go to step 4.

The complete code that implements the pseudo code is cited in Listing 3.1.

Listing 3.1 The complete code of the project GuessInt2

```
 1 /*
 2  * GuessInt2.java - The main class of the project GuessInt2.
 3  */
 4 package guessint;
 5
10 public class GuessInt2 {
11
12     private String gameDescription;
13
14     public GuessInt2() {
15         gameDescription = "This is a game GuessInt. The game initializer "
16                 + "thinks of an integer between 1 and 100.\n"
17                 + "The game player guesses what the integer is.\n"
18                 + "The player who spent the least number of guesses "
19                 + "wins the game.\n";
20         System.out.println(gameDescription);
21         new GamePanel();
22     }
23
27     public static void main(String[] args) {
28         new GuessInt2();
29     }
30 }

 1 /*
 2  * GamePanel.java - A game manager for coordinating the two partners.
 3  */
```

```
 4  package guessint;
 5
10  public class GamePanel {
11
12      private Initializer initializer;
13      private Player player;
14      private int playerInt;
15      private boolean guessCorrect;
16      private int numGuess;
17
18      public GamePanel() {
19          guessCorrect = false;
20          numGuess = 0;
21          initPartner();
22      }
23
24      private void initPartner() {
25          initializer = new Initializer();
26          player = new Player();
27
28          startGame();
29      }
30
31      public void startGame() {
32          initializer.initGame();
33          playGame();
34      }
35
36      public void playGame() {
37          while (!guessCorrect) {
38              numGuess++;
39              playerInt = player.playingGame();
40              guessCorrect = initializer.receiveGuess(playerInt);
41          }
42          terminateGame();
43      }
44
45      public void terminateGame() {
46          System.out.println("Game terminates");
47          System.out.println("\nTotally, you guessed " + numGuess + " times.");
48      }
49  }
```

```
 1  /*
 2   * Initializer.java - The game initializer.
 3   */
 4  package guessint;
 5
10  public class Initializer {
11
12      private int givenInt;
13      private boolean match;
14
15      public Initializer() {
16      }
```

```java
17
18      public void initGame() {
19          givenInt = (int) (Math.random() * 100) + 1; // [1, 100]
20          match = false;
21
22          System.out.println("I already initialized the game with an integer "
23                  + "between 1 and 100 in my mind");
24          System.out.println("Please start your guess. Good luck!\n");
25      }
26
27      public boolean receiveGuess(int receivedGuess) {
28          match = isGuessCorrect(receivedGuess);
29          return match;
30      }
31
32      public boolean isGuessCorrect(int playerGuess) {
33          boolean correct = false;
34          if (playerGuess == givenInt) {
35              System.out.println("Initializer: your guess " + playerGuess
36                      + " is correct!");
37              correct = true;
38          } else if (playerGuess > givenInt) {
39              System.out.println("Initializer: Your guess " + playerGuess
40                      + " is too large");
41          } else if (playerGuess < givenInt) {
42              System.out.println("Initializer: your guess " + playerGuess
43                      + " is too small");
44          }
45          return correct;
46      }
47 }
```

```java
 1 /*
 2  * Player.java - The game player.
 3  */
 4 package guessint;
 5
 6 import javax.swing.JOptionPane;
 7
12 public class Player {
13
14      private String guessedIntStr;
15      private int guessedInt;
16
17      public Player() {
18      }
19
20      public int playingGame() {
21          guessedIntStr = JOptionPane.showInputDialog(
22                  "Enter an guess between 1 and 100");
23          guessedInt = Integer.parseInt(guessedIntStr);
24          System.out.println("Player: My guess is " + guessedInt);
25          return guessedInt;
26      }
27 }
```

Clearly, the method initPartner() of the class GamePanel. java instantiates two objects of initializer and player. And then, it invokes the method startGame() that in turn invokes the method playGame(). These two methods implement the global sequence of actions. The method playGame() has a statement "while(…) { }" that is a "while" loop for driving the sequence of actions repeatedly until the guessedInt equals the givenInt. This repeated loop is caused by the "go to step 4" inside the step 6 of the pseudo code. We will explain the meaning of the "while" loop soon.

So far, we described the process of analysis and design, as well as the implementation of the project GuessInt2. Now, we turn our attention to understand the codes for learning Java language.

3.3 Getting a Random Integer Using a Random Number Generator

How can the class Initializer.java "think" of an integer given-Int in the range of [1, 100] in mind? The integer givenInt is an arbitrary value between 1 and 100 inclusively. Whenever we need an "arbitrary value," we can invoke a built-in class or method called a random number generator to get a number randomly. Java provides two random number generators. One is a method random() defined in the built-in class Math; the other is a class Random defined in the package java.util. Java built-in class Math provides a huge set of mathematical functions, such as, random(), abs(), and max(), just to name a few. The method random() gives a positive double value of [0.0, 1.0). It means that the random() generator may give a value of 0.0 until 0.999…9, which includes the value of 0.0 but excludes the value of 1.0.

If we ask for a random integer between min = 1 and max = 100 inclusively, then a statement aDouble = (Math. random() * max) will give a possible value of [0.0, (max-1).99…9]. Applying a "cast" operation to convert the aDouble to be an integer anInt = (int)(aDouble), the result will be a possible integer in the range of [0, 99]. And then, add the min to the anInt, the result will be a possible integer [1, 100]. The following equation summarizes the entire process.

```
anInt = (int)(Math.random() * max) + min;
```

It is what we would like to have. But, the equation is derived based on the special case for getting an integer in the range of [1, 100]. If we apply the special equation to other cases, the result could be wrong. For example, we would like to have an integer in the range of [5, 99]. We assign min = 5 and max = 99. But, the above equation gives an integer in the range of [5, 103], which is not what we want. Therefore, the correct general formula should be as follows.

```
randomInt = (int)(Math.random() * (max - min
    + 1)) + min;
randomInt = (int)(Math.random() * 95) + 5;
randomInt in [0, 94] + 5
randomInt in [5, 99] = [min, max]
```

Java also provides another random number generator, the built-in class Random defined in the package of java.util, which has more methods that can generate random numbers in different data types. For our case, we would like to have a positive integer value in the range of [min, max]. One of the methods nextInt(int bound) (the value of bound must be positive) in the built-in class Random will return a random integer directly in the range of [0, bound]. Therefore, the following statements will satisfy our need.

```
Random ran = new java.util.Random();
randomInt = ran.nextInt(max - min + 1) +
    min;
```

3.4 The Control Statement "if-then-else"

We have known that all programs have a sequential nature. That is, programs must be executed starting from the first statement, then second statement, until the last statement sequentially. However, along the way, many conditions may enforce the program to jump, to skip some statements, or to "go to back" of some points. For reaching these purposes, some special statements are designed, which are called control statements. It is just like in our real life, we often consider some special conditions to adjust our regular life schedules. For example, someone may think about a travel plan: If I have a 10 days' vacation, I am going to New York; otherwise, if I have only 5 days, I plan to visit my parents in Chicago. That is, where to go depends on the length condition of the vacation. For checking the condition, Java provides an "if-then-else" statement as one of popular control statements.

The method isGuessCorrect() in the class Initializer.java requires "if" control statement because the results of the comparisons between the integer guessedInt against given-Int could be "too large," "too small," or "equal." These different conditions need different pieces of handling codes. When the method isGuessCorrect() gets the actual parameter of playerGuess, which is the copy of the value guessedInt entered by the player, the method isGuessCorrect() compares the value of the actual parameter with the givenInt to make a judgment whether match or not. It may involve three different results "equal," "larger than," or "less than." Here, the if-then-else statement should be hired to check these different conditions. The structure of the if-then-else statement is as follows.

```
if (condition 1 is true) {
   take action 1;
} else if (condition 2 is true) {
   take action 2;
} else { // both conditions above are false
   take other action;
}
```

In the statement, "if" checks a condition. No matter what value or expression inside the parenthesis, it must be evaluated as a value of true or false. When condition 1 is not true, the execution of the program skips the piece of codes inside the "if" block and jumps to "else if" for checking the condition 2. The entire program is executed sequentially, but some codes won't be executed when its condition is not true. We may also rewrite the method isGuessCorrect() by using a nested if-then-else statement as follows.

```
if (playerGuess == givenInt) {
   ...;
   correct = true;
} else { // not equal
   if (playerGuess > givenInt) {
      ...;
   } else { // if (playerGuess <
            //givenInt)
      ...;
   }
}
```

This nested if statement separates the "match" from the "not match" first. Then, under the "not match" situation, it further checks "larger than" or "less than." Hence, when the "match" is true, it can completely ignore the other two comparisons inside the "else" part. One syntax should be emphasized is the pair of curly brackets. Whenever more than one statement should be grouped together, a pair of curly brackets must be used; otherwise, when the statement is single, the curly brackets could be ignored.

3.5 The Control Statement "while"

The pseudo code has the statement "go to step 4," which indicates that the next step is not continuously go forward from the current step to the next step but should be "go back" to some points before the current step. This "go back" will allow some statements to be executed again. Definitely, the "go back" is under certain conditions. When the condition is true, "go back" will be realized, and some codes will be executed again. When the condition becomes false, "go back" will stop, and the program will go ahead sequentially.

Certainly, the "go back" will cause a block of statements to be repeatedly executed, which forms a so-called loop. Java provides a "while" statement for making such a loop and is called "while loop." We may understand that a "while" statement is an extension of an "if" statement because both of them are based on conditions. Once the condition is true, the block of statements inside the curly brackets of the "while" is executed; otherwise, the statements are skipped, and the execution jumps to the first statement after the end curly bracket of the "while" loop. Definitely, the "while" is different from the "if" since the "while" checks the condition multiple times until it is false. But the "if" checks the condition only once without "go back." The method playGame() in the class GamePanel.java is a typical example as follows.

```
36   public void playingGame() {
37      while (!guessCorrect) {
38         numberGuess++;
39         playerInt = player.playingGame();
40         guessCorrect =
            initializer.receiveGuess(playerInt);
41      }
42      terminateGame();
43   }
```

The code block enclosed in the pair of the curly brackets of the "while" statement would be executed repeatedly depends on the "while" condition. The code block of this "while" loop invokes the "player.playingGame()" method for getting a guess value returned by the method and assigning it to the variable "playerInt," which is in turn passed into the method "initializer.isGuessCorrect(playerInt)" for getting a returning value of "true" or "false." If the variable "guessCorrect" gets a value of "false," it means the player's guess is not matching with the value of givenInt; the "while" permits the code block inside the curly brackets to be executed one more time. Otherwise, the "while" enforces the execution jumping to the end of the "while" to invoke the method terminateGame(). How many loops will the "while" perform? It is unpredictable but totally depending on the player-inputted value of guessedInt.

The code in the loop can be depicted as a flowchart shown in Fig. 3.2.

The flowchart on Fig. 3.2 depicts the pseudo code step 6. A diamond in the flowchart refers to a condition checking. The top diamond checks the "while" condition of "!guessCorrect" for the "while" loop. The variable "guessCorrect" is initialized with a Boolean value of "false." The sign "!" means "not" so that the notation of "!guessCorrect" means "not false," which has the value of "true." Thus, the execution enters the "while" loop to execute the step "input guessedInt," which receives the player's input. And then, the flow reaches the second diamond for checking the condition "guessedInt < givenInt." If it is true, the arrow goes back to the "while" condition that has the value of "!guessCorrect" again. If the condition "guessedInt < givenInt" is false, the execution goes to the next diamond for checking

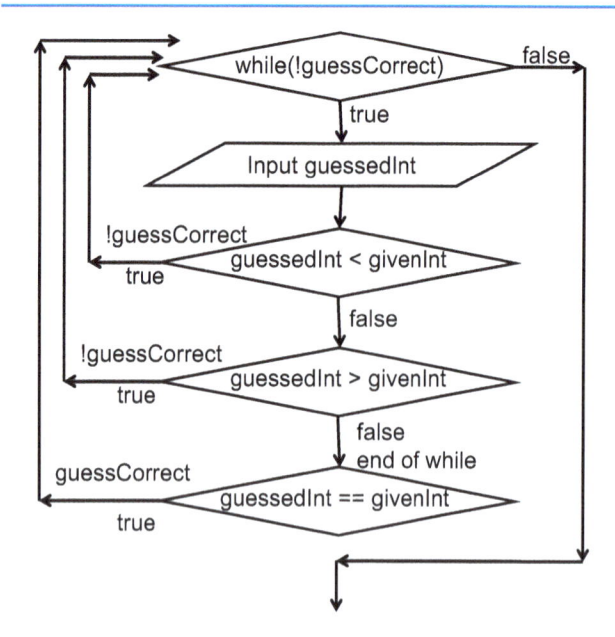

Fig. 3.2 A flowchart of "while" and "if" statements in the method playGame()

"guessedInt > givenInt." Similarly, it ends up either go back to the "while" condition or go to the third diamond. When the execution goes to the third diamond, the condition must be true. It makes the value of "guessCorrect" true. Thus, "!guessCorrect" gives the value of "false." The false condition won't allow the execution entering the loop again but enforce the execution jumping to the statement after the ending curly bracket of the "while" statement. The code that corresponds to the three diamonds for checking the three conditions is implemented inside the method initializer.receiveGuess(playerInt), which checks the three conditions and returns the result "true" or "false" to the variable guessCorrect for controlling the "while" loop. Hence, a flowchart may clearly illustrate the logic of an application for helping programmers writing a correct program or helping users to catch the meaning of the code.

The discussion above gives a key point in writing a "while" loop. The key point is that the condition of the "while" loop must possibly be changed from "true" to "false" by the code block inside the "while" statement. Otherwise, a "while" loop would become an "infinite loop."

3.6 Passing Data by Using Function Invocations

The code of the class GamePanel.java tells that the communications between the objects initializer and player rely on the class GamePanel.java to invoke the related methods available in the two objects. These methods have a "return" statement to return required data from one object to the other.

Clearly, methods could have a return value or no return value. A method has a return value that looks like a function that follows the mathematical notation $y = f(x)$. Consequently, functions are very often designed for passing data.

3.7 Verifying Input Data: The Project GuessInt3

The project GuessInt2 works perfectly only when the player exactly follows the game rule, which asks the player to input "an integer between 1 and 100." However, anything might happen during the time when the player inputting data, such as the input value could be mixed with characters, the value could be out of the range of [1, 100], and so on, especially when the player is a kid who may not know the requirements for inputting the data. That is, whenever a program asks for an input data, programmers do need to verify whether the user inputs a qualified data.

Thus, it is a good practice for ensuring a qualified input data to be sent to a program. For the project GuessInt2, an immediate checking for possible errors should be performed after the player finished his/her input actions before the inputted data are sent to the initializer. In order to realize this checking, a new version GuessInt3 is developed with a new method isQualifiedData() is added. This checking method is better to be added into the class Player.java and is immediately invoked after the player submitted his/her input data. Only when the method isQualifiedData() returns "true," the inputted data can be further sent to the initializer. Otherwise, the program must ask the player to input a data again until the data is qualified.

What should be done? Obviously, a new "while" loop should be involved. We need to modify the step 4 listed in the pseudo code for the version GuessInt3 as follows.

4. GamePanel.java invokes the method player.playingGame() (the step 7 on Fig. 3.1), which asks the player for inputting a *qualified integer* guessedInt and returns the value to the class GamePanel.java (the step 8 on Fig. 3.1).

In order to guarantee a qualified input integer, we implement the isQualifiedData() method in the class Player.java for the new version project GuessInt3. There are two different approaches. One is using a try-catch block; the other is implementing our own checking method.

3.8 Catching Exceptions for Possible Errors When Inputting Data

We have touched the try-catch block when we developed the class ReadFile.java in the previous chapter for catching the FileNotFoundException when opening a file for reading. A try-catch block intends to check an exception with an exception handler so that the program will continue its execution even an error occurred. In project GuessInt3, the player needs to input an integer data. The JOptionPane.ShowInputDialog() accepts an input and returns a String, which will be converted to the type of int. A legal integer string contains only a set of digits or with a negative sign. Java language provides a NumberFormatException for catching any errors against the legal integer, such as empty string, null value, non-digit character, and so on. Therefore, after the statement for getting the input string, the isQualifiedData() method applies the try-catch block for assuring the input data as follows.

```
public boolean isQualifiedData(String inputStr) {
    try {
        guessedInt = Integer.parseInt(inputStr);
    } catch(NumberFormatException ex) {
        System.out.println("\nThe format of the input string " + inputStr +
                " was wrong. Input again.\n");
        return false;
    }

    boolean inRange = isInRange(); // checking guessedInt
    if (inRange) {
        return true;
    } else {
        return false;
    }
}
```

The first step of the method is to call "Integer.parseInt(inputStr);" to convert the inputStr from a String to an integer. The parseInt() method will catch any illegal element and throw the NumberFormatException. If the exception happens, we simply show the message on the screen and hire "return false" to feed the value of false to its caller that will pop up a JOptionPane to enforce the user to input another new data again. Thus, even the user inputted a non-qualified data; the program still continues its execution. If the inputStr has no any errors and is parsed as an integer, then it continuously to be fed into the following method isInRange() for checking its range.

3.9 Developing Our Own Error Detection Methods

The try-catch block is convenient and easy to be used. However, sometimes it cannot give programmers a clear indication what causes the exception. For example, the FileNotFoundException only tells us "file not found" but does not indicate what causes the problem, such as the given file path is wrong, or the file itself does not exist, or something else. Similarly, the NumberFormatException only tells the format of the inputted number is wrong but has no clue to the cause of the exception for the player to correct his/her input error.

This weak point promotes us to develop our own checking routine for catching the cause. The method isInteger(inputStr) shown in Listing 3.2 is such a try. The comments in the method isInteger() clearly indicate the reasons why the inputStr is not a legal integer, which includes empty string, null value, string contains non-digit character, its length exceeds the possible maximum integer, and its value is larger than the possible maximum integer. The showMsg() tells these reasons for the players so that they know what was wrong and will legally to input the data again. Every error case issues a "return false" to immediately terminate the routine and sends a "false" to its caller. For having a complete picture, we cited the new version of the class Player.java that adapted the isInteger() method in Listing 3.2.

Listing 3.2 The class Player.java in the project GuessInt3

```
1 /*
2  * Player.java - A class defines a player.
3  */
4 package guessint;
```

```
 5
 6 import javax.swing.JOptionPane;
 7
12 public class Player {
13
14     private String guessedIntStr;
15     private int guessedInt;
16
17     public Player() {
18     }
19
20     public int playingGame() {
21         boolean qualified = false;
22         while (!qualified) {
23             guessedIntStr = JOptionPane.showInputDialog(
24                     "Enter an integer between 1 and 100");
25             qualified = isQualifiedData(guessedIntStr);
26         }
27         showMsg("Player: My guess is " + guessedInt);
28         return guessedInt;
29     }
30
31     public boolean isQualifiedData(String inputStr) {
32         try {
33             guessedInt = Integer.parseInt(inputStr);
34         } catch (NumberFormatException ex) {
35             System.out.println();
36             isInteger(inputStr);
37             return false;
38         }
39         return isInRange(); // check the range, returns false or true
40     }
41
42     public boolean isInteger(String inputStr) {
43         if (inputStr == null) { // esc key or click Cancel button
44             showMsg("You entered the ESC key or clicked the Cancel button"
45                     + " that aborted the program.");
46             System.exit(0);
47         }
48         if (inputStr.equals("")) { // enter key or click OK without input
49             showMsg("You entered the Return key or clicked the OK button"
50                     + " without data. Input again.");
51             return false;
52         }
53
54         int length = inputStr.length();
55         int i = 0;
56         int maxlength = 10; // max integer has 10 digits
57         String maxnum = String.valueOf(Integer.MAX_VALUE); //2147483647
58         // the length of the input must be less than the max integer
59         if (inputStr.charAt(0) == '-') {
60             maxlength = 11;
61             if (length == 1 || length > maxlength) {
62                 showMsg("You entered a negative integer with zero digit"
63                         + " or its length is larger than the maximum length"
```

3.9 Developing Our Own Error Detection Methods

```java
                        + " of a negative integer. Input again.");
                return false;
            }
            i = 1;
            maxnum = String.valueOf(Integer.MIN_VALUE); //-2147483648
        } else {
            if (length > maxlength) {
                showMsg("You entered a positive integer,"
                        + " its length is larger than the maximum length"
                        + " of a positive integer. Input again.");
                return false;
            }
        }
        // every character must be a digit
        for (int digit = i; digit < length; digit++) {
            char c = inputStr.charAt(digit);
            if (c < '0' || c > '9') {
                showMsg("Your inputted data contains non digit character."
                        + " Input again.");
                return false;
            }
        }
        // the input value must be less than the max integer
        if (length == maxlength) {
            for (; i < length; i++) {
                if (inputStr.charAt(i) < maxnum.charAt(i)) {
                    return true;
                } else if (inputStr.charAt(i) > maxnum.charAt(i)) {
                    showMsg("The value of your input is larger than"
                            + " the possible maximum value"
                            + " of an integer. Input again.");
                    return false;
                }
            }
        }
        return true;
    }

    public boolean isInRange() {
        if ((guessedInt >= 1) && (guessedInt <= 100)) {
            return true;
        } else {
            showMsg("\nYour input is out of the bound of [1, 100]. Input again");
            return false;
        }
    }

    public void showMsg(String msgStr) {
        System.out.println(msgStr);
    }
}
```

A trivial notation is worth to be mentioned here. The special defined method showMsg() hires the output method System.out.println() for showing a message. Why don't we directly use the method System.out.println() instead? The reason is that in the process for developing a program, the System.out.println() is often used for debugging purpose. We may insert the System.out.println() as a debugging statement anywhere for echoing the contents of variables. After completing the debugging, we do need to erase all of these debugging statements. At this moment, it is not easy to distinguish which statement of System.out.println() is showing useful message and which is for debugging purpose. Thus, it is better to prevent us from this confusion by using showMsg() for outputting useful messages.

3.10 Advantages of Try-Catch Approach

Developing our own error detection method is a traditional way; the try-catch block is a new approach supplied by Java. In a comparison, we can tell that the try-catch block organizes the code flow better than the traditional way because it clearly separates the normal code flow from the error handlers. When programs go to more complicated, this point becomes clearer. For example, if we have a chance to develop a method for opening a file and reading an integer from the file. Then we can see that the method needs to catch two kinds of exceptions: FileNotFoundException and NumberFormatException. By using the try-catch block, the code would be organized as follows.

```
try {
    aFile = openFile(filePath);
    inputStr = readInteger(aFile);
    inputInt = Integer.parseInt(inputStr);
} catch (FileNotFoundException fex) {
    fileNotFoundHandler();
} catch (NumberFormatException nex) {
    numberFormatHandler();
}
```

Without using the try-catch block, our codes could be mess. Then, how about the method we developed for clearly indicate the error causes? Actually, we can combine these two approaches together to have a beautiful code flow organization and also to have a clear indication about the mistakes. The combination is to insert our own error detection method as part of the exception handler. In the GuessInt project, we could organize the code as follows.

```
try {
    inputInt = Integer.parseInt(inputStr);
} catch (NumberFormatException nex) {
    isInteger(inputStr);
    return false;
}
```

Thus, whenever the exception is caught, the method isInteger() is also invoked to tell us what exactly caused the exception. Otherwise, the method isInteger() is not necessary to be developed.

Definitely, there are other advantages for using the try-catch block. In addition, we can implement our own exceptions to catch what we like to catch.

3.11 A Principal Strategy for Designing and Implementing an OOP Program

The project GuessInt is our first game project with the OOP style. We went over the entire process for designing and implementing it. Even we have no enough experiences, we would like to draw a principal strategy about how to design and implement an OOP program as a guideline for developing more OOP projects later.

An OOP program consists of classes. The word "class" can be understood from the word "classification." In our real life, people have different careers. Based on careers, people may be classified as student, teacher, lawyer, doctor, firefighter, and so on. Different "class" of people has different expertise or different abilities. Meanwhile, different "class" of people associates with different stories and scenes. When we talk about schools, we deal with a "class" of students and a "class" of teachers; when we talk about hospitals, we deal with a "class" of patients and a "class" of doctors. A "class" of students has a set of same behaviors or a set of same abilities. These behaviors are methods defined for the "class." These methods actually are what students can do. A "class" of students is a group of individual objects of students. In order to identify every individual student, the "class" needs a set of attributes, such as stuId, first-name, last-name, age, and the like for storing different set of values to specify each individual student. Every individual student is an instance of the "class," which is also an object of the "class." Therefore, the objects of the same "class" are distinguished by the set of attributes. Meanwhile, different "class" has different set of methods for specifying what the instances of the "class" can do.

Different games have different stories that define different sequence of actions. The actions should be performed through related objects of corresponding "classes," which have the required behaviors or abilities. Consequently, according to the given story, we need to clearly define the global sequence of actions in a time order and define related classes to offer the abilities for realizing the required actions according to the time order. That is the principal strategy for defining classes for a project. And the global sequence of actions becomes the "core" of the program that should be completely implemented. Usually we will define a "global" class to implement the "core" that invokes different objects with different abilities in order to complete the required actions in the time order. Consequently, the actions defined in the global sequence are dispatched to corresponding classes as their methods.

The project GuessInt just follows this design and implementation principle. It has a class of GamePanel.java to implement the "core," which orders the class Initializer.java to initialize the givenInt; and orders the class Player.java to input the guessedInt. Then, the class GamePanel.java passes the guessedInt to the class Initializer.java and asks the Initalizer.java to compare the two integers for giving the player a hint "too large" and "too small" for continuing guesses or to terminate the program when two integers are equal. For satisfying the required actions, each class implements corresponding methods.

To apply this principal strategy for our game development, we need to provide a story for every game. From the story we are able to identify the global sequence of actions in terms of verbs and the required classes in terms of nouns. And then, according to the "core" and the techniques selected, we dispatch the required actions or abilities from the "core" to the classes. Finally, we create a class to implement the "core" by invoking the capable methods from related classes to perform required actions in time order.

3.12 Java Operators

In our projects, we have learned and used some Java operators. Java operators are the "connections" for linking variables (vocabularies) to form statements (sentences). Thus, deeply understand Java operators are necessary for programming. Java operators mainly are classified as arithmetic operator, relational operator, and logical operator.

3.12.1 Arithmetic Operator

The major arithmetic operators include "addition +," "subtraction −," "multiplication *," "division /," and "mod %." We are familiar with the first four types of arithmetic operators. Here, we mainly explain the operator "mod %."

The operator mod: When we divide an integer dividend with an integer divisor, we get two values, an integer quotient and an integer remainder. The division operation returns the quotient; the mod operation returns the remainder as follows.

```
// integer division
quotient = dividend / divisor
remainder = dividend % divisor;
4 = 100 / 22;
12 = 100 % 22;
```

We can see that the smallest remainder is 0; the largest remainder is (divisor − 1). In the project GuessInt, we need

an integer in the range of [min, max], where min = 1 and max = 100. We derived a formula for it in using the random number generator Math.random(). Based on the mod operation, we have another approach to find an integer in the range of [min, max]. The range [min, max] is equivalent to [(min − min) + min, (max − min) + min] or [(0 + min), (max − min) + min]. We can call a random number generator for getting a random integer with any value of x. And then apply the computation ((x mod (max − min + 1)) + min) to find the value because the computation (x mod (max − min + 1)) will give the smallest remainder 0 and the largest remainder (max − min) and then ((x mod (max − min + 1)) + min) will give the range of [min, (max − min) + min]; it is the required range of [min, max] ([1, 100]). The complete piece of code is as follows.

```
Random ran = new java.util.Random();
// a positive integer
int x = Math.abs(ran.nextInt());
int givenInt = x % (max - min + 1) + min;
```

The operator ++ and --: Java supports special arithmetic operators "++" and "—." The statement "day++" is equivalent to "day = day + 1." The statement "day—" is equivalent to "day = day − 1."

However, we must have a clear mind about the differences between "day++" and "++day" as well as between "day--" and "—day." The "day++" means that using the current value of "day" first and then increasing the value of day by 1. The "++day" means that increasing the day by 1 and then using the value of day. The following two statements would make the difference clearer.

```
int day = 2;
System.out.println("day = " + day++);
System.out.println("day = " + ++day);
```

The first println() prints the current value of 2; and then the value of day is increased by 1 as 3. Then, the second println() invokes "++day" that increases the day by 1 again that makes day holding the value of 4. Therefore, the second println() prints a value of 4. In other words, the two statements of println() will print "day = 2" and "day = 4."

3.12.2 Relational Operator

We have discussed the control statement "if-then-else," which is based on conditions. In order to accurately express conditions, relational operators are needed. For example, an "if-then-else" statement is as follows.

```
if (vacation has 10days) {
    I am going to New York;
```

```
    I will do shopping;
} else if (vacation has 5days) {
    I am going to Chicago;
    I will see my parents;
} else {
    I will stay at home;
}
```

Any condition should be precise and unique. But, all of the three conditional statements are not precise and not unique. If we understand the first condition is equivalent to "vacation == 10 days" and the second condition is equivalent as "vacation == 5 days," then the third condition "else" means either "vacation > 10 days" or "vacation < 10 days" or "vacation > 5 days" or "vacation < 5 days." Human speaking often relies on context; but program code has no context. Hence, in a program, the above condition should be expressed as follows.

```
if ((vacation has less than or equals to 10
   days) and (vacation has more than or equals to
   6days)) {
   I am going to New York;
} else if ((vacation has less than or equals
   to 5days) and (vacation has more than or equals to
   3days)) {
   I am going to Chicago;
} else if (vacation has less than or equals
   to 2days) {
   I will stay at home;
}
```

The example above shows that a condition is true or false very often depends on comparisons or so-called relations. For making concise statements, Java language defines six relational operators.

```
Equal ==
Not equal !=
More than >
Less than <
More than or equal to >=
Less than or equal to <=
```

We should apply these relational operators to make the statements precise and concise.

```
if ((vacation <= 10 days) and (vacation >=
   6days)) {
   I am going to New York;
} else if ((vacation <= 5days) and (vacation
   >=
   3days)) {
   I am going to Chicago;
```

```
} else if (vacation <= 2days) {
   I will stay at home;
}
```

3.12.3 Logical Operator

The example above also shows that a condition may be formed by two or more smaller conditions. This kind of conditions is called "combined condition." A single condition usually uses a Boolean value of "true" of "false." A combined condition is a Boolean expression, which is formed by using logical operators to combine two or more smaller conditions together. The logical operators include "and," "or," and "not," which are corresponding to the sign "&," "|," and "!" in Java.

The operator "not" ("!") actually is for a single value. It appears in the relational operator != (not equal) already. It negates the value of true to be false and negates the false to be true. The "and" ("&") and "or" ("|") operators are used to link two or more conditions to make a combined condition. Their logical meanings are shown in the following three truth tables.

		AND			OR		NOT
T	T	T	T	T	T	T	F
T	F	F	T	F	T	F	T
F	T	F	F	T	T		
F	F	F	F	F	F		

3.12.4 "and" and "or" Symbols in Java

Java defines six symbols for the logical operators as listed in the following table.

Operator	Name	Example	Meaning
&	and	a & b	It is true if both a and b are true
|	or	a | b	It is true if one of a or b is true
!	not	!a	It is true if a is false. It is false if a is true
&&	and	a && b	It is true if both a and b are true
||	or	a || b	It is true if one of a or b is true
^	exclusive-or	a ^ b	It is true if both a and b are true or both are false

There is a difference between the operators "&&" with "&" and the operators "||" with "|." The "&&" and "||" operators mean that if the first condition can determine the combined condition, the second condition is not necessary to be evaluated. For example, the following condition consists of two smaller conditions.

```
if ((condition 1) || (condition 2)) {
    ...
}
```

When condition 1 is true, it can determine the combinational condition is true without checking the second condition so that it saves the checking time and effort. Thus, they are often used in "if-then-else" statements. However, using the "&" and "|" operators, both two conditions must be evaluated and then make the resulting condition. Thus, the single "&" and "|" usually are not used in combinational conditions but usually used in binary computations.

Applying the logical operators, the example above should be written as follows.

```
if ((vacation <= 10) && (vacation >= 6)) {
    System.out.println("I am going to New York");
} else if ((vacation <= 5) && (vacation >= 3)) {
    System.out.println("I am going to Chicago");
} else if (vacation <= 2) {
    System.out.println("I will stay at home");
}
```

The operator "!" looks simple. However, when applying it for negating a combinational condition, it appears not easy. Here, we need to apply the De Morgan's law as follows.

```
!(a && b) = !a || !b
!(a || b) = !a && !b
```

3.13 More Control Statements in Java

Besides "if-then-else" and "while" control statements, Java also provides the following control statements.

3.13.1 The Control Statement "switch"

If the condition in an "if-then-else" statement relates with an integer or a char, the "if-then-else" statement could be replaced with a "switch" statement. The example above refers to the number days in a vacation, which could be converted into a "switch" statement as follows.

```
switch(vacation) {
    case 10:
        System.out.println("I am going to New York");
        break;
    case 5:
        System.out.println("I am going to Chicago");
        break;
    default:
        System.out.println("I will stay at home");
        break;
}
```

However, the switch statement above does not completely express the meaning of the "if-then-else" statement because it does not consider all of other possible number of days: 9, 8, 7, and so on. If we would like to use "switch" statement, we should say:

```
switch(vacation) {
    case 10:
    case 9:
    case 8:
    case 7:
    case 6:
        System.out.println("I am going to New York");
        break;
    case 5:
    case 4:
    case 3:
        System.out.println("I am going to Chicago");
        break;
    case 2:
    case 1:
        System.out.println("I will stay at home");
        break;
}
```

The statement "break" in the code above is a special statement that stops the execution of the remaining code. In other words, without "break" statement, the program will execute from one case to the other. For example, assume that case3 does not have the "break" statement, after executing the code for the case3, the program will continue execute the code for the case2 and case1. The "break" statement is also often used to break a loop. We will see more examples later.

3.13.2 The Control Statement "for"

We have discussed the control statement "while." Assume that I will have a 10 days' vacation and I will go to New York. I would like to set up an alarm clock and let it sound every day for the 10 days. The idea can be described as the following piece of code.

```
int day = 1;
while (day <= 10) {
      Alarm sounds;
      day = day + 1;
}
```

The variable day is initialized as 1 for indicating the first day. The condition (day <= 10) is true because (1 < 10). After alarm sounded, the day is increased by 1 for indicating the second day. Until the 10th day, the value of day is 10. The condition (10 == 10) is still true, the alarm also sounds, and then the day is increased as 11. Thus, the condition (11 <= 10) is false at the 11th day. The control jumps to the end curly bracket that ignores the alarm. From this example, we can see that for controlling a "while" loop, we need three statements: (1) a condition initializing statement, (2) a condition checking statement, and (3) a condition changing statement. Among them the condition changing statement is especially important. In case we forget changing the condition, say we forget the statement "day = day + 1;," the while condition will always be true; the while loop will loop forever. This is termed as "infinite loop."

For avoiding the possible "infinite loop," a "for" loop is invented. The "while" loop above can be converted to a "for" loop as follows.

```
for (int day = 1; day <= 10; day++) {
   Alarm sounds;
}
```

We can see that a "for" loop collects the three statements: condition initializing, checking, and changing into one statement so that none of them would be forgotten.

Clearly, both the "while" and "for" loops above will loop ten times continuously. What if accidentally I would be sick in the middle of the vacation time period? I have to go home immediately. It implies that the loop has to be broken in the middle. For breaking a loop, the statement "break" should be employed. The code becomes the following.

```
for (int day = 1; day <= 10; day++) {
   Alarm sounds;
   if (sick) {
      I go home;
      break;
   }
}
```

The "break" statement will break the nearest loop, which is the "for" loop.

3.14 The Modifier "Static" (Why main() Method Is a Static Method?)

When we would like to have a random number, we invoke the method Math.random(), which consists of two parts. The first part is a class name "Math" since the first character "M" is a capital letter; the second part is a method random() defined in the class Math. We have learned that for invoking a method defined in a class, we do need to instantiate an object of the class then using the dot notation to let the object invoke a method. But here, why can we directly use the class name "Math" (not an object) to invoke the method random()?

The class "Math" is a built-in class in Java APIs. The class Math contains methods for performing basic numeric operations such as the elementary exponential, logarithm, square root, and trigonometric functions. If we open the document of the class Math, we can see the following method definitions.

```
public static double abs(double a);
public static double acos(double a);
public static double sin(double a);
...
```

It shows that all of methods defined in the class Math have a modifier "static." The modifier "static" indicates that the methods associate with the class Math but not associate with a specific instance of that class. Therefore, a static method can be invoked by using the class name directly without instantiation of an object of that class. For a better understanding, we may think about it in an opposite way. When an object is instantiated, a piece of memory is allocated for it. After the object won't be used, the garbage collection will automatically clean it up sometimes later. In that sense, we may understand that an object is a "dynamic" thing. When a method is declared as "static," it does not follow a specific object to be dynamically created and cleaned. Hence, the static methods defined in a class can be invoked using the class name directly.

The built-in class String also defines some methods with a modifier "static," such as follows.

```
public static String valueOf(
   boolean aBoolean);
public static String valueOf(char aChar);
public static String valueOf(int anInt);
public static String valueOf(
   double aDouble);
...
public static String valueOf(Object anObj);
```

These static methods above can accept a parameter with different data types and returns a String representation.

Therefore, the first statement below is not valid, but the second statement is valid.

```
String aDoubleStr = 12.34;
// it causes compile-time error
String aDoubleStr = String.valueOf(12.34);
// it is valid
```

Variables can also be defined as static. Under that case, the static variable associates with the class not with an object of that class. For example, a student class has an attribute "name." Different student objects of that class have different values for the same attribute "name." If the class defines a static attribute "year," then all student objects of this class have the same attribute "year" for specifying all of students of this class belong to the same year. Physically, a static variable is allocated in a different memory location other than the memory location for dynamic variables.

Now we can explain why the method main() is a static method. As we know that main() method is the execution starting point of an application. When the application just starts execution, no any object is available. That is, no any object exists and can be used to invoke the method main(). Only when the main() method is defined as static, it can be invoked by the interpreter through the main class name before creating any objects. Therefore, the main() method has always been defined as a static method.

3.15 Summary

Developing games in-text is a wonderful practice for learning the foundations of Java programming language and programming skills. Games consist of objects and fulfill interactive actions among the objects. Mimicking the interactions among objects greatly enhances our feeling about objects, which is the soul of OOP programming.

Games also embed a lot of conditions and repetition structures that provide chances for us to practice control statements and related operators. For implementing the game GuessInt, control statements "if" and "while" are introduced. In additional sections, the other control statements, such as "switch" and "for," are also studied. The control statements require different operators, especially relational operators and logical operators. Games also require players for inputting data, which definitely require error detections and exception handlings. The try-catch block is a perfect structure for handling exceptions. Our own developed error detection methods can also smoothly incorporate with try-catch blocks.

We expanded the ideas learned from the example game project and tried to draw a principal strategy for designing and implementing OOP programs. We will apply the principal strategy for our development of games on the way.

3.16 Exercises

Self-Reviewing Questions

1. Why do we say, "The project GuessInt1 is not a good coding in OOP programming"? What do you think?
2. What are interactions between the object initializer and the object player?
3. What functions does the class GamePanel.java play?
4. What is a random number generator? Java provides two kinds of random number generators. What are they? What is the difference between them?
5. What general formula will generate a random number in a required range, say [9, 88]?
6. Do you have any algorithm that can be applied for finding the correct answer most quickly (using the least number of guesses) when playing the game GuessInt?
7. What statements can change the execution order when a program is in execution?
8. Make an example to form a single condition and a combinational condition.
9. What is the De Morgan's law? Could you make an example for using it?
10. What is the difference between a "while" loop and a "for" loop?
11. What is the result of 233/55? What is the result of 233 % 55?
12. What is the output of the following "for" loop?

    ```
    int count = 5;
    for (int i = 0; i < 5; i++) {
        System.out.println((i * count++) + " "
            + ++count);
    }
    ```

13. How many loops do the following "for" loop make? Could you find out a formula for calculating it?

    ```
    for (int z = 15; z < 1000; z++) { ... }
    ```

14. A "while" loop is listed as follows. Please give an initial value for the variables ax and bz, respectively, so that the while loop will be started and also complete the code for changing the values of ax and bz in order to avoid an "infinite loop."

    ```
    int ax;
    int bz;
    while ((ax < 5) && (bz > 10)) {
        ...
        ax ...; // ax++ or ax-?
        bz ...; // bz++ or bz-?
    }
    ```

15. Convert the "while" loop above to be a "for" loop.

16. If we would like to negate the condition (!((ax < 5) && (bz > 10))), what is the result?
17. What should be the output of the following println() statements?

    ```
    int anInt = 11;
    System.out.println("The output = ", anInt++);
    System.out.println("The output = ", ++anInt);
    System.out.println("The output = ", anInt--);
    System.out.println("The output = ", --anInt);
    ```

18. Trace the output of the following piece of code:
    ```
    System.out.print("The output = ");
    for (int i = 0; i < 3; i++) {
       for (int j = 2; j < 5; j++) {
          for (int k = 4; k < 7; k++) {
             System.out.println(
                (i + j + k) + "—");
          }
       }
    }
    System.out.println();
    ```

Projects

1. A dice can give a value in the range of [1, 6]. Write a program to simulate the action of throwing a dice for five times and print the result on the console for each throwing.
2. Given the following two Strings. Write a program to make a String str3 that has the content of "Hello, Java" by using the following two given Strings.

   ```
   String str1 = "We say Hello almost every day";
   String str2 = "We have Java course three
       times per week";
   ```

3. The small project TryBoolean is included in the folder of this chapter. Its source code is as follows. Write down the results corresponding to the println() statements in the source code, and then run the project for verifying your answers.

```
 1 /*
 2  * TryBoolean.java - The main class of the project TryBoolean.
 3  */
 4 package tryboolean;
 5
10 public class TryBoolean {
11
12     private double x;
13     private double y;
14     private int z = 5;
15
16     public TryBoolean() {
17        x = 4.6;
18        y = 5.2;
19        printResult();
20     }
21
22     private void printResult() {
23        System.out.println(x > y);
24        System.out.println(++x > y++);
25        System.out.println(x++ > y);
26        System.out.println(x > y);
27
28        for (int i = 0; i < 5; i++) {
29           System.out.println((i * z++) + " " + ++z);
30        }
31     }
32
36     public static void main(String[] args) {
37        new TryBoolean();
38     }
39 }
```

3.16 Exercises

4. The small project TryRandom is included in the folder of this chapter. Its source code is cited as follows. Input the range for the integer givenInt, and then run the project to verify whether the returned random value is in the ranges.

```java
1  /*
2   * TryRandom.java - The main class of the project TryRandom.
3   */
4  package tryrandom;
5
6  import java.util.Random;
7  import javax.swing.JOptionPane;
8
13 public class TryRandom {
14
15     private int givenInt;
16     private Random random2;
17     private int min;
18     private int max;
19
20     public TryRandom() {
21         min = Integer.parseInt(JOptionPane.showInputDialog(
22                 "Enter the lower bound integer min: (e.g. 5)"));
23         max = Integer.parseInt(JOptionPane.showInputDialog(
24                 "Enter the upper bound integer max: (e.g. 88"));
25         System.out.println("The range is " + "[" + min + "," + max + "]");
26
27         givenInt = (int) (Math.random() * (max-min+1)) + min;
28         System.out.println("givenInt1 = " + givenInt);
29
30         random2 = new Random();
31         givenInt = random2.nextInt(max-min+1) + min;
32         System.out.println("givenInt2 = " + givenInt);
33
34         givenInt = Math.abs(random2.nextInt()) % (max-min+1) + min;
35         System.out.println("givenInt3 = " + givenInt);
36     }
37
38     /**
39      * @param args the command line arguments
40      */
41     public static void main(String[] args) {
42         new TryRandom();
43     }
44 }
```

5. The small project TrySwitch is included in the folder of this chapter, which implements some switch statement. Please run the project and verify the result.

6. Write a program for generating a table of multiplications such as the following (or in a better format that you design).

1	2	3	4	5	6	7	8	9
2	4	6	8	10	12	14	16	18
3	6	9	12	15	18	21	24	27
4	8	12	16	20	24	28	32	36
...
8	16	24	32	40	48	56	64	72
9	18	27	46	45	54	63	72	81

7. Write a project GuessDoing that pre-stored information as following examples one-by-one. And then, the program displays the environment and time and let the player guessing what correct action best matches with the environment and time.

    Evening, sit in front of a table: "take a shower," "read a book," or "fall sleep"

    Evening, sit in a sofa: "watch TV," "cook a dish," or "eat fruits"

    Day time, sit in a sofa: "play Ping-Pong," "smoke a cigar," or "make a phone call"

    ...

8. Write a project GuessWord to provide a word with missing characters for the player to guess the complete word, for example, H___o: "Hello." And counting for the correction rate (correct answers/total number of words.)

9. Write a project NumberCrunching to provide a mathematical computation for the player to answer the result, For example, 4 + 5: 9. Counting the correction rate (correct answers/total number of computations.)

10. Write a project to mimic or simplify the TV show "Family Feud."

UML and Its Usage: A Game WheelFortune In-Text

This chapter intends to initialize the introduction about the unified modeling language (UML). The UML supports class diagram, sequence diagram, state machine diagram, and others. In this book, we mainly apply class diagrams for visually describing classes and their relationships, apply sequence diagrams for illustrating the dynamic behaviors among objects, and also apply state machine diagrams for exploring the game states and their transitions in order to structure a guideline for designing games. This chapter also goes through the construction of a new game to investigate the data structure Array and ArrayList, as well as the algorithms for searching and sorting an array.

The objectives of this chapter include:
1. Unified modeling language (UML).
2. Four major relationships among classes.
3. Project WheelFortune: a game in-text.
4. Applying UML for designing the project.
5. Applying Array and ArrayList for the implementation.
6. An array of three players.
7. An array of characters on the board.
8. An array of Strings on the wheel.
9. Searching for a match on an array of characters.
10. Sorting an array of players based on the total-score.
11. Checking of special cases and error cases.
12. The weak points of output in text format.

The project PrintXmasCard in Chap. 2 consists of three classes. The project GuessInt in Chap. 3 has four classes. We can imagine that the more complicated projects the more classes will be involved. When the number of classes increases, the relationships among classes would also be more complicated. We need tools to visually illustrate the classes and their relationships in our mind. The UML (unified modeling language) is such a tool. This chapter intends to initialize the introduction on the UML language and apply it for designing our projects.

4.1 The Unified Modeling Language (UML)

A standard graphical language named as Unified Modeling Language (UML) can be applied for specifying, visualizing, constructing, and documenting the artifacts of software systems in OOP paradigm. It provides diagrams to represent projects and forms a blueprint for the construction of each project. Due to its graphical nature, the drawing diagrams visualize abstractive concepts and ideas that make design and implementation of projects much easier.

In general, the UML supports class diagram, sequence diagram, state machine diagram, and others. For this book, we mainly apply class diagrams for describing classes and their relationships. We also apply sequence diagrams for illustrating the dynamic behaviors among objects and state machine diagrams for demonstrating the game states and their transitions for giving a guideline in designing games.

The UML defines a set of symbols for specifying relationships among classes. We would like to mainly adopt four of them, which include "is-a," "uses," "has," and "implements" as shown in Fig. 4.1. The meaning of these symbols will be explained when they will be met.

4.2 A Game WheelFortune In-Text

Now, we are going to apply the UML class diagram for modeling a new game of WheelFortune in-text, which mimics the TV game show Wheel-Of-Fortune but only partially implements the show in text format without any graphical user interface and animation.

The story of the game Wheel-Of-Fortune is well known. We simplify it and rephrase it here for our purpose. The story of our project WheelFortune says, a game initializer (the anchor of the TV game show) initializes a sentence, such as, a phrase, a citation, and so on and keeps it unseen. An empty text board is formed to fit and prepare for displaying the

© Springer Nature Switzerland AG 2018
C.-w. Xu, *Learning Java with Games*, https://doi.org/10.1007/978-3-319-72886-5_4

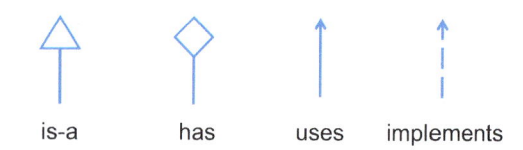

Fig. 4.1 The UML defined major relationships among classes

characters in the given sentence. Three players join the game. One of them is the current player who turns a wheel that has a set of scores and some unfortunate cases, such as "Bankrupt" on it. When the wheel stops turning, the current player inputs a character for guessing the unseen characters of the given sentence. If his/her guessed character matches with a character or multiple instances of the character in the unseen sentence, the matched character will be displayed on the text board at the matched position(s) and he/she will earn a current score, which is the multiplication of the score on the wheel with the number of matches, and then he/she will continue to turn the wheel and accumulate all scores as a total score until a mismatch happens.

The mismatch enforces the current player to give up the playing authority to the next player, who becomes the current player. Anyone might have a chance to hit on the "Bankrupt" slot when he/she turns the wheel, which will erase the total score he/she earned so far. As long as the entire sentence is completed, the game is finished. The player with the highest total score wins the game. In order to ease the manipulation of characters, all of characters are converted to upper case inside the program. In addition, the player always earns a score no matter he/she guessed a vowel or a consonant. (The real TV game asks the player to buy vowels.)

According to the story of the game WheelFortune described above, we may draft the global sequence of actions briefly without considering any abnormal or error cases as follows.

1. The game needs an initializer, three players, a board, and a wheel.
2. The initializer initializes a sentence.
   (a) The board displays a number of empty squares equals to the number of characters in the sentence including blank characters and punctuations.
3. If the sentence hasn't been matched completely:
   (a) The current-player turns the wheel and gets a wheel-score.
   (b) The current-player inputs a guess-character.
4. The initializer receives the guess-character.
   (a) The initializer matches the guess-character with the sentence character-by-character.
   (b) If matching occurs, the index of the matching position in the sentence is recorded into a list idxList.
5. If the length of the idxList > 0:
   (c) The current-player earns a current-score = numMatch * wheel-score.
   (d) The global-score of the current-player + current-score.
   (e) The matched characters are shown on the board.
   (f) Go to step 3.
6. Else (if the length of the idxList == 0) // no match
   (a) The next player becomes the current-player.
   (b) Go to step 3.

Comparing with the game GuessInt in-text discussed in the previous chapter, the new game WheelFortune in-text actually is similar but has the following new features.

1. A sentence string is the guessing target, which is a collection of characters.
2. A board, which displays the collection of characters in the sentence.
3. A wheel, which stores a set of integers in String format including a "Bankrupt."
4. Three players, which refer to three instances of a same class.

A single variable can only store a single value of a certain type. Here, the sentence string, the board, the wheel, and the players on the above list are "a set of" multiple values of a certain data type. All of them raise a new question: How to store the set of multiple values in a variable?

4.3 A Linear Data Structure: Array

In order to store a set of multiple values in a variable, we need a data structure instead of a single variable. A data structure is a structure of multiple memory locations. A simple data structure termed as Array is a linear data structure. Taking the three players as an example, they are represented by three instances of a same class Player.java because they have the same set of behaviors and the same set of attributes.

In order to store the three player objects, two different ways could be used. One way is to declare three variables with the same data type of Player as follows.

```
private Player playerBrown;
private Player playerSmith;
private Player playerCruz;
```

The manner of the storage of the three players looks like Fig. 4.2 (left) shows because the three variables represent three different locations in memory. Due to the three memory locations are not related, if the current player is playerBrown, then who is the next player? We have no suitable

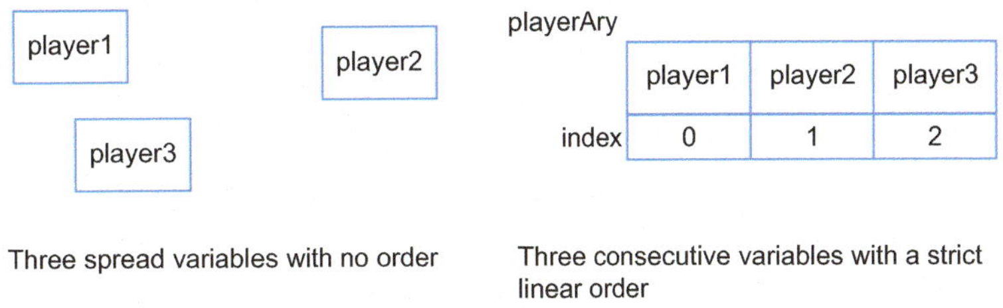

4.3 A Linear Data Structure: Array

Fig. 4.2 A logical representation of an array in Java

algorithms for making such kind of searching. Especially, the number of players could be increased to 20, 100, or more in other cases.

Therefore, we need a new approach to allocate a set of consecutive memory locations where each of them can store one player and each of them can be accessed individually with an order, then the manipulation of the set of players will be much easier. This sequence of consecutive memory locations forms a so-called Array. That is, an array is not a single memory location but a set of consecutively related memory locations. Because they are allocated consecutively, the array name, say playerAry, is the mnemonic starting address of the array, then the first player is stored in the address (playerAry + 0 * object-size); the second player is stored in the address (playerAry + 1 * object-size); and so on. The integers 0, 1, ... appear in the addresses are termed as "index." Due to the fact that an array is a sequence of consecutive memory locations, it is termed as one-dimensional linear data structure, which could be depicted as Fig. 4.2 (right).

The same idea can be extended to store a set of multiple data in any same kind of primitive data type or reference data type, such as a set of int, a set of double, a set of same objects, and the like. Now, if we would like to store three objects of players, we can apply the following statement to declare an array with the reference data type of Player.

```
private Player[] playerAry;
```

The pair of square brackets [] represents an Array data structure. The Player[] means that the array has the data type of the class Player.java. The declaration above is read as "a variable playerAry is a Player array" or "a Player array of playerAry." At this moment, the variable playerAry has no memory allocated yet; thus, we use the term of "declare." For allocating a set of consecutive physical memory locations for the array, we employ the following Java statement with the term of "define."

```
Player[] playerAry = new Player[3];
```

The "new Player[3]" indicates that we need three consecutive memory locations of one instance of class Player each. The value of 3 is also called the length of the array. As mentioned above, every unit of the array has its own index.

The index always starts from 0 so that the three locations in the array is playerAry[0], playerAry[1], and playerAry[2]. When an array has a length of n, its first index is 0 and its last index is (n − 1). Any index exceeding the boundary of [0, (n − 1)] causes a run time error. Therefore, an array data structure allows us to manipulate a set of memory locations with a linear order through the indexes instead to manipulate a group of distributed memory locations. In such a way, we can design corresponding algorithms to easily access any element in the array.

In order to assign data to the array playerAry, we should assign an object to a unit of the array individually.

```
playerAry[0] = new Player();
playerAry[1] = new Player();
playerAry[2] = new Player();
```

Instead, we often adopt a "for" loop for assigning data to an array as follows.

```
for (int k = 0; k < playerAry.length; k++) {
    playerAry[k] = new Player();
}
```

This example illustrates that a "for" loop is suitable for manipulating an array because the length of an array is fixed that provides a countable value for controlling the "for" loop. Whenever possible, we think of a "for" loop when we manipulate an array.

Be careful, a String is also consists of a sequence of characters; but it is not a character array and a character array is not a String. However, due to the similarity, they can be converted each other and they have some similar methods for performing similar functions.

Now, it is clear that an array contains the same data type, has a certain fixed length, and organizes a set of data to be easily accessed through an index. Unfortunately, its advantage of a fixed length sometimes becomes a drawback. What if we have no idea about how many units should be allocated for the array at its definition time? If we allocate the array with a guess, then it might be too short such that the array won't be able to store all of data; it also might be too long such that it wastes the precious memory.

4.4 A Linear Data Structure ArrayList Comes Handy

For overcoming the drawback, another kind of one-dimensional linear data structure called ArrayList<type> comes handy. The "type" inside the angle brackets refers to the data type of the elements stored in the arrayList. We are not required to know the length of the ArrayList in advance for allocating it since the computer system can automatically adjust the length of an arrayList according to the needs without the intervention of human programmers. For example, when we would like to store a set of players in an arrayList and we have no idea how many of them should be, we can simply say:

```
ArrayList<Player> playerList = new
    ArrayList<>();
playerList.add(player1);
// the player1 has the index of 0
playerList.add(player2);
// the player2 has the index of 1
…
playerList.add(playerN);
// the playerN has the index of (N - 1)
```

For accessing the stored data, the built-in method get(index) can be used as follows.

```
Player aPlayer = playerList.get(0);
// here, 0 is the index
```

Consequently, an Array is usually used in cases with known length; and an ArrayList is usually used in cases of unknown length. Programmers should keep this difference in mind. Definitely, they can be selected according to the preferences of the programmers.

4.5 Initializing the Game: The Project WheelFortune1

The data structures Array and ArrayList paved the road for implementing the game of WheelFortune in-text. The story of the game WheelFortune described above naturally reminds us about the game GuessInt that we discussed and implemented in Chap. 3. We start the first version WheelFortune1 that has a similar structure as the game GuessInt2. The structure is made of two kinds of objects: the initializer and the player as well as the interactions between them. Even though the game WheelFortune1 has three players, at anytime only the current-player plays the game such that we can start our development by dealing with one player only and leave other two players in later versions. The familiarized structure with the interactive actions is briefly expressed as follows.

Initializer	Player
1. Makes a sentence	2. CurrPlayer inputs a qualified char
3. Match of the char with the sentence?	4. Match, go to 2; mismatch, nextPlayer go to 2

Therefore, the game WheelFortune1 differs from the game GuessInt2 only in one issue mainly. In the game GuessInt2, the initializer issues an integer; the player also enters an integer. The comparison is integer to integer. However, in the game WheelFortune1, the initializer gives a sentence, which is a String type; but the player inputs a character, which is a char type. As long as the player enters a character, it has to be searched from the sentence. As mentioned, a String is different from a char array. Fortunately, a String also consists of characters. The built-in class String has a method charAt() (see Chap. 2) that can be adopted for searching the individual char inputted by the player. The searching result could be no match, one match, or multiple matches. In addition, the matching position, i.e., the indexes of the matches, should be recorded in order to display the matched character on the board. Due to the fact that the number of matches is an unknown value for every guess, thus, recording the matching indexes requires an ArrayList<Integer>.

As the first version of the game, the project WheelFortune1 ignores the board and related functions and also ignores the wheel and associated actions. The project only implements the partial global sequence of actions listed in Sect. 4.2, which deals with the initializer and the current-player.

Consequently, the project WheelFortune1 is very close to the project GuessInt2. It deals with four classes. We apply the UML class diagram to depict the four classes and the relationships among them as shown in Fig. 4.3.

The UML class diagram indicates that the main class WheelFortune.java "uses" the class GamePanel.java. Here, "uses" means that the class WheelFortune.java instantiates an object of the class GamePanel.java and "uses" its functionality to complete the tasks assigned to it. And then, the

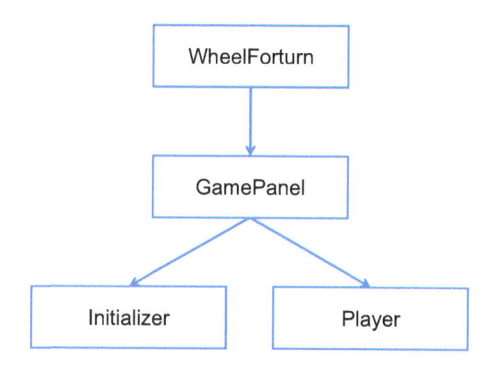

Fig. 4.3 The UML class diagram of the project WheelFortune1

4.5 Initializing the Game: The Project WheelFortune1

class GamePanel.java "uses" the classes Initializer.java and Player.java. It means that the GamePanel.java class further "uses" the functionalities of the two objects and provides a communication space to allow them work together for realizing the goal of the game. The pseudo code of the game WheelFortune1 could be drafted as follows.

1. The project WheelFortune1 has four classes: WheelFortune.java, GamePanel.java, Initializer.java, and Player.java.
2. The main class WheelFortune1.java instantiates an object gamePanel of the class GamePanel.java.
3. The class GamePanel.java does the following.
   (a) It instantiates an object initializer of the class Initializer.java and an object of the class Player.java.
   (b) It invokes initializer.initSentence() to initialize a sentence as "Hello World."
   (c) It invokes player.inputGuess() to let the player inputting a guessedChar.
   (d) It passes the guessedChar to the method initializer.receiveGuess(), which searches the guessedChar along the given sentence for matching. Whenever a match occurs, the matching index in the sentence is added into the arrayList idxList. After finishing the matching process, the method returns the idxList to the class GamePanel.java.
   (e) If the idxList is empty, it means no match; the program finishes its execution.
   (f) Else if the idxList is not empty that indicates at least one match happened, the player continues his/her playing by going to the step 3.c.

Reading over the pseudo code above, we can tell that the project WheelFortune1 is very similar with the project GuessInt2. The class GamePanel.java implements the "core" of the program, and the "core" has a "while" loop since the step 3.f has a "go to 3.c" action. The corresponding methods that perform the real functions are dispatched to the classes Initializer.java and Player.java, respectively. The major new feature is performed by the method initializer.receiveGuess() that searches the sentence string for finding the matches with the guessedChar. Listing 4.1 only displays the code of the class Initializer.java for demonstrating this new idea.

Listing 4.1 The code of the class Initializer.java in the project WheelFortune1

```
1  /*
2   * Initializer.java - A class defines the initializer.
3   */
4  package wheelfortune;
5
6  import java.util.ArrayList;
7
12 public class Initializer {
13
14     private String sentence;
15     private int sentenceLen;
16
17     public Initializer() {
18     }
19
20     public int initSentence() {
21         sentence = "Hello World"; // assume
22         sentence = sentence.toUpperCase();
23         sentenceLen = sentence.length();
24         showMsg("Game is ready. Start playing");
25         return sentenceLen;
26     }
27
28     public ArrayList<Integer> receiveGuess(char inputChar) {
29         inputChar = Character.toUpperCase(inputChar);
30         ArrayList<Integer> idxList = new ArrayList();
31         for (int i = 0; i < sentenceLen; i++) {
32             if (sentence.charAt(i) == inputChar) {
33                 idxList.add(i);
```

```
34              }
35          }
36          return idxList;
37      }
38
39      public void showMsg(String msg) {
40          System.out.println(msg);
41      }
42 }
```

The method initializer.receiveGuess(inputChar) demonstrates the matching process. The sentence is a String, but the parameter inputChar is a single char. The built-in method charAt() in the built-in class String is invoked to get a single character from the sentence and compares it with the inputChar. If (sentence.charAt(index) == inputChar), then add the "index" into the arrayList idxList for keeping track of the matching position for later use. A "for" loop switches the index from 0 to (sentence.length() – 1) for comparing the inputChar with every character in the sentence. As long as the "for" loop finishes, the arrayList idxList will hold all of the indexes, where the matches occur.

The method initializer.receiveGuess() is designed as a function, which returns the arrayList idxList to the caller gamePanel. The gamePanel checks the length of the idxList and makes the following report on the console as shown in Fig. 4.4. Whenever the guessedChar is mismatched, the program is terminated.

4.6 The Game Has Three Players: The Project WheelFortune2

In reality, three players join the game. The three players have different names and different genders, but they have the same behaviors. One class defines a set of attributes and a set of methods. The same set of attributes of name and gender can store different values for representing three different players. The same set of methods supports the same behaviors or abilities of every player. Therefore, three player objects are three instances of the same class Player.java. We

```
Game is ready. Start playing
The player Brown is playing:
The guessed char h matches 1 character(s) in the sentence.
The guessed char l matches 3 character(s) in the sentence.
The guessed char p matches 0 character in the sentence.
The game is terminated
```

Fig. 4.4 A simple output in text from the project WheelFortune1

can define an array that has the same reference data type for storing the three player objects.

Consequently, for adding the three players, we do need to add the following new actions.

1. Initializing three players and storing them into the array playerAry.
2. Assigning one of them as the current-player.
3. When needed, switching the next player to be the current-player.

These new actions are listed in the global sequence of actions in Sect. 4.2 as part of step 1 and step 6.a.

4.7 Initializing Three Players

For adding the three players into the game WheelFortune2, the original class Player.java designed for the game GuessInt should be modified with a set of attributes of name, gender, number of playing, and score, as well as having more methods. The constructor of the class GamePanel.java initializes integer variables numPlayer = 3 and currPlayer = 0 (assigning the player with the index 0 as the current player). And the method initPlayer() defines an array "Player[] playerAry = new Player[numPlayer];." Immediately, it uses a "for" loop to initialize the three players. Inside the "for" loop, it applies "new" operator to instantiate an object of player and invoke the method initPlayerData() to initialize the set of attributes with different set of values for every player object. And then, it stores every instance of the players to the playerAry. The method initPlayerData() hires the JOptionPane.showInputDialog() as an input mechanism to issue the related prompts and accept input data. The try-catch block is still employed for exception checking. The code of the class GamePanel.java that contains the two methods initPlayer() and initPlayerData() is shown in Listing 4.2.

Listing 4.2 The code of the two methods initPlayer() and initPlayerData() in the class GamePanel.java of the project WheelFortune2

```java
1  /*
2   * GamePanel.java - A class to be the coordinator of initializer and player.
3   */
4  package wheelfortune;
5
6  import java.util.ArrayList;
7  import javax.swing.JOptionPane;
8
13 public class GamePanel {
14
15     private Initializer initializer;
16     private Player[] playerAry;
17     private int numPlayer;
18     private int currPlayer;
19
20     public GamePanel() {
21         numPlayer = 3;
22         currPlayer = 0;
23         initComponent();
24     }
25
26     private void initComponent() {
27         initPlayer(); // three players with name, ...
28         initializer = new Initializer();
29         initializer.initSentence();
30
31         startGame();
32     }
33
34     public void initPlayer() {
35         playerAry = new Player[numPlayer];
36         for (int i = 0; i < numPlayer; i++) {
37             playerAry[i] = new Player();
38             playerAry[i].setName(initPlayerData(i, "name"));
39             playerAry[i].setSex(initPlayerData(i, "sex"));
40             playerAry[i].setNumPlay(0);
41             playerAry[i].setScore(0);
42         }
43     }
44
45     public String initPlayerData(int idx, String title) {
46         boolean hasInput = false;
47         String titleStr = "";
48         char isEmpty;
49
```

```java
        String numTh = "first";
        switch (idx) {
            case 0:
                numTh = "first ";
                break;
            case 1:
                numTh = "second ";
                break;
            case 2:
                numTh = "third ";
                break;
        }
        while (!hasInput) {
            titleStr = JOptionPane.showInputDialog(
                    "Enter " + numTh + "player's " + title);
            try {
                isEmpty = titleStr.charAt(0);
                hasInput = true;
            } catch (StringIndexOutOfBoundsException siex) {
                showMsg("You did not input the " + title + ". Input again.");
            } catch (NullPointerException npex) {
                showMsg("You clicked Cancel.");
                abortGame();
            }
        }
        return titleStr;
    }

    public void startGame() {
        ArrayList<Integer> idxList; // one letter may have multiple matches
        boolean guessValid;
        char playerGuess;

        while (currPlayer < 3) { // allows next player
            guessValid = true;
            showMsg("The current player " + playerAry[currPlayer].getName()
                    + " is playing:");
            while (guessValid) { // current player continues
                playerGuess = playerAry[currPlayer].inputGuess();
                idxList = initializer.receiveGuess(playerGuess);
                if (idxList.isEmpty()) { // guess has no match,
                    showMsg("The guessed char " + playerGuess
                            + " matches 0 character in the sentence.");
                    guessValid = false; // next player takes turn
                } else {
                    showMsg("The guessed char " + playerGuess
                            + " matches " + idxList.size()
                            + " character(s) in the sentence.");
                }
            }
            currPlayer = (currPlayer + 1) % numPlayer; // switch to next player
        }
    }
```

```
103
104     public void abortGame() {
105         showMsg("The game is aborted");
106         System.exit(0);
107     }
108
109     public void showMsg(String msg) {
110         System.out.println(msg);
111     }
112 }
```

4.8 Assigning the Current-Player

An extra effort is the definition of current player. It is easy when the three players are held by the playerAry. We only need to assign an index for indicating one of players as the current-player. Actually, it has been done in the constructor GamePanel() of the class GamePanel.java (line 22 in Listing 4.2), where we initialize the index 0 as the current-player. And then, the next current-player will be currPlayer + 1. Of course, after the index of 2, the next index must be back to 0. This circular sequence can be obtained by using a "mod" operation as follows.

```
currPlayer = (currPlayer + 1) % numPlayer;
// numPlayer = 3
```

Where currPlayer is an index with the initial value of 0. The implementation appears in the method startGame().

4.9 The Output of the Project WheelFortune2

The output of the project WheelFortune2 is made by using the method showMsg(), which prints text information on the console as cited below. The output shows that when a mismatch occurs, the next player becomes the current player. The program continues its execution until either one of players "rejects" to enter more guess or all of characters in the sentence have been matched over.

```
Game is ready. Start playing
The current player Smith is playing:
The guessed char w matches 1 character(s) in the sentence.
The guessed char p matches 0 character in the sentence.
The current player Brown is playing:
The guessed char o matches 2 character(s) in the sentence.
The guessed char m matches 0 character in the sentence.
The current player John is playing:
The guessed char l matches 3 character(s) in the sentence.
The guessed char b matches 0 character in the sentence.
The current player Smith is playing:
You clicked Cancel. The program is terminated.
BUILD SUCCESSFUL (total time: 4 minutes 28 seconds)
```

4.10 Initializing the Board and the Wheel: The Project WheelFortune3

As mentioned in the global sequence of actions, the game WheelFortune requires two more objects. One is the "board" that displays the matched characters guessed by the players. The other is the "wheel" that is turned by the current-player for giving a wheel-score or a "Bankrupt" symbol. The entire game has only one board and one wheel. That is, both of them are global objects and are also instantiated by the class GamePanel.java. Therefore, the UML class diagram of the project WheelFortune3 is as in Fig. 4.5.

Reaching this point, the project WheelFortune3 should completely implement the entire global sequence of actions outlined in Sect. 4.2. In order to easier access and better improve the pseudo code, we repeat the global sequence of actions here with some modifications.

1. The class GamePanel.java instantiates the initializer of the class Initializer.java, the board of the class Board.java, the wheel of the class Wheel.java, and the array of three players of the class Player.java.
2. Without considering any special cases including "Bankrupt" and error cases, the class GamePanel.java
   (a) Invokes wheelScore = playerAry[currPlayer].turnWheel() to get a wheel-score
   (b) Invokes inputChar = playerAry[currPlayer].inputGuess() to get a guessedChar
   (c) Invokes idxList = initializer.receiveGuess(inputChar) to return an idxList that held the indexes of matching positions

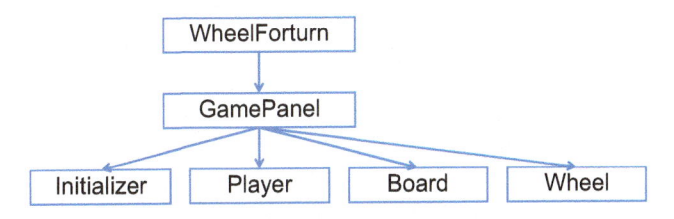

Fig. 4.5 The UML class diagram of the project WheelFortune3

i. If (idxList is empty), mismatch happens, changes currPlayer to next player, go to step 2.a.
ii. Else, match happens,
   1. Calculate the currScore = idxList.size() * wheelScore and then totalScore = playerAry[currPlayer].getTotalScore() + currScore. Finally, invoke playerAry[currPlayer].setTotalScore(totalScore).
   2. Show matched characters on the board using board.insertCharAry() and board.showBoard().
3. If (all characters in the sentence are matched), game terminates.
4. Else, go to step 2.

Clearly, the class GamePanel.java implements the "core," which invokes methods defined in other classes to perform the sequence of actions. The codes of the two new classes Board.java and Wheel.java are cited in Listing 4.3.

Listing 4.3 The codes of the two new classes Board.java and Wheel.java in the project WheelFortune3

```
 1  /*
 2   * Board.java -- A class defines a board for displaying the matched characters.
 3   */
 4  package wheelfortune;
 5
 6  import java.util.ArrayList;
 7
12  public class Board {
13
14      private int strLen;
15      private char[] currAry;
16
17      public Board() {
18      }
19
20      public void initBoard(int oriStrLen) {
21          strLen = oriStrLen;
22          currAry = new char[strLen];
23          initCharAry(currAry); // init it with ' ' char
24      }
25
26      public boolean insertCurrAry(ArrayList<Integer> idxAry, char inputChar) {
27          boolean exist = false;
28          inputChar = Character.toUpperCase(inputChar);
29          for (Integer idx : idxAry) {
30              if (currAry[idx] == (inputChar)) {
31                  exist = true;
32                  break;
33              } else {
34                  currAry[idx] = inputChar;
35              }
36          }
37          return exist;
38      }
39
40      public void showBoard() {
41          showTop();
42          fillCurrentAry(currAry);
43          showBottom();
44          showLineEnd();
45      }
```

```java
46
47      public void showTop() {
48          for (int i = 0; i < strLen; i++) {
49              showUnit("-----");
50          }
51          showLineEnd();
52          for (int i = 0; i < strLen; i++) {
53              showUnit("|     |");
54          }
55          showLineEnd();
56      }
57
58      public void showBottom() {
59          for (int i = 0; i < strLen; i++) {
60              showUnit("|     |");
61          }
62          showLineEnd();
63          for (int i = 0; i < strLen; i++) {
64              showUnit("-----");
65          }
66          showLineEnd();
67      }
68
69      public void fillCurrentAry(char[] current) {
70          for (int i = 0; i < strLen; i++) {
71              showUnit("| " + current[i] + " |");
72          }
73          showLineEnd();
74      }
75
76      public void showUnit(String drawStr) {
77          System.out.print(drawStr);
78      }
79
80      public void showLineEnd() {
81          System.out.println();
82      }
83
84      public void initCharAry(char[] ary) {
85          for (int i = 0; i < strLen; i++) {
86              ary[i] = ' ';
87          }
88      }
89
90      public char[] getCurrAry() {
91          return currAry;
92      }
93  }

1   /*
2    * Wheel.java - A class defines the wheel.
3    */
4   package wheelfortune;
5
```

```java
10 public class Wheel {
11
12     private String[] wheel;
13     private int wheelLen;
14
15     public Wheel() {
16         wheelLen = 10;
17         wheel = new String[wheelLen];
18         initWheel();
19     }
20
21     private void initWheel() {
22         int ranInt;
23         for (int i = 0; i < wheelLen; i++) {
24             ranInt = (int) ((Math.random() * 1000) + 100); // [100, 1100)
25             if (i == 5) {
26                 wheel[i] = "Bankrupt";
27             } else {
28                 wheel[i] = Integer.toString(ranInt);
29             }
30         }
31     }
32
33     public String wheelTurns() {
34         int ranIdx = (int)(Math.random() * 10); // [0, 9]
35         return wheel[ranIdx];
36     }
37 }
```

4.11 Mimicking the Wheel Turning

The class Wheel.java implements a very simple wheel, which is a String array. We define the wheel as a String array because one of data in the array is the String "Bankrupt." For keeping the same data type in one array, all of other integers are also converted as the type of String. In addition, designing the wheel as an array of String would make any extensions of the wheel easy. For example, the number of slots on the wheel could be enlarged or shrunk. Any other cases, such as "Special Gift," "Special Penalty," and the like, could be added freely.

We assume that the total number of slots of the wheel is 10 and the position with the index of [5] holds the "Bankrupt" and other slots store randomly generated integers. The method wheelTurns() in the class Wheel.java simulates the wheel turning by picking up a random number as the index, and the String at the position pointed to by the index is the wheel-score. When the current-player invokes the method player.turnWheel(), it calls wheel.wheelTurns() for returning a wheel-score in the type of String. If the String is not "Bankrupt," the String is converted to be an int; otherwise, it converts the "Bankrupt" to be the int of −1. The value is returned to the class GamePanel.java as the wheelScore for the current-player including the −1 as the indicator of "Bankrupt." Unfortunately, in this text game we have to omit any kind of "real turning" action for the wheel.

The wheel object of the class Wheel.java is instantiated in the class GamePanel.java since it is a global component. However, the players should be able to touch the object wheel for turning it. That is, the class Player.java needs a new method turnWheel() that should be able to invoke the method wheel.wheelTurns() defined in another object wheel. For that reason, a special channel of communication for allowing the player to touch the object of the wheel should be set up. Thus, a variable "wheel" is declared in the class Player.java, and a setter method setWheel() is added to allow the class GamePanel.java passing the object wheel through the setter method into the class Player.java. This is a very useful way for passing an object of a class to the other class. The code is shown in Listing 4.4.

4.12 The Board Displays the Matched Characters

Listing 4.4 The partial code of the class Player.java in the project WheelFortune3

```
 1 /*
 2  * Player.java - A class defines a player.
 3  */
...
12 public class Player {
13
22 ...
23     public int turnWheel() {
24         String wheelScoreStr;
25         int wheelScore;
26         wheelScoreStr = wheel.wheelTurns();
27         if (!(wheelScoreStr.equals("Bankrupt"))) {
28             wheelScore = Integer.parseInt(wheelScoreStr);
29         } else {
30             wheelScore = -1;
31         }
32         return wheelScore;
33     }
34
87 ...
88     public void setWheel(Wheel wheel) {
89         this.wheel = wheel;
90     }
91 }
```

This is a special case illustrating the relationship between classes, which sometimes is different from the relationship in our mind. We might think of "the player turns the wheel" so that we might let the class Player.java instantiating an object of wheel. If we would design the class Player.java in this way, then when we instantiate three objects of player, every player has his/her own wheel and everyone would turn his/her own wheel instead of a globally shared wheel. Obviously, it is not true in reality because the entire game has only one wheel shared by three players. Therefore, we have only one global wheel object that is instantiated by the class GamePanel.java and is passed to every player.

4.12 The Board Displays the Matched Characters

The class Board.java draws a board in text fashion as shown in Fig. 4.6. The code looks complicated and the display seems "ugly." It is a limitation of drawing in text.

Because the board needs to display all of characters of the given sentence one by one, the class Board.java defines an empty charAry and an empty board with the same number of characters as in the given sentence. The charAry is for holding the matched characters internally, and the board is for displaying the matched characters stored in the charAry

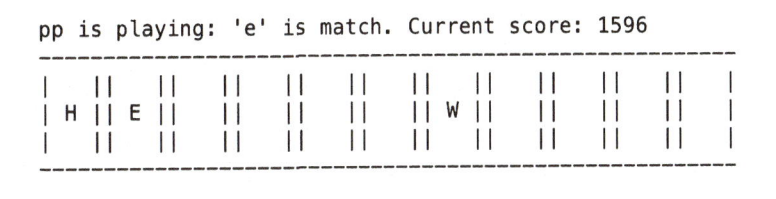

Fig. 4.6 The board displays the matched guessed character(s)

```
pp is playing: 'e' is match. Current score: 1596
------------------------------------------------------------
|   || || || || || || || || || || |
| H || E || || || || || W || || || || |
|   || || || || || || || || || || |
------------------------------------------------------------

pp is playing:
```

on the console. The number of characters is obtained from the given sentence by invoking the method sentence. length(). Every unit on the empty board has a rectangle shape and is constructed by using characters "-" and "|." Due to the fact that the arrayList idxList held the indexes of the matching positions in the sentence, the code applies the stored indexes in the idxList to find out the corresponding characters from the sentence and insert those matched characters into the charAry, and then in turn that characters in the charAry are displayed at the corresponding rectangles of the board.

4.13 Initializing the Given Sentence Through Reading a Text File

So far the given sentence is temporarily assumed as "Hello World." It is hard-coded and cannot be applied to real games. To solve the "hard-coded" problem, the project needs an input mechanism for getting the given sentence. As we know, there are two approaches. One is let the initializer to input a given sentence using the JOptionPane; the other is getting a sentence by reading a text file. We have used the second approach in Chap. 2 and have created a class ReadFile.java. Here we selected the second approach again in order to further understand the functionality of the class ReadFile.java. By adding the class ReadFile.java, the UML class diagram of the project WheelFortune4 should be modified as shown in Fig. 4.7, where the class Initializer.java "uses" the class ReadFile.java for inputting a sentence.

The class ReadFile.java was coded in Chap. 2 with a simplified assumption. That is, there is only one text file and the text file contains only one line string. Now, we are going to enhance the class ReadFile.java in considering two more general facts: (1) There are multiple text files, and the class ReadFile.java needs to allow the user to select one of them. (2) One text file could contain multiple lines, and every line is a sentence such that the class ReadFile.java needs to randomly pick up one of lines for a new game.

We implemented a project TestReadFile in trying to handle the new situations by modifying the class ReadFile.java as cited in Listing 4.5.

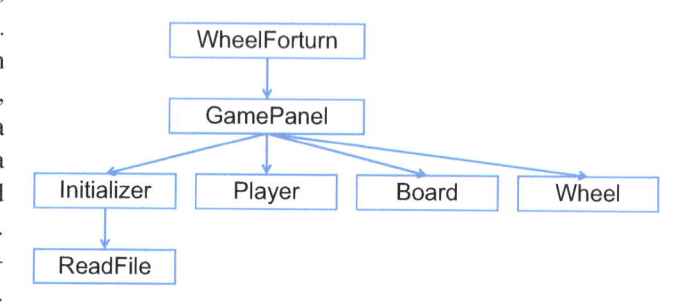

Fig. 4.7 The new UML class diagram of the project WheelFortune4

Listing 4.5 The class ReadFile.java in the project TestReadFile and WheelFortune4

```
1  /*
2   * ReadFile.java - A class for opening a file and reading a line from it.
3   */
4  package wheelfortune;
5
6  import java.io.BufferedReader;
7  import java.io.FileNotFoundException;
8  import java.io.FileReader;
9  import java.io.IOException;
10 import java.net.URL;
11 import javax.swing.JOptionPane;
12
17 public class ReadFile {
18
19     FileReader inputFile;
20     String filePath;
21     String fileName;
22
23     public ReadFile() {
24     }
25
26     public void selectFile() {
27         Object[] selectionValues = {"wheel1.txt", "wheel2.txt"};
28         String initialSelection = "";
```

```java
29           Object selection = JOptionPane.showInputDialog(null,
30                   "Select the file you would like to use",
31                   "Select a file", JOptionPane.QUESTION_MESSAGE, null,
32                   selectionValues, initialSelection);
33           filePath = "../txt/" + selection;
34           URL url = getClass().getResource(filePath);
35           fileName = url.getPath();
36
37           try {
38               //Create object of FileReader
39               inputFile = new FileReader(fileName);
40           } catch (FileNotFoundException fex) {
41           }
42       }
43
44       public String readContent() {
45           BufferedReader bufferedReader = new BufferedReader(inputFile);
46           String line = null;
47           int numLines = 3;
48           int lineNum;
49           int count;
50
51           lineNum = (int) (Math.random() * numLines);
52           try {
53               count = 0;
54               while ((line = bufferedReader.readLine()) != null) {
55                   if (count == lineNum) { // reach the random line
56                       break;
57                   }
58                   count++;
59               }
60               bufferedReader.close();
61           } catch (IOException ioex) {
62           }
63           return line;
64       }
65   }
```

The new code of the class ReadFile.java has two methods selectFile() and readContent(). The method selectFile() defines an Object[] array for storing two file names "Object[] selectionValues = {"wheel1.txt", "wheel2.txt"};" and then the method employs one of the methods JOptionPane.showInputDialog() to display the two text file names stored in the array on the dialog GUI for allowing the user to select one of them. Of course, the number of file names can be extended according to the needs. The method readContent() uses the variable "numLines = 3" to indicate that the text file contains three lines such that the random number generator generates an integer lineNum in the range of [0, (3 − 1)] for randomly picking up one of three lines as the given sentence for the game.

Clearly, the new ReadFile.java satisfies the new requirements. However, everything is built in the class code. The user loses the flexibility. For example, if the user would like to add another new text file, say wheel3.txt, into the subdirectory txt, the user has no way to add it into the Object[] array by modifying the code. When the number of lines in the text file is changed from 3 to other number, the reader also has no authority to change the code.

In order to return the flexibility to the user, the project TestReadFile2 modified the code of the class ReadFile.java as shown in Listing 4.6. The new code allows the user to input the text file name and the line numbers in the text file.

Listing 4.6 Another code of the class ReadFile.java in the project TestReadFile2

```
 1 /*
 2  * ReadFile.java - A class for opening a file and reading a line from it.
 3  */
 4 package wheelfortune;
 5
 6 import java.io.BufferedReader;
 7 import java.io.FileNotFoundException;
 8 import java.io.FileReader;
 9 import java.io.IOException;
10 import java.net.URL;
11 import javax.swing.JOptionPane;
12
17 public class ReadFile {
18
19     private FileReader inputFile;
20     String filePath;
21     String fileName;
22
23     public ReadFile() {
24     }
25
26     public void selectFile() {
27         String aFileName = JOptionPane.showInputDialog(
28                 "Please enter a file name for reading (e.g. wheel1.txt)");
29         filePath = "../txt/" + aFileName;
30         URL url = getClass().getResource(filePath);
31         fileName = url.getPath();
32
33         try {
34             // Create object of FileReader
35             inputFile = new FileReader(fileName);
36         } catch (FileNotFoundException fex) {
37         }
38     }
39
40     public String readContent() {
41         BufferedReader bufferedReader = new BufferedReader(inputFile);
42         String line = null;
43         int numLines;
44         int lineNum;
45         int count;
46
47         String lineNumStr = JOptionPane.showInputDialog(
48                 "How many lines in the file? (an integer)");
49         numLines = Integer.parseInt(lineNumStr);
50         lineNum = (int) (Math.random() * numLines);
51         try {
52             count = 0;
53             while ((line = bufferedReader.readLine()) != null) {
54                 if (count == lineNum) { // reach the random line
55                     break;
56                 }
57                 count++;
```

```
58              }
59              bufferedReader.close();
60         } catch (IOException ioex) {
61         }
62
63         return line;
64     }
65 }
```

Which one is better to be adopted depends on the entire program structure and the preference of the programmers and users. We selected the code of the class ReadFile.java listed in Listing 4.5 for the project WheelFortune4 due to its easy to be used.

4.14 Considering Special Cases and Error Cases: The Project WheelFortune4

After making the project WheelFortune3 works on all of regular cases, we need to consider all of special cases and possible error cases as listed below.

1. If the current-player turns the wheel and gets a "Bankrupt," his/her total score has to be erased as zero and next player takes turn.
2. If the current-player's guessedChar does not match with any character in the sentence, ignore the wheel-score and next player takes turn.
3. If the current-player's guessedChar matches with a character in the sentence but the character has already been guessed and verified by the previous players, the matched situation and the wheel-score must be ignored. And then, the next player should become the current player.
4. If current-player does not enter any character (the player does not enter any character into the input slot of the JOptionPane but hits the return key), it also counts as an error case. The next player takes turn.

For considering all of these possible abnormal cases listed above, the additional actions should be inserted into the global sequence of actions with italic font as follows.

1. The project has an initializer, three players, a board, a wheel, and a readFile.
2. The initializer reads a sentence from a selected text file through the readFile.
   (a) The board displays a set of empty rectangles according to the length of the sentence.
3. If the sentence hasn't been matched completely:
   (a) The current-player turns the wheel and gets a wheel-score.
      - *If the wheel-score = "Bankrupt," erase the total score earned by the current-player.*
      - *The next player becomes the current-player.*
      - *Go to step 3.*
   (b) The current-player inputs a guess-character.
      - *If the guess-character is empty (the player does not enter a character but hit return), the next player becomes the current-player.*
      - *Go to step 3.*
   (c) Searching the sentence for the guess-character.
   (d) The index of a matching position of the sentence is stored into an arrayList idxList.
4. If the length of the idxList = 0:
   (a) The next player becomes the current-player.
   (b) Go to step 3.
5. Else if the length of the idxList > 0:
   (a) *If the matched character has been guessed already:*
      - *The next player becomes the current player.*
      - *Go to step 3.*
   (b) Else (if the matched character has not been guessed already)
      - The current-player earns a current-score = numMatch * wheel-score.
      - The total-score of the current-player + current-score.
      - The matched characters are shown on the board.
6. If all characters in the sentence are matched:
   (a) Set the complete-match true to terminate the loop.
   (b) Terminate the game.
7. Else
   (a) Go to step 3.

The modifications on the global sequence of actions will be reflexed on the modifications of the "core" in the new version. According to the sequence of actions above, the new version WheelFortune4 has an enhanced class GamePanel.java that implements the "core" with all of possible error cases.

In addition, the method terminateGame() is also enhanced with a sorting method sortAry() for arranging the three players in an descending order based on the total scores earned by the three players so that the game winner is always the player in the position of playerAry[0] after the sorting action. Meanwhile, the class Initializer.java goes through the object readFile to read in a new sentence from an existing file each time when a new game starts. The new codes of the class GamePanel.java and Initializer.java are shown in Listing 4.7.

Listing 4.7 The new codes of the classes GamePanel.java and Initializer.java in the project WheelFortune4

```
  1  /*
  2   * GamePanel.java - A class to be the coordinator of initializer and player.
  3   */
  4  package wheelfortune;
  5
  6  import java.util.ArrayList;
  7  import javax.swing.JOptionPane;
  8
 13  public class GamePanel {
 14  ...
 69
 70      public void startGame() {
 71          ArrayList<Integer> idxList; // one letter may have multiple matches
 72          boolean gameDone = false;
 73          boolean guessValid;
 74          char playerGuess;
 75          int wheelScore;
 76          boolean exist;
 77
 78          showMsg("Game is ready. Start playing");
 79          while (!gameDone) { // allows next player
 80              currPlayer = playerAry[currPlayerIdx];
 81              guessValid = true;
 82              while (guessValid) { // current player continues
 83                  showMsgSameLine(currPlayer.getName() + " is playing: ");
 84                  wheelScore = currPlayer.turnWheel();
 85                  showMsgSameLine("wheel score is " + wheelScore + ". ");
 86                  // player gets bankrupt, break
 87                  if (wheelScore < 0) { // bankrupt
 88                      currPlayer.setTotalScore(0);
 89                      showMsgSameLine(currPlayer.getName() + " is Bankrupt.");
 90                      showMsg(" Current score: " + currPlayer.getTotalScore());
 91                      break; // next player takes turn
 92                  }
 93                  // player does not bankrupt
 94                  playerGuess = currPlayer.inputGuess();
 95                  idxList = initializer.receiveGuess(playerGuess);
 96                  // player's guessed char mismatch, break
 97                  if (idxList.isEmpty()) {
 98                      showMsgSameLine("'" + playerGuess + "' is mismatch.");
 99                      showMsg(" Current score: " + currPlayer.getTotalScore());
100                      break; // next player takes turn
101                  }
102                  // player's guessed char match
103                  // insert the matched char into board for displaying
104                  exist = board.insertCurrAry(idxList, playerGuess);
105                  // the guessed char exists already, break
106                  if (exist) {
107                      showMsgSameLine("'" + playerGuess + "' exists already.");
108                      showMsg(" Current score: " + currPlayer.getTotalScore());
109                      break; // next player takes turn
110                  }
111                  // the guessed char does not exist, the best case
```

4.14 Considering Special Cases and Error Cases: The Project WheelFortune4

```
112                    // calculate current-player's total-score
113                    wheelScore = idxList.size() * wheelScore;
114                    showMsgSameLine("'" + playerGuess + "' is match.");
115                    // add wheel-score to player's total score
116                    currPlayer.setTotalScore(
117                            currPlayer.getTotalScore() + wheelScore);
118                    showMsg(" Current score: " + currPlayer.getTotalScore());
119                    // show the board
120                    board.showBoard();
121                    // is the sentence completely matched?
122                    if (initializer.getSentence().equals(
123                            new String(board.getCurrAry()))) {
124                        gameDone = true;
125                        break;
126                    }
127                }
128                if (gameDone) {
129                    break; // game is completed
130                } else { // turn to the next player
131                    currPlayerIdx = (currPlayerIdx + 1) % numPlayer;
132                }
133            }
134            terminateGame();
135        }
136
137        public void terminateGame() {
138            showMsg("The game is completed.");
139            sortAry(playerAry);
140            showMsg("Sorted players' scores are: ");
141            for (Player player : playerAry) {
142                showMsg(String.format("%-10s %6d",
143                        player.getName(), player.getTotalScore()));
144            }
145
146            showMsg("Congratulation " + playerAry[0].getName()
147                    + "! You won the game!");
148        }
149
150        public void sortAry(Player[] ary) {
151            Player temp;
152            for (int i = 0; i < ary.length - 1; i++) {
153                for (int j = i + 1; j < ary.length; j++) {
154                    if (ary[i].getTotalScore() < ary[j].getTotalScore()) {
155                        temp = ary[i];
156                        ary[i] = ary[j];
157                        ary[j] = temp;
158                    }
159                }
160            }
161        }
162
163        public void showMsgSameLine(String msg) {
164            System.out.print(msg);
165        }
166
```

```
167     public void showMsg(String msg) {
168         System.out.println(msg);
169     }
170 }
```

```
1  /*
2   * Initializer.java - A class defines the initializer.
3   */
4  package wheelfortune;
5
6  import java.util.ArrayList;
7
12 public class Initializer {
13
14     private String sentence;
15     private int sentenceLen;
16     private ReadFile readFile;
17
18     public Initializer() {
19         readFile = new ReadFile();
20     }
21
22     public String initSentence() {
23         readFile.selectFile();
24         sentence = readFile.readContent();
25         System.out.println(sentence);
26         sentenceLen = sentence.length();
27         sentence = sentence.toUpperCase();
28         return sentence;
29     }
30
31     public ArrayList<Integer> receiveGuess(char inputChar) {
32         inputChar = Character.toUpperCase(inputChar);
33         ArrayList<Integer> idxList = new ArrayList();
34         for (int i = 0; i < sentenceLen; i++) {
35             if (sentence.charAt(i) == inputChar) {
36                 idxList.add(i);
37             }
38         }
39         return idxList;
40     }
41
42     public String getSentence() {
43         return sentence;
44     }
45
46     public void showMsg(String msg) {
47         System.out.println(msg);
48     }
49 }
```

4.15 The Driving Force of the Game

Clearly, the "core" of the game is implemented in the method startGame() of the class GamePanel.java. The "core" includes two nested "while" loops that drive the game. The condition of the inner "while" is "guessValid." That is, the inner "while" asks the current-player for turning the wheel and inputting a guess-character. Then it checks all of the special cases and error cases. When it finds "Bankrupt" or mismatch, or the guessedChar already exists, it "breaks" the "while" loop and lets the next player to be the current player. Only when everything is valid, it adds the score for the current-player and displays the correctly matched character guessed by the current-player on the board. The outer "while" checks whether the entire sentence has been completely guessed. If not, it goes to the inner "while" loop; otherwise, the outer "while" loop is terminated for invoking the terminateGame() method to terminate the game.

In contrast to the method terminateGame(), another method abortGame() is implemented for treating a special case. The special case is that when the initializer or the current-player is asked for inputting data but the "Cancel" button on the JOptionPane is clicked. That is, the game needs inputting data for continuous running; however the initializer or the player refused to provide the data. The game won't be able to continue and has to be aborted. Aborting the game is different from terminating the game. Therefore, the class GamePanel.java codes two different methods abortGame() and terminateGame().

For every special case or error case, a statement "break" is used. A "break" means to break the "closest" loop. For example, if "Bankrupt" happens, a "break" is issued to break the inner "while" loop. The execution of a "break" includes ignoring all of the remaining statements inside the curly brackets of the loop and continuing the execution of the statements after the ending curly bracket.

4.16 Terminating the Game

As mentioned above, when the game is regularly terminated, a method terminateGame() will be invoked. The terminateGame() method is not only terminating the game but also outputting the playing result for showing who is the winner of the game. The winning player is the player who earns the highest totalScore. Fortunately, the three players are stored in the array playerAry[], and every player has his/her record of the totalScore. We may either apply a searching algorithm for finding out the player who holds the highest totalScore or apply a sorting algorithm to sort the entire array into the descending order such that the winner is the player with the index of [0] in the array playerAry[]. We adopted the sorting algorithm approach because it not only tells the game winner for the game players but also demonstrates the fundamental idea about sorting for readers.

We haven't learned any sorting algorithm yet. Because the array has only three elements, we can intuitively illustrate a sorting algorithm for sorting the array. Assuming that an array has only two elements. We can compare the first element with the second one. If the first one is larger than the second one, the array has been sorted in a descending order already. If the first one is smaller than the second one, we can swap them to move the second one onto the first position and move the first one onto the second position so that the two elements are in a descending order. Suppose that we call it as a "compare and swap." Now, actually we have three elements in the array. We need to apply the "compare and swap" three times. The first time, we "compare and swap" the first two elements and make them in a descending order. The second time, we "compare and swap" the current first with the third element to make them in a descending order. These two steps ensure the largest element among the three has been at the first position already. And then, the third "compare and swap" makes the remaining two elements (the current second and the current third elements) in a descending order.

The implementation of the algorithm above is shown in the method sortAry() (lines 150–161 in Listing 4.7) of the class GamePanel.java. The code consists of two nested "for" loops. The outer "for" loop picks up the first element, and then the inner "for" loop in turn picks up the remaining second element and then the third element in the array. The statement in the body of the nested loop "compare and swap" the first element with the second one and keeps the larger one at the first position; then the statement "compare and swap" the current first one with the third one and keeps the larger one at the first position. When the inner "for" loop finishes its iteration, the largest element among all of the three values in the array is kept at the first position. As long as the inner "for" loop finishes its iteration, the outer "for" loop picks up the current second element and "compare and swap" with the third element picked up by the inner "for" loop and keeps the second largest element at the second position. In other words, the first iteration of the inner "for" loop makes the largest element of the array resides in the first position; the second iteration of the inner "for" loop makes the second largest element at the second position. The remaining smallest element is on the third position. Extending the length of the array to n, the outer "for" loop starts from the first element and ends at the $(n-1)$th element, and the inner "for" loop starts from the second element and ends at the nth element; after the inner "for" loop iterated $(n-1)$ times, all of elements in the array are sorted in a descending order.

There is a variety of sorting algorithms, which will be covered in a course of "Data Structures." Here, we design the sorting algorithm based on our logical thinking.

4.17 An Important Notice

Both the story of the game WheelFortune and the corresponding pseudo code indicated that the game has an initializer and three players. The major tasks of the players are playing the game, including turning the wheel, inputting the guess-character, and so on. All of other functions, such as setting the sentence, inputting the information of players, and the like, are the initializer's tasks. However, for reading a sentence from a file needs to select a file; for inputting the information of three players requires typing. When we designed the computer as the initializer, the initializer would not do all of those functions that should be done by humans. In other words, some functions, such as select a file, input the players' names, and the like, have to be done by a human initializer. Thus, when we design a game, sometimes we have to imagine that a human initializer works on the initialization part of the game for providing some initialization data, unless we may apply the random number generator or file reading mechanism for performing all of these functions. The human initializer could be the game player or his/her partners.

4.18 Summary

Chapter 3 and this chapter discussed two games in-text. They prepared us to have a fundamental view on the OOP programming technology and to have a basic understanding what a game is. The objects and interactions among objects are the soul of a game. An object comes from a class. A class is an abstraction of an object in a program. Multiple objects work together must involve interactive actions and communications. For an easy modeling and a clear description about the classes as well as the relationships among classes, a tool is needed. It is that the UML class diagram.

The game WheelFortune promotes the learning of the data structure Array and ArrayList, which is one of the simple but important data structures that are adopted anywhere. The algorithm associates with Array and ArrayList are rich and worth to be studied.

However, a game in-text displays the output only on the console with plain text. Like the game WheelFortune in-text, its board is "ugly" and is not easy to be made. Even worse, its wheel is never shown up. Therefore, a game in-text is hard to simulate our real world. What we need is a graphical display that may really mimic the scenes as in TV shows. For reaching this goal, we would like to turn our study from the text to the graphical technique in order to realize real video games.

4.19 Exercises

Self-Reviewing Questions

1. What are similarities and what are differences between the game WheelFortune and the game GuessInt? Could you use two UML class diagrams to describe them?
2. The game uses both Array and ArrayList data structures. What condition requires us to select Array or ArrayList?
3. How to compare the guessed character with the sentence and make a record about the matched position?
4. Why do we need a special method showMsg()? May we use System.out.println() directly instead?
5. Do you find any variations of the simple "for" loop in the code of the game? Do you understand the meaning of the new version of "for" loop?
6. In order to format the outputs of the println(), what symbols do we use?
7. Without looking at the book, write down your pseudo code for outlining the game WheelFortune.
8. How to select a word from four existing words through JOptionPane.showInputDialog()?
9. Which is valid and which is invalid in the following definitions?

    ```
    String aStr = 12.34;
    String aStr = "12.34";
    String aStr = "" + 12.34;
    String aStr = String.valueOf(12.34);
    ```

10. A static method or variable can be conveniently invoked by using the class name directly without instantiating an object. May we define all of methods or all of variables as static? Why do you say so?
11. What special cases and error cases are involved in the game WheelFortune?
12. Make two examples: one is for showing "is-a" relationship and the other is for showing "uses" relationship.

Projects

1. According to the description about Array, we can declare array and assign values to the array with different approaches, such as follows.

    ```
    int[] myInt = {1, 3, 5, 7, 9};   Or

    int[] myInt = new int[5];
    myInt[0] = 1;
    ...
                                     Or
    ```

4.19 Exercises

```
for (int k = 0; k < 5; k++) {
   myInt[k] = k * 2 + 1;
}
```

Write a test program to verify these statements.

2. A course has five students. Every student has a first name, a last name, and a score. Write a program to allow the teacher inputting required data for every student and store all of data and five students into an array. After finishing the input portion, the program allows the teacher to make a choice either based on students' scores or last-names for sorting them in an ascending order. And finally the program prints all of students' information on the console.

3. What is difference between Array and ArrayList? Write a program to store "Hello" into an array and into an arrayList, respectively. And then, the program prints the contents of the array and the arrayList on the screen.

4. Write a program that prints a set of rectangles using characters '-' and '|.' The program allows the user to input an integer as the number of rectangles. The program should be able to handle all of special cases or possible errors.

5. Write a program that asks the user to input a string. And then, the program counts the number of characters of the string and prints it on the console.

6. Write a program that accepts an input string from the user. And then, the program counts and prints the numbers of each character in the string. For example,
   'b' : 3
   'h' : 2 ...

7. Write a program that declares an int array with 15 elements, initializes the array with random numbers in the range of [5, 115], and outputs the largest integer and the smallest integer of the array.

8. Write a program that declares an integer arrayList and accepts a user input integer as the length of the arrayList. And then the program initializes the arrayList with random numbers in the range of [2, 87]. Finally, the program outputs the average value of the integers in the arrayList.

9. Implement a project with a name of "EchoFile." Create a text file in a subdirectory "txt" under the folder "Source Package" of the project and open the file for editing some strings, then close it. And then, ask the program to open and read the contents of the text file and echo the contents of the file on the console.

10. Extend the project "EchoFile" described in the previous question to include three text files. The project allows the user to select one of them for reading and echoing.

11. Modify the project "EchoFile" described in the previous question for defining a String array with a length of three. Store the three text file names onto the array, and display the three file names on the console. The project then asks the user to input an integer of 1, 2, or 3 as an index to get the corresponding file name from the array and opens the corresponding text file for reading and echoing.

12. Design and implement the following game DiceFortune. The story of the game says, "Two players are initially assigned a same amount of money, say 100 dollars. When a 'play' starts, the two players throw two dices interchangeably five times. The player whose average value of the five throws is larger wins this 'play'. The loser pays the amount of money that equals to the average value of his/her five throws to the winner. Once a player gets a throw value of 12, he/she can stop the throw and his/her average value of five throws counts as 12. The other player continues his/her throws. If the other player also gets a throw value of 12, this 'play' is finished without a winner. Otherwise, if the other player does not have any value of 12, the former player wins this 'play'. Whenever one of players loses all of money, the game is terminated." The design stage should include a UML diagram and a pseudo code.

Part II
Games Based on Event-Driven: Chaps. 5–10

5. GUI Programming with Graphical Drawing: A Project PaintXmasCard

Video games need to show their output graphically in using a graphical user interface (GUI), which requires GUI programming. In general, GUI programming is based on two techniques. One is the graphical drawing; the other is the software components with event handling. This chapter concentrates on the former technique. It discusses a project PaintXmasCard with five different versions for illustrating the text drawing, image drawing, and fundamental geographical shape drawing. The latter technique is deferred to later chapters.

The objectives of this chapter include:
1. GUI programming in Java.
2. Containers and components.
3. Constructing a basis for GUIs.
4. Inheritance: "is-a" relationship.
5. Graphical drawing and computations.
6. Painting a Christmas card.
7. Painting images.
8. Painting decorations.
9. Super() method and keywords of "super" and "this."
10. Override and overload methods.

Video games need to show their outputs graphically, that is, they need a graphical user interface (GUI). In the previous chapter, we have experienced the difficulties in displaying outputs of the game WheelFortune in-text without graphical technique. Now, we should start the discussions on the GUI programming for equipping all of video games.

In general, fundamental GUI programming is based on two techniques. One is the graphical drawing; the other is the software components with event handling. The former mainly is for displaying the output portion of a game; the latter is for realizing the input portion of a game. For simplifying the discussion, this chapter concentrates on the graphical drawing. The software components and their layouts, as well as the event handling, are deferred to later chapters.

5.1 Java Provides a Rich Capacity for GUI Programming

The initial step of GUI programming is to display objects graphically. No doubt, it just likes to make an oil painting in our real life. An oil painting needs a canvas with a frame and a set of resources. For mimicking the setting and resources, Java APIs provide a variety of built-in classes that offer capacities for realizing graphical programming. These classes belong to two packages of java.awt and javax.swing, respectively. At the beginning, the package java.awt displays the graphical components through underlying operating system. This tightly coupled design is not flexible enough for implementing complicated graphics. Later a new package javax.swing comes, which displays components by Java language itself. All classes defined in javax.swing have a capital "J" as the initial of the class names to distinguish them from the classes in the package of java.awt. Nowadays, we are more interested in classes defined in the package of javax.swing. However, some classes defined in the package java.awt are still involved very often.

The built-in classes defined in the package javax.swing could be classified as container classes and component classes. The major container classes are JFrame, JApplet, JPanel, and JDialog. Specifically, the JFrame usually functions as the root class of a stand-alone Java application; and the JApplet acts as the root class of a Java applet, which is a component of the web. This book mainly discusses Java applications so that we are using the class JFrame only. The class JPanel is an intermediate-level container because it can contain other components and at the same time itself can be contained in a higher-level container, such as the JFrame or the JApplet. Both built-in classes JFrame and JPanel have built-in graphics context that supports graphical drawing. Especially a JPanel is used most popularly as a canvas due to its nature of an intermediate container. And then the class JFrame plays the role of a frame to contain the canvas made of a JPanel.

Consequently, for developing games we select the built-in class JPanel as the canvas for painting and displaying components in GUIs and select the built-in class JFrame as the frame and the root class for applications. Definitely, painting process not only requires a canvas and some painting tools but also requires an excellent sense for laying out objects and their structures.

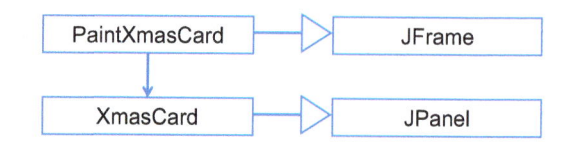

Fig. 5.1 The UML class diagram for making a GUI with a frame and a canvas

5.2 Constructing a Basis for GUIs

As discussed above, for painting a graphical scene, we need a frame that contains a canvas. We also learned that the package javax.swing has a built-in class JFrame that performs functions to be a frame; and another built-in class JPanel can be adopted as a canvas. However, every different game requires its own special frame and special canvas. How to match the general functionalities possessed by the built-in classes with the special requirements issued by different specific games? OOP programming offers a so-called "inheritance" technique for providing a perfect solution.

A simplified speaking is that we are going to create a user-defined class that inherits all of the properties and behaviors from the built-in class JFrame such that the user-defined class also has the functionality to be a frame. Meanwhile, the user-defined class can be further developed to contain any special features issued by the specific game. The relationship between the built-in class JFrame and the user-defined class is termed as "is-a." It is that the user-defined class "is-a" the built-in class. The user-defined class is a subclass of the built-in class and the built-in class is a parent class of the user-defined class. Similarly, when we need a class to play a role of a canvas, we can define a subclass to inherit all of properties and behaviors of the parent class JPanel. In a UML class diagram, this "is-a" relationship is indicated by a symbol as shown in Fig. 5.1 (the symbol was introduced in Chap. 4).

Figure 5.1 shows that the user-defined class PaintXmasCard.java "is-a" the built-in class JFrame and the user-defined class XmasCard.java class "is-a" the built-in class JPanel. We also call the class PaintXmasCard.java as a subclass of the class JFrame and the class JFrame as the parent class of the class PaintXmasCard.java. So does for the relations between the classes XmasCard.java and JPanel.

Even though we did not write any code for these two subclasses, the "is-a" relationship indicates that the subclass PaintXmasCard.java now has all of the abilities defined in the parent class JFrame and is able to play a role of a frame for the project. Similarly, the XmasCard.java subclass possesses all of the properties of the parent class JPanel and acts as a canvas for the project. Those subclasses are not only can inherit all of the properties from the parent classes but also they can be tailored by programmers to satisfy the needs of the specific new project. This is the power of the "is-a" relationship.

The execution result of the UML class diagram in Fig. 5.1 is as Fig. 5.2 shows. It constructs the basis for all of GUIs. The source code of the GUI is listed in Listing 5.1.

Listing 5.1 The source code of the GUI basis on the project TestGUIBasis

```
1  /*
2   * TestGUIBasis.java -- A frame is a subclass of JFrame.
3   */
4  package testguibasis;
5
6  import javax.swing.JFrame;
7  import javax.swing.WindowConstants;
8
13 public class TestGUIBasis extends JFrame {
14
15     private ACanvas anyCanvas;
16
17     @SuppressWarnings("OverridableMethodCallInConstructor")
18     public TestGUIBasis() {
19         setDefaultCloseOperation(WindowConstants.EXIT_ON_CLOSE);
20         setTitle("Test a GUI basis");
21         setSize(500, 400);
```

5.2 Constructing a Basis for GUIs

```
22
23          anyCanvas = new ACanvas();
24          add(anyCanvas);
25
26          setVisible(true);
27      }
28
32      public static void main(String[] args) {
33          new TestGUIBasis();
34      }
35  }
```

```
1   /*
2    * ACanvas.java - A canvas is a subclass of JPanel
3    */
4   package testguibasis;
5
6   import javax.swing.JPanel;
7
12  public class ACanvas extends JPanel {
13
14      public ACanvas() {
15      }
16  }
```

The code of the class ACanvas.java shows that it is a subclass of JPanel. The keyword "extends" expresses that it inherits the parent class JPanel or it "is-a" JPanel. The class does not have any special codes, but it needs to import the javax.swing.JPanel built-in class from Java APIs. The code of the class TestGUIBasis.java also "extends" the built-in class JFrame. It adds three statements to set up its own properties. The statement (line 19) "setDefaultCloseOperation(WindowConstants.EXIT_ON_CLOSE);" means that it needs a default operation "Close" to close the frame when the user of the project clicks the red dot button on the left most position of the window. The statement "setTitle("Test a GUI basis");" (line 20) sets up the title for the project. And then, the statement "setSize(500, 400);" is to set up the size of the frame with a width of 500 pixels and a height of 400 pixels. And then, it uses the additional two statements (lines 23–24) to instantiate an object of the canvas and adds the canvas with it. Finally, the statement "setVisible(true);" (line 26) visualizes the entire GUI. Actually, the class JFrame itself is a subclass of another built-in class Window. That is why eventually the GUI appears as a window on the screen when the project runs.

In OOP paradigm, this "is-a" relationship is equivalent to the term inheritance. A subclass inherits all of properties and behaviors of a superclass that makes the subclass "is-a" superclass. In our real world, it is a popular phenomenon. For example, a Student class could be a superclass for the subclasses of UndergraduateStudent and GraduateStudent. In addition, two classes of PhDCandidate and MasterStudent could be subclasses of the superclass GraduateStudent. These relationships can be depicted as an inheritance hierarchy as shown in Fig. 5.3. Both undergraduate student and graduate student "is-a" student respectively so that they inherit attributes and behaviors defined in the class Student; but they can also be extended to include their own special attributes and behaviors. Apparently, this inheritance makes OOP programming powerful and easy. Furthermore, the inheritance programming is a perfect strategy for increasing

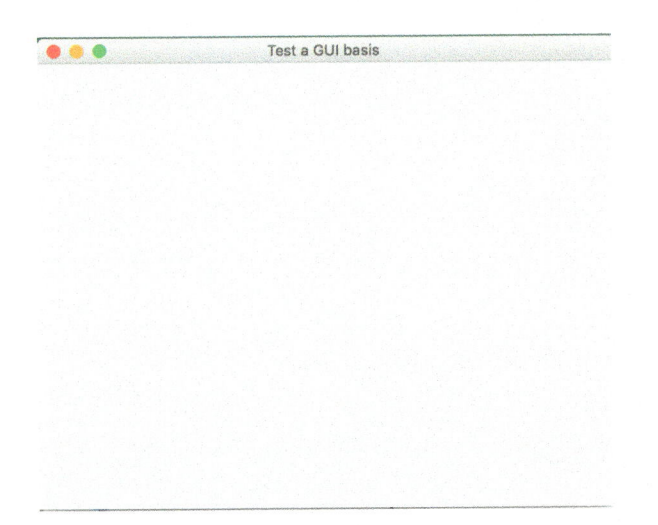

Fig. 5.2 A screenshot of the frame and the empty canvas for GUIs

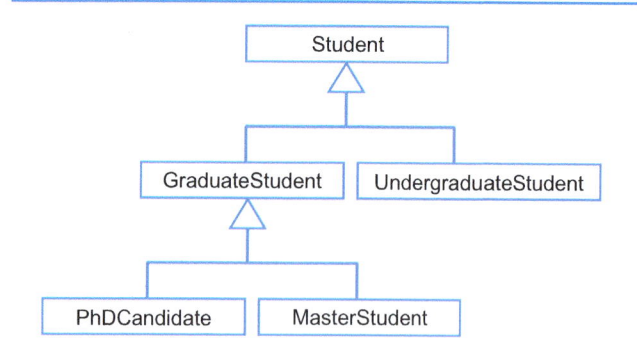

Fig. 5.3 An inheritance hierarchy of Student

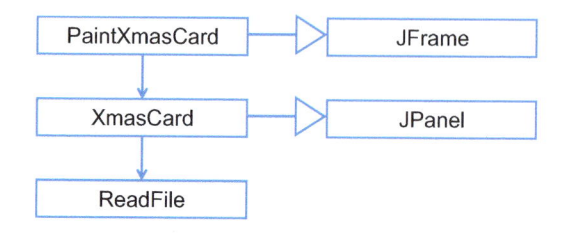

Fig. 5.4 The UML class diagram of the project PaintXmasCard1

the reusability and maintainability of classes. We will apply it for our game programming extensively.

5.3 Building Up a GUI Foundation: The Project PaintXmasCard1

The project PrintXmasCard introduced in Chap. 2 illustrates the programming process for making a Christmas card in text. Obviously, the output of the project PrintXmasCard is not exciting since it is based on text. Now, instead of "print," we change our term to "paint." That is, we are going to apply the GUI programming for painting a Christmas card, which will make a totally different look-and-feel.

The new project PaintXmasCard1 has the similar general structure as the PrintXmasCard project developed in Chap. 2. Both of them have three classes: the main class, XmasCard.java, and ReadFile.java. Of course, the project PaintXmasCard1 needs two more superclasses of JFrame and JPanel for its GUI.

The UML class diagram of the project PaintXmasCard1 is shown in Fig. 5.4, which indicates that the class PaintXmasCard.java "uses" the class XmasCard.java as its canvas for painting and, in turn, the class XmasCard.java "uses" the class ReadFile.java for reading a season greeting from a text file. The class ReadFile.java is identical to the class ReadFile.java in the WheelFortune4 project discussed in Chap. 4. The codes of the XmasCard.java class in this project PaintXmasCard1 are logically identical to the corresponding class in the project PrintXmasCard3 in Chap. 2. The only difference is that the original method printCard() in the project PrintXmasCard3 is replaced by the method paint() in this project PaintXmasCard1. The source code of the XmasCard.java class in this project is cited in Listing 5.2. This is a good example for demonstrating that a properly implemented class can be widely reused or adapted.

Listing 5.2 The code of the class XmasCard.java in the project PaintXmasCard1

```
1  /*
2   * XmasCard.java - A canvas for painting a Christmas card.
3   */
4  package paintxmascard;
5
6  import java.awt.Color;
7  import java.awt.Font;
8  import java.awt.Graphics;
9  import javax.swing.JOptionPane;
10 import javax.swing.JPanel;
11
16 public class XmasCard extends JPanel {
17
18     private String recName;
19     private String merryXmas;
20     private String signature;
21     ReadFile readFile;
22
23     @SuppressWarnings("OverridableMethodCallInConstructor")
24     public XmasCard() {
```

5.4 A Built-In Graphics Context

```
25            inputRecName();
26            inputMerryXmas();
27            inputSignature();
28            repaint();
29        }
30
31        private void inputRecName() {
32            recName = JOptionPane.showInputDialog("Enter recipient's name: ");
33        }
34
35        private void inputMerryXmas() {
36            readFile = new ReadFile();
37            readFile.selectFile();
38            merryXmas = readFile.readContent();
39        }
40
41        private void inputSignature() {
42            signature = JOptionPane.showInputDialog("Enter sender's name: ");
43        }
44
45        @Override
46        public void paint(Graphics g) {
47            g.setColor(Color.red);
48            g.setFont(new Font("Time", Font.BOLD, 24));
49            g.drawString(recName, 50, 100);
50            g.setFont(new Font("Algerian", Font.BOLD, 30));
51            g.drawString(merryXmas, 80, 150);
52            g.setFont(new Font("Time", Font.BOLD, 24));
53            g.drawString(signature, 50, 200);
54        }
55 }
```

The output of the project PaintXmasCard1 is shown in Fig. 5.5. It is clear that the output of the project PaintXmasCard1 is totally different from the output of the project PrintXmasCard due to that it is based on the GUI programming.

5.4 A Built-In Graphics Context

The new features made by this new application are implemented in the XmasCard.java class because the class XmasCard.java extends the built-in class JPanel for making itself as a canvas for painting. The built-in class JPanel has a built-in graphics context, which supports the method paint(Graphics g). The class XmasCard.java inherits the graphics context so that it uses the paint() method with the codes (lines 45–54) to make a beautiful Christmas card as its output.

The code shows that the Graphics g has a rich set of graphics capabilities, such as g.setColor(), g.setFont(), and the like, which can accept different parameters to make the output with different styles. We should familiarize ourselves with those built-in methods. Taking the g.setFont() method

Fig. 5.5 The output of the project PaintXmasCard1. The different fonts render different styles. (Left) Font "Edwardian Script ITC"; (Right) Font "Algerian"

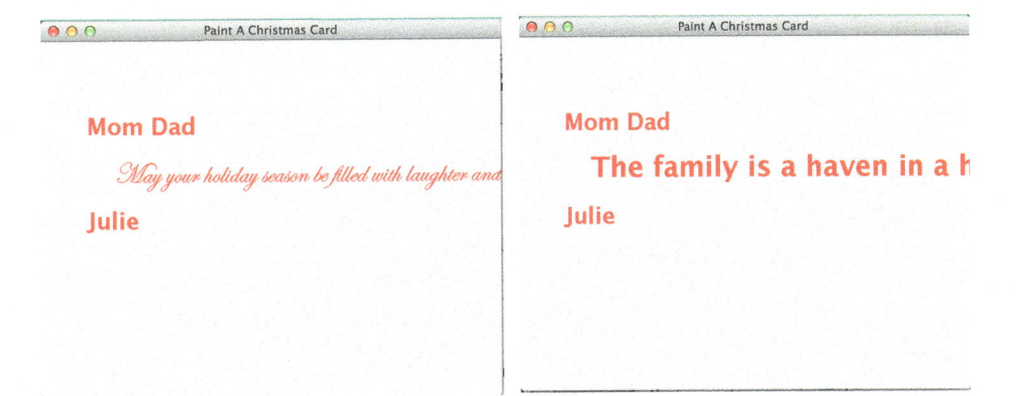

as an example, the complete call of the method is "g.setFont(new Font("Time", Font.BOLD, 24));" The statement indicates that the method g.setFont() accepts an object as its parameter. The object is instantiated by a "new Font()" call, which invokes the constructor of the built-in class Font. The constructor asks for three parameters: the font name, the font style (plain, bold, or italic), and the font size. The Font class uses the information to map a character to a glyph and render the glyph on Graphics and Component object. When we change the font name, we can see different rendering results as shown in Fig. 5.5. In comparison with the project PrintXmasCard3 in Chap. 2, the painting ability of the project PaintXmasCard1 produces a much better look-and-feel.

5.5 Computations Involved: The Project PaintXmasCard2

However, the output shown in Fig. 5.5 also reveals some problems that we need to solve. For example, the season greeting is beautiful but it exceeds the boundary of the panel. In order to solve some possible problems like that and to design and realize reusable program units, we do need to carefully involve some computations.

When we would like to layout components on the canvas, we need to know the positions where the components should appear. Graphical systems commonly use axes to measure and to position components. A canvas usually uses a 2D coordinate system, which consists of two axes x and y as shown in Fig. 5.6. This coordinate system takes the up-left corner as the origin with the (x, y) values of (0, 0). The x-axis is toward the right direction and the y-axis is downward the bottom.

Figure 5.6 (left) shows a canvas made by the MS Windows operating system and (right) shows a canvas made by the Mac OS operating system. The MS Windows' screenshot has a dark blue bar that appears on the top of the canvas and three thin bars that appear around the canvas. The top bar is the title bar for displaying the title of the JFrame; the three thin bars are edges of the canvas. But, the Mac OS screenshot has a top bar only. When we use the statement setSize(500, 400) in the class PaintXmasCard.java, it defines the total width of the canvas with 500 pixels and the total height of the canvas with 400 pixels. That is, the height of the 400 pixels along the y-axis includes the height of the top bar. It implies that the real height of the canvas should be (400 − height of the top bar). In considering the coordinates of the real boundaries, we need to understand Fig. 5.6, which has two red rectangles: the outer rectangle shows the boundaries and the inner rectangle shows a displaying area. The two rectangles are based on the following definitions.

We define a constant TITLE_HEIGHT = 18 (in MS Windows) or = 22 (in Mac OS) for measuring the height of the title bar and a constant EDGE_WIDTH = 5 (in MS Windows) or = 0 (in Mac OS) for measuring the width of an edge; and a MARGIN constant is for the displaying area. The boundary rectangle is drawn based on the following computations:

```
//the origin (0, 0) starts from the right side of
//the left edge
MINX = 0;
MAXX = total-width (500) - 2*EDGE_WIDTH;
MINY = 0;
MAXY = total-height (400) - TITLE_HEIGHT -
    EDGE_WIDTH;
```

The displaying area is defined by the following computations, where the constant MARGIN represents the distance between the edges and the displaying area:

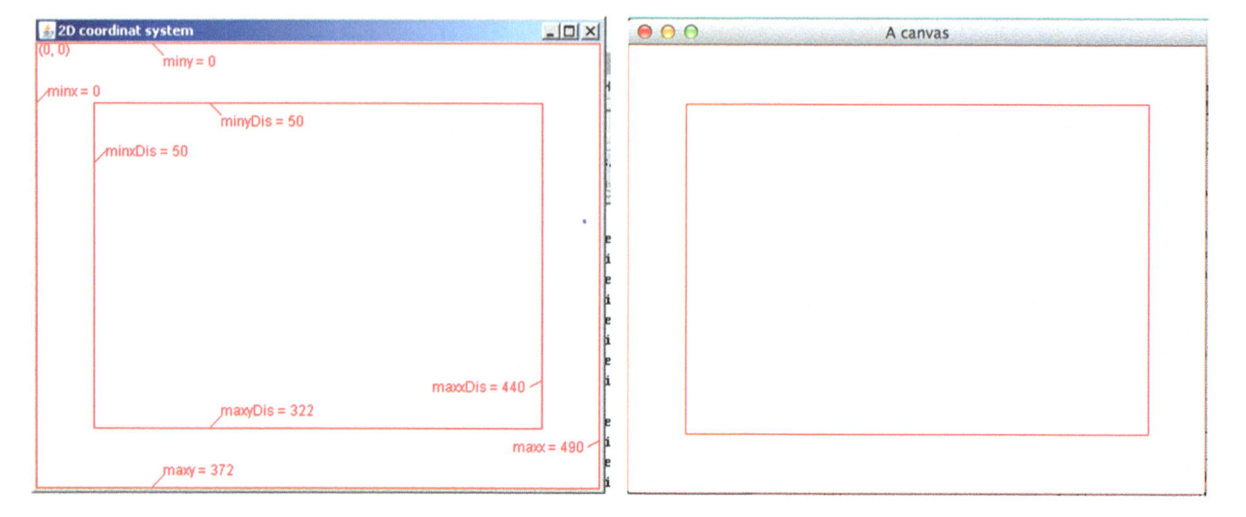

Fig. 5.6 The coordinate system and the displaying field: (Left) MS Windows; (Right) Mac OS

5.6 Arranging the Output Nicely

```
MINX_DIS = MINX + MARGIN; // minx_display
MAXX_DIS = MAXX - MARGIN;
MINY_DIS = MINY + MARGIN;
MAXY_DIS = MAXY - MARGIN;
```

That is, based on the definition above, we defined two coordinate systems. One of them corresponds to the MARGIN = 0; the other corresponds to the MARGIN = a certain value. Some screens, such as the screen for displaying the output of a game, are usually based on the MARGIN = 0 case, where the constants MINX, MAXX, MINY, and MAXY are involved. Some other screens, such as a Christmas card screen, are based on the case of MARGIN that has a certain value, where the constants MINX_DIS, MAXX_DIS, MINY_DIS, and MAXY_DIS are used. In order to make the programming easier and clearer, we will create a class Consts.java to define these constants as static attributes such that the class Consts.java can be used for all of projects that need the graphical drawings. Please see the project CanvasOfGUIs of this chapter for details.

5.6 Arranging the Output Nicely

After we understand the coordinate system described in the previous section, we can arrange the components positions in advance by going through related computations. Let us go back to the project PaintXmasCard1. Assume that the recipient's name would be arranged with the starting point of (MINX_DIS, MINY_DIS). Due to the fact that the starting point of a string is defined on the left-bottom corner of the first letter in the string, the real coordinates for the starting point of the recipient's name should be (MINX_DIS, MINY_DIS + height-of-character). Assume that the signature of the card sender would be positioned in the right-bottom corner of the displaying area and correspondingly the real coordinates of the starting point of the signature should be (MAXX_DIS − width-of-signature, MAXY_DIS) as shown in Fig. 5.7.

Clearly, the remaining task is to find out the values of "height-of-character" and "width-of-signature." For that, we need to know how to measure the string width and character height for a given string. Obviously, both the width and height of a string depend on the font defined for the string since different font defines different type, style, and size that affect the width of the entire string and the height of individual character of the string.

The built-in class FontMetrics provides the measurements. The following piece of codes gives the width of the string and the height of a character under a given font.

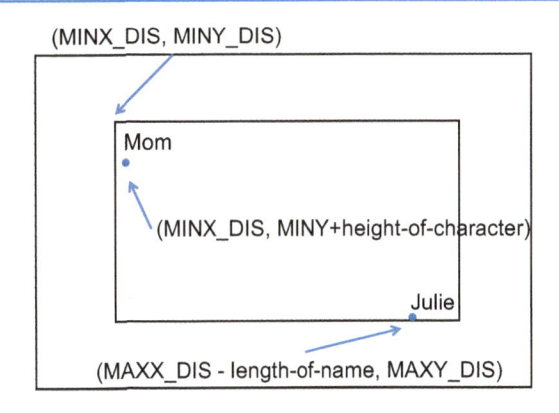

Fig. 5.7 The computations for defining the position of a string

```
g.setFont(myFavoriteFont);
FontMetrics fm = g.getFontMetrics();
int signatureWidth = fm.stringWidth(
    signatureStr);
int charHeight = fm.getAscent();
// the ascent of a character
```

Applying the width of the string and the height of a character, the coordinates of the starting point of the recipient's name string and the starting point of the signature string can be determined.

A little bit of more complicated is how to control the painting of the season greeting string for preventing them from out of the boundary of the displaying field as shown in Fig. 5.5. Since the season greeting string is read from a file randomly, we have no idea about the length of the season greeting string in advance. Fortunately, we know that the entire season greeting string will be held in the String variable merryXmas, and we also know that the width of the displaying area is areaWidth = MAXX_DIS − MINX_DIS. Based on the areaWidth, we can divide the entire merryXmas string into substrings, and the width of every substring should be able to fit into the areaWidth. Based on this idea, the pseudo code for dividing the greeting string into substrings could be described as follows.

1. Divide the entire string into a set of words in terms of blank character between words.
2. Concatenate maximum number of words into a substring such that the total width of the substring is maximum but still less than or equal to the areaWidth.

Another built-in class StringTokenizer supports the implementation of the step 1 above. The methods defined in the class StringTokenizer can divide a string into tokens whenever the delimiter of each token is defined. The following code is an example for showing the usage of the StringTokenizer.

```
StringTokenizer st = new
   StringTokenizer("This is a string", " ,/");
while (st.hasMoreTokens()) {
   System.out.println(
      st.nextToken());
}
```

Definitely, an object of the class StringTokenizer should be instantiated. The constructor of the StringTokenizer() asks for two parameters. The first parameter "This is a string" is the string that we would like to divide. The second parameter is known as delimiters that is a set of characters for separating the string into tokens. In this example, the set of delimiters is " ,/", which includes a blank, a comma, and a slash character. If the string "This is a string" contains four words and every word is separated by a blank character, then the System.out.println(st.nextToken()) will print four tokens (words) into four lines. This separating process is controlled by a while loop "while(st.hasMoreTokens())." The statement "while" will keep looping as long as the st.hasMoreTokens() returns true. The true means that another "next token" exists. The "st.nextToken()" method inside the curly bracket of the "while" loop will return the next word individually. We can use this mechanism to get every individual word from the entire string. The flowchart of the "while" loop is depicted in Fig. 5.8. This is the first step in the pseudo code above.

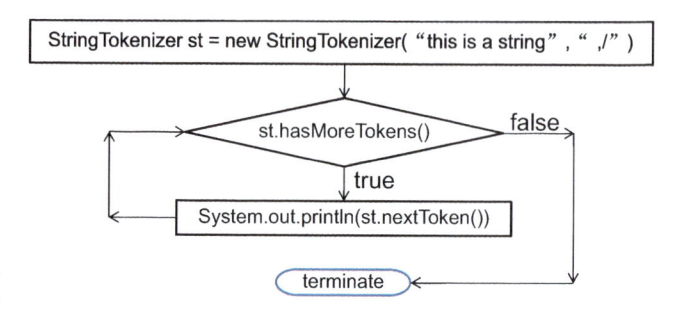

Fig. 5.8 A flowchart of the "while" loop

For implementing the second step of the pseudo code, we declare a variable subStr for concatenating word by word. We keep track of the width of the subStr plus the width of the next word. If the summation of the two widths is less than or equal to the width of the areaWidth, it means that the next word can be concatenated with the substring currently held by the variable subStr. As long as the summation of the two widths is larger than the areaWidth, the subStr should stop to concatenate the next word, and its value will be painted immediately on the Christmas card because at this moment the subStr has reached its maximum width but still can fit into the width of the field areaWidth. In addition, the next word should be assigned to the next substring occurrence. All these new activities enforce the changes of the XmasCard.java class as shown in Listing 5.3.

Listing 5.3 The code of the class XmasCard.java in the project PaintXmasCard2

```
1  /*
2   * XmasCard.java - A canvas for painting a Christmas card.
3   */
4  package paintxmascard;
5
6  import java.awt.Color;
7  import java.awt.Font;
8  import java.awt.FontMetrics;
9  import java.awt.Graphics;
10 import java.util.StringTokenizer;
11 import javax.swing.JOptionPane;
12 import javax.swing.JPanel;
13
18 public class XmasCard extends JPanel {
19
20     private String recName;
21     private String merryXmas;
22     private String signature;
23     private ReadFile readFile;
24     private int x, y;
25
26     public XmasCard() {
27         inputRecName();
28         inputMerryXmas();
```

5.6 Arranging the Output Nicely

```
29              inputSignature();
30              repaint();
31          }
32
33          private void inputRecName() {
34              recName = JOptionPane.showInputDialog("Enter recipient's name: ");
35          }
36
37          private void inputMerryXmas() {
38              readFile = new ReadFile();
39              readFile.selectFile();
40              merryXmas = readFile.readContent();
41          }
42
43          private void inputSignature() {
44              signature = JOptionPane.showInputDialog("Enter sender's name: ");
45          }
46
47          @Override
48          public void paint(Graphics g) {
49              g.setColor(Color.red);
50              paintRecName(g);
51              paintMerryXmas(g);
52              paintSignature(g);
53          }
54
55          private void paintRecName(Graphics g) {
56              g.setFont(new Font("Time", Font.BOLD, 24));
57              FontMetrics fm = g.getFontMetrics();
58              int charHeight = fm.getAscent();
59              y = Consts.MINY_DIS + charHeight;
60              g.drawString(recName, Consts.MINX_DIS, y);
61          }
62
63          private void paintMerryXmas(Graphics g) {
64              int displayWidth = Consts.MAXX_DIS - Consts.MINX_DIS;
65              g.setFont(new Font("Edwardian Script ITC", Font.BOLD, 30));
66              FontMetrics fm = g.getFontMetrics();
67              int charHeight = fm.getAscent();
68
69              // concatinate words into a subStr
70              StringTokenizer st
71                      = new StringTokenizer(merryXmas, " ");
72              String subStr = "";
73              y = y + charHeight;
74              while (st.hasMoreTokens()) {
75                  String nextT = st.nextToken();
76                  int subStrW = fm.stringWidth(subStr) + fm.stringWidth(nextT);
77                  if (subStrW <= displayWidth) {
78                      subStr = subStr + nextT + " ";
79                  } else {
80                      y = y + Consts.NEXTLINE;
81                      g.drawString(subStr, Consts.MINX_DIS, y);
82                      subStr = nextT + " ";
83                  }
```

```
84          }
85          if (!subStr.equals(" ")) {
86              y = y + Consts.NEXTLINE;
87              g.drawString(subStr, Consts.MINX_DIS, y);
88          }
89      }
90
91      private void paintSignature(Graphics g) {
92          g.setFont(new Font("Time", Font.BOLD, 24));
93          FontMetrics fm = g.getFontMetrics();
94          int startX = Consts.MAXX_DIS - fm.stringWidth(signature);
95          int charHeight = fm.getAscent();
96          y = y + Consts.NEXTLINE + charHeight;
97          g.drawString(signature, startX, y);
98      }
99 }
```

The new code of the class XmasCard.java in the project PaintXmasCard2 shows several modified methods including paintRecName(), paintMerryXmas(), and paintSignature(). Specifically, the method paintMerryXmas() implements the algorithm that divides the entire season greeting into substrings for fitting into the areaWidth as just discussed. The output of the project PaintXmasCard2, displayed in Fig. 5.9 (left), looks different from the output shown in Fig. 5.5 because the project PaintXmasCard2 paints the season greeting string according to a rational computation.

The project PaintXmasCard2 also introduces a new class Consts.java that defines all of the constants required for properly arranging components on the GUI based on the computations described above. The code of the class Consts.java is shown in Listing 5.4.

Listing 5.4 The code of the class Consts.java in the project PaintXmasCard2

```
1  /*
2   * Consts.java -- A class that defines constants for the project.
3   * Defining a Consts class makes the access of constants easier and
4   * makes the change of constants much convenient.
5   */
6  package paintxmascard;
7
12 public class Consts {
13
14     public Consts() {
15     }
```

Fig. 5.9 (Left) The output of the project PaintXmasCard2; (Right) the output of the project PaintXmasCard3

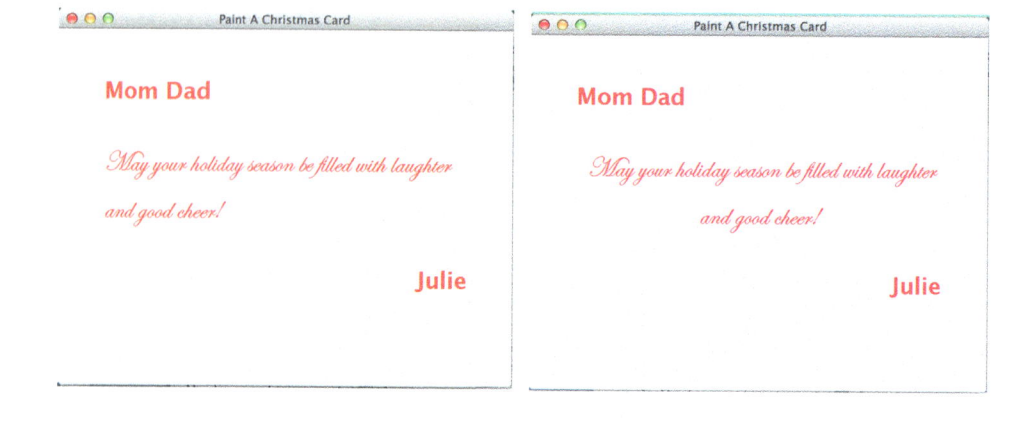

```
16
17      // values need to be set (for Mac)
18      public static final int TOP_BAR_HEIGHT = 22; // for Windows: 18
19      public static final int EDGE_WIDTH = 0; // for Windows: 4
20      public static final int CV_WIDTH = 500;
21      public static final int CV_HEIGHT = 400;
22
23      // when MARGIN = 0
24      public static final int FIELD_HEIGHT = CV_HEIGHT-TOP_BAR_HEIGHT;
25      public static final int MINX = 0;
26      public static final int MAXX = CV_WIDTH - 2 * EDGE_WIDTH;
27      public static final int MINY = 0;
28      public static final int MAXY = FIELD_HEIGHT - EDGE_WIDTH;
29
30      // when MARGIN > 0
31      public static final int MARGIN = 50; // depends on the application
32      public static final int MINX_DIS = MINX + MARGIN;
33      public static final int MAXX_DIS = MAXX - MARGIN;
34      public static final int MINY_DIS = MINY + MARGIN;
35      public static final int MAXY_DIS = MAXY - MARGIN;
36      public static final int NEXTLINE = 50; // the distance between two lines
37  }
38
```

5.7 Aligning Substrings Along the Center: The Project PaintXmasCard3

A better improvement exists if we are going to arrange the substrings of the season greeting string along the center of the x-axis of the displaying field. We may further develop the pseudo code as follows.

1. Find the center x-coordinate along the width of the displaying area: xCenter = (MAXX_DIS − MINX_DIS) / 2;

2. The x-coordinate of the starting point of every substring will be equal to
   xStart = xCenter − (widthOfSubstring) / 2
   or
   xStart = (MAXX_DIS − MINX_DIS) / 2 − (widthOfSubstring) / 2

These computations are added in the paintMerryXmas() method as displayed in Listing 5.5, which paints the output as shown in Fig. 5.9 (right).

Listing 5.5 The new code of the method paintMerryXmas() in the class XmasCard.java of the project PaintXmasCard3

```
64      private void paintMerryXmas(Graphics g) {
65          int displayWidth = Consts.MAXX_DIS - Consts.MINX_DIS;
66          g.setFont(new Font("Edwardian Script ITC", Font.BOLD, 30));
67          FontMetrics fm = g.getFontMetrics();
68          int charHeight = fm.getAscent();
69
70          // concatinate words into a subStr and paint it centerized
71          StringTokenizer st
72              = new StringTokenizer(merryXmas, " ");
73          String subStr = "";
74          y = y + charHeight;
75          while (st.hasMoreTokens()) {
76              String nextT = st.nextToken();
77              int subStrW = fm.stringWidth(subStr) + fm.stringWidth(nextT);
```

```
78              if (subStrW <= displayWidth) {
79                  subStr = subStr + nextT + " ";
80              } else {
81                  y = y + Consts.NEXTLINE;
82                  int subStrWidth = fm.stringWidth(subStr);
83                  int midW = subStrWidth / 2;
84                  int startX = (Consts.MAXX_DIS - Consts.MINX_DIS) / 2 - midW;
85                  g.drawString(subStr, Consts.MINX_DIS + startX, y);
86                  subStr = nextT + " ";
87              }
88          }
89          // for painting the last piece if any
90          if (!subStr.equals(" ")) {
91              y = y + Consts.NEXTLINE;
92              int subStrWidth = fm.stringWidth(subStr);
93              int midW = subStrWidth / 2;
94              int startX = (Consts.MAXX_DIS - Consts.MINX_DIS) / 2 - midW;
95              g.drawString(subStr, Consts.MINX_DIS + startX, y);
96          }
97      }
```

5.8 Adding an Image into the Christmas Card: The Project PaintXmasCard4

Nowadays, adding a photo onto a Christmas card is a preferred design for many people, especially for many families. Whenever you use a camera to take a photo, it is a digital image. The Graphics class has a g.drawImage() method that can be hired to draw an image easily. The class Graphics provides several methods with the same name drawImage(), but every of them has different number of parameters or different type of parameters. This set of methods that has the same method title but with different number or different type of parameters is known as "overload" method. Each of them is designed for a specific purpose.

The simplest one is the method g.drawImage(img, x, y, null), which draws an image img at the coordinates (x, y), where (x, y) is the top-left corner of the image. The last parameter "null" refers to a so-called imageObserver, which is designed for loading images from networks. Here, we can simply ignore it and mark it as null. The parameter img in the drawImage() method refers to an object of digital image.

Usually images are an external file to the program itself, just like the text file that contains the season greeting strings. As we have discussed, we prefer to load text files into a folder inside the file structure of the project. Similarly, we also prefer to load images into a folder inside the file structure of the project. Therefore, we create a subdirectory with the name of "images" under the folder "Source Packages" in the project PaintXmasCard4 to collect all images to be used by the project. And then, we copy an example image with the name of "Winter.jpg" into the "images" folder. The extension of the filename "jpg" refers to the type of JPEG, which is one of the image formats. The other image formats mainly include GIF and PNG. The resulting structure is as shown in Fig. 5.10.

Similar with the ReadFile.java class, we define a class ReadImage.java to read images from the folder "images" into the PaintXmasCard4 project. For holding the image, a variable is needed. The type of variable for holding an image has been evolved several times in Java language. The most popular type today is BufferedImage. The code of the new class ReadImage.java is shown in Listing 5.6.

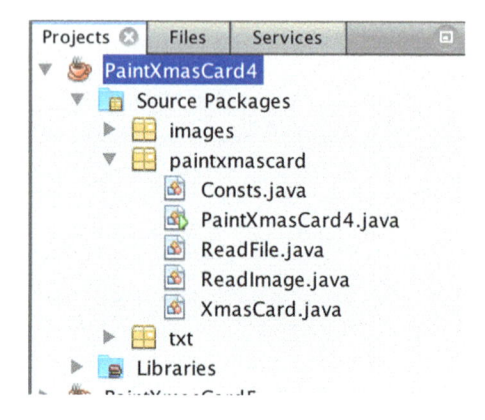

Fig. 5.10 The screenshot of the structure of the project PaintXmasCard4

5.8 Adding an Image into the Christmas Card: The Project PaintXmasCard4

Listing 5.6 The classes ReadImage.java and part of class XmasCard.java that read an image in the project PaintXmasCard4

```
 1 /*
 2  * ReadImage.java - A class to read an image into the project.
 3  */
 4 package paintxmascard;
 5
 6 import java.awt.image.BufferedImage;
 7 import java.io.IOException;
 8 import javax.imageio.ImageIO;
 9
10 public class ReadImage {
11     private BufferedImage img;
12
13     public ReadImage() {
14         try {
15             img = ImageIO.read(getClass().getResource(
16                     "../images/Winter.jpg"));
17         } catch (IOException ex) {
18         }
19     }
20
21     public BufferedImage getImage() {
22         return img;
23     }
24 }
```

```
 1 /*
 2  * XmasCard.java - A canvas for painting a Christmas card.
 3  */
 4 package paintxmascard;
 5
...
14
15 public class XmasCard extends JPanel {
16
17     private String recName;
18     private String merryXmas;
19     private String signature;
20     private ReadFile readFile;
21     private ReadImage readImage;
22     private int x, y;
23     // due to CV_WINDTH is doubled, left side of MAXX_DIS is changed
24     private int leftMAXX_DIS;
25
26     public XmasCard() {
27         leftMAXX_DIS = Consts.CV_WIDTH / 2 - Consts.MARGIN;
28         inputRecName();
29         inputMerryXmas();
30         inputSignature();
31         inputImage();
32         repaint();
33     }
34
...
```

```
 48
 49      private void inputImage() {
 50          readImage = new ReadImage();
 51      }
 52
 53      @Override
 54      public void paint(Graphics g) {
 55          g.setColor(Color.red);
 56          paintRecName(g);
 57          paintMerryXmas(g);
 58          paintSignature(g);
 59          paintImage(g);
 60      }
 61
...
113
114      private void paintImage(Graphics g) {
115          BufferedImage img = readImage.getImage();
116          int imgMinx = Consts.CV_WIDTH / 2 + Consts.MARGIN;
117          int imgMiny = Consts.MINY_DIS;
118          int imgMaxx = Consts.MAXX - Consts.MARGIN;
119          int imgMaxy = Consts.MAXY_DIS;
120          int imgW = imgMaxx - imgMinx;
121          int imgH = imgMaxy - imgMiny;
122          g.drawImage(img, imgMinx, imgMiny, imgW, imgH, null);
123      }
124  }
```

The following statement shown in the class ReadImage.java (lines 15–16) is used for reading the image:

```
img = ImageIO.read(getClass().getResource(
    "../images/Winter.jpg"));
```

Java 2D supports a class javax.imageio.ImageIO, which has a method read() that loads the external image format into the BufferedImage format. The parameter of the method read() is the url of the external image file. Since we follow the same strategy for reading a text file under the subdirectory "txt" inside the file structure of the project, the relative file path for the image "Winter.jpg" under the subdirectory "images" is similar with the text file as "../images/Winter.jpg." The "getClass().getResource("../images/Winter.jpg");" returns the url of the image file and the image Winter.jpg is loaded into the variable img with the data type of BufferedImage.

The output of this new version shown in Fig. 5.11 verifies the success of the image reading. Definitely, the image can be better replaced with a family photo. The wide Christmas card can be folded along the center of the x-axis to make a new kind of Christmas card.

5.9 Decorating the Christmas Card: The Project PaintXmasCard5

The graphics context Graphics g can also draw different geometrical shapes, such as line, oval, rectangle, curve, and so on. The project PaintXmasCard5 further demonstrates these capabilities for adding a decoration on the Christmas card as shown in Fig. 5.12.

The decoration consists of rectangles and circles with a small dash line between them. The computations for making the decoration are as follows:

1. Define the size of 10 for both the rectangles and circles and the length of 5 for the dash line; and then define one rectangle plus a dash line or one circle plus a dash line as a unit so that the width of the unit is 10 + 5 = 15.
2. Calculate how many units can be placed along the decoration area by using the unit width divides the total width of the decoration area.
3. Use a "for" loop to draw one rectangle with a dash line and then one circle with a dash line alternatively and without the dash line for the last rectangle or circle.

5.9 Decorating the Christmas Card: The Project PaintXmasCard5

Fig. 5.11 Load an image into the Christmas card

Fig. 5.12 Add a decoration onto the Christmas card

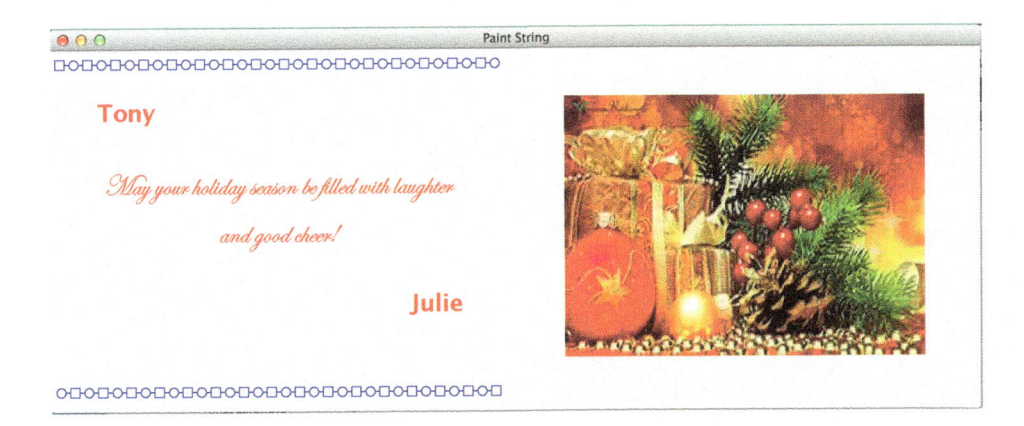

Definitely, we can design any kinds of decorations by fully using the primitive graphical drawing capabilities supplied by the class Graphics. Or we can load in more images and tailor them into different shapes as decorations.

Based on the outline of the computations above, the new method paintDecoration() is added into the XmasCard.java class. The detailed implementation is shown in Listing 5.7.

Listing 5.7 The method paintDecoration() in XmasCard.java class of PaintXmasCard5

```
135     // draw a dash for a unit and calculate the value of x for next drawing
136     private int aDash(Graphics g, int x, int dWidth, int i,
137             int numUnits, int midY) {
138         x = x + dWidth;
139         if (i < numUnits - 1) { // don't draw a dash for the last unit
140             g.drawLine(x, midY, x + dWidth / 2, midY);
141             x = x + dWidth / 2;
142         }
143         return x;
144     }
145
146     private void paintDecoration(Graphics g) {
147         int dWidth = 10; // width of a unit in the decoration
148         int dHeight = 10; // height of a unit in the decoration
149         int dMargin = 10;
150         int x = 5; // starting x
151         int locY = dMargin; // starting y
152         int midY = locY + dHeight / 2; // y coordinate of the small dash
```

```
153        int lengthDash = dWidth / 2; // length of one dash
154        int numUnits =
155                ((maxxDis + Consts.MARGIN) - (minxDis - Consts.MARGIN)) /
156                (dWidth + lengthDash);
157
158        g.setColor(Color.blue);
159        // top decoration
160        y = locY;
161        for (int i = 0; i < numUnits; i++) {
162            if (i % 2 == 0) { // i == 0, 2, 4, ... are rectangles
163                g.drawRect(x, y, dWidth, dHeight);
164                x = aDash(g, x, dWidth, i, numUnits, midY);
165            } else { //  i == 1, 3, 5, ... are circles
166                g.drawOval(x, y, dWidth, dHeight);
167                x = aDash(g, x, dWidth, i, numUnits, midY);
168            }
169        }
170        // bottom decoration
171        x = 5;
172        y = maxyDis + Consts.MARGIN - dMargin - dHeight;
173        midY = y + dHeight / 2;
174        for (int i = 0; i < numUnits; i++) {
175            if (i % 2 == 0) { // i == 0, 2, 4 ... are circles
176                g.drawOval(x, y, dWidth, dHeight);
177                x = aDash(g, x, dWidth, i, numUnits, midY);
178            } else { // i == 1, 3, 5 ... are rectangles
179                g.drawRect(x, y, dWidth, dHeight);
180                x = aDash(g, x, dWidth, i, numUnits, midY);
181            }
182        }
183    }
```

All these paintings are rich but are static. If we would like to make them animated, we need new techniques that will be covered later.

5.10 Superclass and Subclass

The GUI programming and the example project PaintXmasCard demonstrate the OOP inheritance concept and practice. A class can be derived from an existing class as a subclass or a derived class. The "existing" class becomes a parent class or a superclass. So far, we only said that the subclass thus inherits the attributes and the methods defined in the superclass and the subclass can add its own new features for satisfying all of needs required by different cases.

Therefore, the inheritance greatly enhances the reusability and maintainability of software components. For better understanding and applying inheritance, here we further discuss some terms related with superclass and subclass.

5.10.1 Access Modifiers: Private, Public, and Protected

Listing 5.8 shows an example project TestInheritance, which has three classes. The ChildClass inherits the ParentClass. The main class instantiates an object of the ChildClass; at the same time, an object of the ParentClass is also instantiated. Clearly, the ChildClass inherits the attributes and the methods defined in the ParentClass.

5.10 Superclass and Subclass

Listing 5.8 The source code of the example project TestInheritance

```
 1  /*
 2   * TestInheritance.java -- A class that instantiates an object of
 3   * ChildClass.java for testing the inheritance.
 4   */
 5  package testinheritance;
 6
11  public class TestInheritance {
12      private static ChildClass childObj;
13
17      public static void main(String[] args) {
18          childObj = new ChildClass(60, 20);
19          System.out.println("Parent age = " + childObj.getParentAge());
20          System.out.println("Child age = " + childObj.getAge());
21          System.out.println("Parent money = " + childObj.getParentMoney());
22      }
23  }
```

```
 1  /*
 2   * ParentClass.java -- A parent class.
 3   */
 4  package testinheritance;
 5
10  public class ParentClass {
11
12      private int parentAge;
13      private double money;
14
15      public ParentClass(int parentAge) {
16          this.parentAge = parentAge;
17          this.money = 1000.00;
18      }
19
20      public int getAge() {
21          return this.parentAge;
22      }
23
24      public void setAge(int age) {
25          this.parentAge = age;
26      }
27
28      protected double getMoney() {
29          return money;
30      }
31
32      protected void setMoney(double money) {
33          this.money = money;
34      }
35  }
```

```
 1  /*
 2   * ChildClass.java -- A class that inherits the ParentClass.
 3   */
 4  package testinheritance;
```

```
 5
10  public class ChildClass extends ParentClass {
11
12      private int childAge;
13
14      public ChildClass(int parentAge, int childAge) {
15          super(parentAge);
16          this.childAge = childAge;
17      }
18
19      @Override
20      public int getAge() {
21          return this.childAge;
22      }
23
24      @Override
25      public void setAge(int age) {
26          this.childAge = age;
27      }
28
29      public int getParentAge() {
30          return super.getAge();
31      }
32
33      public double getParentMoney() {
34          return getMoney();
35      }
36  }
```

However, the accessibility of the attributes and the methods in the ParentClass depend on the access modifiers defined for every attribute and every method. In general, the private attributes and private methods defined in the ParentClass cannot be accessed by the object of the ChildClass since "private" means only the defining class, the ParentClass, can access these private members. In contrast, both ChildClass and ParentClass can access the public attributes and public methods defined in the ParentClass. However, no matter which object invokes the attributes or the methods, the values stored in the attributes and behaviors coded in the methods are the same since physically both classes access to the same memory locations and execute the same piece of codes. Whenever we would like to distinguish some attributes, the two classes should have their own defined attributes and methods. For example, when we would like to store different ages for them, the ParentClass needs an attribute of parentAge (line 12 in ParentClass) and the ChildClass needs to declare another attribute childAge (line 12 in ChildClass).

What is meant by the access modifier "protected"? Let us look at an example in our daily life. If a parent has certain amount of money, he/she would like to have a definition of "private double money" for keeping track of his/her own money confidentially. Because of the "private" modifier, even his/her children won't be able to access the private money. However, eventually the parent would like to allow his/her children to inherit the money. One solution is to change the "private" to be "public." Definitely it doesn't make sense because "public" not only allows his/her children but also allows "everybody" to directly access the "public money." Another solution is to keep the "private double money" but define a method "public double getMoney()" for allowing his/her children to access the "private money." The result is the same as the previous solution because anybody can invoke "public double getMoney()" for getting the "private money."

The "protected double money" comes handy. When the parent changed the "private" to be "protected," it not only permits his/her children directly accessing the "protected money" but also prohibits "everybody" to access the "protected money." Unfortunately, this approach violates another principle that is called "encapsulation" associated with the OOP programming. The "encapsulation" means all of data in a class won't be able directly accessed by "anybody" including any subclass. Consequently, a better solution is to define a "protected double getMoney()" method (lines 28–30 in ParentClass) to permit his/her children but prohibit "everybody" go through the protected getter method to access the "private money" (lines 33–35 in ChildClass).

5.10.2 Constructor super() and Keywords "Super" and "This"

When we encode the ChildClass, a method super() can be used to invoke the constructor of the ParentClass. In the cases when the ParentClass has a default constructor that does not have parameters, the explicit call "super();" could be ignored because the no-argument super constructor will be invoked automatically and implicitly. If someone would like to ensure the no-argument constructor of the ParentClass is successfully invoked, he/she should add a "super();" call as the first statement in the constructor of the subclass ChildClass manually. The call must appear as the first statement since the object "parent" must be initialized before the object of "child".

In contrast, when the ParentClass has an attribute parentAge and the ChildClass has an attribute childAge, meanwhile the constructor of the ParentClass defines a parameter (line 15 in ParentClass) and then the ChildClass should define a constructor that has two parameters (line 14 in ChildClass). One parameter refers to the parentAge, and the other refers to the childAge. In addition, the constructor of the ChildClass needs to invoke the constructor of the ParentClass via super() call with the actual parameter of parentAge for initializing the attribute parentAge defined in the ParentClass (line 15 in ChildClass).

Besides the super() method for calling the constructor of the ParentClass, a keyword "super" is defined for representing the object of the ParentClass. As long as the ChildClass needs to invoke a method defined in the ParentClass, the "super" can be used to invoke the method through the dot notation "super.theMethod()" (lines 29–31 in ChildClass). Another keyword "this" is defined to represent this object itself.

5.10.3 Override Method

A subclass inherits the properties of the superclass and also can be extended or tailored to include new features. The methods getAge() and setAge() defined in the ParentClass (lines 20–26) are inherited by the ChildClass (lines 19–27). However, these two methods are tailored for accessing the childAge. In other words, these two methods have the same titles but with different behaviors. These methods are called "override" methods. They are required to add the sign "@Override."

Actually, we have used "override" method in the project PaintXmasCard. The typical one is that paint() method. When the subclass XmasCard.java extends its superclass JPanel, it inherits the paint() method from the JPanel class. Of course, we can change the name of the paint() to be different one. However, the system defines a method repaint() that will implicitly invoke the paint() method. In order to follow this system setting, we cannot change the method name of paint(). Therefore, we should override it for making the paint() method to serve what we need. The label "@Override" is also a marker for distinguishing a method in the subclass from the original method defined in its parent class. The original method defined in the superclass and the "override" method in the subclass has the exactly same title and same number and type of parameters.

5.10.4 Overload Method

Another kind of methods is termed as "overload" methods, which is different from the "override" methods. For example, the Graphics class supports some "overload" methods that have the same method's name but with different number and/or different type of parameters. The method drawImage() is one of them.

```
public abstract boolean drawImage(Image img,
        int x, int y, ImageObserver observer)
public abstract boolean drawImage(Image img,
        int x, int y, int width, int height,
        ImageObserver observer)
public abstract boolean drawImage(Image img,
        int x, int y, Color bgcolor,
        ImageObserver observer)
public abstract boolean drawImage(Image img,
        int x, int y, int width, int height,
        Color bgcolor, ImageObserver observer)
public abstract boolean drawImage(Image img,
        int dx1, int dy1, int dx2, int dy2,
        int sx1, int sy1, int sx2, int sy2,
        ImageObserver observer)
public abstract boolean drawImage(Image img,
        int dx1, int dy1, int dx2, int dy2,
        int sx1, int sy1, int sx2, int sy2,
        Color bgcolor,
        ImageObserver observer)
```

Defining "overload" methods can avoid the cumbersome in using different method names for each of the methods in the set. We can find many other examples, such as the method valueOf() defined in the class String as cited in Chap. 3.

In short, "override" methods refer to the methods in the superclass and the subclass, which have the same method name with the same number and the same type of formal parameters. In the contrast, "overload" methods refer to the methods in the same class, which have the same method name but different number and/or different type of formal parameters.

5.11 Mastering Built-In Classes Used in the Project PaintXmasCard

The different version of the projects PaintXmasCard adopts several useful built-in classes, which highlight the importance of Java APIs. Mastering the built-in classes defined in Java APIs is one of the main tasks in learning Java programming. Here, we list some of these useful built-in classes for further study. They include:

- Top-level container class JFrame and intermediate-level container class JPanel for constructing a basis for GUIs
- Graphics class for providing fundamental graphical drawing methods, such as drawLine(), drawRect(), drawOval(), drawString(), drawImage(), setColor(), setFont(), and so on
- File class for permanently storing texts, such as season greeting strings, in order to supply text resources
- FileReader class for creating an object of a file through the file name
- BufferedReader class for structuring a stream to read a file
- BufferedImage class for holding and manipulating images
- FontMetrics class for measuring the length of strings and height of characters
- StringTokenizer class for splitting a string into tokens

5.12 Summary

Games in-text version developed in the previous chapters are not very exciting since the outputs of them are not beautiful and not flexible. We would like to have GUIs (graphical user interfaces) with better look-and-feel to allow users enjoy the playing of games. Especially for video games, GUI is the heart and soul since GUI provides not only an output mechanism for graphically displaying the game scenes but also an input mechanism for game players to input data or to control the game.

This chapter introduced the software structure of GUI and the built-in containers JFrame and JPanel with their built-in graphics context. The project PaintXmasCard illustrates the graphical drawing capabilities of the built-in graphics context including drawing strings, images, and primitive geometrical shapes. Nevertheless, arranging components on a GUI involves some computations because every component needs a definition of coordinates of its starting position in a beautiful layout.

However, graphical drawings are static. Video games require dynamic game scenes. For adding dynamic performance on GUIs, we need to learn more techniques. The coming chapter will introduce one of them in terms of the software components and their functionalities.

5.13 Exercises

Self-Reviewing Questions

1. What is your feeling in comparing outputs in graphics with outputs in text?
2. What software structure is needed for making a graphical user interface in general?
3. How to define a displaying area for a GUI? What factors are required to consider?
4. How to define the coordinates of the central point of the displaying area?
5. Why do we need the built-in class FontMetrics and the built-in class StringTokenizer?
6. If a season greeting is too long to fit in the displaying area along the y-axis, what can we do to arrange it nicely?
7. Could you add a family photo into a Christmas card? Could you add two, three, or four family photos into a Christmas card?
8. In the method paintDecoration(), could you apply a "while" loop for replacing the "for" loop?
9. What is the semantics meaning of the statement "getClass().getResouce()" in loading an image in the class ReadImage.java?
10. What are the differences between the "overload" and "override" methods?
11. Why do we need "overload" and "override" methods?
12. Besides the examples in the book, what other sets of overloaded methods exist?
13. Make an example of an inheritance hierarchy with at least three layers and use the UML class diagram to illustrate it.
14. May we use substring() method defined in the class String to replace the functionality of the class StringTokenizer?

Projects

1. Design and implement a new decoration for the Christmas card.
2. Write a program to test all of overloaded methods drawImage() defined in the class Graphics.
3. Write a program to arrange a season greeting align the center of a Christmas card in both x- and y-axis of the canvas.
4. Write a program to display a circle at the center of a canvas.
5. Write a program to display a snowman that consists of three ovals at the center of the canvas.
6. Usually a 2D coordinate system divides a canvas into four quarters. The origin of the entire coordinate system

5.13 Exercises

Fig. 5.13 (Left) The output of the TrySymPoint; (Right) The output of the TrySymTri

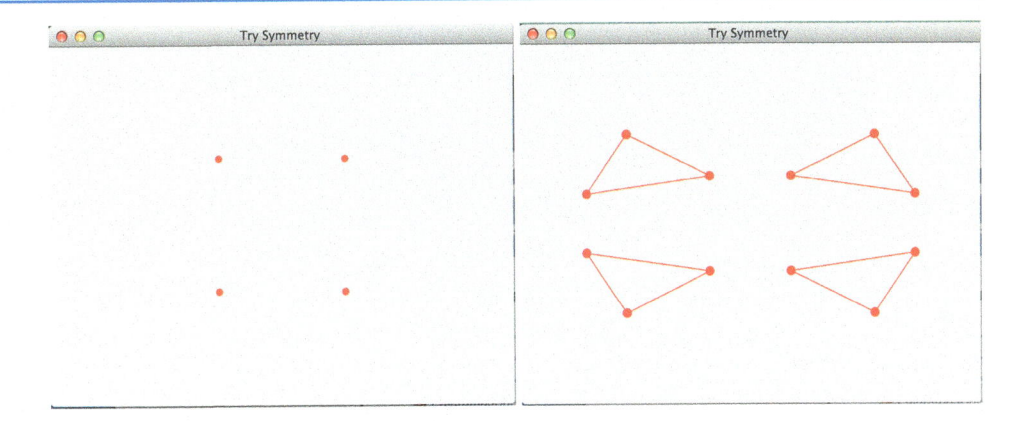

is in the middle point of the canvas. Write a program TrySymPoint that adopts a random number generator to generate a pair of (x, y) as the center coordinates of a small circle inside the top-left quarter and paints the circle on the center point of (x, y). And then reflex the small circle symmetrically on the other three quarters as shown in Fig. 5.13 (left).

7. With the same setting as above, write a program TrySymTri that adopts a random number generator to generate three pairs of (x, y) as the center coordinates of three small circles inside the top-left quarter and paints a triangle with the three small circles. And then reflex the triangle symmetrically on the other three quarters as shown in Fig. 5.13 (Right).
8. Design and implement a birthday card using a GUI.
9. Design and implement a "sorry card" using a GUI.
10. Design and implement a new version of the project PaintXmasCard that stores multiple images in the directory "images" and allow the user to select one of them to be shown on a Christmas card.
11. Design and implement a new version of the project PaintXmasCard that asks the user for inputting the absolute file path of an image to display it on a Christmas card.

Java Software Components and Event Handling: Projects CalculatorApp and ImageSlider

A game GUI is not only for outputting game scenes but also for accepting players' controlling actions. These actions go through Java software components, events, and event listeners to form action-event chains for controlling the game. Furthermore, the action-event chain is developed to be the action-event-update-repaint chain for updating and repainting dynamic scenes.

The objectives of this chapter include:
1. A GUI consists of software components: CalculatorApp.
2. Applying layout managers for arranging components.
3. The communications between components and logics.
4. An action-event chain: action, source, event, and event listener.
5. Implementing event listeners for embedding control logics.
6. Alternative approaches for implementing an event listener.
7. Semantic events and low-level events.
8. An action-event-update-repaint chain: ImageSlider.
9. Interfaces and abstract classes.

The Christmas card constructed in the previous chapter is based on the drawing capability of the built-in graphics context Graphics g. However, the painted output is only static scenes. In order to visualize dynamic scenes of a game, a game GUI usually includes Java software components that support a panel for game players to input data, to watch the games' status, and to trigger events for driving the game with dynamic behaviors. This chapter starts learning the Java software components and their event-handling abilities.

6.1 A GUI Consists of Java Software Components: A Software Calculator

A software calculator is an easy understandable example for illustrating the features and techniques of Java software components in certain depth because it is a well-known device that almost everyone knows it and uses it so that we don't need to make much effort for describing and explaining it. Meanwhile, a software calculator is purely made by Java software components so that we can concentrate our discussions on the new topic.

Figure 6.1 shows the GUI of a simple software calculator. A GUI of such a calculator mainly deals with three issues, which include (1) what kinds of components are needed, (2) how to arrange these components, and (3) more important and more complicated is how to build up the connection between the visible components and unseen logics and functionalities behind the GUI.

Intuitively, the GUI of the calculator consists of a set of buttons and a console for displaying the computation formula and the result. The Java APIs provide all of these software components. The super class of all software components is the built-in class JComponent. The subclasses are components that form a huge set. The most popular components include JButton, JLabel, JTextArea, JTextField, JCheckBox, and JRadioButton, just to name a few. The superclass and major subclasses form a hierarchical structure as depicted in Fig. 6.2.

In order to organize multiple software components as our expected, Java also provides a set of layout managers such that we can nicely organize components without our own calculations.

6.2 The Design of the GUI

First of all, in order to ease the organization of all components, it would be better to divide the entire GUI into several sub-areas as shown on the right side of Fig. 6.1. We divide the entire GUI into two portions. The "top portion" is a console for displaying the operand1, the operand2, a line, and the computation result. The "bottom portion" of the GUI is for placing all buttons. We further divide the "bottom portion" into an "up board" and a "down board." The "up board"

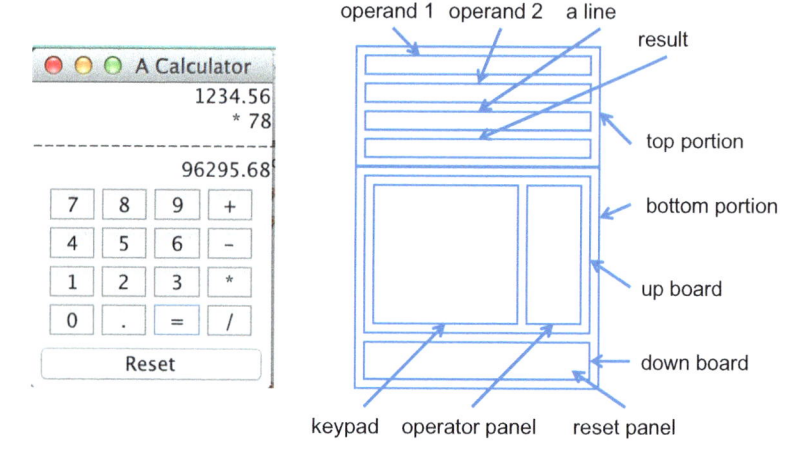

Fig. 6.1 The GUI of a simple calculator in the project CalculatorApp

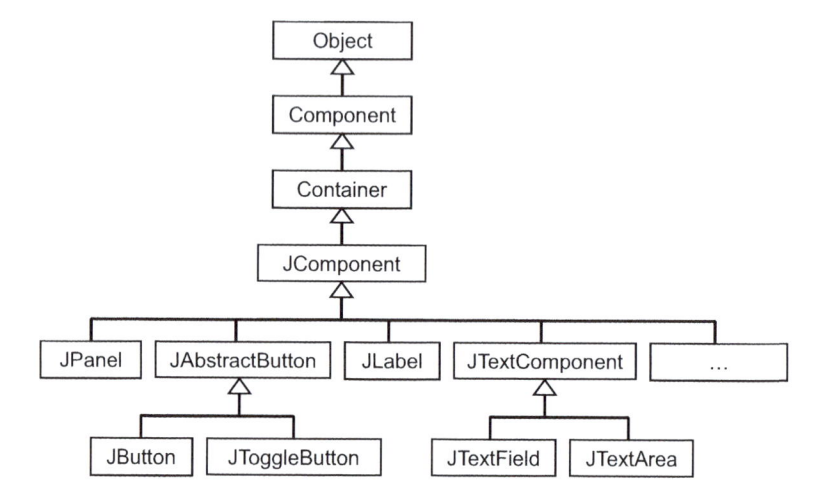

Fig. 6.2 The partial software component inheritance hierarchy

is further split into the "keypad" on the left side and the "operator panel" on the right side. The "keypad" organizes the ten-digit buttons plus the dot button and the equal sign button. The "operator panel" is for the four calculation functions: add, sub, mul, and div buttons. The "down board" has only a reset button.

6.3 Arranging Components Using Layout Managers

Continuously, we are going to fill required components into the smaller sub-areas, and some sub-areas are grouped as a larger area. Certainly, the intermediate container JPanel is suitable for building up such kind of structure. Taking the "up board on the bottom portion" as an example. The up board contains the "keypad" sub-area and the "operator panel" sub-area. The "keypad" consists of 12 buttons including ten-digit buttons, a dot button, and an equal sign button. All of them are organized in four rows and three columns. The GridLayout manager is suitable for this case. The code is as follows.

```
JPanel kp = new JPanel(); // kp -- keypad
kp.setLayout(new GridLayout(4, 3, 5, 5));
```

The first statement instantiates an object kp of the JPanel. The second statement allows the object kp to invoke the method setLayout() and accepts an object of the GridLayout as its actual parameter. For instantiating the object of the GridLayout, four integers "4, 3, 5, 5" are passed in. The first value of 4 defines four rows; the second value of 3 defines three columns; the third value of 5 defines the gaps between components along the x direction; the fourth value of 5 defines the gaps between components along the y direction. Its effect is depicted in Fig. 6.3 (1). The following step is to instantiate 12 objects of JButtons and add them into the "keypad" kp one by one. Along the adding order, the 12 buttons are placed from left to right and from top to bottom onto the 12 positions arranged by the GridLayout manager. Similarly, the "operator panel" contains four buttons for the four calculation functions. An object op of the JPanel is instantiated, and the GridLayout manager is applied again to arrange the four buttons into four rows and one column with the statement "new GridLayout(4,1,5,5)," which is depicted

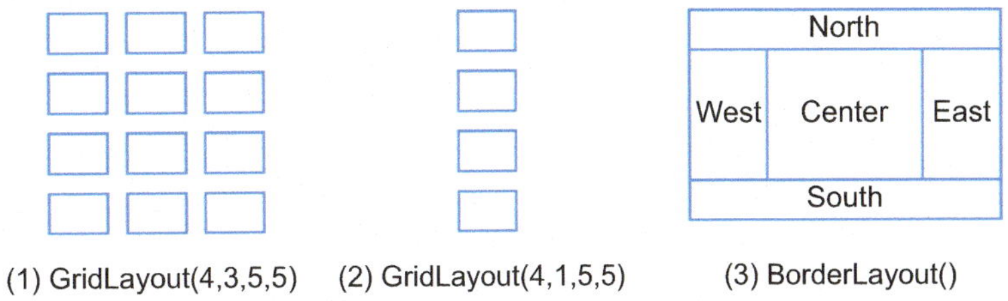

6.3 Arranging Components Using Layout Managers

Fig. 6.3 The GridLayout and the BorderLayout managers

(1) GridLayout(4,3,5,5)   (2) GridLayout(4,1,5,5)   (3) BorderLayout()

in Fig. 6.3 (2). And then, both the objects of the "keypad" kp and the "operator panel" op are added onto the "up board" ub, which is another object of a JPanel. That is, the two smaller panels kp and op are added onto a bigger panel ub.

After that, the implementation continues to make the "top portion," which arranges four JTextField components. The first one is for displaying the operand1; the second is for displaying the operator and the operand2; the third one is for displaying a ling; and the last one is for filling the computational result. Among them, the line is filled in advance. Other three text fields initially are blank, and when the user clicks related buttons for making the operand1 and the operand2, the related digits are filled in the corresponding text fields. For holding these four JTextFields, a new object topPortion of a JPanel is instantiated, and a GridLayout manager arranges the four JTextFields into four rows and one column by invoking the statement "new GridLayout(4, 1)" without setting gaps between components.

The last step is to set up the layout manager BorderLayout to divide the entire GUI into five areas as shown in Fig. 6.3 (3). And then, the method add() is invoked three times to add the topPortion to the NORTH part, to add the "up board" ub to the CENTER part, and finally to add the JButton bReset to the SOUTH part, respectively.

The code cited in Listing 6.1 just follows these ideas to arrange all of required software components onto their positions. Going through the code, we should understand the functionality of JPanels, layout managers, JButtons, and JTextFields.

Listing 6.1 The partial code of the class CalculatorFace.java that shows the GUI part of the calculator in the project CalculatorApp

```
1  /*
2   * CalculatorFace.java -- A class defines the GUI of the calculator
3   */
4  package calculatorgui;
5
6  import java.awt.BorderLayout;
7  import java.awt.Dimension;
8  import java.awt.GridLayout;
9  import javax.swing.JButton;
10 import javax.swing.JPanel;
11 import javax.swing.JTextField;
12
13 public class CalculatorFace extends JPanel {
14
15     private JPanel topPortion;
16     private JButton bZero = new JButton("0");
17     private JButton bOne = new JButton("1");
18     private JButton bTwo = new JButton("2");
19     private JButton bThree = new JButton("3");
20     private JButton bFour = new JButton("4");
21     private JButton bFive = new JButton("5");
22     private JButton bSix = new JButton("6");
23     private JButton bSeven = new JButton("7");
24     private JButton bEight = new JButton("8");
25     private JButton bNine = new JButton("9");
26     private JButton bDot = new JButton(".");
27     private JButton bEqual = new JButton("=");
```

```java
28      private JButton bAdd = new JButton("+");
29      private JButton bSub = new JButton("-");
30      private JButton bMul = new JButton("*");
31      private JButton bDiv = new JButton("/");
32      private JButton bReset = new JButton("Reset");
33      private JTextField dispOperand1;
34      private JTextField dispOperand2;
35      private JTextField dispLine;
36      private JTextField dispResult;
37
38      public CalculatorFace() {
39          initComponents();
40      }
41
42      private void initComponents() {
43          // the top board of the bottom portion
44          JPanel ub = new JPanel(); // ub -- up board
45          JPanel pp = new JPanel(); // pp -- pad panel
46          pp.setLayout(new GridLayout(4, 3, 5, 5));
47          bSeven.setPreferredSize(new Dimension(30, 20));
48          pp.add(bSeven);
49          bEight.setPreferredSize(new Dimension(30, 20));
50          pp.add(bEight);
51          bNine.setPreferredSize(new Dimension(30, 20));
52          pp.add(bNine);
53          bFour.setPreferredSize(new Dimension(30, 20));
54          pp.add(bFour);
55          bFive.setPreferredSize(new Dimension(30, 20));
56          pp.add(bFive);
57          bSix.setPreferredSize(new Dimension(30, 20));
58          pp.add(bSix);
59          bOne.setPreferredSize(new Dimension(30, 20));
60          pp.add(bOne);
61          bTwo.setPreferredSize(new Dimension(30, 20));
62          pp.add(bTwo);
63          bThree.setPreferredSize(new Dimension(30, 20));
64          pp.add(bThree);
65          bZero.setPreferredSize(new Dimension(30, 20));
66          pp.add(bZero);
67          bDot.setPreferredSize(new Dimension(30, 20));
68          pp.add(bDot);
69          bEqual.setPreferredSize(new Dimension(30, 20));
70          pp.add(bEqual);
71          ub.add(pp);
72
73          JPanel cp = new JPanel(); // cp -- calculation panel
74          cp.setLayout(new GridLayout(4, 1, 5, 5));
75          bAdd.setPreferredSize(new Dimension(30, 20));
76          cp.add(bAdd);
77          bSub.setPreferredSize(new Dimension(30, 20));
78          cp.add(bSub);
79          bMul.setPreferredSize(new Dimension(30, 20));
80          cp.add(bMul);
81          bDiv.setPreferredSize(new Dimension(30, 20));
82          cp.add(bDiv);
```

```
 83         ub.add(cp);
 84
 85         // the topPortion
 86         dispOperand1 = new JTextField(20);
 87         dispOperand1.setHorizontalAlignment(JTextField.RIGHT);
 88         dispOperand1.setBorder(null);
 89         dispOperand2 = new JTextField();
 90         dispOperand2.setHorizontalAlignment(JTextField.RIGHT);
 91         dispOperand2.setBorder(null);
 92         dispLine = new JTextField("--------------------------------");
 93         dispLine.setHorizontalAlignment(JTextField.RIGHT);
 94         dispLine.setBorder(null);
 95         dispResult = new JTextField();
 96         dispResult.setHorizontalAlignment(JTextField.RIGHT);
 97         dispResult.setBorder(null);
 98         topPortion = new JPanel();
 99         topPortion.setLayout(new GridLayout(4, 1));
100         topPortion.add(dispOperand1);
101         topPortion.add(dispOperand2);
102         topPortion.add(dispLine);
103         topPortion.add(dispResult);
104
105         // organize all components
106         this.setLayout(new BorderLayout());
107         this.add(topPortion, BorderLayout.NORTH);
108         this.add(ub, BorderLayout.CENTER);
109         this.add(bReset, BorderLayout.SOUTH);
110     }
111 }
```

This section demonstrates the process how to design and organize components into a GUI, which includes instantiating JPanels and components, setting up layout managers, organizing individual components into a smaller group, and merging smaller groups into bigger groups. As long as we familiarize ourselves with the components and layout managers, the process is very straightforward. This implementation process relies on a nice design in advance. Of course, here we have not touched the functions of these components yet, which deal with event listeners and event handlers.

6.4 More Layout Managers

So far, we learned two layout managers: GridLayout and BorderLayout. Other popular layout managers include FlowLayout and CardLayout as shown in Fig. 6.4. The FlowLayout arranges multiple components one by one along a row from left to right. When one component reaches the right edge of the area, it turns to the next row. The CardLayout manager arranges multiple components in an overlapping fashion like a deck of cards. The Card1 is on the front, then Card2 is underneath Card1, then Card3 is underneath Card2,

and so on. We will learn its application later. There are some other layout managers, such as GridBagLayout, BoxLayout, GroupLayout, and SpringLayout.

6.5 A UML Sequence Diagram Illustrates an Action-Event Chain

Why do we need to adopt these Java software components? These software components will link the game players' actions with hidden events and event listeners. In other words, the software components are the communication points between the GUI and the logic behind scenes. Actually, almost everyone experiences event and event handling every

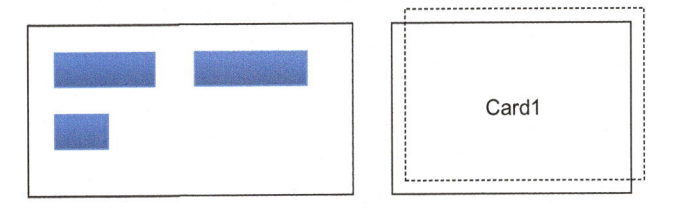

Fig. 6.4 (Left) The FlowLayout manager; (Right) the CardLayout manager

day. When we turn on a computer or a cell phone and click certain buttons, the scene on the screen is changed. When we open a browser and key in a ".com" address on the URL field or a search field with a press on the <return> key, a new web page is showing up. That is, when an action of a mouse clicks on a button component or a key presses on a text field component, the action triggers an event. As long as an event listener receives the event, it executes a predefined event handler for performing certain functions that change the scenes of the output screen.

A mouse click or a key press on a component is termed as an "action." The action with the software component together creates a related event. The button that receives a mouse click or the text field that receives a key press is termed as the event "source component." After a source component is pre-registered with an event listener, once the listener receives an event, it triggers a related event handler embedded with the event listener to perform certain pre-defined functions. Thus, action, source component, pre-registered event listener with its event handler form an action-event chain to allow external users inputting their actions for controlling the application. The action-event chain mainly consists of register-trigger-execute three steps.

The UML language not only provides a class diagram for describing the relationships among classes statically but also provides a sequence diagram for depicting dynamic functions among objects. Figure 6.5 is a sequence diagram that depicts an action-event chain in general.

In Fig. 6.5, a colon plus a class name with an underline represents an object of the class. The figure uses an object of JButton to represent a source component; an object of Event represents an ActionEvent; an object of EventListener represents an ActionListener. The action-event chain is depicted in Fig. 6.5 as follows. "1. register" means that the button registers with an object of ActionListener that implements an event handler. "2. action" means once an external action, such as a click on the button, occurs, an object of ActionEvent is created (is marked as "3. create event") and is sent to the object of ActionListener, which triggers the event handler defined in the ActionListener (is marked as "4. trigger handler"). Finally "5. perform function" indicates that the event handler performs the predefined function as a response for the button click action. In general, all of event handlings go through this chain to allow users to input their actions on software components for controlling embedded event handlers in applications. In programming paradigm, this is termed as event-driven programming, which builds dynamic behaviors for applications.

6.6 Making the Software Calculator Work

The class CalculatorFace.java cited in Listing 6.1 builds up the GUI of the software calculator as shown in Fig. 6.6 (left). After applying the register-trigger-execute three steps, in which every software component associates with a pre-defined event handler, we make the calculator working as Fig. 6.6 (right) illustrates. The linkages that link the components on the GUI with the unseen event handlers are the action-event chains. The code for implementing these chains is cited in Listing 6.2.

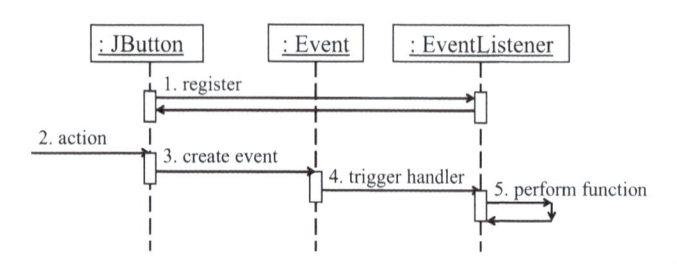

Fig. 6.5 The UML sequence diagram depicts an action-event chain

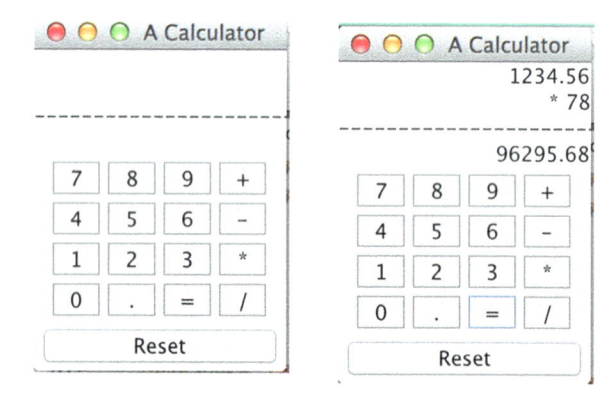

Fig. 6.6 (Left) The GUI of the software calculator; (Right) The function of the software calculator

Listing 6.2 The partial code of the class CalculatorFace.java for registering components with related event listeners in the project CalculatorApp

```
126        // assign action listeners to components
127        private void addAction() {
128            bZero.addActionListener(new DigitActionListener());
129            bOne.addActionListener(new DigitActionListener());
130            bTwo.addActionListener(new DigitActionListener());
131            bThree.addActionListener(new DigitActionListener());
132            bFour.addActionListener(new DigitActionListener());
133            bFive.addActionListener(new DigitActionListener());
134            bSix.addActionListener(new DigitActionListener());
135            bSeven.addActionListener(new DigitActionListener());
136            bEight.addActionListener(new DigitActionListener());
137            bNine.addActionListener(new DigitActionListener());
138            bDot.addActionListener(new DigitActionListener());
139            bAdd.addActionListener(new DigitActionListener());
140            bSub.addActionListener(new DigitActionListener());
141            bMul.addActionListener(new DigitActionListener());
142            bDiv.addActionListener(new DigitActionListener());
143            bEqual.addActionListener(new DigitActionListener());
144            bReset.addActionListener(new DigitActionListener());
145        }
```

The code in Listing 6.2 reveals a pattern. This is, every button invokes a built-in method "addActionListener()" to add an object of "new DigitActionListener()." The UML class diagram of the project CalculatorApp shown in Fig. 6.7 gives us a clue. A special new feature shown in the diagram is the dashed line with a triangle sign, which represents an "implements" relationship between the class CalculatorFace.java and the ActionListener. It says that the class CalculatorFace.java "implements" an event listener ActionListener. The built-in class ActionListener is defined as a special kind of class called "Interface," which is "special" because an "Interface" is different from a "regular" class. An "Interface" only declares methods without coding the body of the methods. In fact, the real Interface ActionListener only declares one method actionPerformed() without method body. Consequently, the method should be "implemented."

The "implementing an Interface" means to fill in the methods with their bodies according to the needs of the application. The implementation has different approaches. A popular approach is to create an inner class. That is, inside the class CalculatorFace.java, we create a class DigitActionListener that "implements" the Interface ActionListener as cited in Listing 6.3.

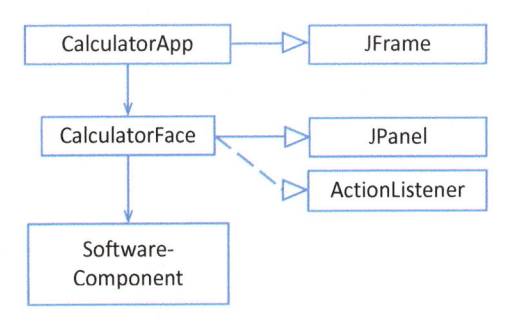

Fig. 6.7 The UML class diagram of the project CalculatorApp

Listing 6.3 The partial code of the class CalculatorFace.java that defines the inner class DigitActionListener for implementing the Interface ActionListener

```
162     // implementing the action listener
163     class DigitActionListener implements ActionListener {
164
165         @Override
166         public void actionPerformed(ActionEvent evt) {
167             String aLetter = "";
168             Object obj = (Object) evt.getSource();
169             if (obj.equals(bZero)) {
170                 aLetter = "0";
171                 getOp = false;
172             } else if (obj.equals(bOne)) {
173                 aLetter = "1";
174                 getOp = false;
175             } else if (obj.equals(bTwo)) {
176                 aLetter = "2";
177                 getOp = false;
178             } else if (obj.equals(bThree)) {
179                 aLetter = "3";
180                 getOp = false;
181             } else if (obj.equals(bFour)) {
182                 aLetter = "4";
183                 getOp = false;
184             } else if (obj.equals(bFive)) {
185                 aLetter = "5";
186                 getOp = false;
187             } else if (obj.equals(bSix)) {
188                 aLetter = "6";
189                 getOp = false;
190             } else if (obj.equals(bSeven)) {
191                 aLetter = "7";
192                 getOp = false;
193             } else if (obj.equals(bEight)) {
194                 aLetter = "8";
195                 getOp = false;
196             } else if (obj.equals(bNine)) {
197                 aLetter = "9";
198                 getOp = false;
199             } else if (obj.equals(bDot)) {
200                 aLetter = ".";
201                 getOp = false;
202             } else if (obj.equals(bAdd)) {
203                 assignOp("+");
204             } else if (obj.equals(bSub)) {
205                 assignOp("-");
206             } else if (obj.equals(bMul)) {
207                 assignOp("*");
208             } else if (obj.equals(bDiv)) {
209                 assignOp("/");
210             }
211
212             // accumulate digits for ope1 and ope2
213             if (getOpe1 && !getOpe2) { // first operand
```

```
214            if (!getEqual) {
215                ope1 = ope1 + aLetter;
216            }
217            dispOperand1.setText(ope1);
218        } else if (!getOpe1 && getOpe2) { // second operand
219            if (!getEqual && !getOp) { // cp won't be added
220                ope2 = ope2 + aLetter;
221            }
222            dispOperand2.setText(op + " " + ope2);
223        }
224
225        // equal sign triggers computations and reset
226        if (obj.equals(bEqual)) {
227            if (!(ope1.equals("")) && !(op.equals(""))
228                && !(ope2.equals(""))) {
229                getEqual = true;
230                double ope1Value = Double.parseDouble(ope1);
231                double ope2Value = Double.parseDouble(ope2);
232                if (op.equals("+")) {
233                    doAdd(ope1Value, ope2Value);
234                } else if (op.equals("-")) {
235                    doSub(ope1Value, ope2Value);
236                } else if (op.equals("*")) {
237                    doMul(ope1Value, ope2Value);
238                } else if (op.equals("/")) {
239                    doDiv(ope1Value, ope2Value);
240                }
241            }
242        } else if (obj.equals(bReset)) {
243            initReset();
244        }
245    }
246
```

Therefore, inside the "outer" class of CalculatorFace.java, we define a class in using "class DigitActionListener implements ActionListener {}" (line 163). The new class DigitActionListener is part of the class CalculatorFace.java; thus, it is an inner class that is inside an "outer" class and can be seen as a member of the "outer" class. Because it is an inner class, the object of the inner class can be instantiated by other members of the "outer" class, and the object of the inner class can also access the other members of the "outer" class. More specific, the object of the inner class "new DigitActionListener()" can be registered with any software components defined inside the "outer" class, and the object of the inner class DigitActionListener can also directly access the software components defined in the "outer" class.

The class DigitActionListener implements the Interface ActionListener by adding codes into the method actionPerformed(ActionEvent evt) (line 166). Whenever a button, say bZero, is clicked, an ActionEvent is generated and is sent to the actionPerformed() through the parameter evt, and then the statement "Object obj = (Object) evt.getSource();" (line 168) will find the source button through the method evt.getSource() and assign it to the variable obj. The source component should be the button bZero. Correspondingly, the variable aLetter will be assigned a value of "0" (line 170). The value of "0" will be added into an operand.

6.7 The Register-Trigger-Execute for Making an Action-Event Chain

In order to make a complete picture, we take the button zero as an example for repeating the three steps register-trigger-execute in making an action-event chain.

0. Create the button bZero (line 16 in Listing 6.1).
   An object of the JButton is instantiated and assigned to the variable bZero.

```
private JButton bZero = new JButton("0");
```

The method initComponent() assigns the object button bZero with a preferred size and adds it onto the "keypad" kp. Later, the "keypad" kp is added onto the "up board" ub for making a proper position for the button bZero.

1. Register bZero with an object ActionListener (line 128 in Listing 6.2).

   The method addActionListener() adds an object of the DigitActionListener with bZero.

   ```
   bZero.addActionListener(
       new DigitActionListener());
   ```

2. Trigger the event handler actionPerformed() (line 166 in Listing 6.3).

   When a mouse clicks on the button bZero, an ActionEvent is generated and is sent to the action listener DigitActionListener that was registered with the button bZero, and the event triggers the event handler method.

   ```
   actionPerformed(ActionEvent evt) {}
   ```

3. Execute the event handler actionPerformed() (lines 169–171 in Listing 6.3).

   The predefined event handler actionPerformed() invokes the following code:

   ```
   Object obj = (Object) evt.getSource();
   if (obj.equals(bZero)) {
       aLetter = "0";
       getOp = false;
   }
   ```

   Eventually, the statement "aLetter = "0"" assigns the digit of 0 to the variable aLetter.

Following the same chain, all of software components on the "keypad" go through the same sequence of register-trigger-execute steps. Thus, the similar codes are repeated many times.

The four buttons in the "operator panel" also go through the sequence of register-trigger-execute steps, but the functions of their event handlers are different from the digit buttons. The four operator buttons associate with the four operation methods doAdd(), doSub(), doMul(), and doDiv(), respectively. After operand1 and operand2 are available, as long as the special button bEqual is clicked, the two operands and the corresponding operation function are invoked to perform the calculations for making a computational result, which is then displayed on the text field dispResult. So does the "reset button" that will invoke a special method initReset() for re-initializing all of data when it is clicked.

6.8 Controlling the Sequence of Actions for Making a Computation

The initialization of source components and registration of event listener is a mechanical and repeated work. After the GUI provides all of required buttons and the function of every button is supported with its event listener, our concern turns to the controls of the sequence of actions for making a computation. As a common sense, a computation needs four steps: input an operand1, select an operator, input an operand2, and then click the equal sign to have the computation result. It follows the input, computation, and output sequence.

A user of the software calculator may have the common sense described above or may not. But, the device should be able to guarantee the correct sequence of actions for making a correct computation result. The logic is built in the event handler inside the event listener. The sequence of controls is arranged by Boolean variables getOpe1, getOpe2, getOp, and getEqual. (1) When a new computation begins, the method initReset() initializes getOpe1 (get operand1) true, getOpe2 (get operand2) false, getOp (get operator) false, and getEqual (get equal sign) false. Under this setting, only digit button clicks are accepted in order to form the operand1, and all of other non-digit button clicks are ignored. (2) When one of operator +, −, *, or / button is clicked, the getOp and getOpe2 are turned to be true, and getOpe1 is set to be false. This new setting allows the user to enter the operand2. (3) When the bEqual button is clicked, both operand1 and operand2 are converted from a String to a double number. And then, depending on the operator, a corresponding operation function is invoked to perform the computation, and the result is displayed. (4) The click on the reset button will re-initialize all of variables to start a new computation. The implementation of these controls is shown in Listing 6.3.

6.9 Major Semantic Events and Their Event Listeners

The events associated with the software components are classified with the term of "semantic events." Different source components and different actions generate different events and require different event listeners for listening the corresponding events. The major events and related source components with certain actions are listed as follows.

ActionEvent	JButton (click), JTextField (press <return>), JRadioButton (click), JCheckBox (check), JMenuItem (select)
ItemEvent	JRadioButton (click), JCheckBox (check), JComboBox (click)
ListSelectionEvent	JList (click)
AdjustmentEvent	JScrollBar (move)
ChangeEvent	JSlider (move)

As long as knowing the kind of event XXXX, the corresponding event listener should be XXXXListener. For example, the ItemEvent listener is ItemListener.

The other kind of events associated with hardware components, such as key and mouse, is classified as "low-level events," which will be discussed later.

6.10 Alternative Approaches for Implementing Event Listeners

The project CalculatorApp adopted the inner class approach for implementing the event listener. Due to the fact that the inner class has the same scope as all of attributes and methods defined in the "outer" class, the inner class can conveniently access any software components defined inside the "outer" class whenever needed.

Surely, we have other alternative approaches to implement an ActionListener, such as (1) let the CalculatorFace.java class directly implement the ActionListener for defining the class CalculatorFace.java with the title of "public class CalculatorFace extends JPanel implements ActionListener {}," (2) code the listener as an anonymous inner class, and (3) make the class DigitActionListener as an independent public class.

The project CalculatorAppAlt1 follows the first alternative approach as listed in Listing 6.4, where we only cite the definition of the event listener because all of other codes are the same as in Listing 6.3.

Listing 6.4 The partial code of the class CalculatorFace.java that directly implements the ActionListener in the project CalculatorAppAlt1

```
1  /*
2   * CalculatorFace.java -- A class defines the GUI of the calculator
3   */
14 …
15 public class CalculatorFace extends JPanel implements ActionListener {
16
125 …
126     // assign action listeners to components
127     private void addAction() {
128         bZero.addActionListener(this);
129         bOne.addActionListener(this);
130         bTwo.addActionListener(this);
…
138         bDot.addActionListener(this);
139         bAdd.addActionListener(this);
140         bSub.addActionListener(this);
141         bMul.addActionListener(this);
142         bDiv.addActionListener(this);
143         bEqual.addActionListener(this);
144         bReset.addActionListener(this);
145     }
146
161 …
162     // implementing the action listener declared in the interface ActionListener directly
163     @Override
164     public void actionPerformed(ActionEvent evt) {
165         String aLetter = "";
166         Object obj = (Object) evt.getSource();
167         if (obj.equals(bZero)) {
168             aLetter = "0";
169             getOp = false;
170         } else if (obj.equals(bOne)) {
171             aLetter = "1";
172             getOp = false;
173         } …
240         } else if (obj.equals(bReset)) {
241             initReset();
242         }
243     }
244
253 …
277 }
```

This approach allows the public class CalculatorFace.java to "implement" the Interface ActionListener and directly code the event handler actionPerformed() as one of methods. And then a component registers the object of the listener as "this" (lines 128–144) because "this" object of the class CalculatorFace.java itself implements the action listener. This alternative way works fine and is also one of the popular approaches.

The second alternative approach is to implement the ActionListener as an anonymous inner class, which means that the class that implements the ActionListener is an inner class without an explicit name. It is defined and instantiated in a single expression using the "new" operator as follows.

```
bReset.addActionListener(
    new ActionListener() {
        public actionPerformed(
            ActionEvent evt) {
            initReset();
        }
    }
);
```

The code above means that we can register an ActionListener with the button bReset using the "new" operator to directly instantiate an object of the Interface ActionListener with the implementation of the event handler such that the ActionListener has no name. It is a concise way to implement an ActionListener. In addition, the code is straight and easy to follow. However, it can only be used one time for the specific button bReset; other buttons cannot share the event handler defined inside the anonymous inner class. In other words, one anonymous event listener can only serve one component. It is not convenient enough as the inner class DigitActionListener implemented in the class CalculatorFace.java, which can be shared by all of buttons.

The third alternative approach is to move the inner class DigitActionListener out of the CalculatorFace.java class as an independent regular public class DigitActionListener.java. Due to the separation, all of the software components originally defined inside the "outer" class CalculatorFace.java have to be copied and transferred into the independent event listener class DigitActionListener.java so that all of components have to be duplicated. It not only creates extra works but also makes a tightly coupled software structure. These weak points make this approach rarely used.

6.11 Flexibility of Event Handling: A Project ImageSlider

Certainly, a button click not only can produce a digit or invoke a method as did in the project CalculatorApp but also can perform dynamic actions. Here, we make a simple project ImageSlider for demonstrating this feature.

The simple ImageSlider is similar with the photo slider in market. But, this ImageSlider is simple since it only has one function, which can move an image to the right direction or to the left direction according to a click on the right button or on the left button.

The pseudo code (the global sequence of actions) of the project could be as follows.

1. The project requires five objects: main, sliderPanel, showBoard, readImage, and software components rightBtn and leftBtn.
2. The readImage reads in a set of scenery images and stores them into an ArrayList. In addition, it also reads in a rightArrow image and a leftArrow image.
3. The showBoard displays one of scenery images on the board at a time.
4. The sliderPanel uses the BorderLayout manager to arrange the left arrow image on a button inside the WEST part, the right arrow image on a button inside the EAST part, and the showBoard inside the CENTER part.
5. When the left button is clicked, all of the images in the ArrayList are moved to left one position. That is, the current index is increased by one. And when the right button is clicked, the current index is decreased by one.

Based on this description, the UML class diagram can be shown as Fig. 6.8.

6.12 Showing a Static Scene: The Project ImageSlider1

Usually we start a new project from its static behaviors and then add the dynamic behaviors into it. The project ImageSlider1 only statically shows one image at the showBoard, which "is-a" JPanel and is added at the CENTER part of the sliderPanel as in Fig. 6.9 (left). The project illustrates the arrangement of major components. The code is similar with that in the project PaintXmasCard4 in the previous chapter. It is clear and simple so that we leave the code reading for readers.

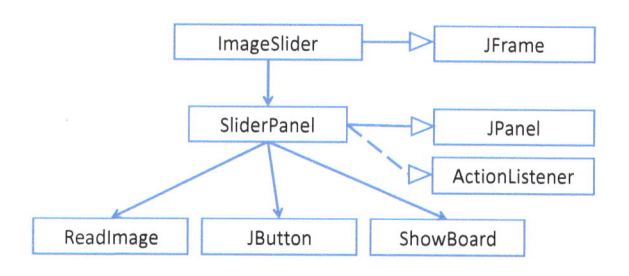

Fig. 6.8 The UML class diagram of the project ImageSlider

Fig. 6.9 (Left) The GUI of the ImageSlider1; (Right) the GUI of the ImageSlider2

6.13 Adding Dynamic Behaviors: The Project ImageSlider2

Then, we download a set of scenery images and a left arrow image as well as a right arrow image from Google/images and store them into a folder "images" inside the project ImageSlider2. After that, we completely implement the pseudo code listed above for adding two buttons and their action listeners. The code of each class is shown and explained as follows.

The class ReadImage.java is an extension of the original one in the previous chapter. The extension makes the class possible to read in multiple images instead of only read in one image. The method initImage() reads in the set of scenery images and stores them into an arrayList sceneryList. The reason for defining an ArrayList is that the program should be flexible enough for reading any number of images for different cases. Fortunately, all of the scenery images have the same name with an additional sequence number so that we can easily access them with the code. In addition, the class also reads in two images of a left arrow and a right arrow. The stored images will be accessed by other classes; thus, three getter methods getImage(), getLeftArrow(), and getRightArrow() are ready to be used. The getter method getImage() has a parameter of index so that other classes can specify an index for getting any required image from the arrayList sceneryList. The code of the class ReadImage.java is shown in Listing 6.5.

Listing 6.5 The code of the class ReadImage.java in the project ImageSlider2

```
1  /*
2   * ReadImage.java -- a class to read an image into the project
3   */
4  package imageslider;
5
6  import java.awt.Image;
7  import java.awt.image.BufferedImage;
8  import java.io.IOException;
9  import java.util.ArrayList;
10 import javax.imageio.ImageIO;
11
12 public class ReadImage {
13
14     private BufferedImage img;
15     private ArrayList<BufferedImage> sceneryList;
16     private Image rightArrow;
```

```
17      private Image leftArrow;
18
19      public ReadImage() {
20          sceneryList = new ArrayList<>();
21          initImage();
22      }
23
24      private void initImage() {
25          try {
26              for (int idx = 0; idx < 6; idx++) {
27                  img = ImageIO.read(getClass().getResource(
28                          "../images/scenery" + (idx + 1) + ".jpeg"));
29                  sceneryList.add(img);
30              }
31              rightArrow = ImageIO.read(getClass().getResource(
32                      "../images/rightArrow.png"));
33              leftArrow = ImageIO.read(getClass().getResource(
34                      "../images/leftArrow.png"));
35          } catch (IOException ex) {
36          }
37      }
38
39      public ArrayList<BufferedImage> getSceneryList() {
40          return sceneryList;
41      }
42
43      public BufferedImage getImage(int idx) {
44          return sceneryList.get(idx);
45      }
46
47      public Image getRightArrow() {
48          return rightArrow;
49      }
50
51      public Image getLeftArrow() {
52          return leftArrow;
53      }
54  }
```

The class ShowBoard.java is constructed for displaying the current image that is one of the images stored in the sceneryList. The class "is-a" JPanel; hence it has the graphics context Graphics g and the method paint() for painting the image. When the class gets the current image, it supports a method calcPosition() to zoom the current image for fitting the image into the size of the board. The zoom scale is proportional to the larger one between the width and the height of the real image. When the width of the current image is larger than the height of the current image, we would like to make the width of the zoomed image imgWidth fits with the width of the board held in the variable boardW and the height of the zoomed image imgHeight is zoomed corresponding to the same scale. Similarly, when the height of the current image is larger than the width of the current image, we zoom the image for making the imgHeight equals to the height of the board held in the variable boardH and the imgWidth is zoomed accordingly. Finally, the zoomed image is painted on the board by the method paint(). The code of the class is cited in Listing 6.6.

Listing 6.6 The code of the class ShowBoard.java in the project ImageSlider2

```
1  /*
2   * ShowBoard.java - A class defines the show panel for showing an image.
3   */
4  package imageslider;
5
6  import java.awt.Dimension;
7  import java.awt.Graphics;
8  import java.awt.image.BufferedImage;
9  import javax.swing.JPanel;
10
15 public class ShowBoard extends JPanel {
16
17     private ReadImage readImage;
18     private BufferedImage theShowImg;
19     private int boardW;
20     private int boardH;
21     private double zoomRatio;
22     private int imgWidth;
23     private int imgHeight;
24     private int xCoor, yCoor;
25     private int imgIdx;
26
27     public ShowBoard() {
28         boardW = Consts.CV_WIDTH - 2 * Consts.BUTTON_W;
29         boardH = Consts.CV_HEIGHT - Consts.TOP_BAR_HEIGHT;
30         this.setPreferredSize(new Dimension(boardW, boardH));
31     }
32
33     public void initShowImg() {
34         // for getting the first image; one time
35         imgIdx = readImage.getSceneryList().size() / 2; // the middle index
36     }
37
38     public void findShowImg() {
39         theShowImg = readImage.getImage(imgIdx);
40         calcPosition();
41     }
42
43     public void calcPosition() {
44         // zoom the image to fit in the board
45         if (theShowImg.getWidth() >= theShowImg.getHeight()) {
46             zoomRatio = (boardW * 1.0) / theShowImg.getWidth();
47             imgWidth = boardW;
48             imgHeight = (int) (theShowImg.getHeight() * zoomRatio);
49             xCoor = 0; // x starting point relative to the board
50             yCoor = boardH / 2 - imgHeight / 2; // y starting point
51         } else { // if height > width
52             zoomRatio = (boardH * 1.0) / theShowImg.getHeight();
53             imgHeight = boardH;
54             imgWidth = (int) (theShowImg.getWidth() * zoomRatio);
55             yCoor = 0;
56             xCoor = boardW / 2 - imgWidth / 2;
57         }
```

```
58      }
59
60      @Override
61      public void paint(Graphics g) {
62          g.drawImage(theShowImg, xCoor, yCoor, imgWidth, imgHeight, this);
63      }
64
65      public void setReadImage(ReadImage readImage) {
66          this.readImage = readImage;
67      }
68
69      public int getImgIdx() {
70          return imgIdx;
71      }
72
73      public void setImgIdx(int imgIdx) {
74          this.imgIdx = imgIdx;
75      }
76 }
```

The class SliderPanel.java is the "global" class for implementing the "core" of the program. The class initializes all of objects of the corresponding classes in its method initComponent(). When the method initReadImage() is invoked, the ReadImage.java class reads in all of images from the folder "images" inside the project and stores them in the arrayList sceneryList. When the method initShowBoard() is invoked, the boardW and boardH are calculated. And the object of the readImage is passed into the class ShowBoard.java to allow the board to access the sceneryList. And then, the method showBoard.initShowImg() is invoked to find the middle index of the sceneryList and immediately the method showBoard.findShowImg() gets the image in the middle position of the sceneryList as the current image. And then, the board is added onto the CENTER part of the sliderPanel. We select the image in the middle position as the first image because the images may be moved to the right direction or to the left direction. The middle image is a good starting position. Certainly, it is not a very important issue because any image could be selected as the first image to be shown.

Listing 6.7 The code of the class SliderPanel.java in the project ImageSlider2

```
 1 /*
 2  * SliderPanel.java - A class defines the canvas panel for the image slider.
 3  */
 4 package imageslider;
 5
 6 import java.awt.BorderLayout;
 7 import java.awt.Dimension;
 8 import java.awt.Graphics;
 9 import java.awt.Image;
10 import java.awt.event.ActionEvent;
11 import java.awt.event.ActionListener;
12 import java.awt.image.BufferedImage;
13 import javax.swing.ImageIcon;
14 import javax.swing.JButton;
15 import javax.swing.JPanel;
16
21 public class SliderPanel extends JPanel implements ActionListener {
22
23      private ReadImage readImage;
```

6.13 Adding Dynamic Behaviors: The Project ImageSlider2

```
24      private ShowBoard showBoard;
25      private JButton leftBtn;
26      private JButton rightBtn;
27
28      public SliderPanel() {
29          initComponent();
30      }
31
32      private void initComponent() {
33          setLayout(new BorderLayout());
34          initReadImage();
35          initShowBoard();
36          initButtons();
37      }
38
39      public void initReadImage() {
40          readImage = new ReadImage();
41      }
42
43      public void initShowBoard() {
44          showBoard = new ShowBoard();
45          showBoard.setReadImage(readImage); // showBoard accesses readImage
46          showBoard.initShowImg();
47          showBoard.findShowImg();
48          add(showBoard, BorderLayout.CENTER);
49      }
50
51      public void initButtons() {
52          leftBtn = new JButton();
53          leftBtn.setPreferredSize(new Dimension(
54                  Consts.BUTTON_W, (int) (Consts.BUTTON_W * 1.5)));
55          BufferedImage leftArrow = zoomImage(readImage.getLeftArrow());
56          leftBtn.setIcon(new ImageIcon(leftArrow));
57          leftBtn.setBorder(null);
58          add(leftBtn, BorderLayout.WEST);
59          leftBtn.addActionListener(this);
60
61          rightBtn = new JButton();
62          rightBtn.setPreferredSize(new Dimension(
63                  Consts.BUTTON_W, (int) (Consts.BUTTON_W * 1.5)));
64          BufferedImage rightArrow = zoomImage(readImage.getRightArrow());
65          rightBtn.setIcon(new ImageIcon(rightArrow));
66          rightBtn.setBorder(null);
67          add(rightBtn, BorderLayout.EAST);
68          rightBtn.addActionListener(this);
69      }
70
71      public BufferedImage zoomImage(Image arrow) {
72          BufferedImage bufferedArrow = (BufferedImage) arrow;
73          BufferedImage newArrow;
74
75          double ratio = (Consts.BUTTON_W * 1.0) / bufferedArrow.getWidth();
76          int newW = (int) (bufferedArrow.getWidth() * ratio);
77          int newH = (int) (bufferedArrow.getHeight() * ratio);
78          newArrow = new BufferedImage(newW, newH, BufferedImage.TYPE_INT_ARGB);
```

```
79          Graphics g = newArrow.createGraphics();
80          g.drawImage(arrow, 0, 0, newH, newH, null);
81          g.dispose();
82          return newArrow;
83      }
84
85      @Override
86      public void actionPerformed(ActionEvent evt) {
87          int listSize = readImage.getSceneryList().size();
88          if (evt.getSource() == rightBtn) {
89              int newIdx = showBoard.getImgIdx() - 1; // move idx to left
90              if (newIdx == -1) {
91                  newIdx = listSize - 1; // the last index of the list
92              }
93              showBoard.setImgIdx(newIdx % listSize);
94              showBoard.findShowImg();
95              showBoard.repaint();
96          } else if (evt.getSource() == leftBtn) {
97              showBoard.setImgIdx((showBoard.getImgIdx() + 1)
98                      % listSize); // move idx to right
99              showBoard.findShowImg();
100             showBoard.repaint();
101         }
102     }
103 }
```

After that, the class SliderPanel.java starts building the dynamic behaviors of the project by adding two buttons and implementing the corresponding action listener. The leftBtn loads the image icon leftArrow, and the rightBtn loads the image icon rightArrow. In order to fit the images with the size of the button, the method zoomImage() applies the same zoom scale for zooming two arrow images. The two buttons register with the event handler actionPerformed() and are placed onto the WEST and EAST parts of the BorderLayout manager, respectively.

The dynamic behaviors of the project rely on the event handler actionPerformed(). As discussed above, the current image is fetched from the sceneryList with an index. The event handler actionPerformed() just manipulates the index for realizing the dynamic behaviors. When the rightBtn is clicked, the index of the current image is changed to be the (current index − 1), and when the leftBtn is clicked, the index of the current image is switched to be the (current index + 1). Suppose that the sceneryList holds ten images. The first image to be shown has the index of 5. When the leftBtn is clicked, the index of the current image is changed to be (5 + 1). The computation (5 + 1) % 10 is still 6. That is, the showBoard will show the image of index 6 in the sceneryList. Immediately, the repaint() method is called to invoke the paint() method for painting the new image. When the current image has the index of 9 and the leftBtn is clicked again, (9 + 1) % 10 = 0, the current index is automatically changed to be 0, which circulates the index to the beginning of the sceneryList. However, the rightBtn will give a different condition. One click on the rightBtn causes (current index − 1). When the value reaches 0, one more click will make the current index becoming −1. Thus, under that case, we have to manually assign the last index of 9 to be the current index.

From the action of clicking a button to an event, to an event handler that updates the index of the image, and then to the image that is painted on the GUI, they form an action-event-update-repaint chain. This chain makes the GUI dynamically changing the scene. Actually, this chain is the foundation of the animation technique for video games.

This example illustrates that the button click may end up with some dynamic behaviors. Unfortunately, we can only see the image is switched, but we cannot see the "sliding" effect. However, we can imagine that if every button click only moves the current image with a small distance, a sequence of continuous button clicks would produce a "sliding" feeling due to the quick update-repaint effects. The exercises suggest some modifications that allow us to see a kind of "sliding" effect, which will prepare us to better understanding the animation technique later.

6.14 Interface and Event Listener

As mentioned, Interface is a special class that only declares methods that do not have body codes. Event listeners are such an Interface. Why do we need such kind of Interface?

In our real world, a device always provides some input panel or some input handset for users to control the device.

For example, a calculator has a digit keypad to allow users to input data for a computation. A TV unit supports a remote controller that also has a digit keypad for users to select TV channels. A telephone also provides a digit keypad for users to key in phone numbers. These digit keypads are the "interface" between the devices and their users. We might design and manufacture a digit keypad as a standard interface but adapt specific circuits behind the interface for specific devices such that different devices may share a standard interface but perform each specific function.

Similarly, a class defines a set of attributes and a set of methods. Usually the attributes are "private" such that nobody can directly access them. However, the set of public methods forms a "software interface" so that the external world could go through the "software interface" to touch the private properties and the abilities of the class. That is, a class also has an interface for allowing the user to access its specific data and behaviors.

When Java defines a set of built-in software components, such as a button and the like, nobody knows the button would be used in a calculator or in a TV remote controller. That implies that the function that the button should perform has to be deferred until someone uses the button for a particular kind of devices, such as a calculator or a remote controller. In other words, the implementation of the function that should be performed has to be postponed until we know the button is placed on a calculator or on a remote controller. For supporting such kind of flexibility, we can define the event associated with the button click but leave the event handlers undefined. These event handlers are wrapped inside a class such that the class only declares the event handlers as methods but without defining a particular method body for performing a particular function. The real implementation of the methods is deferred until coding a particular application. This kind of classes becomes a standard interface, and its real functionality can be tailored for satisfying the requirements of real applications. Consequently, they got a special name of "Interface."

The ActionListener that we have used in the project CalculatorApp is just one of this kind of Interfaces that declares a method actionPerformed() as follows.

```
public Interface ActionListener {
   public void actionPerformed(
      ActionEvent e);
}
```

The same ActionListener can provide different responses for either a button click or a <Enter> key press. The real function of the method actionPerformed() depends on the particular purpose of a particular button in a particular application. In short, an Interface defines common characteristics as a template that supports a rule-based programming such that programmers can implement event handlers through adding different sets of statements for performing different functions.

Definitely, Interface is not only defined for event listeners. Whenever we would like to declare common characteristics of some objects, we can define an Interface. The methods in an Interface are implicitly "public" because an "interface" is formed from a set of public methods. In Java a subclass can only have one superclass but can implement multiple Interfaces. Thus, Interfaces enhance the inheritance ability and increase the flexibility of Java programs.

In addition, this kind of methods that have no "body" obtained a special name as "abstract" method. As long as a method has a modifier of "abstract," the implementation of its function can be deferred until needed.

Hence, defining an Interface should follow certain "rules," which include (1) all attributes are public and static constants, (2) all methods are public and abstract methods, and (3) it has no constructor. Here, we ignore the discussions about the default methods and static methods that can be contained by Interfaces.

6.15 Abstract Method and Abstract Class

As mentioned above, an Interface contains a set of methods without implementation, such as the method of actionPerformed() in the Interface ActionListener cited above. This kind of methods is termed as "abstract method." The implementation of abstract methods can be deferred until needed.

The abstract methods are not only defined in Interfaces; they can be defined in any classes. When a class contains abstract method(s), the class is an "abstract class," and the class needs a modifier "abstract" in front of its name. An abstract class cannot be instantiated as an object. An abstract class differs from an Interface since it may contain methods with implementations. But, an Interface does not contain any methods with implementations.

Why do we need abstract classes? Abstract classes can define common characteristics for a group of closely related subclasses, which have common features but need different implementations. The abstract methods can be declared for "cheating" compiler during compile time and can be implemented later to perform functions during run time. Thus, it has a broad usage. We will heavily use abstract classes in video game projects later.

6.16 More Software Components: JRadioButton and JCheckBox

We only deal with software component JButton and JTextField so far. We will see more software components gradually. Here, we would like to introduce the new software component JCheckBox and its usage through a very simple project.

Both JCheckBox and JRadioButton are subclasses of the superclass JToggleButton. Both are used for selections. However, JRadioButton is usually used for making a single choice among multiple possible options, and JCheckBox is usually used for multiple selections. That is, if we do have a group of objects with the same type and we would like to select one of them at a time exclusively, we can adopt JRadioButton. Since the choice is exclusive, we need to place multiple radio buttons into a same group. The player can only select one of them at a time. Contrast with it, the user may need to have multiple choices inclusively, such as in conducting a survey, where one question may have multiple answers. Under that case, the suitable software components are JCheckBox. The following project TryCheckBox is an example for demonstrating the usage of JCheckBox.

Listing 6.8 The code of the project TryCheckBox

```
1 /*
2  * TryCheckBox.java - The main class of the project.
3  */
4 package trycheckbox;
5
6 import javax.swing.JFrame;
7
12 public class TryCheckBox extends JFrame {
13
14     public TryCheckBox() {
15         setTitle("A survey");
16         setDefaultCloseOperation(JFrame.EXIT_ON_CLOSE);
17         setSize(500, 400);
18
19         SurveyStu survey = new SurveyStu();
20         add(survey);
21
22         setVisible(true);
23     }
24
27     public static void main(String[] args) {
28         new TryCheckBox();
29     }
30 }
```

```
1 /*
2  * SurveyStu.java - A class defines a survey sheet.
3  */
4 package trycheckbox;
5
6 import java.awt.Dimension;
7 import java.awt.GridLayout;
8 import java.awt.Insets;
9 import javax.swing.ButtonGroup;
10 import javax.swing.JCheckBox;
11 import javax.swing.JLabel;
12 import javax.swing.JPanel;
13 import javax.swing.border.EmptyBorder;
14
19 public class SurveyStu extends JPanel {
20
21     private JPanel oneQu;
22     private JPanel qu1;
```

```
23        private JPanel qu2;
24        private JLabel questionLbl;
25        private ButtonGroup quGroup;
26        private JCheckBox CB1;
27        private JCheckBox CB2;
28        private JCheckBox CB3;
29        private JCheckBox CB4;
30
31        public SurveyStu() {
32            qu1 = initOneQu("1. Which language do you know (all applicable) ",
33                    "Java", "C++", "C", "C#");
34            add(qu1);
35
36            qu2 = initOneQu("2. Which course have you taken (all applicable) ",
37                    "Math", "Physics", "Biology", "Java programming");
38            add(qu2);
39        }
40
41        private JPanel initOneQu(String qu, String a1, String a2, String a3, String a4) {
42            oneQu = new JPanel();
43            oneQu.setPreferredSize(new Dimension(450, 120));
44            oneQu.setLayout(new GridLayout(5, 1));
45            EmptyBorder eb = new EmptyBorder(new Insets(5, 10, 5, 10));
46            oneQu.setBorder(eb);
47            questionLbl = new JLabel(qu);
48            CB1 = new JCheckBox(a1);
49            CB2 = new JCheckBox(a2);
50            CB3 = new JCheckBox(a3);
51            CB4 = new JCheckBox(a4);
52
53            oneQu.add(questionLbl);
54            oneQu.add(CB1);
55            oneQu.add(CB2);
56            oneQu.add(CB3);
57            oneQu.add(CB4);
58
59            return oneQu;
60        }
61    }
```

When we execute this project, we can select multiple choices among multiple possible options. The fundamental usage is shown in lines 48–51.

The usage of the JRadioButton will be demonstrated in the next chapter. Actually, the single selection and multiple selections are not a built-in property of the JRadioButton and JCheckBox, but they are a convention or a programming preference.

6.17 Summary

Event programming is one of important techniques for constructing a game. Java provides many different event listeners corresponding to different source components and user's input actions. Every event listener is an Interface that declares a set of methods without implementation. The event programming consists of four steps: (1) to design proper source components and to determine proper actions on the source components, (2) based on the source component and the action type to find out the corresponding event and select a proper event listener, (3) to implement the declared methods in the event listener as event handlers according to the required functions to be performed, and (4) to register the event listeners with the event source components. After finishing this action-event chain, once the expected event occurs on the event source component, the registered event handler is triggered to perform the suitable functions for the application.

There are different implementation approaches for implementing an event listener. Among them, two approaches are most popular. One is the inner class approach; the other is letting the "outer" class implement the event listener. The anonymous inner class approach has its advantages, but it cannot be shared by multiple components. The public class approach is rarely used.

The example project CalculatorApp in this chapter deals with the components statically arranged. The project ImageSlider further adds update-repaint chain for changing the scenes on the GUI, which prepares us to better understand the animation technique discussed later.

6.18 Exercises

Self-Reviewing Questions

1. What are software components? Make four examples of them.
2. Draw an inheritance hierarchy of software components defined in Java.
3. What are layout managers?
4. What major layout managers are defined in Java?
5. What are an event, an event listener, and an event handler? Make an example for explaining the answer.
6. Make an example to explain the steps for building up an action-event chain.
7. The project CalculatorApp contains many repeated codes. Abstracting a piece of codes associated with the button bSeven only in order to see the function and the code more clearly.
8. What is an inner class? Why do we like to use an inner class to implement an event handler?
9. What are other alternative approaches for implementing an event listener? What are the advantages and disadvantages of each alternative approach? Why do you say so?
10. What is an action-event-update-repaint chain? Does it differ from the action-event chain?
11. What is an Interface? Why do we need to define Interfaces? When are we going to use Interfaces?
12. Define an Interface RemoteController for mimicking a TV remote controller.
13. What is an "abstract method"?
14. What is an "abstract class"?

Projects

1. Write a program to arrange ten buttons as the following pattern by using layout managers.

2. Write a program to replace the inner class approach in the CalculatorApp project by using the anonymous event listener alternative approach.
3. Extend the project CalculatorApp to add a function of mod (%) operation.
4. Develop a project to mimic the interface of a scientific calculator.
5. Select three to five buttons defined in the scientific calculator to implement corresponding functions.
6. Develop a project to mimic the interface of a TV remote controller.
7. In order to get the "sliding" feeling, we may modify the project ImageSlider as follows. (1) To divide the width boardW of the showBoard into 4 (or more) sections. One click on the left button only moves the image to the left direction one section. That is, it needs four (or more) continuous clicks on the left button in order to completely move the current image out of the left edge. Apply the same design for the clicks of the right button. (2) To add a loop statement that will continuously move the image section-by-section instead of several clicks.
8. Extend the simple ImageSlider to pre-store multiple sets of images into multiple ArrayLists. For example, a sceneryList is for scenery images; a familyList is for family photos; another friendList is for friends; and the like. And then add a set of JRadioButtons or a JComboBox to allow the user to select one of sets of images for sliding at a time (Check the usage of the JRadioButton demonstrated in the next chapter, section 7.10, if necessary).

6.18 Exercises

9. Develop a project MakeQuiz for making a quiz sheet with multiple-choice questions. The questions are predesigned and pre-stored in multiple text files. (1) The project allows a teacher to indicate a number of questions he/she needs for making a quiz sheet and also allows him/her to select one of text files for reading in the specified number of questions. (2) And then, the project reads in the number of questions from the selected file randomly for making a quiz sheet and is displayed on a panel. Every question has multiple choices formed by a set of JCheckBox or JRadioButton (which one should be used depends on the number of answers allowed for each question). (3) The project accepts a student's answers and grades the score for the quiz. The main purpose of the project is to familiarize with the software component JCheckBox or JRadioButton and its event listener (Check the usage of the JRadioButton demonstrated in the next chapter, section 7.10, if necessary).

7 Event-Driven: Adding a GUI for the Game Anagram In-Text

The Java software components and the event driven technique support a GUI for games. The GUI is not only showing the output of a game but also plays an input role. This chapter illustrates these features of a GUI by developing a game Anagram from a pure in-text version to a GUI version. The input portion of the GUI equips the game with software components for allowing the player to input data and actions in order to trigger events for updating the state of the game. The output portion of the GUI provides a board for repainting the updated scenes dynamically. Switching a same game from a text version to a GUI version intuitively explores the features of the event-driven technique clearer and deeper.

The objectives of this chapter include:
1. Applying GUI and event-driven for games.
2. A game of Anagram in-text.
3. A game of Anagram with a GUI.
4. A UML sequence diagram illustrates dynamic activities.
5. An action-event-update-repaint chain realizes dynamic behaviors.
6. A new method paintComponent().
7. A new graphics context Graphics2D g2d.
8. The usage of JRadioButton and JComboBox.

Graphical painting opens a door for offering a visible graphical interface to display outputs of applications. The project PaintXmasCard developed in Chap. 5 illustrated this feature. And then, the event and event-handling technique opens another door to allow players to input data and actions for driving applications with dynamic behaviors as demonstrated in the projects CalculatorApp and ImageSlider on the previous chapter. As a combination, a GUI may consist of an input portion organized by software components and an output portion that displays dynamic scenes. The merge of the graphical drawing and event-driven technique allows us to develop a variety of games with dynamic activities. These games earn not only benefits from the input actions issued by players to manually drive the internal computations and game rules for changing game states but also benefits from the output portion to visualize the dynamic scenes. This kind of games is under event-driven but has not adopted animation technique yet.

In comparison with games in-text, this kind of event-driven games provides a GUI for making input and output, which is more beautiful and more dynamic. We are going to apply this new technique for equipping a new game Anagram in-text with a GUI. From this transition, the differences between a game in-text and a game based on event-driven would be better explored.

7.1 The Story of the Game Anagram

A game Anagram is a word-playing game. The game gets a given word, scrambles the order of characters in the given word, and displays it as a scrambled word. The player is trying to reorganize the scrambled characters of the scrambled word and guess what the original given word is.

Clearly, a simple text version game AnagramText is similar with the GuessInt discussed in Chap. 3 in many aspects. Definitely, the purpose of developing this new game Anagram is not to duplicate the old aspects but to bring the games in-text into a new stage. After the implementation of the pure text version, we further facilitate the game with a GUI and apply the event-driven technique for emphasizing the special features of the new technique and further awareness of the new look-and-feel brought by the new GUI.

7.2 A Text Version of the Game Anagram: The Project AnagramText

Based on the description above, a pseudo code of a game AnagramText can be drafted as follows.

1. Pre-store a set of words in to text files. Considering the huge number of words, we may create multiple text files for storing different sets of words for making every text

file shorter in order to speed up the reading process. For illustrating this idea, we created two text files. One is wordaj.txt for storing words with the initial letters of 'a' to 'j.' The other is wordkz.txt for storing words with the initial letters of 'k' to 'z.'

2. The game initializer selects one of the two text files and reads in a word from the selected text file as a givenWord, and then the givenWord is scrambled and is displayed as a scrambledWord on the console.
3. The game player enters a guessedWord that exactly consists of all of the characters provided by the scrambledWord.
4. The initializer receives the guessedWord and compares it with the givenWord. If the guess is correct, the player earns a score; else the player loses some points.
5. If the player selects "yes" to start a new "play," go to step 2; otherwise, the game is terminated.

The pseudo code provides a basis for designing a UML class diagram for the project AnagramText as shown in Fig. 7.1. Clearly, the class AnagramText.java is the main class of the project. It "uses" the class GameControl.java as a controller for running the game. A method playGame() in the class GameControl.java employs a "while" loop as a driver to repeatedly invoke the related methods defined in the two classes Initializer.java and Player.java.

7.3 A UML Sequence Diagram of the Project AnagramText

A UML class diagram only illustrates the classes and the relationships among the classes. A UML sequence diagram will further depict the dynamic communications among the objects of corresponding classes. In other words, such a sequence diagram depicts the global sequence of actions of an application. We have introduced a UML sequence diagram in the previous chapter, which depicts the dynamic behaviors of an action-event chain. For the project AnagramText, the dynamic behaviors among the objects can be expressed in a UML sequence diagram as shown in Fig. 7.2.

Figure 7.2 shows that the project AnagramText has five objects corresponding to five classes. The object of the class Anagram.java instantiates an object of the class GameControl.java that in turn instantiates an object of the class Initializer.java and an object of the class Player.java. After that, a method in the class GameControl.java implements the "core" of the program for driving the required actions until the game is terminated.

Based on the pseudo code, the UML class diagram, and the UML sequence diagram, the codes of the five classes including AnagramText.java, GameControl.java, Initializer.java, Player.java, and ReadFile.java of the project AnagramText are listed in Listing 7.1.

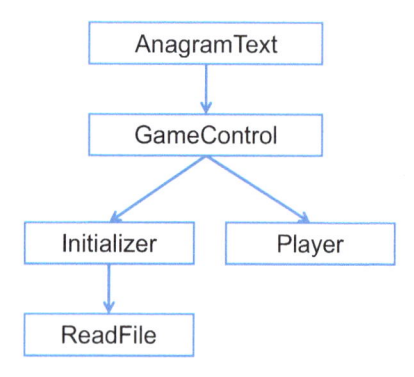

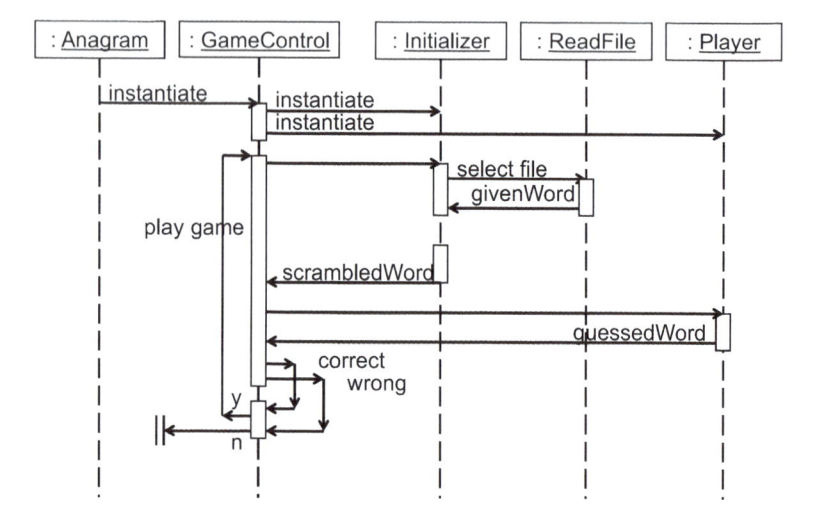

Fig. 7.1 The UML class diagram of the project AnagramText

Fig. 7.2 The UML sequence diagram of the game AnagramText

7.3 A UML Sequence Diagram of the Project AnagramText

Listing 7.1 The code of the game AnagramText without the class ReadFile.java

```
 1  /*
 2   * AnagramText.java - The main class of the game AnagramText
 3   */
 4  package anagramtext;
 5
10  public class AnagramText {
11
12      public AnagramText() {
13          GameControl gameControl = new GameControl();
14      }
15
19      public static void main(String[] args) {
20          new AnagramText();
21      }
22  }
```

```
 1  /*
 2   * GameControl.java - A class that implements the controls.
 3   */
 4  package anagramtext;
 5
 6  import javax.swing.JOptionPane;
 7
12  public class GameControl {
13
14      private Initializer initializer;
15      private Player player;
16      private String givenWord;
17      private char[] scrambledWord;
18      private char[] charAry;
19      private String guessedWord;
20
21      public GameControl() {
22          initComponent();
23      }
24
25      private void initComponent() {
26          initializer = new Initializer();
27          player = new Player();
28          playGame();
29      }
30
31      public void playGame() {
32          boolean guessMore = true;
33          while (guessMore) {
34              makeScrambledWord();
35              guessedWord = player.guessWord();
36              if (guessedWord.equals(givenWord)) {
37                  showMsg("Congratulation!!! Your guess is correct");
38              } else {
39                  showMsg("Sorry! Your guess is incorrect");
40              }
```

```
41              guessMore = moreGuess();
42          }
43      }
44
45      public void makeScrambledWord() {
46          givenWord = initializer.readGivenWord();
47          charAry = givenWord.toCharArray();
48          scrambledWord = initializer.scrembleWord(charAry);
49          initializer.printAry(scrambledWord);
50      }
51
52      public boolean moreGuess() {
53          boolean guessAgain = false;
54          Object[] selectionValues = {"Yes", "No"};
55          String initialSelection;
56          initialSelection = "Yes";
57          Object selection = JOptionPane.showInputDialog(null,
58                  "Would you like to play again?",
59                  "Select a file", JOptionPane.QUESTION_MESSAGE, null,
60                  selectionValues, initialSelection);
61
62          try {
63              if (selection.equals("Yes")) {
64                  guessAgain = true;
65              } else {
66                  System.out.println("The user terminates the program.");
67              }
68          } catch (NullPointerException nullex) {
69              System.out.println("You clicked Cancel.");
70              System.out.println("Program is aborted by the user.");
71              System.exit(0);
72          }
73          return guessAgain;
74      }
75
76      public void showMsg(String msgStr) {
77          System.out.println(msgStr);
78      }
79 }

 1 /*
 2  * Initializer.java - A class implements the game initializer.
 3  */
 4 package anagramtext;
 5
 6 import java.util.Random;
 7
12 public class Initializer {
13
14     private ReadFile readFile;
15
16     public Initializer() {
17     }
18
19     public String readGivenWord() {
```

7.3 A UML Sequence Diagram of the Project AnagramText

```
20            String givenWord;
21            readFile = new ReadFile();
22            readFile.selectFile();
23            givenWord = readFile.readContent();
24            return givenWord;
25        }
26
27        public char[] scrembleWord(char[] givenAry) {
28            int num = givenAry.length;
29            Random random = new Random();
30            random.nextInt();
31            for (int i = 0; i < num; i++) {
32                int destIdx = i + random.nextInt(num - i);
33                swap(givenAry, i, destIdx);
34            }
35            return givenAry;
36        }
37
38        private static void swap(char[] givenAry, int i, int destIdx) {
39            char theChar = givenAry[i];
40            givenAry[i] = givenAry[destIdx];
41            givenAry[destIdx] = theChar;
42        }
43
44        public void printAry(char[] ary) {
45            for (int i = 0; i < ary.length; i++) {
46                System.out.print(ary[i]);
47            }
48            System.out.println();
49        }
50 }
51
```

```
 1 /*
 2  * Player.java - A class implements a player.
 3  */
 4 package anagramtext;
 5
 6 import javax.swing.JOptionPane;
 7
12 public class Player {
13
14     public Player() {
15     }
16
17     public String guessWord() {
18         String guessedWord = "";
19         char inputChar;
20         boolean hasInput = false;
21
22         while (!hasInput) {
23             guessedWord = JOptionPane.showInputDialog(
24                     "Please enter a word for guessing");
25             try {
26                 inputChar = guessedWord.charAt(0);
```

```
27                hasInput = true;
28            } catch (StringIndexOutOfBoundsException siex) {
29                showMsg("You did not input any char. Input again.");
30            } catch (NullPointerException npex) {
31                showMsg("You clicked Cancel. The program is aborted.");
32                System.exit(0);
33            }
34        }
35        return guessedWord;
36    }
37
38    public void showMsg(String msg) {
39        System.out.println(msg);
40    }
41 }
```

```
 1 /*
 2  * ReadFile.java - A class for opening a file and read a line from it.
 3  */
 4 package anagramtext;
 5
 6 import java.io.BufferedReader;
 7 import java.io.FileNotFoundException;
 8 import java.io.FileReader;
 9 import java.io.IOException;
10 import java.net.URL;
11 import javax.swing.JOptionPane;
12
17 public class ReadFile {
18
19     FileReader inputFile;
20     String filePath;
21     String fileName;
22
23     public ReadFile() {
24     }
25
26     public void selectFile() {
27         Object[] selectionValues = {"wordaj.txt", "wordjz.txt"};
28         String initialSelection;
29         initialSelection = "wordaj.txt";
30         Object selection = JOptionPane.showInputDialog(null,
31                 "Select the file you would like to use",
32                 "Select a file", JOptionPane.QUESTION_MESSAGE, null,
33                 selectionValues, initialSelection);
34         filePath = "../txt/" + selection;
35
36         try {
37             URL url = getClass().getResource(filePath);
38             fileName = url.getPath();
39             //Create object of FileReader
40             inputFile = new FileReader(fileName);
41         } catch (NullPointerException nullex) {
42             System.out.println("You clicked Cancel.");
43             System.out.println("Program is aborted by the user.");
```

```
44              System.exit(0);
45          } catch (FileNotFoundException fex) {
46              System.out.println("The file is not found.");
47              System.exit(0);
48          }
49      }
50
51      public String readContent() {
52          BufferedReader bufferReader = new BufferedReader(inputFile);
53          String aWord = null;
54          int numLines = 10;
55          int lineNum;
56          int count;
57
58          lineNum = (int) (Math.random() * numLines);
59          try {
60              count = 0;
61              while ((aWord = bufferReader.readLine()) != null) {
62                  if (count == lineNum) { // reach the random line
63                      break;
64                  }
65                  count++;
66              }
67              bufferReader.close();
68          } catch (IOException ioex) {
69          }
70          return aWord;
71      }
72  }
```

The code approves that in general the project AnagramText is very similar with the game GuessInt; in particular the class ReadFile.java is almost the same as the same class adopted in the game WheelFortune4 in Chap. 4 but with a more complete exception checking.

Following the UML sequence diagram in Fig. 7.2, the object corresponding to the class GameControl.java initializes the objects of initializer and player, and then it starts its method playGame() to invoke the method makeScrambledWord(), which in turn calls the initializer.readGivenWord() method to select one of two text files and to read in a given word, and then immediately invokes the initializer.scrembleWord() method for scrambling the given word and printing the scrambled word on the console. When the player sees the scrambled word, he/she enters a guessedWord through the method player.guessWord().

Promptly, the gameControl checks the guessedWord against the givenWord, and the game shows the comparison result "correct" or "wrong." And then, it asks the player whether willing to have a new play or not. If the player answers "yes," a "while" loop brings the execution back to the beginning for selecting a file and reading in a new givenWord. In case the answer is "no," the game terminates.

A possible error case may occur when the user inputs the guessedWord in using the method JOptionPane.showInputDialog(). The user may click the OK button or hit the <Enter> key without inputting any character. Under these cases, the program asks the user to input a guessedWord again. If the user clicks the Cancel button, it can be understood as that the user refuses to input data for playing the game, the program is aborted. The method JOptionPane.showInputDialog() is also invoked when the user selects a text file or answers the question whether to play the game again; if the user also clicks the Cancel button, then the program is also aborted. Clearly, the GameControl.java class controls the sequence of "core" actions. The codes of the remaining classes are straightforward. They are left for readers as a reading exercise.

7.4 Adding a GUI to the Game Anagram: The Project AnagramGUI

Now, we are going to add a GUI into the game and apply the event-driven technique for developing the new version of AnagramGUI. The GUI of the new game is shown in Fig. 7.3,

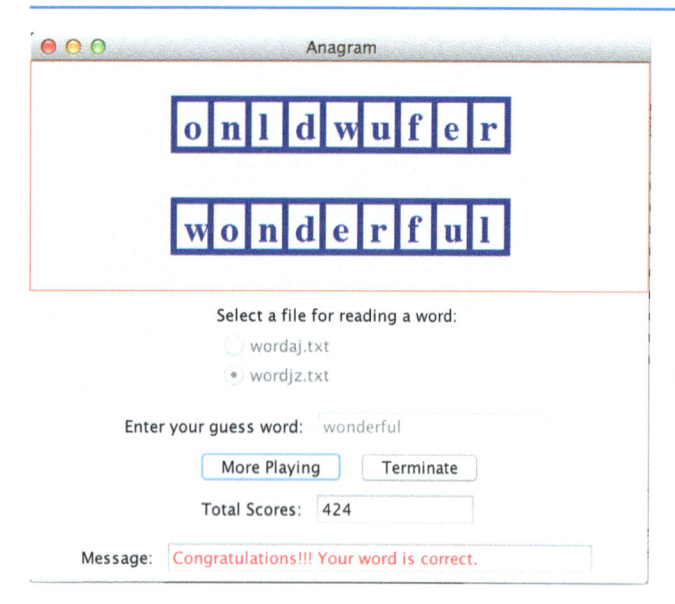

Fig. 7.3 A GUI of the project AnagramGUI

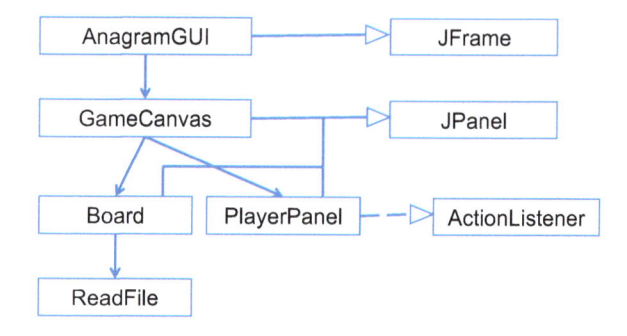

Fig. 7.4 The UML class diagram of the project AnagramGUI

which consists of two parts. A board on the top is for the output; a playerPanel on the bottom is for the player to input data and controls. Due to the fact that the game is text based, the board only paints text, and the playerPanel only contains a set of software components. Definitely, the GUI makes the game looks different in comparison with the version of AnagramText.

Because of the GUI, the UML class diagram of the project AnagramGUI is modified as in Fig. 7.4. The class diagram illustrates that the main class AnagramGUI.java "is-a" JFrame that "uses" the class GameCanvas.java, which "is-a" JPanel. This part has the same structure as in the project PaintXmasCard in Chap. 5, which is the common software structure of all applications that have a GUI. The class GameCanvas.java contains two smaller JPanels that wraps the classes Board.java and PlayerPanel.java, respectively. For simplifying the structure, the class Board.java merges the original Initializer.java class; and the class PlayerPanel.java merges the original class Player.java. That is why the original classes Initializer.java and Player.java are "disappeared" in the new project. And then, the class Board.java "uses" the class ReadFile.java to read in a givenWord.

7.5 The Class PlayerPanel.java Implements the Sequence of Actions

Surely, the project AnagramGUI is an event-driven program since the player controls the game through the software components arranged in the class PlayerPanel.java. As long as the player inputs actions on the software components, the action listeners registered with the corresponding source software components will execute the event handlers to drive the game step-by-step. Consequently, the class PlayerPanel.java becomes the "global" class that performs the global sequence of actions. The UML sequence diagram of the project AnagramGUI is as Fig. 7.5 shows. The code of the class PlayerPanel.java is cited in Listing 7.2.

Listing 7.2 The code of the class PlayerPanel.java in the project AnagramGUI

```
1  /*
2   * PlayerPanel.java - A class defines the player's panel for the player to
3   * input data and controls.
4   */
5  package anagramgui;
6
7  import java.awt.BorderLayout;
8  import java.awt.Color;
9  import java.awt.Dimension;
10 import java.awt.GridLayout;
11 import java.awt.Insets;
12 import java.awt.event.ActionEvent;
13 import java.awt.event.ActionListener;
14 import javax.swing.ButtonGroup;
```

7.5 The Class PlayerPanel.java Implements the Sequence of Actions

Fig. 7.5 The UML sequence diagram of the project AnagramGUI

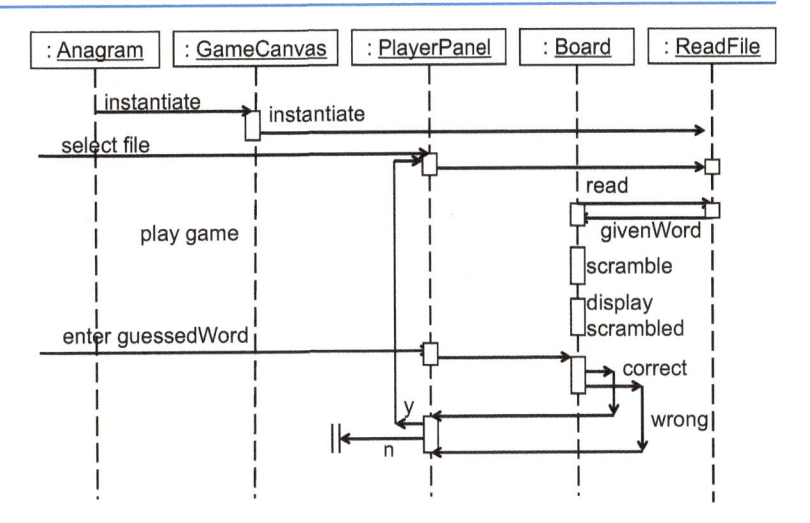

```
15 import javax.swing.JButton;
16 import javax.swing.JLabel;
17 import javax.swing.JPanel;
18 import javax.swing.JRadioButton;
19 import javax.swing.JTextField;
20 import javax.swing.border.EmptyBorder;
21
26 public class PlayerPanel extends JPanel {
27
28      private ButtonGroup fileGroup;
29      private JLabel fileLbl;
30      private JRadioButton fileajRBtn;
31      private JRadioButton filekzRBtn;
32
33      private JLabel guessedWordLbl;
34      private JTextField guessedWordTxt;
35      private JButton morePlayBtn;
36      private JButton terminateBtn;
37
38      private JLabel msgLbl;
39      private JTextField msgTxt;
40
41      private JLabel scoreLbl;
42      private JTextField scoreTxt;
43
44      private JPanel selFileP;
45      private JPanel playP;
46      private JPanel playerP;
47      private JPanel scoreP;
48      private JPanel msgP;
49
50      private ReadFile readFile;
51      private Board board;
52
53      public PlayerPanel() {
54          this.setPreferredSize(new Dimension(
55                  Consts.CV_WIDTH, Consts.PLAYER_PANEL_H));
56          this.setLayout(new BorderLayout());
57          initPlayerPanel();
```

```java
58      }
59
60      private void initPlayerPanel() {
61          ActionListener myActionListener = new MyActionListener();
62
63          // Select a file for reading a given word
64          selFileP = new JPanel();
65          selFileP.setLayout(new GridLayout(3, 1));
66          EmptyBorder eb = new EmptyBorder(new Insets(30, 150, 5, 30));
67          selFileP.setBorder(eb);
68          fileLbl = new JLabel("Select a file for reading a word: ");
69          fileGroup = new ButtonGroup();
70          fileajRBtn = new JRadioButton("wordaj.txt");
71          fileajRBtn.setActionCommand("wordaj.txt");
72          fileajRBtn.addActionListener(myActionListener);
73          filekzRBtn = new JRadioButton("wordkz.txt");
74          filekzRBtn.setActionCommand("wordkz.txt");
75          filekzRBtn.addActionListener(myActionListener);
76          fileGroup.add(fileajRBtn);
77          fileGroup.add(filekzRBtn);
78          selFileP.add(fileLbl);
79          selFileP.add(fileajRBtn);
80          selFileP.add(filekzRBtn);
81
82          // Player plays the game and gets a score
83          playerP = new JPanel();
84          EmptyBorder eb2 = new EmptyBorder(new Insets(5, 30, 5, 30));
85          playerP.setBorder(eb2);
86          guessedWordLbl = new JLabel("Enter your guess word: ");
87          guessedWordTxt = new JTextField(15);
88          guessedWordTxt.addActionListener(myActionListener);
89          morePlayBtn = new JButton("More Playing");
90          morePlayBtn.addActionListener(myActionListener);
91          terminateBtn = new JButton("Terminate");
92          terminateBtn.addActionListener(myActionListener);
93          playerP.add(guessedWordLbl);
94          playerP.add(guessedWordTxt);
95          playerP.add(morePlayBtn);
96          playerP.add(terminateBtn);
97
98          scoreP = new JPanel();
99          scoreLbl = new JLabel("Total Scores: ");
100         scoreTxt = new JTextField(10);
101         scoreP.add(scoreLbl);
102         scoreP.add(scoreTxt);
103
104         playP = new JPanel();
105         playP.setLayout(new BorderLayout());
106         playP.add(playerP, BorderLayout.CENTER);
107         playP.add(scoreP, BorderLayout.SOUTH);
108
109         // A message panel
110         msgP = new JPanel();
111         msgLbl = new JLabel("Message: ");
112         msgTxt = new JTextField(28);
113         msgTxt.setForeground(Color.red);
```

7.5 The Class PlayerPanel.java Implements the Sequence of Actions

```
114            msgP.add(msgLbl);
115            msgP.add(msgTxt);
116
117            this.add(selFileP, BorderLayout.NORTH);
118            this.add(playP, BorderLayout.CENTER);
119            this.add(msgP, BorderLayout.SOUTH);
120
121            setMsg("Please select a file for reading a given word.");
122        }
123
124        class MyActionListener implements ActionListener {
125
126            @Override
127            public void actionPerformed(ActionEvent evt) {
128                if ((evt.getSource() == fileajRBtn)
129                        || (evt.getSource() == filekzRBtn)) {
130                    readFile.selectFile(evt.getActionCommand());
131                    board.initGivenWord();
132                    filekzRBtn.setEnabled(false);
133                    fileajRBtn.setEnabled(false);
134                    guessedWordTxt.setEnabled(true);
135                    guessedWordTxt.setText("");
136                    guessedWordTxt.requestFocus();
137                    setMsg("Please enter your word.");
138                } else if (evt.getSource() == guessedWordTxt) {
139                    board.receiveGuess(guessedWordTxt.getText());
140                    guessedWordTxt.setEnabled(false);
141                } else if (evt.getSource() == morePlayBtn) {
142                    // reset the board displaying
143                    fileajRBtn.setEnabled(true);
144                    filekzRBtn.setEnabled(true);
145                    board.setInitPaint(true);
146                    board.repaint();
147                    setMsg("Please select a file for reading a given word.");
148                } else if (evt.getSource() == terminateBtn) {
149                    System.exit(0);
150                }
151            }
152        }
153
154        public void setReadFile(ReadFile readFile) {
155            this.readFile = readFile;
156        }
157
158        public void setBoard(Board board) {
159            this.board = board;
160        }
161
162        public void setMsg(String msg) {
163            msgTxt.setText(msg);
164        }
165
166        public void setScoreTxt(String score) {
167            this.scoreTxt.setText(score);
168        }
169 }
```

The class PlayerPanel.java employs the following software components to form a control panel for the player to input data and actions.

1. A ButtonGroup groups two JRadioButtons for allowing the player to select one of two text files for reading a givenWord. The two files are wordaj.txt and wordkz.txt, which are copied from the project AnagramText. Here, we switched the selection action from the initializer to the player because the selection requires an external action.
2. A JTextField for the player to type in his/her guessedWord.
3. Two JButtons have the labels of "More Playing" and "Terminate," respectively. The former supports the player to play next anagram; the latter is for terminating the game.
4. A JLabel with a label "Total Score" and a JTextField displays the current total score.
5. A JTextField for showing playing instructions or game statuses.

The method initPlayerPanel() in the class PlayerPanel.java arranges all of these required software components. Fortunately, all of these software components associate with the same ActionEvent so that we only need to have one inner class MyActionListener to implement the ActionListener with one event handler actionPerformed() for supporting all of actions on these software components. The object evt of the ActionEvent provides the evt.getSource() method to identify the action source component for performing corresponding functions.

Let us take the text file selection as an example and we duplicate the program of the event handler actionPerformed() in the inner class MyActionListener for this action as follows.

```
129    if ((evt.getSource() == fileajRBtn)
130         || (evt.getSource() == filekzRBtn)) {
131        readFile.selectFile(
              evt.getActionCommand());
132        board.initGivenWord();
133        filekzRBtn.setEnabled(false);
134        fileajRBtn.setEnabled(false);
135        guessedWordTxt.setEnabled(true);
136        guessedWordTxt.setText("");
137        guessedWordTxt.requestFocus();
138        setMsg("Please enter your word.");
139    } else if …
```

The piece of code carries out the following functions. (1) The if statement makes sure the action is a click on the JRadioButton fileajRBtn or on the JRadioButton filekzRBtn. (2) The method evt.getActionCommand() gets the action command associates with the clicked JRadioButton. The action command is the corresponding file name that was the actual parameter passed into the method setActionCommand() of the JRadioButton. The returned file name is passed into the readFile.selectFile() method as the actual parameter such that the file will be opened for reading. (3) The method board.initGivenWord() then reads a word from the text file. (4) The methods setEnabled() are called to enable or disable corresponding software components in order to enforce the player playing a correct sequence of actions.

The point (4) above is important. As we know the global sequence of actions has its sequential nature. We should follow the sequential order to implement the application. However, when the player inputs data or controls, the player could click any software component in any arbitrary order. How can we enforce the player to follow the correct sequential order? In the previous chapter, when we develop the project CalculatorApp, we discussed this question. Because all of software components on the GUI of the CalculatorApp should be always opened for the user to click, we employed Boolean variables to guide the user's clicks to follow the required order. In this AnagramGUI project, when one software component is setEnabled(false), the component is disabled not only its functionality but also its visibility. Hence, the fileajRBtn.setEnabled(false) will disable the function of the JRadioButton fileajRBtn so that the button will be blurred out and a click on the button won't cause any reaction. We can follow the required sequence of actions to make sure only one software component is able to accept the player's action at a time such that the player won't have any possibility to make any incorrect inputting order.

As mentioned above, the GUI has a playerPanel for the player to issue input and a board for displaying the output of the game. Actually it is not completely true because the scores and the messages are part of outputs; however, they are also shown on the text fields on the playerPanel. When the player clicks the button "More Playing," the file selection is triggered and enabled, which is also a part of output, but it also appears on the playerPanel. In other words, some software components, for example, a text field, could be counted as one of input components; but sometimes it can also be used for showing outputs. Therefore, thoroughly familiarizing ourselves with the functionality of every kind of software components is important.

7.6 The Class Board.java Displays the Scrambled Word and the Guessed Word

Before the game starts, the board needs to paint two empty blocks of rectangles. At this moment, a given word is not available yet. The two empty blocks are painted with a predefined eight empty characters temporarily.

When the player is ready to play, firstly he/she selects one of two text files by clicking one of two JRadioButtons.

7.6 The Class Board.java Displays the Scrambled Word and the Guessed Word

Due to the existence of software components for inputs, we are no longer to use the JOptionPane. After selecting one of the text files, the board reads in a givenWord from the file, and the board immediately adjusts the lengths of the two empty blocks and paints the scrambledWord on the top block. After the player types in his/her guessedWord and presses the <Enter> key, the event handler of the JTextField invokes the method defined in the class Board.java to paint the guessedWord on the bottom block. The detailed code of the class Board.java is cited in Listing 7.3.

Listing 7.3 The code of the class Board.java in the project AnagramGUI

```
1  /*
2   * Board.java - A class defines a board for displaying.
3   */
4  package anagramgui;
5
6  import java.awt.BasicStroke;
7  import java.awt.Color;
8  import java.awt.Dimension;
9  import java.awt.Font;
10 import java.awt.Graphics;
11 import java.awt.Graphics2D;
12 import java.awt.Stroke;
13 import java.util.Random;
14 import javax.swing.JPanel;
15
20 public class Board extends JPanel {
21
22     private ReadFile readFile;
23     private PlayerPanel playerPanel; // for communication
24
25     private String givenWord;
26     private int wordLen;
27     private char[] scrambledWord;
28     private String guessedWord;
29     private char[] guessedWordAry;
30     private boolean hasGuessed = false;
31     private int totalScore = 0;
32     private boolean initPaint = true;
33
34     private char[] currAry;
35     private int cx; // center point (x) of board
36     private int bx, by; // starting point (x, y) for painting
37     private int sx, sy; // starting point (x, y) of each character
38
39     public Board() {
40         this.setPreferredSize(new Dimension(Consts.CV_WIDTH, Consts.BOARD_H));
41         wordLen = 8; // assume the wordLen = 8 initially
42         repaint();
43     }
44
```

```java
45      public void initGivenWord() {
46          hasGuessed = false;
47          givenWord = readFile.readContent();
48          //System.out.println(givenWord);
49          givenWord = givenWord.toLowerCase();
50          currAry = givenWord.toCharArray();
51          scrambledWord = scrambleWord(currAry);
52          wordLen = givenWord.length();
53          repaint();
54      }
55
56      public char[] scrambleWord(char[] givenAry) {
57          int num = givenAry.length;
58          Random random = new Random();
59          random.nextInt();
60          for (int i = 0; i < num; i++) {
61              int destIdx = i + random.nextInt(num - i);
62              swap(givenAry, i, destIdx);
63          }
64          return givenAry;
65      }
66
67      private static void swap(char[] givenAry, int i, int destIdx) {
68          char theChar = givenAry[i];
69          givenAry[i] = givenAry[destIdx];
70          givenAry[destIdx] = theChar;
71      }
72
73      public void receiveGuess(String aGuessedWord) {
74          try {
75              this.guessedWord = aGuessedWord;
76              guessedWord = guessedWord.toLowerCase();
77              guessedWordAry = guessedWord.toCharArray();
78              hasGuessed = true;
79              if (guessedWord.equals(givenWord)) {
80                  playerPanel.setMsg("Congratulations!!! Your word is correct.");
81                  totalScore += Consts.SCORE + wordLen * 2;
82                  playerPanel.setScoreTxt("" + totalScore);
83              } else {
84                  playerPanel.setMsg("Sorry! Your word is incorrect.");
85                  totalScore -= Consts.SCORE;
86                  playerPanel.setScoreTxt("" + totalScore);
87              }
88              repaint();
89          } catch (StringIndexOutOfBoundsException siex) {
90              playerPanel.setMsg("You did not enter a word.");
91              totalScore -= Consts.SCORE;
92              playerPanel.setScoreTxt("" + totalScore);
93          } catch (NullPointerException nullex) {
94              playerPanel.setMsg("You click the Cancel that aborts the game.");
95              System.exit(0);
96          }
97      }
98
```

7.6 The Class Board.java Displays the Scrambled Word and the Guessed Word

```
 99     @Override
100     public void paintComponent(Graphics g) {
101         super.paintComponent(g);
102         Graphics2D g2d = (Graphics2D) g;
103
104         bx = (int) (Consts.CV_WIDTH / 2)
105                 - (int) ((wordLen * 1.0 / 2) * Consts.CHAR_BLOCK_W);
106         // showing the board area
107         g2d.setColor(Color.RED);
108         g2d.drawRect(0, 0, Consts.CV_WIDTH, Consts.BOARD_H);
109
110         Stroke solid = new BasicStroke(5.0f);
111         g2d.setStroke(solid);
112
113         g2d.setColor(Color.BLUE);
114         g2d.setFont(new Font("Times", Font.BOLD, 30));
115
116         if (initPaint) {
117             paintEmpty(g2d);
118             initPaint = false;
119         } else {
120             paintScrambledWord(g2d);
121             if (hasGuessed) {
122                 paintGuessedWord(g2d);
123             }
124         }
125     }
126
127     public void paintEmpty(Graphics2D g2d) {
128         // paint an empty board for the scrambled word
129         by = Consts.BLOCK_Y;
130         for (int i = 0; i < wordLen; i++) {
131             g2d.drawRect(bx + i * Consts.CHAR_BLOCK_W, by, Consts.CHAR_BLOCK_W,
132                     Consts.CHAR_BLOCK_H);
133         }
134         // paint an empty board for the guessedWord
135         by = Consts.BLOCK_Y + 2 * Consts.CHAR_BLOCK_H;
136         for (int i = 0; i < wordLen; i++) {
137             g2d.drawRect(bx + i * Consts.CHAR_BLOCK_W, by, Consts.CHAR_BLOCK_W,
138                     Consts.CHAR_BLOCK_H);
139         }
140     }
141
142     public void paintScrambledWord(Graphics2D g2d) {
143         paintEmpty(g2d); // two empty blocks must always be there
144
145         // paint the scrambled word
146         sx = bx + 8;
147         sy = Consts.BLOCK_Y;
148         for (int k = 0; k < wordLen; k++) {
149             if (scrambledWord[k] != ' ') {
150                 g2d.drawString(Character.toString(scrambledWord[k]),
151                         sx + k * Consts.CHAR_BLOCK_W,
152                         sy + (int) (Consts.CHAR_BLOCK_H * 0.8));
153             }
154         }
155     }
156
```

```
157    public void paintGuessedWord(Graphics2D g2d) {
158        sx = bx + 8;
159        sy = Consts.BLOCK_Y + 2 * Consts.CHAR_BLOCK_H;
160        try {
161            for (int k = 0; k < wordLen; k++) {
162                if (guessedWordAry[k] != ' ') {
163                    g2d.drawString(Character.toString(guessedWordAry[k]),
164                            sx + k * Consts.CHAR_BLOCK_W,
165                            sy + (int) (Consts.CHAR_BLOCK_H * 0.8));
166                }
167            }
168        } catch (ArrayIndexOutOfBoundsException ex) {
169            // this try block prevents the case if the length of
170            // the guessedWord is shorter than the wordLen that
171            // comes from the scrambledWord
172        }
173    }
174
175    public void setReadFile(ReadFile readFile) {
176        this.readFile = readFile;
177    }
178
179    public void setPlayerPanel(PlayerPanel playerPanel) {
180        this.playerPanel = playerPanel;
181    }
182
183    public void setInitPaint(boolean initPaint) {
184        this.initPaint = initPaint;
185    }
186 }
```

Apparently, the major functions of the class Board.java include (1) to draw two empty blocks of rectangles on the board, (2) to read in a givenWord through the object readFile, (3) to scramble the givenWord as a scrambledWord, (4) to display the scrambledWord on the top block, (5) to display the guessedWord on the bottom block after receiving the player inputted guessedWord from the object playerPanel, and (6) to compare the two words givenWord with guessedWord and send the comparing result correct or incorrect to the class PlayerPanel.java and at the same time calculate the score for the player.

The first function is implemented in the method paintEmpty(), which consists of two parts. The first part uses a "for" loop to draw a block with same number of empty rectangles as the "wordLen" on the top of the board for displaying the scrambledWord later. The second part employs the same "for" loop to draw another block with the same number of empty rectangles on the bottom of the board for displaying the guessedWord later. Here, each empty rectangle in the block is used to fill in one character.

The second and third functions are implemented in the method initGivenWord(), which invokes the method readFile.readContent() for reading a word from the selected file. The word is a String. In order to scramble the characters of the word, the method converts the String to an array of char, char[] currAry, and stores all of characters in the lower case. And then, the method immediately passes the char[] currAry into the function scrambleWord(char[] givenAry) as the actual parameter. The method accepts the char array and hires a "for" loop to pick up every char in the array one by one and swap it with another char selected randomly. After the "for" loop, every char in the givenWord is placed at a randomly selected position several times such that the word is scrambled.

The fourth function is implemented in the method paintScrambledWord(). Be careful, the method itself only paints all of characters of the scrambledWord. But, the four lines of each rectangle around each character should be repainted again. Therefore, the method paintEmpty() has to be invoked again for making the set of rectangles.

The fifth function is implemented in the method paintGuessedWord(), which simply paints the guessedWord in the empty rectangles of the bottom block. However it should prevent a possible abnormal case that the length of the guessedWord may be shorter than the length of the given scrambledWord caused by the player, who could give up his/her guess without inputting any character or stop inputting enough number of characters when he/she has no idea about the correct guessing. We apply a try-catch block to allow the program continuing its execution when the case would occur.

The sixth function is implemented in the method receiveGuess(), which accepts the player inputted guessedWord and compares it with the givenWord. If they are equal, the method sends a message to the playerPanel for "Congratulations" and increases the total score; otherwise, the method sends a message "Sorry" to the playerPanel and decreases the total score. Here, the score counting rule is simple. For a correct guess, the total is increased with Consts.SCORE + wordLen * 2 in considering the difficulty level is proportional to the length of the word. For a failure of a guess, the total score is decreased Consts.SCORE points. The value of Consts.SCORE is 10. This rule for the calculation of the score is defined arbitrary.

An interesting point here is the control of the painting process. The paintComponent() method in the game AnagramGUI invokes all of methods for painting, which includes the methods paintEmpty(), paintScrambledWord(), and paintGuessedWord(). However, the time sequence for invoking these three methods should be perfectly controlled. (1) Before reading in the givenWord, the paintEmpty() should be invoked to paint the two empty blocks. (2) After the word is scrambled, the paintScrambledWord() should be invoked for painting the scrambled word only. (3) After receiving the guessedWord, the method paintGuessedWord() paints the guessedWord and still keeps the scrambledWord on the board. For the three different paintings, the repaint() method should be called three times. One call is in the constructor Board() of the class Board.java; the other is in the method initGivenWord(); and the third call is in the method receiveGuess(). The three calls for the repaint() method happen at three different time periods but invoke the same method paintComponent(). In order to distinguish the three different paintings, we defined two Boolean variables initPaint and hasGuessed. The "if (initPaint)" allows the function (1) to be performed. The "else" allows the function (2) to be executed. The "if (hasGuessed)" allows the function (3) to be completed.

The paintComponent() method has two details that are worth to be noticed. (1) The painting of the rectangles and words is supported by some computations. The idea is that we would like to place the entire block of rectangles on the center of the board along the x-axis. Thus, the coordinate x of the starting point of the top block bx is equal to the center x of the board minus the half-width of the word. The block consists of small rectangles. Each rectangle is for showing one character. For that, we convert a word from a String to an array of char. For adjusting the position of each char in one rectangle, the variables sx and sy are set. (2) In order to define the pen width for painting the rectangles and characters, a built-in class BasicStroke is involved. The parameters of its constructor BasicStroke() include line-width, end-cap, line-join, and more. Here, we only pass in the line-width for defining the width of the stroke.

7.7 The Class GameCanvas.java Sets Up Communication Paths Among Classes

The major function of the class GameCanvas.java is to instantiate all of objects of classes and set up communication paths for them. The code of the GameCanvas.java class is cited in Listing 7.4.

Listing 7.4 The code of the class GameCanvas.java in the project AnagramGUI

```
1  /*
2   * GameCanvas.java - A class that sets up communication paths between related
3   * classes.
4   */
5  package anagramgui;
6
7  import java.awt.BorderLayout;
8  import java.awt.Dimension;
9  import javax.swing.JPanel;
10
15 public class GameCanvas extends JPanel {
16
```

```java
17      private ReadFile readFile;
18      private Board board;
19      private PlayerPanel playerPanel;
20
21      public GameCanvas() {
22          setPreferredSize(new Dimension(Consts.CV_WIDTH,
23                  Consts.BOARD_H + Consts.PLAYER_PANEL_H));
24          this.setLayout(new BorderLayout());
25
26          initComponent();
27      }
28
29      private void initComponent() {
30          initReadFile();
31          initBoard();
32          initPlayerPanel();
33      }
34
35      public void initReadFile() {
36          readFile = new ReadFile();
37      }
38
39      public void initBoard() {
40          board = new Board();
41          board.setReadFile(readFile);
42          add(board, BorderLayout.NORTH);
43      }
44
45      public void initPlayerPanel() {
46          playerPanel = new PlayerPanel();
47          add(playerPanel, BorderLayout.SOUTH);
48          playerPanel.setReadFile(readFile);
49          playerPanel.setBoard(board);
50          board.setPlayerPanel(playerPanel);
51      }
52  }
```

The communications among objects very often form a network. Therefore, the paths of communications should be set up carefully. For instance, we need to consider the following communication paths for the project AnagramGUI. (1) The playerPanel should be able to get in touch with the readFile for selecting one of two files. (2) The board needs to invoke the methods defined in the readFile for getting a givenWord. (3) The playerPanel should also be able to send the guessedWord to the board for displaying. (4) The board also needs to invoke the methods defined in the playerPanel to feedback the comparison result between the two words givenWord and guessedWord.

Because the class GameCanvas.java instantiates all of objects, it is the good place for setting up the communication paths among the objects. After it instantiates the object of readFile in the method initReadFile() and instantiates the object board in the method initBoard(), it immediately invokes the method board.setReadFile(readFile) to accept the readFile into the object board in order to realize the path (2) listed in the previous paragraph for allowing the board to read in a word from the readFile. And further, after the method initPlayerPanel() instantiates the object playerPanel, it invokes the method playerPanel.setReadFile(readFile) to pass the object readFile into the object playerPanel for setting up the path (1) listed above. Meanwhile, it also invokes the method playerPanel.setBoard(board) for passing the object board into the object playerPanel for making the communication path (3) mentioned above. Finally, it invokes the method board.setPlayerPanel(playerPanel) for passing the object playerPanel into the object board in order to form the path (4) above. Due to the fact that the "core" of the program is moved to the class PlayerPanel.java, the class GameCanvas.java is just for performing these setting functions.

7.8 Graphics and Graphics2D; paint() and paintComponent()

The pseudo code and the detailed implementation of the project AnagramGUI bring in a new method paintComponent() instead of using the method paint() for painting the board. In addition, the method paintComponent() uses a new graphics context Graphics2D g2d instead of Graphics g.

The Graphics2D class is the subclass of the class Graphics. The subclass Graphics2D extends the functionality of the superclass Graphics and provides more sophisticated control over geometry, coordinate transformations, color management, and text layout. The built-in class BasicStroke is an example here. The two blue blocks of rectangles shown in the board have a "thick" line width. It is made by the following code.

```
Stroke solid = new BasicStroke(5.0f);
g2d.setStroke(solid);
```

The first statement "Stroke solid = new BasicStroke(5.0f);" instantiates an object solid through the constructor BasicStroke(), which is an overloaded method and can accept different number of parameters. Here, we only pass in an actual parameter "5.0f" for specifying the line width. Then, the second statement "g2d.setStroke(solid);" makes the drawing line has a width of 5 pixels. The object g of the class Graphics doesn't have this ability; but the object g2d does. Consequently, we would like to upgrade g to g2d.

The method paint() is defined in the java.awt.Component class. The paintComponent() is defined in the class javax.swing.JComponent. We have learned that the javax.swing package provides lightweight components that are rendered by the Java language itself and is good for sophisticated drawings. Especially, the method paintComponent() adopts the so-called double-buffering technique such that it can eliminate the flicker problem, which is important for video games. We will explain the double-buffering technique in detail when we will learn the animation technique later. For these considerations, we apply the method paintComponent() to replace the method paint() since then.

This game uses paintComponent() method with the built-in graphics context Graphics2D for taking the advantages of both. However, the usage of Graphics2D should follow certain pattern as shown below.

```
public void paintComponent(Graphics g) {
    // override the definition in the superclass
    super.paintComponent(g);
    // cast the Graphics g to be g2d
    Graphics2D g2d = (Graphics2D) g;
    // using g2d to invoke methods
    g2d.setColor(Color.RED);
    …
}
```

7.9 Dynamic Activities of the Game AnagramGUI

Clearly, the dynamic activities of the game AnagramGUI are based on player's actions through the set of software components. We have explored an action-event-update-repaint chain from the project ImageSlider in the previous chapter. The dynamic behaviors of the project AnagramGUI is also made with the same chain. This chain starts from a particular action on a particular source component for generating a particular event, and the event is transferred to a particular event handler inside its event listener that is preregistered with the particular source component. The execution of the particular event handler causes a preset update of the scenes of the game, and then a repaint() method is invoked to call the paintComponent() method for repainting the updated output on the GUI that changes the scene on the GUI dynamically. Such a chain is implemented in the class Board.java as described in the previous section. We repeat mention this chain here would like to emphasize the importance of the chain for making games in using the event-driven technique and for better understanding the principle of animation technique later.

The dynamic behaviors of the game in two different versions of project AnagramText and AnagramGUI are the same. But, the project AnagramText has a "while" loop defined in the class GameControl.java for driving the game; and the project AnagramGUI provides the class PlayerPanel.java with software components for the player to manually drive the game. The former is a continuous driven based on a continuous loop, and the latter is a discrete driven based on a sequence of discrete actions.

7.10 Replacing the JRadioButton with a JComboBox

In the previous chapter, we introduced the usage of the software component JCheckBox that is usually used in the cases where users select multiple choices among multiple possible options.

The project AnagramGUI introduced the usage of the software component JRadioButton when the player would like to select one of two text files for reading as shown in Fig. 7.3. The fundamental usage of the JRadioButton is as follows.

```
fileajRBtn = new JRadioButton("wordaj.txt");
filekzRBtn = new JRadioButton("wordkz.txt");

fileGroup = new ButtonGroup();
fileGroup.add(fileajRBtn);
fileGroup.add(filekzRBtn);
```

```
        selFileP = new JPanel();
        selFileP.setLayout(new GridLayout(3, 1));
        selFileP.add(new JLabel("Select a file for reading a word: "));
        selFileP.add(fileajRBtn);
        selFileP.add(filekzRBtn);
```

The codes above can be divided into three steps. The first step is to instantiate every required JRadioButton. Then, important is the second step, which makes a "fileGroup = new ButtonGroup();" and add every individual JRadioButton into the group. This is the key step to determine only one of JRadioButtons can be selected exclusively. The third step is to set up all of JRadioButtons onto a JPanel for displaying. The more detailed real codes are implemented in the method initPlayerPanel() of the class PlayerPanel.java (lines 63–80 in Listing 7.2).

Fortunately, we have only two text files such that we only need to arrange two JRadioButtons on the GUI. Imagine that if a selection should be done from 10 files, we have to set up 10 JRadioButtons, which would occupy a big dimension of physical size for arranging the 10 JRadioButtons. Even worse, if a choice should be done among an uncertain number of text files, then the size of the JPanel for holding the JRadioButtons has to be allocated uncertainly.

A JComboBox comes handy for handling these cases since a JComboBox only requires one fixed physical size, but it can accommodate any number of items. Here, we are going to use a JComboBox to replace the JRadioButton for illustrating the usage of the software component JComboBox.

When we would like to replace the two JRadioButtons fileajRBtn and filekzRBtn with one JComboBox, the code should be as follows, where a JComboBox is used and the variable fileGroup is no longer needed since the function of the variable fileGroup is only to ensure a single selection, but the JComboBox is just designed in such way.

```
64      // select a file for reading in a word
65      selFileP = new JPanel();
66      selFileP.setPreferredSize(new Dimension(
67              selFileP.getPreferredSize().width, 85));
68      // insets: top, left, bottom, right
69      EmptyBorder eb = new EmptyBorder(new Insets(30, 130, 5, 130));
70      selFileP.setBorder(eb);
71      // for controlling the width of the JComboBox,
72      // flowLayout is suitable
73      selFileP.setLayout(new FlowLayout());
74      fileLbl = new JLabel("Select a file for reading a word: ");
75      fileNames = new String[]{"wordaj.txt", "wordkz.txt"}; // any number of files
76      cBox = new JComboBox(fileNames);
77      Dimension d = cBox.getPreferredSize();
78      cBox.setPreferredSize(new Dimension(120, d.height)); // width = 120
79      cBox.addActionListener(myActionListener);
80      selFileP.add(fileLbl);
81      selFileP.add(cBox);
```

For properly arranging a software component on the GUI, its width and its height should be controllable. In using the JRadioButton, we used the GridLayout manager for placing two JRadioButtons. However, the GridLayout manager is not suitable for arranging the JComboBox. We have to change the layout manager to be FlowLayout and adjust the settings of EmptyBorder, selFileP.setPreferredSize(), and cBox.setPreferredSize().

After settling down the JComboBox, the GUI is as Fig. 7.6 shows. The left screenshot shows the software component JComboBox, which physically only occupies one slot. The right screenshot shows the opened JComboBox,

7.10 Replacing the JRadioButton with a JComboBox

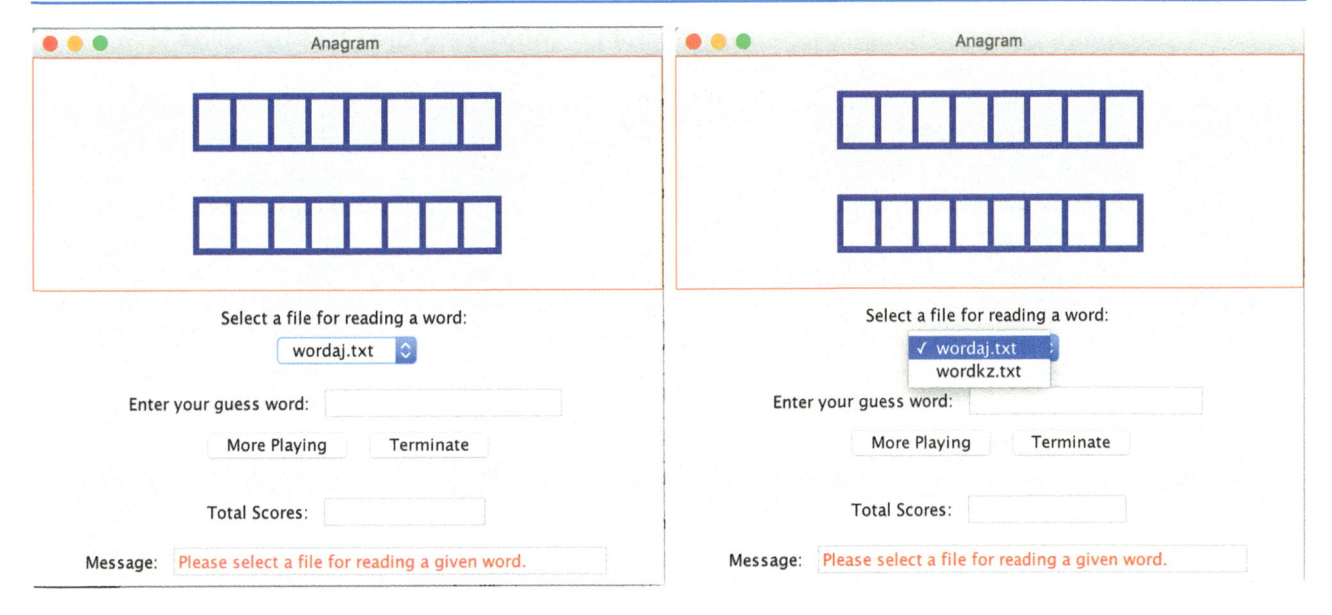

Fig. 7.6 The GUI in the project AnagramGUICombo: (Left) the JComboBox; (Right) the opened JComboBox

which may contain any number of items. Here, it only lists two text files. For adding more items, we only need to add more file names into the String[] array fileNames on line 75 of the code shown above. It is easy and won't affect the space the JComboBox needs.

The function of the JComboBox is to allow the player for selecting one of text files on the drop-down list. Once the player clicks on one of file names in the list, an ActionEvent will be generated. Thence, we need to implement an ActionListener. This is similar with the JRadioButton.

The code of the event handler actionPerformed() for handling the action event of the JRadioButton is implemented in the inner class MyActionListener() inside the class PlayerPanel.java as cited below.

```
129    if ((evt.getSource() == fileajRBtn)
130            || (evt.getSource() == filekzRBtn)) {
131        readFile.selectFile(evt.getActionCommand());
132        board.initGivenWord();
133        filekzRBtn.setEnabled(false);
134        fileajRBtn.setEnabled(false);
135        guessedWordTxt.setEnabled(true);
136        guessedWordTxt.setText("");
137        guessedWordTxt.requestFocus();
138        setMsg("Please enter your word.");
139    }
```

We should modify it to handle the click on the JComboBox as follows.

```
129    if (evt.getSource() == cBox) {
130        readFile.selectFile((String) cBox.getSelectedItem());
131        board.initGivenWord();
132        cBox.setEnabled(false);
133        guessedWordTxt.setEnabled(true);
134        guessedWordTxt.setText("");
135        guessedWordTxt.requestFocus();
136        setMsg("Please enter your word.");
137    }
```

The key statement is "(String) cBox.getSelectedItem()" that returns the text file name selected by the player from the drop-down list in the JComboBox. For more detailed codes, please refer to the project AnagramGUICombo.

In fact, the software component JCheckBox can also be used to replace the JRadioButton. However, traditionally the JCheckBox is suitable for multiple selections, which is not compatible with the "select one file" case even it can also be coded for a single selection.

Under this case, the JComboBox has its advantages over the JRadioButton. However, under many other cases, for example, a set of multiple-choice questions on a test sheet, we still prefer JRadioButton or JCheckBox since they can clearly show all of multiple choices on the surface without hiding them in a drop-down list like the JComboBox does.

7.11 Modifying the Class ReadFile.java

For making testing easier, we used JOptionPane.showInputDialog() with an Object[] array to allow the user selecting one of text files for reading in a sentence in the game WheelFortune in Chap. 4 and for reading in a word in the game AnagramText of this chapter. Under these two cases, the file selection happens inside the class ReadFile.java. However, in the game AnagramGUI, we provided two JRadioButtons for showing two text files. That means that the file selection is happened outside of the class ReadFile.java. And then, the selected file name should be passed into the class ReadFile.java. That new code structure enforced us to modify the class ReadFile.java as shown in Listing 7.5.

Listing 7.5 The partial code of modified class ReadFile.java in the project AnagramGUI

```
 1 /*
 2  * ReadFile.java - A class for opening a file and read a line from it.
 3  */
 4 package anagramgui;
 5
 6 ...
11
16 public class ReadFile {
17
18 ...
24
25     public ReadFile() {
26     }
27
28     public void selectFile(String selection) {
29         filePath = "../txt/" + selection;
30
31         try {
32             url = getClass().getResource(filePath);
33             fileName = url.getPath();
34             //Create object of FileReader
35             inputFile = new FileReader(fileName);
36             numLines = countNumLines();
37         } catch (NullPointerException nullex) {
38             System.out.println("Program is aborted by the user.");
39             System.exit(0);
40         } catch (FileNotFoundException fex) {
41             System.out.println("The file is not found.");
42             System.exit(0);
43         }
44     }
45
46     public int countNumLines() {
47         bufferedReader = new BufferedReader(inputFile);
48         int num = 0;
```

7.12 Summary

```
49          try {
50              while ((bufferedReader.readLine()) != null) {
51                  num++;
52              }
53              inputFile.close(); // close file for rewinding its pointer
54              bufferedReader.close();
55          } catch (IOException ioex) {
56          }
57          return num;
58      }
59
60      public String readContent() {
61          String aWord = null;
62          try {
63              //Create object of FileReader since inputFile was closed
64              inputFile = new FileReader(fileName);
65              bufferedReader = new BufferedReader(inputFile);
66          } catch (FileNotFoundException fex) {
67          }
68          int lineNum;
69          int count;
70
71          lineNum = (int) (Math.random() * numLines);
72          try {
73              count = 0;
74              while ((aWord = bufferedReader.readLine()) != null) {
75                  if (count == lineNum) { // reach the random line
76                      break;
77                  }
78                  count++;
79              }
80              inputFile.close();
81              bufferedReader.close();
82          } catch (IOException ioex) {
83          }
84          return aWord;
85      }
86  }
```

The method selectFile() is no longer to provide a file selection code for the user but is modified to have a formal parameter "String selection" in order to accept a selected file name passed in. The method selectFile() is called in the class PlayerPanel.java as follows.

```
readFile.selectFile(evt.getActionCommand());
```

The actual parameter evt.getActionCommand() holds the file name associated with the JRadioButton that was clicked by the player. This example demonstrates that the class ReadFile.java is reused, but sometimes we need to modify the code for satisfying new environment.

In addition, the new code added a new method countNumberLines() that is used to open the selected file and count exactly how many number of lines in the selected text file. In previous codes, the number of lines is hard-coded. Now, the method selectFile() will invoke this new method to get the real number of lines and assign it to a global variable numLines, and then the method readContent() will randomly pick up one line from the numLines. The new method makes the class ReadFile.java more real and more flexible.

7.12 Summary

The GUIs of these event-driven games usually consist of a board and a playerPanel. The board shows the game output, and the playerPanel provides input mechanism for players to enter their inputs. The players input actions go through events and event handlers to update the states of the game; and then the method repaint() invokes the method paintComponent() for painting the updated output scenes on the GUI. Implementing and managing this action-event-update-repaint chain is the heart of this kind of games.

For further understanding this kind of games, we are going to develop another new game Blackjack with more complicated functions in next chapter.

7.13 Exercises

Self-Review Questions

1. The GUI of games in using event-driven technique usually includes a board and a playerPanel. What are major functions played by these two parts?
2. Is it possible to implement a game with a board but without a playerPanel? Why?
3. Why player's inputs are important for this kind of games?
4. On the GUI, the board and the playerPanel are two pieces. How to make them work together?
5. What communication paths are required in the project AnagramGUI?
6. How to set up all of the communication paths in the project AnagramGUI?
7. The class Board.java involves three repaint() calls for painting different parts of the board. What are they?
8. How to control these three calls discussed above in different time periods?
9. Write down the sequence of method invocations in the game AnagramGUI for making a clear mind about the action-event-update-repaint chain.
10. Draw a UML sequence diagram to illustrate the dynamic behaviors in the game of WheelFortune in-text developed in Chap. 4.
11. Write a sequence of steps for summarizing the process starting from instantiating a JRadioButton object until echoing its current status (clicked or unclicked).
12. Searching and browsing the Internet for finding out the differences between the components JTextField and JTextArea.

Projects

1. Write a program for accepting a givenWord inputted by the player and showing it on a board as the first line. And then, the program scrambles the givenWord as a scrambledWord and displays it on the board as the second line.
2. Apply the logic and GUI of the game AnagramGUI for designing and implementing a game with the name of GuessWord. The game displays a word with some missing characters and asks the player to guess the word with a complete and correct spelling. The game may provide three difficulty levels, such as easy, medium, and hard. The different difficulty levels imply missing different percentages of characters in a given word.
3. Apply the event-driven technique for designing and implementing a game with the name of NumberCrunch. The game allows the player to select a number of computational equations he/she would like to take, and then the game displays a mathematical computational equation, such as "22 + 55 = ," "−25 * 66 = ," and the like, to ask the player for answering the computational result. The given equations could be integer or double, positive or negative, and the computations include +, −, *, /, and %. As long as the player enters an answer, the game responses the correctness and displays a ratio of the number of correct answers over the total number of equations issued and immediately gives another computational equation. When the number of equations issued is equal to the number the player would like to answer, the game shows the time spend for answering these questions. Based on the correct ratio and the total time spend, the game gives a score for the player. And then, the game allows the player to select New Game or Exit. The game may have three difficulty levels for providing smaller or larger values for the given equations. For example, easy level gives one-digit numbers "2 * 5 = "; medium level gives two-digit numbers "35 * 88 = "; and hard level gives three-digit numbers "234 * 543 = ." The system built-in method System.currentTimeMillis() can be used to measure a beginTime and an endTime. And the time spend is the difference of the two times.

Event-Driven with an Update-Repaint Chain: A Game Blackjack

8

The game Blackjack further illustrates the event-driven strategy. Its GUI also consists of two portions. The output board not only displays text but also shows more complicated graphics and images. The input panel arranges software components for supporting the player's inputted data and actions. Following an abstract game model, the game clearly sets apart the game GUI from the game logic and closely links them together through event listeners and event handlers. It is that the abstract game model constructs a loosely coupled software system, which should be a designing guidance for constructing any games. In addition, the game adapts the truth table for determining "when to show what."

The objectives of this chapter include:
1. A new game based on event-driven technique: Blackjack.
2. Adopting a divide-and-conquer approach for the implementation.
3. Blackjack1 implements the card and deck.
4. The "has" relationship: a composite class Deck.java "has" a class Card.java.
5. Blackjack2 adds two players and three actions "new," "hit," and "stand."
6. Blackjack3 completes the game with a new "bet" action.
7. A set of action-event-update-repaint chains forms the logics and rules.
8. A truth table is employed for determining "when to show what."

The previous chapter developed a game AnagramGUI. It is a kind of games based on event-driven technique. This chapter intends to give another example of this kind of games with the name of Blackjack. It is also based on the event-driven technique and has a GUI with a board for showing the output of the game and a playerPanel for accepting inputted data and actions issued by the player.

However, the game Blackjack has its special features. It is a card game so that it deals with two new classes Card.java and Deck.java, which prepare us for more card games later. The output scene contains both texts and images and shows different scenes in different game stages. The logic of the game is much more complicated than the game AnagramGUI. Thus, the game will enhance our understanding on the event-driven technique and the action-event-update-repaint chain. Through the game, we will further study the abstract game model and apply it for constructing loosely coupled software system.

8.1 A Game Blackjack

A new project Blackjack is another good example for games with a GUI and events. It is a famous gambling game with cards for two players. One player is named dealer; the other is named gambler. The story of the game Blackjack says each card has a value: a card numbered 2–10 is worth its face value; Jacks, Queens, and Kings each counts as 10; Aces can count as either 1 or 11 up to the player's choice. When a game starts, the dealer gets a hand of two cards, one of them faces down and the other faces up. The gambler also gets a hand of two cards but with both face up. The gambler can express "hit" to get additional cards face up until the gambler expresses "stand" that stops getting more cards. After that, the dealer's hidden card is revealed. If the value of the dealer's hand is 16 or less, the dealer must hit; if the dealer's hand has a value of 17 or more, the dealer must stand.

Once the value of a hand equals 21, the owner of the hand has a "Blackjack" and wins the game. If the value of one hand exceeds 21, which is called "bust," the owner loses the game. If both hands of two players have the equal value, which is called "push," no one wins the game. If the values of both hands are not exceeding 21 and not equal, the owner who has the larger value wins the game.

8.2 A Brainstorm on the Design

According to the experiences gained from the game AnagramGUI, we also design the GUI of the game Blackjack with a board and a playerPanel. The board shows the hands of both players with the hand's values. The playerPanel arranges buttons and other software components. We also may learn from the games discussed before to assign the computer playing the role of the dealer and the human player as the gambler. However, in considering both the dealer and the gambler who have the same actions "hit," "stand," and the like, we can design one class Player.java to instantiate two of them. The difference between them is that the gambler can make his/her decisions by looking at his/her hand's value on the board and clicking corresponding buttons to play the game; but, the dealer's decisions are controlled through built-in rules based on his/her hand's value.

Some facts will increase the complexity of the game. (1) The value of Aces could be counted either as 1 or 11. How to perform the calculation? (2) The winning of a game depends on the comparisons of two hand's values. What rule should be built in to compare the two hand's values, which include the possible two different counts of Aces? (3) The dealer's actions, "hit" or "stand," are controlled through the codes. What rules should be designed for that? (4) In order to make the game more interesting, a "bet" action is added that would require extra design and implementation. (5) In different stages of playing, the board needs to display different scenes. How to control different stages of playing in a sequence of time periods?

We are going to develop version by version to solve these problems gradually. At the same time, we may encounter some detailed problems that have to be solved, too.

8.3 Preparing a Deck of Cards: The Project Blackjack1

The first step, the project Blackjack1, is to prepare a deck of cards. We draft a pseudo code as follows.

1. A class Card.java defines a single card.
   (a) A single card is an image. For placing the card image in a position, the class needs a rectangle with attributes of x, y, width, height, cardBack, cardFront, value, and a Boolean faceUp. The width and the height of the card image are constants.
   (b) The constructor of the class Card.java reads in a cardBack image for representing a new object of a card is instantiated.
   (c) A method paintCard() paints the card on the GUI when it is invoked.
   (d) Setter methods are defined for other classes to set up all of related attributes.
2. A class Deck.java collects 52 cards.
   (a) A method initDeck() reads in 52 cards and stores them in a ArrayList as a deck.
   (b) A method shuffleCard() shuffles the 52 cards in the deck.
   (c) A method dealCard() always deals the first card from the deck. When the remaining number of cards equals to or less than 15, the deck of cards is renewed.
3. A class Board.java "is-a" JPanel.
   (a) A method paintComponent() invokes aCard.paintCard() for displaying the aCard.
4. A class PlayerPanel.java "is-a" JPanel to be developed later.
5. A class GameCanvas.java "is-a" JPanel.
   (a) An initComponent() method instantiates an object board of the class Board.java and an object playerPanel of the class PlayerPanel.java and adds them into this JPanel for making a GUI. And then, the method also instantiates a deck of cards of the class Deck.java and asks the deck for dealing a card, which is placed on the board. The paintComponent() method of the board paints the card face up for indicating the deck of cards is ready for using.
6. A class Consts.java defines a set of required constants.

Corresponding to the pseudo code, the UML class diagram and the execution result of the project Blackjack1 are shown in Fig. 8.1. The GUI on the right side proves the design and the implementation work fine. For saving space, the detailed codes will be shown later. If interested, readers can read all of codes from the included project Blackjack1.

8.4 The Relationship "has" Between the Class Deck.java and the Class Card.java

The UML class diagram of the game shown on Fig. 8.1 illustrates that the class Deck.java "has" the class Card.java. The "has" means "contains." In the real world, an object of deck contains or consists of a set of objects card in general; or a deck contains or consists of 52 cards in particular. In other words, the class Deck.java is a class that "has" another class as its component.

Clearly, as a component, the class Card.java mainly describes one card, such as its geometric shape, its position, its image, its value, and so on. As a composite class, the class Deck.java needs a data structure for holding multiple cards and some methods for manipulating the set of cards, such as shuffle cards, deal a card, and the like. The codes of both classes from the project Blackjack3 are shown in Listing 8.1.

8.4 The Relationship "has" Between the Class Deck.java and the Class Card.java

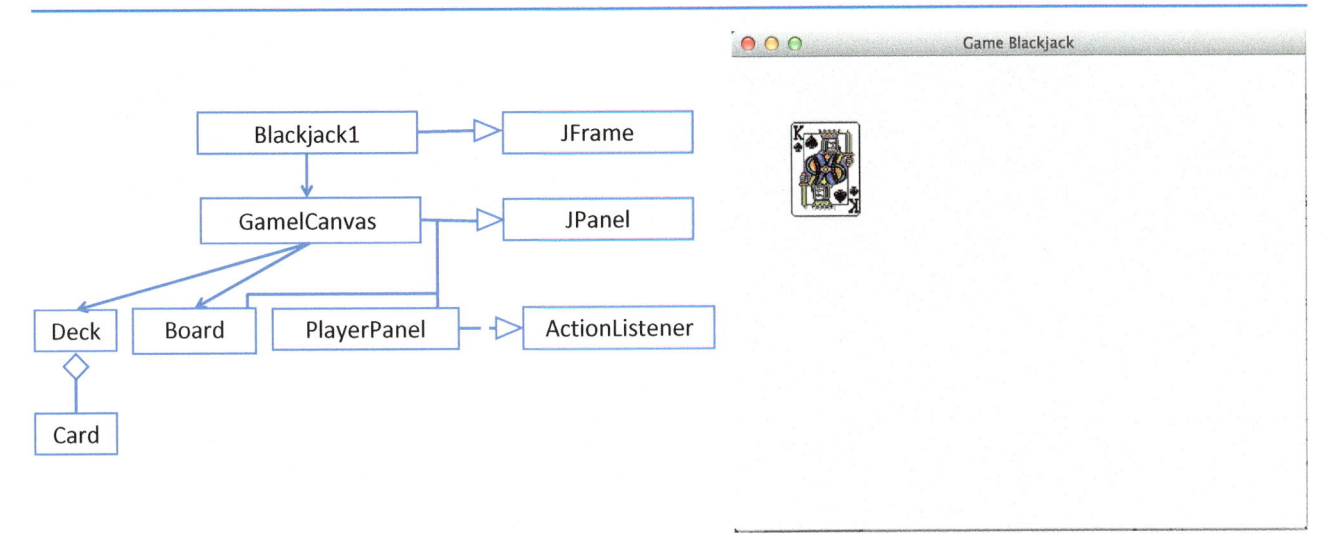

Fig. 8.1 (*Left*) The UML diagram; (*Right*) the GUI of the project Blackjack1

Listing 8.1 The codes of both classes Card.java and Deck.java in the project Blackjack3

```java
1  /*
2   * Card.java - A class defines one card.
3   */
4  package blackjack;
5
6  import java.awt.Graphics2D;
7  import java.awt.Image;
8  import java.io.IOException;
9  import javax.imageio.ImageIO;
10
15 public class Card {
16
17     private int x, y;
18     private int width = 60, height = 80;
19     private Image cardBack;
20     private Image cardFront;
21     private boolean faceUp;
22     private int value;
23
24     public Card() {
25         faceUp = false;
26         try {
27             cardBack = ImageIO.read(getClass().getResource("../cards/Back.gif"));
28         } catch (IOException ex) {
29         }
30     }
31
32     public void paintCard(Graphics2D g2d) {
33         if (faceUp) {
34             g2d.drawImage(cardFront, x, y, width, height, null);
35         } else {
36             g2d.drawImage(cardBack, x, y, width, height, null);
37         }
38     }
```

```java
39
40     public int getX() {
41         return x;
42     }
43
44     public void setX(int x) {
45         this.x = x;
46     }
47
48     … // other getters and setters
75 }
```

```java
1  /*
2   * Deck.java - A class defines a deck of cards.
3   */
4  package blackjack;
5
6  import java.awt.*;
7  import java.io.IOException;
8  import java.util.ArrayList;
9  import javax.imageio.ImageIO;
10
15 public class Deck {
16
17     private ArrayList<Card> deck;
18     private Card card;
19
20     public Deck() {
21         deck = new ArrayList();
22         initDeck();
23     }
24
25     private void initDeck() {
26         deck.clear();
27         for (int i = 0; i < Consts.DECK_LEN; i++) {
28             card = initNewCard(i);
29             deck.add(card);
30         }
31         shuffleCard();
32     }
33
34     public Card initNewCard(int idx) {
35         Image img = null;
36         int aValue;
37         try {
38             img = ImageIO.read(getClass().getResource(
39                     "../cards/" + (idx + 1) + ".gif"));
40         } catch (IOException ex) {
41         }
42         Card aCard = new Card();
43         aCard.setCardFront(img);
44         // set a value for a card
45         aValue = idx % 13;
46         if (aValue >= 10) {
47             aValue = 10; // Jack, Queen, and King
```

```java
48          } else if (aValue == 0) {
49              aValue = 11; // A
50          } else {
51              aValue += 1; // 2 to 10
52          }
53          aCard.setValue(aValue);
54
55          return aCard;
56      }
57
58      private void shuffleCard() {
59          int randIdx1, randIdx2;
60          for (int i = 0; i < 1000; i++) {
61              randIdx1 = ((int) (Math.random() * 10000)) % Consts.DECK_LEN;
62              randIdx2 = ((int) (Math.random() * 10000)) % Consts.DECK_LEN;
63              swapCard(randIdx1, randIdx2);
64          }
65      }
66
67      public void swapCard(int idx1, int idx2) {
68          Card tCard;
69          tCard = deck.get(idx1);
70          deck.set(idx1, deck.get(idx2));
71          deck.set(idx2, tCard);
72      }
73
74      public Card dealCard() {
75          Card theCard;
76          theCard = deck.get(0);
77          deck.remove(0);
78          if (deck.size() <= Consts.DECK_RENEW) {
79              initDeck();
80          }
81          return theCard;
82      }
83
84      public ArrayList<Card> getDeck() {
85          return deck;
86      }
87  }
```

8.5 Adding Players and Applying Game Rules: The Project Blackjack2

Now, we need to add more objects for the game. The first is to add a dealer and a gambler. The second is to add the software components on the playerPanel for the gambler to play the game. The third is to build in rules with the event handler for controlling the dealer's actions. The last is to judge who is the winner of the game based on the status of each player. The UML class diagram and the GUI of the project Blackjack2 are shown in Fig. 8.2.

8.6 The Class Player.java Determines the Current Status of Each Player

In the games addressed in previous chapters, such as GuessInt and AnagramGUI, the initializer and the player had different behaviors. Therefore, two classes Initializer.java and Player.java were needed for instantiating two different objects. However, in this game Blackjack, the two players, the dealer and the gambler, have the same playing actions, such as "hit," "stand," "bust," and the like. Thence, we let the "global" class GameCanvas.java to complete the initialization and let the two players to share one class Player.java. The code of the class Player.java is cited in Listing 8.2.

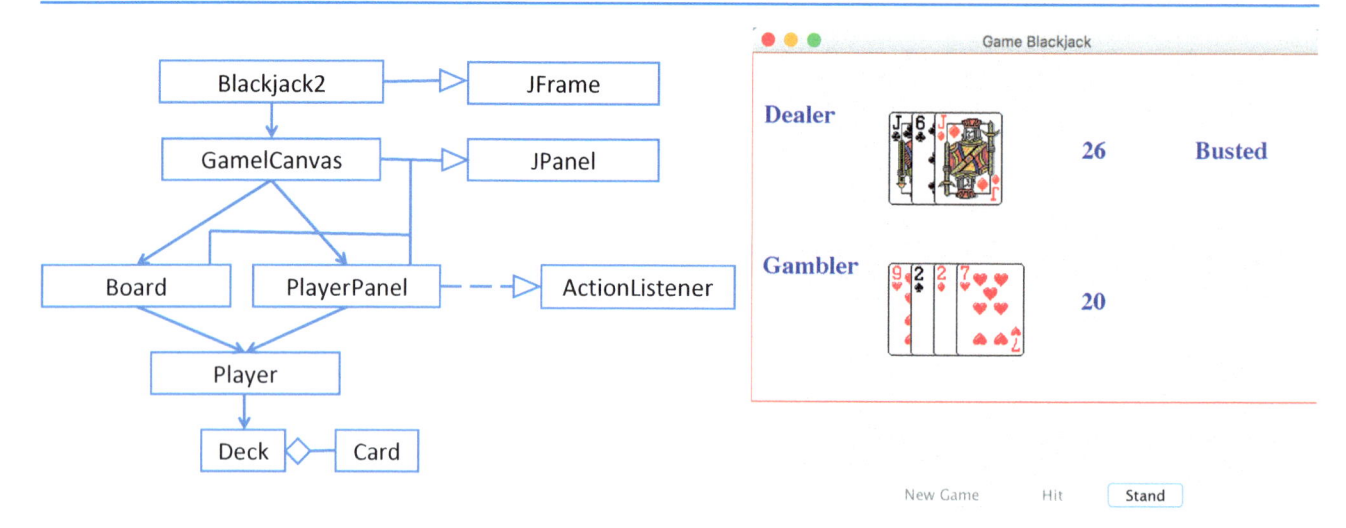

Fig. 8.2 (*Left*) The UML class diagram; (*Right*) the GUI of the project Blackjack2

Listing 8.2 The class Player.java in the project Blackjack2

```
 1  /*
 2   * Player.java - A class defines a player.
 3   */
 4  package blackjack;
 5
 6  import java.awt.Graphics2D;
 7  import java.util.ArrayList;
 8
13  public class Player {
14
15      private String name;
16      private ArrayList<Card> hand;
17      private int handValue1;
18      private int handValue2;
19      private int numAce;
20      private int status;
21
22      private Deck deck; // for dealing a card to hands
23
24      public Player() {
25          initPlayer();
26      }
27
28      private void initPlayer() {
29          hand = new ArrayList<>();
30          numAce = 0;
31          handValue1 = 0;
32          handValue2 = 0;
33          status = Consts.COMPARE1;
34      }
35
```

8.6 The Class Player.java Determines the Current Status of Each Player

```java
36      public void assignHand(boolean faceUp, int y) {
37          Card card = deck.dealCard();
38          card.setFaceUp(faceUp);
39          // assign the coordinate (x, y) for painting
40          if (hand.isEmpty()) {
41              card.setX(Consts.INIT_X);
42          } else {
43              int tempX = (hand.get(hand.size() - 1)).getX();
44              card.setX(tempX + Consts.CARD_GAP);
45          }
46          card.setY(y);
47          hand.add(card);
48          // calculate hand values
49          if (card.getValue() == 11) { // i.e. the card is an Ace
50              numAce++;
51          }
52          handValue1 += card.getValue(); // the total value of the hand
53          if (numAce > 0) {
54              handValue2 = handValue1 - numAce * 10;
55          }
56          // determine current status
57          if ((handValue1 == 21) || (handValue2 == 21)) {
58              status = Consts.BLACKJACK;
59          } else if ((handValue1 > 21) && (handValue2 > 21)) {
60              status = Consts.BUSTED;
61          } else if ((handValue1 > 21) && (handValue2 == 0)) {
62              status = Consts.BUSTED;
63          } else if ((handValue1 > 21) && (handValue2 < 21)) {
64              status = Consts.COMPARE2;
65          } else if (handValue1 < 21) { // handValue2 default < 21
66              status = Consts.COMPARE1;
67          }
68      }
69
70      public void paintHand(Graphics2D g2d) {
71          for (int i = 0; i < hand.size(); i++) {
72              hand.get(i).paintCard(g2d);
73          }
74      }
75
76      public int getHandValue1() {
77          return handValue1;
78      }
79
80      public int getHandValue2() {
81          return handValue2;
82      }
83
84      public void setName(String name) {
85          this.name = name;
86      }
87
88      public ArrayList<Card> getHand() {
89          return hand;
90      }
91
```

```
 92        public void setDeck(Deck deck) {
 93            this.deck = deck;
 94        }
 95
 96        public int getStatus() {
 97            return status;
 98        }
 99
100        public void setStatus(int status) {
101            this.status = status;
102        }
103    }
```

The class Player.java has an ArrayList to hold a hand of cards. The method assignHand() is used to invoke the method deck.dealCard() for putting one new card at a time to the hand. When the hand gets a new card, (1) it assigns the coordinates (x, y) of a new card for painting it on the GUI later; (2) it calculates the value of the hand. Since an Ace may count as a value of 1 or a value of 11, thus, one hand has two values stored in the variables of handValue1 and handValue2. The handValue1 counts the value of an Ace as 11; the handValue2 counts the value of an Ace as 1.

That is, when a card is added into a hand, if the card has a value of 11, it is an Ace since the value in a single Ace card is assigned as 11 by the class Card.java. At the same time, the numAce is increased by one. The handValue1 accumulates all of values of all cards in the current hand. If numAce == 0, the handValue2 is zero; otherwise, both handValue1 and handValue2 have a value and "handValue2 = handValue1 – numAce * 10."

According to the definition above, when handValue2 is zero, the board only shows handValue1; otherwise, both values are shown so that the gambler can choose one of them. For the dealer, we apply the rules of the game implemented as codes to make a decision for him/her. We will see the codes later in the class PlayerPanel.java.

The method assignHand() also determines the current status of the player based on the value of the hand. The status of a player is determined by the rules described in the story of the game. The implementation of the rules deals with a set of if-then-else statements as follows.

```
// determine current status
if ((handValue1 == 21) || (handValue2 == 21)) {
    status = Consts.BLACKJACK;
} else if ((handValue1 > 21) && (handValue2 > 21)) {
    status = Consts.BUSTED;
} else if ((handValue1 > 21) && (handValue2 == 0)) {
    status = Consts.BUSTED;
} else if ((handValue1 > 21) && (handValue2 < 21)) {
    status = Consts.COMPARE2;
} else if (handValue1 < 21) { // handValue2 default < 21
    status = Consts.COMPARE1;
}
```

The code above means that:

If one of the values is equal to 21, the player has the status of "Blackjack."

If both values are larger than 21, the status is "Busted."

If handValue1 is larger than 21 and handValue2 is 0, the status is also "Busted."

If handValue1 is larger than 21 but handValue2 is less than 21, then handValue2 should be used to compare with the hand value of another player because handValue1 has no meaning already; thus the status is marked as "COMPARE2."

If handValue1 is less than 21, then handValue2 definitely is less than 21 since "handValue2 = handValue1 – numAce * 10";

therefore only handValue1 is meaningful to be used to compare with the hand value of another player, and then the status is marked as "COMPARE1."

The class Player.java has another method paintHand(Graphics2D g2d) that is for painting the hand of cards on the GUI. The class also provides some getter and setter methods for other classes to access the corresponding attributes.

8.7 The Class PlayerPanel.java Implements the "core" of the Program

The gambler plays the game through the software components placed on the playerPanel. Hence, the class PlayerPanel.java implements all of functions required for driving the game as shown in Listing 8.3.

Listing 8.3 The class PlayerPanel.java in the project Blackjack2

```
1  /*
2   * PlayerPanel.java - A class defines the player's panel.
3   */
4  package blackjack;
5
6  import java.awt.event.ActionEvent;
7  import java.awt.event.ActionListener;
8  import javax.swing.JButton;
9  import javax.swing.JPanel;
10
15 public class PlayerPanel extends JPanel {
16
17     private Player dealer;
18     private Player gambler;
19     private Board board;
20
21     private JButton newGameBtn;
22     private JButton hitBtn;
23     private JButton standBtn;
24
25     public PlayerPanel() {
26         initPlayerPanel();
27     }
28
29     private void initPlayerPanel() {
30         ActionListener myActionListener = new MyActionListener();
31
32         newGameBtn = new JButton("New Game");
33         newGameBtn.addActionListener(myActionListener);
34         newGameBtn.setEnabled(false);
35         add(newGameBtn);
36         hitBtn = new JButton("Hit");
37         hitBtn.addActionListener(myActionListener);
38         add(hitBtn);
39         standBtn = new JButton("Stand");
40         standBtn.addActionListener(myActionListener);
41         add(standBtn);
42
43         initGame();
44     }
45
46     private void initGame() {
47         //newGame.setEnabled(true) cannot be included for the first time
```

```
48            newGameBtn.setEnabled(true);
49            hitBtn.setEnabled(false);
50            standBtn.setEnabled(false);
51        }
52
53        private void clickedNewGame() {
54            board.setNewGameFlag(true);
55            newGameBtn.setEnabled(false);
56            hitBtn.setEnabled(true);
57            standBtn.setEnabled(true);
58        }
59
60        private void dealerHitStand() {
61            // dealer: hit or stand
62            if (dealer.getHandValue2() == 0) { // if no Ace
63                if (dealer.getHandValue1() <= 16) { // hit
64                    while (dealer.getHandValue1() <= 16) {
65                        dealer.assignHand(true, Consts.DEALER_Y);
66                    }
67                } else if (dealer.getHandValue1() >= 17) { // stand
68                }
69            }
70            if (dealer.getHandValue2() != 0) { // if has Ace
71                if (dealer.getHandValue1() == 21) { // based on value1
72                    // Blackjack, stand
73                } else if (dealer.getHandValue1() <= 16) { // hit
74                    while (dealer.getHandValue1() <= 16) {
75                        dealer.assignHand(true, Consts.DEALER_Y);
76                    }
77                } else if (dealer.getHandValue1() >= 17) { // stand
78                }
79                if (dealer.getHandValue1() > 21) { // based on value2
80                    if (dealer.getHandValue2() <= 16) { // hit
81                        while (dealer.getHandValue2() <= 16) {
82                            dealer.assignHand(true, Consts.DEALER_Y);
83                        }
84                    } else if (dealer.getHandValue2() >= 17) { // stand
85                    }
86                }
87            }
88            board.setStandFlag(true);
89            board.setHitFlag(true);
90        }
91
92        private void determineFinalStatus() {
93            // determines final status
94            int dS = dealer.getStatus();
95            int gS = gambler.getStatus();
96            if ((dS == Consts.BLACKJACK) && (gS == Consts.BLACKJACK)) {
97                dealer.setStatus(Consts.PUSHED);
98                gambler.setStatus(Consts.PUSHED);
99            } else if ((dS == Consts.BUSTED) && (gS == Consts.BUSTED)) {
100                dealer.setStatus(Consts.PUSHED);
101                gambler.setStatus(Consts.PUSHED);
102            }
```

8.7 The Class PlayerPanel.java Implements the "core" of the Program

```java
103            dS = dealer.getStatus();
104            gS = gambler.getStatus();
105
106            // COMPARE: four combinations
107            if (((dS == Consts.COMPARE1) || (dS == Consts.COMPARE2))
108                    && ((gS == Consts.COMPARE1) || (gS == Consts.COMPARE2))) {
109                int dV1 = dealer.getHandValue1();
110                int dV2 = dealer.getHandValue2();
111                int gV1 = gambler.getHandValue1();
112                int gV2 = gambler.getHandValue2();
113                if ((dS == Consts.COMPARE1) && (gS == Consts.COMPARE1)) {
114                    if (dV1 > gV1) {
115                        dealer.setStatus(Consts.WON);
116                    } else if (dV1 < gV1) {
117                        gambler.setStatus(Consts.WON);
118                    } else { // (dV1 == gV1)
119                        dealer.setStatus(Consts.PUSHED);
120                        gambler.setStatus(Consts.PUSHED);
121                    }
122                } else if ((dS == Consts.COMPARE1) && (gS == Consts.COMPARE2)) {
123                    if (dV1 > gV2) {
124                        dealer.setStatus(Consts.WON);
125                    } else if (dV1 < gV2) {
126                        gambler.setStatus(Consts.WON);
127                    } else { // (dV1 == gV2)
128                        dealer.setStatus(Consts.PUSHED);
129                        gambler.setStatus(Consts.PUSHED);
130                    }
131                } else if ((dS == Consts.COMPARE2) && (gS == Consts.COMPARE1)) {
132                    if (dV2 > gV1) {
133                        dealer.setStatus(Consts.WON);
134                    } else if (dV2 < gV1) {
135                        gambler.setStatus(Consts.WON);
136                    } else { // (dV2 == gV1)
137                        dealer.setStatus(Consts.PUSHED);
138                        gambler.setStatus(Consts.PUSHED);
139                    }
140                } else if ((dS == Consts.COMPARE2) && (gS == Consts.COMPARE2)) {
141                    if (dV2 > gV2) {
142                        dealer.setStatus(Consts.WON);
143                    } else if (dV2 < gV2) {
144                        gambler.setStatus(Consts.WON);
145                    } else { // (dV2 == gV2)
146                        dealer.setStatus(Consts.PUSHED);
147                        gambler.setStatus(Consts.PUSHED);
148                    }
149                }
150            }
151        }
152
153        class MyActionListener implements ActionListener {
154
155            @Override
156            public void actionPerformed(ActionEvent evt) {
157                if (evt.getSource() == newGameBtn) {
```

```
158                dealer.assignHand(false, Consts.DEALER_Y);
159                dealer.assignHand(true, Consts.DEALER_Y);
160
161                gambler.assignHand(true, Consts.GAMBLER_Y);
162                gambler.assignHand(true, Consts.GAMBLER_Y);
163                clickedNewGame();
164            } else if (evt.getSource() == hitBtn) {
165                gambler.assignHand(true, Consts.GAMBLER_Y);
166                board.setHitFlag(true);
167            } else if (evt.getSource() == standBtn) {
168                hitBtn.setEnabled(false);
169                // reveal the first facedown card
170                Card theCard = dealer.getHand().get(0);
171                theCard.setFaceUp(true);
172
173                dealerHitStand();
174                determineFinalStatus();
175            }
176            board.repaint();
177        }
178    }
179
180    public void setDealer(Player dealer) {
181        this.dealer = dealer;
182    }
183
184    public void setGambler(Player gambler) {
185        this.gambler = gambler;
186    }
187
188    public void setBoard(Board board) {
189        this.board = board;
190    }
191 }
```

Referring to the code of the class PlayerPanel.java cited in Listing 8.3, the class PlayerPanel.java installs three buttons: "New Game," "Hit," and "Stand" as shown in Fig. 8.2 (right). The corresponding event handlers are implemented inside the inner class MyActionListener(). The event handlers of the three buttons perform the following functions.

1. When the button "New Game" is clicked, two players receive a hand of two cards, respectively. The dealer's hand has one card facedown and one card faceup. The gambler's hand has both cards faceup. And immediately, the clickedNewGame() method is invoked to call board. setNewGameFlag(true) for announcing the board to display the value of the gambler's hand but keep the value of the dealer's hand as unknown. Meanwhile, the method also setEnabled(false) for the "New Game" button and setEnabled(true) for the "Hit" button and "Stand" button.
2. When the button "Hit" is enabled and clicked ones, a new card is dealt to the gambler's hand and board. setHitFlag(true) is invoked to allow the board updating the value of the gambler's hand as well as the current status of the gambler.
3. When the button "Stand" is enabled and clicked, the gambler stops his/her actions. At the same time, the dealer starts "hit" or "stand" actions according to the codes of the method dealerHitStand(). Firstly, the facedown card in the dealer's hand is faced up, and the value of the dealer's hand is displayed. Secondly, according to the rules of the game, if the initial value of the dealer's hand is equal to or less than 16, the dealer's "hit" action starts to continuously deal cards to the dealer's hand until the hand's value equals to or larger than 17 and the dealer is "stand." If the initial value of the dealer's hand equals to or larger than 17, no cards are dealt to the dealer's hand. Under that case, the dealer does not have "hit" process but automatically falls in "stand." And then, the status of the dealer is displayed.
4. After finishing the displaying of individual player's status, the determineFinalStatus() method finally is invoked

8.9 The GUI and the Event-Driven in the Project Blackjack3 — 167

to determine who is the winner of the game, where "dS" stands for dealer's status and "gS" stands for gambler's status.

The possible statuses of each player are defined in the class Consts.java as constants of BLACKJACK, BUSTED, PUSHED, WON, COMPARE1, and COMPARE2. (1) When both players have the same status of BLACKJACK or both have the same status of BUSTED, the final status should be PUSHED. (2) If only one of them is BLACKJACK, the owner is WON. If only one of them is BUSTED, then the other player is WON. (3) When both of them have the status of either COMPARE1 or COMPARE2, we have to complete four different comparisons for assuring who is the winner. Finally, the method board.repaint() is invoked to call the method paintComponent() of the class Board.java to retrieve the final status and paint corresponding remark on the board.

8.8 Adding Chips for Gamblers to Bet: The Project Blackjack3

As a gambling game, it is more interesting to have chips for betting. At the beginning, the gambler should input his/her total amount of money for playing the game. And then, the gambler places chips for representing his/her bets. Suppose that the chips have five kinds: $25, $100, $500, $1000, and $5000. We add corresponding five buttons on the class PlayerPanel.java for the gambler to bet. Every click on any one of the five chip buttons, the amount of the chip is inserted into an Arraylist with the name of chips, which is defined in the class Player.java. At the same time, the chip is displayed on the board. The entire process still follows the general action-event-update-repaint chain as usual. A complete UML class diagram and a complete GUI for the project Blackjack3 are shown in Fig. 8.3.

8.9 The GUI and the Event-Driven in the Project Blackjack3

Clearly, the GUI of the game Blackjack is still consisting of two portions: a board and a playerPanel. The board displays the dealer and gambler's hands, the hand's values, the chips, and the final status. The playerPanel provides buttons and textFields for the gambler to input data and actions. All of the displays on the board follow the button clicks accordingly.

For better understanding the design of the software structure and the implementation of the game, we would like to revisit Fig. 1.7 in Chap. 1, which is duplicated here as Fig. 8.4. The figure describes that an entire game consists of two parts: game GUI and game logic. The linkages between them are inputState and outputState. Physically, the inputState is the click actions on the set of buttons with corresponding events, and the outputState is the results of the executions of the corresponding event handlers. The execution of any event handler is triggered by a button click on the GUI, which in turn updates the states of the game and output a new scene on the GUI.

Definitely we have to develop the class PlayerPanel.java for adding more buttons and text fields as well as attaching more corresponding event handlers. In addition, we need to add one more flag betFlag for controlling the class Board.java to display the chips. Besides that, the setEnabled() method is employed to enable or disable the software components in order to enforce them to be controlled following the requirements of the global sequence of actions. The enhanced class PlayerPanel.java in the project Blackjack3 is displayed in Listing 8.4.

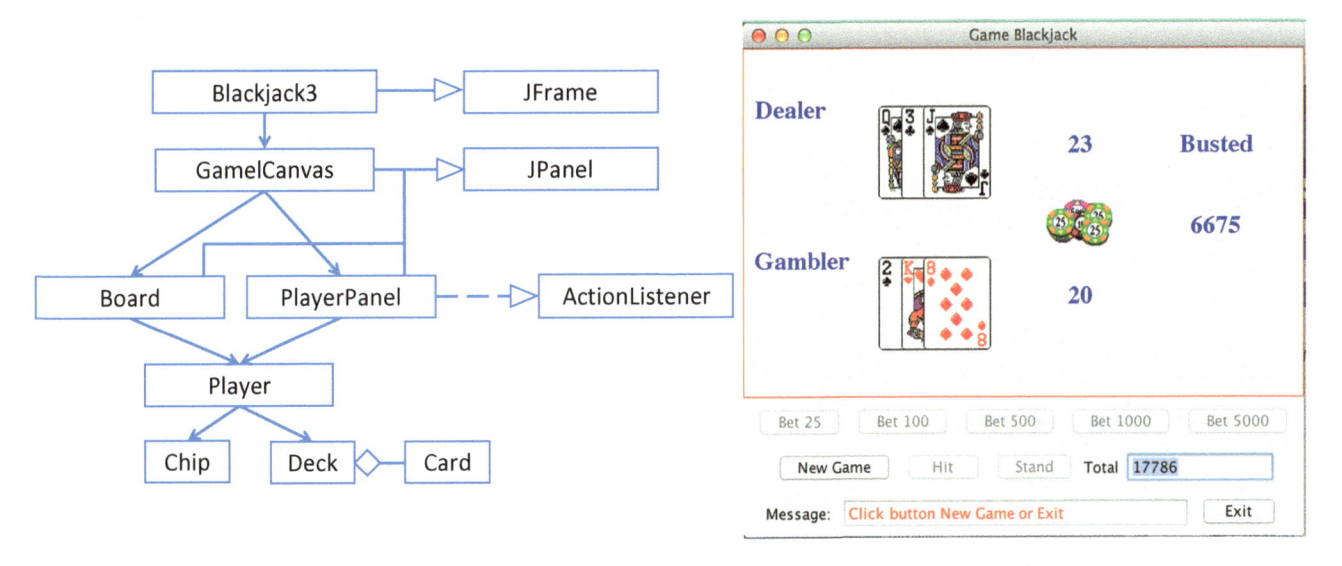

Fig. 8.3 (*Left*) The UML class diagram; (*Right*) the GUI of the project Blackjack3

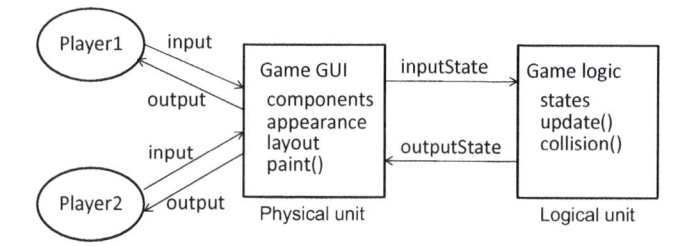

Fig. 8.4 An abstract model of games with two players

Listing 8.4 The class PlayerPanel.java in the project Blackjack3

```java
/*
 * PlayerPanel.java - A class defines the player's panel.
 */
package blackjack;

import java.awt.Color;
import java.awt.GridLayout;
import java.awt.event.ActionEvent;
import java.awt.event.ActionListener;
import javax.swing.JButton;
import javax.swing.JLabel;
import javax.swing.JPanel;
import javax.swing.JTextField;

public class PlayerPanel extends JPanel {

    private Player dealer;
    private Player gambler;
    private Board board;

    private JPanel betP;
    private JPanel actionP;
    private JPanel msgP;

    private JButton newGameBtn;
    private JButton hitBtn;
    private JButton standBtn;
    private JButton bet25Btn;
    private JButton bet100Btn;
    private JButton bet500Btn;
    private JButton bet1000Btn;
    private JButton bet5000Btn;
    private JLabel totalLbl;
    private JTextField totalTxt;
    private JButton exitBtn;
    private JLabel msgLbl;
    private JTextField msgTxt;
    private boolean newBet = true; // a flag for one bet
    private int preChipValue;

    public PlayerPanel() {
        initPlayerPanel();
    }

```

8.9 The GUI and the Event-Driven in the Project Blackjack3

```java
49      private void initPlayerPanel() {
50          ActionListener myActionListener = new MyActionListener();
51          setLayout(new GridLayout(3, 1));
52
53          betP = new JPanel();
54          bet25Btn = new JButton("Bet 25");
55          bet25Btn.addActionListener(myActionListener);
56          bet100Btn = new JButton("Bet 100");
57          bet100Btn.addActionListener(myActionListener);
58          bet500Btn = new JButton("Bet 500");
59          bet500Btn.addActionListener(myActionListener);
60          bet1000Btn = new JButton("Bet 1000");
61          bet1000Btn.addActionListener(myActionListener);
62          bet5000Btn = new JButton("Bet 5000");
63          bet5000Btn.addActionListener(myActionListener);
64          betP.add(bet25Btn);
65          betP.add(bet100Btn);
66          betP.add(bet500Btn);
67          betP.add(bet1000Btn);
68          betP.add(bet5000Btn);
69          add(betP);
70
71          actionP = new JPanel();
72          newGameBtn = new JButton("New Game");
73          newGameBtn.addActionListener(myActionListener);
74          newGameBtn.setEnabled(false);
75          actionP.add(newGameBtn);
76          hitBtn = new JButton("Hit");
77          hitBtn.addActionListener(myActionListener);
78          actionP.add(hitBtn);
79          standBtn = new JButton("Stand");
80          standBtn.addActionListener(myActionListener);
81          actionP.add(standBtn);
82          totalLbl = new JLabel("Total");
83          actionP.add(totalLbl);
84          totalTxt = new JTextField(10);
85          totalTxt.setText("Enter amount");
86          totalTxt.addActionListener(myActionListener);
87          actionP.add(totalTxt);
88          add(actionP);
89
90          msgP = new JPanel();
91          msgLbl = new JLabel("Message: ");
92          msgTxt = new JTextField(25);
93          msgTxt.setForeground(Color.red);
94          exitBtn = new JButton("Exit");
95          exitBtn.addActionListener(myActionListener);
96          msgP.add(msgLbl);
97          msgP.add(msgTxt);
98          msgP.add(exitBtn);
99          add(msgP);
100         msgTxt.setText("Enter your total amount and press <Enter>");
101
102         initGame(); // before entering the total amount
103     }
104
```

```java
class MyActionListener implements ActionListener {

    @Override
    public void actionPerformed(ActionEvent evt) {
        if (evt.getSource() == totalTxt) {
            gambler.setTotalAmount(Integer.parseInt(totalTxt.getText()));
            newGameBtn.setEnabled(true); // start new game
            msgTxt.setText("Click button New Game or Exit");
        } else if (evt.getSource() == newGameBtn) {
            resetGame();
            dealer.assignHand(false, Consts.DEALER_Y);
            dealer.assignHand(true, Consts.DEALER_Y);

            gambler.assignHand(true, Consts.GAMBLER_Y);
            gambler.assignHand(true, Consts.GAMBLER_Y);
            clickedNewGame();
        } else if (evt.getSource() == hitBtn) {
            newBet = false;
            gambler.assignHand(true, Consts.GAMBLER_Y);
            // if Busted happens before hitting stand button
            int status = gambler.getStatus();
            checkGamblerStatus(status);
        } else if (evt.getSource() == standBtn) {
            hitBtn.setEnabled(false);
            // reveal the first facedown card
            Card theCard = dealer.getHand().get(0);
            theCard.setFaceUp(true);

            dealerHitStand();
            determineFinalStatus();
        } else if (evt.getSource() == bet25Btn) {
            gamblerBet(25);
        } else if (evt.getSource() == bet100Btn) {
            gamblerBet(100);
        } else if (evt.getSource() == bet500Btn) {
            gamblerBet(500);
        } else if (evt.getSource() == bet1000Btn) {
            gamblerBet(1000);
        } else if (evt.getSource() == bet5000Btn) {
            gamblerBet(5000);
        } else if (evt.getSource() == exitBtn) {
            System.exit(0);
        }
        board.repaint();
        if (gambler.getTotalAmount() >= 0) { // if having money
            totalTxt.setText("" + gambler.getTotalAmount());
        }

        if (board.isStandFlag() == true) { // finally, init a new game
            // allow new game
            if (gambler.getTotalAmount() >= 25) { // may have a bet on $25
                newGameBtn.setEnabled(true);
            } else {
                newGameBtn.setEnabled(false); // disable newGameBtn
                msgTxt.setText("You have no money to play a new game. Exit");
```

8.9 The GUI and the Event-Driven in the Project Blackjack3

```
160                    }
161                    initGame();
162                }
163            }
164        }
165
166        private void checkGamblerStatus(int status) {
167            if (status == Consts.BUSTED) {
168                msgTxt.setText("Click Stand button to see dealer's status");
169            } else {
170                msgTxt.setText("Bet or click button Hit or Stand");
171            }
172        }
173
174        private void dealerHitStand() {
175            if (dealer.getHandValue2() == 0) { // if no Ace
176                if (dealer.getHandValue1() <= 16) { // hit
177                    while (dealer.getHandValue1() <= 16) {
178                        dealer.assignHand(true, Consts.DEALER_Y);
179                    }
180                } else if (dealer.getHandValue1() >= 17) { // stand
181                }
182            }
183            if (dealer.getHandValue2() != 0) { // if has Ace
184                if (dealer.getHandValue1() == 21) { // based on value1
185                    // Blackjack, stand
186                } else if (dealer.getHandValue1() <= 16) { // hit
187                    while (dealer.getHandValue1() <= 16) {
188                        dealer.assignHand(true, Consts.DEALER_Y);
189                    }
190                } else if (dealer.getHandValue1() >= 17) { // stand
191                }
192                if (dealer.getHandValue1() > 21) { // based on value2
193                    if (dealer.getHandValue2() <= 16) { // hit
194                        while (dealer.getHandValue2() <= 16) {
195                            dealer.assignHand(true, Consts.DEALER_Y);
196                        }
197                    } else if (dealer.getHandValue2() >= 17) { // stand
198                    }
199                }
200            }
201            board.setStandFlag(true);
202        }
203
204        private void determineFinalStatus() {
205            int dS = dealer.getStatus();
206            int gS = gambler.getStatus();
207            if ((dS == Consts.BLACKJACK) && (gS == Consts.BLACKJACK)) {
208                // reset the statuses
209                dealer.setStatus(Consts.PUSHED);
210                gambler.setStatus(Consts.PUSHED);
211                sayHa();
212            } else if ((dS == Consts.BUSTED) && (gS == Consts.BUSTED)) {
213                // reset the statuses
214                dealer.setStatus(Consts.PUSHED);
```

```java
                gambler.setStatus(Consts.PUSHED);
                sayHa();
            } else if ((dS == Consts.BLACKJACK) && (gS != Consts.BLACKJACK)) {
                sayBad();
            } else if ((dS != Consts.BLACKJACK) && (gS == Consts.BLACKJACK)) {
                sayGood();
            } else if ((dS == Consts.BUSTED) && (gS != Consts.BUSTED)) {
                gambler.setStatus(Consts.WON);
                sayGood();
            } else if ((dS != Consts.BUSTED) && (gS == Consts.BUSTED)) {
                dealer.setStatus(Consts.WON);
                sayBad();
            } // COMPARE: four combinations
            else if (((dS == Consts.COMPARE1) || (dS == Consts.COMPARE2))
                    && ((gS == Consts.COMPARE1) || (gS == Consts.COMPARE2))) {
                // without Blackjack or Busted
                int dV1 = dealer.getHandValue1();
                int dV2 = dealer.getHandValue2();
                int gV1 = gambler.getHandValue1();
                int gV2 = gambler.getHandValue2();
                if ((dS == Consts.COMPARE1) && (gS == Consts.COMPARE1)) {
                    compHandValues(dV1, gV1);
                } else if ((dS == Consts.COMPARE1) && (gS == Consts.COMPARE2)) {
                    compHandValues(dV1, gV2);
                } else if ((dS == Consts.COMPARE2) && (gS == Consts.COMPARE1)) {
                    compHandValues(dV2, gV1);
                } else if ((dS == Consts.COMPARE2) && (gS == Consts.COMPARE2)) {
                    compHandValues(dV2, gV2);
                }
            }
        }

    public void compHandValues(int dV, int gV) {
        if (dV == gV) {
            dealer.setStatus(Consts.PUSHED);
            gambler.setStatus(Consts.PUSHED);
            sayHa();
        } else {
            if (dV > gV) {
                dealer.setStatus(Consts.WON);
                sayBad();
            } else {
                gambler.setStatus(Consts.WON);
                sayGood();
            }
        }
    }

    private void gamblerBet(int chipValue) {
        if (!newBet) { // if the previous bet is fail
            // return the previous bet value back to the totalAmount
            gambler.setTotalAmount(gambler.getTotalAmount() + preChipValue);
            newBet = true; // continue a new bet
        }
        int remainTotal = gambler.assignChips(chipValue);
```

8.9 The GUI and the Event-Driven in the Project Blackjack3

```
270             if (remainTotal > 0) { // it is the normal case
271                 hitBtn.setEnabled(true);
272                 standBtn.setEnabled(true);
273                 board.setBetFlag(true);
274                 msgTxt.setText("More bet or click button Hit or Stand");
275             } else if (remainTotal == 0) {
276                 // no more bet, but hit or stand are allowed
277                 disableBet();
278                 hitBtn.setEnabled(true);
279                 standBtn.setEnabled(true);
280                 msgTxt.setText("No more bet can be made");
281             } else { // if remainTotal < 0, the bet cannot go through
282                 preChipValue = chipValue; // keep the bet value for returning back
283                 newBet = false; // a new bet is fail since money is not enough
284                 // don't allow "hit" or "stand"
285                 hitBtn.setEnabled(false);
286                 standBtn.setEnabled(false);
287                 // show the information
288                 msgTxt.setText("Your money is not enough. RE-BET or Exit");
289                 totalTxt.setText("" + (gambler.getTotalAmount() + chipValue)
290                         + " < " + chipValue);
291             }
292         }
293
294         private void sayGood() {
295             // won the bets
296             gambler.setTotalAmount(gambler.getTotalAmount()
297                     + 2 * gambler.getChipsValue());
298             msgTxt.setText("Congratulations!!! You won! New Game or Exit");
299         }
300
301         private void sayBad() {
302             // lost the bets
303             msgTxt.setText("Sorry! You lost! New Game or Exit");
304         }
305
306         private void sayHa() {
307             // return the bets
308             gambler.setTotalAmount(gambler.getTotalAmount()
309                     + gambler.getChipsValue());
310             msgTxt.setText("Ha, No one won the game. New Game or Exit");
311         }
312
313         private void initGame() {
314             //newGame.setEnabled(true) cannot be included for the first time
315             hitBtn.setEnabled(false);
316             standBtn.setEnabled(false);
317             disableBet();
318         }
319
320         private void disableBet() {
321             bet25Btn.setEnabled(false);
322             bet100Btn.setEnabled(false);
323             bet500Btn.setEnabled(false);
324             bet1000Btn.setEnabled(false);
```

```
325            bet5000Btn.setEnabled(false);
326        }
327
328    private void resetGame() {
329        initGame();
330        dealer.initPlayer();
331        gambler.initPlayer();
332        board.setReset();
333    }
334
335    private void clickedNewGame() {
336        board.setNewGameFlag(true);
337        newGameBtn.setEnabled(false);
338        hitBtn.setEnabled(true);
339        standBtn.setEnabled(true);
340        bet25Btn.setEnabled(true);
341        bet100Btn.setEnabled(true);
342        bet500Btn.setEnabled(true);
343        bet1000Btn.setEnabled(true);
344        bet5000Btn.setEnabled(true);
345
346        msgTxt.setText("Bet or click button Hit or Stand");
347    }
348
349    public void setDealer(Player dealer) {
350        this.dealer = dealer;
351    }
352
353    public void setGambler(Player gambler) {
354        this.gambler = gambler;
355    }
356
357    public void setBoard(Board board) {
358        this.board = board;
359    }
360 }
```

The "bet" action directly relates with the total amount that the gambler has. As a gambler, he/she should have enough amount money for playing the game. However, a bet action affects the current remaining of the total amount that the gambler will have. That is, whether a bet may go through depends on the current remaining of the total amount. Therefore, after one bet action, the remaining of the total amount would have three different cases. (1) The remaining is positive. The bet can be realized, which is a regular case. (2) The remaining is zero. The current bet can be made. But, no more bets could be performed. Thus, all of bet buttons have to be disabled. But, the hitBtn and the standBtn should be enabled. (3) The remaining is negative. The current bet should be blocked. The hitBtn and the standBtn have to be disabled to prevent the gambler from continuing on following actions. In addition, special indications should be shown on the textField of the totalAmount and the msgTxt. The gambler may issue a "RE-BET" with a smaller bet value in next step. If the gambler is re-betting, the previous bet value has to be returned to the totalAmount, and a new calculation should be done for checking the three conditions listed above. All of these considerations are implemented in the method gamblerBet().

When the gambler clicks on different software components, the class PlayerPanel.java accepts the gambler's actions to update the game statuses, which cause the class Board.java to follow the dynamic actions for displaying updated scenes, and related software components are also affected to be disabled or enabled. The following six cases can be understood as six action-event-update-repaint chains that summarize the dynamic behaviors of the game and form the logics and rules of the game. Meanwhile, the implementation of the class PlayerPanel.java in Listing 8.4 and the class Board.java in Listing 8.5 are the realization of these chains. Thus, the following six cases are also the pseudo code of these two classes.

1. When a new game starts, the initial scene looks like the following: on the playerPanel, all buttons are disabled; only the textField of the total amount is enabled in order to ask the gambler for entering an initial total amount. On the board, two labels "Dealer" and "Gambler" are displayed.
2. After the gambler enters the total amount on the text field and presses the key <Enter>, only the button "NewGame" is enabled. All of other buttons keep disabled.
3. When the button "NewGame" is clicked, the button "NewGame" is disabled, and all of other buttons are enabled. The newGameFlag in the class Board.java sets true. On the board, two labels and two hands of cards are displayed; gambler's handValue is shown, but dealer's handValue is hidden. If the gambler has a special status Blackjack or Busted, then the status is also shown.
4. When the button "Hit" is clicked, the gambler gets a new card, and the handValue is changed. The hitFlag in the class Board.java is set true. On the board, two labels, two hands, the gambler's handValue, and the gambler's special status Blackjack or Busted should be displayed.
5. When the button "Stand" is clicked, the dealer hand is changed according to the rule for the dealer. The standFlag in the class Board.java is set true. At the same time, the two labels, two hands, two handValues, and final status should be shown on the board.
6. When any bet button is clicked, the betFlag in the class Board.java is set true. On the board, the chips and their total value are displayed.

8.10 Determining "when to show what" by Using Truth Tables

These six requirements are clearly implemented in the class PlayerPanel.java with software components, actions, events, and event listeners. However, the scenes displayed on the board are kind of confused by "when to show what." In the project Blackjack2, we implement the class Board.java based on our logic thinking. The code works fine. However, we have to spend much time and efforts to go over the trial-failure process. We would be better to have a "tool" for making a clear mind and a clear decision without possible failures. Here, we introduce the truth table approach for helping the design and implementation. A truth table usually is used for designing hardware components. Because a truth table is based on the binary on/off, it is also suitable for our Boolean flags' values of true/false.

Figure 8.5 has two separated tables. The truth table on the left side includes three flags, and the truth table on the right side only deals with one flag. Regularly, the left truth table should include all of the four flags. However, since the betFlag can be independent from other flags, we separate it to another table for simplifying the left truth table. On the left truth table, the left column lists three flags: "n" represents the newGameFlag, "h" represents the hitFlag, and "s" represents the standFlag. A digit 1 indicates the flag is true; a digit 0 indicates the flag is false. The right column lists what should be shown on the board, which is represented by a single or double letters. "l" stands for two labels of dealer and gambler; "h" stands for two hands; "dv" stands for dealer's handValue; "gv" stands for gambler's handValue; "ds" stands for dealer's special status; "gs" stands for gambler's special status, which is Blackjack or Busted; and "fs" stands for the final statuses of both the dealer and gambler. A digit 1 means display it; a digit 0 means do not display it.

On the left truth table, the three Boolean variables on the left column generate eight ($2^3 = 8$) combinations. Horizontally, (1) the pattern 000 on the left column corresponds to the pattern 1000000 on the right column. The pattern 000 means all of three flags are false, which corresponds to the initial situation, where no any button is clicked. The pattern 1000000 means that on the board, only two labels should be displayed. These are the cases 1 and 2 of the six cases listed above; (2) the pattern 100 on the left column means that only the newGameFlag is true, which implies only the button NewGame is clicked. The pattern 1101010 on the right column means that two labels, two hands, the gambler's handValue, and in case the gambler's special status should be displayed on the board. This is the case 3 of the six cases; (3) the pattern 110 on the left column means that the newGameFlag and hitFlag are true and the pattern 1101010 on the right column means two labels, two hands, and the gambler's handValue as well as its special status if any should be displayed on the board. It is the case 4 of the six cases; (4) the 111 pattern on the left column means that the newGameFlag, hitFlag, and standFlag are true. The pattern 1111111 on the right column means two labels, two

n	h	s	l	h	dv	gv	ds	gs	fs	b	c	cv
0	0	0	1	0	0	0	0	0	0	0	0	0
0	0	1	1	1	1	1	0	0	0	1	1	1
0	1	0	1	1	0	1	0	0	0			
0	1	1	1	1	1	1	0	0	0			
1	0	0	1	1	0	1	0	1	0			
1	0	1	1	0	0	0	0	0	0			
1	1	0	1	1	0	1	0	1	0			
1	1	1	1	1	1	1	1	1	1			

Fig. 8.5 Truth tables correspond to button clicks and displays

hands, both the dealer's and the gambler's handValues, and their final statuses should be displayed on the board. This corresponds to the case 5 of the six cases listed above. All of other combinations are "don't care" cases. That is, they are some impossible combinations such that they can be ignored. For example, the pattern 010 is impossible because when the newGameFlag is false, the hitFlag is impossible to be true.

After we listed all of these cases, the conclusions can be drawn by vertically looking at the truth table. In other words, we can clearly answer the question "when to show what" now. Formally, the Boolean algebra is applied to simplify the truth table for conducting the conclusions. In order to avoid the explanation about the Boolean algebra, here we base on logical derivations to draw our conclusions.

We can find the following listing from the left truth table.

```
000      => l
100      => l, h, gv, gs
110      => l, h, gv, gs
111      => l, h, gv, gs, dv, ds, fs
```

Looking at all four lines, the letter "l" always appears. It means that the two labels ("l") should be always displayed regardless which cases. The second, third, and fourth lines indicate that as long as the newGameFlag is true, the two hands ("h"), gambler's handValue ("gv"), and gambler's special status (gs) should be displayed without caring of the hitFlag and the standFlag. The fourth line indicates that when standFlag is true, the dealer's handValue ("dv"), the dealer's special status ("ds"), and the final statuses ("fs") should be shown. Therefore, the hitFlag can be ignored since its value of 1 or 0 won't affect the board display. According to these conclusions, the implementation of the method paintComponent() in the class Board.java becomes easy, and its code becomes concise as cited in Listing 8.5. The benefits of using the truth table is obvious when we compare this code with the code of the paintComponent() in the Blackjack2.

The right truth table has only one variable betFlag. The table reflexes the case 6 of the six cases summarized above.

Listing 8.5 The implementation of the method paintComponent() in the class Board.java of the project Blackjack3

```
1  /*
2   * Board.java - A class defines the board for displaying the game scene.
3   */
4  package blackjack;
5
6  import java.awt.Color;
7  import java.awt.Font;
8  import java.awt.Graphics;
9  import java.awt.Graphics2D;
10 import javax.swing.JPanel;
11
16 public class Board extends JPanel {
17
18     private Player dealer;
19     private Player gambler;
20     private boolean newGameFlag;
21     // private boolean hitFlag;
22     private boolean standFlag;
23     private boolean betFlag;
24
25     public Board() {
26         initBoard();
27     }
28
29     private void initBoard() {
30         newGameFlag = false;
31         standFlag = false;
32         betFlag = false;
33     }
```

8.10 Determining "when to show what" by Using Truth Tables

```
34
35      @Override
36      public void paintComponent(Graphics g) {
37          super.paintComponent(g);
38          Graphics2D g2d = (Graphics2D) g;
39
40          g2d.setColor(Color.RED);
41          g2d.drawRect(Consts.MINX, Consts.MINY, Consts.CV_WIDTH, Consts.BOARD_H);
42          g2d.setColor(Color.BLUE);
43          g2d.setFont(new Font("Times", Font.BOLD, 22));
44          g2d.drawString("Dealer", 10, 60);
45          g2d.drawString("Gambler", 10, 190);
46
47          if (newGameFlag) {
48              // show two hands
49              dealer.paintHand(g2d);
50              gambler.paintHand(g2d);
51              // show gambler's handValue
52              if (gambler.getHandValue2() == 0) {
53                  g2d.drawString("" + gambler.getHandValue1(),
54                          Consts.VALUE_X, Consts.GAMBLER_V_Y);
55              } else { // value2 is not 0, show both
56                  g2d.drawString("" + gambler.getHandValue1()
57                          + "(" + gambler.getHandValue2() + ")",
58                          Consts.VALUE_X, Consts.GAMBLER_V_Y);
59              }
60              // show gambler's special status
61              int specStatus = gambler.getStatus();
62              if (specStatus == Consts.BLACKJACK) {
63                  g2d.drawString("Blackjack", Consts.STATUS_X, Consts.GAMBLER_S_Y);
64              } else if (specStatus == Consts.BUSTED) {
65                  g2d.drawString("Busted", Consts.STATUS_X, Consts.GAMBLER_S_Y);
66              }
67          }
68          if (standFlag) {
69              // show dealer's handValue
70              if (dealer.getHandValue2() == 0) {
71                  g2d.drawString("" + dealer.getHandValue1(),
72                          Consts.VALUE_X, Consts.DEALER_V_Y);
73              } else {
74                  g2d.drawString("" + dealer.getHandValue1()
75                          + "(" + dealer.getHandValue2() + ")",
76                          Consts.VALUE_X, Consts.DEALER_V_Y);
77              }
78              // show dealer's special status
79              int specStatus = dealer.getStatus();
80              if (specStatus == Consts.BLACKJACK) {
81                  g2d.drawString("Blackjack", Consts.STATUS_X, Consts.DEALER_S_Y);
82              } else if (specStatus == Consts.BUSTED) {
83                  g2d.drawString("Busted", Consts.STATUS_X, Consts.DEALER_S_Y);
84              }
85              // show final status
86              int dS = dealer.getStatus();
87              int gS = gambler.getStatus();
88
```

```
 89              if (dS == Consts.WON) {
 90                  g2d.drawString("Won", Consts.STATUS_X, Consts.DEALER_S_Y);
 91              } else if (dS == Consts.PUSHED) {
 92                  g2d.drawString("Pushed", Consts.STATUS_X, Consts.DEALER_S_Y);
 93                  g2d.drawString("Pushed", Consts.STATUS_X, Consts.GAMBLER_S_Y);
 94              } else if (gS == Consts.WON) {
 95                  g2d.drawString("Won", Consts.STATUS_X, Consts.GAMBLER_S_Y);
 96              }
 97          }
 98          // show chips and chips value
 99          if (betFlag) {
100              gambler.paintChips(g2d);
101          }
102      }
103
...
128      public void setReset() {
129          newGameFlag = false;
130          standFlag = false;
131          betFlag = false;
132      }
133 }
```

8.11 The Class GameCanvas.java Sets Up Communication Paths

Due to the fact that this game Blackjack is also an event-driven application, the class PlayerPanel.java implements the "core" of the program; the major function of the class GameCanvas.java is to initialize all of objects and set up communication paths among them. The code of the class GameCanvas.java is shown in Listing 8.6.

Listing 8.6 The code of the class GameCanvas.java in the project Blackjack3

```
 1 /*
 2  * GameCanvas.java -- A class defines game canvas.
 3  */
 4 package blackjack;
 5
 6 import java.awt.BorderLayout;
 7 import javax.swing.JPanel;
 8
13 public class GameCanvas extends JPanel {
14
15     private Player dealer;
16     private Player gambler;
17     private Deck deck;
18     private Board board;
19     private PlayerPanel playerPanel;
20
21     public GameCanvas() {
22         setLayout(new BorderLayout());
23         initComponent();
24     }
25
```

```
26    private void initComponent() {
27        deck = new Deck();
28        board = new Board();
29        playerPanel = new PlayerPanel();
30        playerPanel.setBoard(board);
31
32        initPlayer();
33        add(board, BorderLayout.CENTER);
34        add(playerPanel, BorderLayout.SOUTH);
35    }
36
37    public void initPlayer() {
38        dealer = new Player();
39        dealer.initPlayer();
40        dealer.setName("dealer");
41        dealer.setDeck(deck);
42
43        gambler = new Player();
44        gambler.initPlayer();
45        gambler.setName("gambler");
46        gambler.setDeck(deck);
47
48        board.setDealer(dealer);
49        board.setGambler(gambler);
50        playerPanel.setDealer(dealer);
51        playerPanel.setGambler(gambler);
52    }
53 }
```

The method initComponent() instantiates all of objects of all classes. The playerPanel controls actions of the board; therefore the board object is passed into the playerPanel to enable the playerPanel to access the board whenever needed. The method initPlayer() instantiates two players, the dealer and the gambler, and pass the object of deck into both the dealer and the gambler for dealing cards to both players. In addition, the playerPanel needs to get statuses from both players; thus, the two objects of dealer and gambler have to be passed into the playerPanel.

The project Blackjack is little bit of more complex than the project AnagramGUI. We should carefully analyze all of action-event chains in the designing stage and then exceedingly map the action-event chains with source software components and event listeners while updating and repainting the output scenes.

The truth table is a helpful tool for analyzing and organizing the interactions between the inputs and the outputs. The truth table can exhaustively list all of causes and effects so that the program can completely consider all of cases without ignorance.

8.12 Summary

The event-driven means that the flow of execution is determined by events. Both of the project Blackjack and the project AnagramGUI are based on the event-driven technique. Both of them have similar GUI structure and software structure. The GUI consists of two portions, one is the board and the other is the playerPanel. The former shows the game output, and the latter provides input mechanism for players to enter data and controls. The players' actions go through events and event handlers to update the states of the game; and then the method repaint() invokes the method paintComponent() for painting the updated scenes on the GUI. Managing this action-event-update-repaint chain is the heart of this kind of games.

8.13 Exercise

Self-Review Questions

1. Why both dealer and gambler may share one class Player.java?
2. What dynamic behaviors both dealer and gambler have?
3. Why do we need to provide buttons for the gambler to play the game but without providing buttons for the dealer to play the game?
4. How to handle Aces that have two different face values?
5. How to enforce the gambler to follow the sequence of actions in playing the game?

6. How to calculate the amount of money the gambler has in considering all of cases?
7. How to determine who is the winner of a play when both the dealer and the gambler have a current status of either COMPARE1 or COMPARE2?
8. What different data should be displayed on the board at different times?
9. What do you think about using the truth tables for designing and implementing the displays on the board?
10. The truth table actually is also applied to the status checking for the implementation of the method determineFinalStatus() in the class PlayerPanel.java. Please recall this process to see what is your truth table and conclusion.
11. The classes Card.java and Deck.java would be reusable in other card games. What attributes and methods are defined in these two classes?
12. Draw a UML sequence diagram to illustrate the dynamic behaviors in the Blackjack.

Projects

1. Assume that a card game has four players. Write a program to prepare a deck of cards, and deal the deck of cards into four hands with faceup, and show them on a board for the four players sitting on the four directions of EAST, SOUTH, WEST, and NORTH.
2. A simple card game says two players have a hand of half of the deck of cards, respectively. Each of them takes a turn to put one card on the table. As long as one of them, say the first player, puts down a Jack, or a Queen, or a King, the other player, that is the second player, is allowed to respond one, or two, or three cards correspondingly. If one of these responded cards is a Jack, or a Queen, or a King, then the first player has to respond so. Otherwise, if the responded cards don't have any Jack, Queen, or King, the first player collects the pile of the cards on the table. Who eventually collects all of cards wins the game. Write a program to implement this game. (Or, the game could be designed as a human player against a computer player.)

Key Control: A Game Sudoku

9

Java broadly divides events into two categories. The events generated by software components are termed as semantic events. The events generated by hardware mouse or keys are termed as low-level events. We have learned software components generated events and applied them for the developments of event-driven games in previous chapters. Now we turn our attention to apply the low-level events for controlling games. The game Sudoku is a famous numerical game played by a single player. It is taken as an example for exposing the event listeners of keys in this chapter.

The objectives of this chapter include:
1. Lower-level events: key control and mouse control.
2. The story of the game Sudoku.
3. A new data structure: 2D array.
4. A composite class Board.java.
5. Applying the brute-force algorithm for creating a Sudoku board.
6. The keyEvent, KeyListener, and KeyAdapter.
7. Setting "focus" for accepting key events.
8. A key-event-update-repaint chain supports player's actions.

We mentioned in Chap. 6 that events have two kinds. One is so-called semantic event that is associated with software components. The other kind of events is called low-level events that associate with the hardware peripheral devices mouse and keys. Both the game AnagramGUI and the game Blackjack in previous chapters demonstrate some common features that are based on the event-driven technique with software components. Their GUIs have one piece for displaying the output of the game and another piece for players to input data and actions through software components.

Now, we are turning to expose the games of the event-driven technique with the low-level events. These games have more than 90% controls performed by using mouse or keys. Their GUIs have only one piece. The major components on the GUIs are other than Java software components as we have seen so far. The GUI not only displays the dynamically changed scenes but also allows the player to input data and actions through the other kinds of components on the GUI. The remaining 10% controls may still rely on some Java software components. This chapter takes the game Sudoku as an example for illustrating the special features of this kind of games under key controls.

9.1 The Story of the Game Sudoku

The game Sudoku is a famous and popular game played by a single player. Besides the video version, many published books dedicated for painting the game of Sudoku and allow people to use pencils to play the game just like playing the word puzzles.

The game Sudoku defines a board with 9×9 cells. The board thus has nine rows, nine columns, and nine mini-boards as shown in Fig. 9.1. A mini-board is a square that contains 3×3 cells. The entire board contains nine pieces of such mini-board as the bold lines indicated on Fig. 9.1. Usually, we assign the first mini-board to the top-left one, the second to the top-middle one, the third to the top-right one, the fourth to the middle-left one, and so on. When a new play starts, the board shows partial of the 9×9 cells with digits and remaining cells with blanks. The player is asked to fill in the blank cells with proper digits so that each of digits 1–9 is "uniquely appearing once only" alone each row, each column, and each mini-board.

Based on the story, the major steps for building and playing the game Sudoku can be depicted as in Fig. 9.2, which drafts major tasks that should be accomplished for making the game. We will follow the order to explain every step in details.

9.2 Two-Dimensional Array

As Fig. 9.1 shows, the board of the game Sudoku is composed of 9 × 9 small cells. A small cell is a square. All of the small cells arranged as nine rows and nine columns, which form a so-called two-dimensional array. We have learned data structure 1D array, which is a sequence of consecutive units of memory locations for storing a same type of data. A 2D array is similar but consists of multiple sequences of 1D arrays.

If we say a line of chairs in a classroom looks like a 1D array, then the entire classroom that has multiple lines of chairs can be understood as a 2D array. Every line has a set of chairs along the line direction that forms a row and the set of chairs along the cross-line direction that forms a column. Thus, every chair can be accessed by two indexes [row][col]. In other words, a single chair can be located by a row index and a column index. Assume that there are five lines and eight chairs per line and then all students sit on every chair that can be defined as a 2D array with the type of student object of the class Student.java as depicted in Fig. 9.3.

For defining such a 2D array of students, the following statement is required:

```
Student[][] allStudent = new Student[5][8];
// 5 rows and 8 columns
```

where Student[][] with two square brackets indicates that it is a 2D array. The first square bracket is the index of rows; the second square bracket is the index of columns. Assume that we would like to assign every student with a score of integer type, we need to add an attribute "private int score;" in the class Student.java, and we can initialize every student with a score of 0. Due to that it is a 2D array, two nested "for" loops are used for making the initialization.

```
for (int row = 0; row < 5; row++) {
    for (int col = 0; col < 8; col++) {
        allStudent[row][col].setScore(0);
    }
}
```

The execution of the two nested "for" loops is as follows. The outer "for" loop starts and sets the variable row = 0. Then, the inner "for" loop starts and sets the variable col = 0. And then, the statement inside the inner "for" loop, "allStudent[0][0].setScore(0);," is executed. It assigns the value of 0 to the student sits in the first row and the first column. After that, the inner "for" loop makes col++ and the "allStudent[0][1].setScore(0);" is executed. That is, the student sits at the

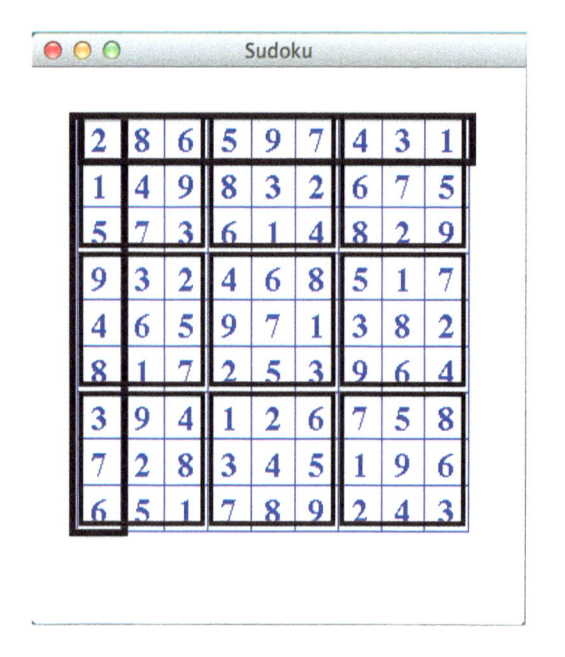

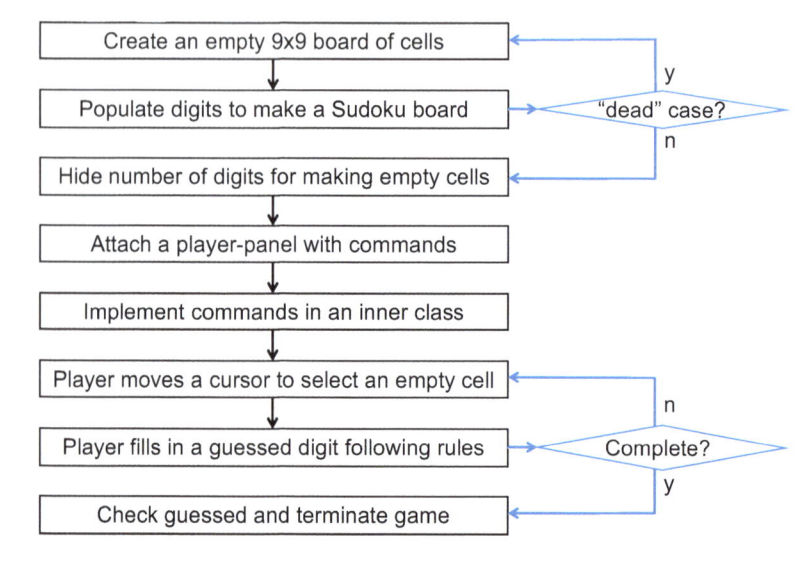

Fig. 9.1 The board of the game Sudoku (row, column, and mini-board)

Fig. 9.2 A flowchart with the major building and playing steps for the game Sudoku

first row, and the second column gets the initial value of 0. Then, the inner "for" loop continues to increase the col with 1; the statement "allStudent[0][2].setScore(0);" assigns the value of 0 to the student sits at the first row and the third column until the col = 7. In the following step, the inner "for" loop increases the value of col as 8 that makes the condition "col < 8" false; the inner "for" loop finishes its loop. The execution loops back to the outer "for" loop, which increases row by 1 and makes its value as 1, which assures the condition "row < 5"; the execution enters the inner "for" loop again. The inner "for" loop then loops from "col = 0" until "col = 7." The execution loops back to the outer "for" loop again for making "row = 2." Repeating this pattern, the final step is the execution of "allStudent[4][7].setScore(0);."

Be careful about two things. (1) What are the row and the column? The statement "five lines of eight chairs per line" means that every row has eight students and totally has five rows. That is, the index along one row is 0, 1, … 7 column; and the index along a column is 0, 1, … 4 row. (2) What is the execution order of the two nested "for" loops? The code above should be read as "go to the first row, assign a 0 to the first column, to the second column, … until to the eighth column. And then, go to the second row, assign a 0 to the first column, to the second column, … until to the eighth column. Continuously, go to the third row, assign a 0 to the first column…." In other words, the inner loop goes first for completely assigning eight zeros to all positions in the first row; then the outer loop moves the index to the second row, and so on. This is so-called row major. If switching the order of the outer loop with the inner loop, it becomes "column major." Logically, they are the same. However, physically the data storage depends on the design of the programming language. If the programming language is designed as "row major," then assign values to the memory using "row major" that is matching with the allocation of the memory locations. That is, all of the assigned digits are consecutive as shown in Fig. 9.4 (left). In contrast, if we are using the "column major" approach for assigning data, then the order of the digits appears "jump across" as shown in Fig. 9.4 (right). Surely, the latter case will cause "chaos" and slow down the access of data stored in the 2D array.

9.3 A Composite Class Board.java: The Project Sudoku1

Clearly, the first step for developing the game Sudoku is to build up the board. As discussed in Chap. 8, the object of deck contains objects of cards. The class Deck.java is a composite class. Here, the object board is also a composite object since it "has" 9 × 9 small object of cells. A cell is an object of a class Cell.java that defines a set of attributes x, y, width, height, color, and digit. The pair of (x, y) defines the coordinates of the top-left corner of the cell. The width and height defines the size of each cell. The attributes color and digit are used to assign different color and different digit for each cell. And then, we define a class Board.java that instantiates 9 × 9 cells with an initial digit value of 0. The "9 × 9" means nine cells along every row and the board has nine such rows. Together they form a two-dimensional array of nine rows and nine columns.

Following the principal description above, the UML class diagram shown in Fig. 9.5 indicates that the project Sudoku1 has a GameCanvas.java that "uses" a Board.java and the Board.java "has" Cell.java. The code of the classes Board.java and Cell.java in the project Sudoku1 is as shown in Listing 9.1.

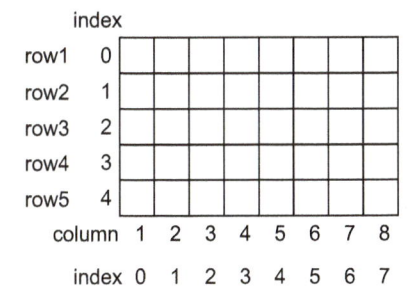

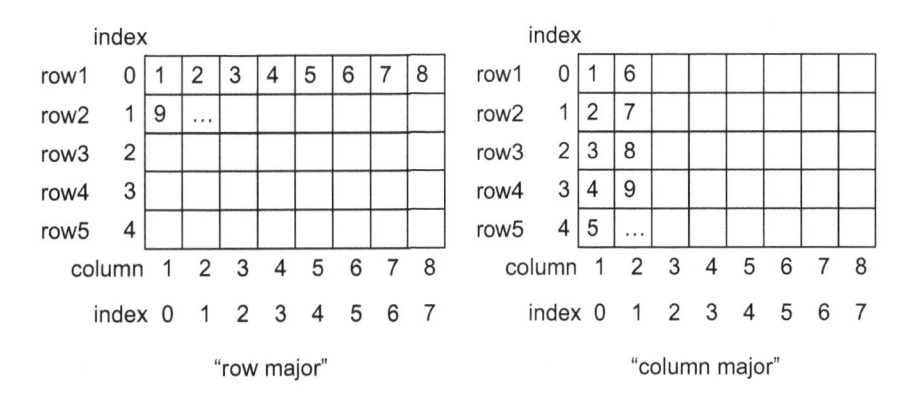

Fig. 9.3 A 2D array for students

Fig. 9.4 (*Left*) Data assigning order in "row major" and (*Right*) in "column major"

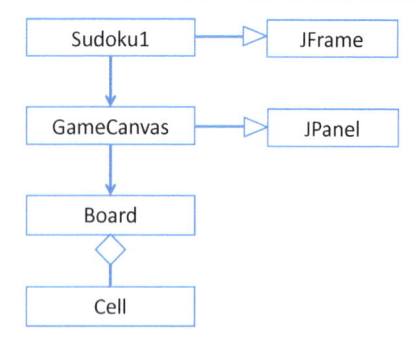

Fig. 9.5 The UML class diagram of the project Sudoku1

Listing 9.1 The class Board.java and the class Cell.java in the project Sudoku1

```
 1  /*
 2   * Board.java - A class defines the board for the game Sudoku.
 3   */
 4  package sudoku;
 5
 6  import java.awt.Graphics2D;
 7
12  public class Board {
13
14      private Cell[][] sudokuBoard;
15
16      public Board() {
17          sudokuBoard = new Cell[Consts.MAX_CELLS][Consts.MAX_CELLS];
18          initBoard();
19      }
20
21      private void initBoard() {
22          Cell aCell;
23          int x, y; // coordinates (x, y) of one cell
24          int xInit = Consts.LEFT_M;
25          int yInit = Consts.TOP_M;
26
27          for (int row = 0; row < Consts.MAX_CELLS; row++) {
28              y = yInit + row * Consts.CELL_H;
29              for (int col = 0; col < Consts.MAX_CELLS; col++) {
30                  x = xInit + col * Consts.CELL_W;
31                  aCell = new Cell();
32                  aCell.setX(x);
33                  aCell.setY(y);
34                  sudokuBoard[row][col] = aCell;
35              }
36          }
37      }
38
39      public void paintBoard(Graphics2D g2d) {
40          for (int row = 0; row < Consts.MAX_CELLS; row++) {
41              for (int col = 0; col < Consts.MAX_CELLS; col++) {
42                  sudokuBoard[row][col].paintCell(g2d);
43              }
```

```
44        }
45    }
46 }
```

```
 1 /*
 2  * Cell.java - A class defines one cell in the board for the game Sudoku.
 3  */
 4 package sudoku;
 5
 6 import java.awt.Color;
 7 import java.awt.Font;
 8 import java.awt.Graphics2D;
 9
14 public class Cell {
15
16     private int x;
17     private int y;
18     private int width;
19     private int height;
20     private Color color;
21     private int digit;
22
23     public Cell() {
24         width = Consts.CELL_W;
25         height = Consts.CELL_H;
26         color = Color.BLUE;
27         digit = 0;
28     }
29
30     public void paintCell(Graphics2D g2d) {
31         g2d.setColor(color);
32         g2d.drawRect(x, y, width, height);
33         g2d.setFont(new Font("TimesRoman", Font.BOLD, 22));
34         g2d.drawString("" + digit, x + Consts.CELL_LEFT, y + Consts.CELL_TOP);
35     }
36
37     public void setX(int x) {
38         this.x = x;
39     }
40
41     public void setY(int y) {
42         this.y = y;
43     }
44 }
```

Clearly, the class Cell.java defines one cell that has two constants of width and height, a blue color, and a digit of 0. The method initBoard() in the class Board.java uses two nested "for" loops to arrange 9 × 9 cells as a 2D array. Every step is to instantiate an object of cell of the class Cell.java, define its coordinates (x, y), and assign the cell object to the 2D array of sudokuBoard. In addition, the class Cell.java has a method paintCell() that paints one cell on the board with its assigned x, y, width, height, color, and digit. The class Board.java has a method paintBoard() that goes through two nested "for" loops to invoke the paintCell() method of the class Cell.java for placing the 9 × 9 cells to form the entire board.

9.4 Applying the Brute-Force Algorithm for Populating the Board: The Project Sudoku2

After making the board, the following task is to assign digits [1, 9] into every cell on the board. According to the story of the game Sudoku, all digits involved are [1, 9]; but every digit can only uniquely appear once along each row, along each column, and within each mini-board. This is the principal task of the "populate the board." It can be done in applying mathematical formulae, which requires a deep understanding of related mathematics. Here, we adopt the brute-force approach to generate-and-test such a board. The brute-force approach systematically enumerates all possible candidates for the required pattern and checks whether each candidate satisfies the requirement. If yes, the populating is successfully done. Otherwise, it enters a "dead case," and a new generate-and-test will restart from beginning until a successful populating achieved.

The principle of the generate-and-test for making a Sudoku board is briefly described as follows. A random number generator generates a digit of 1–9, say 6, and attempt to insert it in the first cell [0, 0]. If it is valid along the first row, then insert it at the cell. Continuously, the random number generator creates a second digit of 1–9, say 3, it is valid along the first row, then insert it in the location [0, 1]. Suppose that the third random digit is 3 again, it is invalid for the first row since the row has a 3 already, the second generated digit 3 is threw away. Then, the fourth random digit is generated. If it is 6, which exists in the first row already, it should be ignored. Assume that the next random digit is 9; it can be inserted at the position [0, 2]. Continuing this generate-and-test, nine digits will fill in the first row. Then, the same procedure is applied for the second row. However, the validation must be extended to verify not only the row but also along every column and every mini-board. In other words, every randomly generated digit must be validated along every row, every column, and every mini-board. In case that the generate-and-test enters a "dead case," the algorithm will restart from the beginning cell [0, 0]. In order to better understand and apply the principle, we develop a series of smaller projects as follows to implement it.

9.4.1 A Project TestPopulate1 for Validating Every Row

We add a new class BoardPopulate.java into the project TestPopulate1 for populating digits in the board. The first attempt is to validate every row. According to the procedure described above, a "while" loop is employed for implementing the following tasks: (1) to create a random digit, (2) to test it on one row, and (3) to loop back if the digit is already in the row or to insert the digit in the row and terminate the loop if the digit is unique so far. The method for validating one row is to compare the new generated digit with every digit already in the same row: a match indicates invalid; no match indicates valid. Thus, the code of the BoardPopulate.java class is coded as in Listing 9.2.

Listing 9.2 The class BoardPopulate.java in the project TestPopultate1

```
1  /*
2   * BoardPopulate.java - A class for populating data with the board.
3   */
4  package testpopulate;
5
6  import java.util.Random;
7
12 public class BoardPopulate {
13
14     private Random random;
15     private Board board;
16
17     public BoardPopulate() {
18         random = new Random();
19     }
20
21     public void populateBoard() {
22         int aDigit = 0;
23         boolean stop = false;
24         int count = 0;
25
```

```
26          for (int row = 0; row < Consts.MAX_CELLS; row++) {
27              for (int col = 0; col < Consts.MAX_CELLS; col++) {
28                  while (!stop) {
29                      aDigit = Math.abs(random.nextInt() % 9) + 1;
30                      if (validRow(aDigit, row, col)) {
31                          stop = true;
32                      }
33                  }
34                  insertDigit(aDigit, row, col);
35                  stop = false;
36              }
37          }
38      }
39
40      private boolean validRow(int aValue, int row, int col) {
41          Cell[][] aBoard = board.getSudokuBoard();
42          for (int i = 0; i < Consts.MAX_CELLS; i++) {
43              if (aBoard[row][i].getDigit() == aValue) {
44                  return false;
45              }
46          }
47          return true;
48      }
49
50      private void insertDigit(int aValue, int row, int col) {
51          board.getSudokuBoard()[row][col].setDigit(aValue);
52      }
53
54      public void setBoard(Board board) {
55          this.board = board;
56      }
57  }
```

The method populateBoard() has two nested "for" loops. The "while" loop inside the inner "for" loop is just for validating the digit randomly generated. When (!stop) is true, the "while" loop invokes the method random.nextInt() for generating an integer random number, which then "% 9" for creating a digit [0, 8]. The function Math.abs() guarantees the digit is positive, and then the (digit + 1) makes a positive digit [1, 9], which is assigned to the variable aDigit. And then, the method validRow() is invoked to compare the digit aDigit with every digit already inserted in the current row. Any match means the new generated digit is already inserted in the same row. The method validRow(), thus, returns a Boolean value of false, which enforces the "while" loop to randomly generate another digit and validate it again until the method validRow() returns true, which stops the looping of the "while" loop. Therefore, the two nested "for" loops in the method populateBoard() go through row-by-row for guaranteeing every row satisfying the requirement "each digit appears once only" along the row. One case of the result made by the project TestPopulate1 is shown in Fig. 9.6.

9.4.2 A Project TestPopulate2 for Validating Both of Rows and Columns

When adding more digits to more rows, the columns are formed. Looking at the data shown in Fig. 9.6, every row is valid; however, not every column is valid, such as the column1 has two 3s, two 1s, and two 6s, but has no 2, 5, and 7. Clearly, the validation of columns should also be implemented. The project TestPopulate2 adds the validColumn() method in the class BoardPopulate.java as shown in Listing 9.3.

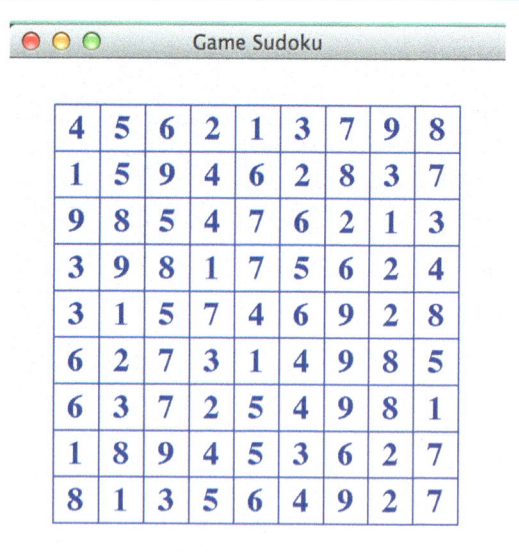

Fig. 9.6 The result of applying the validating row procedure

Listing 9.3 The new class BoardPopulate.java in the project TestPopulate2

```
1  /*
2   * BoardPopulate.java - A class for populating data with the board.
3   */
4  package testpopulate;
5
6  import java.util.Random;
7
12 public class BoardPopulate {
13
14     private Random random;
15     private Cell[][] validBoard;
16     private Board board;
17
18     public BoardPopulate() {
19         random = new Random();
20     }
21
22     public void populateBoard() {
23         int aDigit = 0;
24         boolean stop;
25         int count = 0;
26         boolean forceBreak = false;
27
28         for (int row = 0; row < Consts.MAX_CELLS; row++) {
29             for (int col = 0; col < Consts.MAX_CELLS; col++) {
30                 stop = false;
31                 while (!stop) {
32                     aDigit = Math.abs(random.nextInt() % 9) + 1;
33                     if ((validRow(aDigit, row, col))
34                             && (validColumn(aDigit, row, col))) {
```

9.4 Applying the Brute-Force Algorithm for Populating the Board: The Project Sudoku2

```java
                        stop = true;
                        count = 0;
                    } else {
                        count++;
                        if (count >= 5000) {
                            System.out.println("count >= 5000");
                            stop = true;
                            forceBreak = true;
                        }
                    }
                }
                if (!forceBreak) {
                    insertDigit(aDigit, row, col);
                } else {
                    break;
                }
            }
        }
    }

    private boolean validRow(int aValue, int row, int col) {
        for (int i = 0; i < Consts.MAX_CELLS; i++) {
            if (validBoard[row][i].getDigit() == aValue) {
                //System.out.println("if: " + validBoard[row][i].getDigit());
                return false;
            }
        }
        return true;
    }

    private boolean validColumn(int aValue, int row, int col) {
        for (int i = 0; i < Consts.MAX_CELLS; i++) {
            if (validBoard[i][col].getDigit() == aValue) {
                return false;
            }
        }
        return true;
    }

    private void insertDigit(int aValue, int row, int col) {
        board.getSudokuBoard()[row][col].setDigit(aValue);
    }

    public void setBoard(Board board) {
        this.board = board;
        validBoard = this.board.getSudokuBoard();
    }
}
```

The new method validColumn() performs the similar function as the method validRow() for validating digits along columns. Therefore, the method populateBoard() validates a new generated random digit in both rows and columns. Due to the fact that every new digit must satisfy the requirements in both rows and columns, the "dead case" would be easier to take place, and regenerating a new random digit would occur more frequently such that it may end up as an infinite "while" loop. For preventing the "while" loop from an infinite loop, we declare a variable "count" for counting the number of loops and artificially set up a threshold 5000; whenever the condition "count ≥ 5000" is true, it forces the "while" loop to stop and break the nested "for" loops for giving up the generate-and-test process.

A "dead case" of the project is shown in Fig. 9.7, which indicates that the program runs into a "dead case" situation at the position [4][5]. The reason is that the row 5 (with the index of 4) has the digits 2, 8, 3, 4, and 9, and the column 6 (with the index of 5) has the digits 1, 6, 5, and 7. Every digit of 1–9 is already on the current row and the current column. The next digit must repeat one of them so that no any possible digit in the range of [1, 9] could be found to make the digit "uniquely appears once only" at the position [4][5].

9.4.3 A New Approach for Treating "Dead Case" in the Project TestPopulate3

The observation above gives us a new approach for controlling the "while" loop. Instead of arbitrary picking up a threshold of 5000 to prevent the "while" loop from an infinite loop, we can design an array alreadyTested[] to collect the randomly generated digits that have been already tested so far. This collection performs two functions. Firstly, if a new randomly generated digit is the same as one of the digits in the collection, it means that this new generated digit has been tested and inserted already so that it has to be ignored. Secondly, when the collection includes all of digits 1–9, it indicates a "dead case" is occurred definitely. The program does not need to waste time to continue generating more digits until "count ≥ 5000."

A new question immediately raised is what a solution can be taken for handling a "dead case"? The solution is to re-initialize the board and apply the generate-and-test again until a success board is completed. The new code is displayed in Listing 9.4.

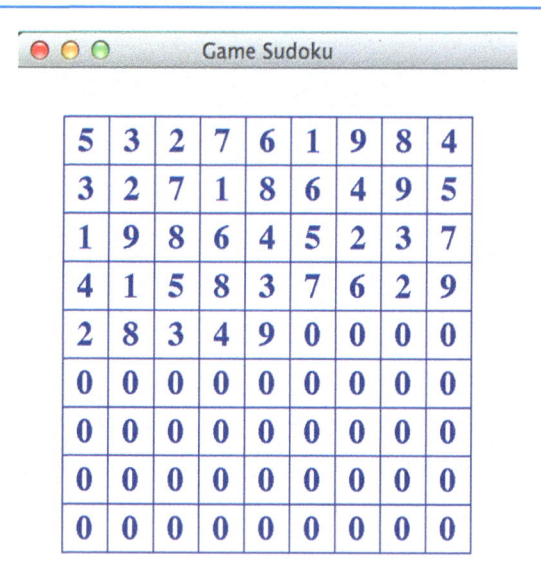

Fig. 9.7 More validations may force the population entering a "dead case"

Listing 9.4 The new code in the class BoardPopulate.java in the project TestPopulate3

```
1  /*
2   * BoardPopulate.java - A class for populating data with the board.
3   */
4  package testpopulate;
5
6  import java.util.Random;
7
12 public class BoardPopulate {
13
14      private Random random;
15      private Cell[][] validBoard;
16      private int[] alreadyTested;
17      private boolean allTested; // all 9 digits have been tested
18      private Board board;
19
```

9.4 Applying the Brute-Force Algorithm for Populating the Board: The Project Sudoku2

```java
20      public BoardPopulate() {
21          random = new Random();
22          alreadyTested = new int[9];
23      }
24
25      public void populateBoard() {
26          int aDigit = 0;
27          boolean stop;
28
29          for (int row = 0; row < Consts.MAX_CELLS; row++) {
30              for (int col = 0; col < Consts.MAX_CELLS; col++) {
31                  initAry(alreadyTested);
32                  allTested = false;
33                  stop = false;
34                  while (!stop) { // the loop may fully fill alreadyTested ary
35                      aDigit = Math.abs(random.nextInt() % 9) + 1;
36                      if ((isNewDigit(aDigit, alreadyTested)) && (!allTested)) {
37                          if ((validRow(aDigit, row, col))
38                                  && (validColumn(aDigit, row, col))) {
39                              stop = true;
40                          }
41                      } else if (allTested) {
42                          stop = true;
43                      }
44                  }
45                  if (!allTested) {
46                      insertDigit(aDigit, row, col);
47                  } else { // "dead case" is true
48                      board.initBoard();
49                      row = 0;
50                      col = -1;
51                  }
52              }
53          }
54      }
55
56      private boolean isNewDigit(int aValue, int[] ary) {
57          if (ary[ary.length - 1] != 0) { // the array has been fully filled
58              allTested = true;
59              return false;
60          }
61          for (int i = 0; i < ary.length; i++) {
62              if (ary[i] == aValue) {
63                  return false;
64              } else if (ary[i] == 0) {
65                  ary[i] = aValue;
66                  break;
67              }
68          }
69          return true;
70      }
71
72      private boolean validRow(int aValue, int row, int col) {
73          for (int i = 0; i < col; i++) { // check digits before the column
74              if (validBoard[row][i].getDigit() == aValue) {
```

```
75                 return false;
76             }
77         }
78         return true;
79     }
80
81     private boolean validColumn(int aValue, int row, int col) {
82         for (int i = 0; i < row; i++) { // the remaining digits are 0s
83             if (validBoard[i][col].getDigit() == aValue) {
84                 return false;
85             }
86         }
87         return true;
88     }
89
90     private void insertDigit(int aValue, int row, int col) {
91         board.getSudokuBoard()[row][col].setDigit(aValue);
92     }
93
94     public void initAry(int[] ary) {
95         for (int i = 0; i < Consts.MAX_CELLS; i++) {
96             ary[i] = 0;
97         }
98     }
99
100    public void setBoard(Board board) {
101        this.board = board;
102        validBoard = this.board.getSudokuBoard();
103    }
104 }
```

The method isNewDigit() implements the two functions mentioned in the previous paragraph. It checks the case of (ary[ary.length-1] != 0) in order to verify whether the array alreadyTested[] is full. Since the length of the array alreadyTested[] is 9, the statement "ary[ary.length − 1] != 0" refers to the condition "alreadyTested[8] != 0." If it is true, it implies that the value stored in the alreadyTested[8] is a digit other than a 0. That is, all nine digits have been tested and no more generated digit is possible to make both the row and the column valid. Consequently, it sets "allTested = true" to indicate a "dead case" happened. Meanwhile, it checks whether the digit is a new digit or not. These two Boolean variables are used in the method populateBoard() to control the row and the column validations. When a "dead case" occurred, the board.initBoard() is called to renew a board for a new process of generate-and-test. Eventually, a satisfied board is made. If we add a statement "System.out.println("renew a board");" inside the else block of the populateBoard() method, we can see how many "dead cases" occurred before a successful board is born.

9.4.4 A Project TestPopulate4 for Validating All Requirements

Now, we have an experience to continue adding the third testing into the populateBoard() method. As the story of the game said, the board also needs to guarantee each of nine digits in every mini-board is also "uniquely appearing once only." A mini-board is a 3 × 3 2D array, and the entire board has nine mini-boards. Thus, we need a method copyMiniBoard() to get every mini-board out from the board and apply another method validMiniBoard() to implement the validating procedure for every mini-board. These two methods are cited in Listing 9.5.

9.4 Applying the Brute-Force Algorithm for Populating the Board: The Project Sudoku2

Listing 9.5 The two new methods added into the class BoardPopulate.java in the project TestPopulate4

```
 1  /*
 2   * BoardPopulate.java - A class for populating data with the board.
 3   */
90  …
91      private boolean validMiniBoard(int aValue, int row, int col) {
92          Cell[][] vMini = copyMiniBoard(row, col);
93          int digit;
94          for (int mRow = 0; mRow < 3; mRow++) { // treat a 2D array as a 1D
95              for (int mCol = 0; mCol < 3; mCol++) {
96                  digit = vMini[mRow][mCol].getDigit();
97                  if ((digit != 0) && (digit == aValue)) {
98                      return false;
99                  }
100             }
101         }
102         return true;
103     }
104
105     private Cell[][] copyMiniBoard(int row, int column) {
106         Cell[][] aMini = new Cell[3][3];
107         if (row < 3 && column < 3) {
108             for (int mRow = 0; mRow < 3; mRow++) {
109                 System.arraycopy(validBoard[mRow], 0, aMini[mRow], 0, 3);
110             }
111         } else if (column > 2 && column < 6 && row < 3) {
112             for (int mRow = 0; mRow < 3; mRow++) {
113                 for (int mCol = 0; mCol < 3; mCol++) {
114                     aMini[mRow][mCol] = validBoard[mRow][mCol + 1 * 3];
115                 }
116             }
117         } else if (column > 5 && row < 3) {
118             for (int mRow = 0; mRow < 3; mRow++) {
119                 for (int mCol = 0; mCol < 3; mCol++) {
120                     aMini[mRow][mCol] = validBoard[mRow][mCol + 2 * 3];
121                 }
122             }
123         } else if (row > 2 && row < 6 && column < 3) {
124             for (int mRow = 0; mRow < 3; mRow++) {
125                 System.arraycopy(validBoard[mRow + 1 * 3], 0, aMini[mRow], 0, 3);
126             }
127         } else if (row > 2 && row < 6 && column > 2 && column < 6) {
128             for (int mRow = 0; mRow < 3; mRow++) {
129                 for (int mCol = 0; mCol < 3; mCol++) {
130                     aMini[mRow][mCol] = validBoard[mRow + 1 * 3][mCol + 1 * 3];
131                 }
132             }
133         } else if (row > 2 && column > 5 && row < 6) {
134             for (int mRow = 0; mRow < 3; mRow++) {
135                 for (int mCol = 0; mCol < 3; mCol++) {
136                     aMini[mRow][mCol] = validBoard[mRow + 1 * 3][mCol + 2 * 3];
137                 }
138             }
139         } else if (row > 5 && column < 3) {
```

```
140            for (int mRow = 0; mRow < 3; mRow++) {
141                System.arraycopy(validBoard[mRow + 2 * 3], 0, aMini[mRow], 0, 3);
142            }
143        } else if (row > 5 && column > 2 && column < 6) {
144            for (int mRow = 0; mRow < 3; mRow++) {
145                for (int mCol = 0; mCol < 3; mCol++) {
146                    aMini[mRow][mCol] = validBoard[mRow + 2 * 3][mCol + 1 * 3];
147                }
148            }
149        } else {
150            for (int mRow = 0; mRow < 3; mRow++) {
151                for (int mCol = 0; mCol < 3; mCol++) {
152                    aMini[mRow][mCol] = validBoard[mRow + 2 * 3][mCol + 2 * 3];
153                }
154            }
155        }
156        return aMini;
157    }
158 ...
173 }
```

The method validMiniBoard() has the similar format as the other two validation methods validRow() and validColumn(). The major effort of the method validMiniBoard() is to "cut" out a mini-board from the global board structure. A mini-board is a 3 × 3 2D array; thus, the entire board can be divided into nine mini-boards. As long as a cell provides its row and column indexes, the mini-board that contains the cell can be found. The method copyMiniBoard() immediately "copies out" the mini-board and validates it. For example, a cell has indexes [3][5], which implies that the cell is in the mini-board that starts from the cell with indexes [3][3] to the cell with indexes [3][5] as the first row, [4][3] to [4][5] as the second row, and [5][3] to [5][5] as the third row. The method validMiniBoard() uses a 3 × 3 array to copy out this mini-board and then validates this mini-board.

Reaching this point, the class BoardPopulate.java has been completed. That is, a board that contains 9 × 9 cells and every digit in the current row, the current column, and the current mini-board is "uniquely appearing once only." The project Sudoku2 simply copies the class BoardPopulate.java from the project TestPopulate4 and reuses it.

After a validated board is generated, the game program will randomly hide a certain number of digits from the board for making a Sudoku board. The number of hidden cells depends on the difficulty level, which is selected by the game player. And then, the player starts playing the game by key in guessed digits on the blank cells. The game asks the player using keys to perform these actions. Clearly, we need to discuss the key event and key event listeners before going ahead to complete the implementation of the game.

9.5 Key Event and Key Event Listener

The low-level events generated by mouse or keys are special important for video games because players who play a game for changing the game scenes most often rely on mouse and keys, especially for this kind of games that have no software components involved.

In general, mouse is the best device to navigate a two-dimensional space. Keys are ideally for inputting text and letting the player control multiple activities concurrently. Sometimes it is not obvious which input device, keyboard or mouse, is better for a game. One solution is to permit both forms of input and let the player to select it. But try to stay away from requiring players to manipulate both mouse and keys simultaneously. In particular, our example game Sudoku requires keys only.

Java provides an Interface KeyListener for listening key events. The listener declared three methods as follows:

```
public Interface KeyListener {
    public void keyTyped(KeyEvent e);
    public void keyPressed(KeyEvent e);
    public void keyReleased(KeyEvent e);
}
```

The keyPressed() refers to an action associated with a key is pressed. The keyReleased() refers to an action associated with a key is released. The keyTyped() refers to type a Unicode character, which is associated with only those keys that represent the Unicode characters. For further distinguishing the keyTyped() from the keyPressed(), just keep in mind that the purpose of using the keyTyped() is to get the typed character. Thus, the function keyEvent.getKeyChar() should be used to return the character, which can further recognize the character is in uppercase or in lowercase. But the purpose of using the keyPressed() is to know which key is pressed by calling keyEvent.getKeyCode(), which does not care what the character is, and the character is in uppercase or in lowercase. In addition, the pressed key can be recognized even the pressed key is not a character key, such as the direction keys. In other words, when we would like to know the character associated with the key, we use the event handler keyTyped(). If we don't care of the character but care of which key is pressed, we would like to use the event handler keyPressed(). Vice versa, if a key won't generate a character, only the event handler keyPressed() is useful.

We learned Interface in previous chapters, and we learned Interface declares methods without implementation. The definitions of KeyListener also follow these general settings. However, the key event listener KeyListener differs from the action event listener ActionListener in that the KeyListener declares multiple methods.

Once we are going to implement an Interface that has multiple abstract methods, we may encounter a problem. For example, the Interface KeyListener has three methods. If we only need to implement the method keyPressed(), even we don't care about the other methods, we still have to define all of them, at least code them with an empty body. This causes "inconvenience" feeling sometimes. For simplifying this matter, Java provides a corresponding class KeyAdapter, which "pre-implements" the Interface for providing empty body for all of methods such that we only need to fill in codes to the necessary methods that we are interested in and don't need to care about other methods that we are not going to use. In other words, if we only interest in the keyPressed() method, we only need to construct a subclass by extending the class KeyAdapter and override the keyPressed() method without the necessity to define all of other methods. Java provides a corresponding adapter for each of those event listeners that declared multiple methods. This saves programmers' efforts a lot.

As said, besides the Interface KeyListener, Java also supplies a class KeyAdapter for saving programmers efforts. That is, we can adopt any one of alternative approaches either to "implement" the Interface for coding the related key event handlers or to "extend" the class KeyAdapter. Because we have learned these implementing techniques already, we will directly apply them for our project Sudoku3 without further explanations.

9.6 Setting Up Focus for Accepting a Key Event

A special issue that we have to pay a special attention in using the key control mechanism is the "focus." When we press a key, usually the key character appears on the screen. That is, key event is a "global" event. As a control mechanism, we have to clearly indicate which area or which component should accept the object of the KeyEvent when a key is pressed. Thus, besides an action-event chain, we need to invoke a special method setFocusable(true) to specify which component has "focus" to receive the key event. In case, we can add one more method requestFocusInWindow() for the component. We will see related statements in the project codes. We should pay a special attention about it. Otherwise, we may waste a lengthy time for debugging our codes when we forget to properly set up a "focus" for a specific component to receive a keyEvent.

9.7 Implementing the Key-Event-Update-Repaint Chain: The Project Sudoku3

After understanding the functions of KeyEvent, the KeyListener, and the KeyAdapter, we are ready to apply the technique for supporting players' actions on the game Sudoku because this game is designed in using keys only. In order to be played, the project Sudoku3 implements the following tasks:

1. The board initializes 9 × 9 digits, and then the board hides a certain number of digits as empty lots for player to fill in his/her guessed digits. The number of digits should be hidden depending on the difficulty levels. Assume that we define three levels of difficulty: "easy" with hiding of 5–15 digits, "medium" with hiding of 16–30, and "hard" with hiding of 31–50. The cells that have missing digits are randomly selected. When the game starts, game sets the easy level as default. Then, the player can press keys E or e, M or m, H or h for specifying the difficulty level.
2. The game provides a cursorMark that can be moved on the board. The player moves it to an empty cell by using up, down, left, and right keys.
3. The key "C" or "c" is designed as a "check" command for checking whether the guessed digits are correct or wrong.
4. The key "N" or "n" performs the function of "New Game."
5. The key "Q" or "q" allows the player to "Quit" the game.

Clearly, besides the Sudoku board, we need a place to tell the game player about all of these settings. Therefore, we designed a GUI as shown in Fig. 9.8, which is divided into two parts. The left side of the GUI displays the game board. The right side of the GUI is the place for displaying all of the key commands. Correspondingly extra functions should be implemented for supporting these commands. All of required classes are summarized in the UML class diagram shown in Fig. 9.9.

For realizing all of these designs, the project Sudoku3 needs to develop the following classes or class components.

Fig. 9.8 The GUI of the project Sudoki3

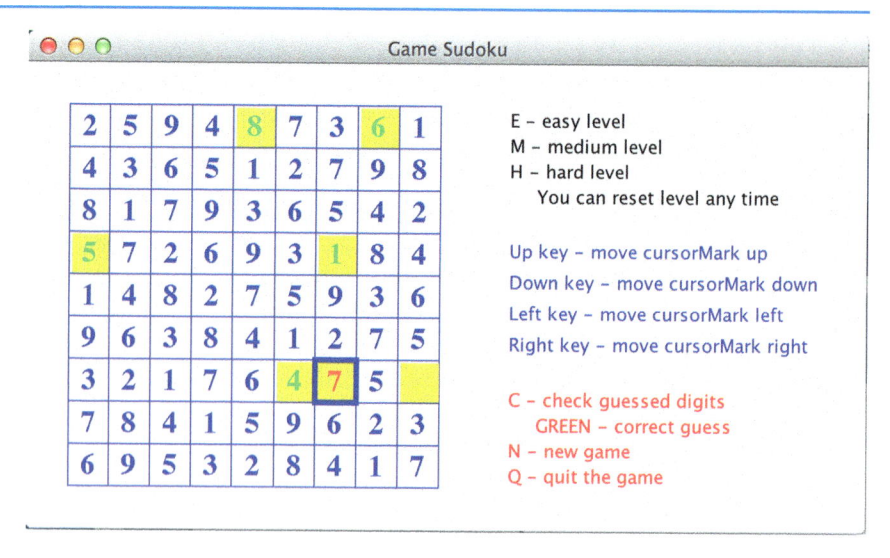

9.7.1 Adding a New Class NotePanel.java for Specifying All of Key Commands

It is only for statically describing commands not for accepting any input control actions. The object of the class is a JPanel and is attached on the right side of the Sudoku board as shown in Fig. 9.8. The code of the class is shown in Listing 9.6.

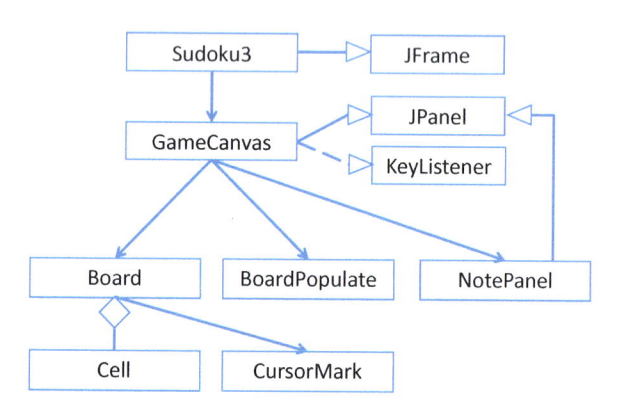

Fig. 9.9 The UML class diagram of the project Sudoku3

Listing 9.6 The partial code of the class NotePanel.java in the project Sudoku3

```
1  /*
2   * NotePanel.java - A class specifies all of key commands.
3   */
4  package sudoku;
5
...
18 public class NotePanel extends JPanel {
19
...
39     @SuppressWarnings("OverridableMethodCallInConstructor")
40     public NotePanel() {
41         setLayout(new GridLayout(3, 1));
42         setPreferredSize(new Dimension(Consts.PLAYER_P_W, Consts.PLAYER_P_H));
43         initLabel();
44     }
45
46     public void initLabel() {
47         EmptyBorder eb = new EmptyBorder(new Insets(30, 0, 30, 30));
48         this.setBorder(eb);
49         emptyLbl = new JLabel("        ");
```

```java
50
51            levelP = new JPanel(new GridLayout(5, 1));
52            easyLbl = new JLabel("E - easy level");
53            mediumLbl = new JLabel("M - medium level");
54            hardLbl = new JLabel("H - hard level");
55            msgLbl = new JLabel("    You can reset level any time");
56            levelP.add(easyLbl);
57            levelP.add(mediumLbl);
58            levelP.add(hardLbl);
59            levelP.add(msgLbl);
60            levelP.add(emptyLbl);
61            add(levelP);
62
63            moveP = new JPanel(new GridLayout(4, 1));
64            upLbl = new JLabel("Up key - move cursorMark up");
65            upLbl.setForeground(Color.BLUE);
66            downLbl = new JLabel("Down key - move cursorMark down");
67            downLbl.setForeground(Color.BLUE);
68            leftLbl = new JLabel("Left key - move cursorMark left");
69            leftLbl.setForeground(Color.BLUE);
70            rightLbl = new JLabel("Right key - move cursorMark right");
71            rightLbl.setForeground(Color.BLUE);
72            moveP.add(upLbl);
73            moveP.add(downLbl);
74            moveP.add(leftLbl);
75            moveP.add(rightLbl);
76            add(moveP);
77
78            commandP = new JPanel(new GridLayout(5, 1));
79            topEmptyLbl = new JLabel("            ");
80            checkLbl = new JLabel("C - check guessed digits");
81            checkLbl.setForeground(Color.RED);
82            colorLbl = new JLabel("    GREEN - correct guess");
83            colorLbl.setForeground(Color.RED);
84            newLbl = new JLabel("N - new game");
85            newLbl.setForeground(Color.RED);
86            quitLbl = new JLabel("Q - quit the game");
87            quitLbl.setForeground(Color.RED);
88            commandP.add(topEmptyLbl);
89            commandP.add(checkLbl);
90            commandP.add(colorLbl);
91            commandP.add(newLbl);
92            commandP.add(quitLbl);
93            add(commandP);
94        }
95 }
```

Clearly, the class NotePanel.java only deals with JLabels for telling the player which key plays what function. The real functions of the key commands will be discussed in the key event listener.

9.7.2 Developing an Inner Class MyKeyAdapter Inside the Class GameCanvas.java

Developing an inner class MyKeyAdapter inside the class GameCanvas.java in order to provide key event handlers for implementing all of the key commands. The key commands include E, M, and H keys for setting the difficulty levels; the UP, DOWN, LEFT, and RIGHT keys for moving the cursorMark to the corresponding directions; the C key for checking the correction of the guessed digit; the N key for starting a new game; and the Q key for quitting the game. All of these functions are performed in corresponding event handlers. The code of the inner class is cited in Listing 9.7.

Listing 9.7 The partial code of the inner class MyKeyAdapter in the GameCanvas.java class of the project Sudoku3

```
1  /*
2   * GameCanvas.java - A class defines the canvas for the game Sudoku.
3   */
86  …
87      class MyKeyAdapter extends KeyAdapter {
88
89          @Override
90          public void keyPressed(KeyEvent evt) {
91              switch (evt.getKeyCode()) {
92                  case KeyEvent.VK_E:
93                      diffLevel = Consts.EASY;
94                      resetBoard(diffLevel);
95                      break;
96                  case KeyEvent.VK_M:
97                      diffLevel = Consts.MEDIUM;
98                      resetBoard(diffLevel);
99                      break;
100                 case KeyEvent.VK_H:
101                     diffLevel = Consts.HARD;
102                     resetBoard(diffLevel);
103                     break;
104                 case KeyEvent.VK_UP:
105                     cursorMark.updatePosition(Consts.UP);
106                     break;
107                 case KeyEvent.VK_DOWN:
108                     cursorMark.updatePosition(Consts.DOWN);
109                     break;
110                 case KeyEvent.VK_LEFT:
111                     cursorMark.updatePosition(Consts.LEFT);
112                     break;
113                 case KeyEvent.VK_RIGHT:
114                     cursorMark.updatePosition(Consts.RIGHT);
115                     break;
116                 case KeyEvent.VK_C:
117                     int score = board.checkGuessed() * diffLevel;
118                     break;
119                 case KeyEvent.VK_N: // new game
120                     resetBoard(Consts.EASY);
121                     break;
122                 case KeyEvent.VK_Q:
123                     System.exit(0);
124                     break;
125             }
126             repaint();
127         }
128
```

9.7 Implementing the Key-Event-Update-Repaint Chain: The Project Sudoku3

```
129        private void resetBoard(int diffLevel) {
130            boardPopulate.setDiffLevel(diffLevel);
131            boardPopulate.populateBoard();
132            initCursorMark();
133
134            // switch back to the playerPanel
135            playerPanel.setVisible(true);
136            // eliminate the termination screen painting
137            gameOver = false;
138        }
139
140        @Override
141        public void keyTyped(KeyEvent evt) {
142            int row = cursorMark.getMoveRow();
143            int col = cursorMark.getMoveCol();
144            char keyChar = evt.getKeyChar();
145            if ((keyChar >= '1') && (keyChar <= '9')) {
146                int digit = (int) keyChar - 48;
147                board.setGuessDigit(row, col, digit);
148                if (guessComplete()) {
149                    gameOver = true;
150                }
151            }
152            repaint();
153        }
154
155        private boolean guessComplete() {
156            Cell aCell;
157            Cell[][] aBoard = board.getSudokuBoard();
158            for (int row = 0; row < Consts.MAX_CELLS; row++) {
159                for (int col = 0; col < Consts.MAX_CELLS; col++) {
160                    aCell = aBoard[row][col];
161                    if ((!aCell.isVisible()) && (aCell.getGuessed() == 0)) {
162                        return false;
163                    }
164                }
165            }
166            return true;
167        }
168    }
169 }
```

The inner class MyKeyAdapter implements two event handlers. One is the KeyPressed(), and the other is KeyTyped(). The keyPressed() is for moving the cursorMark when the up, down, left, or right key is pressed. These same functions can also be realized by using the keyReleased() event handler. However, these two event handlers are slightly different. Using the keyReleased() to implement the moving actions, one key release only moves the cursorMark one cell. But the keyPressed() allows the player to hold down the key for a while to move the cursorMark several cells continuously until the player releases the key. It is the reason that we select the event handler keyPressed() in this implementation.

The other method KeyTyped() implements the typing function. When the game player moves the cursorMark to an empty cell on the board, he/she will type in a guessed digit "1" to "9." For getting the typed character, the keyEvent.getKeyChar() is invoked to return the typed character to the variable keyChar. Because manipulating integers is easier than manipulating characters, the class Cell.java defines an attribute "int digit" to hold the initialized digits and another variable "int guessed" for having the guessed digits. Therefore, if the typed character is in the range of "1" to "9," then the character needs to be converted to its corresponding ASCII integer value, which should have the value of 49–57. And then, the calculation of the ASCII integer value minus 48 gives the integer value of 1–9, which is the integer notation of the guessed digit. Thereafter, the guessed digit is passed to the class Cell.java for displaying it on the empty cell selected.

9.7.3 Creating a New Class CursorMark.java to Implement a cursorMark

Creating a new class CursorMark.java for the player to indicate which empty lot is selected. The cursorMark is a rectangle that can be moved by the player over the sudokuBoard. We simply let the class CursorMark.java extend the built-in class Rectangle and understand the cursorMark as an object attached on the board. Therefore, when the cursorMark is instantiated, we pass the cursorMark object into the object board, set up the bounds of the cursorMark the same as a cell of the sudokuBoard, and place the cursorMark on the cell [0][0] of the sudokuBoard. For implementing these functions, we add a method setCursorMark() in the Board.java class to accept the object cursorMark as follows:

```
77      public void setCursorMark(CursorMark cursorMark) {
78          this.cursorMark = cursorMark;
79          Cell aCell = getSudokuBoard()[0][0];
80          this.cursorMark.setBounds(aCell.getX(), aCell.getY(), aCell.getWidth(),
81                  aCell.getHeight());
82          this.cursorMark.setLocation((int) getSudokuBoard()[0][0].getX(),
83                  (int) getSudokuBoard()[0][0].getY());
84      }
```

The class CursorMark.java provides a method updatePosition() to be invoked by the key event handler keyPressed() defined in the inner class MyKeyAdapter. When the player clicks one of the up, down, left, or right keys, the cursorMark.updatePosition() is invoked to move the cursorMark one position along the corresponding direction. Immediately, the repaint() method invokes the paintComponent() method to paint the sudokuBoard and the cursorMark. When the player moves the cursorMark on an empty cell and press on a digit key, the event handler KeyTyped() in the inner class MyKeyAdapter uses the values of moveRow and moveCol to insert the guessed digit at the selected empty cell. The code of the class CursorMark.java is shown in Listing 9.8.

Listing 9.8 The code of the class CursorMark.java in the project Sudoku3

```
1  /*
2   * CursorMark.java - A class defines a square cursor on the board.
3   */
4  package sudoku;
5
6  import java.awt.BasicStroke;
7  import java.awt.Color;
8  import java.awt.Graphics2D;
9  import java.awt.Rectangle;
10
15 public class CursorMark extends Rectangle {
16
17     private int moveRow, moveCol;
18
19     public CursorMark() {
20         moveRow = 0;
21         moveCol = 0;
22     }
23
```

```java
24      public void paintCursor(Graphics2D g2d) {
25          g2d.setStroke(new BasicStroke(4));
26          g2d.setColor(Color.BLUE);
27          g2d.drawRect((int) getX(), (int) getY(), (int) getWidth(),
28                  (int) getHeight());
29      }
30
31      public void updatePosition(int position) {
32          switch (position) {
33              case Consts.UP:
34                  if (moveRow > 0) {
35                      setLocation((int) getX(), (int) (getY() - getHeight()));
36                      moveRow--;
37                  }
38                  break;
39              case Consts.DOWN:
40                  if (moveRow < (Consts.MAX_CELLS - 1)) {
41                      setLocation((int) getX(), (int) (getY() + getHeight()));
42                      moveRow++;
43                  }
44                  break;
45              case Consts.LEFT:
46                  if (moveCol > 0) {
47                      setLocation((int) (getX() - getWidth()), (int) getY());
48                      moveCol--;
49                  }
50                  break;
51              case Consts.RIGHT:
52                  if (moveCol < (Consts.MAX_CELLS - 1)) {
53                      setLocation((int) (getX() + getWidth()), (int) getY());
54                      moveCol++;
55                  }
56                  break;
57              default:
58                  break;
59          }
60      }
61
62      public int getMoveRow() {
63          return moveRow;
64      }
65
66      public int getMoveCol() {
67          return moveCol;
68      }
69  }
```

The class CursorMark.java handles an update and a repaint dynamic behavior so that it provides two methods updatePosition() and paintCursor() to form an update-repaint chain for displaying the position changing of the cursorMark.

9.7.4 Adding Three Attributes into the Class Cell.java

In order to mark the hidden digits and for showing player's guessed digits on the board, the class Cell.java adds three attributes: an attribute "guessed" with the type of int for memorizing player's guessed digits, another attribute "visible" with the type of Boolean for indicating which cell having a hidden digit, and the third attribute "guessCorrect" with the type of Boolean for marking whether the guessed digit is correct or not. Based on the three new attributes, the method paintCell() employs different colors to display different status. A cell with a white color and a blue digit is a regular cell with the initialized digit. A cell with a yellow color and no digit is an empty lot for the player to fill in a guessed digit. A cell with a yellow color and a red digit holds a guessed digit without verification. After verification, a cell with a yellow color and a green digit indicates a correct guess; a cell with a yellow color and a red digit means an incorrect guess. The code of the method paintCell() is demonstrated in Listing 9.9.

Listing 9.9 The code of the paintCell() in the class Cell.java of the project Sudoku3

```
 1 /*
 2  * Cell.java - A class defines one cell in the board for the game Sudoku.
 3  */
14 public class Cell {
15
16     private int x;
17     private int y;
18     private int width;
19     private int height;
20     private Color color;
21     private int digit;
22     private int guessed;
23     private boolean guessCorrect;
24     private boolean visible;
...
36     public void paintCell(Graphics2D g2d) {
37         // show a rectangle in blue color
38         g2d.setColor(color);
39         g2d.drawRect(x, y, width, height);
40         if (visible) {
41             // show the initialized digit in blue color
42             g2d.setFont(new Font("TimesRoman", Font.BOLD, 22));
43             g2d.drawString("" + digit, x + Consts.CELL_LEFT, y + Consts.CELL_TOP);
44         } else { // invisible
45             // show the empty cell in yellow color
46             g2d.setColor(Color.YELLOW);
47             g2d.fillRect(x + 2, y + 2, width - 2, height - 2);
48             // show the guessed digit
49             if (guessed != 0) {
50                 if (!guessCorrect) { // in red color for haven't checked yet
51                     g2d.setColor(Color.RED);
52                 } else { // in green color for a correct guessed digit
53                     g2d.setColor(Color.GREEN);
54                 }
55                 g2d.drawString("" + guessed, x + Consts.CELL_LEFT, y + Consts.CELL_TOP);
56             }
57         }
58     }
59 ...
111 }
```

9.7.5 Adding a Method paintTerminate() in the Class NotePanel.java

When the player fills in guessed digits completely, the current game is finished. At this moment, the game is better to automatically check all of guessed digits and give the player a score. For a simple calculation, we defined that "score = correct-guessed/total-guessed * 100 * diffLevel," which considers the percentage of correct-guessed and the difficulty level. We arrange the game termination screen on the same place of the notePanel that initially is for displaying the key commands under the consideration of space saving. The GUI screen when game termination is shown in Fig. 9.10.

9.8 Summary

The game Sudoku lets us experience several new techniques for developing games. The 2D array data structure is introduced for implementing the board, which usually is a composite object that consists of smaller objects such as cells. The brute-force algorithm is applied for validating the population of the special required digits. The alreadyTested array is used for checking the "dead case." The KeyEvent and the KeyListener are adopted as a control mechanism for players to move a cursorMark, type in a guessed digit, and execute all of commands. In addition, the switch between the note-panel and the termination-screen also is a notable design. All of these techniques enrich our Java knowledge and programming skills.

Among them, 2D array is one of very important and popular data structures. Especially 2D array of objects will be seen often in many games. Understanding it and mastering its initialization and data insertion will make us to be matured programmers.

9.9 Exercises

Self-Review Questions

1. The game Sudoku is a puzzle game. What other puzzle games do you know?
2. How does a 2D array relate with a 1D array?
3. How to declare a 2D array? How to initialize the 2D array? How to print out the contents of the 2D array?
4. The class Board.java is a composite class. What does "composite class" mean?
5. Why do we need to have the 1D array alreadyTested when we validate the row, column, and mini-board?
6. How to divide the board into mini-boards? How can we determine a mini-board by using the indexes row and col?
7. How to validate a mini-board?
8. How to design the class NotePanel.java? How to switch between the notePanel and the termination screen? May we directly use the existing notePanel to implement the function of the termination screen? (Hint: Without using paint, but using the existing JLabels)
9. What is the computation involved in order to find out different number of hiding cells corresponding to different difficulty level? How to replace random() call by using Math.random() method?
10. How to set up the "focus" for using key controls? Why is it necessary?
11. After creating a Sudoku board, what should be done to support players' actions?
12. May we replace all of key commands by using Java software components?

Projects

1. In order to better understand the principle of the Sudoku board, use paper and pencil to draw a 4 × 4 board, and manually fill in 4 digits [1, 4] in following the principle of "appear once only" along each row, along each column, and in each mini-board. How many different arrangements do you make?
2. Write a project for implementing the 4 × 4 Sudoku as described above for verifying what you found.
3. Several transformed Sudoku boards have been published in books. For example, one of them constructs a Sudoku board as a triangle shape; each side has nine cells so that the entire triangle consists of nine mini-triangles. Find

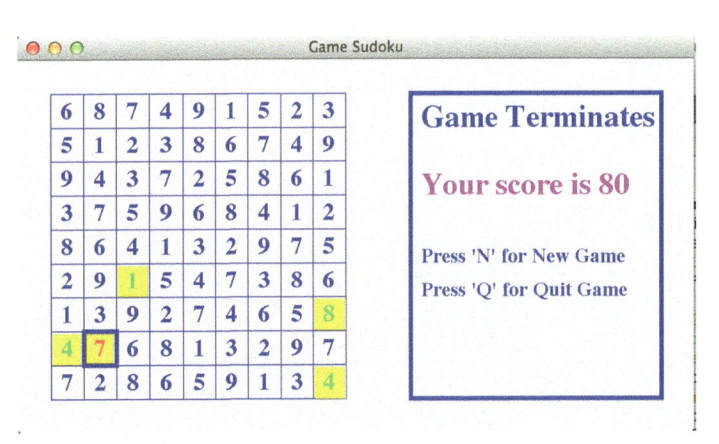

Fig. 9.10 The termination screen of the game Sudoku

one of these transformed Sudoku games, and implement it as a video game.
4. There are many web pages that relate with the game Sudoku. Browse the web pages, and learn more about the principle of the game, and find out any new ideas to improve the design and implementation of the project Sudoku in this chapter.
5. Design and implement a Sudoku game with Java software components instead of key commands.
6. Design and implement a chessboard for the game of international chess as shown in Fig. 9.11. And then, place the chess pieces on proper positions as shown below. (The chess pieces are in the folder "chesspiece." Or find other sets from the Web.)

Fig. 9.11 A chessboard for the international chess

10. Mouse Control: A Card Game Agnes

The other low-level events generated by mouse are adopted for controlling a card game Agnes. In general, mouse is the best device for navigating a two-dimensional space, and mouse event listeners provide a rich set of event handlers. The Agnes is a card game played by a single player. Under the mouse controls, the cards on the GUI are not only for echoing the dynamic behaviors of the game but also play the role of input mechanism.

The objectives of this chapter include:
1. The story of the card game Agnes.
2. One canvas supports both output and input.
3. The data structures of "layout" and "foundation" of the game Agnes.
4. The mouseEvent, MouseListener, and MouseAdapter.
5. Dragging cards from one place to another.
6. Checking abnormal dragging cases.
7. Keeping the dragging cards in front of other cards.

The previous chapter introduced the key controls with the key event and key listener. The control style of keys for the game Sudoku is different from the control style of Java software components used in other games, such as the games AnagramGUI and Blackjack. This chapter switches the topic to discuss another low-level event, that is, the mouse event associated with the mouse control through an example game Agnes.

The game Agnes is a typical card game. The components on the GUI are cards only. The cards as components can be dragged from one place to another following the rule of the game. The movement of cards not only updates the output of the game but also inputs the data for reaching the goal of the game. The entire game is controlled by using mouse only.

10.1 A Card Game Agnes

Card games are one of the popular games. There are many different card games. In Chap. 8 we experienced a card game Blackjack. Thus, we have prepared ourselves to further develop other card games. We pick up one of them called Agnes. It is a card game for one player. It deals with a variety of techniques that are worth to learn.

The original story of the game Agnes is cited as follows:

> Deal 28 cards face up in one row of seven cards, one of six, and so on, down to one card. The 29th card is dealt face up to the center as a foundation card. As they become available, either from the layout or the hand, the other three cards of the same rank will be placed in line with it. The objective of the game is to build ascending, round-the-corner suit sequences onto the foundation cards. The bottom of card of a column in the layout is termed exposed. It may be built on a foundation or packed on another exposed card in the layout, cards are packed in descending sequences of the same color (not necessarily of the same suit), but it should be borne in mind that a sequence may be moved from one column to another only as a whole and only if all the cards of the sequence are of the same suit. If a vacancy occurs through all the cards of a column being moved, it may be filled with any available card, or same-suit sequence of cards, if wished. After all possible moves have been made, cards are dealt face up to the bottom of all the columns, and the game continues until the stock is exhausted. After the third deal has been made from the stock, there will be two cards left in the hand and these may be placed to either a foundation or the layout. [Hamlyn, 2014][1]

We are going to design and implement this card game. Following the implementation step by step, the contents of the original story will be clearer and more meaningful.

---

[1][Hamlyn, 2014] Hamlyn, a division of Octopus Publishing Group Ltd, "The Card Games Bible," Octopus Publishing Group Ltd, 2014

10.2 Preparing Cards for the Game: The Project Agnes1

The first step definitely is to prepare cards for the game. We learned how to prepare a deck of cards from the game Blackjack in Chap. 8. We can reuse both the classes Deck.java and Card.java implemented in the project Blackjack with a slight modification because in the game Agnes, the rank of a card is the same as the face value of the card.

The class Card.java and the class Deck.java have the following functions. The codes of the two classes are shown in Listing 10.1.

1. A class Card.java defines a single card with attributes of x, y, width, and height for placing a card in a proper position. The width and height are defined by the card image. Other two attributes cardFront and cardBack contain the images of the card front and the card back, respectively. A method paintCard() paints a card face up or face down.
2. The class Deck.java is a composite class that contains 52 cards.
   (a) A method initDeck() for reading 52 card images and storing them into an ArrayList in a sorted manner as a deck of cards.
   (b) A method shuffleDeck() shuffles the 52 cards in the deck.
   (c) A method dealCard() always deals the first card from the deck.

Listing 10.1 The codes of the classes Deck.java and Card.java in the project Agnes1

```
 1  /*
 2   * Deck.java - A class defines a deck of cards.
 3   */
 4  package agnes;
 5
 6  import java.awt.Image;
 7  import java.util.ArrayList;
 8  import javax.imageio.ImageIO;
 9
14  public class Deck {
15
16      private ArrayList<Card> deck;
17      private Card card;
18
19      public Deck() {
20          deck = new ArrayList();
21          initDeck();
22          shuffleCard();
23      }
24
25      private void initDeck() { // deck is sorted
26          deck.clear();
27          for (int i = 0; i < Consts.DECK_LEN; i++) {
28              card = initNewCard(i);
29              deck.add(card);
30          }
31      }
32
33      public Card initNewCard(int idx) {
34          Image img = null;
35          try {
36              img = ImageIO.read(getClass().getResource("../cards/" + (idx+1) + ".gif"));
37          } catch (Exception e) {
38          }
39          Card aCard = new Card();
40          aCard.setCardFront(img);
41
42          return aCard;
```

10.2 Preparing Cards for the Game: The Project Agnes1

```
43      }
44
45      private void shuffleCard() {
46          int randIdx1, randIdx2;
47          for (int i = 0; i < 1000; i++) {
48              randIdx1 = (int)(Math.random() * 10000) % Consts.DECK_LEN;
49              randIdx2 = (int)(Math.random() * 10000) % Consts.DECK_LEN;
50              swapCard(randIdx1, randIdx2);
51          }
52      }
53
54      public void swapCard(int idx1, int idx2) {
55          Card tCard;
56          tCard = deck.get(idx1);
57          deck.set(idx1, deck.get(idx2));
58          deck.set(idx2, tCard);
59      }
60
61      public Card dealCard() {
62          Card theCard;
63          theCard = deck.get(0);
64          deck.remove(0);
65          return theCard;
66      }
67
68      public ArrayList<Card> getDeck() {
69          return deck;
70      }
71  }
```

```
1   /*
2    * Card.java - A class defines one card.
3    */
4   package agnes;
5
6   import java.awt.Graphics2D;
7   import java.awt.Image;
8   import javax.imageio.ImageIO;
9
14  public class Card {
15
16      private int x, y;
17      private int width, height;
18      private Image cardBack;
19      private Image cardFront;
20      private boolean faceUp;
21      private int value;
22
23      public Card() {
24          width = Consts.CARD_W;
25          height = Consts.CARD_H;
26          faceUp = false;
27          try {
28              cardBack = ImageIO.read(getClass().getResource("../cards/Back.gif"));
29          } catch (Exception e) {
30          }
31      }
```

```
32
33     public void paintCard(Graphics2D g2d) {
34         if (faceUp) {
35             g2d.drawImage(cardFront, getX(), getY(), width, height, null);
36         } else {
37             g2d.drawImage(cardBack, getX(), getY(), width, height, null);
38         }
39     }
40
41 ... // getter and setter methods
76 }
```

The project Agnes1 is just to paint five cards on the canvas as shown in Fig. 10.1 (right) for assuring the deck of cards works fine. The UML class diagram of the project Agnes1 shown in Fig. 10.1 (left) indicates that the class GameCanvas.java "uses" the class Deck.java and the class Deck.java "has" the class Card.java. The partial code of the class GameCanvas.java is cited in Listing 10.2.

Listing 10.2 The code of the class GameCanvas.java in the project Agnes1

```
1  /*
2   * GameCanvas.java - A class defines a canvas for the game.
3   */
4  package agnes;
5
6  import java.awt.Graphics;
7  import java.awt.Graphics2D;
8  import javax.swing.JPanel;
9
14 public class GameCanvas extends JPanel {
15
16     private Deck deck;
17     private Card aCard;
18
19     public GameCanvas() {
20         initComponent();
21     }
22
23     private void initComponent() {
24         deck = new Deck();
25     }
26
27     @Override
28     public void paintComponent(Graphics g) {
29         super.paintComponent(g);
30         Graphics2D g2d = (Graphics2D) g;
31
32         for (int i = 0; i < 5; i++) { // deal 5 cards for testing
33             aCard = deck.dealCard();
34             aCard.setX(Consts.COL1_X + i * (Consts.CARD_W + Consts.CARD_GAP_X));
35             aCard.setY(Consts.COL1_Y);
36             aCard.setFaceUp(true);
37             aCard.paintCard(g2d);
38         }
39     }
40 }
```

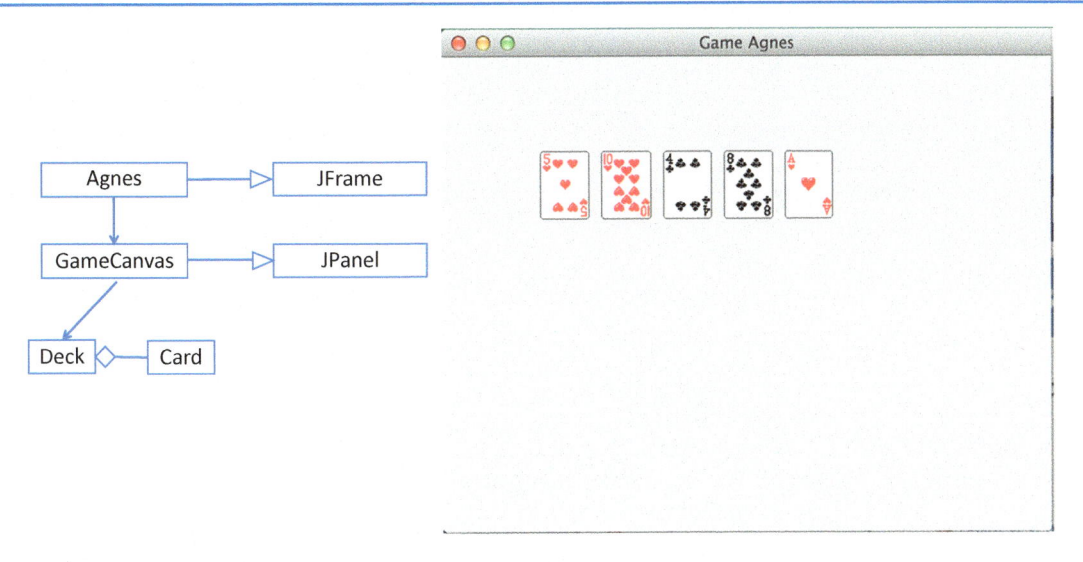

Fig. 10.1 (Left) The UML class diagram; (Right) the GUI of the project Agnes1

Apparently, the class GameCanvas.java has the method initComponent() to instantiate a deck of cards and the method paintComponent() to paint five cards on the canvas.

10.3 Cards on the GUI Form a "Layout" and a "Foundation": The Project Agnes2

The story of the game Agnes said that initially the cards on the GUI of the game Agnes form two structures. One is called "layout" and the other is called "foundation." We arrange the lower portion of the GUI to display the "layout" structure that consists of 7 columns with 28 cards and the upper portion of the GUI to display the structure of "foundation" line with the 29th card as shown in Fig. 10.2 (right). The project Agnes2 is developed to fulfill this task. For that, we add a new class CardLayout.java as listed in Listing 10.3.

Listing 10.3 The new class CardLayuot.java in the project Agnes2

```
 1 /*
 2  * CardLayout.java - A class defines a player.
 3  */
 4 package agnes;
 5
 6 import java.awt.Graphics2D;
 7 import java.util.ArrayList;
 8
13 public class CardLayout {
14
15     private ArrayList[] column;
16     private ArrayList[] foundation;
17
18     private Deck deck; // for dealing a card to column or foundation
19
20     public CardLayout() {
21         column = new ArrayList[Consts.NUM_COL];
22         foundation = new ArrayList[Consts.NUM_SUIT];
23         initDataStruct();
24     }
```

```java
25
26      private void initDataStruct() {
27          for (int col = 0; col < Consts.NUM_COL; col++) {
28              column[col] = new ArrayList<>();
29          }
30          for (int fCol = 0; fCol < Consts.NUM_SUIT; fCol++) {
31              foundation[fCol] = new ArrayList<>();
32          }
33      }
34
35      public void initLayout() {
36          Card aCard;
37          // init the layout with seven columns
38          for (int row = 0; row < Consts.NUM_ROW; row++) {
39              for (int col = 0; col < Consts.NUM_COL - row; col++) {
40                  aCard = deck.dealCard();
41                  aCard.setFaceUp(true);
42                  aCard.setX(Consts.COL1_X + col
43                          * (Consts.CARD_W + Consts.CARD_GAP_X));
44                  if (column[col].isEmpty()) {
45                      aCard.setY(Consts.COL1_Y);
46                  } else {
47                      int tempY;
48                      tempY = ((Card) (column[col].get(
49                              column[col].size() - 1))).getY();
50                      aCard.setY(tempY + Consts.CARD_GAP_Y);
51                  }
52                  column[col].add(aCard);
53              }
54          }
55          // init the foundation
56          aCard = deck.dealCard();
57          aCard.setFaceUp(true);
58          aCard.setX(Consts.FOUNDATION_X);
59          aCard.setY(Consts.FOUNDATION_Y);
60          foundation[0].add(aCard);
61      }
62
63      public void paintLayout(Graphics2D g2d) {
64          Card aCard;
65
66          // paint the layout with seven columns
67          for (int col = 0; col < Consts.NUM_COL; col++) {
68              for (int row = 0; row < column[col].size(); row++) {
69                  aCard = (Card) (column[col].get(row));
70                  aCard.paintCard(g2d);
71              }
72          }
73          // paint the foundation line
74          for (int fCol = 0; fCol < Consts.NUM_SUIT; fCol++) {
75              for (int fRow = 0; fRow < foundation[fCol].size(); fRow++) {
76                  aCard = (Card) foundation[fCol].get(fRow);
77                  if (aCard != null) {
78                      aCard.paintCard(g2d);
79                  }
```

```
80              }
81          }
82      }
83
84      public void setDeck(Deck deck) {
85          this.deck = deck;
86      }
87  }
```

The structure "layout" has seven columns, and every column holds a different number of cards. For representing this structure, the class CardLayout.java declares a variable "column" that is an array of ArrayList. Because one individual ArrayList holds unknown number of cards for one column, then multiple columns require multiple ArrayLists, which form an array of ArrayList. Similarly, the class also declares another variable "foundation" for representing the structure of "foundation," which is also an array of ArrayList since the "foundation" needs to hold four suits of unknown number of cards.

An array of ArrayList looks like 2D structures. However, they are different from a 2D array. In a 2D array, both rows and columns have a fixed known length. But, the array of ArrayList does not have a fixed length on each ArrayList. Fortunately, the initial shape of the "layout" has a regular pattern such that the method initLayout() can adopt two nested "for" loops to deal cards into the 2D data structure. The "layout" requires that the first row has seven cards, the second row has six cards, and until the seventh row has only one card. Thus, the outer "for" loop sets row index from 0 to 6. When row index is 0, the inner "for" loop deals Consts. NUM_COL – row = 7 – 0 = 7 cards for seven columns each. When row index is 1, the inner "for" loop deals Consts. NUM_COL – row = 7 – 1 = 6 cards for the first six columns each. Therefore, every inner "for" loop decreases one card. The "foundation" has only one card when the game is initialized.

Later, the method paintLayout() will be invoked to illustrate all of the cards held in the variable column and in the variable foundation.

All of the cards come from the object deck. Thus, the class CardLayout.java needs a setter method setDeck() to be invoked for passing the object deck into the CardLayout.java class.

Consequently, the functions of the class GameCanvas.java are mainly instantiating objects of cardLayout and deck and also setting up communication paths between them. Listing 10.4 shows the code of the class GameCanvas.java in the project Agnes2.

Listing 10.4 The code of the class GameCanvas.java in the project Agnes2

```
1  /*
2   * GameCanvas.java - A class defines a canvas for the game.
3   */
4  package agnes;
5
6  import java.awt.Graphics;
7  import java.awt.Graphics2D;
8  import javax.swing.JPanel;
9
14 public class GameCanvas extends JPanel {
15
16     private Deck deck;
17     private CardLayout cardLayout;
18
19     public GameCanvas() {
20         initComponent();
21     }
22
```

```
23      private void initComponent() {
24          deck = new Deck();
25          cardLayout = new CardLayout();
26          cardLayout.setDeck(deck);
27          cardLayout.initLayout();
28      }
29
30      @Override
31      public void paintComponent(Graphics g) {
32          super.paintComponent(g);
33          Graphics2D g2d = (Graphics2D) g;
34
35          cardLayout.paintLayout(g2d);
36      }
37  }
```

Besides the instantiation of objects of deck and cardLayout, the method initComponent() also invokes cardLayout.initLayout() to deal cards to the two data structures in the class CardLayout.java. The method paintComponent() invokes cardLayout.paintLayout() to paint the "layout" and the "foundation" for making the GUI of Fig. 10.2 (right).

10.4 Mouse Event and Mouse Event Listener

Mouse is a very popular control mechanism for playing video games. We have learned that when mouse clicks on a software component, such as a JButton, it generates an ActionEvent. But here, we are talking about events generated by mouse itself with the new name of MouseEvent. Mouse has many different actions, such as click, release, move, and so on. That means that the listeners associated with mouse actions need to define multiple event handlers. Java defines three different Interfaces, MouseListener, MouseMotionListener, and MouseWheelListener, to cover all these event handlers. Because tracking the mouse motions involves significantly more system overhead than tracking other mouse events, therefore, a specific MouseMotionListener is defined to uniquely handle mouse motion events. In addition, a mouse has a wheel that generates special mouse wheel events. Thus, a special Interface MouseWheelListener is designed. The definitions of the Interfaces of MouseListener and MouseMotionListener are as follows:

```
public Interface MouseListener {
        public void mouseClicked(MouseEvent e);
        public void mouseEntered(MouseEvent e);
        public void mouseExited(MouseEvent e);
```

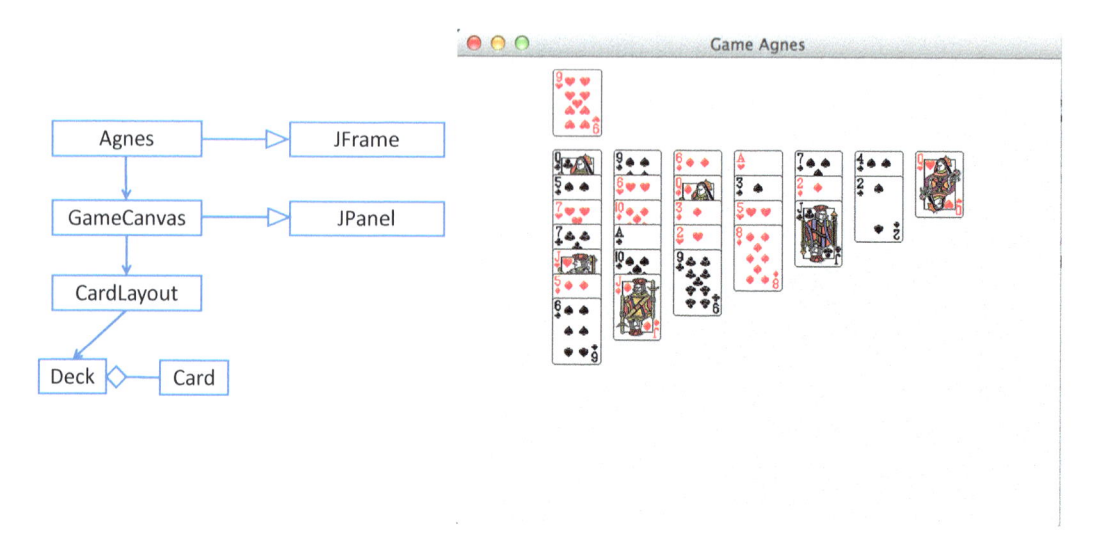

Fig. 10.2 (Left) The UML class diagram; (Right) the initial cards on the GUI form a "layout" and a "foundation"

10.5 Dragging a Card to Anywhere: The Project TestDrag

```
        public void mousePressed(MouseEvent e);
        public void mouseReleased(MouseEvent e);
}

public Interface MouseMotionListener {
        public void mouseDragged(MouseEvent e);
        public void mouseMoved(MouseEvent e);
}
```

Clearly, both MouseListener and MouseMotionListener declare multiple methods. As mentioned before, Java also provides MouseAdapter for the corresponding listeners that have multiple methods. We are going to extend the class MouseAdapter in our projects.

10.5 Dragging a Card to Anywhere: The Project TestDrag

For playing the game Agnes, the player needs to drag a card or a set of cards from a column to other columns or to the foundation line. Therefore, how to use mouse to drag a card from a source position to a destination position is one of the fundamental actions we need to discuss. A mouse drag action means that the player holds down the left button of a mouse on a card and "grabs" the card to bring it to anywhere until the mouse is released.

Surely, the "magic" won't be happened without a support of computations. The principle of the computation is that when a mouse is clicked on a point, the MouseEvent provides event.getX() and event.getY() methods to return the coordinates (x, y) of the clicked point. Therefore, when a mouse is moved to another point, the get methods will dynamically keep track of the updated (x, y) values along the way of moving. If the computation keeps assigning the updated (x, y) to the coordinates of the card by invoking the method aCard.setX(event.getX()) and the method aCard.setY(event.getY()), the card will also be "moved" to the new position following the mouse along the way. For better understanding the principle of the action, we would be better to switch to a series of smaller programs for testing the drag and release actions.

10.5.1 A Project TestDrag1 for Adding a Mouse Listener as an Inner Class

The project Agnes1 displays five cards on the canvas. Taking the advantage of the simplicity of the project Agnes1, we add an inner class into the class GameCanvas.java to either "implement" the Interface MouseMotionListener or "extend" the adapter class MouseAdapter for coding the method mouseDragged(), and then we can test a drag for moving any one of the five cards to anywhere. For realizing this thinking, we simply copy the project Agnes1 and rename it as TestDrag1, and then we implement an inner class MyMouseAdapter to extend the class MouseAdapter inside the GameCanvas.java class. Meanwhile, we need to add the following statement into the constructor or the initializing methods in the class GameCanvas.java:

```
addMouseMotionListener(new MyMouseAdapter());
```

We also define the constants Consts.COL1_X and Consts.COL1_Y for the coordinates (x, y) of top-left corner of the first card. After all, the code of the class GameCanvas.java in the project TestDrag1 is as in Listing 10.5.

Listing 10.5 The partial code of the class GameCanvas.java in the project TestDrag1

```
 1  /*
 2   * GameCanvas.java - A class defines a canvas for the game.
 3   */
29  …
30      @Override
31      public void paintComponent(Graphics g) {
32          super.paintComponent(g);
33          Graphics2D g2d = (Graphics2D) g;
34
35          for (int i = 0; i < 5; i++) {
36              aCard = deck.dealCard();
37              aCard.setX(Consts.COL1_X + i * (Consts.CARD_W + Consts.CARD_GAP_X));
38              aCard.setY(Consts.COL1_Y);
39              aCard.setFaceUp(true);
40              aCard.paintCard(g2d);
41          }
42      }
```

```
43
44      class MyMouseAdapter extends MouseAdapter {
45
46          @Override
47          public void mouseDragged(MouseEvent evt) {
48              aCard.setX(evt.getX());
49              aCard.setY(evt.getY());
50              repaint();
51          }
52      }
53  }
```

Unfortunately, when we run the project, no any card can be dragged.

10.5.2 A Project TestDrag2 for Implementing the Event Handler mouseDragged()

The reason no any card can be dragged is that the five cards shown on the canvas in the project TestDrag1 are painted images. When the method paintComponent() (lines 30–42) starts the "for" loop, the variable aCard gets an object of card from the deck, then the card is assigned a pair of coordinates (x, y) and its image is to be painted on the canvas. In the second loop, the variable aCard gets the second object of card from the deck, at the same time, it lost the first object of card. It also only paints the image of the second object on the canvas. Clearly, the loop only paints the five card images on the canvas but does not hold the five card objects. Actually, we mentioned this problem before, "Don't paint an image as an object but paint an object as an image."

For correcting this mistake, we need to copy the project TestDrag1 to be another project TestDrag2 and modify it to deal with objects of card. For dealing with real objects, the project uses a variable ArrayList<card> aList to hold five card objects from the deck and then show them on the canvas by painting their images. Now, we can drag anyone of them out from the set and move it to anywhere. The code of the class GameCanvas.java in the project TestDrag2 is modified as shown in Listing 10.6.

Listing 10.6 The code of the class GameCanvas.java in the project TestDrag2

```
1  /*
2   * GameCanvas.java - A class defines a canvas for the game.
3   */
4  package testdrag;
5
...
17 public class GameCanvas extends JPanel {
18
19     private Deck deck;
20     private Card aCard;
21     private ArrayList<Card> aList;
22
23     public GameCanvas() {
24         aList = new ArrayList<>();
25         addMouseMotionListener(new MyMouseAdapter());
26         initComponent();
27     }
28
29     private void initComponent() {
30         deck = new Deck();
31         initCard();
32     }
33
34     public void initCard() {
```

```
35          for (int i = 0; i < 5; i++) {
36              aCard = deck.dealCard();
37              aCard.setX(Consts.COL1_X + i * (Consts.CARD_W + Consts.CARD_GAP_X));
38              aCard.setY(Consts.COL1_Y);
39              aCard.setFaceUp(true);
40              aList.add(aCard);
41          }
42      }
43
44      @Override
45      public void paintComponent(Graphics g) {
46          super.paintComponent(g);
47          Graphics2D g2d = (Graphics2D) g;
48
49          for (int i = 0; i < 5; i++) {
50              aCard = aList.get(i);
51              aCard.paintCard(g2d);
52          }
53      }
54
55      class MyMouseAdapter extends MouseAdapter {
56
57          Card clickCard;
58
59          @Override
60          public void mouseDragged(MouseEvent evt) {
61              if ((evt.getY() >= Consts.COL1_Y)
62                      && (evt.getY() <= (Consts.COL1_Y + Consts.CARD_H))) {
63                  int idx = (evt.getX() - Consts.COL1_X)
64                          / (Consts.CARD_W + Consts.CARD_GAP_X);
65                  clickCard = aList.get(idx);
66              }
67              clickCard.setX(evt.getX());
68              clickCard.setY(evt.getY());
69              repaint();
70          }
71      }
72  }
```

The method initComponent() instantiates a deck, and invokes the method initCard() to get five cards from the deck, and stores them into the arrayList aList. The constant Consts.COL1_X defines the x-coordinate of the top-left corner of the first card, and the constant Consts.CARD_GAP_X defines the gap between two adjacent cards. The method paintComponent() then paints the five cards as shown in Fig. 10.3.

When we would like to drag anyone of them, we use mouse to click on it. This action and its event handler are implemented in the method mouseDragged() inside the inner class MyMouseAdapter. When the player clicks on one of the five cards, the coordinates of the clicked point can be obtained from evt.getX() and evt.getY(). Thus, the relative distance between the clicking point and the top-left point of the first card along the x-axis can be found through the calculation (evt.getX() – Consts.COL1_X). If we define "width of one card" = (Consts.CARD_W + Consts.CARD_GAP_X), then (relative distance/"width of one card") will give the index of the clicked card stored in the ArrayList aList. And then, the clicked card can be fetched from the aList by using the value of the index, and the card can be assigned to the variable clickCard. In order to let the clicked card follow the mouse to be dragged to any place, the coordinates of the top-left point of the clickCard should be set up as evt.getX() and evt.getY(). That means the top-left corner of the clickCard should be moved to the clicked point. This movement appears as a slight "shaking" when dragging starts.

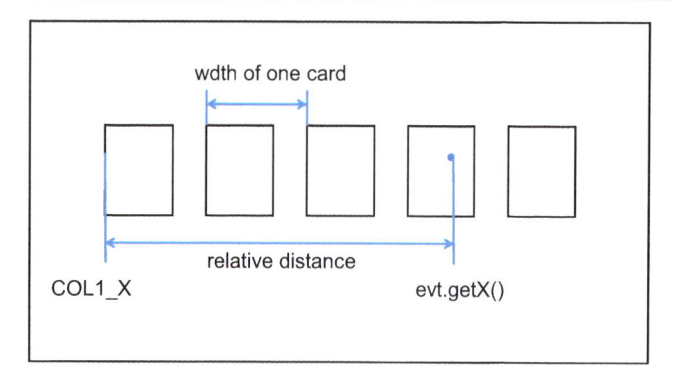

Fig. 10.3 Finding the index of the clickCard in the project TestDrag2

10.5.3 A Project TestDrag3 for Eliminating the "Shaking"

The project TestDrag2 shows that when we start clicking a card for dragging, the clickCard behaves a slight shaking. The reason is that at this moment, the statement clickCard.setX(evt.getX()) sets the value evt.getX() to be the x-coordinate of the left edge of the clickCard. It causes that the left edge of the clickCard shifts from its original position to the clicked point. This shift creates the shaking. For making the reason easy to see, we can assume that at the moment of clicking, the value of evt.getX() is 50 and the left edge of the clickCard is 45. The relative distance between the clicked point and the left edge of the card is 50 − 45 = 5. However, the statement clickCard.setX(50) sets the left edge of the clickCard as 50 such that the card will shift 5 pixels to the right from the original 45 to the new point of 50. It is that the shaking. The similar shifting also happens along the y direction caused by clickCard.setY(evt.getY()).

Surely, we would like to eliminate this shaking for a smooth dragging. That is, we would like to keep the clickCard at its original position without shifting to the clicked point. In order to make it, we need to find out the distance dx, which is the relative distance between the left edge and the clicked point on the clickCard. Certainly, the value of dx = clickCard.getX() − evt.getX(). Similarly, a dy = clickCard.getY() − evt.getY(), which is the distance between the top edge of the clickCard and the clicked point. And then, we apply the values of dx and dy for modifying the statements clickCard.setX(evt.getX() − dx) and clickCard.setY(evt.getY() − dy) to prevent the clickCard from shifting. For making a numerical example, the two statements above work as clickCard.setX(50 − 5) that will keep the left edge of the clickCard as 45 even the clicked point has x value of 50.

However, the drag action is a continuous action. We'd better to understand the codes in the method mouseDragged() like a loop because when mouse moves, the value of evt.getX() is continuously changed along the way of moving. But clickCard.setX() is calculated as follows:

```
clickCard.setX(evt.getX() - dx)
   = clickCard.setX(evt.getX() - (click-
       Card.getX() - evt.getX()))
   = clickCard.setX(clickCard.getX())
```

It keeps the click card always at its original position. In other words, the card won't be dragged. For solving this problem, we need to find out the value of dx at the moment of clicking and keep the value as a constant to allow the clickCard following the evt.getX() to be moved. In the coding, we need to calculate the values of dx only one time at the clicking moment and apply the constant values of dx to clickCard.setX(evt.getX() − a-constant). For that, we add a new Boolean variable firstTime to split the codes into two parts. One part is for the clicking moment with the variable firstTime = true; the other part is for dragging action after setting the value of firstTime = false. The code of the class GameCanvas.java of the project TestDrag3 is cited in Listing 10.7.

Listing 10.7 The partial code of the class GameCanvas.java in the project TestDrag3

```
1  /*
2   * GameCanvas.java - A class defines a canvas for the game.
3   */
56 ...
57     class MyMouseAdapter extends MouseAdapter {
58
59         boolean firstTime = true;
60         Card clickCard;
61         int dx, dy;
62
63         @Override
64         public void mouseDragged(MouseEvent evt) {
65             if (firstTime) { // clicking moment
66                 if ((evt.getY() >= Consts.COL1_Y)
```

10.5 Dragging a Card to Anywhere: The Project TestDrag

```
67                      && (evt.getY() <= Consts.COL1_Y + Consts.CARD_H)) {
68                  int idx = (evt.getX() - Consts.COL1_X)
69                          / (Consts.CARD_W + Consts.CARD_GAP_X);
70                  clickCard = aList.get(idx);
71              }
72              dx = evt.getX() - clickCard.getX(); // make dx a constant
73              dy = evt.getY() - clickCard.getY(); // make dy a constant
74              firstTime = false; // finishing clicking moment and starting dragging
75          }
76          if (clickCard != null) {
77              clickCard.setX(evt.getX() - dx);
78              clickCard.setY(evt.getY() - dy);
79          }
80          repaint();
81      }
82  }
83 }
```

The project works fine now. Unfortunately, when we leave the first dragged card somewhere and try to drag the second card, as long as we click on the second card and start dragging, the first dragged card jumps back under mouse such that we still drag the first dragged card. The reason is that we have only one variable clickCard. It was assigned to the first dragged card; even mouse clicks on the second card with a new click point, the drag action still gets the same first dragged card. For solving the problem, we need to break the linkage between the variable clickCard with the object of the first dragged card. This break should be done when we release mouse from the first dragged card.

10.5.4 A Project TestDrag4 for Implementing the Event Handler mouseReleased()

Fortunately, the MouseListener declares another event handling method with the name of mouseReleased(), which is also included in the definition of the class MouseAdapter. Therefore, we only need to add the method mouseReleased() into the inner class MyMouseAdapter. Nevertheless, we must add the statement addMouseListener(new MyMouseAdapter()) in the class GameCanvas.java in addition to the existing statement addMouseMotionListener(new MyMouseAdapter()) due to the fact that originally the method mouseDragged() is declared in the Interface MouseMotionListener but the method mouseReleased() is declared in another Interface MouseListener.

In the event handler mouseReleased(), we add a new variable removedCard and let the new variable to hold the first dragged card by assigning the variable clickCard to the new variable. And then the clickCard can be released. When painting the contents of the aList, a method adjustList() is invoked to reset the coordinates of every remaining card in the aList so that the paintComponent() method can paint the new content of the aList after removing the first dragged card. We can see that the aList has only four cards left and the removedCard is also shown at a position that is outside of the cards still in the aList. Now, if we click on one of the cards remained in the aList and drag the clicked card, it can be dragged to anywhere. Once we release the mouse, the new contents of the aList and the second dragged card will be shown. However, the first dragged card is disappeared since no any variable keeps the reference to the first dragged card. This new problem will be solved later when we go back to the real project Agnes.

We have to pay attention on the scope of variables under this case. Even if the two event handlers are inside the same inner class MyMouseAdapter, the two methods originally belong to two different Interfaces. All of the shared variables of the two methods should be defined as "global variables" inside the inner class so that the global variables can be shared. The more complete codes of the class GameCanvas.java in the project TestDrag4 are shown in Listing 10.8.

Listing 10.8 The code of the class GameCanvas.java in the project TestDrag4

```
1 /*
2  * GameCanvas.java - A class defines a canvas for the game.
3  */
22
```

```java
23     private boolean firstTime = true;
24     private Card clickCard;
25     private Card removedCard;
26
27     public GameCanvas() {
28         addMouseMotionListener(new MyMouseAdapter());
29         addMouseListener(new MyMouseAdapter());
30         aList = new ArrayList<>();
31         initComponent();
32     }
48 ...
49     @Override
50     public void paintComponent(Graphics g) {
51         super.paintComponent(g);
52         Graphics2D g2d = (Graphics2D) g;
53
54         for (int i = 0; i < aList.size(); i++) {
55             aCard = aList.get(i);
56             aCard.paintCard(g2d);
57         }
58         if (removedCard != null) {
59             removedCard.paintCard(g2d);
60         }
61     }
62
63     class MyMouseAdapter extends MouseAdapter {
64
65         int dx = 0, dy = 0;
66         int clickIdx = 0;
67
68         @Override
69         public void mouseDragged(MouseEvent evt) {
70             if (firstTime) {
71                 if ((evt.getY() >= Consts.COL1_Y)
72                         && (evt.getY() <= Consts.COL1_Y + Consts.CARD_H)) {
73                     clickIdx = (evt.getX() - Consts.COL1_X)
74                             / (Consts.CARD_W + Consts.CARD_GAP_X);
75                     clickCard = aList.get(clickIdx);
76                 }
77                 dx = evt.getX() - clickCard.getX();
78                 dy = evt.getY() - clickCard.getY();
79                 firstTime = false;
80             }
81             if (clickCard != null) {
82                 clickCard.setX(evt.getX() - dx);
83                 clickCard.setY(evt.getY() - dy);
84             }
85             repaint();
86         }
87
88         @Override
89         public void mouseReleased(MouseEvent evt) {
90             removedCard = clickCard;
91             aList.remove(clickCard);
92             adjustList(aList);
```

```
 93
 94                firstTime = true;
 95                repaint();
 96            }
 97
 98            // the coordinates (x, y) of each card should be adjusted for painting
 99            private void adjustList(ArrayList tList) {
100                Card tCard;
101                for (int i = 0; i < tList.size(); i++) {
102                    tCard = (Card) tList.get(i);
103                    tCard.setX(Consts.COL1_X + i * (Consts.CARD_W + Consts.CARD_GAP_X));
104                    tCard.setY(Consts.COL1_Y);
105                }
106            }
107        }
108 }
```

10.6 Dragging and Releasing a Set of Cards: The Project Agnes3

Through the testing projects, we have a better understanding on mouse drag and release events, and we are going to apply them for developing the project Agnes3. The project Agnes2 arranges cards as the "layout" and the "foundation." The following step is to allow the player to drag a set of cards from a source column and release the set on a destination column or drag a single card from the "layout" to the "foundation." Due to the fact that "a set of cards" includes the case of "a single card," thus, in our implementation, we only work on the case of "a set of cards." The number of cards in the set is unknown; therefore, we select the data structure ArrayList to form a tempList for holding "a set of cards" including the case of holding "a single card."

The pseudo code looks like the following:

1. The class GameCanvas.java adds an inner class MyMouseAdapter that "extends" the built-in class MouseAdapter.
2. When the player clicks on a card in a column of the "layout," the event MouseEvent gets the coordinates (x, y) of the clicking point. Based on the value of evt.getX(), the index of the column clickCol can be found through the method theCol(evt.getX()). The required calculations have been discussed in the project TestDrag2. At the same time, the clickCard refers to the single card been clicked.
3. The ArrayList tempList is used to hold the clickCard and the cards follow it along the same column as a set. The player, then, drags the tempList leaving the source column.
4. When the player selects a destination column and releases mouse, the set of cards in the tempList is appended to the "exposed" card on the destination column. In addition, the corresponding set of cards is removed from the source column clickCol.
5. Keep in mind that the values of clickCard and tempList could be null when the player performs invalid clicks, which should be prevented with a validation checking.
6. The GUI is divided into two areas. The top portion is for the "foundation" line; the bottom portion is for the "layout." The tempList can hold a set of cards in order to be moved from a source column to a destination column. But, for adding cards to the "foundation," the player can only move one card at a time. When the player releases the mouse on the top portion, it means to add the card held by the tempList to the "foundation" line. Otherwise, when the player releases the mouse on the bottom portion, it means to add the cards in the tempList to a destination column.

A complete implementation of the inner class based on the pseudo code above will be cited in the following section.

10.7 Implementing the Game Rules: The Projects Agnes4 and Agnes5

The project Agnes3 only implements the actions for dragging and releasing a set of cards. The following project Agnes4 should build up the logic for embedding the game rules and synchronizing the logic with the game playing mechanism. For realizing this goal, the required considerations include: (1) How to handle the remaining cards in the deck after completing the "layout" and the "foundation"? (2) How to verify the movements of cards satisfying the rule of the game? Or say how to check and handle any invalid movements of cards?

After initializing the "layout" and the "foundation," the deck remains 52 − 29 = 23 cards. We would like to place these remaining cards as a stock on the rightmost end of the "foundation" line. All of the remaining cards in the stock are face down. According to the story of the game Agnes, the remaining cards should be dealt to every column one card each when the player requests. For that, we design and implement an event handler mouseClicked() in the inner class MyMouseAdapter, which will be invoked to deal seven cards to seven columns with one card each once the player clicks on the stock.

For the second consideration, we add functions for checking the validations of player's movements. As long as a movement is invalid, the destination column should reject the tempList and the cards in the tempList will be returned back to the original source column automatically. According to the story of the game Agnes, the rules that should be followed include:

1. The cards in the "foundation" line are four suits, and the starting cards of the four suits have the same rank as the 29th card shown on the first suit position.
2. The cards on every suit are in ascending order.
3. When packing a set of cards held by the tempList on the exposed card of the destination column, the first card in the tempList and the exposed card on the destination column should be in a descending order of the same color (but not necessary to be the same suit).
4. A set of cards should be moved from one column to another as a whole, and the cards on the set must belong to the same suit.
5. Vacancy columns can be filled with any available card or any available set of cards.
6. As long as the player clicks on the stock, cards in the stock are dealt from the stock face up to the bottom of every column with one card per column.

From the experiences of playing the game, we find out that the rule (4) makes a too restricted requirement to be accepted for playing the game and the requirement is in conflict with the rule (3). We would like to release the requirement of "the cards on the set must belong to the same suit" so that a set of cards can be packed on an exposed card whenever the rule (3) is satisfied.

Then, we embed all of the rules in the codes. Any violation of rules will cause a rejection by the destination column and the packed cards will be returned back to the source column immediately. For the implementation, we add the rule checking into the event handlers in the inner class MyMouseAdapter, which resides on the GameCanvas.java class, as the following pseudo code indicated:

1. We implement a method cardToColumn() in the inner class MyMouseAdapter for adding the cards in the tempList to a destination column. It returns a Boolean value for indicating the success or failure of the addition. The method cardToColumn() invokes the method sameColor() to check "the same color" and invokes the method descendOrder() to check "the descending order of the rank" between the exposed card in the destination column and the first card in the tempList. When checking is failure, the method sendBackTempList() is invoked to return the tempList back to the original source column.
2. Similarly, we implement another method cardToFoundation() in the inner class MyMouseAdapter for adding the single card in the tempList to the "foundation" line. The method cardToFoundation() invokes the method sameSuit() for checking "the same suit" and invokes the ascendOrder() method for checking "the ascending order of the rank" between the exposed card in the destination foundation suit and the card dragged. For adding a new suit card on an empty foundation column, the method sameRank() is invoked to check "the same rank" of the first card in all four suits. Any violation of the checking will end up with the method sendBackTempList().
3. Whenever a new card is added on the "foundation" line, a method isOver() is invoked to check whether the game is finished by checking whether all of four suits on the "foundation" line have a King as their exposed card.
4. After initializing the structures of "layout" and "foundation," all of the remaining cards in the deck is placed on the right edge of the "foundation" line as a stock. When needed, the player simply clicks on the stock, and the event handler method mouseClicked() in the inner class will deal one card each to the columns in the "layout" part.

A more complete inner class MyMouseAdapter that implements all of the functions listed above is in the project Agnes5, which is cited in Listing 10.9.

Listing 10.9 The partial code of the inner class MyMouseAdapter inside the class GameCanvas.java of the project Agnes5

```
1  /*
2   * GameCanvas.java - A class defines a canvas for the game.
3   */
```

10.7 Implementing the Game Rules: The Projects Agnes4 and Agnes5

```
 68
 69        class MyMouseAdapter extends MouseAdapter {
 70
 71            Card aCard;
 72            int dx, dy; // offset of (x, y) to (evt.getX(), evt.getY())
 73
 74            // the mouseDragged() and mouseReleased() belong to
 75            // two different listeners (variables cannot be shared)
 76            @Override
 77            public void mouseDragged(MouseEvent evt) {
 78                theColumn = cardLayout.getColumn();
 79                // select a tempList to be dragged
 80                if (firstTime) {
 81                    // click the card and find the clickCol
 82                    clickCol = theCol(evt.getX());
 83                    if ((clickCol >= 0) && (clickCol < Consts.NUM_COL)) {
 84                        // get the clicked card and the tempList
 85                        for (int row = (theColumn[clickCol].size() - 1); row >= 0; row--) {
 86                            aCard = (Card) theColumn[clickCol].get(row);
 87                            if (dragTheCard(evt.getX(), evt.getY(),
 88                                    aCard.getX(), aCard.getY())) { // (x, y) is inside the card
 89                                clickCard = aCard;
 90                                tempList = new ArrayList<>();
 91                                tempLen = (theColumn[clickCol].size() - 1) - row + 1;
 92                                for (int i = 0; i < tempLen; i++) {
 93                                    aCard = (Card) theColumn[clickCol].get(row + i);
 94                                    tempList.add(aCard);
 95                                }
 96                                break;
 97                            } else {
 98                                clickCard = null;
 99                            }
100                        }
101                    }
102                    if (clickCard != null) {
103                        // find the offset between the clicked point and the card (x, y)
104                        dx = evt.getX() - clickCard.getX(); // dx and dy must be a constant
105                        dy = evt.getY() - clickCard.getY();
106                    }
107                    firstTime = false;
108                }
109                if (tempList != null) {
110                    // drag the entire tempList around
111                    for (int k = 0; k < tempLen; k++) {
112                        tempList.get(k).setX(evt.getX() - dx);
113                        tempList.get(k).setY((evt.getY() - dy) + k * Consts.CARD_GAP_Y);
114                    }
115                }
116                repaint();
117            }
118
119            @Override
120            public void mouseReleased(MouseEvent evt) {
121                if (tempList != null) {
122                    if (evt.getY() < (Consts.COL1_Y + Consts.CARD_GAP_Y)) {
```

```java
                    // append cards in tempList to the foundation line
                    if (!cardToFoundation(evt.getX(), tempList)) {
                        sendBackTempList(clickCol, tempList);
                    } else // success, check whether game is over
                    if (isOver()) {
                        gameTerminate = true;
                        playerPanel.setGameTerminate(true);
                    }
                } else {
                    // append cards in tempList to the destination column
                    int destCol = theCol(evt.getX()); // the destination column
                    if (!cardToColumn(destCol, tempList)) {
                        sendBackTempList(clickCol, tempList);
                    }
                }
                // prevent a null click
                clickCard = null;
                tempList.clear();
                tempList = null;
            }
            firstTime = true; // after release one card, then select the next
            repaint();
        }

        // find the index of a column based on the evt.getX()
        private int theCol(int evtX) {
            int relativeX = evtX - columnLeft(0);
            return (relativeX / (Consts.CARD_W + Consts.CARD_GAP_X));
        }

        // assure the card or the first card of a tempList is dragged
        private boolean dragTheCard(int evtX, int evtY, int cardX, int cardY) {
            boolean inside = false;
            if ((evtX >= cardX) && (evtX <= cardX + Consts.CARD_W)
                    && (evtY >= cardY) && (evtY <= cardY + Consts.CARD_H)) {
                inside = true;
            }
            return inside;
        }

        // attach the tempList to the destination column
        private boolean cardToColumn(int aCol, ArrayList tList) {
            Card tCard;
            boolean success = false;
            if (!(theColumn[aCol].isEmpty())) { // not empty
                tCard = (Card) tList.get(0);
                if ((sameColor(tCard, exploredCardColumn(aCol)))
                        && (decendingRank(tCard, exploredCardColumn(aCol)))) {
                    for (Object tList1 : tList) {
                        tCard = (Card) tList1;
                        appendColumn(tCard, aCol);
                    }
                    success = true;
                }
            } else { // is empty
```

```java
                    for (Object tList1 : tList) {
                        tCard = (Card) tList1;
                        appendColumn(tCard, aCol);
                    }
                    success = true;
                }
                // always to remove the tempList from the sourc column
                removeFromColumn(clickCol, tempList);
                return success;
            }

            // remove tList from the source column
            private void removeFromColumn(int aCol, ArrayList tList) {
                Card tCard;
                for (Object tList1 : tList) {
                    tCard = (Card) tList1;
                    theColumn[aCol].remove(tCard);
                }
            }

            // append a card to the destination column
            private void appendColumn(Card theCard, int theCol) {
                if (!theColumn[theCol].isEmpty()) {
                    theCard.setX(columnLeft(theCol));
                    theCard.setY(exploredCardColumn(theCol).getY()
                            + Consts.CARD_GAP_Y);
                } else {
                    theCard.setX(columnLeft(theCol));
                    theCard.setY(Consts.COL1_Y + Consts.CARD_GAP_Y);
                }
                theColumn[theCol].add(theCard);
            }

            // assure the same color of the appending card and the exposed card
            private boolean sameColor(Card card1, Card card2) {
                boolean same = false;
                if ((card1.getSuit() == Consts.CARD_CLUBS)
                        && (card2.getSuit() == Consts.CARD_CLUBS)
                        || (card2.getSuit() == Consts.CARD_SPADES)) {
                    same = true;
                } else if ((card1.getSuit() == Consts.CARD_SPADES)
                        && (card2.getSuit() == Consts.CARD_CLUBS)
                        || (card2.getSuit() == Consts.CARD_SPADES)) {
                    same = true;
                } else if ((card1.getSuit() == Consts.CARD_DIAMONDS)
                        && (card2.getSuit() == Consts.CARD_DIAMONDS)
                        || (card2.getSuit() == Consts.CARD_HEARTS)) {
                    same = true;
                } else if ((card1.getSuit() == Consts.CARD_HEARTS)
                        && (card2.getSuit() == Consts.CARD_DIAMONDS)
                        || (card2.getSuit() == Consts.CARD_HEARTS)) {
                    same = true;
                }
                return same;
            }
```

```
233
234        // assure the two cards in a descending order
235        private boolean decendingRank(Card card1, Card card2) {
236            boolean withOrder = false;
237            if (card1.getValue() == (card2.getValue() - 1)) {
238                withOrder = true;
239            }
240            return withOrder;
241        }
242
243        // send the tempList back to the source column
244        private void sendBackTempList(int sCol, ArrayList tList) {
245            Card tCard;
246            for (Object tList1 : tList) {
247                tCard = (Card) tList1;
248                appendColumn(tCard, sCol);
249            }
250        }
251
252        // attach the tempList to the foundation
253        private boolean cardToFoundation(int evtX, ArrayList tList) {
254            boolean success = false;
255            int fCol, theCol = 0;
256            Card fCard, tCard;
257            // assure the destination foundation
258            fCol = theCol(evtX);
259            if ((fCol >= 0) && (fCol < Consts.NUM_SUIT)) {
260                theFoundation = cardLayout.getFoundation();
261                int aLen = theFoundation[fCol].size();
262                if (aLen > 0) {
263                    fCard = (Card) theFoundation[fCol].get(aLen - 1);
264                    if ((fCard.getSuit() == clickCard.getSuit())
265                            && (fCard.getValue() == (clickCard.getValue() - 1))) {
266                        for (Object tList1 : tList) {
267                            tCard = (Card) tList1;
268                            appendFoundation(tCard, fCol);
269                        }
270                        success = true;
271                    } else {
272                    } // ignore it
273                } else { // an empty slot
274                    for (int col = 0; col < Consts.NUM_SUIT; col++) {
275                        if (!theFoundation[col].isEmpty()) {
276                            theCol = col;
277                            break;
278                        }
279                    }
280                    if (sameRank((Card) theFoundation[theCol].get(0),
281                            (Card) tList.get(0))) {
282                        for (Object tList1 : tList) {
283                            tCard = (Card) tList1;
284                            appendFoundation(tCard, fCol);
285                        }
286                        success = true;
287                    }
```

10.7 Implementing the Game Rules: The Projects Agnes4 and Agnes5

```java
                }
            }
            removeFromColumn(clickCol, tList);
            return success;
        }

        // append a card to the foundation
        private void appendFoundation(Card aCard, int aCol) {
            // no matter it is empty or not
            aCard.setX(columnLeft(aCol));
            aCard.setY(Consts.FOUNDATION_Y);
            theFoundation[aCol].add(aCard);
        }

        private boolean sameRank(Card card1, Card card2) {
            boolean rank = false;
            if (card1.getValue() == card2.getValue()) {
                rank = true;
            }
            return rank;
        }

        // get the x-coordinate of the left edge of a column
        private int columnLeft(int col) {
            return (Consts.COL1_X + col * Consts.CARD_W
                    + col * Consts.CARD_GAP_X);
        }

        // get the x-coordinate of the right edge of a column
        private int columnRight(int col) {
            return (columnLeft(col) + Consts.CARD_W);
        }

        // get the exposed card of a column
        private Card exploredCardColumn(int col) {
            int size = theColumn[col].size();
            return (Card) (theColumn[col].get(size - 1));
        }

        // get the exposed card of a column
        private Card lastCardFoundation(int col) {
            int size = theFoundation[col].size();
            return (Card) (theFoundation[col].get(size - 1));
        }

        private boolean isOver() {
            boolean over = false;
            int count = 0;
            for (int fCol = 0; fCol < Consts.NUM_SUIT; fCol++) {
                if (!theFoundation[fCol].isEmpty()) {
                    if ((lastCardFoundation(fCol).getValue() == 13)) {
                        count += 1;
                    }
                }
            }
```

```
343                if (count == Consts.NUM_SUIT) {
344                    over = true;
345                }
346                return over;
347            }
348
349            // deal one card from the stock to every column
350            @Override
351            public void mouseClicked(MouseEvent evt) {
352                theColumn = cardLayout.getColumn();
353                int deckX = columnLeft(0) + (Consts.NUM_COL - 1)
354                        * (Consts.CARD_W + Consts.CARD_GAP_X);
355                if ((evt.getX() >= deckX) && (evt.getX() <= deckX + Consts.CARD_W)
356                        && (evt.getY() >= Consts.FOUNDATION_Y)
357                        && (evt.getY() <= Consts.FOUNDATION_Y + Consts.CARD_H)) {
358                    for (int col = 0; col < Consts.NUM_COL; col++) {
359                        aCard = deck.dealCard();
360                        if (aCard != null) {
361                            aCard.setFaceUp(true);
362                            appendColumn(aCard, col);
363                        }
364                    }
365                }
366                repaint();
367            }
368        }
369
370        public void setPlayerPanel(PlayerPanel playerPanel) {
371            this.playerPanel = playerPanel;
372        }
373    }
```

10.8 Adding a Class PlayerPanel.java: The Project Agnes5

When a game is finished or in the middle stage of playing, usually the player needs two additional controls, which could be implemented by using two buttons. One is a "New Game" button for initializing a new play, and the other is a "Quit" button to quit the game if wished. Meanwhile, we also would like to have a place for displaying a message "You Won!!! Congratulations!!!" when one game is successful. Consequently, we add a new class PlayerPanel.java to the new version Agnes5. The class PlayerPanel.java is a small panel and could be added on the GUI. However, we would like to hide the new added playerPanel from the GUI unless when a game playing is finished or the player moves mouse entering the panel area. Two reasons support this design: (1) the two buttons are rarely used and (2) the GUI is better to be clean. The switching function of hiding or showing the playerPanel is implemented in an inner class HidePanelMouseAdapter in the PlayerPanel.java class with two event handlers mouseEntered() and mouseExited().

The pseudo code for implementing the class PlayerPanel.java is as follows:

1. The class has three software components: a JLabel for displaying the message "You won!!! Congratulations!!!," a JButton "New Game," and another JButton "Quit."
2. When one play is finished, the panel and the three software components show up automatically. The player may click the button "New Game" for starting a new game or click the button "Quit" for leaving the game.
3. During the time period when the player plays the game, regularly the panel with all of components won't be visible unless the player moves mouse entering the area so that the panel will be visible for the player to either interrupt the current game and start a new game or quit from the game.

The new added inner classes in the class PlayerPanel.java are shown in Listing 10.10.

Listing 10.10 The new inner classes HidePanelMouseAdapter and MyActionListener in the class PlayerPanel.java of the project Agnes5

```
 1  /*
 2   * PlayerPanel.java - A class defines a player's panel for buttons of "New Game"
 3   * and "Quit".
 4   */
64  …
65      class HidePanelMouseAdapter extends MouseAdapter {
66          @Override
67          public void mouseEntered(MouseEvent evt) {
68              newGameBtn.setVisible(true);
69              quitBtn.setVisible(true);
70          }
71
72          @Override
73          public void mouseExited(MouseEvent evt) {
74              newGameBtn.setVisible(false);
75              quitBtn.setVisible(false);
76          }
77      }
78
79      class MyActionListener implements ActionListener {
80          @Override
81          public void actionPerformed(ActionEvent evt) {
82              if (evt.getSource() == newGameBtn) {
83                  if (gameCanvas != null) {
84                      gameCanvas.renewGame();
85                  }
86              } else if (evt.getSource() == quitBtn) {
87                  System.exit(0);
88              }
89          }
90      }
95  …
96      public void setGameTerminate(boolean gameTerminate) {
97          this.gameTerminate = gameTerminate;
98          if (this.gameTerminate) {
99              msgLbl.setVisible(true);
100             newGameBtn.setVisible(true);
101             quitBtn.setVisible(true);
102         } else {
103             msgLbl.setVisible(false);
104             newGameBtn.setVisible(false);
105             quitBtn.setVisible(false);
106         }
107     }
108 }
```

10.9 Always Showing the Dragged Cards on Top: The Project Agnes6

So far, the game works fine. Only one problem bothers the player. The problem is that when the player drags a set of cards and move over other existing cards in other columns, the dragged cards may go under the existing cards and become invisible. The reason is that the cards on the GUI have "layer." When cards are placed on the canvas, every card has its layer, which is also called z-order. That is, one card may be on top of other cards or under some other cards, which is "layer" along the z direction. Java provides a

JLayeredPane to allow programmers in controlling the layers of components, especially for overlapped components. However, it is not easy to be applied for controlling layers among so many cards with dynamic movements.

For solving the problem, we apply a "tricky" approach, which comes from observations. We can see that all cards on the same column are overlapped nicely, that is, the later added cards are on the front of the cards added earlier. More than that, when we drag a set of cards from a column and move the set of cards over some existing cards in other columns, the set of cards may be behind some existing cards; however, as long as we release mouse, the set of cards will jump to the front. These phenomena indicate that the "add" operations make the new added cards appear in front of existing cards that will be overlapped. Based on that observation, we implement a set of codes that is disguising to "add" the dragged cards on a new column whenever the dragged cards go over the edge of the new column so that the dragged cards appear on the front of the existing cards on the going over columns. Of course, if these going over columns are not the destination column, these "disguising added" cards should be removed later. The following piece of codes is an example for illustrating this idea:

```
Card dragCard;
dragCard = tempList.get(0); // to get the first card in the tempList
if (dragCard.getY() >= Consts.COL1_Y) { // dragCard is in the layout part
    overCol = theCol(dragCard.getX() + Consts.CARD_W);
    if ((overCol > beginCol) || (overCol < beginCol)) {
        overColumnList.add(overCol); // recording which column is "overCol"
        topColumn(overCol, tempList); // "add" the tempList on the overCol
        beginCol = overCol; // set beginCol to be overCol for continuous drag
    }
}

private void topColumn(int aCol, ArrayList tList) {
    Card tCard;
    if (aCol < Consts.NUM_COL) {
        for (int i = 0; i < tList.size(); i++) {
            tCard = (Card) tList.get(i);
            theColumn[aCol].add(tCard);
        }
    }
}
```

We can imagine that a tempList is dragged from left to right. The code above starts with a variable dragCard that refers to the first card of the tempList. If the dragCard is on the area of "layout" part (not in the "foundation" line), when the dragCard moves over a column overCol, the right edge of the dragCard would cover the left edge of the column. If the overCol is not the beginCol (the source column of the dragCard), an ArrayList overColumnList would record the index of the overCol for later use, and the method topColumn() is invoked to add the tempList on the overCol, which will make the cards in the tempList appearing in the front of the cards on the overCol. Immediately, the code assigns the beginCol to the overCol for making the overCol as the beginCol preparing for the continuous dragging. That is, if the tempList is continuously to be dragged to the right direction, the current overCol is counted as the beginCol and the next column would be the new overCol. This piece of codes adds the cards in the tempList on the overCol for making the cards in the tempList appear on the top of the overCol. Because the ArrayList overColumnList remembers which overCol has added the cards of the tempList, later when mouse is released to finish the dragging and add the tempList on the destination column, the overColumnList will tell those recorded overCols to remove the disguising added cards of the tempList so that the cards are not really added to those overCols. This piece of codes only checks the condition when the tempList is dragged from columns on the left side of the GUI to columns on the right side (it only checks the right edge of the dragCard) because when cards are dragged from right to left, the dragged cards won't appear under other existing cards.

The reason is that the cards on the right columns were added later than the cards on the left columns such that they have higher layer orders already.

Dragging cards from the card "layout" to the "foundation" line is more complicated than that situation as described above since the dragged cards could be from right to left, or from left to right, or from bottom to top. We have to check the dragged cards from all of three directions, but the principle is the same. After adding these codes, the game behaves "perfect." Please run the projects Agnes5, which does not have the codes described above, and Agnes6, which added the piece of codes above, to watch the differences and better understand the effects of the piece of codes for the implementation of the "trick."

10.10 Summary

The game Agnes explores the mouse-event-update-repaint chains for supporting the mouse controls. Java provides three different listeners for organizing the mouse event handlers. The game Agnes illustrated the usage of the mouse event handlers mouseDragged(), mouseReleased(), mouseClicked(), mouseEntered(), and mouseExited(). It demonstrates that mouse is a powerful controller for playing games.

The implementation of the game Agnes also tells that programming occasionally needs some tricky codes for solving some special problems. The tricky ideas are gained from experiences and programming skills. Even though they are not academic algorithms, they could be solutions adapted in practices.

We have experienced both semantic events and low-level events. They are very important for creating dynamic actions in video games. They should be learned from practices.

10.11 Exercises

Self-Review Questions

1. What are the definitions of the Interface MouseListener, MouseMotionListener, and MouseWheelListener?
2. What is the definition of the class MouseAdapter? What is the difference between listener and adapter?
3. After we added the inner class MyMouseAdapter into the class GameCanvas.java in the project Agnes1, we could not drag the cards on the canvas. Why? And later we solve the problem in the project Agnes2. How?
4. What is the functionality of the event handler mouseDragged()?
5. Why do we need to have the Boolean variable firstTime for separating the codes in the event handler mouseDragged() into two parts in the game Agnes?
6. What functionality is implemented in the event handler mouseReleased()?
7. What special requirements should be followed for declaring the shared variables among mouseDragged() and mouseReleased()?
8. What is a data structure of "array of ArrayList" for the "layout" structure of the game Agnes? Why do we need to have two nested "for" loops for dealing cards into the "layout"?
9. We developed an inner class MyMouseAdapter for supporting mouse event in the game Agnes. Do we have other alternative approaches for the implementation of the MouseAdapter?
10. In the game Agnes, we used the following two statements. Why?

```
addMouseListener(new MyMouseAdapter());
addMouseMotionListener(new
    MyMouseAdapter());
```

11. Draw a UML class diagram for the projects Agnes4 and Agnes5, respectively.
12. Draw a UML class diagram and a UML sequence diagram for the project Agnes6.

Projects

1. In our example projects, we did not use the event handler methods mousePressed() and mouseMoved(). Develop a test example project for using these two methods.
2. Imagine that "mouse drag" is equivalent to "mouse pressed + mouse moved." Could you apply this idea to replace the mouseDragged() method in the game Agnes? Write a test program to verify your ideas.
3. Modify the project ImageSlider discussed in Chap. 6 by removing the left button and the right button. Instead, use mouse to slide the images. That is, drag the current image to the left or to the right for sliding the current image.
4. A popular card game is called Solitaire. The story of the game says arrange cards in a "layout" as shown in Fig. 10.4. All of the cards are face down with only the exposed card on every column is face up. The objective of the game is to collect four full suits on the "foundation" line starting from Ace until King. Only when the following rules are satisfied, a dragged set of cards from a source column can be appended on an exposed card of a destination column: (1) the first card of the set of cards is one less than the exposed card, and (2) the two cards

have different colors. When a column has no exposed card, the last face-down card can be turned as face up. When the player clicks on the stock, one click opens one card face up. And the player can use any one of them for playing the game. And then, one click on the stock, all of face-up cards should be face down and piled back to the stock. Design and implement the game.
5. There are many different card games. Pick up a card game you prefer and implement it.
6. Further develop the game international chess listed in the exercise of the previous chapter to allow two players to move the chess pieces with mouse for playing the game.

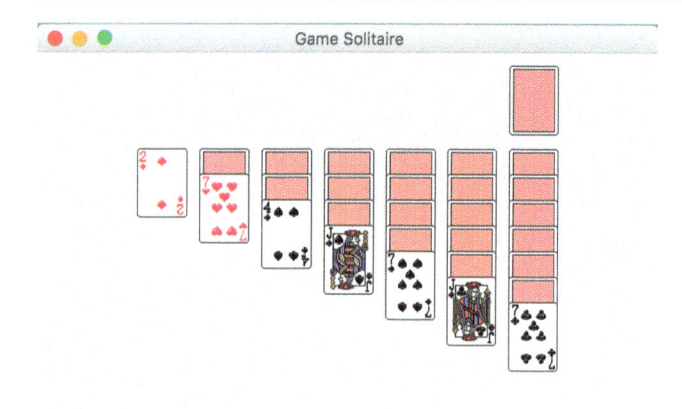

Fig. 10.4 The initial card layout of the game Solitaire (the "foundation" line is empty)

Part III
Games Based on Animation: Chaps. 11–21

Animation Programming: A Digital Clock and an Analog Clock

All of the event-driven games support different action-event update-repaint chains that are under the players' controls to discretely drive the games for dynamically updating and repainting their output scenes. If we can continuously drive the chains, the output scenes can also be continuously changed, which makes an illusion of animation. Java provides a built-in class Thread that can be constructed as a "game loop" that continuously drives an update-repaint chain for realizing the illusion of animation. This chapter goes through a digital clock and an analog clock to discover the "game loop" for introducing the programming on sprite-based animation.

The objectives of this chapter include:
1. The concept of animation.
2. A "clue": animation = while loop + update-repaint chain.
3. Animating a digital clock: from the "clue" to a technique.
4. The concept of "thread."
5. Java built-in class Thread and its usage.
6. Applying the animation technique for ticking an analog clock.
7. A computation for converting angles to coordinates.
8. Constructing a superclass of existing subclasses.
9. Auto time setting.

So far, we applied event-driven technique for programming games. No matter what the techniques are based on software components, or keys, or mouse, their action-event, or key-event, or mouse-event chains contain the same update-repaint part that updates the output scene and repaints them for realizing the dynamic behaviors of the games. Due to the fact that the human player's actions are discrete, that is, the driving force of events is discrete, the updated and repainted output scenes are also discrete. As long as we can find a mechanism that will continuously drive the update-repaint functions, the dynamic behaviors of the game will also become continuous.

A plenty of components in video games requires continuous dynamic behaviors. A simple bouncing ball is an intuitive example. The ball automatically and continuously changes its position inside a window. When it touches an edge of the window, the ball is bounced back and moves to another direction. Such a component gains a special term of "sprite" in the game field. A set of sprites in a game dynamically changes their positions, colors, shapes, etc. and interactively acts each other on a game scene. The game players intend to control their behaviors for realizing a story. It is that a video game.

The continuous dynamic behavior gives an illusion of animation. The technique of animation can be understood through cartoons or movies. A cartoon or a movie consists of a set of pre-drawn static pictures or a set of static photos. Every picture or every photo has the same object that is located in a slightly different position. When the set of pictures or photos is continuously shown in a certain speed, the slightly different positions give an illusion of a movement of the object. This is what the term "animation" means. Another kind of animations is made through animated objects themselves. That is, an animated object updates its position, and immediately the object in the updated position is repainted on the scene so that we can see an animation of the object. In order to distinguish these two kinds of animations, the former is termed as "frame-based animation," and the latter is termed as "sprite animation." The high-speed computers make it possible to rapidly change the position of an object and reshow the object on the updated position for giving an illusion of a movement of the object. Hence, today's video games are mainly based on the sprite animation. Consequently, before implementing a video game with sprites, we do need to learn how to animate an object.

11.1 Programming Continuous Dynamic Behaviors

As we have analyzed in Chap. 1, simulating dynamic behaviors is one of the necessary knowledge and skills for developing video games because almost all of objects on the GUI of games have dynamic behaviors. We have experienced many different dynamic behaviors from the example games in previous chapters. However, those dynamic behaviors are "discrete" since they are based on event-driven such that they happened only when player's actions applied. Now, we are going to further discuss new kind of dynamic behaviors that are "continuous."

Actually, the example game projects discussed on previous chapters have given us the clue for making continuous animation. We have demonstrated that the driving force of games in-text is a "while" loop in the "core"; the driving force in event-driven games is the player's manual inputs through an action-event chain or an action-event-update-repaint chain. What if we merge them together for using a continuous loop to drive an update-repaint chain? The update-repaint chain updates the position of an object and repaints the object. It is that an animation with a continuous dynamic behavior. If it is a correct clue, the remaining efforts for us are studying the techniques that can realize the clue.

Bearing the concept above in mind, we can see that a digital clock shows a different time with a numerical value every second; an analog clock displays its second hand, minute hand, and hour hand at different positions, respectively, in every second. That is, a dynamic behavior always associates with some properties of an object, and the values of the properties are continuously changed with a certain speed. In the light of the fact, if we can select some properties from an object, continuously update the values of the selected properties, and then keep repainting the updated object, we may express the object's continuous dynamic behaviors visually. This is the fundamental understanding for the animation programming.

For making the animation technique easier to be understood, we start our learning from a daily-life object, a digital clock, because for showing its ticks, we only need to paint a text string without dealing with any calculation and complicated paintings. After we understand the principle of animation, we are going to apply the technique for animating more sophisticated dynamic behaviors of other objects.

11.2 How to Tick: The Projects ADigitClock1 and ADigitClock2

Based on the GUI technique, we can write a program for displaying the simplest digital clock, which only shows a face of a digital clock without ticking. Its output is shown in Fig. 11.1 and the code is cited in Listing 11.1. This is the first version of a digital clock with the project name of ADigitClock1. When the project runs, it shows the current value of date and time only once without ticking. That is, it only shows a static scene without dynamic behaviors.

Listing 11.1 The project ADigitClock1

```
1  /*
2   * ADigitClock -- A project that implements a digit clock but it doesn't tick
3   */
4  package adigitclock;
5
6  import javax.swing.JFrame;
7
12 public class ADigitClock extends JFrame {
13
14     public ADigitClock() {
15         setDefaultCloseOperation(JFrame.EXIT_ON_CLOSE);
16         setTitle("A digit clock");
17         setSize(420, 100);
18
19         ClockCv cv = new ClockCv();
20         add(cv);
21
22         setVisible(true);
23     }
24
```

11.2 How to Tick: The Projects ADigitClock1 and ADigitClock2

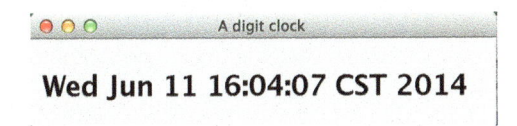

Fig. 11.1 A face of a digital clock without ticking

```
25     public static void main(String[] args) {
26         new ADigitClock();
27     }
28 }
```

```
1  /*
2   * ClockCv.java -- A class defines a digit clock, which cannot tick
3   */
4  package adigitclock;
5
6  import java.awt.Font;
7  import java.awt.Graphics;
8  import java.util.Date;
9  import javax.swing.JPanel;
10
15 public class ClockCv extends JPanel {
16     private Date theDate;
17
18     public ClockCv() {
19         theDate = new Date();
20     }
21
22     @Override
23     public void paint(Graphics g) {
24         g.setFont(new Font("TimeRoman", Font.BOLD, 24));
25         g.drawString(theDate.toString(), 10, 50);
26     }
27 }
```

Clearly, the face of the digital clock is made by the drawing coded in the paint() method of the class ClockCv.java. Why doesn't it tick? We might find out the problem from the code, which shows that the value of the date and time is obtained by calling "theDate = new Date()," but the program only invokes the statement ones so that the value won't be able to change continuously. Naturally we may find a solution for that problem based on the animation "clue" described above. The solution is to add a "while" loop to repeatedly update the value of the variable theDate and repaint it. This is the project ADigitClock2 and its code is shown in Listing 11.2.

Listing 11.2 The project ADigitClock2

```
1  /*
2   * ClockCv.java -- A class defines a digit clock, which cannot tick
3   */
4  package adigitclock;
5
6  import java.awt.Font;
```

```
 7  import java.awt.Graphics;
 8  import java.util.Date;
 9  import javax.swing.JPanel;
10
15  public class ClockCv extends JPanel {
16
17      private Date theDate;
18
19      public ClockCv() {
20          start();
21      }
22
23      private void start() {
24          while (true) {
25              theDate = new Date();
26              repaint();
27          }
28      }
29
30      @Override
31      public void paint(Graphics g) {
32          g.setFont(new Font("TimeRoman", Font.BOLD, 24));
33          g.drawString(theDate.toString(), 10, 50);
34      }
35  }
```

The project ADigitClock2 adds a "while" loop in the method start() of the ClockCv.java class, which tries to repeatedly update the variable theDate and invokes the method paint() to repaint the new updated value. Surprisingly, the execution result of the ADigitClock2 project is even worse than the project ADigitClock1 because nothing shows up (run the project ADigitClock2 to see). Why? For understanding the problem, we need to talk about process and mini-process in a multiprogramming environment.

11.3 Process and Mini-Process

A program in execution is termed as a process. A process is allocated in a block of main memory of a computer. The block of memory is known as the process's address space. The process starts, runs, and calls methods, until it terminates. All these form a sequence of control. In other words, a process occupies an address space and has its own control sequence.

A multiprogramming environment can support multiple processes running at the "same time." Chapter 1 mentioned that a computer has only one CPU. How can one CPU run multiple processes at the same time? Actually, these multiple processes are not running simultaneously, but they are running concurrently by sharing one CPU. A queuing model is often used to illustrate the controls of multiple processes as shown in Fig. 11.2. Every computer has only one CPU. At any time, the CPU only executes one process, and other processes should be waiting in the job queue. A long-time running process may be preempted by the operating system and be put back to the tail of the job queue so that the CPU can be shared by executing other processes from the job queue. It is the concurrent running that only one process in using the CPU at a time and multiple processes take a turn to share the same CPU.

Based on the description above, it is clear that each process deals with an own locus of control sequence, which is termed as a "thread." Multiple processes form multiple threads of control. Nowadays, programs usually have a GUI for users. Assume that the GUI of a program supports

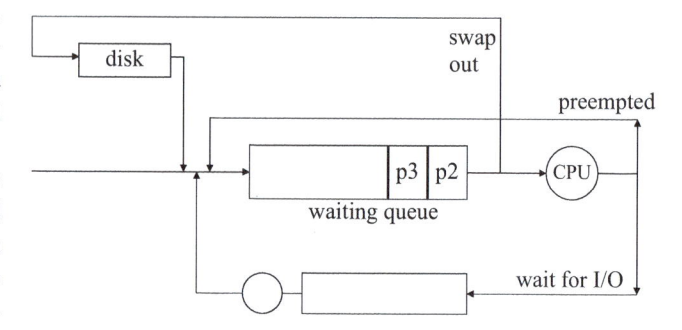

Fig. 11.2 A queuing model for illustrating the execution of multiple processes

multiple buttons and allows the user to click on any one of the buttons at any time, which is implemented in our example game projects in previous chapters. A button click means a new control sequence starts because the click would trigger an event handler that may change the behaviors of the process. For instance, when a program is in the middle way of its execution, whenever the user clicks the "Exit" or "Quit" button on the program's GUI, the program should stop its execution immediately. This is the event-driven programming that we have seen. An event-driven program means that it has multiple entry points: the main method is the starting entry point; every button has its own event handling routine that refers to its own sequence of control. It looks like a video player device that has start, stop, pause, resume, forward, and reverse multiple entry points. A click on any function button causes a switch among the multiple entry points. It is a similar scenario as multiple processes go through the querying model shown in Fig. 11.2. The difference is that these multiple sequences of control associate with the multiple function buttons inside one program, that is, inside one address space. These multiple sequences of control inside one program are termed as "lightweight process" in order to distinguish them from individual processes, which are termed as "heavyweight process." These multiple sequences of control are concurrent mini-processes inside one process address space.

Enlarge our view to a networked environment like the Web. Multiple users could access the same application (say an e-commerce page) at the same time. Every user activates an instance of the web page. Every instance involves one independent control sequence, that is, an independent thread. A concurrent server should be able to support multiple threads for controlling these multiple instances. Consequently, multi-threading is needed for an operating system, for a concurrent server in a network, and for an event-driven program that supports multiple entry points.

After understanding these concepts, let us go back to the project ADigitClock2 to explore the reason why the added "while" loop won't show the time ticks. Actually, the added "while" loop performs the function to repeatedly update the date and time and then invoke a repaint() call to display the new value of the date and time. However, the paint() method relies on the graphics context, which is another set of resources that resides on the graphical board hardware of the computer with its own control sequence. It looks like a mini-process that needs to share the CPU with the main control sequence. Unfortunately, the "while" loop in the main control sequence monopolizes all the resources in the system so that the mini-process paint() cannot be executed. In other words, the main control sequence won't allow the mini-process paint() to share the CPU so that the paint() method won't be able to perform its drawing function for repainting the new values of date and time. The following experience may make this scenario more understandable. If we add a statement System.out.println(theDate) into the "while" loop, then, when the project executes, the println() shows the updated value of the date and time in a text format repeatedly on the console window because the "while" loop includes the statement System.out.println() as part of the main control sequence, which is not another mini-process outside of the main control sequence. Clearly, the paint() is different from the println(). The paint() belongs to another mini-process that has its own control sequence. In other words, the project ADigitClock2 actually has two control sequences. One is the main control sequence and the other is the paint() control sequence. It requires a specific separate thread to support the paint() control sequence such that it can share the unique CPU with the main control sequence to allow the two threads running concurrently.

However, mini-processes or threads are different from processes. Threads that are lightweight processes inside a heavyweight process are not quite as independent as different heavyweight processes. All threads inside one heavyweight process are exactly inside the same address space, which means they share the same global variables, open files, child processes, timers, signals, etc. Therefore, one thread can read, write, or even completely wipe out another thread's stack. There is no protection between threads. But, each heavyweight process has its own address space, and the address space is protected.

11.4 The Java Built-In Class Thread

That is the reason why the Java programming language provides the built-in class Thread to support the multiple mini-process programming. The Java Thread class provides the following major methods: start(), run(), sleep(), join(), yield(), etc.

The start() method starts the thread execution, and it automatically invokes the method run(). There is no guarantee which moment the run() method will be begun after the start() method is invoked. However, in general this delay is at most only a few milliseconds after the start() method returns. The run() method body contains the code to be executed by the thread. When run() method returns, the thread is finished. Therefore, usually a repeated operation or a lengthy operation is placed in the run() method. A thread could be paused for a certain time period by calling the sleep() method. A statement sleep(50) means sleep for 50 ms. The yield() method is similar with the sleep() method, but it is used without the specific time indication. Both sleep() and yield() methods will pause the execution of the current thread in order to allow other threads with the same priority or greater priority (not lesser priority) to execute. The method join() can be used to synchronize the activities of different threads.

Fig. 11.3 The life cycle of a thread

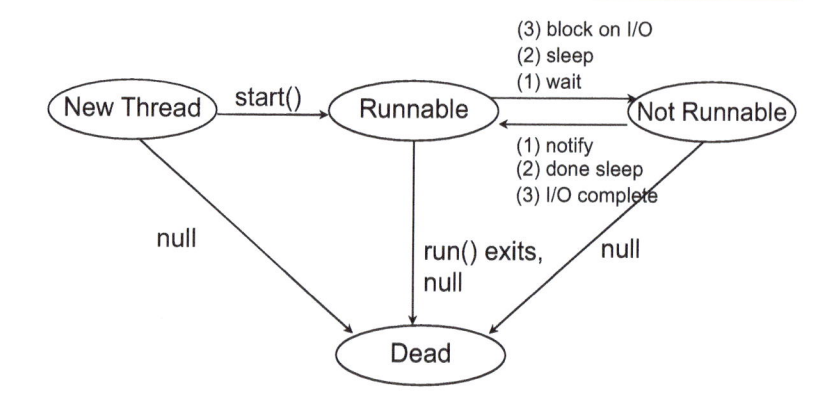

For example, ThreadA calls the join() method on ThreadB, which will cause ThreadA to be blocked until ThreadB has completed, and then ThreadA will continue. A Thread can be interrupted or assigned with a null value to be stopped at the current instruction.

Merging all of these methods together, we can depict thread's life cycle as shown in Fig. 11.3. As the figure indicates, after a New-Thread.start(), it automatically involves the method run().

11.5 How to Use the Class Thread?

There are two ways for using the class Thread. The first approach is to derive a subclass from the Thread class and override the run() method. A possible pseudo code could be drafted as follows:

```
public class MyThread extends Thread {
    public void run() {
        while(true) {
            do something;
            the thread sleeps for a while;
            // to allow other processes sharing
            // the CPU
        }
    }
}
```

The class MyThread can be invoked by another piece of code in another class as follows:

```
MyThread myThread = new MyThread();
myThread.start(); // the start() will auto-
    // matically invoke the run() defined above
```

Suppose that the "another class" is referred as main class. The above code means that the main class can access the run() method through the object of myThread.

The second approach is to implement an Interface Runnable. We have learned that an Interface is a special kind of class. It declares a set of abstract methods, which have no implementations. Besides the class Thread, Java also provides an Interface Runnable, which declares a method run().

If a class is a subclass of a superclass already, that is, the class "extends OtherClass" already, then it cannot "extend Thread" since Java only allows one superclass. In other words, under that case, the first approach discussed above cannot be adopted for creating a new thread. We have to use the second approach to create a thread. It means that the class has to "implements Runnable" instead. Then, we need to implement the method run() with what we would like to do. A possible pseudo code of this second approach could be:

```
public class MySub extends SuperClass imple-
    ments Runnable {
    public void run() {
        while(true) {
            do something;
            the thread sleeps for a while;
            // to allow other processes sharing
            // the CPU
        }
    }
}
```

Continuously, the class MySub will be invoked by other pieces of code as follows:

```
MySub ms = new MySub();
Thread myThread = new Thread(ms);
myThread.start();
```

Very often, these two separated pieces of code are merged into one class as follows:

```
public class MySub extends SuperClass imple-
    ments Runnable {
    Thread animThread = null;
```

```
    public void start() {
        if (animThread == null) {
            animThread = new Thread(this);
            animThread.start();
        }
    }

    // The implementation of the method run()
    //declared in the Interface Runnable
    public void run() {
        while(true) {
            do something;
            the thread sleeps for a while;
            // to allow other processes sharing
            // the CPU
        }
    }
    ….
}
```

Apparently, creating a thread is very similar with creating an event listener. When the main class implements the Interface Runnable, the method run() is directly implemented inside the main class. The statement "animThread = new Thread(this);" means that the new object animThread can access the method run() through the object "this." It is similar with the case when the main class directly implements the event listener ActionListener, where the event handler method actionPerformed() is implemented inside the main class. Under that case, the statement "bZero.addActionListener(this);" is used to allow the object bZero accessing the event handler method through the object "this" because "this" contains the event handler.

11.6 Applying Thread for Ticking the Digital Clock: The Project ADigitClock3

Now, we are ready to demonstrate the usage of a thread for ticking the digital clock. The third version of the project ADigitClock3 realizes the functionality as listed in Listing 11.3. The output of the project is shown in Fig. 11.4 (left).

Listing 11.3 The class ClockCv.java in the project ADigitClock3

```
1  /*
2   * ClockCv.java -- A class defines a digital clock, which now ticks by
3   * applying a thread.
4   */
5  package adigitclock;
6
7  import java.awt.Font;
8  import java.awt.Graphics;
9  import java.util.Date;
10 import javax.swing.JPanel;
11
16 public class ClockCv extends JPanel implements Runnable {
17
18     private Date theDate;
19     private Thread animation;
20
21     public ClockCv() {
22         start();
23     }
24
25     private void start() {
26         if (animation == null) {
27             animation = new Thread(this);
28             animation.start();
```

Fig. 11.4 (*Left*) A digital clock with the trail problem; (*Right*) a perfect clock

```
29          }
30      }
31
32      @Override
33      @SuppressWarnings("SleepWhileInLoop")
34      public void run() {
35          try {
36              while (true) {
37                  theDate = new Date();
38                  repaint();
39                  Thread.sleep(1000);
40              }
41          } catch (InterruptedException ex) {
42          }
43      }
44
45      @Override
46      public void paint(Graphics g) {
47          g.setFont(new Font("TimeRoman", Font.BOLD, 24));
48          g.drawString(theDate.toString(), 10, 50);
49      }
50 }
```

The method run() implements the abstract method run() declared in the Interface Runnable. The statement "animThread = new Thread(this)" instantiates a Thread object "animThread" and accepts "this" object as a parameter such that the object animThread can access the run() method inside the object "this." Then the following statement "animThread.start()" will invoke the run() method for executing the statements inside the run(). The run() method has a "while" loop that invokes three steps. (1) The first step is "theDate = new Date()," which assigns the current value of date and time to the variable theDate. That is, this statement updates the value of the variable theDate in every loop. (2) The second step is to invoke the method repaint() that is a built-in system method for invoking the method paint(). This call will repaint the new value of theDate on the canvas. (3) The third one is calling Thread.sleep(100) to enforce the thread sleeping for a certain time; here the time period is 100 ms. This sleep will allow other threads to share the unique CPU. Obviously, the working principle of the run() method realizes the "clue" mentioned above to repeatedly update the value of date and time and then paint the new value on the canvas for illustrating a ticking illusion.

Why the project ADigitClock3 works fine but the project ADigitClock2 doesn't work? The reason is that the project ADigitClock3 employs a thread that separates the "while + update-repaint chain" from the main thread. In addition, the sleep() call allows this thread share the unique CPU with the main control sequence such that we can see the painting of the updated values when we run the project ADigitClock3.

11.7 Trail and Flicker Problems: The Projects ADigitClock4 and ADigitClock5

Note: This section may count as a historical review since the new version of Java has eliminated the trail and flicker problems. That is, the code of the project ADigitClock3 works fine. Consequently, readers can skip this section. However, the paintComponent() method supports more functions than the method paint(). The code of ADigitClock5 is preferred.

Unfortunately, the output of the project ADigitClock3 in Fig. 11.4 (left) illustrates a so-called "trail" problem. The trail problem makes the time "second" part of the clock as two black rectangles. It is caused by that the repeatedly painting different values at the same position so that the different values are overlapped and "screwed up" as a black rectangle. If the clock runs for a while, then all of time digits will also be screwed up as black squares.

Actually, the solution is simple if the program can clean up the old painting before painting a new value. Thus, the project ADigitClock4 adds a new piece of code into the paint() method, which uses the background color to repaint the displaying area for "erasing" the old painting and then paints the new date and time on the cleaned canvas as shown in Listing 11.4.

11.7 Trail and Flicker Problems: The Projects ADigitClock4 and ADigitClock5

Listing 11.4 The method paint() in the class ClockCv of the project ADigitClock4

```
49      @Override
50      public void paint(Graphics g){
51          // make a special background color
52          g.setColor(new Color(50, 255, 50));
53          g.fillRect(0, 0, 420, 100);
54
55          g.setColor(Color.BLACK);
56          g.setFont(new Font("TimeRoman", Font.BOLD, 24));
57          g.drawString(theDate.toString(), 10, 50);
58      }
59  }
```

Obviously, this process goes through a sequence of actions: sets up the background color, erases the old painting with the background color, sets up the foreground color of the new painting, and paints the new values with the foreground color. In addition, a painting itself is a process just like a human drawing something on a paper, which takes a period of time starting from the first stroke until the last one on the screen. All of these are repeatedly and quickly switched in a very short time period, especially in cases of sophisticated paintings, which cause a new problem termed as "flicker" problem. When a flicker takes place, the screen may have some moving black lines appeared that looks weird.

For solving the flicker problem, a "double-buffering" technique has been developed. The technique hires a second buffer internally to allow the repeated sequence of switching actions described above occurring on the second buffer instead directly on the screen buffer. When a new painting is completed on the second buffer, one copy action copies the finished new painting from the second buffer to the screen so that no any dynamic actions appear on the screen. In other words, the second buffer absorbs the flicker and avoids the flicker directly appearing on the screen.

In the old days, programmers should implement the double-buffering technique in their own coding. Since Java 2D, Java implements the double-buffering technique in the new method paintComponent(), which has been introduced in Chap. 7 and used in previous chapters. In other words, the method paintComponent() does not only have stronger graphical capability than the method paint() but also is equipped with the double-buffering new technique. We are going to use the method paintComponent() instead of paint() method to take advantage of the built-in double-buffering technique for eliminating the flicker problem. The usage of the method paintComponent() is illustrated in the code in Listing 11.5. In using the method paintComponent(), a special attention is worth to be mentioned again. That is, the following two statements should be added as the first and the second statements in the method paintComponent().

```
super.paintComponent(g);
Graphics2D g2d = (Graphics2D) g;
```

These two statements switch the graphics context to Graphics2D. The Graphics2D supports more powerful drawing capabilities than Graphics. We have used the method paintComponent() for a while. Here, we returned to paint() method to emphasize the double-buffering technique and the benefits in using the method paintComponent(). The project ADigitClock5 results in a perfect digital clock without the problems of trail and flicker as shown in Fig. 11.4 (right).

Listing 11.5 The class ClockCv.java in the project ADigitClock5

```
1  /*
2   * ClockCv.java -- A class defines a digit clock, which ticks by applying
3   * a thread and invokes paintComponent() for taking advantage of the
4   * double buffer technique.
5   */
6  package adigitclock;
7
8  import java.awt.Color;
9  import java.awt.Font;
```

```java
10  import java.awt.Graphics;
11  import java.awt.Graphics2D;
12  import java.util.Date;
13  import javax.swing.JPanel;
14
19  public class ClockCv extends JPanel implements Runnable {
20
21      private Date theDate;
22      private Thread tickThread;
23
24      public ClockCv() {
25          start();
26      }
27
28      private void start() {
29          if (tickThread == null) {
30              tickThread = new Thread(this);
31              tickThread.start();
32          }
33      }
34
35      @Override
36      public void run() {
37          try {
38              while (true) {
39                  updateValue();
40                  repaint();
41                  Thread.sleep(1000);
42              }
43          } catch (InterruptedException ex) {
44          }
45      }
46
47      public void updateValue() {
48          theDate = new Date();
49      }
50
51      @Override
52      public void paintComponent(Graphics g){
53          super.paintComponent(g);
54          Graphics2D g2d = (Graphics2D) g;
55
56          // make a special background color
57          g2d.setColor(new Color(0, 255, 100));
58          g2d.fillRect(0, 0, 420, 100);
59
60          g2d.setColor(Color.BLACK);
61          g2d.setFont(new Font("TimeRoman", Font.BOLD, 24));
62          g2d.drawString(theDate.toString(), 10, 50);
63      }
64  }
```

11.8 Animation Technique

It is clear that the ticks of a digital clock are based on the thread that updates the value of date and time and repaints the new updated value. Besides that, an extra Thread.sleep() is added for pausing the current thread in order to give itself an opportunity to share the CPU with other threads. These actions are grouped in the "while" loop inside the method run() so that all of update-repaint functions will perform continuously, which realizes an applicable animation technique.

This while loop inside the method run() has a special name as a "game loop" because it is adapted in all of game programs for realizing required animations. Imagine that if we apply the game loop for updating the value of a position parameter of an object and repaint the object, then the object will appear at a new position in every loop. Under a certain number of update-repaint per second, the object will appear in a sequence of continuous new positions, which will give an illusion of a new kind of dynamic behavior – the object moves along the screen. This is an animation.

As mentioned before, there are two kinds of animation. One of them is frame based; the other is sprite based. The frame-based animation needs a set of pre-drawn figures, and each figure drew the same object with a slightly different position. Showing the set of frames continuously with a rate of certain number of frames per second, it produces an illusion of animation just like cartoons or movies. The sprite-based animation is using a computer to create a static object and then continuously change the object's attributes, such as position, shape, and the like. The independently animated objects in game world are termed as "sprite" so that this kind of animation is named sprite-based animation.

11.9 A Better Illustration of the Animation Technique

The project ADigitClock only displays a string with updated values at the same position. Now, let us go to see how an analog clock ticks, which would better illustrate the animation technique. The GUI of the analog clock is shown in Fig. 11.5 (left). Its UML class diagram is as in Fig. 11.5 (right). The class diagram indicates that the class ClockCv.java "uses" the following three classes: ClockFace.java, MinuteHand.java, and SecondHand.java.

When an analog clock ticks, the two hands should be able to move. Their movements are closer to real animations. The new project AnalogClock differs from the digital clock project in two aspects. (1) It animates real objects. (2) The changing property is the angle of the two hands, but the painting is based on coordinates (x, y), which require a special treatment.

11.10 A GUI of an Analog Clock: The Project AnalogClock1

Apparently, the GUI shown in Fig. 11.5 (left) is not a complete analog clock because it shows only the hands for minute and second. Due to the fact that the behaviors of the hour hand are similar with the two hands, we leave the hour hand later on purpose.

Programming an analog clock can be divided into two steps. The first step is to realize its static scene, and the second step is to add its dynamic behaviors. No matter which step, the first question is how to handle the property in angles because the 2D coordinate system has only the coordinates (x, y) without directly displaying of angles. The principle for converting an angle to coordinates (x, y) is shown in Fig. 11.6.

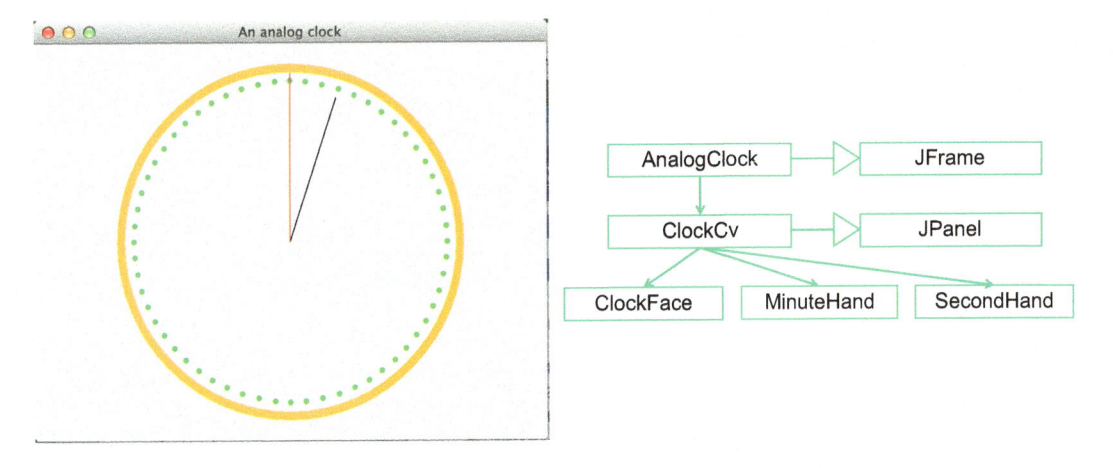

Fig. 11.5 (*Left*) A static scene of an analog clock; (*Right*) its UML class diagram

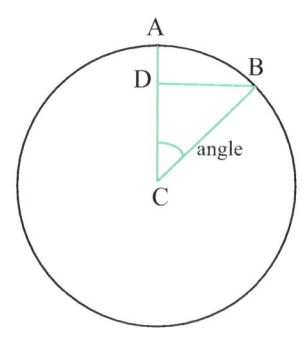

Fig. 11.6 The computation for converting angles to coordinates

Assume that the line CA is directly pointing to the 12 direction, which has an angle of 0. Then, the line CA turns an angle and reaches the position of the line CB. The lengths of both CA and CB are the radiuses of the circle. That is, the coordinates of point A are (centerX + 0, centerY − radius), and the coordinates of point B are (centerX + DB, centerY − DC). By looking at the triangle DCB, clearly the lengths of DB and DC are as follows:

```
// sin() and cos() accept radian
DB = (int)(Math.sin(angle in radian) * radius);
DC = (int)(Math.cos(angle in radian) * radius);
```

where (angle in radian) = angle * 2PI/360 and radius is a known value. That makes the painting of line CB easy since both centerX and centerY are known values, too.

```
g2d.drawLine(centerX, centerY, (centerX + DB),
    (centerY − DC));
```

Based on this analysis and following the UML class diagram shown in Fig. 11.5 (right), the static scene of the analog clock is implemented as in Listing 11.6.

Listing 11.6 The classes of the project AnalogClock1

```
1  /*
2   * AnalogClock1.java - The main class of a project that simulates an analog clock.
3   */
4  package analogclock;
5
6  import javax.swing.JFrame;
7
12 public class AnalogClock1 extends JFrame {
13
14     private ClockCv cv;
15
16     public AnalogClock1() {
17         super();
18         setDefaultCloseOperation(JFrame.EXIT_ON_CLOSE);
19         setTitle("An analog clock");
20         setSize(Consts.CV_WIDTH, Consts.CV_HEIGHT);
21
22         cv = new ClockCv();
23         add(cv);
24
25         setVisible(true);
26     }
27
28     public static void main(String[] args) {
29         new AnalogClock1();
30     }
31 }
```

```
1  /*
2   * ClockCv.java -- A class controls an analog clock.
3   */
```

11.10 A GUI of an Analog Clock: The Project AnalogClock1

```java
 4 package analogclock;
 5
 6 import java.awt.Graphics;
 7 import java.awt.Graphics2D;
 8 import javax.swing.JPanel;
 9
14 public class ClockCv extends JPanel {
15
16     private ClockFace clockFace;
17     private MinuteHand minuteHand;
18     private SecondHand secondHand;
19     // the radius of the clock frame. A global variable for every component
20     private int radiusClock;
21
22     public ClockCv() {
23         initComponent();
24     }
25
26     private void initComponent() {
27         initClockFace();
28         initMinuteHand();
29         initSecondHand();
30     }
31
32     public void initClockFace() {
33         clockFace = new ClockFace();
34         // radiusClock is calculated inside ClockFace.java
35         radiusClock = clockFace.getRadiusClock();
36     }
37
38     public void initMinuteHand() {
39         // radius of the minute hand is based on radiusClock
40         minuteHand = new MinuteHand(radiusClock);
41     }
42
43     public void initSecondHand() {
44         // radius of the second hand is based on radiusClock
45         secondHand = new SecondHand(radiusClock);
46     }
47
48     @Override
49     public void paintComponent(Graphics g) {
50         super.paintComponent(g);
51         Graphics2D g2d = (Graphics2D) g;
52
53         clockFace.paintFace(g2d);
54         minuteHand.paintMinuteHand(g2d);
55         secondHand.paintSecondHand(g2d);
56     }
57 }

 1 /*
 2  * ClockFace.java - A class defines the clock face of an analog clock.
 3  */
 4 package analogclock;
```

```
 5
 6 import java.awt.Color;
 7 import java.awt.Graphics2D;
 8
13 public class ClockFace {
14
15     private int radiusClock;
16     private int numCircles; // for making the clock frame thicker
17     private Color circleColor;
18     private int radiusDotCircle;
19     private int numDots;
20     private int dotRadius;
21     private Color dotColor;
22     private int da; // distance in angle between dots
23
24     public ClockFace() {
25         if (Consts.CV_WIDTH > Consts.CV_HEIGHT) {
26             radiusClock = (Consts.MAXY_DIS - Consts.MINY_DIS) / 2;
27         } else {
28             radiusClock = (Consts.MAXX_DIS - Consts.MINX_DIS) / 2;
29         }
30         numCircles = 8; // clock frame consists of 8 circles
31         circleColor = Color.ORANGE;
32         // distance between the dot circle and the frame is 10
33         radiusDotCircle = radiusClock - (int) (radiusClock * 0.10);
34         numDots = 60;
35         dotRadius = 3;
36         dotColor = Color.GREEN;
37         da = 6; // 6 degrees
38     }
39
40     public void paintFace(Graphics2D g2d) {
41         // paint the frame of the analog clock with 8 circles
42         g2d.setColor(circleColor);
43         for (int i = 0; i < numCircles; i++) {
44             g2d.drawOval(Consts.CENTERX - (radiusClock - i),
45                     Consts.CENTERY - (radiusClock - i),
46                     2 * (radiusClock - i), 2 * (radiusClock - i));
47         }
48
49         // paint the 60 dots
50         g2d.setColor(dotColor);
51         for (int j = 0; j < numDots; j++) {
52             int dotCx = Consts.CENTERX
53                     + (int) (Math.sin(da * j * Consts.RADIAN) * radiusDotCircle);
54             int dotCy = Consts.CENTERY
55                     - (int) (Math.cos(da * j * Consts.RADIAN) * radiusDotCircle);
56             g2d.fillOval(dotCx - dotRadius, dotCy - dotRadius,
57                     2 * dotRadius, 2 * dotRadius);
58         }
59     }
60
61     public int getRadiusClock() {
62         return radiusClock;
63     }
64 }
```

11.10 A GUI of an Analog Clock: The Project AnalogClock1

```java
/*
 * MinuteHand.java - A class defines the minute hand of an analog clock.
 */
package analogclock;

import java.awt.Color;
import java.awt.Graphics2D;

public class MinuteHand {

    private int radiusClock;
    private int radiusMinute;
    private Color minuteColor;
    private double minuteTurnAngle;
    private int minuteMoveX;
    private int minuteMoveY;

    public MinuteHand(int radiusClock) {
        this.radiusClock = radiusClock;
        radiusMinute = (int) (this.radiusClock * 0.85);
        minuteColor = Color.BLACK;
        // initialize the minute hand
        minuteTurnAngle = 18; // assume that its initial position is at 18 degrees
        minuteMoveX = (int) (Math.sin(minuteTurnAngle * Consts.RADIAN)
                * radiusMinute);
        minuteMoveY = (int) (Math.cos(minuteTurnAngle * Consts.RADIAN)
                * radiusMinute);
    }

    public void paintMinuteHand(Graphics2D g2d) {
        g2d.setColor(minuteColor);
        int minuteCx = Consts.CENTERX + minuteMoveX;
        int minuteCy = Consts.CENTERY - minuteMoveY;
        g2d.drawLine(Consts.CENTERX, Consts.CENTERY, minuteCx, minuteCy);
    }
}
```

```java
/*
 * SecondHand.java - A class defines the second hand of an analog clock.
 */
package analogclock;

import java.awt.Color;
import java.awt.Graphics2D;

public class SecondHand {

    private int radiusClock;
    private int radiusSecond;
    private Color secondColor;
    private int secTurnAngle;
    private int secMoveX;
    private int secMoveY;
```

```
21
22      public SecondHand(int radiusClock) {
23          this.radiusClock = radiusClock;
24          radiusSecond = (int) (this.radiusClock * 0.95);
25          secondColor = Color.RED;
26          // initialize the second hand
27          secTurnAngle = 0;
28          secMoveX = (int) (Math.sin(secTurnAngle * Consts.RADIAN) *
29                  radiusSecond);
30          secMoveY = (int) (Math.cos(secTurnAngle * Consts.RADIAN) *
31                  radiusSecond);
32      }
33
34      public void paintSecondHand(Graphics2D g2d) {
35          g2d.setColor(secondColor);
36          int secCx = Consts.CENTERX + secMoveX;
37          int secCy = Consts.CENTERY - secMoveY;
38          g2d.drawLine(Consts.CENTERX, Consts.CENTERY, secCx, secCy);
39      }
40 }
```

The class ClockCv.java has two major methods. The method initComponent() instantiates three objects of the three classes: clockFace, minuteHand, and secondHand. The other method paintComponent() invokes three painting methods defined in the three classes for painting the three objects. The class ClockFace.java mainly paints a clock frame that is represented by eight circles arranged consecutively in order to make the frame thicker and paints 60 dots along a circle for representing 60 s. The class MinuteHand.java receives the clock radius and sets the radius of the minute hand as 85% of the clock radius. Then, the class arbitrary assumes that the initial position of the minute hand is at 18°. Based on this given angle, the code converts the angle to coordinates of (x, y) and provides a paintMinuteHand() method to display the minute hand. Similarly, the class SecondHand.java also receives the clock radius and sets the radius of the second hand as 95% of the clock radius. The second hand directly points to the 12 position so that its initial position has an angle of 0°. A method paintSecondHand() is available for painting the object of the second hand.

11.11 Constructing a Superclass for Two Subclasses: The Project AnalogClock2

Looking at the codes of the two classes MinuteHand.java and SecondHand.java in the project AnalogClock1, we can see that they have the same set of attributes and methods; the only difference is that one has a title of "minute" and the other has a title of "second"; and some attributes have different values, such as radiusMinute vs. radiusSecond, minuteTurnAngle vs. secondTurnAngle, and the like. These similarities of the two classes in both codes and semantic meanings indicate that we can design a superclass for them. In order to create a superclass, we can move all of the common codes in terms of their semantic meanings into a new superclass and then make the original two classes as two subclasses that inherit the common properties and methods from the superclass. The resulting codes are shown in Listing 11.7.

Listing 11.7 The superclass ClockHand.java and two subclasses MinuteHand.java and SecondHand.java in the project AnalogClock2

```
1 /*
2  * ClockHand.java - A class defines the superclass clock hands of an analog clock.
3  */
4 package analogclock;
5
6 import java.awt.Color;
7 import java.awt.Graphics2D;
8
```

```java
13 public class ClockHand {
14
15     private int radiusClock;
16     private int radiusHand;
17     private double handPercent;
18     private Color handColor;
19     private int turnAngle;
20     private int moveX;
21     private int moveY;
22
23     public ClockHand(int radiusClock) {
24         this.radiusClock = radiusClock;
25     }
26
27     public void initHand() {
28         radiusHand = (int) (this.radiusClock * handPercent);
29         moveX = (int) (Math.sin(turnAngle * Consts.RADIAN) * radiusHand);
30         moveY = (int) (Math.cos(turnAngle * Consts.RADIAN) * radiusHand);
31     }
32
33     public void paintHand(Graphics2D g2d) {
34         g2d.setColor(handColor);
35         int tipX = Consts.CENTERX + moveX;
36         int tipY = Consts.CENTERY - moveY;
37         g2d.drawLine(Consts.CENTERX, Consts.CENTERY, tipX, tipY);
38     }
39
40     public double getHandPercent() {
41         return handPercent;
42     }
43
44     public void setHandPercent(double handPercent) {
45         this.handPercent = handPercent;
46     }
47
48     public int getTurnAngle() {
49         return turnAngle;
50     }
51
52     public void setTurnAngle(int turnAngle) {
53         this.turnAngle = turnAngle;
54     }
55
56     public Color getHandColor() {
57         return handColor;
58     }
59
60     public void setHandColor(Color handColor) {
61         this.handColor = handColor;
62     }
63 }
```

```
1  /*
2   * MinuteHand.java - A class defines the minute hand of an analog clock.
3   */
4
5  package analogclock;
6
7  import java.awt.Color;
8
13 public class MinuteHand extends ClockHand {
14
15     public MinuteHand(int radiusClock) {
16         super(radiusClock);
17         setHandPercent(0.85);
18         setTurnAngle(18);
19         setHandColor(Color.BLACK);
20         initHand();
21     }
22 }
```

```
1  /*
2   * SecondHand.java - A class defines the second hand of an analog clock.
3   */
4
5  package analogclock;
6
7  import java.awt.Color;
8
13 public class SecondHand extends ClockHand {
14
15     public SecondHand(int radiusClock) {
16         super(radiusClock);
17         setHandPercent(0.95);
18         setTurnAngle(0);
19         setHandColor(Color.RED);
20         initHand();
21     }
22 }
```

Both the classes MinuteHand.java and SecondHand.java "extend" the ClockHand.java superclass. They inherit all of the properties and methods. They separately assign the different initial values to their own attributes. Once we have the ClockHand.java as a superclass, adding an hour hand into the clock becomes much easy.

11.12 Applying Animation to Tick the Analog Clock: The Project AnalogClock3

After we have the static GUI ready, the second step is to explore the dynamic behaviors of the analog clock. We know that one circle of the clock face is 360° and the second hand goes through one circle and counts 60 s. Thus, the secondHand moves 360/60 = 6° per second. At the same time, when the secondHand completes one circle with 360°, the minuteHand turns 6° because 1 min is equivalent to 60 s. Consequently, the minuteHand moves 6/60 = 0.1° in every second. Thus, we can add these two values TICK_ANGLE = 6 and MINUTE_ANGLE = 0.1 into the class Consts.java. Similarly, the hourHand moves 360/12 = 30° in 1 h and 1 h counts 3600 s. In other words, the hourHand moves (30/3600)° in the time period of 1 s.

Due to the fact that both the classes MinuteHand.java and SecondHand.java are the subclasses of the superclass ClockHand.java, we only need to add a method updateHand() into the superclass ClockHand.java, and both the two subclasses can inherit the same method. Furthermore, the class ClockCv.java implements Interface Runnable, instantiates a Thread animThread, codes a method run(), and lets the method updateComponent() to invoke the two methods minuteHand.updateHand() and secondHand.updateHand(). The game loop drives the two hands animated nicely. The new added codes are listed in Listing 11.8.

11.12 Applying Animation to Tick the Analog Clock: The Project AnalogClock3

Listing 11.8 The new added codes for dynamic behaviors in the project AnalogClock3

```
 1  /*
 2   * ClockCv.java -- A class controls an analog clock.
 3   */
...
14  public class ClockCv extends JPanel implements Runnable {
15
...
49
50      private void start() {
51          if (animThread == null) {
52              animThread = new Thread(this);
53              animThread.start();
54          }
55      }
56
57      @Override
58      public void run() {
59          try {
60              while (true) {
61                  updateComponent();
62                  repaint();
63                  Thread.sleep(1000);
64              }
65          } catch (InterruptedException ex) {
66
67          }
68      }
69
70      public void updateComponent() {
71          minuteHand.updateHand();
72          secondHand.updateHand();
73      }
74
75      @Override
76      public void paintComponent(Graphics g) {
77          super.paintComponent(g);
78          Graphics2D g2d = (Graphics2D) g;
79
80          clockFace.paintFace(g2d);
81          minuteHand.paintHand(g2d);
82          secondHand.paintHand(g2d);
83      }
84  }
```

```
 1  /*
 2   * ClockHand.java - A class defines the superclass clock hands of an analog clock.
 3   */
...
13  public class ClockHand {
14
...
34      public void updateHand() {
35          setTurnAngle(getTurnAngle() + getAnglePerSec());
```

```
36              if (getTurnAngle() == 360) {
37                  setTurnAngle(-360);
38              }
39              moveX = (int) (Math.sin(getTurnAngle() * Consts.RADIAN) * radiusHand);
40              moveY = (int) (Math.cos(getTurnAngle() * Consts.RADIAN) * radiusHand);
41          }
42
43          public void paintHand(Graphics2D g2d) {
44              g2d.setColor(getHandColor());
45              int tipX = Consts.CENTER_X + moveX;
46              int tipY = Consts.CENTER_Y - moveY;
47              g2d.drawLine(Consts.CENTER_X, Consts.CENTER_Y, tipX, tipY);
48          }
49
50          … // getters and setters
81      }
```

```
1   /*
2    * MinuteHand.java - A class defines the minute hand of an analog clock.
3    */
4
5   package analogclock;
6
7   import java.awt.Color;
8
13  public class MinuteHand extends ClockHand {
14
15      public MinuteHand(int radiusClock) {
16          super(radiusClock);
17          setHandPercent(0.85);
18          setTurnAngle(18);
19          setHandColor(Color.BLACK);
20          setAnglePerSec(Consts.MINUTE_ANGLE);
21          initHand();
22      }
23  }
```

```
1   /*
2    * SecondHand.java - A class defines the second hand of an analog clock.
3    */
4
5   package analogclock;
6
7   import java.awt.Color;
8
13  public class SecondHand extends ClockHand {
14
15      public SecondHand(int radiusClock) {
16          super(radiusClock);
17          setHandPercent(0.95);
18          setTurnAngle(0);
19          setHandColor(Color.RED);
20          setAnglePerSec(Consts.TICK_ANGLE);
21          initHand();
22      }
23  }
```

11.13 Setting Clock Time Automatically: The Project AnalogClock4

Now we are going to complete the project by developing a new version of AnalogClock4. Firstly, we add an hour hand for the analog clock. The successful construction of the superclass ClockHand.java and the derivations of two subclasses of MinuteHand.java and SecondHand.java demonstrate the power of inheritance in OOP programming. Based on the experience, we can easily derive a new class HourHand.java for adding an hour hand because it is nothing else but a subclass of the super ClockHand.java, just like the minute hand. Therefore, in the new version, we simply make a copy of the class MinuteHand.java and rename it as HourHand.java with initial values of the properties for the hour hand. The clock face now is as shown on Fig. 11.7.

However, the initial time of the clock is still arbitrary set. If we would like to make it a useful analog clock, we need a mechanism to adjust the time with the real time in the real world. Therefore, we are going to design and implement an auto-setting mechanism. We can get the real time in the real world by instantiating an object of the Java built-in class GregorianCalendar, which is a concrete subclass of Calendar and provides the standard calendar system used by most of the world.

For getting the real time, the project AnalogClock4 adds a new class AutoSetButton.java as shown in Listing 11.9.

Listing 11.9 The new class AutoSetButton.java in the project AnalogClock4

```
 1  /*
 2   * AutoSetButton.java - A class defines an auto-setting button
 3   * for automatically sets up the analog clock.
 4   */
 5  package analogclock;
 6
 7  import java.awt.event.ActionEvent;
 8  import java.awt.event.ActionListener;
 9  import java.util.Calendar;
10  import java.util.GregorianCalendar;
11  import java.util.SimpleTimeZone;
12  import java.util.TimeZone;
13  import javax.swing.JButton;
14  import javax.swing.JPanel;
15
20  public class AutoSetButton extends JPanel {
21
22      private JButton autoSetButton;
23      private ClockCv clockCv;
24
25      public AutoSetButton(ClockCv clockCv) {
26          this.clockCv = clockCv;
```

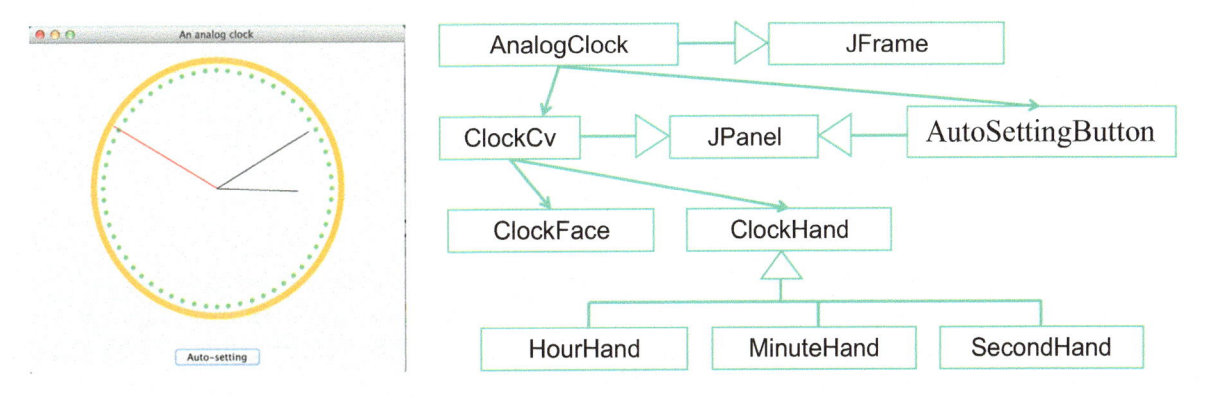

Fig. 11.7 (*Left*) The GUI; (*Right*) the UML class diagram of the project AnalogClock4

```java
            autoSetButton = new JButton("Auto-setting");
            add(autoSetButton);
            autoSetButton.addActionListener(new AutoSetListener());
        }

    class AutoSetListener implements ActionListener {

        @Override
        public void actionPerformed(ActionEvent evt) {
            if (evt.getSource() == autoSetButton) {
                // get the supported ids for GMT-05:00 (Eastern Standard Time)
                String[] ids = TimeZone.getAvailableIDs(-5 * 60 * 60 * 1000);
                // if no ids were returned, something is wrong. get out.
                if (ids.length == 0) {
                    System.exit(0);
                }

                // create a Eastern Standard Time time zone
                SimpleTimeZone est = new SimpleTimeZone(
                        -5 * 60 * 60 * 1000, ids[0]);
                // set up rules for Daylight Saving Time
                est.setStartRule(Calendar.APRIL, 1, Calendar.SUNDAY,
                        2 * 60 * 60 * 1000);
                est.setEndRule(Calendar.OCTOBER, -1, Calendar.SUNDAY,
                        2 * 60 * 60 * 1000);

                // create a GregorianCalendar with the Eastern Daylight time
                // zone and the current date and time
                GregorianCalendar gcalendar = new GregorianCalendar(est);
                int hour = gcalendar.get(Calendar.HOUR);
                int minute = gcalendar.get(Calendar.MINUTE);
                int second = gcalendar.get(Calendar.SECOND);

                int secondDegree = second * Consts.TICK_ANGLE;
                // minute degree should include the second's angle
                double minuteDegree = minute * 360 / 60
                        + secondDegree * 1.0 / 60; // convert to double
                // hour degree should include the minute's angle
                double hourDegree = hour * 360 / 12
                        + minuteDegree * 1.0 / 60;

                clockCv.getHourHand().setTurnAngle(hourDegree);
                clockCv.getMinuteHand().setTurnAngle(minuteDegree);
                clockCv.getSecondHand().setTurnAngle(secondDegree);
            }
        }
    }
}
```

Clearly, the class AutoSetButton.java "is-a" JPanel, and it contains a JButton. The inner class AutoSetListener "implements" the ActionListener with the actionPerformed() event handler. At any time, when the user clicks the auto-setting button, the event handler reacts the click action to instantiate an object of the built-in class GregorianCalendar. For getting a real local time, the code sets up the time zone "Eastern Standard Time" (New York time) that is (GWT – 05:00) and passes it as a parameter into the constructor of the built-in class GregorianCalendar(est) to get all the values of day, time, hour, minute, second, etc. Among them, we are interested in the values of hour, minute, and second, which are further converted into angle degrees and set up three hands geometrically. No doubt, it would be better if we can add an input mechanism to allow the user to input or select his/her local time zone. It could be an exercise for readers.

In order to avoid seriously modifying the code of the previous version AnalogClock3, we simply "append" an object autoSetButton in the main class AnalogClock4.java by adding a BorderLayout manager to set the clockCv on the CENTER and the autoSetButton on the SOUTH so that the original GUI and codes won't be modified a lot. The code is as shown in Listing 11.10. The resulting GUI and the UML class diagram of the project AnalogClock4 are shown in Fig. 11.7.

Listing 11.10 The class AnalogClock4.java "appends" the autoSetButton in the project AnalogClock4

```
1  /*
2   * AnalogClock4.java - The main class of a project that simulates an analog clock.
3   */
4  package analogclock;
5
6  import java.awt.BorderLayout;
7  import javax.swing.JFrame;
8
13 public class AnalogClock4 extends JFrame {
14
15     private ClockCv cv;
16
17     @SuppressWarnings("OverridableMethodCallInConstructor")
18     public AnalogClock4() {
19         super();
20         setDefaultCloseOperation(JFrame.EXIT_ON_CLOSE);
21         setTitle("An analog clock");
22         setSize(Consts.CV_WIDTH, Consts.CV_HEIGHT + Consts.BUTTON_H);
23
24         cv = new ClockCv();
25         add(cv, BorderLayout.CENTER);
26         AutoSetButton autoSetButton = new AutoSetButton(cv);
27         add(autoSetButton, BorderLayout.SOUTH);
28
29         setVisible(true);
30     }
31
32     @SuppressWarnings("ResultOfObjectAllocationIgnored")
33     public static void main(String[] args) {
34         new AnalogClock4();
35     }
36 }
```

11.14 Summary

This chapter discussed the animation programming. It starts from the dynamic behavior of a digital clock. For ticking the clock, a separated thread, i.e., a locus of control sequence besides the main control sequence, is required. A thread is a mini-process, which can be created by employing the Java built-in class Thread. After constructing the applicable animation technique, the project ADigitClock successfully animates the date and time to display a dynamic ticking. Furthermore, an analog clock is also developed that further approved the beauty and power of the animation technique.

Java built-in class Thread makes sprite animation easy. The run() method of a thread mainly performs three actions: update the value of a selected attribute of an object, paint the object according to the new updated value of the attribute, and pause for a while to allow other threads sharing the

CPU. The repetition of these three actions forms a so-called game loop that enhances the discrete update-repaint chain to be continuous update-repaint engine for driving sprite-based animations in video games. The thread supports concurrency inside one program. It is one of key techniques for game programming.

Reaching this point, the three major techniques, GUI, event handling, and animation, are covered. It prepared us to start our video games with animation.

11.15 Exercises

Self-Review Questions

1. What is the frame-based animation?
2. What is the sprite-based animation?
3. What is the principle of the animation technique?
4. Give an example in your daily life for explaining what concurrency is and what simultaneity is.
5. Give an example for explaining what multi-threading is.
6. What are the similarities and differences between processes and threads?
7. What are the two major approaches for using the Java built-in class Thread?
8. What are the major three steps in a "game loop"? Why do we need the three steps?
9. What special features does the method paintComponent() have? Why do we prefer the method paintComponent() to the method paint()?
10. What are the major differences between the project ADigitClock and the project AnalogClock?
11. How to derive a superclass based on existing subclasses? And how to derive a subclass from a superclass?
12. How to get the real time in the real world?

Projects

1. Further develop the analog clock to allow the user to set up the local time zone.
2. Design and implement a clock board that has two digital clocks and two analog clocks. The four clocks display four different times of four important cities in the world.
3. Add an alarm to make the analog clock as an alarm clock (if you don't know how to add sound yet, you may allow the alarm to display a string instead).
4. Design and implement a project that can move a square UP from the center of the canvas, and when it reaches a predefined distance, the square is automatically moved down to the center of the canvas. Then it repeats the same action for the directions of DOWN, LEFT, and RIGHT. Furthermore, the users are able to change its moving direction by using the four arrow keys or other four keys such as key W for UP, key Z for DOWN, key A for LEFT, and key S for RIGHT. The changed moving direction will be effective only when the square comes back to the center of the canvas.
5. Design and implement a photo slider that automatically slides a set of pre-stored photos or pictures one by one either to the left or to the right controlled by the users.
6. Design and implement a hello banner that moves a string "Hello, World!" from right to left. When the last character moves out of the left edge of the displaying area, the first character just enters the displaying area from the right edge (Fig. 11.8).
7. Design and implement a banner board that moves a set of banners from right to left. The board has a control panel to allow the users to add or delete banners and to change the font name, font size, font style, and color of each individual banner.

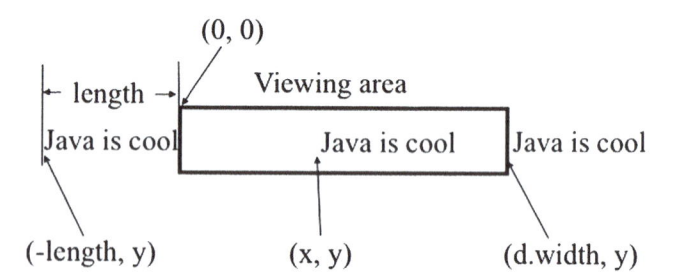

Fig. 11.8 The measures of a banner

12. Merging Visualization, Event Driven, and Animation: A Game WheelVideo

No doubt, the animation technique is directly related with the development of video games. We are going to make a transition from event-driven-based games to animation-based games. As an example, this chapter intends to apply the animation technique for enhancing the game WheelForture in-text (Chap. 4) to be a video game as WheelVideo. The GUI of the new video game has three pieces: a board, a player panel, and an animated wheel. The three pieces cover the three general techniques of visualization, event driven, and animation. They are needed for almost all of video games. The synchronization of the three pieces is illustrated through a UML sequence diagram.

The objectives of this chapter include:
1. Equipping the game WheelVideo with a GUI.
2. The GUI consists of three pieces that are made by different techniques.
3. Painting a string along the radius direction.
4. Painting a wheel with multiple sections.
5. The principle for rotating the wheel in using the animation technique.
6. Pausing and resuming the game loop.
7. The class PlayerPanel.java supports player's actions.
8. The class GameCanvas.java sets up communication paths among classes.
9. A UML sequence diagram explores dynamic behaviors of the game.

We have discussed and demonstrated three techniques: visualization, event driven, and animation. They are the most important techniques for programming video games. This chapter intends to illustrate the merging power of the three techniques for developing the game WheelFortune in-text discussed in Chap. 4 to be a video game WheelVideo. The GUI of the game WheelVideo includes a board, a rotating wheel, and a players' control panel for mimicking the real TV game Wheel-Of-Fortune. The board uses the painting technique; the rotating wheel is constructed with the animation technique; and the player panel is supported by the event-driven technique.

The text game WheelFortune in-text is centrally controlled, which has a "while" loop for driving every object to contribute its functionality. By adding a GUI that consists of three pieces, the game seems a distributed object system. All of independent objects have their own functions, and they work together by passing requests and data through the paths of communications. Thus, the project behaves different from its text version. Its design and implementation enhance our skills about event-driven programming with animations; meanwhile, it also enriches our concepts and knowledge about the object-oriented programming.

12.1 Adding a GUI to the Game WheelFortune In-Text: The Project WheelVideo1

The game WheelVideo has a similar story as the game WheelFortune in-text. However, they have different look-and-feel since the WheelVideo has a GUI. The first version WheelVideo1 only constructs the GUI with a static scene. All of dynamic behaviors of the game will be implemented in the next version of WheelVideo2.

The WheelVideo1 replaces the text board in the game WheelFortune in-text with a painting board for displaying characters guessed by the players, replaces the driving force from a "while" loop to be event driven, and also replaces the static wheel array with a rotating wheel driven by animation. For these replacements in the initialization stage, we may draft a pseudo code as follows:

1. A class Board.java is a JPanel, which paints an empty displaying block of rectangles corresponding to a given sentence and later fills in characters one-by-one guessed by the players.

2. A class PlayerPanel.java is another JPanel, which organizes a bunch of software components for displaying player's names and scores, and also provides text fields and buttons for players to input data and actions.
3. A class WheelGUI.java is also a JPanel, which paints a wheel with a set of scores. It then rotates the wheel with the animation technique.
4. A class GameCanvas.java is a bigger JPanel that organizes the three smaller JPanels of the three classes Board.java, PlayerPanel.java, and WheelGUI.java as one piece of GUI as shown in Fig. 12.1.

Due to these changes, the UML class diagram of the project WheelVideo1 is shown in Fig. 12.2 (right). For a comparison, the UML class diagram of the text game of WheelFortune3 is also cited as Fig. 12.2 (left). The two UML class diagrams tell us that these two games actually have a similar structure with the similar set of classes; however, the entire WheelFortune3 is text based, but every corresponding class in the game WheelVideo1 employs different technique as mentioned above.

12.2 The Class WheelGUI.java Constructs the Wheel with a Special Painting

We have learned the painting and event-driven techniques and applied them for several games. Therefore, the new fashion and the new technique in this game clearly appear on the new wheel. It thus is the focus we are going to discuss first.

The original class Wheel.java in the project WheelFortune in-text is a simple String array. It was an unseen component. However, the project WheelVideo1 needs a special painting for making a "complicated" wheel on the GUI as shown in Fig. 12.1. For explaining the principle of the painting, we develop a simpler project TestRotatePaint and then apply the new painting technique for making the wheel in the class WheelGUI.java.

12.2.1 Painting a String Along the Radius Direction Around the Center of a Circle

The project TestRotatePaint is to paint a string "Zero" along the radius direction with a certain degree around the central point of a circle as shown in Fig. 12.3. The first string "Zero" is painted along the perpendicular direction with a degree of zero. This painting has to be done one character a position along a radius direction with different values of radius. A piece of code for painting one string is as follows:

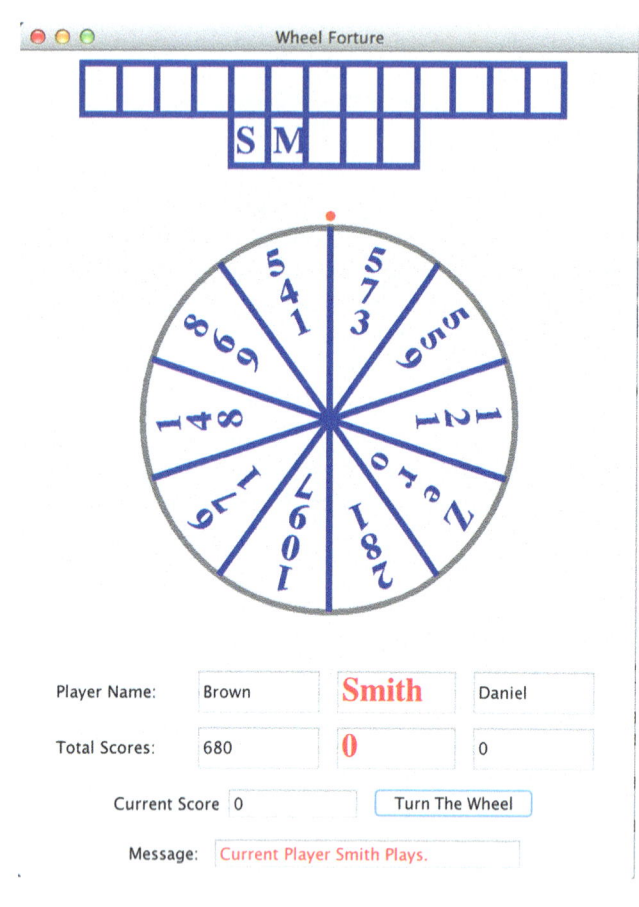

Fig. 12.1 The static scene of the GUI for the game WheelVideo1

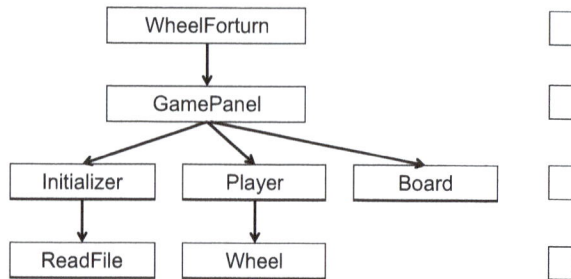

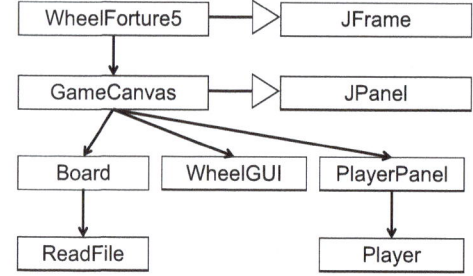

Fig. 12.2 (*Left*) The UML class diagram of the project WheelFortune3 in-text; (*right*) the UML class diagram of the project WheelVideo1

12.2 The Class WheelGUI.java Constructs the Wheel with a Special Painting

Fig. 12.3 Painting a string along the radius direction

```
String aStr = "Zero";
int charRadius = 100;
for (int j = 0; j < aStr.length(); j++) {
    g2d.drawString(aStr.substring(j, j +
        1), cx, (cy - charRadius));
    charRadius -= 25;
}
```

The String variable aStr currently holds the String "Zero." The variable charRadius defines the relative distance along the circle radius for each character. The first value of 100 is the radius for the first character "Z." The "for" loop sets up the index j from 0 to the aStr.length(), which counts for every character in the aStr. Entering the "for" loop, j = 0 and j+1 = 1 and the statement aStr.substring(j, j+1) get the first substring "Z" from the variable aStr. Thus, the statement g2d.drawString() draws the "Z" at the coordinates (cx, cy − charRadius), where the pair of (cx, cy) is the coordinates of the center of the circle. The following statement "charRadius -= 25;" minus 25 from the original 100 to make the radius 75 for the second substring, and then the second loop paints the second substring "e" at the radius 75. Similarly, the remaining loops continuously paint the remaining substrings of aStr at radius of 50 for "r" and 25 for "o."

Finishing the painting of the first "Zero," the program needs to turn a certain degree around the center of the circle for painting the second "Zero" and, then, the program turns the same angle again for painting the third "Zero." The built-in method g2d.rotate() can perform this function. The method is defined as follows:

```
g2d.rotate(Math.toRadians(degree), cx, cy);
```

The first parameter of the method g2d.rotate() requires the angle in the radians unit such that the degree has to be converted to the radians by invoking the Math.toRadians() method. The pair of (cx, cy) is the coordinates of the center of the circle.

Now, we can put them together for painting the string "Zero" along the radius direction with a rotation of certain degree. The complete piece of code is as below:

```
String aStr = "Zero";
int degrees = 0;
for (int i = 0; i < 5; i++) { // paint 5 strings at different angles
    g2d.rotate(Math.toRadians(degrees), cx, cy);
    // paint one string "Zero" at a certain angle
    int charRadius = 100;
    for (int j = 0; j < aStr.length(); j++) {
        g2d.drawString(aStr.substring(j, j + 1), cx, (cy - charRadius));
        charRadius -= 25;
    }
    degrees = 20;
}
```

The value of the variable "degrees" is the angle from the current position rotates to the next position. It is a relative value, not an accumulated total value from the position of 0 because the five paintings are inside one "for" loop and inside one paintComponent() call. Readers can find the complete code from the project TestRotatePaint.

12.2.2 Painting the Wheel in the Project WheelVideo1: The Class WheelGUI.java

After understanding the principle of painting a string along the radius direction around the center of a circle, we can implement the wheel for the project WheelVideo1. We design the wheel of the game consists of ten strings. We would like to paint 10 radius lines and then paint each of ten strings between two lines.

The pseudo code for painting the entire wheel can be drafted as follows: (1) initializing an String array wheel[10] with a String "Zero" at the wheel[5] and then inserting nine integer strings with random values in the range of [100, 1000) into the remaining nine slots, (2) drawing a circle as the edge of the wheel, (3) dividing the wheel into ten slots with 36° each and setting up the angle from one radius line to the starting point of a string with the variable rotateToStr = 13° and the angle from the starting point of the string to the next radius line with a variable rotateToLine = 36 − 13 = 23°, and (4) drawing 1 radius line and an integer string at one slot for the ten integer strings stored in the array wheel[]. The code of the class WheelGUI.java is shown in Listing 12.1.

Listing 12.1 The class WheelGUI.java in the project WheelVideo1

```
1  /*
2   * WheelGUI.java - A class defines the wheel component.
3   */
4  package wheelvideo;
5
6  import java.awt.BasicStroke;
7  import java.awt.Color;
8  import java.awt.Font;
9  import java.awt.Graphics;
10 import java.awt.Graphics2D;
11 import java.awt.Stroke;
12 import javax.swing.JPanel;
13
18 public class WheelGUI extends JPanel {
19
20     private final String wheel[];
21     private final int wheelLen = 10; // assume that
22     private int cx, cy;
23     private int wheelRadius;
24     private final int pRadius = 4; // radius of the red point
25     private final double rPercent = 0.8; // radius percent for leaving margine
26
27     public WheelGUI() {
28         wheel = new String[wheelLen];
29         initWheel();
30     }
31
32     private void initWheel() {
33         if (Consts.CV_WIDTH > Consts.CV_HEIGHT) {
34             wheelRadius = (int) ((Consts.MAXY - Consts.MINY) / 2 * rPercent);
35         } else {
36             wheelRadius = (int) ((Consts.MAXX - Consts.MINX) / 2 * rPercent);
37         }
38         int ranInt;
39         for (int i = 0; i < wheelLen; i++) {
40             ranInt = (int) ((Math.random() * 1000) + 100); // [100, 1100)
41             if (i == 5) {
42                 wheel[i] = "Zero";
43             } else {
44                 wheel[i] = Integer.toString(ranInt); // all are Strings
45             }
46         }
```

12.3 The Class Board.java Constructs a Displaying Board

```java
47              cx = (int) (Consts.MAXX - Consts.MINX) / 2;
48              cy = (int) (Consts.MAXY - Consts.MINY) / 2;
49          }
50
51          @Override
52          public void paintComponent(Graphics g) {
53              super.paintComponent(g);
54              Graphics2D g2d = (Graphics2D) g;
55
56              // paint the stop-indicator
57              g2d.setColor(Color.RED);
58              g2d.fillOval(cx - pRadius, cy - wheelRadius - 5 - 2 * pRadius,
59                      2 * pRadius, 2 * pRadius);
60              // paint the wheel circle
61              g2d.setColor(Color.GRAY);
62              Stroke solid = new BasicStroke(5.0f);
63              g2d.setStroke(solid);
64              g2d.drawOval(cx - wheelRadius, cy - wheelRadius, 2 * wheelRadius,
65                      2 * wheelRadius);
66
67              // paint the wheel
68              g2d.setColor(Color.BLUE);
69              drawWheel(g2d);
70          }
71
72          public void drawWheel(Graphics2D g2d) {
73              g2d.setFont(new Font("Times", Font.BOLD, 30));
74              // rotate the angle for painting strings and lines
75              int rotateToStr = 13;
76              int rotateToLine = 23;
77              for (int i = 0; i < wheelLen; i++) {
78                  // paint number strings: rotate the angle from the line to the number
79                  g2d.rotate(Math.toRadians(rotateToStr), cx, cy);
80                  int charRadius = (int) (wheelRadius * rPercent);
81                  String aStr = wheel[i];
82                  for (int j = 0; j < aStr.length(); j++) {
83                      g2d.drawString(aStr.substring(j, j + 1), cx, (cy - charRadius));
84                      charRadius -= 25;
85                  }
86                  // paint lines: rotate the angle from the number string to the next line
87                  g2d.rotate(Math.toRadians(rotateToLine), cx, cy);
88                  g2d.drawLine(cx, cy, cx, cy + wheelRadius);
89              }
90          }
91      }
```

Clearly, the method initWheel() implements the step (1) in the pseudo code, and the method paintComponent() realizes the other steps of the pseudo code. No doubt, the wheel is a static painting only at this moment.

12.3 The Class Board.java Constructs a Displaying Board

The class Board.java constructs the displaying board for painting a block of empty rectangles at the central position along the x direction. Fortunately, the AnagramGUI game

(Chap. 7) has implemented a board with the same requirement. In addition the project PaintXmasCard (Chap. 5) has discussed how to divide a long sentence into shorter substrings and arrange them at the center position of a board. The board in this game WheelVideo1 is a combination of these two cases. Thus, the code of the class Board.java is directly cited in Listing 12.2.

Listing 12.2 The code of the class Board.java in the project WheelVideo1

```
 1 /*
 2  * Board.java - A class defines a board for displaying the sentence.
 3  */
 4 package wheelvideo;
 5
 6 import java.awt.BasicStroke;
 7 import java.awt.Color;
 8 import java.awt.Dimension;
 9 import java.awt.Font;
10 import java.awt.Graphics;
11 import java.awt.Graphics2D;
12 import java.awt.Stroke;
13 import java.util.StringTokenizer;
14 import javax.swing.JPanel;
15
20 public class Board extends JPanel {
21
22     private String sentenceStr;
23     private int sentenceLen;
24     private ReadFile readFile;
25
26     private int cx, cy; // center point (x, y)
27     private char[] currAry;
28     private int px, py; // paint panel starting point (x, y)
29     private int bWidth, bHeight; // width and height of each char
30     private int sx, sy; // paint string starting point (x, y)
31     private double marginPerc = 0.98; // making margins
32     private boolean hasNextLine = false;
33
34     public Board() {
35         this.setPreferredSize(new Dimension(Consts.CV_WIDTH, Consts.BOARD_H));
36         initSentence();
37         initBoard();
38     }
39
40     private void initSentence() {
41         readFile = new ReadFile();
42         readFile.selectFile();
43         sentenceStr = readFile.readContent();
44         sentenceStr = sentenceStr.toUpperCase();
45         sentenceLen = sentenceStr.length();
46     }
47
48     private void initBoard() {
49         cx = (int) ((Consts.MAXX_DIS - Consts.MINX_DIS) / 2);
50         cy = (int) (Consts.BOARD_H / 2);
```

12.3 The Class Board.java Constructs a Displaying Board

```java
51            px = 10;
52            py = 10;
53            bWidth = 30;
54            bHeight = 40;
55            sx = px + 4;
56            sy = py + 30;
57            currAry = new char[sentenceLen];
58            initCharAry(); // init it with empty char
59        }
60
61        @Override
62        public void paintComponent(Graphics g) {
63            super.paintComponent(g);
64            Graphics2D g2d = (Graphics2D) g;
65
66            Stroke solid = new BasicStroke(5.0f);
67            g2d.setStroke(solid);
68
69            g2d.setColor(Color.BLUE);
70            g2d.setFont(new Font("Times", Font.BOLD, 30));
71
72            // the maximum number of characters can be displayed along the width
73            int numCharDisp = (int) (((Consts.MAXX_DIS - Consts.MINX_DIS)
74                    * marginPerc) / bWidth);
75            // concatenate words into a subStr and paint it centered
76            String subStr = "";
77            int numCharSubStr = subStr.length();
78            int row = 0;
79            int nextLineIdx = 0;
80            StringTokenizer st
81                    = new StringTokenizer(sentenceStr, " ");
82            while (st.hasMoreTokens()) {
83                String nextT = st.nextToken();
84                numCharSubStr = numCharSubStr + nextT.length();
85                if (numCharSubStr <= numCharDisp) {
86                    subStr = subStr + nextT + " "; // add a blank between two words
87                    numCharSubStr += 1;
88                } else {
89                    hasNextLine = true; // enter here means that the second line exist
90                    paintOneRow(g2d, subStr, row, nextLineIdx);
91
92                    // parameters for the next line
93                    nextLineIdx = subStr.length(); // index of the second line
94                    // start the subStr in the next line
95                    subStr = nextT + " ";
96                    numCharSubStr = subStr.length();
97                    row++; // counting for number of lines
98                }
99            }
100           // painting the last piece if any (after "while" finishes)
101           // the last piece could be the first row or the second row
102           if (!subStr.equals(" ")) {
103               paintOneRow(g2d, subStr, row, nextLineIdx);
104           }
105       }
106
```

```java
    public void paintOneRow(Graphics2D g2d, String subStr, int row, int nextLineIdx) {
        // paint the board: px = (center x - half of subStr width)
        // "- 1" is to minus the added blank character
        px = cx - (int) (((subStr.length() - 1) / 2) * bWidth);
        sx = px + 4;

        if (!hasNextLine) { // if only has one line, it should be at the middle
            py = cy - (int) (bHeight / 2);
        }
        sy = py + 30; // the coordinates of the bottom-left point
        paintEmptyPanel(g2d, subStr, row);
        paintSubStr(g2d, subStr, row, nextLineIdx);
    }

    public void paintEmptyPanel(Graphics2D g2d, String subStr, int row) {
        for (int i = 0; i < subStr.length() - 1; i++) {
            g2d.drawRect(px + i * bWidth, py + row * bHeight,
                    bWidth, bHeight);
        }
    }

    public void paintSubStr(Graphics2D g2d, String subStr, int row, int nextLineIdx) {
        for (int k = 0; k < subStr.length() - 1; k++) {
            int idx = k + nextLineIdx; // comes from the first line
            if (currAry[idx] != ' ') {
                g2d.drawString(Character.toString(currAry[idx]),
                        sx + k * bWidth, sy + row * bHeight);
            }
        }
    }

    public void initCharAry() {
        for (int i = 0; i < sentenceLen; i++) {
            currAry[i] = ' ';
        }
    }
}
```

The code of the class Board.java shows that it has a method initSentence() to invoke the methods defined in the class ReadFile.java to read in a sentence from a text file for initializing the variable sentenceStr and to hold the length of the sentence in the variable sentenceLen. And then, another method initBoard() sets up several coordinates (x, y) for painting an empty block of rectangles preparing for filling in guessed characters issued by the game players later. Internally, a char array currAry[] that has the same length as the sentence is declared to hold the correctly guessed characters that matched with the characters in the given sentence. And then the characters stored in the currAry[] are painted in the corresponding empty blocks on the board.

The major method paintComponent() of the class Board.java is going to paint an empty displaying block on the central position of the board. As mentioned, the related algorithm and practice have been seen in previous chapters. Here, we briefly summarize the major functions defined in the method paintComponent() as a reminder. (1) It hires the built-in class BasicStroke to set up the line width and set up the color blue for painting the block and characters. At the same time, it also sets up the font for the characters. The font size should match with the values of bWidth and bHeight defined for each "box" that is for holding a character. (2) It, then, measures the maximum number of characters that could be placed along the width of the board as follows:

```
numCharDisp = (int) (((Consts.MAXX_DIS - Consts.MINX_DIS) * marginPerc) / bWidth);
```

After that, it employs the built-in class StringTokenizer to split the sentence into tokens (words) and concatenate the words into a subStr such that the length of the subStr is less than or equal to the numCharDisp. And then, it looks for the starting x-coordinate px of the subStr by using the central x-coordinate cx minus the half-length of the subStr. (3) The height of the board only permits at most three lines of characters, which posts a requirement to all of sentences in the text files that the lengths of all of sentences must be less than or equal to (2 * numCharDisp). (4) Finally, it invokes the paintOneRow() method, which in turn invokes paintEmptyPanel() to paint the empty displaying block without characters at the initialization stage and invokes the method paintSubStr() to paint the characters stored in the array currAry[] later when players issue guessed characters.

However, this game board needs to paint a sentence, but the board in the AnagramGUI game is for painting a word. Usually a sentence is longer than a word; it may end up with multiple rows. Thus, besides placing every substring at the center position along the x direction, we also would like to arrange the entire sentence near the middle position along the y direction. The code sets py = 10 is for the case of a long sentence that will last two or more rows. Once the sentence is short and only forms one row, the code applies the statement "py = cy - (int) (bHeight / 2);" to adjust the starting y coordinate for making the entire sentence closing to the middle position along the y direction.

We would also like to reuse the same method paintOneRow() for painting either single row or multiple rows. For that, we add a Boolean variable hasNextLine and initialize it as false. For the case of multiple rows, after the first row has been painted, the code sets "hasNextLine = true" such that the method paintOneRow() continues to paint the second row. This is a kind of skill that can extend the reusability of codes.

The class Board.java also reuses the class ReadFile.java for reading in a sentence from a text file. The class ReadFile.java has been reused for couple of times. The code used in the game AnagramGUI (Chap. 7) is the most complete one. But, in the AnagramGUI game, two JRadioButtons were used for selecting one of two text files. However, this approach may limit the flexibility when the number of text files would be more than two. Therefore, for this game, we simply use a JOptionPane for asking the users to type in a file name. The method selectFile() contains this statement. In addition, the other two methods countNumLines() and readContent() are exactly same as the class ReadFile.java in the game AnagramGUI. Readers can find the complete code of the class ReadFile.java from the project WheelVideo1.

12.4 The Class PlayerPanel.java Provides a Control Panel for Players

The class PlayerPanel.java is based on the event-driven technique to provide a control panel for players. As Fig. 12.1 shows, it lists three players' names and total scores and hires the red color and bigger font to indicate the current player. The more important is that it provides a "Turn The Wheel" button for the current player to click on it in order to rotate the wheel. At the initialization stage, the class only statically composes related software components on the GUI. The code of the class PlayerPanel.java is shown in Listing 12.3.

Listing 12.3 The code of the class PlayerPanel.java in the project WheelVideo1

```
 1  /*
 2   * PlayerPanel.java - A class defines a panel for players.
 3   */
 4  package wheelvideo;
 5
 6  import java.awt.BorderLayout;
 7  import java.awt.Color;
 8  import java.awt.Dimension;
 9  import java.awt.Font;
10  import java.awt.GridLayout;
11  import java.awt.Insets;
12  import javax.swing.JButton;
13  import javax.swing.JLabel;
14  import javax.swing.JOptionPane;
15  import javax.swing.JPanel;
16  import javax.swing.JTextField;
17  import javax.swing.border.EmptyBorder;
18
23  public class PlayerPanel extends JPanel {
24
```

```java
25      private Player[] playerAry;
26      private int numPlayer;
27      private int currPlayerIdx;
28
29      private JLabel nameLabel;
30      private JTextField playerName1;
31      private JTextField playerName2;
32      private JTextField playerName3;
33      private JLabel tScoreLabel;
34      private JTextField totalScore1;
35      private JTextField totalScore2;
36      private JTextField totalScore3;
37
38      private JLabel cScore;
39      private JTextField currScore;
40      private JButton turnWheel;
41
42      private JLabel msgLabel;
43      private JTextField msg;
44
45      private JPanel playerP;
46      private JPanel scoreP;
47      private JPanel msgP;
48
49      public PlayerPanel() {
50          this.setPreferredSize(new Dimension(
51                  Consts.CV_WIDTH, Consts.PLAYER_PANEL_H));
52          this.setLayout(new BorderLayout());
53          initPlayer();
54          initPlayerPanel();
55      }
56
57      private void initPlayer() {
58          numPlayer = 3;
59          currPlayerIdx = 0;
60          playerAry = new Player[numPlayer];
61          for (int i = 0; i < numPlayer; i++) {
62              playerAry[i] = new Player();
63              playerAry[i].setName(initPlayerData(i, "name"));
64              playerAry[i].setSex(initPlayerData(i, "sex"));
65              playerAry[i].setTotalScore(0);
66          }
67      }
68
69      public String initPlayerData(int idx, String title) {
70          String numTh = "first";
71          switch (idx) {
72              case 0:
73                  numTh = "first ";
74                  break;
75              case 1:
76                  numTh = "second ";
77                  break;
78              case 2:
79                  numTh = "third ";
```

12.4 The Class PlayerPanel.java Provides a Control Panel for Players

```java
80                      break;
81              }
82              return JOptionPane.showInputDialog(
83                      "Enter " + numTh + " player's " + title);
84      }
85
86      private void initPlayerPanel() {
87              playerP = new JPanel();
88              EmptyBorder eb = new EmptyBorder(new Insets(5, 30, 5, 30));
89              playerP.setBorder(eb);
90              playerP.setLayout(new GridLayout(2, 4, 8, 5));
91
92              nameLabel = new JLabel("Player Name: ");
93              playerP.add(nameLabel);
94              playerName1 = new JTextField(10);
95              playerP.add(playerName1);
96              playerName2 = new JTextField(10);
97              playerP.add(playerName2);
98              playerName3 = new JTextField(10);
99              playerP.add(playerName3);
100             tScoreLabel = new JLabel("Total Scores: ");
101             playerP.add(tScoreLabel);
102             totalScore1 = new JTextField(10);
103             playerP.add(totalScore1);
104             totalScore2 = new JTextField(10);
105             playerP.add(totalScore2);
106             totalScore3 = new JTextField(10);
107             playerP.add(totalScore3);
108
109             scoreP = new JPanel();
110             cScore = new JLabel("Current Score");
111             scoreP.add(cScore);
112             currScore = new JTextField(8);
113             scoreP.add(currScore);
114             turnWheel = new JButton("Turn The Wheel");
115             scoreP.add(turnWheel);
116
117             msgP = new JPanel();
118             msgLabel = new JLabel("Message: ");
119             msg = new JTextField(28);
120             msgP.add(msgLabel);
121             msgP.add(msg);
122             msg.setForeground(Color.red);
123
124             this.add(playerP, BorderLayout.NORTH);
125             this.add(scoreP, BorderLayout.CENTER);
126             this.add(msgP, BorderLayout.SOUTH);
127
128             showData();
129     }
130
131     public void showData() {
132             Font newFont = new Font("Times", Font.BOLD, 26);
133             JTextField modelText = new JTextField();
134             Font defaultFont = modelText.getFont();
135             switch (currPlayerIdx) {
```

```
136                case 0:
137                    playerName1.setForeground(Color.red);
138                    playerName1.setFont(newFont);
139                    playerName1.setText(playerAry[0].getName());
140                    totalScore1.setForeground(Color.red);
141                    totalScore1.setFont(newFont);
142                    totalScore1.setText("" + playerAry[0].getTotalScore());
143
144                    playerName2.setForeground(Color.black);
145                    playerName2.setFont(defaultFont);
146                    playerName2.setText(playerAry[1].getName());
147                    totalScore2.setForeground(Color.black);
148                    totalScore2.setFont(defaultFont);
149                    totalScore2.setText("" + playerAry[1].getTotalScore());
150
151                    playerName3.setForeground(Color.black);
152                    playerName3.setFont(defaultFont);
153                    playerName3.setText(playerAry[2].getName());
154                    totalScore3.setForeground(Color.black);
155                    totalScore3.setFont(defaultFont);
156                    totalScore3.setText("" + playerAry[2].getTotalScore());
157                    break;
158                case 1:
159                    playerName1.setForeground(Color.black);
160                    playerName1.setFont(defaultFont);
161                    playerName1.setText(playerAry[0].getName());
162                    totalScore1.setForeground(Color.black);
163                    totalScore1.setFont(defaultFont);
164                    totalScore1.setText("" + playerAry[0].getTotalScore());
165
166                    playerName2.setForeground(Color.red);
167                    playerName2.setFont(newFont);
168                    playerName2.setText(playerAry[1].getName());
169                    totalScore2.setForeground(Color.red);
170                    totalScore2.setFont(newFont);
171                    totalScore2.setText("" + playerAry[1].getTotalScore());
172
173                    playerName3.setForeground(Color.black);
174                    playerName3.setFont(defaultFont);
175                    playerName3.setText(playerAry[2].getName());
176                    totalScore3.setForeground(Color.black);
177                    totalScore3.setFont(defaultFont);
178                    totalScore3.setText("" + playerAry[2].getTotalScore());
179                    break;
180                case 2:
181                    playerName1.setForeground(Color.black);
182                    playerName1.setFont(defaultFont);
183                    playerName1.setText(playerAry[0].getName());
184                    totalScore1.setForeground(Color.black);
185                    totalScore1.setFont(defaultFont);
186                    totalScore1.setText("" + playerAry[0].getTotalScore());
187
188                    playerName2.setForeground(Color.black);
189                    playerName2.setFont(defaultFont);
```

12.5 The Project TestWheel Rotates the Wheel with the Animation Technique

```
190                playerName2.setText(playerAry[1].getName());
191                totalScore2.setForeground(Color.black);
192                totalScore2.setFont(defaultFont);
193                totalScore2.setText("" + playerAry[1].getTotalScore());
194
195                playerName3.setForeground(Color.red);
196                playerName3.setFont(newFont);
197                playerName3.setText(playerAry[2].getName());
198                totalScore3.setForeground(Color.red);
199                totalScore3.setFont(newFont);
200                totalScore3.setText("" + playerAry[2].getTotalScore());
201                break;
202         }
203         msg.setText("Current Player "
204                 + playerAry[currPlayerIdx].getName() + " Plays.");
205     }
206 }
```

The class GameCanvas.java "uses" the three classes (Board.java, WheelGUI.java, and PlayerPanel.java) to form a GUI as shown in Fig. 12.1, which displays a static scene.

No doubt, a brand new task is to make the wheel turning around. For exploring the principle of rotating, we develop a project TestWheel in using the animation technique.

12.5 The Project TestWheel Rotates the Wheel with the Animation Technique

The project WheelVideo2 will further activate the entire game for allowing players to play it. The major tasks include (1) to rotate the wheel for generating a wheel score and (2) to realize dynamic communications among the three pieces for making the game work.

12.5.1 The Project TestWheel1 Turns a Radius Line Circulating Around a Circle

We start our discussion with a simpler object in the project TestWheel1 as shown in Fig. 12.4 (left). Clearly, the GUI indicates that the project TestWheel1 mainly needs two classes. One of them named as RadiusLine.java that is for the object radius line. The other is using the same name WheelGUI.java that is for rotating the radius line. One more

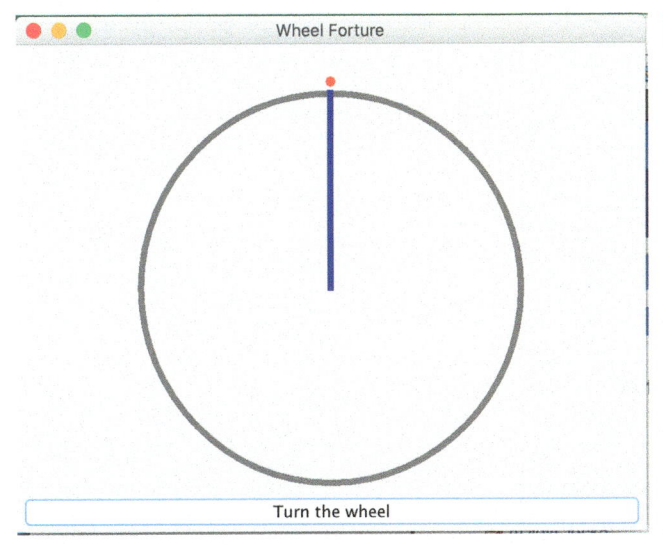

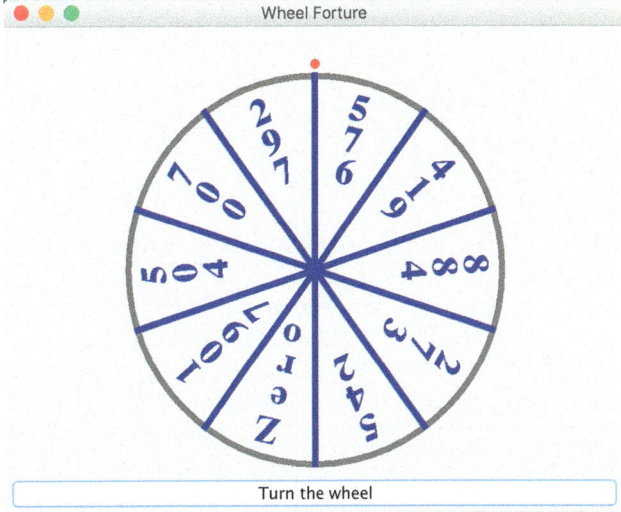

Fig. 12.4 (*Left*) The GUI of the project TestWheel1; (*right*) the GUI of the project TestWheel2

class GameCanvas.java instantiates an object of the class WheelGUI.java with the radius line and arranges it on the top. It also instantiates an object of the JButton with a label of "Turn the wheel" and places it on the bottom.

In order to rotate the object radiusLine, the class WheelGUI.java implements the Interface Runnable, which implies that the class is going to implement the run() method defined in the built-in class Thread. As mentioned before, the run() method will be automatically ignited by a method Thread.start(). Therefore, the class WheelGUI.java defines a method start() to instantiate an object animThread of the class Thread and issue animThread.start() for executing the method run(). The method run() implements a game loop that is a while(turnWheel) loop, which invokes three methods: updateAll(), repaint(), and Thread.sleep(period). It is the core of the animation technique. The codes of the class WheelGUI.java and the class RadiusLine.java are shown in Listing 12.4.

Listing 12.4 The codes of the classes WheelGUI.java and RadiusLine.java in the project TestWheel1

```
1  /*
2   * WheelGUI.java - A class uses a Thread to rotate a radius line.
3   */
4  package testwheel;
5
6  import java.awt.Graphics;
7  import java.awt.Graphics2D;
8  import javax.swing.JPanel;
9
14 public class WheelGUI extends JPanel implements Runnable {
15
16     private final RadiusLine radiusLine;
17     private boolean turnWheel = false;
18     private Thread animThread;
19     private int period;
20
21     public WheelGUI() {
22         radiusLine = new RadiusLine();
23     }
24
25     public void start() {
26         if (animThread == null) {
27             animThread = new Thread(this);
28             animThread.start();
29         }
30     }
31
32     @Override
33     public void run() {
34         try {
35             while (turnWheel) {
36                 updateAll();
37                 repaint();
38                 Thread.sleep(period);
39             }
40         } catch (InterruptedException iex) {
41         }
42     }
43
44     public void updateAll() {
45         radiusLine.updateLine();
```

```java
46          period = (int) (period * 1.1);
47          if (period >= 1000) { // a defined threshold for stopping the radiusLine
48              stopLine();
49          }
50      }
51
52      @Override
53      public void paintComponent(Graphics g) {
54          super.paintComponent(g);
55          Graphics2D g2d = (Graphics2D) g;
56
57          radiusLine.paintLine(g2d);
58      }
59
60      public void stopLine() {
61          turnWheel = false;
62          animThread.interrupt();
63          animThread = null;
64      }
65
66      public void reStart() {
67          // reset variables and call start() again
68          turnWheel = true;
69          period = 50;
70          radiusLine.reStartLine();
71          start();
72      }
73 }
```

```java
1  /*
2   * RadiusLine.java -- A class that defines an object of radiusLine.
3   */
4  package testwheel;
5
6  import java.awt.BasicStroke;
7  import java.awt.Color;
8  import java.awt.Graphics2D;
9  import java.awt.Stroke;
10
15 public class RadiusLine {
16
17     private final int cx;
18     private final int cy;
19     private int wheelRadius;
20     private int rotateAngle;
21     private int dAngle; // increase angle for g2d.rotate()
22     private final int pRadius = 4; // radius of the red point
23     private final double rPercent = 0.8; // radius percent for leaving margine
24
25     public RadiusLine() {
26         if (Consts.CV_WIDTH > Consts.CV_HEIGHT) {
27             wheelRadius = (int) ((Consts.MAXY - Consts.MINY) / 2 * 0.8);
28         }
29         cx = (int) (Consts.MAXX - Consts.MINX) / 2;
30         cy = (int) (Consts.MAXY - Consts.MINY) / 2;
```

```
31      }
32
33      public void updateLine() {
34          rotateAngle += dAngle;
35      }
36
37      public void paintLine(Graphics2D g2d) {
38          // paint the stop-indicator
39          g2d.setColor(Color.RED);
40          g2d.fillOval(cx - pRadius, cy - wheelRadius - 5 - 2 * pRadius,
41                  2 * pRadius, 2 * pRadius);
42          // paint the wheel circle
43          g2d.setColor(Color.GRAY);
44          Stroke solid = new BasicStroke(5.0f);
45          g2d.setStroke(solid);
46          g2d.drawOval(cx - wheelRadius, cy - wheelRadius, 2 * wheelRadius,
47                  2 * wheelRadius);
48
49          // paint the radius line
50          g2d.setColor(Color.BLUE);
51          // rotate the coordinate system around the center point
52          g2d.rotate(Math.toRadians(rotateAngle), cx, cy);
53          drawLine(g2d);
54      }
55
56      public void drawLine(Graphics2D g2d) {
57          g2d.drawLine(cx, cy, cx, cy + wheelRadius);
58      }
59
60      public void reStartLine() {
61          // continue the rotate from the starting angle
62          rotateAngle = 0;
63          //System.out.println("starting angle = " + rotateAngle);
64          // randomly selects dAngle for making the wheel stopped randomly
65          // avoiding dAngle == 36 since it makes the rotating line seems stoped
66          dAngle = (int) (Math.random() * 33) + 2; // [2, 35)
67          System.out.println("dAngle = " + dAngle);
68      }
69 }
```

The purpose of the game loop is to rotate the radiusLine. The radiusLine is painted in using the following statements in the method paintLine() of the class RadiusLine.java.

```
49      // paint the radius line
50      g2d.setColor(Color.BLUE);
51      // rotate the coordinate system around the center point
52      g2d.rotate(Math.toRadians(rotateAngle), cx, cy);
53      drawLine(g2d);
```

The code 50 sets the color blue. The code 52 g2d.rotate() rotates the coordinate system of the radiusLine with a rotateAngle. And the code 53 draws the line. Clearly, the rotation is made by the method g2d.rotate(), and the rotated position is determined by the value of rotateAngle.

The value of the rotateAngle is updated in the method updateLine() through the statement "rotateAngle += dAngle," which increases the value of rotateAngle with a variable dAngle. That is, every time the game loop invokes the method updateAll() defined in the class WheelGUI.java, which in turn invokes the method radiusLine.updateLine(), the value of rotateAngle will be increased dAngle degree so that every repaint() will paint the radiusLine at a new position, which creates an illusion of circulating. Meanwhile, the method updateAll() of the class WheelGUI.java also increases the value of "period" that enlarges the sleep duration of the thread, which slows down the circulating speed of the radiusLine until the condition "period ≥ 1000" true that causes the method stopLine() to be invoked. The process of slowing down until stop mimics the wheel turning process.

Once the method stopLine() is invoked, it makes turnWheel = false, interrupts the animThread, and sets it as null. Only when the player clicks the JButton, its event listener invokes the method wheelGUI.reStartWheel() for re-initializing all of variables related with the thread, and in turn it also calls the method radiusLine.reStartLine() to re-initialize all of variables related with the radiusLine. And then, it calls the method start() of the class WheelGUI.java for triggering the execution of the game loop again.

In the method radiusLine.reStartLine(), the "rotateAngle = 0" statement makes every rotate start from the origin 0°. The statement "dAngle = (int)((Math.random() * 33) + 2);" assigns the value of dAngle with a random integer in the range of (2, 35). The different value of dAngle will show us that the radius line is rotated with different angle every time.

One point should be clear. In the project TestRotatePaint, after painting a string along the radius direction, the g2d.rotate() is called to turn an angle and then to paint the second string. The turning angle is a relative value to the previous one. But, in the project TestWheel1, the method g2d.rotate() rotates the angle rotateAngle that is an absolute value "rotateAngle += dAngle." Actually, they are the same. In the former case, every rotate is relative to the previous one; but it is also absolute to the origin 0°. Since five rotations happened inside one paintComponent(), it is not so obvious. In the latter case, one call on the method paintComponent(), it erases the original paint first and then paints a new object with the rotate angle that also has the absolute value relative to the origin 0°.

12.5.2 The Project TestWheel2 Turns the Wheel Circulating Around a Circle

Obviously, the principle for turning the radiusLine is based on the g2d.rotate() method with the continuously updated value of rotateAngle. The continuous update-repaint keeps painting the radiusLine at an updated position. Every call to the method paintComponent() will erase the previous painting and then repaint the radiusLine at the new position. It gives us an animated radiusLine rotating around the circle.

Understanding the principle described above makes the wheel turning easy. We simply replace the class RadiusLine.java with the class TheWheel.java and replace the method drawLine() with the method drawWheel() defined in the class TheWheel.java to paint the wheel as shown in Fig. 12.4 (right). The code of the class TheWheel.java will be copied to the project WheelVideo2. The detailed code will be shown there.

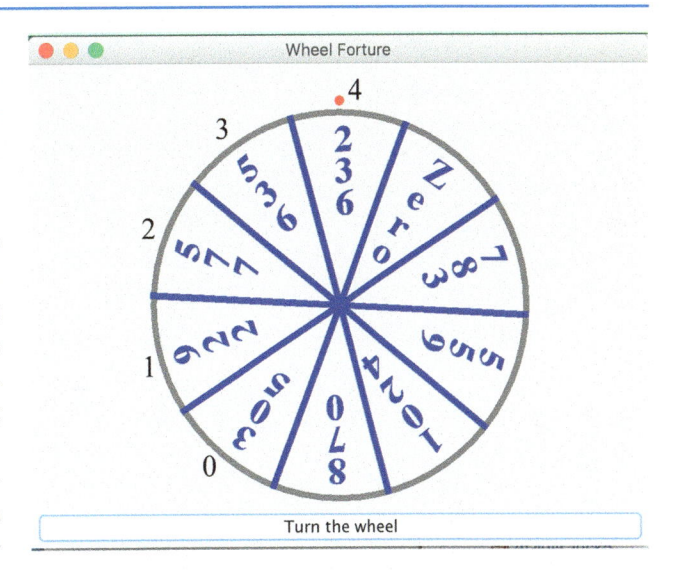

Fig. 12.5 The wheel score is at the section pointed to by the red point when the wheel stops

The purpose of turning the wheel is to give the current player a wheel score, which is the score in the section that is pointed to by the red point when the wheel stops. The score can be determined through the following analysis.

We will take the case shown on Fig. 12.5 as an example. The wheel is based on the array wheel[]. (1) When a game is started, the value of the wheel[0] = 305. The left line of the section wheel[0] is pointed to by the red point. (2) After the rotating, when the wheel stops, the left line of the section wheel[0] is at the position as shown in Fig. 12.5. (3) The total degrees of the rotation are accumulated in the variable rotateAngle. Thus, the current degree of the left line of the wheel[0] is "currAngle = rotateAngle % 360." (4) The indexes of each section are labeled in Fig. 12.5. The index of the section that is pointed to by the red point is "index = ((360 − currAngle)/36)." Then the score in the section is wheel[index]. We insert some System.out.println() statements in the code of the project TestWheel2 for displaying these values above. They print correct results. Readers can run the project to verify the analysis.

12.6 The Collaborations of Classes in the Project WheelVideo2

Now, we turn to discuss the dynamic behaviors and the communications among all of classes in the project WheelVideo2. The three pieces on the GUI physically are separated. But, they collaborate for one goal through communications. The major dynamic actions and their coordination are depicted in the UML sequence diagram shown in Fig. 12.6. In the diagram, the object wheelGUI represents both the object wheelGUI itself and the object of theWheel in order to

Fig. 12.6 A UML sequence diagram describes communications among the three pieces

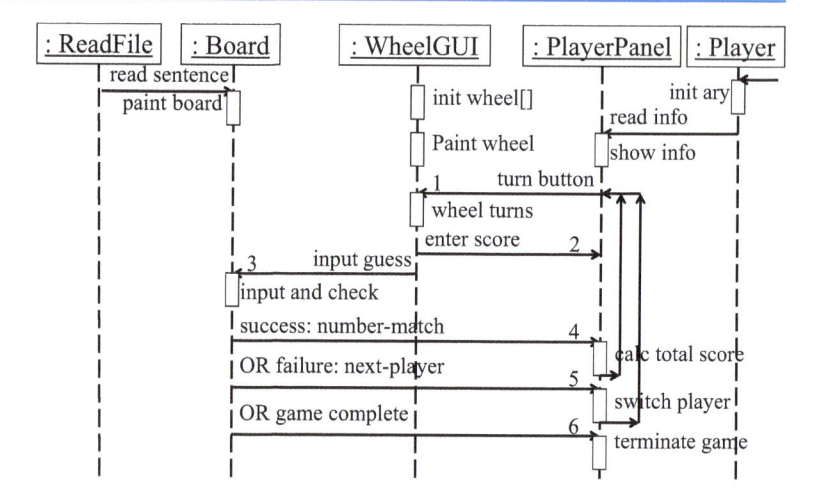

simplify the description. Actually, the WheelGUI.java class only implements the game loop for driving the rotation of the class TheWheel.java. The diagram uses an arrow that leaves an object and reaches another object to represent a dynamic action that is sent out from the former object and is accepted by the latter object.

12.6.1 The Class PlayerPanel.java Plays the Role of a Control Center

Since the class PlayerPanel.java is the control panel, the dynamic actions start from there. The required dynamic methods are added into the class PlayerPanel.java first, which are cited in Listing 12.5.

Listing 12.5 The new methods that perform the dynamic behaviors in the class of the PlayerPanel.java in the project WheelVideo2

```
1   /*
2    * PlayerPanel.java - A class defines the player's panel.
3    */
4   package wheelvideo;
5
...
25  public class PlayerPanel extends JPanel {
26
...
51
52      private WheelGUI wheelGUI;
53
...
212
213     class MyActionListener implements ActionListener {
214
215         @Override
216         public void actionPerformed(ActionEvent evt) {
217             if (evt.getSource() == turnWheel) {
218                 wheelGUI.reStart();
219             }
220         }
221     }
222
223     public void setWheelGUI(WheelGUI wheelGUI) {
224         this.wheelGUI = wheelGUI;
```

```java
225         }
226
227         public void terminateGame() {
228             sortAry(playerAry);
229             // show winner information with red color
230             currPlayerIdx = 0;
231             showData();
232             msg.setText("Congratulation " + playerAry[0].getName()
233                     + "! You won the game!");
234         }
235
236         public void sortAry(Player[] ary) {
237             Player temp;
238             for (int i = 0; i < playerAry.length - 1; i++) {
239                 for (int j = i + 1; j < playerAry.length; j++) {
240                     if (ary[i].getTotalScore() < ary[j].getTotalScore()) {
241                         temp = ary[i];
242                         ary[i] = ary[j];
243                         ary[j] = temp;
244                     }
245                 }
246             }
247         }
248
249         public int getCurrPlayerIdx() {
250             return currPlayerIdx;
251         }
252
253         public void setCurrPlayerIdx(int currPlayerIdx) {
254             this.currPlayerIdx = (currPlayerIdx % numPlayer);
255             showData();
256         }
257
258         public void setCurrScoreInt(int currScoreInt) {
259             this.currScoreInt = currScoreInt;
260             if (currScoreInt == -1) {
261                 currScore.setText("Zero");
262                 playerAry[currPlayerIdx].setTotalScore(0);
263                 msg.setText("Current Player " + playerAry[currPlayerIdx].getName()
264                         + " Bankrupt!");
265                 setCurrPlayerIdx(currPlayerIdx + 1);
266             } else {
267                 currScore.setText("" + currScoreInt);
268             }
269         }
270
271         public void setNumMatch(int numMatch) {
272             int thisCurrScore = numMatch * currScoreInt;
273             currScore.setText("" + thisCurrScore);
274             int currTotalScore = playerAry[currPlayerIdx].getTotalScore();
275             playerAry[currPlayerIdx].setTotalScore(currTotalScore + thisCurrScore);
276             showData();
277         }
278 }
```

After we completed the task to rotate the wheel in using the animation technique and demonstrated it in the small project TestWheel2, immediately, we moved the inner class MyActionListener from the project TestWheel2 into the class PlayerPanel.java in the project WheelVideo2 and registered the action listener with the JButton with the label "Turn The Wheel" on the GUI of the control panel. The dynamic behavior of the game starts from the arrow 1 with the label of "turn button" in the sequence diagram, which represents the action when the current player clicks on the button. This action ignites the game loop to rotate the wheel.

12.6.2 The Class WheelGUI.java Turns the Wheel in Using the Animation Technique

Both the class WheelGUI.java and the class TheWheel.java implemented in the project TestWheel2 are copied to the project WheelVideo2. Therefore, the UML class diagram of the project WheelVideo2 should be as Fig. 12.7 shows.

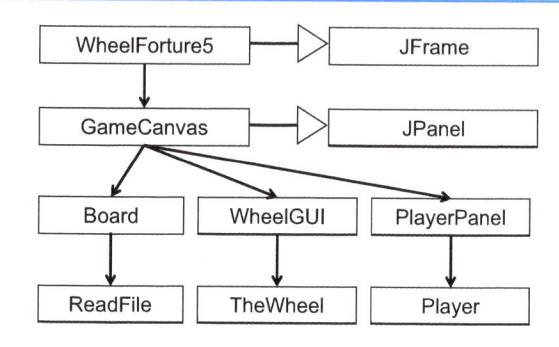

Fig. 12.7 The UML class diagram of the project WheelVideo2

When the method wheelGUI.reStart() is activated, it makes the game loop working for rotating the wheel. The rotating principle and the game loop have been discussed with the projects TestWheel1 and TestWheel2. The codes of the classes WheelGUI.java and TheWheel.java are shown in Listing 12.6.

Listing 12.6 The codes of the classes WheelGUI.java and TheWheel.java in the project WheelVideo2

```
 1 /*
 2  * WheelGUI.java - A class rotates the wheel in using the animation technique.
 3  */
 4 package wheelvideo;
 5
 6 import java.awt.Graphics;
 7 import java.awt.Graphics2D;
 8 import javax.swing.JPanel;
 9
14 public class WheelGUI extends JPanel implements Runnable {
15
16     private final TheWheel theWheel;
17     private boolean turnWheel = false;
18     private Thread animThread;
19     private int period;
20     private String strCurrScore;
21
22     private Board board;
23     private PlayerPanel playerPanel;
24
25     public WheelGUI() {
26         theWheel = new TheWheel();
27     }
28
29     public void start() {
30         if (animThread == null) {
31             animThread = new Thread(this);
32             animThread.start();
33         }
```

12.6 The Collaborations of Classes in the Project WheelVideo2

```java
34        }
35
36        @Override
37        public void run() {
38            try {
39                while (turnWheel) {
40                    updateAll();
41                    repaint();
42                    Thread.sleep(period);
43                }
44            } catch (InterruptedException iex) {
45                // statements that should be executed after the thread is
46                // interrupted must be placed here
47                strCurrScore = theWheel.stopStatistic();
48                sendCurrScore(strCurrScore);
49            }
50        }
51
52        public void updateAll() {
53            theWheel.updateWheel();
54            period = (int) (period * 1.1);
55            if (period >= 1200) { // a defined threshold for stoping the theWheel
56                stopWheel();
57            }
58        }
59
60        @Override
61        public void paintComponent(Graphics g) {
62            super.paintComponent(g);
63            Graphics2D g2d = (Graphics2D) g;
64
65            theWheel.paintWheel(g2d);
66        }
67
68        public void stopWheel() {
69            turnWheel = false;
70            animThread.interrupt();
71            animThread = null;
72            // these statement won't guarantee the wheel stops at the position
73            // it should be stopped. Thus, no any other statements can be
74            // correctly executed at this method. Other statements should be
75            // added to the catch block of the game loop
76        }
77
78        public void reStart() {
79            // reset variables and call start() again
80            turnWheel = true;
81            period = 50;
82            theWheel.reStartWheel();
83            start();
84        }
85
86        public void sendCurrScore(String score) {
87            int intCurrScore;
88
```

```
89              if (score.equals("Zero")) {
90                  intCurrScore = -1;
91              } else {
92                  intCurrScore = Integer.parseInt(score);
93              }
94              playerPanel.setCurrScoreInt(intCurrScore);
95              if (intCurrScore != -1) { // if current score is Bankrupt, no guess
96                  board.inputGuess();
97              }
98          }
99
100         // to allow the player inputs the guess char
101         public void setBoard(Board board) {
102             this.board = board;
103         }
104
105         // to pass the current score to playerPanel
106         public void setPlayerPanel(PlayerPanel playerPanel) {
107             this.playerPanel = playerPanel;
108         }
109 }
```

```
1  /*
2   * TheWheel.java - A class that defines the wheel component.
3   */
4  package wheelvideo;
5
6  import java.awt.BasicStroke;
7  import java.awt.Color;
8  import java.awt.Font;
9  import java.awt.Graphics2D;
10 import java.awt.Stroke;
11
16 public class TheWheel {
17
18     private final int cx;
19     private final int cy;
20     private int wheelRadius;
21     private int rotateAngle;
22     private int dAngle; // increase angle for g2d.rotate()
23     private final int pRadius = 4; // radius of the red point
24     private final double rPercent = 0.8; // radius percent for leaving margine
25     private final int rotateToStr = 13; // rotate the angles for painting strings
26     private final int rotateToLine = 23; // rotate the angles for painting lines
27     private final int wheelLen = 10; // assume the wheel has 10 integers
28     private final String[] wheel;
29
30     public TheWheel() {
31         if (Consts.CV_WIDTH > Consts.CV_HEIGHT) {
32             wheelRadius = (int) ((Consts.MAXY - Consts.MINY) / 2 * 0.8);
33         }
34         cx = (int) (Consts.MAXX - Consts.MINX) / 2;
35         cy = (int) (Consts.MAXY - Consts.MINY) / 2;
36
```

12.6 The Collaborations of Classes in the Project WheelVideo2

```java
37            // add all of integers into wheel[]
38            wheel = new String[wheelLen];
39            int ranInt;
40            for (int i = 0; i < wheelLen; i++) {
41                ranInt = (int) ((Math.random() * 1000) + 100); // [100, 1100]
42                if (i == 5) {
43                    wheel[i] = "Zero";
44                } else {
45                    wheel[i] = Integer.toString(ranInt);
46                }
47            }
48            System.out.println("wheel[0] = " + wheel[0]);
49        }
50
51        public void updateWheel() {
52            rotateAngle += dAngle;
53            //System.out.println("rotateAngle = " + rotateAngle);
54        }
55
56        public void paintWheel(Graphics2D g2d) {
57            // paint the stop-indicator
58            g2d.setColor(Color.RED);
59            g2d.fillOval(cx - pRadius, cy - wheelRadius - 5 - 2 * pRadius,
60                    2 * pRadius, 2 * pRadius);
61            // paint the wheel circle
62            g2d.setColor(Color.GRAY);
63            Stroke solid = new BasicStroke(5.0f);
64            g2d.setStroke(solid);
65            g2d.drawOval(cx - wheelRadius, cy - wheelRadius, 2 * wheelRadius,
66                    2 * wheelRadius);
67
68            // paint the wheel
69            g2d.setColor(Color.BLUE);
70            // rotate the coordinate system around the center point
71            g2d.rotate(Math.toRadians(rotateAngle), cx, cy);
72            drawWheel(g2d);
73        }
74
75        public void drawWheel(Graphics2D g2d) {
76            g2d.setFont(new Font("Times", Font.BOLD, 30));
77            for (int i = 0; i < wheelLen; i++) {
78                // paint number strings: rotate the angle from the line to the number
79                g2d.rotate(Math.toRadians(rotateToStr), cx, cy);
80                int charRadius = (int) (wheelRadius * rPercent);
81                String aStr = wheel[i];
82                for (int j = 0; j < aStr.length(); j++) {
83                    g2d.drawString(aStr.substring(j, j + 1), cx, (cy - charRadius));
84                    charRadius -= 25;
85                }
86                // paint lines: rotate the angle from the number string to the next line
87                g2d.rotate(Math.toRadians(rotateToLine), cx, cy);
88                g2d.drawLine(cx, cy, cx, cy + wheelRadius);
89            }
90        }
91
```

```
92      public String stopStatistic() {
93          // For checking the calculations, all of System.out.println()
94          // statements can be released for printing related information.
95          //System.out.println("rotateAngle = " + rotateAngle);
96          // the over turning angle A = (total rotated angles % 360)
97          // due to the opposite direction against the red point
98          // the over turning angle in the clock wise direction B = 360 - A
99          // the index of the slot in the wheel theIndex = B / 36
100         int theIndex = (360 - (rotateAngle % 360)) / 36;
101         //System.out.println("theIndex = " + theIndex);
102         // the score is wheel[theIndex]
103         //System.out.println("wheel[theIndex] = " + wheel[theIndex]);
104         return wheel[theIndex];
105     }
106
107     public void reStartWheel() {
108         // continue the rotate from the angle where the wheel stopped
109         rotateAngle = rotateAngle % 360;
110         //System.out.println("starting angle = " + rotateAngle);
111         // randomly selects dAngle for making the wheel stopped randomly
112         // avoiding dAngle == 36 since it makes the rotating line seems stoped
113         dAngle = (int) (Math.random() * 33) + 2; // [2, 35)
114         //System.out.println("dAngle = " + dAngle);
115     }
116 }
```

The code of the method reStartWheel() in the class WheelGUI.java is slightly different from the method reStartLine(). We keep the statement "dAngle = (int)((Math.random() * 33) + 2);" in order to rotate the wheel with different dAngle so that the wheel would stop at different angle for getting different wheel score. However, we modify the statement "rotateAngle = rotateAngle % 360;." The value of "rotateAngle % 360" actually gives the angle when the wheel is stopped from rotating such that the next turning will start from where the wheel stopped.

When the wheel stops turning, the red indicator points to a slot on the wheel, which is the wheel score earned by the current player. The wheel score is sent to the PlayerPanel.java for displaying. The sending action is represented by the arrow 2 with the label of "enter score" in the sequence diagram.

One "coding secret" is worth to be noticed. The sending score should be coded after the wheel stops turning. Logically, the first place for adding the sending code is the last statement in the method stopWheel(). However, the added sending code will cause the wheel stops at a position that is different from the position it should be stopped. This unstable coding indicates that the method stopWheel() is not a safe place for adding the sending code. After testing we found that the correct place for adding the sending code is the "catch (InterruptedException iex) {}" block in the game loop. The reason is that the method stopWheel() invokes the statement "animThread.interrupted()" call. However, this call does not mean the animThread is interrupted completely. Only the catch block guarantees the complete interruption of the thread. This case also tells us the importance of practice. Sometimes, only "logic" might not support a correct solution; but "practice" verifies it.

The wheel score could be a string integer or a "Zero" notation. The string integers should be converted to integer values; the "Zero" string is converted to be -1. The score value is sent to the method playerPanel.setCurrScoreInt() for the current player. If the integer -1 is received, the total score of the current player should be reset to 0. Otherwise, the wheel score is saved for calculating the total score after the current player enters his/her guessed character. The arrow 3 with the label "input guess" in the diagram indicates that the wheelGUI invokes the method board.inputGuess() to accept the current player's guess.

12.6.3 The Class Board.java Handles Guessed Character and Displays Guesses

The method board.inputGuess() receives a guessed character and sends the guessed character directly to the method board.insertCurrAry(). These two methods check the guessed character and result in one of five possible cases, which correspond to the arrow 4 (correct), the arrow 5 (error1, error2, error3), or the arrow 6 (game complete) in the UML sequence diagram.

1. "If (error1)" refers to the error "the character is empty," which means that the current player clicks OK button but without entering any character. It could be understood as the current player "gives up" his/her chance for playing the game. Thus, the class Board.java sends a signal to the class PlayerPanel.java for switching the next player as the current player.
2. "Else (erroe2)" refers to the case that the guessed character does not match with any character in the given sentence. The class Board.java sends a signal to the class PlayerPanel.java for switching the current player to the next player.
3. "Else (error3)" occurs when the current player enters a guessed character that has been made by previous players already. The class Board.java ignores this new guessed character and sends a signal to the PlayerPanel.java class for switching the current player.
4. "Else (correct)," the method counts the number of instances of the matched character in the sentence and stores the value in the variable numMatch. Meanwhile, it also inserts the character into the matching positions in the char array currAry[]; and then the method sends the value of numMatch to the class PlayerPanel.java. In addition:
   (a) The class Board.java paints the contents of the char array currAry[] into the displaying block of rectangles on the board.
   (b) If the content of the currAry[] is exactly the same as the sentence, the Board.java signals the class PlayerPanel.java to terminate the game, which refers to the arrow 6 in the sequence diagram.

After finishing all of the checking, the value of numMatch is sent to the class PlayerPanel.java indicated by the arrow 4 in the sequence diagram. When the playerPanel receives the value, it performs a calculation of (numMatch * wheel-score) to find out the subtotal of the current score and add it with the total score for the current player. If the game is not completed yet, the current player continues to turn the wheel for a next guess. In cases of errors, the current player will be switched to the next player. All of these cases form a "loop" in the sequence diagram shown in Fig. 12.6. The new added methods in the class Board.java is shown in Listing 12.7.

Listing 12.7 The new methods of the class Board.java in the project WheelVideo2

```
1  /*
2   * Board.java - A class defines a board for displaying.
3   */
4  package wheelvideo;
5
...
21 public class Board extends JPanel {
22
...
35     private PlayerPanel playerPanel;
36
...
65     public void inputGuess() {
66         char guessChar;
67         try {
68             String guessStr
69                 = JOptionPane.showInputDialog("Please enter a char for guessing");
70             guessChar = guessStr.charAt(0);
71             if (insertCurrAry(guessChar)) { // guess success
72                 repaint();
73                 if (sentenceStr.equals(new String(currAry))) {
74                     playerPanel.terminateGame();
75                 }
76             } else { // guess failure, switch to next player
77                 playerPanel.setCurrPlayerIdx(playerPanel.getCurrPlayerIdx() + 1);
78             }
79         } catch (StringIndexOutOfBoundsException siex) {
80             // current player inputs an empty char, switch to next player
```

```java
81                playerPanel.setCurrPlayerIdx(playerPanel.getCurrPlayerIdx() + 1);
82        }
83    }
84
85    public boolean insertCurrAry(char inputChar) {
86        numMatch = 0;
87        boolean success = false;
88        inputChar = Character.toUpperCase(inputChar);
89        for (int i = 0; i < sentenceLen; i++) {
90            if (sentenceStr.charAt(i) == inputChar) {
91                if (currAry[i] == (inputChar)) { // exist already
92                    break;
93                } else { // char match and it does not exist already
94                    numMatch++;
95                    currAry[i] = inputChar;
96                    success = true;
97                }
98            }
99        }
100        playerPanel.setNumMatch(numMatch);
101        return success;
102    }
103
104    @Override
105    public void paintComponent(Graphics g) {
106        super.paintComponent(g);
107        Graphics2D g2d = (Graphics2D) g;
108
118        ...
148    }
149
150    public void paintOneRow(Graphics2D g2d, String subStr, int row, int nextLineIdx) {
151        ...
162    }
163
164    public void paintEmptyBoard(Graphics2D g2d, String subStr, int row) {
165        ...
169    }
170
171    public void paintSubStr(Graphics2D g2d, String subStr, int row, int nextLineIdx) {
172        ...
179    }
180
181    public void initCharAry() {
182        for (int i = 0; i < sentenceLen; i++) {
183            currAry[i] = ' ';
184        }
185    }
186
187    public char[] getCurrAry() {
188        return currAry;
189    }
190
191    public void setPlayerPanel(PlayerPanel playerPanel) {
192        this.playerPanel = playerPanel;
193    }
194 }
```

12.6.4 The Class GameCanvas.java Sets Up All of Communication Paths

Due to the needs of communications, all of the objects pointed to by the arrows in the sequence diagram in Fig. 12.6 should be passed into the classes that issue the arrows. Therefore, the object playerPanel should be passed into the class WheelGUI.java; the object board should be passed into the class WheelGUI.java; and the object playerPanel should be passed into the class Board.java. The class GameCanvas.java performed these settings through the following statements.

```
1  /*
2   * GameCanvas.java - A class defines the canvas.
3   */
4  package wheelvideo;
5  …
14 public class GameCanvas extends JPanel {
15
27 …
28     private void initComponent() {
29         initBoard();
30         initWheelGUI();
31         initPlayerPanel();
32     }
33
34     public void initBoard() {
35         board = new Board();
36         add(board, BorderLayout.NORTH);
37     }
38
39     public void initWheelGUI() {
40         wheelGUI = new WheelGUI();
41       this.add(wheelGUI, BorderLayout.CENTER);
42         wheelGUI.setBoard(board);
43     }
44
45     public void initPlayerPanel() {
46         playerPanel = new PlayerPanel();
47         add(playerPanel, BorderLayout.SOUTH);
48         playerPanel.setWheelGUI(wheelGUI);
49         board.setPlayerPanel(playerPanel);
50         wheelGUI.setPlayerPanel(playerPanel);
51     }
52
53 …
60 }
```

12.7 Summary

This chapter developed the text game WheelFortune to be a video game of WheelVideo by adding three pieces on the GUI and setting up communications among them to realize the dynamic behaviors of the game. It illustrates an important principle that a game in text is a kind of central control; but a game in video version involves a kind of distributed control. Because the GUI has three pieces, the control signals have to be passed from one object to the other. In order to make these communications, the object of a class has to be passed into an object of the other class. This is a simple approach for setting up data paths for communications. However, this approach constructs a tightly coupled software structure.

For describing dynamic behaviors and the communications among classes, a nice tool is the UML sequence diagram. The diagram depicts objects and their interactive activities by using arrows with time lines. It not only indicates who interacts with whom but also expresses the time relationship among all activities. It makes us a clear mind about both space and time.

The project WheelVideo is a mixture of graphical visualization, event driven, and animation techniques. It approves that all of techniques that we learned are important for game programming.

12.8 Exercises

Self-Review Questions

1. What is the essential difference between the text version and the video version of the game WheelFortune in-text and the game WheelVideo?
2. How to merge three pieces of GUIs into one complete GUI? What kind of class every piece should be?
3. How to paint a string along the radius direction?
4. How to use the method g2d.rotate() to rotate an angle in painting multiple strings along the radius direction?
5. What is the principle of a game loop?
6. How to implement a game loop?
7. Which piece of GUI does need a game loop? Which does not need a game loop? Why?
8. How to control the speed of a game loop?
9. How to stop the game loop and how to restart the game loop?
10. How to paint the empty displaying block at the center of the GUI board?

11. How to paint the complete wheel with ten sectors?
12. How to draw a UML sequence diagram for describing dynamic interactions among classes?

Projects

1. Design and implement a project to simulate a spinning and flowing UFO around a GUI.
2. Design and implement an analog clock that adopts the method g2d.rotate() instead of converting an angle to a pair of coordinates (x, y).
3. Design and implement an animated solar system as depicted in Fig. 12.8 (left). Figure 12.8 (right) is a UML class diagram as a reference.

Fig. 12.8 (*Left*) A model of the solar system; (*right*) a UML class diagram

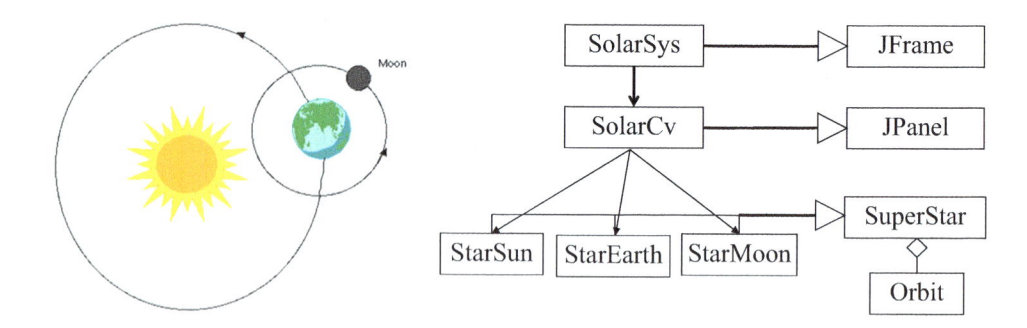

Animated Sprites and Collisions: A Game Pong

13

The game components that animated continuously and independently are termed as sprites in the game field. The animated sprits collide each other and collide with other objects. These collisions trigger embedded collision detection and collision handlers for dynamically changing the game states and output scenes. The collision detection and collision handlers actually are collision-event-update-repaint chains, which have the similar functions as the action-event-update-repaint chains. The player of the game just follows the game rules to control the animated sprites in order to avoid the collisions or to engage the collisions. The simple video game Pong is our first game example to start the introduction of sprites and their collisions for illustrating these new concepts and new techniques.

The objectives of this chapter include:
1. A simple video game Pong.
2. A brief introduction of JavaBeans model.
3. A GUI of the game Pong.
4. Animating the bouncing ball with a game loop.
5. Collision detection.
6. Playing the game Pong with keys.
7. A score counting mechanism.
8. Using score to control the speed of the ball.

The previous chapter developed the project WheelVideo, which practiced the animation technique for turning the wheel, applied event-driven technique for players to control the wheel turning and character guessing. The project is under the control of a mixture of both event-driven and animation techniques.

Further, we are going to see games that are more "pure" animation driven. These games mainly are sprite based. As mentioned before, a sprite is an object that independently and continuously animated. The animation of sprites causes collisions with each other or with either static or dynamic objects. The collisions trigger events that update the game states for the changes of game scenes. This kind of games is driven by animation and relies on sprites' collisions to trigger new events. Since the animation is "continuous," the collisions are also "continuous." Therefore, this kind of games differs from the "discrete" controls issued by players. It brings a brand new direction for games.

Programming this kind of video games mainly go through three steps. The first step is to analyze the game story for finding required objects and apply GUI programming for organizing the objects as components. The second step is to apply the animation technique for animating the dynamic components as sprites. The animated sprites collide with each other or with other objects. Taking advantages of collisions, we build up event handling mechanisms to allow collisions triggering new events according to the story of the video game. And the third step is to let the video games provide certain input mechanisms to allow the player of the game to control the collisions either guiding collisions or avoiding collisions in order to reach the goal of the game. Occasionally, some software components are built for players to control the starting, aborting, or quitting actions. These games are mainly driven by the "game loop." This chapter intends to start developing a simple game Pong for illustrating these new features.

13.1 The Story of the Game Pong

The game Pong is a simple game and played by a single player. It was an example for explaining what a game is in Chap. 1. The story of the game Pong says a ball is a sprite that animates inside a playing field. When the ball collides with the top, left, or bottom edges of the playing field, it will be bounced back. On the right edge side of the playing field, a paddle is added in parallel with the right edge. The paddle can be moved up or down by the game player. The player moves the paddle to bounce the ball back and prevents the ball from hitting the right edge of the playing field. Once the paddle successfully bounces the ball back, the player earns a score. As long as the ball is lost by the paddle and hits on the right edge of the playing field, the game is over.

13.2 Constructing the GUI: The Project Pong1

From the story of the game, we should construct a GUI with three objects: a red ball, a playing field, and a paddle as shown in Fig. 13.1.

A pseudo code for implementing the GUI could be as follows.

1. A canvas that is contained in a frame with a width of 500 pixels and a height of 400 pixels.
2. A red ball is statically placed at the center of the canvas.
3. A playing field is built around the four edges of the canvas.
4. A paddle exists at the right side against the right edge in parallel.

Following the pseudo code, the project Pong1 starts the construction of a static GUI. Before beginning, we would be better to repeat the following sentence again, "Don't paint images as objects but paint objects as images."

In order to arrange the three objects on the GUI, a UML class diagram is formed as shown in Fig. 13.2. It expresses that the main class Pong.java "is-a" JFrame and the class PongCanvas.java "is-a" JPanel. The class PongCanvas.java "uses" three classes Ball.java, FieldWall.java, and Paddle.

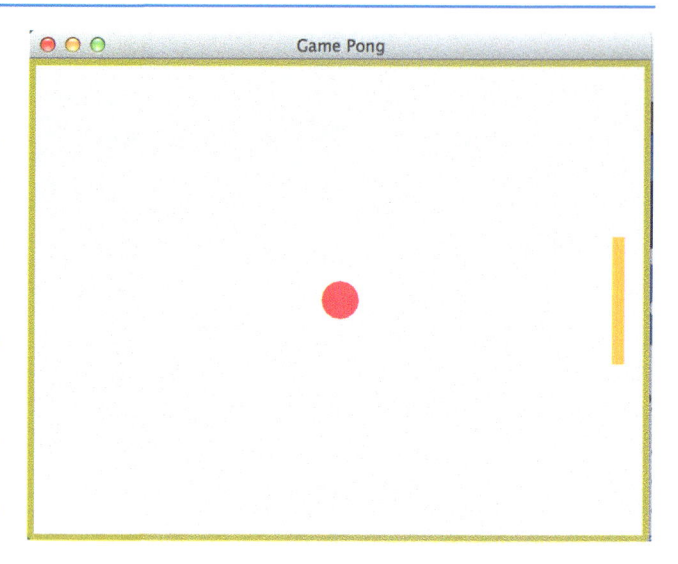

Fig. 13.1 The GUI of the game Pong

java. The class FieldWall.java "has" the class WallUnit.java. As usual, the classes Pong.java and PongCanvas.java make a canvas. And then the class PongCanvas.java instantiates three objects of the corresponding classes and arranges them to form a GUI. The implementation of the class PongCanvas.java is cited in Listing 13.1.

Listing 13.1 The class PongCanvas.java in the project Pong1

```
1  /*
2   * PongCanvas.java -- A canvas for the game Pong.
3   */
4  package pong;
5
6  import java.awt.Graphics;
7  import java.awt.Graphics2D;
8  import javax.swing.JPanel;
9
14 public class PongCanvas extends JPanel {
15
16      private FieldWall theWall;
17      private Ball theBall;
18      private Paddle thePaddle;
19
20      public PongCanvas() {
21          initComponent();
22      }
23
24      private void initComponent() {
25          theWall = new FieldWall();
26          theBall = new Ball();
27          thePaddle = new Paddle();
28      }
29
```

```
30      @Override
31      public void paintComponent(Graphics g) {
32          super.paintComponent(g);
33          Graphics2D g2d = (Graphics2D) g;
34
35          // draw a boundcing wall of the playing field
36          theWall.paintFieldWall(g2d);
37
38          // draw a red ball at the center of the canvas
39          theBall.paintBall(g2d);
40
41          // draw a paddle on the right side of the playing field
42          thePaddle.paintPaddle(g2d);
43      }
44  }
```

Before going to see the detailed code of every class, we can see that the class PongCanvas.java has the method initComponent() to instantiate the three objects from three classes: FieldWall.java, Ball.java, and Paddle.java. And then, its paintComponent() method invokes three painting methods implemented in the three classes for showing the three objects at the proper positions on the GUI, respectively.

13.3 A Brief Introduction on JavaBeans Model

The three classes FieldWall.java, Ball.java, and Paddle.java are components of the GUI in the game Pong. As a component, we would like to apply the principle of JavaBeans model for coding them. The JavaBeans is the component model in Java. That is, if we understand that a program, no matter how complicated of it, is made of components, then we can write the program component by component and "link" them together to form a unit or a system. This programming approach will increase software reusability and promote an easy maintainability due to its loosely coupled infrastructure. JavaBeans programming model can make the component programming much easier.

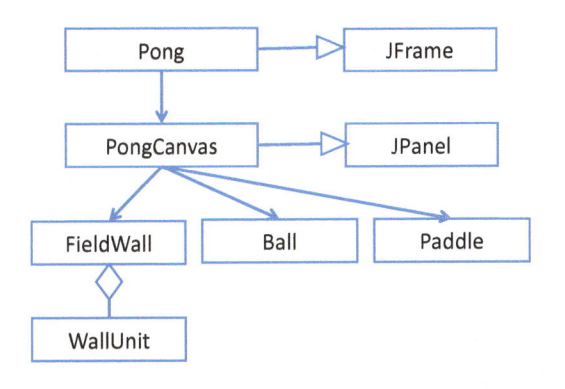

Fig. 13.2 The UML class diagram of the project Pong1

A JavaBean is a class that follows certain conventions. The conventions can be briefly summarized as follows. (1) A bean class has a default constructor, that is, the constructor doesn't have any parameters. (2) The bean class has a set of properties that correspond to the set of attributes of the object. (3) Every property has a getter method and a setter method. For a Boolean property, it has a "is" method and a "set" method.

Assume that a property is declared as "private int length;" and its getter and setter methods are coded as follows:

```
public int getLength() {
    return length;
}

public void setLength(int length) {
    this.length = length;
}
```

For a Boolean property "private Boolean done," it has a "public Boolean isDone()" method and a "public void setDone(Boolean done)" method.

Clearly, the names of the methods are the prefix "get" (or "is") and "set" plus the property name with the capitalized first letter. More genetic, these methods are also called accessor and mutator methods. A getter method returns the value of the property, and a setter method assigns the inputted value stored in the parameter to the property. All of getter and setter methods are "public" so that other classes can invoke the public methods to "get" or "set" the corresponding "private" properties. This is termed as "encapsulation" or "data hiding" in object-oriented programming. It encapsulates all of the properties of an object to prohibit them to be directly accessed from external world. The only way to access them is going through the public getter or setter methods.

Because of the regulation of the coding conversions, the intelligent source code editor in the NetBeans IDE or other IDEs can automatically generate codes of getter and setter methods for a specified property. That is, when we create a new JavaBeans class and declare a set of properties, we can right click at the spot where we would like to add the getter and setter methods on the source code editor window, and then a context menu will pop up. On the menu, we can select the menu item "Insert Code…" and then further select "Getter and Setter" or other similar menu items, such as "Getter…" and "Setter…," and then a panel with the declared properties will pop up. On the panel we can further check any properties and press the "generate" button; the corresponding getter and setter methods will be generated and inserted at the clicked spot. Of course, to generate getter and/or setter methods depend on whether the property is a mutable or immutable. If a property is mutable, it means that other objects can change the value of the property, and then the property may have a setter method. Otherwise, the setter method cannot be given. Indeed, whether adding getter or setter method depends on the "needs" of the program.

Every bean class should be "serializable," which is a topic that mainly deals with the transferring beans to other programming environments in a network setting. We are not going to discuss it here.

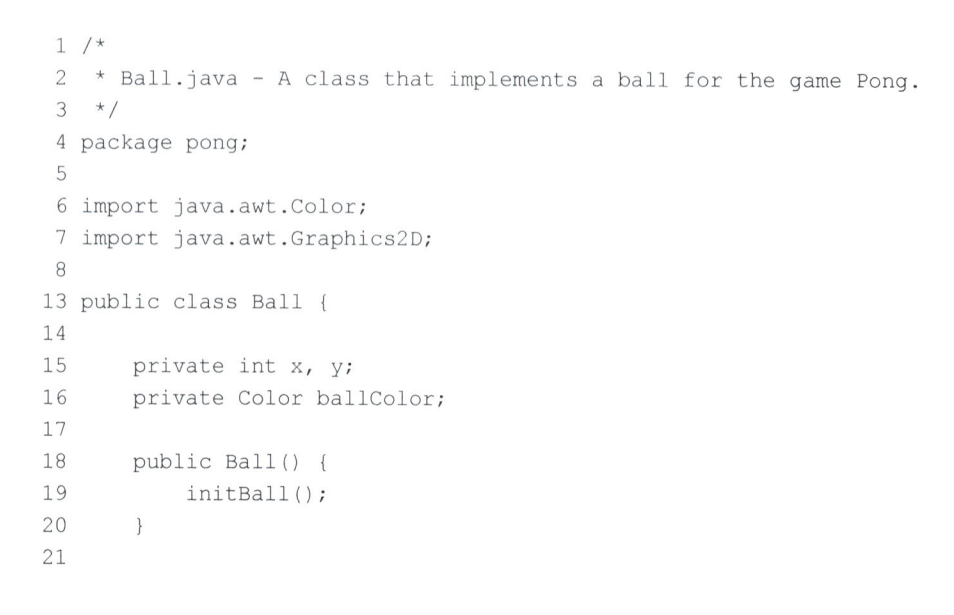

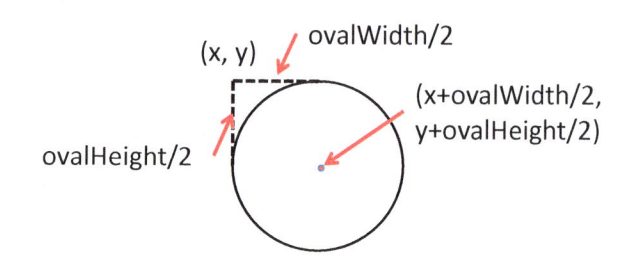

Fig. 13.3 The coordinates of the up-left corner of the bounding rectangle of an oval

13.4 The Class Ball.java Defines the Bouncing Ball in the Project Pong1

Taking advantage of the JavaBeans model, we can easily define a class for a component, such as the class Ball.java in the project Pong1 by using the IDE NetBeans or other IDEs. The process is as follows. We can right click the source package "pong" and select New > Java Class…, then type in the class name "Ball" and click "Finish" button to create a new class Ball.java class.

A ball is simulated as a circle in the 2D environment. Fig. 13.3 shows a circle. What properties are needed for defining the circle? We know that a circle is an oval. An oval is defined by its bounding rectangle. When an oval has (ovalWidth == ovalHeight), it is a circle with a radius = ovalWidth/2. Therefore, for defining a circle, the coordinates (x, y) of the pivot point of its bounding rectangle must be defined. In addition, a circle has a color. Considering the ball has a fixed radius, we can define a constant BALL_RADIUS in the class Consts.java.

Thus, in the class Ball.java, we declare attributes x, y, and ballColor as the properties of a ball. In addition, we define a constant BALL_RADIUS in the class Consts.java. Then we can employee the approach described above to add corresponding getter and setter methods for all of the properties declared. Besides the getter and setter methods, the Ball.java class needs one more method initBall() for initializing its attributes and another method paintBall() for displaying itself. The resulting code of the class Ball.java is cited in Listing 13.2.

Listing 13.2 The class Ball.java in the project Pong1

```
1  /*
2   * Ball.java - A class that implements a ball for the game Pong.
3   */
4  package pong;
5
6  import java.awt.Color;
7  import java.awt.Graphics2D;
8
13 public class Ball {
14
15     private int x, y;
16     private Color ballColor;
17
18     public Ball() {
19         initBall();
20     }
21
```

```
22      private void initBall() {
23          int cvX = (Consts.MAXX - Consts.MINX) / 2;
24          int cvY = (Consts.MAXY - Consts.MINY) / 2;
25          setX(cvX - Consts.BALL_RADIUS);
26          setY(cvY - Consts.BALL_RADIUS);
27          setBallColor(Color.RED);
28      }
29
30      public void paintBall(Graphics2D g2d) {
31          g2d.setColor(getBallColor());
32          g2d.fillOval(x, y, 2 * Consts.BALL_RADIUS, 2 * Consts.BALL_RADIUS);
33      }
34
35      public void setX(int x) {
36          this.x = x;
37      }
38
39      public void setY(int y) {
40          this.y = y;
41      }
42
43      public Color getBallColor() {
44          return ballColor;
45      }
46
47      public void setBallColor(Color ballColor) {
48          this.ballColor = ballColor;
49      }
50  }
```

The computation in the method initBall() is trying to set the center of the ball at the center of the canvas. The center of the canvas is at the coordinates (cvX, cvY). Hence, the coordinate x of the pivot point of the ball is "cvX − Consts.BALL_RADIUS," and the coordinate y of the pivot point of the ball is "cvY − Consts.BALL_RADIUS." The corresponding setter methods setX() and setY() are invoked to assign the values to x and y. And then, the method paintBall() simply invokes g2d.setColor(getBallColor()) and g2d.fillOval(x, y, …) to paint the ball object at the center of the canvas. Surely, inside the same class, the x and y on the method g2d.fillOval(x, y, …) can be replaced by getX() and getY(), respectively.

13.5 The Class FieldWall.java Defines the Field-Wall in the Project Pong1

The class FieldWall.java is a little bit more complicated than the class Ball.java because the object of field-wall consists of four segments of the wall-unit objects. That is, the FieldWall.java "has" four objects of wall-unit, which is an instance of another class WallUnit.java. We need to create the class WallUnit.java, and then the FieldWall.java class separately instantiates four objects of topUnit, bottomUnit, leftUnit, and rightUnit. These four segments are arranged on their own positions to form a complete field-wall. In other words, the object field-wall is a composite object that contains multiple smaller objects of wall-unit. The code of classes FieldWall.java and WallUnit.java are cited in Listing 13.3.

Listing 13.3 The classes FieldWall.java and WallUnit.java in the project Pong1

```
1  /*
2   * FieldWall.java - A class for implementing a field wall that consists
3   * of four wallUnits.
4   */
5  package pong;
6
```

```
 7  import java.awt.Color;
 8  import java.awt.Graphics2D;
 9
14  public class FieldWall {
15
16      WallUnit[] aWall = new WallUnit[4];
17
18      public FieldWall() {
19          initFieldWall();
20      }
21
22      private void initFieldWall() {
23          WallUnit topUnit = new WallUnit();
24          topUnit.setX(Consts.MINX);
25          topUnit.setY(Consts.MINY);
26          topUnit.setWidth(Consts.MAXX - Consts.MINX);
27          topUnit.setHeight(Consts.WALL_THICK);
28          aWall[0] = topUnit;
29          WallUnit bottomUnit = new WallUnit();
30          bottomUnit.setX(Consts.MINX);
31          bottomUnit.setY(Consts.MAXY - Consts.WALL_THICK);
32          bottomUnit.setWidth(Consts.MAXX - Consts.MINX);
33          bottomUnit.setHeight(Consts.WALL_THICK);
34          aWall[1] = bottomUnit;
35          WallUnit leftUnit = new WallUnit();
36          leftUnit.setX(Consts.MINX);
37          leftUnit.setY(Consts.MINY);
38          leftUnit.setWidth(Consts.WALL_THICK);
39          leftUnit.setHeight(Consts.MAXY - Consts.MINY);
40          aWall[2] = leftUnit;
41          WallUnit rightUnit = new WallUnit();
42          rightUnit.setX(Consts.MAXX - Consts.WALL_THICK);
43          rightUnit.setY(Consts.MINY);
44          rightUnit.setWidth(Consts.WALL_THICK);
45          rightUnit.setHeight(Consts.MAXY - Consts.MINY);
46          aWall[3] = rightUnit;
47          for (int i = 0; i < 4; i++) {
48              aWall[i].setUnitColor(Color.decode("#bbaa00"));
49          }
50      }
51
52      public void paintFieldWall(Graphics2D g2d) {
53          for (int i = 0; i < 4; i++) {
54              aWall[i].paintUnit(g2d);
55          }
56      }
57  }

 1  /*
 2   * WallUnit.java - A class that implements a unit of the field wall.
 3   */
 4
 5  package pong;
 6
 7  import java.awt.Color;
```

13.5 The Class FieldWall.java Defines the Field-Wall in the Project Pong1

```java
 8  import java.awt.Graphics2D;
 9
14  public class WallUnit {
15      private int x;
16      private int y;
17      private int width;
18      private int height;
19      private Color unitColor;
20
21      public WallUnit() {
22      }
23
24      public void paintUnit(Graphics2D g2d) {
25          g2d.setColor(getUnitColor());
26          g2d.fillRect(getX(), getY(), getWidth(), getHeight());
27      }
28
29      public int getX() {
30          return x;
31      }
32
33      public void setX(int x) {
34          this.x = x;
35      }
36
37      public int getY() {
38          return y;
39      }
40
41      public void setY(int y) {
42          this.y = y;
43      }
44
45      public int getWidth() {
46          return width;
47      }
48
49      public void setWidth(int width) {
50          this.width = width;
51      }
52
53      public int getHeight() {
54          return height;
55      }
56
57      public void setHeight(int height) {
58          this.height = height;
59      }
60
61      public Color getUnitColor() {
62          return unitColor;
63      }
64
65      public void setUnitColor(Color unitColor) {
66          this.unitColor = unitColor;
67      }
68  }
```

Clearly, the class WallUnit.java is a JavaBean. We declare x, y, width, and height for constructing a wall-unit as a rectangle. In addition, another property of unitColor can be used to select a color for the object. And then, the source code editor generates all of getter and setter methods for the set of properties.

The class FieldWall.java has four objects of wall-unit such that it declares a variable aWall as an Array as follows:

```
WallUnit[] aWall = new WallUnit[4];
```

Thus, the initFieldWall() method instantiates four objects of wall-unit individually and assigns each of objects into the array aWall with the statement "aWall[0] = topUnit" and the like.

The array makes coding much easier. We can use aWall[0] which refers to an object and use aWall[1] which refers to another object without the naming "topUnit" or "bottomUnit." Especially it is convenient to involve a "for" loop for manipulating a set of same type of objects if possible. The two "for" loops in the class FieldWall.java are good examples. The first "for" loop assigns the same color to four different objects by using only one statement, and the second "for" loop also only uses one statement to paint four different objects.

13.6 The Class Paddle.java Defines the Paddle in the Project Pong1

Similarly, the class Paddle.java is also based on the JavaBeans model. It declares three properties: x, y, and paddleColor. In addition, the class Consts.java defines two constants of PADDLE_WIDTH and PADDLE_HEIGHT. The method initPaddle() performs a calculation trying to place the paddle at the center position along the y direction in parallel with the right edge of the playing field. And the method paintPaddle() is to paint the object of paddle, which is simulated as a rectangle. Its code is cited in Listing 13.4.

Listing 13.4 The class Paddle.java in the project Pong1

```
1  /*
2   * Paddle.java - A class that implements a paddle for the game Pong.
3   */
4  package pong;
5
6  import java.awt.Color;
7  import java.awt.Graphics2D;
8
13 public class Paddle {
14
15     private int x, y;
16     private Color paddleColor;
17
18     public Paddle() {
19         initPaddle();
20     }
21
22     private void initPaddle() {
23         setX(Consts.MAXX - Consts.PADDLE_MARGIN);
24         setY((Consts.MAXY - Consts.MINY) / 2 - Consts.PADDLE_HEIGHT / 2);
25         setPaddleColor(Color.ORANGE);
26     }
27
28     public void paintPaddle(Graphics2D g2d) {
29         g2d.setColor(getPaddleColor());
30         g2d.fillRect(x, y, Consts.PADDLE_WIDTH, Consts.PADDLE_HEIGHT);
31     }
32
33     public void setX(int x) {
34         this.x = x;
35     }
36
```

```
37      public void setY(int y) {
38          this.y = y;
39      }
40
41      public Color getPaddleColor() {
42          return paddleColor;
43      }
44
45      public void setPaddleColor(Color paddleColor) {
46          this.paddleColor = paddleColor;
47      }
48  }
```

It is clear that the JavaBeans model makes the component programming much easier. For every component, we only need to define its properties and then take advantages of the IDE to generate getter and setter methods. In addition, the composite class FieldWall.java "has" four components of WallUnit.java to be a bigger component. And finally the class PongCanvas.java "uses" these components to form a GUI for the game.

13.7 Animating the Ball Sprite: The Project Pong2

The GUI of the game Pong gives us all required objects. Among them, the ball should be animated as a sprite with the name of "bouncing ball." Besides the ball, the paddle should be able to move up and down under the control of the game player.

The bouncing ball is a sprite that moves independently and continuously. In other words, the ball should be driven by a "game loop." As we have learned that a "game loop" is made through a Thread, hence, in general, a pseudo code for constructing a "game loop" is as follows:

1. Creating an object animThread of Thread and the method call animThread.start() will start the execution of the method run().
2. The method run() has a "while" loop, which invokes three methods:
   (a) The first method updates the position of the ball. We select the pivot point of the bounding rectangle of the ball with the coordinates (x, y) as the position parameter. Updating the x with a value of dx and updating the y with a dy in every step. The values of dx and dy are selected to make the ball animated smoothly. Whenever the ball hits on the top, left, and bottom wall-units, or hits on the paddle, the ball should be bounced back.
   (b) The second method repaint() invokes the method paintComponent() for repainting the ball in the updated position.
   (c) The third method is Thread.sleep() to pause the thread for a while.

The run() method with the "game loop" is added in the class PongCanvas.java due to the following considerations. (1) The class PongCanvas.java instantiates all of objects. The "game loop" can easily access any one of objects. (2) The "game loop" updates the position property (x, y) of the ball and then immediately invokes the painting method to show the ball with the new position on the GUI. The painting method paintComponent() is implemented in the PongCanvas.java class already. Hence, adding the "game loop" in this way will keep the UML class diagram unchanged. (3) A new method updateBall() should be added to allow the game loop to update the position property of the ball. It could be added into the class PongCanvas.java or into the class Ball.java. This time, we made a mind to add it into the class PongCanvas.java so that we only need to modify the class PongCanvas.java without touching other classes.

13.8 Applying the Collision Detection Technique: The Project Pong2

The ball is animated. For keeping the ball moving inside the playing field, the ball should be bounced back whenever it touches any one of wall-units of the field-wall. Therefore, after every updating for the position of the ball, we do need to check whether the ball collides with any wall-unit of the field-wall. This is called collision detection. Definitely, collision detection is a big topic. Here, we only consider collisions happened among 2D geometrical objects without considering physics principles of collisions as in the real world. The ball is an object with a circle shape. One wall-unit of the field-wall is another object with a shape of rectangle. No matter what kinds of shape, every object has a bounding rectangle as shown in Fig. 13.4. As long as two bounding rectangles get in touch with each other, they are collided. Based on this understanding, for non-accurate

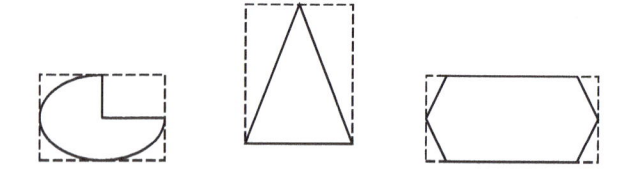

Fig. 13.4 The bounding rectangle represents the object

simple collision detection, we can employ the bounding rectangle to represent an object.

A piece of pseudo code for this kind of collision detection is straightforward.

```
Boolean collision = false;
Rectangle objARect = new Rectangle(xA, yA, widthA,
    heightA);
Rectangle objBRect = new Rectangle(xB, yB,
    widthB, heightB);
if (objARect.intersects(objBRect)) {
    collision = true;
}
```

Where, the class Rectangle is a built-in class in Java APIs. The method intersects() is defined in the built-in class Rectangle. The method intersects() returns "true" means two bounding rectangles objARect and objBRect have at least a cross point, that is, they are collided. This approach is suitable for detecting collisions between the ball and a wall-unit of the field-wall. When a collision takes place between the ball and any wall-unit of the field-wall, the ball should change its moving direction to the opposite way. In the calculations, the bouncing back can be realized by negating the value of dx and/or dy depending on the collision direction. Similarly, when the ball collides with the paddle, a same procedure can also be applied for the collision detection because the paddle is also a rectangle.

In the process of designing collision detection, we create two new ideas:

1. Replace our own class WallUnit.java by using the built-in class Rectangle. The project Pong1 implements the field-wall as an array of four wall-units defined in the class WallUnit.java, which holds the properties of x, y, width, height, and color for every wall-unit. And then, the class FieldWall.java instantiates four wall-units with different parameters. However, when we implement the collision detection between the ball and the wall-units, we need to have the bounding rectangle of every wall-unit. In fact, the shape of the bounding rectangle of a wall-unit is exactly same as that of wall-unit itself. It is redundant to instantiate four bounding rectangles again. For avoiding the redundancy, we can directly employ the built-in class Rectangle for replacing the class WallUnit.java. In other words, the class WallUnit.java could be deleted. This kind of redesign and re-implementation often happens in the iterative modifications of codes to improve the implementation better and better as discussed in Chap. 1.

2. Which class is better to hold the method for the collision detection? Because the method is to check whether the ball collides with the field-wall object or the paddle object, the method is better to be implemented inside a class that is able to involve all of these objects that could be collided. Obviously, the better selection is the class PongCanvas.java, which instantiates all of component objects, including the three objects of ball, field-wall, and paddle.

Adopting these new ideas, the modified codes in the project Pong2 are as in Listing 13.5.

Listing 13.5 The modified classes FieldWall.java and the class PongCanvas.java in the project Pong2

```
1  /*
2   * FieldWall.java - A class for implementing a field-wall that consists
3   * of four rectangles.
4   */
5  package pong;
6
7  import java.awt.Color;
8  import java.awt.Graphics2D;
9  import java.awt.Rectangle;
10
15 public class FieldWall {
16
17     Rectangle[] aWall = new Rectangle[4];
18
19     public FieldWall() {
20         initFieldWall();
21     }
22
```

13.8 Applying the Collision Detection Technique: The Project Pong2

```
23      private void initFieldWall() {
24          // top wall unit
25          aWall[0] = new Rectangle(Consts.MINX, Consts.MINY,
26                  (Consts.MAXX - Consts.MINX), Consts.WALL_THICK);
27          // bottom wall unit
28          aWall[1] = new Rectangle(Consts.MINX, Consts.MAXY - Consts.WALL_THICK,
29                  (Consts.MAXX - Consts.MINX), Consts.WALL_THICK);
30          // left wall unit
31          aWall[2] = new Rectangle(Consts.MINX, Consts.MINY,
32                  Consts.WALL_THICK, Consts.FIELD_HEIGHT);
33          // right wall unit
34          aWall[3] = new Rectangle(Consts.MAXX - Consts.WALL_THICK, Consts.MINY,
35                  Consts.WALL_THICK, Consts.FIELD_HEIGHT);
36      }
37
38      public void paintFieldWall(Graphics2D g2d) {
39          g2d.setColor(Color.decode("#bbaa00"));
40          for (int i = 0; i < 4; i++) {
41              g2d.fillRect(aWall[i].x, aWall[i].y, aWall[i].width, aWall[i].height);
42          }
43      }
44
45      public Rectangle[] getaWall() {
46          return aWall;
47      }
48
49      public void setaWall(Rectangle[] aWall) {
50          this.aWall = aWall;
51      }
52  }
```

```
1  /*
2   * PongCanvas.java -- A canvas for the game Pong.
3   */
4  package pong;
5
6  import java.awt.Graphics;
7  import java.awt.Graphics2D;
8  import java.awt.Rectangle;
9  import javax.swing.JPanel;
10
15 public class PongCanvas extends JPanel implements Runnable {
16
17     private FieldWall theWall;
18     private Ball theBall;
19     private Paddle thePaddle;
20     private Thread anim = null;
21
22     public PongCanvas() {
23         initComponent();
24         start();
25     }
26
27     private void initComponent() {
28         theWall = new FieldWall();
```

```java
29          theBall = new Ball();
30          thePaddle = new Paddle();
31      }
32
33      private void start() {
34          if (anim == null) {
35              anim = new Thread(this);
36              anim.start();
37          }
38      }
39
40      @Override
41      public void run() {
42          try {
43              while (true) {
44                  updateBall();
45                  detectCollision();
46                  repaint();
47                  Thread.sleep(60);
48              }
49          } catch (InterruptedException ex) {
50          }
51      }
52
53      public void updateBall() {
54          theBall.setX(theBall.getX() + theBall.getDx());
55          theBall.setY(theBall.getY() + theBall.getDy());
56      }
57
58      public void detectCollision() {
59          // make a bounding rectangle of the ball
60          Rectangle ballRect = new Rectangle(theBall.getX(), theBall.getY(),
61                  2 * Consts.BALL_RADIUS, 2 * Consts.BALL_RADIUS);
62          // whether the ball hits on any unit of the bouncing wall
63          for (int i = 0; i < 4; i++) {
64              if ((theWall.getaWall()[i]).intersects(ballRect)) {
65                  switch (i) {
66                      case 0: // top
67                      case 1: // bottom
68                          theBall.setDy(-theBall.getDy());
69                          break;
70                      case 2: // left
71                          theBall.setDx(-theBall.getDx());
72                          break;
73                      case 3: // right, lose points 30
74                          resetGame();
75                          break;
76                  }
77              }
78          }
79          // whether the ball collides the paddle
80          Rectangle paddleRect = new Rectangle(thePaddle.getX(), thePaddle.getY(),
81                  Consts.PADDLE_WIDTH, Consts.PADDLE_HEIGHT);
82          if (paddleRect.intersects(ballRect)) {
83              theBall.setDx(-theBall.getDx());
```

```
 84              }
 85          }
 86
 87          public void resetGame() {
 88              // define it later
 89          }
 90
 91          @Override
 92          public void paintComponent(Graphics g) {
 93              super.paintComponent(g);
 94              Graphics2D g2d = (Graphics2D) g;
 95
 96              // draw a bouncing wall of the playing field
 97              theWall.paintFieldWall(g2d);
 98              // draw a red ball at the center of the canvas
 99              theBall.paintBall(g2d);
100              // draw a paddle on the right side of the playing field
101              thePaddle.paintPaddle(g2d);
102          }
103     }
```

The class PongCanvas.java implements a "game loop." Inside the "game loop," a method updateBall() updates the coordinates (x, y) of the pivot point of the ball. Immediately, the method detectCollision() is invoked to check whether the ball collides with any wall-unit of the field-wall. If the ball collides with the top or bottom wall-unit, the method negates the dy value; if the ball collides with the left wall-unit, the method negates the dx value. The negation of the dx or dy causes the ball bouncing back and moving in the opposite direction. In addition, the method detectCollision() also checks whether the ball collides with the paddle. After updating the ball, repaint() method invokes the paintComponent() method to paint the ball again. This repeated update-repaint function creates an illusion of a bouncing ball.

13.9 Allowing the Player to Move the Paddle with Keys: The Project Pong3

The "game loop" animates the bouncing ball and collision changes the moving direction of the ball. Definitely, the ball will move to the right direction by any chance. According to the story of the game Pong, the paddle is added in parallel with the right edge of the playing field, and the paddle should be able to move up or down under the control of the player for bouncing the ball back in order to prevent the ball from hitting the right edge. Otherwise, the ball is counted as lost and the game is over.

For controlling the paddle up and down, the up key and down key are a suitable choice. Thus, we are going to apply the keys as the control mechanism, which we have discussed in Chap. 9. The pseudo code for adding this function is as follows. Its implementation is cited in Listing 13.6.

1. Adding an inner class MyKeyAdapter that extends built-in class KeyAdapter in the class PongCanvas.java.
2. Implementing the event handler keyPressed() method in the inner class MyKeyAdapter.
3. The method keyPressed() invokes the method evt.getSource() that returns the event source—down key or up key:
   (a) If the returning value indicates the key "Down" is pressed, it moves the paddle down ten pixels in each press. When the bottom of the paddle reaches the bottom wall-unit of the field-wall, no more movement can be made.
   (b) If the returning value indicates the key "Up" is clicked, it moves the paddle up ten pixels in each press. When the top of the paddle reaches the top wall-unit of the field-wall, no more movement can be made.
   (c) We select the keyPressed() as the event handler to allow the player being able to continuously move the paddle by keeping pressing the key until he/she releases the key.
4. Once the paddle moves one step, the method repaint() calls the paintComponent() method to paint all of objects at the new positions on the GUI.
5. Due to the fact that it is a key listener, we must remember to add a special statement setFocusable(true) in the constructor of the class PongCanvas.java.

Listing 13.6 The code of the class PongCanvas.java with the inner class MyKeyAdapter in the project Pong3

```java
 1 /*
 2  * PongCanvas.java -- A canvas for the game Pong.
 3  */
 4 package pong;
 5
 6 import java.awt.Graphics;
 7 import java.awt.Graphics2D;
 8 import java.awt.Rectangle;
 9 import java.awt.event.KeyAdapter;
10 import java.awt.event.KeyEvent;
11 import javax.swing.JPanel;
12
17 public class PongCanvas extends JPanel implements Runnable {
18
19     private FieldWall theWall;
20     private Ball theBall;
21     private Paddle thePaddle;
22     private Thread anim = null;
23
24     public PongCanvas() {
25         setFocusable(true);
26         addKeyListener(new MyKeyAdapter());
27         initComponent();
28         start();
29     }
30
31     private void initComponent() {
32         theWall = new FieldWall();
33         theBall = new Ball();
34         thePaddle = new Paddle();
35     }
36
37     private void start() {
38         if (anim == null) {
39             anim = new Thread(this);
40             anim.start();
41         }
42     }
43
44     @Override
45     public void run() {
46         try {
47             while (true) {
48                 updateBall();
49                 detectCollision();
50                 repaint();
51                 Thread.sleep(60);
52             }
53         } catch (InterruptedException ex) {
54         }
55     }
56
```

13.9 Allowing the Player to Move the Paddle with Keys: The Project Pong3

```java
57      public void updateBall() {
58          theBall.setX(theBall.getX() + theBall.getDx());
59          theBall.setY(theBall.getY() + theBall.getDy());
60      }
61
62      public void detectCollision() {
63          // make a bounding rectangle of the ball
64          Rectangle ballRect = new Rectangle(theBall.getX(), theBall.getY(),
65                  2 * Consts.BALL_RADIUS, 2 * Consts.BALL_RADIUS);
66          // whether the ball hits on any unit of the bouncing wall
67          for (int i = 0; i < 4; i++) {
68              if ((theWall.getaWall()[i]).intersects(ballRect)) {
69                  switch (i) {
70                      case 0: // top
71                      case 1: // bottom
72                          theBall.setDy(-theBall.getDy());
73                          break;
74                      case 2: // left
75                          theBall.setDx(-theBall.getDx());
76                          break;
77                      case 3: // right, lose points 30
78                          resetGame();
79                          break;
80                  }
81              }
82          }
83          // whether the ball collides the paddle
84          Rectangle paddleRect = new Rectangle(thePaddle.getX(), thePaddle.getY(),
85                  Consts.PADDLE_WIDTH, Consts.PADDLE_HEIGHT);
86          if (paddleRect.intersects(ballRect)) {
87              theBall.setDx(-theBall.getDx());
88          }
89      }
90
91      public void resetGame() {
92          // define it later
93      }
94
95      @Override
96      public void paintComponent(Graphics g) {
97          super.paintComponent(g);
98          Graphics2D g2d = (Graphics2D) g;
99
100         // draw a boundcing wall of the playing field
101         theWall.paintFieldWall(g2d);
102         // draw a red ball at the center of the canvas
103         theBall.paintBall(g2d);
104         // draw a paddle on the right side of the playing field
105         thePaddle.paintPaddle(g2d);
106     }
107
108     // an inner class for implementing the key event adapter
109     // for catching the up or down keys to move the paddle
110     class MyKeyAdapter extends KeyAdapter {
111
```

```
112         @Override
113         public void keyPressed(KeyEvent evt) {
114             switch (evt.getKeyCode()) {
115                 case KeyEvent.VK_DOWN:
116                     if ((thePaddle.getY() + Consts.PADDLE_HEIGHT)
117                             < (Consts.MAXY - Consts.WALL_THICK)) {
118                         thePaddle.setY(thePaddle.getY() + 10);
119                     }
120                     break;
121                 case KeyEvent.VK_UP:
122                     if (thePaddle.getY() > (Consts.MINY + Consts.WALL_THICK)) {
123                         thePaddle.setY(thePaddle.getY() - 10);
124                     }
125                     break;
126                 default:
127             }
128             repaint();
129         }
130     }
131 }
```

13.10 Adding a Score Counting Mechanism: The Project Pong3

A video game usually has a score counting function for evaluating the performance of the game player in order to promote the player playing better and also could be served as a measurement for the competitions among players. In this game, we design a simple score counting mechanism that will increase the score with 5 points every time when the player controls the paddle to successfully bounce the ball back. When the player won't bounce the ball back and the ball is lost, the game is finished and a method resetGame() should be invoked to reset the ball back to the initial state. Here, we simply insert the statement System.exit(0) into the method resetGame() to quit from the game and postpone the implementation of the method resetGame() to the next chapter in a combination with other considerations. The current score should be always displayed on the playing field with a new paintCurrScore() method. These codes are added into the PongCanvas.java class as shown in Listing 13.7.

Listing 13.7 The score counting mechanism in the class PongCanvas.java of the project Pong3

```
 1 /*
 2  * PongCanvas.java -- A canvas for the game Pong.
 3  */
 4 package pong;
 5
...
14
19 public class PongCanvas extends JPanel implements Runnable {
20
21     private FieldWall theWall;
22     private Ball theBall;
23     private Paddle thePaddle;
24     private Thread anim = null;
25     private int currScore;
26     private int hitPaddle;
27
```

```
28      public PongCanvas() {
29          setFocusable(true);
30          addKeyListener(new MyKeyAdapter());
31          initComponent();
32          start();
33      }
34
...
104     public void resetGame() {
105         System.exit(0);
106     }
107
108     @Override
109     public void paintComponent(Graphics g) {
110         super.paintComponent(g);
111         Graphics2D g2d = (Graphics2D) g;
112
113         // draw a boundcing wall of the playing field
114         theWall.paintBouncingWall(g2d);
115         // draw a red ball at the center of the canvas
116         theBall.paintBall(g2d);
117         // draw a paddle on the right side of the playing field
118         thePaddle.paintPaddle(g2d);
119
120         // paint the game score
121         paintCurrScore(g2d);
122     }
123
...
148     public void paintCurrScore(Graphics2D g2d) {
149         currScore = Consts.SCORE_UNIT * hitPaddle;
150         g2d.setFont(new Font("TimesRoman", Font.BOLD, 20));
151         g2d.setColor(Color.red);
152         g2d.drawString("Score: " + currScore, 25, 25);
153     }
154 }
```

For counting the score, two variables hitPaddle and currScore are declared. In the method detectCollision(), there is a statement for checking whether the ball collides with the paddle. If yes, not only the ball is bounced back but also the value of the variable hitPaddle is increased by one. When the method paintComponent() is invoked, it calls the paintCurrScore() method, which calculates the score in the statement "currScore = Consts.SCORE_UNIT * hitPaddle" and paints the currScore on the GUI. Once the player loses the ball, the method resetGame() is invoked to quit the game.

13.11 Increasing the Degree of Playing Difficulty: The Project Pong4

The counting mechanism is not only can be used to measure the playing skill of the player or to server the purpose of competition but also can be used to change the playing difficulty level of a game. For example, we may preset two thresholds, say 10 and 25. When the score exceeds the threshold of 10, the ball speed will automatically increase to certain percentage of the original speed in order to raise the degree of playing difficulty. Similarly, when the score reaches 25, another speed increment may happen again automatically.

The moment to increase the ball speed is when the score reaches a certain value. Because the score counting mechanism is inside the class PongCanvas.java, the related codes are also implemented in the class PongCanvas.java. We know that changing the speed of the bouncing ball has two ways. One way is to change the moving distance dx or dy of the ball; the other way is to change the sleep time period of the Thread inside the game loop. Therefore, a pseudo code could be as follows.

1. After the score is increased, a method checkScore() checks the current value of the score. If the value is >= Consts.THRESHOLD1, then it increases the speed of the ball by one of the following approaches:
    (a) Increase the value of dx and dy.
    (b) Reduce the sleeping time of the thread to increase the speed of the game loop.
2. The class PongCanvas.java adds the new method checkScore(). The paintCurrScore() method invokes the method checkScore() after it calculates the currScore.

We implemented this idea as follows:

```
public void paintCurrScore(Graphics2D g2d) {
    currScore = Consts.SCORE_UNIT * hitPaddle;
    ...
    checkScore(currScore);
}

public void checkScore(int currScore) {
    if (currScore >= Consts.THRESHOLD1)) {
        theBall.setDx((int)(theBall.getDx() * 2));
        theBall.setDy((int)(theBall.getDy() * 1.6));
    }
}
```

However, it won't work successfully. Why? Whenever the condition (currScore >= Consts.THRESHOLD1) is true, it always true. Thus, the checkScore() continuously increases the speed whenever it is invoked so that the ball "flies." We need a switch that can open the checking before the condition is true and close the checking after the condition has been true. The switch is a Boolean variable. Because there are two thresholds, we declare two Boolean variables and initialize them as "threshould1 = false;" and "threshould2 = false;" They mean that the threshold1 and the threshold2 have not been reached yet. Furthermore, we modify the method checkScore() as follows:

```
public void checkScore(int currScore) {
    if ((!threshold1) && (currScore >=
        Consts.THRESHOLD1)) {
        theBall.setDx((int)(theBall.getDx() * 2));
        theBall.setDy((int)(theBall.getDy() * 1.6));
        threshold1 = true;
    } else if ((!threshold2) && (
        currScore >= Consts.THRESHOLD2)) {
        theBall.setDx((int)(theBall.getDx() * 2.2));
        theBall.setDy((int)(theBall.getDy() * 2.2));
        threshold2 = true;
    }
}
```

The (!threshold1) opens the check for the following condition. Once the second condition is true, the speed of the ball is increased, the statement "threshold1 = true" closes the possible checking forever until the threshold2 is reached. The ball's speed will be increased again. But, the statement "threshold2 = true" will make no more increment of the ball's speed. What if a program has ten thresholds? We can define an array of switches to handle it.

As the pseudo code mentioned, we have another approach to increase the speed of the ball. It is to reduce the sleeping time of the thread so that the speed of the game loop will be increased. We can simply replace the approach for increasing the values of dx and dy with a new calculation to reduce the value of the variable sleepTime as follows:

```
public void checkScore(int currScore) {
    if ((!threshold1) && (currScore >=
        Consts.THRESHOLD1)) {
        sleepTime = (int)(sleepTime / 2);
        threshold1 = true;
    } else if ((!threshold2) &&
        (currScore >= Consts.THRESHOLD2)) {
        sleepTime = (int)(sleepTime / 2);
        threshold2 = true;
    }
}
```

The statement "if" checks for two conditions. We place the condition "(!threshold1)" at the first position because if the first condition is false, the second condition is not to be checked. Therefore, the Boolean value of the variable threshold1 is a real "switch" that either opens or closes the validation of the second condition. The new added methods in the class PongCanvas.java is cited in Listing 13.8.

Listing 13.8 The new added codes in the class PongCanvas.java in the project Pong4

```java
1  /*
2   * PongCanvas.java -- A canvas for the game Pong.
3   */
4  package pong;
5
...
19 public class PongCanvas extends JPanel implements Runnable {
20
...
27     private int sleepTime = 60;
28     private boolean threshold1;
29     private boolean threshold2;
30
31     public PongCanvas() {
32         initComponent();
33         start();
34     }
35
...
107    @Override
108    public void paintComponent(Graphics g) {
109        super.paintComponent(g);
110        Graphics2D g2d = (Graphics2D) g;
111
118 ...
119        // paint the game score
120        paintCurrScore(g2d);
121    }
122
...
147    public void paintCurrScore(Graphics2D g2d) {
148        currScore = Consts.SCORE_UNIT * hitPaddle;
149        g2d.setFont(new Font("TimesRoman", Font.BOLD, 20));
150        g2d.setColor(Color.red);
151        g2d.drawString("Score: " + currScore, 25, 25);
152        checkScore(currScore);
153    }
154
155    public void checkScore(int currScore) {
156        if ((!threshold1) && (currScore >= Consts.THRESHOLD1)) {
157            theBall.setDx((int) (theBall.getDx() * 2));
158            theBall.setDy((int) (theBall.getDy() * 1.6));
159            threshold1 = true;
160        } else if ((!threshold2) && (currScore >= Consts.THRESHOLD2)) {
161            theBall.setDx((int) (theBall.getDx() * 2.2));
162            theBall.setDy((int) (theBall.getDy() * 2.2));
163            threshold2 = true;
164        }
165    }
166 }
```

13.12 Summary

The game Pong is a simple video game based on animation technique. This game gives us a real example for understanding the built-in class Thread, the game loop, the sprite, the collision, the collision detection, the player's control, the score counting, the approach for increasing the degree of playing difficulty, and so on. All of these concepts and programming skills will be broadly applied for implementing almost all of video games based on the animation. One of special features of games based on the animation technique is that the new scenes of the game is not made by player's actions but is created by sprite collisions. That is, the game canvas equips a game loop that drives the sprite to be continuously animated and collided. Therefore, the execution of the game is continuously independent of the player's "discrete" actions.

The original definition of "sprite" refers to the components in a video game, which is animated independently and continuously. The bouncing ball is a typical sprite in the game Pong. How about other objects, such as the field-wall? It is a static object, not a sprite. In order to make our programming easier, we "define" the concept that all of components of a video game are sprites. Some of them have an animation speed if they are real sprites; some of them have a speed of zero if they are static objects. This understanding makes a "unified" treatment on all of components. We will apply this concept in our video games that we are going to develop.

The game Pong will be continuously discussed in the next chapter.

13.13 Exercises

Self-Review Questions

1. What are relationship among the terms "animation," "collision," and "playing a game"?
2. How to animate an object? Make an example with a piece of code for illustrating it.
3. What is a "game loop"? What are the major steps in the game loop?
4. Make an example in our real world to explain what a collision is.
5. Write a piece of code to demonstrate the fundamental idea of collision detection.
6. Make an example to explain some collisions are needed and some collisions should be avoided.
7. Why collisions are important in a video game? Make an example to explain it.
8. What are the advantages of the JavaBeans model? Does the model have any disadvantages?
9. What computation is involved to stop the movement of the paddle when the paddle reaches the bottom wall-unit when pressing the down key?
10. What statement(s) is(are) required to use the key control mechanism?
11. What are the differences between the event driven and animation? Do they have similarity in certain points?
12. Why do games usually have a score counting mechanism?

Projects

1. The game Pong in this chapter defines "the game is terminated once the ball is lost." Modify this definition to be "the game is terminated when the ball lost three times" and implement the new definition.
2. Create a small project for illustrating programming skills for applying the JavaBeans model (e.g., a course that involves a teacher and a set of students).
3. Design and implement a project that illustrates an explosion when a bomb hits on the background.
4. Design and implement a project that illustrates the scene for launching a rocket.
5. Replace the key control with mouse control for moving the paddle in the game Pong.
6. Modify the project Pong4 by changing the sleepTime for increasing the speed of the bouncing ball.

14 Multiple Screens: An Extension of the Game Pong

Besides the GUI screen, usually a game requires other multiple screens, such as, splash screen, setting screen, instruction screen, and the like. How to organize these multiple screens such that only one of them will be visible at a time? This chapter extends the game Pong with an additional splash screen for demonstrating the suitability of the CardLayout manager for that purpose. In addition, the game Pong is further extended with more features, such as, increasing the number of bouncing balls with different animation speeds, changing the objective of the game from bouncing balls to catching balls, in order to explore the significance of the word "extension".

The objectives of this chapter include:
1. A game usually has multiple screens.
2. Arranging multiple screens using CardLayout.
3. A structure of multiple classes in using CardLayout.
4. Adding a splash screen for the game Pong.
5. Extensions of the game Pong.
6. Increasing the number of balls.
7. Modifying the story of the game Pong.
8. Constructing reusable units.

The previous chapter introduced the game Pong, built up its GUI, and implemented the dynamic behaviors of the game by animating the bouncing ball, detecting collisions for triggering new actions, controlling the paddle, as well as constructing the score-counting mechanism.

In order to make a game more complete with more interesting behaviors, this chapter intends to introduce two concepts, "multiple screens" and "extensions," for enriching the game Pong. Certainly, these two concepts are applicable to all of video games.

The "extensions" means to add more features into the basis of a game. What extensions could be? It depends on our understanding of the game and our imaginations. The "multiple screens" means a complete game usually has multiple screens beside the GUI screen in the game. What are these multiple screens? How to construct multiple screens for a game? We are going to discuss the concept and its implementations.

14.1 A Game Usually Has Multiple Screens

Usually video games have multiple screens. Figure 14.1 illustrates some of them. Besides the GUI (the "Game scenes" in Fig. 14.1) of a game, usually a game needs a "Splash screen" for explaining the story of the game; a "Menu screen" for telling important commands or actions; an "Instruction screen" for indicating how to play the game; a "Setting screen" for allowing players to preset some parameters, such as the difficulty level, sound on or off, and the like; a "Game over" screen for showing the final scene or the final score of the current playing; and a "Game finish" screen for counting some statistics data of all of playing so far, such as the highest score, the lowest score, the average score, and so on.

The existence of multiple screens requires us to develop multiple classes corresponding to each of the screens. Additionally, it raises a new question about how to arrange the multiple screens and how to switch from one screen to the other when needed.

14.2 Applying the CardLayout for Structuring Multiple Screens

Fortunately, we have learned how to implement card games in previous chapters. A set of cards can be organized as a card deck. At any time, only the card at the top is visible. On the card games, the action "deal a card" is restricted to only deal the first card on the deck. Actually, any card in the deck can be pulled out and placed at the top. Applying this principle, we can also organize multiple screens in the similar fashion. That is, we can stack multiple screens as a "deck" and only the screen at the top is visible. In addition, any screen in the "deck" can be pulled out and placed on the top to be visible.

© Springer Nature Switzerland AG 2018
C.-w. Xu, *Learning Java with Games*, https://doi.org/10.1007/978-3-319-72886-5_14

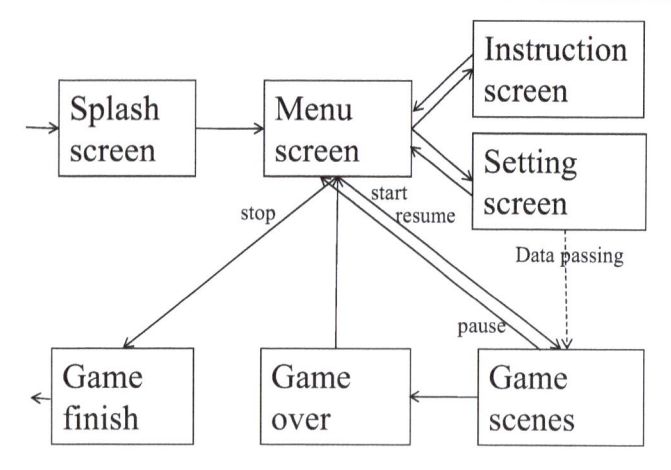

Fig. 14.1 Multiple screens in a game

Java supplies a CardLayout manager to support this style of arrangement. The layout manager CardLayout is different from other layout managers. The other layout managers attempt to show all of components in the container at once; the CardLayout displays only one of the components at a time.

In a card game, a card is a simple object. A deck is a composite class that contains a set of cards. Similarly, a screen is a JPanel. One JPanel is assigned to play the role of a composite class that employs a CardLayout manager to "contain" other multiple screens of JPanel as components. We may assign every screen with a mnemonic name and add them into the "container" to form a "deck" such that any screen can be pulled out through its mnemonic name. If we add screens into the "deck" without mnemonic name, then they can only be shown in a fixed order in using methods, such as previous(), next(), and the like.

14.2.1 Organizing Screens with an Extra "Container": TestCardLayout1

As an example, we assume that a project has three screens. They are three classes SplashScreen.java, SettingPanel.java, and GameCanvas.java. No doubt, everyone of these three classes "is-a" JPanel with a method paintComponent() since every screen should be a canvas for displaying related information. For making them simple, here every screen only shows its own mnemonic name. How to organize them as a deck by using the CardLayout manager?

The project TestCardLayout1 implements the approach that uses an extra container. Because at any time only one of the three screens is visible and we would like to have ability to select either one of them, we design three buttons that correspond to the three classes. When the user clicks one of buttons, the corresponding screen will be shown on the top of the screen deck. Consequently, we have two sets of components. One set consists of the three buttons; the other consists of the three screens.

The project TestCardLayout1 thus uses a class ScreenDeck.java that "is-a" JPanel to hire an intermediate JPanel with the name of "buttons" for arranging the three buttons. And it hires another intermediate JPanel with the name of "screenStack", which adopts the CardLayout manager for organizing the three screens. The class ScreenDeck.java uses the BorderLayout manager to arrange the set of buttons on its NORTH part and place the set of screens on its CENTER part.

As a result, the GUI of the project TestCardLayout1 is as shown in Fig. 14.2 (Right). We can see three buttons are shown on the top of the GUI and the first card of the screen deck appears on the bottom of the GUI. Whenever one of buttons is clicked, the corresponding screen will be pulled up to be visible. This action is realized under the control of the event handlers implemented in the class ScreenDeck.java

The UML class diagram of the project TestCardLayout1 is shown on Fig. 14.2 (Left). The classes SplashScreen.java, SettingPanel.java, and GameCanvas.java are the three screens. Due to the fact that the two intermediate JPanels "buttons" and "screenStack" are objects that are not shown in the UML class diagram. Thereafter, the UML class diagram only shows the ScreenDeck.java "has" the three classes. The partial codes of the project are shown in Listing 14.1.

Listing 14.1 The codes of the classes **ScreenDeck.java** and **SplashScreen.java** in the project TestCardLayout1 (The codes of classes **SettingPanel.java** and **GameCanvas.java** are similar with the code of the class **SplashScreen.java** in this example project)

```
1  /*
2   * ScreenDeck.java -- A class that uses a CardLayout to organize three
3   * screens corresponding to three classes as a screen "deck".
4   */
5  package testcardlayout;
6
7  import java.awt.BorderLayout;
```

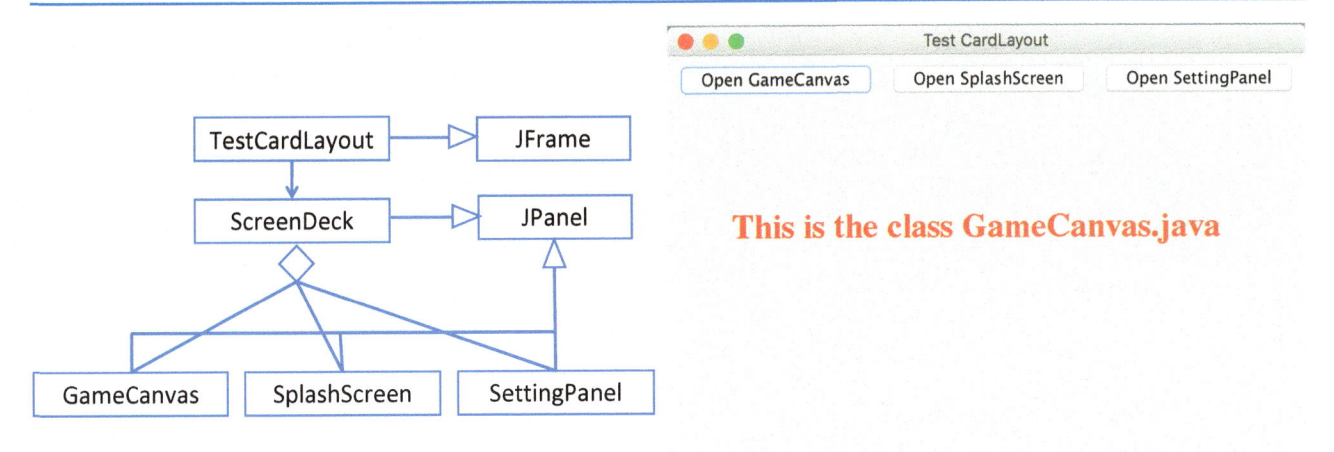

14.2 Applying the CardLayout for Structuring Multiple Screens

Fig. 14.2 (*Left*) The UML class diagram of the project TestCardLayout1. (*Right*) The GUI

```java
 8  import java.awt.CardLayout;
 9  import java.awt.event.ActionEvent;
10  import java.awt.event.ActionListener;
11  import javax.swing.JButton;
12  import javax.swing.JPanel;
13
18  public class ScreenDeck extends JPanel implements ActionListener {
19
20      private JPanel screenStack;
21      private JPanel buttons;
22      private CardLayout cardLayout;
23      private JButton canvasBtn;
24      private JButton splashBtn;
25      private JButton settingBtn;
26
27      public ScreenDeck() {
28          initComponent();
29      }
30
31      private void initComponent() {
32          setLayout(new BorderLayout());
33          initButtons();
34          initScreenStack();
35      }
36
37      private void initButtons() {
38          buttons = new JPanel();
39          canvasBtn = new JButton("Open GameCanvas");
40          canvasBtn.addActionListener(this);
41          buttons.add(canvasBtn);
42
43          splashBtn = new JButton("Open SplashScreen");
44          splashBtn.addActionListener(this);
45          buttons.add(splashBtn);
46
```

```
47              settingBtn = new JButton("Open SettingPanel");
48              settingBtn.addActionListener(this);
49              buttons.add(settingBtn);
50
51              add(buttons, BorderLayout.NORTH);
52          }
53
54          public void initScreenStack() {
55              screenStack = new JPanel();
56              cardLayout = new CardLayout();
57              screenStack.setLayout(cardLayout);
58
59              GameCanvas gameCanvas = new GameCanvas();
60              screenStack.add(gameCanvas, "GameCanvas");
61
62              SplashScreen splashScreen = new SplashScreen();
63              screenStack.add(splashScreen, "SplashScreen");
64
65              SettingPanel settingPanel = new SettingPanel();
66              screenStack.add(settingPanel, "SettingPanel");
67
68              add(screenStack, BorderLayout.CENTER);
69          }
70
71          @Override
72          public void actionPerformed(ActionEvent evt) {
73              CardLayout cl = (CardLayout) screenStack.getLayout();
74              if (evt.getSource() == canvasBtn) {
75                  cl.show(screenStack, "GameCanvas");
76              } else if (evt.getSource() == splashBtn) {
77                  cl.show(screenStack, "SplashScreen");
78              } else {
79                  cl.show(screenStack, "SettingPanel");
80              }
81          }
82
83 }
```

```
 1 /*
 2  * SplashScreen.java -- A JPanel for mimicking a screen in a screen "deck".
 3  */
 4 package testcardlayout;
 5
 6 import java.awt.Color;
 7 import java.awt.Font;
 8 import java.awt.Graphics;
 9 import java.awt.Graphics2D;
10 import javax.swing.JPanel;
11
16 public class SplashScreen extends JPanel {
17
18     @SuppressWarnings("OverridableMethodCallInConstructor")
19     public SplashScreen() {
20         repaint();
21     }
```

```
22
23      @Override
24      public void paintComponent(Graphics g) {
25          super.paintComponent(g);
26          Graphics2D g2d = (Graphics2D) g;
27
28          g2d.setColor(Color.RED);
29          g2d.setFont(new Font("Times", Font.BOLD, 26));
30          String script1
31                  = "This is the class SplashScreen.java";
32          g2d.drawString(script1, 50, 100);
33      }
34  }
```

The method initButtons() of the class ScreenDeck.java declares a variable JPanel buttons to "contain" three JButtons. The method initScreenStack() declares a variable JPanel screenStack with a CardLayout manager to "contain" the three screen JPanels as a deck. Every screen has its mnemonic name. Due to the screen "GameCanvas" is added first, it becomes the default visible screen to be shown on the GUI first.

For showing other screens, the ScreenDeck.java class implements the ActionListener registered with the three buttons on the NORTH part. When the player clicks one of the buttons, the event handler invokes the method cardLayout.show() for showing the corresponding screen. The visible screen simply paints its name for telling which screen is visible at the moment.

14.2.2 Using One of the Existing Screens as the "Container": TestCardLayout2

Observe the structure of the screen "deck" in the project TestCardLayout1, we may find out that:

1. The placement of the three buttons on the NORTH part of the GUI is not a good design because it means that the same set of three buttons is always shown on the GUI. It is not necessary since not every screen requires all of the three buttons and it might make an "unpleasant" GUI. Instead, we may add different sets of buttons into different screens and then remove the set of three buttons.
2. The extra container JPanel screenStack is redundant since the class ScreenDeck.java itself is a JPanel, which can be directly used as the "container."

The project TestCardLayout2 takes the two observations above into consideration and improves the coding of the class ScreenDeck.java as cited in Listing 14.2. Its GUI and UML class diagram is very similar with that of the project TestCardLayout1 as shown in Fig. 14.2.

Listing 14.2 The codes of the classes ScreenDeck.java and SplashScreen.java in the project TestCardLayout2 (The codes of classes SettingPanel.java and GameCanvas.java are similar with the class SplashScreen.java)

```
1   /*
2    * ScreenDeck.java -- A class that implements the screen "deck".
3    */
4   package testcardlayout;
5
6   import java.awt.CardLayout;
7   import javax.swing.JPanel;
8
13  public class ScreenDeck extends JPanel {
14
15      private CardLayout cardLayout;
16
17      @SuppressWarnings("OverridableMethodCallInConstructor")
```

```
18      public ScreenDeck() {
19          cardLayout = new CardLayout();
20          setLayout(cardLayout);
21          initScreenDeck();
22      }
23
24      public void initScreenDeck() {
25          GameCanvas gameCanvas = new GameCanvas();
26          add(gameCanvas, "GameCanvas");
27          gameCanvas.setParent(this);
28          gameCanvas.setCardLayout(cardLayout);
29
30          SplashScreen splashScreen = new SplashScreen();
31          add(splashScreen, "SplashScreen");
32          splashScreen.setParent(this);
33          splashScreen.setCardLayout(cardLayout);
34
35          SettingPanel settingPanel = new SettingPanel();
36          add(settingPanel, "SettingPanel");
37          settingPanel.setParent(this);
38          settingPanel.setCardLayout(cardLayout);
39
40          cardLayout.show(this, "SplashScreen");
41      }
42 }
```

```
 1 /*
 2  * SplashScreen.java -- A class that implements a splash screen.
 3  */
 4 package testcardlayout;
 5
 6 import java.awt.BorderLayout;
 7 import java.awt.CardLayout;
 8 import java.awt.Color;
 9 import java.awt.Font;
10 import java.awt.Graphics;
11 import java.awt.Graphics2D;
12 import java.awt.event.ActionEvent;
13 import java.awt.event.ActionListener;
14 import javax.swing.JButton;
15 import javax.swing.JPanel;
16
21 public class SplashScreen extends JPanel implements ActionListener {
22
23      private ScreenDeck parent;
24      private CardLayout cardLayout;
25      private JButton settingBtn;
26      private JButton quitBtn;
27
28      @SuppressWarnings("OverridableMethodCallInConstructor")
29      public SplashScreen() {
30          setLayout(new BorderLayout());
31          initButtons();
32          repaint();
33      }
```

```java
34
35      public void initButtons() {
36          JPanel btnP = new JPanel();
37
38          settingBtn = new JButton("Open SettingPanel");
39          settingBtn.addActionListener(this);
40
41          quitBtn = new JButton("Quit");
42          quitBtn.addActionListener(this);
43
44          btnP.add(settingBtn);
45          btnP.add(quitBtn);
46
47          add(btnP, BorderLayout.SOUTH);
48      }
49
50      @Override
51      public void paintComponent(Graphics g) {
52          super.paintComponent(g);
53          Graphics2D g2d = (Graphics2D) g;
54
55          String script1
56                  = "This is the class SplashScreen.java";
57          g2d.setColor(Color.RED);
58          g2d.setFont(new Font("Times", Font.BOLD, 26));
59          g2d.drawString(script1, 50, 100);
60      }
61
62      @Override
63      public void actionPerformed(ActionEvent evt) {
64          if (evt.getSource() == settingBtn) {
65              cardLayout.show(parent, "SettingPanel");
66          } else if (evt.getSource() == quitBtn) {
67              System.exit(0);
68          }
69      }
70
71      public void setParent(ScreenDeck parent) {
72          this.parent = parent;
73      }
74
75      public void setCardLayout(CardLayout cardLayout) {
76          this.cardLayout = cardLayout;
77      }
78  }
```

The new implementation of the project TestCardLayout2 takes the class ScreenDeck.java as the "container" such that the constructor of the class ScreenDeck() sets a CardLayout as the layout manager for making the class ScreenDeck.java as a "container" to form a screen "deck." Following that, the method initScreenDeck() instantiates the three objects gameCanvas, splashScreen, and settingPanel and further invokes the method this.add() to add them into "this" "container" object (the object of the class ScreenDeck.java itself) with a mnemonic name each. The last statement "cardLayout.show(this, "SplashScreen")" pulls out the splashScreen from "this" deck and displays it. All of these codes realize the second observation listed above.

In order to implement the first observation listed above, we are not going to show all of the three buttons with every screen but move buttons to every individual class. Taking the class SplashScreen.java as an example, it only needs two buttons. One button is for switching to the settingPanel and the other is for "Quit" in case the player is not interested in playing the game. Therefore, the SplashScreen.java class sets up the two buttons on the SOUTH part of the screen and implements an event handler actionPerformed() to respond the button click actions. When the button "Open SettingPanel" is clicked, the event handler actionPerformed() should invoke the statement "cardLayout.show(parent, "SettingPanel");" to pull out the settingPanel from the deck and display it on the top of the deck. That statement requires accessing the objects of both "cardLayout" and "parent." The object "cardLayout" is instantiated by the class ScreenDeck.java, and the object "parent" refers to the object of the class ScreenDeck.java itself. Thus, the method screenDeck.initScreenDeck() uses the following two statements to pass these two objects into the class SplashScreen.java.

```
32      splashScreen.setParent(this);
33      splashScreen.setCardLayout(cardLayout);
```

The same statements are also applied to other two screens contained in the cardLayout.

14.3 Adding a Splash Screen: The Project Pong5

After understanding the principle and the usage of the CardLayout manager, we are going to add a real splash screen for the game Pong. In general, a splash screen is a separate screen against the game canvas. The splash screen looks like a cover page of a book that briefly introduces the game. Thus, the new added splash screen mainly describes what the game Pong is and how to play the game Pong. It helps buyers or players to make a decision whether to buy the game or play on it. Fig. 14.3 (Left) shows the UML class diagram of the project Pong5, which has a new class ScreenDeck.java that "contains" two classes SplashScreen.java and GameCanvas.java. Fig. 14.3 (Right) displays the splash screen of the game Pong, which shows that besides the description of the game it also includes two buttons of "Start Game" and "Quit."

Surely, the new class ScreenDeck.java employs a CardLayout manager to organize the two screens as a "deck," and only one of them is shown at a time. Logically, the splash screen usually is shown up first to let the player know what the game is about, and then the player either clicks the "Start Game" button for opening the game canvas or clicks the "Quit" button without any interest to see the game. The codes of the two new classes ScreenDeck.java and SplashScreen.java are cited in Listing 14.3. The gameCanvas screen displays the game scenes as see in the project Pong4 in the previous chapter.

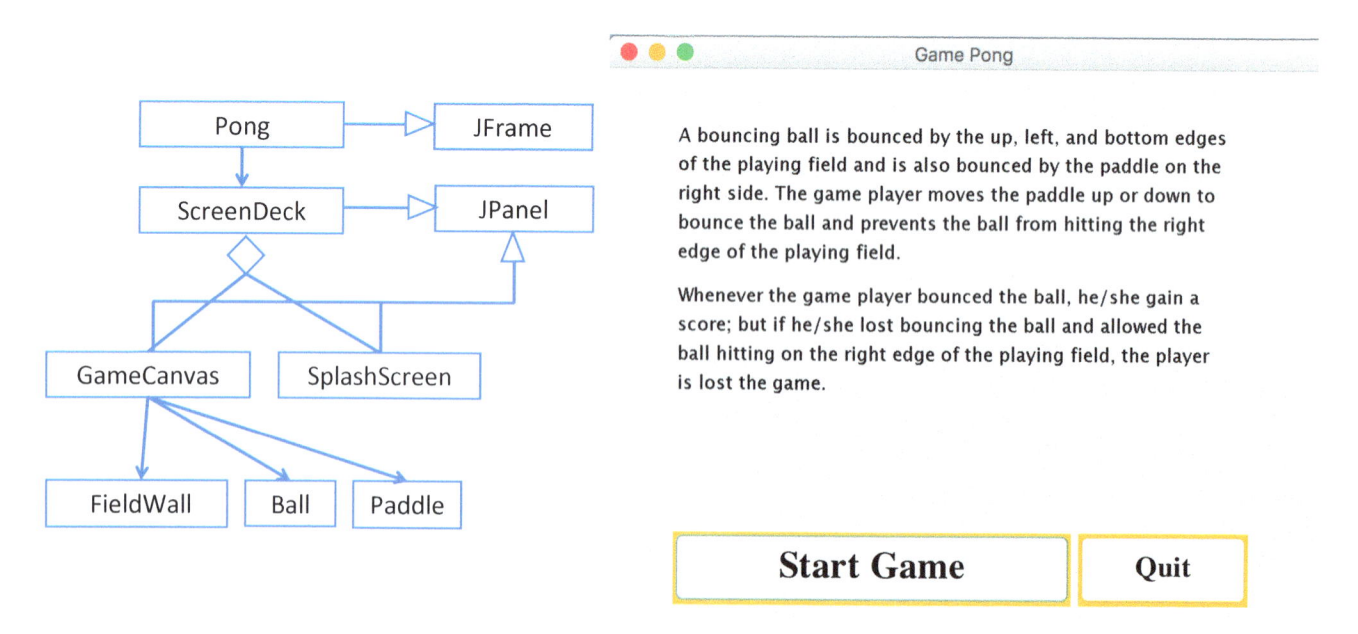

Fig. 14.3 (*Left*) The UML class diagram. (*Right*) The splash screen of the game Pong5

14.3 Adding a Splash Screen: The Project Pong5

Listing 14.3 The two new classes ScreenDeck.java and SplashScreen.java in the project Pong5

```
 1  /*
 2   * ScreenDeck.java -- A class that implements the screenDeck of the game.
 3   */
 4  package pong;
 5
 6  import java.awt.CardLayout;
 7  import javax.swing.JPanel;
 8
13  public class ScreenDeck extends JPanel {
14
15      private CardLayout cardLayout;
16
17      public ScreenDeck() {
18          initComponent();
19      }
20
21      private void initComponent() {
22          cardLayout = new CardLayout();
23          setLayout(cardLayout);
24
25          // instantiate gameCanvas first since it is required by the splashScreen
26          GameCanvas gameCanvas = new GameCanvas();
27          gameCanvas.setParent(this);
28          gameCanvas.setCardLayout(cardLayout);
29          add(gameCanvas, "GameCanvas");
30
31          SplashScreen splashScreen = new SplashScreen();
32          splashScreen.setParent(this);
33          splashScreen.setCardLayout(cardLayout);
34          splashScreen.setGameCanvas(gameCanvas);
35          add(splashScreen, "SplashScreen");
36          cardLayout.show(this, "SplashScreen");
37      }
38  }
```

```
 1  /*
 2   * SplashScreen.java -- A class that implements a splash screen.
 3   */
 4  package pong;
 5
 6  import java.awt.BorderLayout;
 7  import java.awt.CardLayout;
 8  import java.awt.Color;
 9  import java.awt.Dimension;
10  import java.awt.FlowLayout;
11  import java.awt.Font;
12  import java.awt.Graphics;
13  import java.awt.Graphics2D;
14  import java.awt.event.ActionEvent;
15  import java.awt.event.ActionListener;
16  import javax.swing.JButton;
17  import javax.swing.JPanel;
18
```

```java
23 public class SplashScreen extends JPanel implements ActionListener {
24
25     private JButton startBtn;
26     private JButton quitBtn;
27     private JPanel buttonPn;
28     private ScreenDeck parent;
29     private CardLayout cardLayout;
30     private GameCanvas gameCanvas;
31
32     @SuppressWarnings("OverridableMethodCallInConstructor")
33     public SplashScreen() {
34         setLayout(new BorderLayout());
35         initComponent();
36     }
37
38     private void initComponent() {
39         buttonPn = new JPanel();
40         buttonPn.setLayout(new FlowLayout()); //(1, 2, 10, 0));
41         buttonPn.setPreferredSize(new Dimension(Consts.CV_WIDTH, 65));
42
43         startBtn = new JButton("Start Game");
44         startBtn.setPreferredSize(new Dimension(280, 50));
45         startBtn.setFont(new Font("Times", Font.BOLD, 26));
46         startBtn.setOpaque(true);
47         startBtn.setBackground(Color.ORANGE);
48         startBtn.addActionListener(this);
49         buttonPn.add(startBtn);
50
51         quitBtn = new JButton("Quit");
52         quitBtn.setPreferredSize(new Dimension(120, 50));
53         quitBtn.setFont(new Font("Times", Font.BOLD, 20));
54         quitBtn.setOpaque(true);
55         quitBtn.setBackground(Color.ORANGE);
56         quitBtn.addActionListener(this);
57         buttonPn.add(quitBtn);
58         add(buttonPn, BorderLayout.SOUTH);
59     }
60
61     @Override
62     public void paintComponent(Graphics g) {
63         super.paintComponent(g);
64         Graphics2D g2d = (Graphics2D) g;
65
66         // describe the game
67         g2d.drawString(
68                 "A bouncing ball is bounced by the up, left, and bottom edges ", 50, 50);
69         g2d.drawString(
70                 "of the playing field and is also bounced by the paddle on the ", 50, 70);
71         g2d.drawString(
72                 "right side. The game player moves the paddle up or down to ", 50, 90);
73         g2d.drawString(
74                 "bounce the ball and prevents the ball from hitting the right", 50, 110);
75         g2d.drawString(
76                 "edge of the playing field. ", 50, 130);
77         g2d.drawString(
```

14.3 Adding a Splash Screen: The Project Pong5

```java
78                    "Whenever the game player bounced the ball, he/she gain a ", 50, 160);
79            g2d.drawString(
80                    "score; but if he/she lost bouncing the ball and allowed the ", 50, 180);
81            g2d.drawString(
82                    "ball hitting on the right edge of the playing field, the player ", 50, 200);
83            g2d.drawString(
84                    "is lost the game.", 50, 220);
85        }
86
87        @Override
88        public void actionPerformed(ActionEvent evt) {
89            if (evt.getSource() == startBtn) {
90                cardLayout.show(parent, "GameCanvas");
91                // the card requires focus when it is shown
92                gameCanvas.requestFocusInWindow();
93                // reset the game by replacing the ball
94                gameCanvas.setTheBall(new Ball());
95            } else if (evt.getSource() == quitBtn) {
96                System.exit(0);
97            }
98        }
99
100       @Override
101       public ScreenDeck getParent() {
102           return parent;
103       }
104
105       public void setParent(ScreenDeck parent) {
106           this.parent = parent;
107       }
108
109       public CardLayout getCardLayout() {
110           return cardLayout;
111       }
112
113       public void setCardLayout(CardLayout cardLayout) {
114           this.cardLayout = cardLayout;
115       }
116
117       public GameCanvas getGameCanvas() {
118           return gameCanvas;
119       }
120
121       public void setGameCanvas(GameCanvas gameCanvas) {
122           this.gameCanvas = gameCanvas;
123       }
124   }
```

The class ScreenDeck.java mainly organizes the two screens using the CardLayout. Its method initComponent() instantiates the object cardLayout as its layout manager. Then, it instantiates the object gameCanvas and adds it into the cardLayout with the mnemonic name of "GameCanvas." Similarly, it also instantiates the object splashScreen and adds the object into the cardLayout with the mnemonic name of "SplashScreen." Then, it shows the SplashScreen immediately.

Whenever the player clicks the button "Start Game" on the splashScreen, the event handler actionPerformed() implemented in the class SplashScreen.java is going to do three things. (1) It lets the cardLayout show the game canvas. (2) The focus ability is immediately assigned to the gameCanvas in order to allow the player to move the paddle up or down by using the keys control. (3) It resets the ball at the initial position for making a new game scene.

These three actions are performed inside the class SplashScreen.java. However, the first action needs to access the cardLayout and the screenDeck. The second and the third actions require accessing the object gameCanvas. Therefore, the ScreenDeck.java class has to invoke the following three statements for passing the three objects into the class SplashScreen.java.

```
splashScreen.setParent(this);
// "this" is the object of ScreenDeck.java
splashScreen.setCardLayout(cardLayout);
splashScreen.setGameCanvas(gameCanvas);
```

One important issue should be repeated here. It is about the focus on the game canvas. As mentioned before, when the player plays the game, the paddle should be moved up or down in order to bounce the ball back to prevent the ball from "lost." Because the control mechanism is the keys, for accepting key controls, the game screen should get "focus." That is why in the previous versions, the class PongCanvas.java has a setFocusable(true). But, in this new version, there are two screens that are switched as a visible screen and a hidden screen dynamically. Under this case, the static statement setFocusable(true) is no longer working. It needs a dynamic setting whenever the game canvas is to be the visible screen. That is the reason why the statement gameCanvas.requestFocusInWindow() is necessary to be invoked in the method actionPerformed() of the class SplashScreen.java. At the same time, the static statement setFocusable(true) in the class GameCanvas.java is removed.

14.4 Formatting the Texts on the Splash Screen: The Project Pong6

Obviously, the code of the class SplashScreen.java indicates that the description of the game on the splash screen consists of several short strings. The arrangement of them is artificially made. It works but it wastes the developer's time and efforts. We would like to have a piece of code to arrange a long string into several rows automatically. Actually, it is a popular issue that we have discussed in the project PaintXmasCard and in the game WheelVideo. Due to its popularity, we are going to make it as a reusable unit.

As a reusable unit, the related codes could be designed as a method or a class. We think a JavaBean is a better unit since it is easier to be copied or transferred to new projects as a completely wrapped unit. Thus, we create a PaintStrBean.java to perform the function for painting a long string on the center position along the *x*-axis of a painting area. The new class is cited in Listing 14.4.

Listing 14.4 The new class PaintStrBean.java in the project Pong6

```
1  /*
2   * PaintStrBean.java - A bean to paint a string on the center position of
3   * a painting area along the x-coordinate.
4   */
5  package pong;
6
7  import java.awt.FontMetrics;
8  import java.awt.Graphics2D;
9  import java.util.StringTokenizer;
10
15 public class PaintStrBean {
16
17     private int paintAreaMinX;
18     private int paintAreaMaxX;
19     private int paintY;
20
21     public PaintStrBean() {
22     }
23
24     public void paintLongString(Graphics2D g, String paintStr) {
25         // for displaying the description, Consts.java sets MARGIN = 20.
```

14.4 Formatting the Texts on the Splash Screen: The Project Pong6

```
26              // Thus, MAXX_DIS and MINX_DIS are used
27              int areaWidth = paintAreaMaxX - paintAreaMinX;
28
29              FontMetrics fm = g.getFontMetrics();
30              int charHeight = fm.getAscent();
31
32              // concatinate words into a subStr and paint it centerized
33              StringTokenizer st
34                      = new StringTokenizer(paintStr, " ");
35              String subStr = "";
36
37              paintY = paintY + charHeight;
38              while (st.hasMoreTokens()) {
39                  String nextT = st.nextToken();
40                  int subStrW = fm.stringWidth(subStr) + fm.stringWidth(nextT);
41                  if (subStrW <= areaWidth) {
42                      subStr = subStr + nextT + " ";
43                  } else {
44                      paintY = paintY + Consts.NEXTLINE;
45                      int subStrWidth = fm.stringWidth(subStr);
46                      int midW = subStrWidth / 2;
47                      int startX = areaWidth / 2 - midW;
48                      g.drawString(subStr, paintAreaMinX + startX, paintY);
49                      subStr = nextT + " ";
50                  }
51              }
52              // for painting the last piece if any
53              if (!subStr.equals(" ")) {
54                  paintY = paintY + Consts.NEXTLINE;
55                  int subStrWidth = fm.stringWidth(subStr);
56                  int midW = subStrWidth / 2;
57                  int startX = areaWidth / 2 - midW;
58                  g.drawString(subStr, paintAreaMinX + startX, paintY);
59              }
60          }
61
62          public void setPaintAreaMinX(int paintAreaMinX) {
63              this.paintAreaMinX = paintAreaMinX;
64          }
65
66          public void setPaintAreaMaxX(int paintAreaMaxX) {
67              this.paintAreaMaxX = paintAreaMaxX;
68          }
69
70          public int getPaintY() {
71              return paintY;
72          }
73
74          public void setPaintY(int paintY) {
75              this.paintY = paintY;
76          }
77      }
```

The class PaintStrBean.java provides three setter methods to accept three input data. The data of paintAreaMinX and paintAreaMaxX defines the width of the painting area. The data paintY indicates the y-coordinate of the starting letter of the string on the painting area. The body of the method paintLongString() looks familiar. It is coded based on the following pseudo code that we learned before.

1. Find the width of the painting area areaWidth.
2. Set up the font for painting the string and measure the stringWidth and the charHeight by applying the built-in class FontMetrics.
3. Divide the entire string into a set of words by using the built-in StringTokenizer class.
4. Concatenate maximum number of words into a substring until the total width of the substring is still less than or equal to the areaWidth.
5. Paint substring by substring on the center position of the painting area.

The method paintLongString() requires two parameters: Graphics2D g2d and String paintStr. Therefore, before a caller method, say, paintComponent(), invokes the method paintLongString(), the caller method should prepare a suitable g2d with a preferred font and pass it into the paintLongString() method. Meanwhile, the painted string paintStr is also passed. And then, the method paintLongString() implements the pseudo code above for painting the long string. The modified class SplashScreen.java is shown in Listing 14.5. Figure 14.4 shows an example of the result.

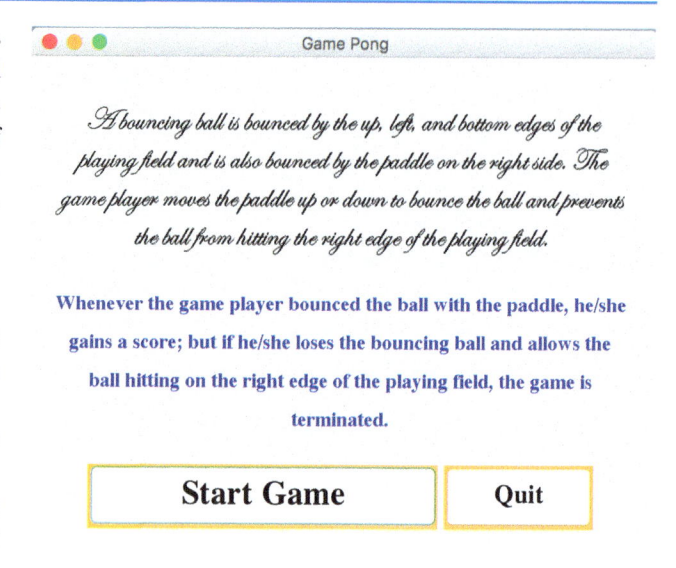

Fig. 14.4 A better-formatted splash screen in the project Pong6

Listing 14.5 The modified class SplashScreen.java in the project Pong6

```
 1 /*
 2  * SplashScreen.java -- A class that implements a splash screen.
 3  */
 4 package pong;
 5
...
22  */
23 public class SplashScreen extends JPanel implements ActionListener {
24
25     private JButton startBtn;
26     private JButton quitBtn;
27     private JPanel buttonPn;
28     private ControlPanel parent;
29     private CardLayout cardLayout;
30     private GameCanvas gameCanvas;
31     private int paintY;
32
33     public SplashScreen() {
34         setLayout(new BorderLayout());
35         initComponent();
36     }
37
```

14.4 Formatting the Texts on the Splash Screen: The Project Pong6

```
38      private void initComponent() {
39          ...
59      }
60
61      @Override
62      public void paintComponent(Graphics g) {
63          super.paintComponent(g);
64          Graphics2D g2d = (Graphics2D) g;
65
66          // describe the game
67          String script1
68                  = "A bouncing ball is bounced by the up, left, and bottom edges "
69                  + "of the playing field and is also bounced by the paddle on the "
70                  + "right side. The game player moves the paddle up or down to "
71                  + "bounce the ball and prevents the ball from hitting the right "
72                  + "edge of the playing field. ";
73          String script2
74                  = "Whenever the game player bounced the ball with the paddle, "
75                  + "he/she gains a score; but if he/she loses the bouncing ball "
76                  + "and allows the ball hitting on the right edge of the playing "
77                  + "field, the game is terminated.";
78
79          PaintStrBean paintBean = new PaintStrBean();
80          paintBean.setPaintAreaMinX(Consts.MINX_DIS);
81          paintBean.setPaintAreaMaxX(Consts.MAXX_DIS);
82
83          paintY = Consts.MINY_DIS - 15;
84          paintBean.setPaintY(paintY);
85          g2d.setFont(new Font("Edwardian Script ITC", Font.BOLD, 24));
86          paintBean.paintLongString(g2d, script1);
87
88          paintY = paintBean.getPaintY() + 10; // make a gap between two scripts
89          paintBean.setPaintY(paintY);
90          g2d.setFont(new Font("Times", Font.BOLD, 16));
91          g2d.setColor(Color.BLUE);
92          paintBean.paintLongString(g2d, script2);
93      }
94
95      @Override
96      public void actionPerformed(ActionEvent evt) {
97          if (evt.getSource() == startBtn) {
98              cardLayout.show(parent, "GameCanvas");
99              // the card requires focus when it is shown
100             gameCanvas.requestFocusInWindow();
101             // reset the game by replacing the ball
102             gameCanvas.setTheBall(new Ball());
103         } else if (evt.getSource() == quitBtn) {
104             System.exit(0);
105         }
106     }
107
...     // getters and setters
132 }
```

In using the class PaintStrBean.java, we don't need to worry about the length of the string that we would like to paint.

14.5 Extending the Game Pong

The "extension" of a game is also an important concept and practice. After building up a basis of a game, we may extend the game with multiple new features to make the game more fun. Take the game Pong as an example, we may extend it with the following new features.

1. The game will generate two or more bouncing balls with different speeds and different moving patterns for increasing the degree of playing difficulty of the game.
2. And more, we may oppose the objective of the original game Pong. The original idea of the game Pong is to use the paddle for bouncing the ball back. Instead, we can design an opposite action to catch the ball. That is, instead of the paddle, we design a movable hole on the right edge of the field-wall. The player moves the hole to allow the bouncing ball to go through the hole; otherwise, the solid part of the right edge will bounce the ball back. When a ball is caught, the game automatically generates another ball with a higher speed.
3. After every certain time period, even the game has some uncaught balls, the game still generates a new bouncing ball with different speed and different moving pattern to let the player to catch them. The number of uncaught balls would be increased for making catching more difficult.

14.6 Increasing the Number of Ball Sprites: The Project Pong7

As mentioned above, we can extend the game Pong to increase the number of balls. As a simple step, we only generate two bouncing balls with different speeds and different moving patterns, which can be adjusted by setting different initial values of dx and dy.

For generating two different balls, we need to modify the class Ball.java for making it as a generic class that can be instantiated multiple times for making multiple instances by assigning different sets of values to the attributes. The modified code of the class Ball.java is shown in Listing 14.6. We can see that the class is very close to a "pure" JavaBeans. It only defines a set of attributes and their getter and setter methods. All of attributes are accessed through its getter and setter methods by the class that "uses" it.

Listing 14.6 The modified class Ball.java in the project Pong7

```
1  /*
2   * Ball.java - A class that implements a ball for the game Pong.
3   */
4  package ponggame;
5
6  import java.awt.Color;
7  import java.awt.Graphics2D;
8
13 public class Ball {
14
15     private int x, y;
16     private int radius;
17     private Color ballColor;
18     private int dx, dy;
19     private boolean lost;
20
21     public Ball() {
22     }
23
24     public void updateBall() {
25         setX(getX() + getDx());
26         setY(getY() + getDy());
27     }
28
29     public void paintBall(Graphics2D g2d) {
30         g2d.setColor(getBallColor());
31         g2d.fillOval(getX(), getY(), 2 * getRadius(), 2 * getRadius());
32     }
```

14.6 Increasing the Number of Ball Sprites: The Project Pong7

```
33
34      public int getX() {
35          return x;
36      }
37
38      public void setX(int x) {
39          this.x = x;
40      }
41
42      public int getY() {
43          return y;
44      }
45
46      public void setY(int y) {
47          this.y = y;
48      }
49
50      public int getRadius() {
51          return radius;
52      }
53
54      public void setRadius(int radius) {
55          this.radius = radius;
56      }
57
58      public Color getBallColor() {
59          return ballColor;
60      }
61
62      public void setBallColor(Color ballColor) {
63          this.ballColor = ballColor;
64      }
65
66      public int getDx() {
67          return dx;
68      }
69
70      public void setDx(int dx) {
71          this.dx = dx;
72      }
73
74      public int getDy() {
75          return dy;
76      }
77
78      public void setDy(int dy) {
79          this.dy = dy;
80      }
81
82      public boolean isLost() {
83          return lost;
84      }
85
86      public void setLost(boolean lost) {
87          this.lost = lost;
88      }
89 }
```

Surely, the major modifications are in the class GameCanvas.java, which instantiates two objects ball1 and ball2 of the class Ball.java and assigns them different initial values through related setter methods. If we understand the object ball1 is the original ball, then the new object ball2 has the same behaviors as the ball1 because they have the same set of methods, such as updateBall(), detectCollision(), paintComponent(), and the like. Especially the new added method callResetGame() ensures that it will invoke the method resetGame() only after both ball1.isLost() and ball2.isLost() occurred. The modified class GameCanvas.java is listed in Listing 14.7.

The method resetGame() is going to show the splash screen only. The real function for resetting the game is performed only when the button "Start Game" is clicked, which triggers the action event listener defined in the class SplashScreen.java. The action event handler invokes the method gameCanvas.initBall(), which collects all variables that are required to be reset for a new game. This is one of programming skills that we should pay attention since the skill is needed for almost all of games to renew a new game.

Listing 14.7 The modified class GameCanvas.java in the project Pong7

```
1  /*
2   * GameCanvas.java -- A canvas for the game Pong.
3   */
4  package ponggame;
5  …
20 public class GameCanvas extends JPanel implements Runnable {
21
22     private FieldWall theWall;
23     private Ball ball1;
24     private Ball ball2;
25 …
34
35     public GameCanvas() {
36         addKeyListener(new MyKeyAdapter());
37         initComponent();
38         start();
39     }
40
41     private void initComponent() {
42 …
44         initBall();
45     }
46
47     public void initBall() {
48         int cvX = (Consts.MAXX-Consts.MINX) / 2;
49         int cvY = (Consts.MAXY-Consts.MINY) / 2;
50         ball1 = new Ball();
51         ball1.setRadius(Consts.BALL_RADIUS1);
52         ball1.setX(cvX - ball1.getRadius());
53         ball1.setY(cvY - ball1.getRadius());
54         ball1.setBallColor(Color.RED);
55         ball1.setDx(3);
56         ball1.setDy(2);
57         ball1.setLost(false);
58         ball2 = new Ball();
59         ball2.setRadius(Consts.BALL_RADIUS2);
60         ball2.setX(cvX - ball2.getRadius());
61         ball2.setY(cvY - ball2.getRadius());
62         ball2.setBallColor(Color.BLUE);
```

14.6 Increasing the Number of Ball Sprites: The Project Pong7

```
 63            ball2.setDx(2);
 64            ball2.setDy(3);
 65            ball2.setLost(false);
 66            currScore = 0;
 67            hitPaddle = 0;
 68            threshold1 = false;
 69            threshold2 = false;
 70
 71            sleepTime = 60;
 72        }
 73
 74        private void start() {
 75    ...
 79        }
 80
 81        @Override
 82        public void run() {
 83            try {
 84                while (true) {
 85                    ball1.updateBall();
 86                    ball2.updateBall();
 87    ...
 90                }
 91            } catch (InterruptedException ex) {
 92            }
 93        }
 94
 95        public void detectCollision() {
 96            // make a bounding rectangle of the ball
 97            Rectangle ballRect1 = new Rectangle(ball1.getX(), ball1.getY(),
 98                    2 * Consts.BALL_RADIUS1, 2 * Consts.BALL_RADIUS1);
 99            Rectangle ballRect2 = new Rectangle(ball2.getX(), ball2.getY(),
100                    2 * Consts.BALL_RADIUS2, 2 * Consts.BALL_RADIUS2);
101            // whether the ball hits on any unit of the bouncing wall
102            for (int i = 0; i < 4; i++) {
103                if ((theWall.getaWall()[i]).intersects(ballRect1)) {
104                    switch (i) {
105                        case 0: // top
106                        case 1: // bottom
107                            ball1.setDy(-ball1.getDy());
108                            break;
109                        case 2: // left
110                            ball1.setDx(-ball1.getDx());
111                            break;
112                        case 3: // right, game is over
113                            ball1.setLost(true);
114                            callResetGame();
115                            break;
116                    }
117                }
118            }
119            for (int i = 0; i < 4; i++) {
120                if ((theWall.getaWall()[i]).intersects(ballRect2)) {
121                    switch (i) {
122                        case 0: // top
```

```java
                        case 1: // bottom
                            ball2.setDy(-ball2.getDy());
                            break;
                        case 2: // left
                            ball2.setDx(-ball2.getDx());
                            break;
                        case 3: // right, game is over
                            ball2.setLost(true);
                            callResetGame();
                            break;
                    }
                }
            }
        // whether the ball collides the paddle
        Rectangle paddleRect = new Rectangle(thePaddle.getX(), thePaddle.getY(),
            Consts.PADDLE_WIDTH, Consts.PADDLE_HEIGHT);
        if (paddleRect.intersects(ballRect1)) {
            hitPaddle++;
            ball1.setDx(-ball1.getDx());
        }
        if (paddleRect.intersects(ballRect2)) {
            hitPaddle++;
            ball2.setDx(-ball2.getDx());
        }
    }

    public void callResetGame() {
        if ((ball1.isLost()) && (ball2.isLost())) {
            resetGame();
        }
    }

    public void resetGame() {
        hitPaddle = 0;
        cardLayout.show(parent, "SplashSheet");
    }

    @Override
    public void paintComponent(Graphics g) {
...
        // draw a red ball at the center of the canvas
        ball1.paintBall(g2d);
        ball2.paintBall(g2d);
...

        // paint the game score
        paintCurrScore(g2d);
    }

    // an inner class for implementing the key event adapter
    // for catching the up or down keys to move the paddle
    class MyKeyAdapter extends KeyAdapter {
        @Override
        public void keyPressed(KeyEvent evt) {
...
```

```
197         }
198     }
199
200     public void paintCurrScore(Graphics2D g2d) {
201 …
206     }
207
208     public void checkScore(int currScore) {
209 …
216     }
217
218 … getters and setters
234 }
```

Certainly, another approach is to declare an array of Ball for holding all of objects of the class Ball.java. And then applying a "for" loop to let every ball object invokes related methods.

14.7 Modifying the Game Story for Catching the Ball Sprites: The Project Pong8

Another extension is to modify the story of the game Pong. The new story says a bouncing ball is bounced by four edges of the game playing field. But, the right edge has a hole that can be moved by the game player to catch the bouncing ball. When the player catches a ball, the game generates a new ball with a different size, a different bouncing speed, and a different moving pattern. When the player catches a ball, the score increases 10 points; when the player misses a catch and the ball is bounced back by the right edge, the score is decreased 5 points. As long as the ball lost for five times, the game is over.

For implementing the new story, some codes should be modified.

1. A new class Hole.java replaces the class Paddle.java. They are very similar, just the shape and initial position have some modifications. The code is shown in Listing 14.8.

Listing 14.8 The class Hole.java in the project Pong8

```
 1 /*
 2  * Hole.java - A class that implements a hole.
 3  */
 4 package ponggame;
 5 …
13 public class Hole {
14
15     private int x, y;
16     private Color color;
17
18     public Hole() {
19         initHole();
20     }
21
22     private void initHole() {
23         setX(Consts.MAXX - Consts.HOLE_WIDTH);
24         setY((Consts.MAXY - Consts.MINY) / 2 - Consts.HOLE_HEIGHT / 2);
25         setColor(Color.RED);
26     }
27
```

```
28    public void paintHole(Graphics2D g2d) {
29        g2d.setColor(getColor());
30        g2d.fillRect(getX(), getY(), Consts.HOLE_WIDTH, Consts.HOLE_HEIGHT);
31    }
32
33 … getters and setters
56 }
```

2. Whenever a ball is caught, a new ball should be initialized. In considering every ball should have different animation speed and pattern, we use the random number generator to generate different initial values for the dx and dy and also generate either positive sign or negative sign for the values of dx or dy. The randomly generated sign depends on the statement "(int)Math.round(Math.random());", which gives a value of 0 or 1 since Math.random() returns a value in the range of [0, 1); the Math.round() will round the values that are less than 0.5 to be 0 and round the values that are larger than 0.5 to be 1. When the rounded value is 0, a negative sign is assigned to the value of dx or dy; otherwise, a positive sign is assigned to the value of dx or dy. Consequently, every new ball starts from the center position of the canvas, but each of them may go to different directions. The new code of the method initBall() in the class Ball.java is shown in Listing 14.9.

Listing 14.9 The class Ball.java in the project Pong8

```
 1  /*
 2   * Ball.java - A class that implements a ball for the game Pong.
 3   */
 4  …
14
15      private int x, y;
16      private Color ballColor;
17      private int dx, dy;
18      private int radius;
19      private boolean active;
20      private boolean visible;
21
22      public Ball() {
23          initBall();
24      }
25
26      private void initBall() {
27          int cvX = (Consts.MAXX - Consts.MINX) / 2;
28          int cvY = (Consts.MAXY - Consts.MINY) / 2;
29          setRadius((int) (Math.random() * Consts.BALL_RADIUS) + 5);
30          setX(cvX - getRadius());
31          setY(cvY - getRadius());
32          setDx((int) (Math.random() * Consts.BALL_DX) + 2); // [2, 7]
33          int sign = (int) Math.round(Math.random());
34          if (sign == 0) {
35              setDx(-getDx());
36          }
37          setDy((int) (Math.random() * Consts.BALL_DY) + 2); // [3, 5]
38          sign = (int) Math.round(Math.random());
39          if (sign == 0) {
40              setDy(-getDy());
41          }
```

14.7 Modifying the Game Story for Catching the Ball Sprites: The Project Pong8

```
42              setBallColor(Color.BLUE);
43              setActive(true);
44              setVisible(true);
45          }
46
47          public void updateBall() {
48              if (isActive()) {
49                  setX(getX() + getDx());
50                  setY(getY() + getDy());
51              }
52          }
53
54          public void paintBall(Graphics2D g2d) {
55              if (isVisible()) {
56                  g2d.setColor(getBallColor());
57                  g2d.fillOval(getX(), getY(), 2 * radius, 2 * radius);
58              }
59          }
60      … getters and setters
124     }
```

The class Ball.java also adds two Boolean variables of "active" and "visible." The true value of "active" means the ball can be updated, and the true value of "visible" means the ball can be painted. When a ball is caught by the hole, the ball should be disappeared, which is made by assigning a value of false to these two Boolean variables.

3. For implementing the catch action, we still apply the collision detection between the hole and the ball. When they collide, we set the variables "active" and "visible" to be false. They will make the ball "disappear." The modified detectCollision() method in the class GameCanvas.java is shown in Listing 14.10.

Listing 14.10 The modified method detectCollision() in the project Pong8

```
1   /*
2    * GameCanvas.java -- A canvas for the game Pong.
3    */
4   package ponggame;
5   …
20  public class GameCanvas extends JPanel implements Runnable {
21
22  …
33      public GameCanvas() {
34          addKeyListener(new MyKeyAdapter());
35          initComponent();
36          start();
37      }
38
39      private void initComponent() {
40          theWall = new FieldWall();
41          hole = new Hole();
42          currScore = 0;
43          catchBall = 0;
44          numPenalty = 0;
45          initBall();
46      }
47
```

```java
48      public void initBall() {
49          theBall = new Ball();
50          if (catchBall >= Consts.MAX_BALL) {
51              currScore = 0;
52              catchBall = 0;
53              numPenalty = 0;
54          }
55      }
56
57  ...
77      public void detectCollision() {
78          // make a bounding rectangle of the ball
79          Rectangle ballRect = new Rectangle(theBall.getX(), theBall.getY(),
80                  2 * Consts.BALL_RADIUS, 2 * Consts.BALL_RADIUS);
81          // whether the ball hits on any unit of the bouncing wall
82          for (int i = 0; i < 4; i++) {
83              if ((theWall.getaWall()[i]).intersects(ballRect)) {
84                  switch (i) {
85                      case 0: // top
86                      case 1: // bottom
87                          theBall.setDy(-theBall.getDy());
88                          break;
89                      case 2: // left
90                          theBall.setDx(-theBall.getDx());
91                          break;
92                      case 3: // right, lose points 30
93                          if (!collideHole(ballRect)) {
94                              theBall.setDx(-theBall.getDx());
95                              numPenalty++;
96                              System.out.println("numPenalty = " + numPenalty);
97                          }
98                          break;
99                  }
100             }
101         }
102     }
103
104     public boolean collideHole(Rectangle ballRect) {
105         boolean collide = false;
106         // whether the ball collides the hole
107         Rectangle holeRect = new Rectangle(hole.getX(),
108                 hole.getY(), Consts.HOLE_WIDTH, Consts.HOLE_HEIGHT);
109         if (holeRect.intersects(ballRect)) {
110             catchBall++;
111             theBall.setActive(false);
112             theBall.setVisible(false);
113             collide = true;
114             if (catchBall >= Consts.MAX_BALL) {
115                 resetGame();
116             }
117
118             initBall(); // generating a new ball object
119         }
120         return collide;
121     }
122 ...
197 }
```

14.8 Summary

A video game usually has multiple screens. Besides the main game canvas, the game needs other screens for describing the game, instructing the players, or setting parameters of the game. The game displays these multiple screens one at a time. Consequently, the layout manager CardLayout is hired for arranging them, which organizes a set of screens like a deck of cards. The usage of the CardLayout manager is a little bit complicated. We need more practices for mastering it.

Another important aspect is the "extension" of a game. After finishing a basis of a video game, it usually can be extended by adding more special features into the basis. This chapter demonstrated some extensions for the game Pong. This is one of the precious characteristics in developing games for learning Java since it opens a door for brainstorm, for imagination, and for problem solving.

The game Pong is simple because it has only one sprite. The project Pong7 has two balls. That is, it has two sprites. We may raise some questions, what if we would like to have 10 balls or even 100 balls? Do we need to repeat some piece of codes 10 times or 100 times? How to add new sprites into an existing game implementation? This is a new topic we should consider in the next chapter.

14.9 Exercises

Self-Review Questions

1. Why does a game usually have multiple screens? What function usually should be implemented in each of them?
2. What is a proper order for the multiple screens?
3. How to organize multiple screens?
4. What should be done in order to switch between the game canvas and the splash screen?
5. Why is the "extension" important in the development of a game?
6. What extensions does the game Pong have? Are there any other new extensions?
7. Are there any extensions that could be done for other games, such as WheelVideo and so on?
8. In the project Pong6, we set two thresholds for increasing the ball speed. How to check the thresholds?
9. In the project Pong7, the game generates two balls. What classes should be affected?
10. Why do we say the class PaintStrBean.java is a reusable software unit?

Projects

1. Assume that there are four screens, a splash screen, a setting screen, a game canvas, and a game finish screen. Write a piece of code to organize these screens in using the CardLayout manager.
2. Based on the project Pong7, add one more ball into the game and make it work.
3. Based on the project Pong8, add one more ball into the game and make it work.
4. Modify the project PaintXmasCard by using the JavaBean PaintStrBean.java.
5. Revisit the project WheelFortune in text to make the class ReadFile.java as a reusable JavaBean.
6. Add a new screen SettingPanel.java in the game Pong. The setting panel allows the player to set some parameters for the game, such as the initial speed, the number of balls, the thresholds for increasing the ball speed, and the like.
7. So far, the fieldWall in all of versions of game Pong consists of four rectangles. Now, extend the fieldWall by adding some circles such that when the bouncing ball collides with those circles, the collision point should determine the bouncing direction as shown in Fig. 14.5. Extending a version of the game Pong with these circles and modify the collision handlers.
8. Modify the idea of circles above as some holes. When the bouncing ball falls into the holes, the score of the game will increase or decrease certain points and the game generates a new ball to continue the game.

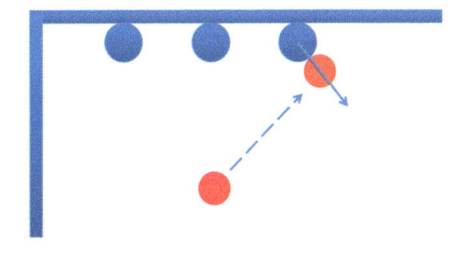

Fig. 14.5 The unit of fieldWall has some circles

A Three-Layer Software Structure for Games: A Game PongStruTwo

The extensions of the game Pong explore a fact that the number of sprites and their behaviors, as well as the complexity of the game could be dynamically changed during the game in execution. For example, the game Pong7 asks for two bouncing balls. What if a game asks for adding 10 or 100 sprites? We not only need new techniques but also require a stable software structure for accommodating these changes. Based on the inheritance, abstract class, abstract method, and polymorphism of OOP, a three-layer software structure is constructed as a template for developing video games in order to handle such requirements.

The objectives of this chapter include:
1. Unifying all of static and dynamic components as sprite.
2. How to store different types of sprites into one linear data structure?
3. Applying inheritance hierarchy for converting different types as a same type.
4. Abstracting common properties to design abstract classes.
5. Using abstract classes to construct a sprite inheritance hierarchy.
6. Dynamic binding searches for an implementation in an inheritance hierarchy.
7. Polymorphism allows a superclass accommodating multiple forms of subclasses.
8. Applying polymorphism for animating all sprites.
9. Constructing a three-layer software structure for games.
10. The open-closed principle for software structure.

The project Pong7 in the previous chapter extended the game Pong with two balls. It promotes us to ask some questions. What if we would like to have 10 or even 100 ball sprites? What if we would like to add more other kinds of sprites? How to insert more sprites into an existing game? Clearly, we cannot simply instantiate 10 or 100 balls and repeatedly duplicate some pieces of codes 10 times or 100 times. It is also hard to redesign and re-implement an existing game in order to insert some new sprites. The solution for solving these questions lies on software architecture that allows us to easily extend a game and to insert sprites as many as we wish. In other words, we should not only pay much attention to the programming skills but also should pay many efforts for thinking and designing the higher-level software architecture for games. This is the topic of this chapter, and we will end up with a three-layer software structure framework for games.

Before going there, we do need to unify our understanding about sprites. The term "sprite" is used commonly in the game world to refer to the screen representations of objects, such as figures or elements that have the capability of moving independently of one another. According to the definition, the game Pong has only one sprite, the ball sprite. Then, how about other objects, such as the field-wall, the paddle, and the like? Here, we suggest that we are going to understand that any objects in a video game are sprites. Even some static objects, we also treat them as sprites but with a moving speed of zero. This understanding allows us to unify the implementation of any objects in a game. Based on this idea, we can say that the game Pong has three sprites: the ball, the paddle, and the field-wall.

15.1 A Ball Sprite

We would like to recall how did we handle a ball sprite. For implementing a ball sprite, at the beginning, we can make a ball sprite with a speed of zero (a static ball) and let it sit at the center of the canvas. The ball object is an instance of the class Ball.java, which should define a set of attributes and a set of methods. The set of attributes include the coordinates (x, y) of the up-left corner point of its bounding rectangle, the (2*radius) for its width and height, and the color of the ball. The behaviors of the ball object under the static case only needs methods initBall() and paintBall(). Besides that, the class includes a pair of getter and setter methods for every attribute.

In order to display the static ball at the center of the screen, the project starts from the main class, which "is-a" JFrame, and a class GameCanvas.java, which "is-a" JPanel. The class GameCanvas.java inherits the built-in graphics context with the paintComponent() method from the JPanel. The method paintComponent() invokes the ball.paintBall() method defined in the class Ball.java to paint the ball object at the required position.

Continuously, the project adds a Thread to form a game loop, which animates the ball object to be a dynamic ball sprite. The game loop performs three actions: (1) updating the ball's coordinates (x, y), (2) repainting the ball for displaying it on the updated position, and (3) pausing for a while to allow other threads sharing the unique CPU. Corresponding to these three steps, the class Ball.java adds a pair of new attributes dx and dy and a new method updateBall() to update the coordinates of the ball. And then, the game loop continuously invokes the methods updateBall() and repaint() to make an illusion of animation. This is a sprite-based animation. In order to prevent the ball from animating out of game screen, the method detectCollision() checks the collisions among the ball and the four units of the field-wall to bounce the ball back and makes the ball as a bouncing ball.

15.2 Adding Another Kind of Animated Sprite

The project Pong7 extends the game Pong for adding one more ball sprite, which is a same kind of sprite. As another extension, definitely we can add a different kind of sprite instead. For example, we may add a new blue bouncing rectangle instead of another bouncing ball. No doubt, for creating the blue bouncing rectangle, a new class Rect.java should be added under that case. For having a more generic notation, we rename the Ball.java as BallSprite.java and rename the Rect.java as RectSprite.java such that the new version of the game Pong, now, has a BallSprite.java and a RectSprite.java. Furthermore, we rename the methods in the class BallSprite.java from initBall() to initSprite(), from updateBall() to updateSprite(), and from paintBall() to paintSprite(). And then, do the same modifications for the class RectSprite.java.

Intuitively, the pseudo code for adding the new rectSprite can be described as follows:

1. Create a class RectSprite.java, which defines a set of attributes and a set of behaviors, as well as a set of getter and setter methods. The attributes for defining a rectangle actually are the same as defining a ball. They include the coordinates (x, y), the width, and the height, as well as the color. The new attributes for bouncing the rectangle include dx and dy. The same, the class needs a initSprite() method to initialize the sprite. In addition, the two methods updateSprite() and paintSprite() are needed and to be invoked by the game loop for animating the rectangle sprite.
2. The class GameCanvas.java instantiates an object of rectSprite in addition to the object of ballSprite.
3. In the class GameCanvas.java, the method initComponent() instantiates two objects of ballSprite and rectSprite with required attributes. And then, the updateComponent() method invokes two updateSprite() methods from the two objects and the method paintComponent() also invokes two paintSprite() methods from the two sprites.
4. In order to bounce the rectSprite, a method rectDetectCollision() is added in the class GameCanvas.java, which is very similar as the method ballDetectCollision().
5. For switching from the "splashScreen" to the "gameCanvas," we can click the button "Start Game." But, for switching from the "gameCanvas" to "splashScreen," we have to make sure both ballSprite and rectSprite are lost before invoking the resetGame() method as we did in the project Pong7.

15.3 What If More Types of Sprites?

We can continue this effort to add more sprites into the game Pong. Suppose that we would like to have total 100 same kind or different kinds of bouncing sprites in the game Pong, the method initComponent() in the GameCanvas.java has to instantiate all of 100 instances from the corresponding classes, and the method updateComponent() needs to have at least 100 statements to invoke the updateSprite() method in every object as shown in the following pseudo code.

```
public void updateComponent() {
    sprite1.updateSprite();
    sprite2.updateSprite();
    ...
    sprite100.updateSprite();
}
```

As the same, the paintComponent() method also needs to involve 100 statements for painting every object. They would form a long and tedious code. Obviously, we don't like this kind of coding. We do need a new software structure to get away from this kind of coding.

We have learned the linear data structure Array and ArrayList. Both of them can hold a set of objects and only a single "for" loop is needed to access every object stored in the Array or the ArrayList. That is, if we may use the linear data structure to hold the 100 sprites, then one "for" loop may replace all of the 100 statements. However, the structure of Array has its limitations, such as the size of an array cannot be changed to fit the case where the number of sprites is unknown. The better choice is the other linear data structure ArrayList. No matter which one, the prerequisite of using a linear data structure is that all of elements stored in the structure must be the same type. However, the 100 different sprites could be different types. How can we make different types of sprites to be stored in an Array or an ArrayList that requires all of sprites have the same type?

15.4 Inheritance Converts Different Types of Sprites to Be the Same Type

The inheritance of OOP supports a solution to make the different types of sprites to be the same type. The inheritance means that a subclass "is-a" its superclass. Now, assume that sprite1 to sprite100 are all geometrical shapes, such as ballSprite, rectSprite, triSprite, and the like. Then a class Sprite2D could be derived as the superclass of all the geometrical shape sprites as shown in Fig. 15.1.

We experienced the inheritance principle and applied it in the project AnalogClock in Chap. 11, where we derived a superclass ClockHand.java from the two subclasses MinuteHand.java and SecondHand.java by moving common attributes among the subclasses to the superclass ClockHand.java and leave the differences in the subclasses. And then, derive a subclass HourHand.java from the superclass ClockHand.java.

Here, we would like to apply the principle and the process again for converting different kinds of sprites to have a common superclass. For example, both the BallSprite.java and the RectSprite.java classes have the same attributes of coordinates (x, y), width, height, color, and dx and dy. These common attributes can be moved to the superclass Sprite2D.java. But leave the different implementations of the method initSprite(), updateSprite(), and paintSprite() in the subclasses, respectively. Due to the fact that the inheritance hierarchy indicates that every subclass, such as BallSprite.java, RectSprite.java, and so on, "is-a" superclass Sprite2D.java, the linear data structure can be defined by using the superclass as the element type, so as ArrayList<Sprite2D>, and the linear data structure can hold all of those different kinds of sprites that belong to the inheritance hierarchy. Consequently, a single "for" loop can be used to access every instance of all sprites stored in the linear data structure instead of a long listing of individual sprite calls.

15.5 It Is Necessary to Specify the Type When Getting Out of a Sprite from a Group

Unfortunately, a new problem is encountered when the project would like to update each sprite, which has to access the different method defined in every individual subclass as follows. The code causes a compile time error.

```
for (int i = 0; i < arrayList.size(); i++) {
    arrayList.get(i).updateSprite();
    // compile error occurs
}
```

The problem is that the statement arrayList.get(i) will return an object of Sprite2D and the dot notation intends to invoke the method updateSprite(); however, the class Sprite2D does not define the method updateSprite(). As we know both the BallSprite.java and RectSprite.java classes defined the updateSprite() method but their implementations are different. One is for updating a ball object; the other is for updating a rectangle object. Thus, the two different updateSprite() methods implemented in two different subclasses cannot be "moved" up to the superclass Sprite2D.

Hence, during the compile time, when the compiler checks the type of the object arrayList.get(i) for matching the method updateSprite() with the definition of the class Sprite2D, the matching is failure. In order to successfully pass the compile time checking, the real type of the object, the BallSprite or the RectSprite, should be identified.

For making the concept clearer, we can take an example from our daily life. We have an inheritance hierarchy in our daily life as shown in Fig. 15.2.

It says that a car is a vehicle; a bicycle is a vehicle. But a vehicle is what? It is not a real object. We need to verify that if an object is a car, then it can be treated as a vehicle. If an

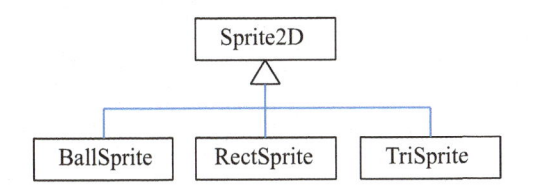

Fig. 15.1 An inheritance hierarchy of sprites with geometrical shapes

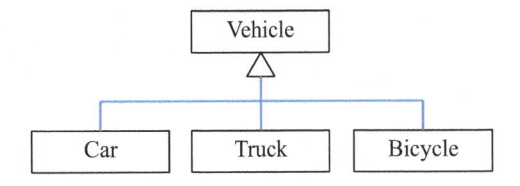

Fig. 15.2 An inheritance hierarchy on vehicle

object is a candy, it cannot be treated as a vehicle. Imagine that a huge container is used to store vehicles only. Then, we can place a car and a bicycle into the container without hesitation since both the car and the bicycle are a vehicle. Later, we will take an object out from the huge container and ask how many wheels of the object have. At that time, we have to verify if the object is a car, the answer is 4; but if the object is a bicycle, the answer should be 2. That is, without the verification for distinguishing the vehicle is a car or the vehicle is a bicycle, we cannot correctly answer the number of wheels.

In OOP technology, when a subclass extends its superclass, the subclass inherits all of features from its superclass. In addition, some features that are specific to the subclass can be added to the subclass. That is, an instance of a subclass is always an instance of its superclass; but an instance of the superclass is not necessary to be the same as an instance of its subclass. In other words, an instance of a BallSprite.java is always an instance of the Sprite2D.java; but an instance of the Sprite2D.java is not necessary an object of the class BallSprite.java. It is equivalent to say, an instance of a subclass can substitute for an instance of its superclass; however using an instance of superclass to substitute an instance of subclass may result in a compile error. Consequently, an explicit casting is required. It implies that the following casting is expected in a piece of code.

```
Super s;
Sub sub;
// an instance of subclass is an instance of superclass
s = new Sub();
// casting is necessary
sub = (Sub) new Super();
```

Therefore, under the assumption of ArrayList<Sprite2D>, to assign an object ballSprite to the arrayList, such as "arrayList.add(ballSprite)", is acceptable because an instance of a subclass is an instance of its superclass. However, to get an object out from the arrayList and assign it to a variable with the type of subclass, an explicit casting is required by the compiler during the compile time. That is, the correct statement should be "BallSprite ballSprite = (BallSprite)arrayList.get(i)". It is the same when getting an object of subclass from the arrayList<superclass> and invoking a method defined in the subclass, an explicit casting is also required. Furthermore, in order to have a correct casting, the "instanceof" operator should be applied to verify it. All of these requirements turn the code back to a long list for dealing with each individual sprite as following piece of pseudo code shows.

```
public void updateComponent() {
    for (int i = 0; i < arrayList.size(); i++) {
        Sprite2D anObj = arrayList.get(i);
        if ((anObj instanceof BallSprite) {
            // if the object is the type of BallSprite
            ((BallSprite)anObj).updateSprite();
        } else if (anObj instanceof RectSprite) {
            // if the object is the type of RectSprite
            ((RectSprite)anObj).updateSprite();
        }
    }
}
```

If we have 100 different kinds of objects stored in the arrayList, then when we need to get every individual object out of the arrayList, the 100 if statements and castings won't be able avoided.

15.6 Replacing Concrete Classes by Abstract Classes with Abstract Methods

Fortunately, the "abstract class" can be applied to solve the problem shown above. As we have learned, an abstract class contains abstract methods that have no implementations. The implementation of such an abstract method can be postponed to the subclasses of the abstract class when needed. That is, the abstract class separates the method specification from the implementation. An abstract method defined in an abstract superclass can be implemented in a concrete subclass.

In our case, we know that every sprite class has methods initSprite(), updateSprite(), and paintSprite(). Clearly, these methods are also the common features of all subclasses so that they can be migrated up to their superclass Sprite2D.java. However, it is impossible to implement these methods in the superclass Sprite2D.java since the superclass has so many different kinds of subclasses and every subclass has its own specific needs for the implementations of these methods. The only way to keep these methods in the superclass Sprite2D.java is to define them as abstract methods and defer their implementations to all of its subclasses, such as BallSprite.java, RectSprite.java, and the like. It is equivalent to say that we have to redefine the class Sprite2D.java as an abstract class AbsSprite2D.java with three abstract methods initSprite(), updateSprite(), and paintSprite(); and then correspondingly redefine the linear data structure to become ArrayList<AbsSprite2D>. According to the OOP technology, the real methods that are implemented in subclasses are called "override" the abstract methods declared in the superclass.

Based on this discussion, an object obtained from the arrayList.get(i) has two types. One is so-called declared type, which is AbsSprite2D since the declaration of the arrayList is ArrayList<AbsSprite2D>. The other type is so-called actual type, which could be one of the subclasses, such as BallSprite.java, RectSprite.java, and the like. The declared type AbsSprite2D has the abstract methods initSprite(), updateSprite(), and paintSprite(). During compile time, the compiler performs type checking; the methods are found in the superclass so that an explicit casting can be ignored without causing compile time errors.

At the same time, the actual type, BallSprite or RectSprite, has the real implementation of these methods. During runtime, the JVM searches for the implementation of the methods from the bottom of the inheritance hierarchy up to the root. As long as an implementation is found, the search stops and the first found implementation will be executed. It is termed as "dynamic binding," which allows a variable of superclass referring to an object of a subclass. Such a superclass accommodates multiple forms of subclasses is the so-called polymorphism in the OOP technology.

Under the supporting of these technologies, the elimination of the long list in the method updateComponent() can be realized with simplified code as follows.

```
ArrayList<AbsSprite2D> arrayList =
    new ArrayList<AbsSprite2D>();
public void updateComponent() {
    for (int i = 0; i < arrayList.size();
        i++) {
        arrayList.get(i).updateSprite();
    }
}
```

The above code is correct because during compile time, the arrayList.get(i) returns a type of AbsSprite2D that defines an abstract method updateSprite() so that it won't cause any compile time error; and during run time, the dynamic binding binds the implemented updateSprite() method defined in one of the subtype classes, which executes the correct method. Consequently, the code shown above is simplified as expected. Similarly, the paintComponent() method can apply the same strategy for using a "for" loop to invoke the method paintSprite() defined in every subclass of sprites.

15.7 Applying Abstract Classes for Constructing a Sprite Inheritance Hierarchy

Definitely, the sprites are not only geometrical shapes but also other kinds of sprites, such as images, 3D sprites, and so on. An image sprite can be a subclass of a superclass AbsSpriteImage.java. We further extend the concepts and practices discussed above to define a higher-level root superclass AbsSprite.java to cover all of kinds of sprites, such as

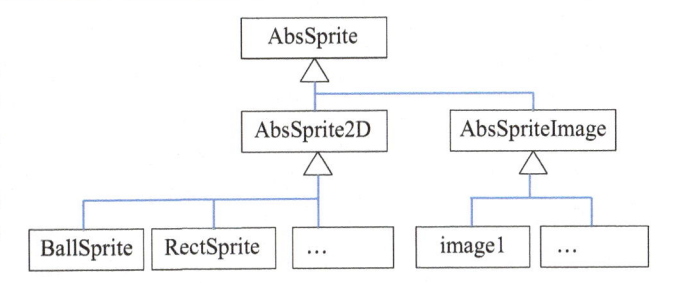

Fig. 15.3 A sprite inheritance hierarchy in games

AbsSprite2D.java, AbsSpriteImage.java, and the like, in games.

The superclass AbsSprite.java is an abstract class because the term "sprite" is a concept not a real object in the real world. The essential features of sprites include states and behaviors. The states are the internal representations of onscreen appearance, such as activity, visibility, priority, updateability, and the like. The behaviors include initializing, updating, painting, and so on. However, almost all of these behaviors are not common features of all sprites. They are common features that belong to different kinds of sprites. Therefore, the root class AbsSprite mainly defines a few states, such as activity, visibility, priority, and so on.

After defining the AbsSprite.java root class, a sprite inheritance hierarchy could be formed as shown in Fig. 15.3. Surely, the UML class diagram can be extended as needed.

15.8 Constructing a Three-Layer Software Structure Framework for Games

An abstract class is not only an excellent tool for constructing an inheritance hierarchy of sprites but also a wonderful means for abstraction. As we have known, an abstract class can separate the specification from the implementation. Therefore, an abstract class can be used to formally specify a class and at the same time to allow developers flexibly implement the class corresponding to the real circumstances. By further applying this technique, we can specify an abstract class AbsGameCanvas.java to be the superclass of the concrete class GameCanvas.java. The abstract superclass AbsGameCanvas.java contains all of common features for all games and leave special features to its concrete subclass GameCanvas.java, which satisfies special requirements in different games.

All these technologies and ideas promote a three-layer software structure framework for games. Its UML class diagram is depicted in Fig. 15.4. Along the vertical direction, the three-layer structure consists of the frame layer on the top, the canvas layer in the middle, and the sprite layer on the bottom. The frame layer also includes a class ScreenDeck.java that organizes multiple screens, such as the splash screen, the game canvas, and the like in using the CardLayout manager.

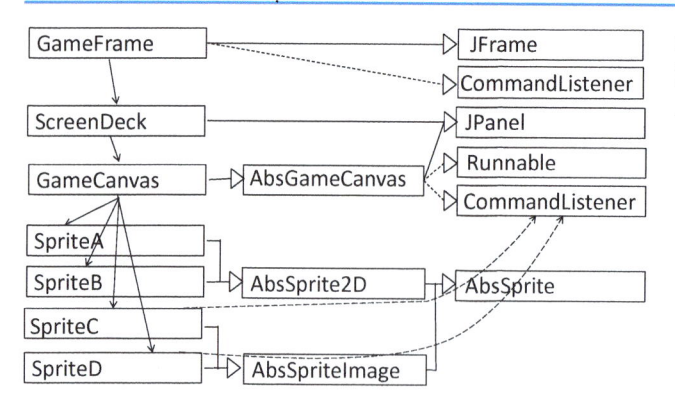

Fig. 15.4 A generic three-layer software structure for games

The class GameCanvas.java makes the major game screen among the multiple screens, which is a special and most important screen that organizes all of sprites in a game. The third layer is based on the sprite inheritance hierarchy that contains all of sprites required by the game. As discussed above, all of sprites are stored in an ArrayList and can be updated and painted in using a single "for" loop no matter how many sprites in the game. Because the three-layer software structure is specially constructed for games, we simplify its name as "three-layer game structure." Along the horizontal direction, the UML class diagram forms three columns that describe the inheritance relationship among all classes in a game. The left column shows all concrete classes in a game; the middle column lists the abstract super classes defined by developers; and the right column lists the built-in super classes and the root class of the sprite inheritance hierarchy.

15.9 Deriving the Abstract Classes AbsSprite.java and AbsSprite2D.java

The abstract class AbsSprite.java is the root class of the entire sprite inheritance hierarchy. All sprites can be classified as active sprites and inactive sprites. The active sprites are animated sprites with dynamic behaviors, and the inactive sprites are static ones. Meanwhile, all of sprites can also be classified as visible sprites and invisible sprites. Therefore, the class AbsSprite.java may have two Boolean variables "active" and "visible" to classify all sprites into these categories. The method updateComponent() invokes the methods updateSprite() defined in every active sprite; the method paintComponent() invokes the methods paintSprite() defined in every visible sprite. In cases, some sprites may switch between active or inactive or may switch between visible or invisible, the variables "active" and "visible" can be conveniently set up with values of true or false according to specific needs. Additionally, it may have a variable "priority" to distinguish a sprite that may have higher priority than the other. The code of the class AbsSprite.java could be as follows.

```java
public abstract class AbsSprite {
    private boolean active;
    private boolean visible;
    private int priority;

    public boolean isActive() {
        return active;
    }

    public void setActive(boolean active) {
        this.active = active;
    }
    …
    // other getter and setter methods
}
```

The abstract class AbsSprite2D.java is the root class of all sprites with 2D geometrical shapes. It may contain all common attributes for specifying a geometrical shape, such as coordinates (x, y), width, height, and color. In addition, for specifying the moving speed along the x-axis and the y-axis, two variables dx and dy can be added. The class may also have the abstract method initSprite() for assigning the initial values to the attributes and other two abstract methods updateSprite() and paintSprite() for specifying the dynamic behaviors of sprites in its inheritance hierarchy.

```java
public abstract class AbsSprite2D extends
    AbsSprite {
    private int x;
    private int y;
    private int width;
    private int height;
    private Color color;
    private int dx;
    private int dy;

    public AbsSprite2D() {
        super();
    }

    public abstract void initSprite();
    public abstract void updateSprite();
    public abstract void paintSprite(
        Graphics2D g2d);
    …    // getter and setter methods
}
```

15.10 Deriving the Abstract Class AbsGameCanvas.java

Based on the experience earned from the development of the game Pong, the class GameCanvas.java is the manager of all active sprites and inactive sprites in the game. It initializes all of them; and then, it forms a game loop to update and paint all active sprites for animating them and paint all of visible sprites for making the scenes. It also detects all possible collisions among sprites and shows the results of the game, such as the scores, the termination message, and so on. The class is also the manager of the entire game for defining some methods like startGame(), pauseGame(), resumeGame(), stopGame(), etc.

All of functions listed in the concrete class GameCanvas.java can be roughly divided into two categories. One kind of functions is common to all games, such as the game loop, the methods updateComponent(), paintComponent(), and so on. The other kind is specific functions for specific games, such as the initComponent() method, and the like. The abstract class AbsGameCanvas.java defines the first kind of functions, and the concrete class GameCanvas.java defines the second kind of functions. This design makes the class AbsGameCanvas.java as a template for all games; only leave the class GameCanvas.java for implementing special needs for the specific game.

Because of the sprite inheritance hierarchy, the class AbsGameCanvas.java is able to create a linear data structure spriteAry for holding all of sprites in a game and implement the methods updateComponent() and paintComponent() in using the global spriteAry to update and paint all of sprites. One point should be emphasized here, the spriteAry stores all of sprites no matter active or inactive and no matter visible or invisible because an inactive sprite could be updated and an invisible sprite might also be painted. We ask the methods updateComponent() and paintComponent() for distinguishing them by checking the Boolean variables "active" and "visible" that every sprite inherited from the root class AbsSprite.java of the inheritance hierarchy. It only leaves the method initComponent() for the concrete class GameCanvas.java since every specific game will involve a set of specific sprites with specific initial routines and values. Consequently, a rudimental class AbsGameCanvas.java may look like the following.

```java
public abstract class AbsGameCanvas extends JPanel implements Runnable {

    private ArrayList<AbsSprite> spriteAry; // assume its type
    private Thread animThread;
    private boolean playing;

    public AbsGameCanvas() {
        spriteAry = new ArrayList<>();
    }

    private void initAnimation() {
        if (animThread == null) {
            animThread = new Thread(this);
            animThread.start();
        }
    }

    @Override
    public void run() {
        try {
            while (isPlaying()) {
                updateComponent();
                repaint();
                Thread.sleep(60);
            }
        } catch (InterruptedException ex) {
        }
    }
}
```

```java
    public void updateComponent() {
        for (AbsSprite element : spriteAry) {
            if (element.isActive()) {
                (element).updateSprite();
            }
        }
    }

    @Override
    public void paintComponent(Graphics g) {
        super.paintComponent(g);
        Graphics2D g2d = (Graphics2D) g;

        for (AbsSprite element : spriteAry) {
            if (element.isVisible()) {
                (element).paintSprite(g2d);
            }
        }
    }

    public void startGame() {
        setPlaying(true);
        initAnimation();
    }

    public void pauseGame() {
        setPlaying(false);
    }

    public void resumeGame() {
        setPlaying(true);
    }

    public void stopGame() {
        setPlaying(false);
        animThread.interrupt();
        animThread = null;
    }

    ... // getter and setter methods
}
```

15.11 Applying the Three-Layer Game Structure: The Project PongStruTwo

The three-layer game structure is constructed to provide a generic guideline and structure for designing and implementing video games that are based on the animation technique. The software structure supports the three abstract classes AbsGameCanvas.java, AbsSprite.java, and AbsSprite2D.java. When we would like to develop a specific game, we need to implement concrete classes. In order to make the new structure easier to be followed, as the first example, we are going to apply the framework for the game PongStruTwo. The project name means a game Pong in using the three-layer software structure with two different sprites: a ball sprite and a rectangle sprite.

15.11.1 The Sprite Layer Defines an Inheritance Hierarchy

According to the unified understanding of sprites, the game Pong totally has four classes of sprites: BallSprite.java,

15.11 Applying the Three-Layer Game Structure: The Project PongStruTwo

RectSprite.java, FieldWall.java, and Paddle.java. They are all of subclasses of the abstract classes AbsSprite.java and AbsSprite2D.java. However, the first two are animated sprites and the last two are static sprites. Therefore, they have different implementations as listed in Listing 15.1.

Listing 15.1 The six classes of AbsSprite.java, AbsSprite2D.java, BallSprite.java, RectSprite.java, Paddle.java, and FieldWall.java in the project PongStruTwo

```
1  /*
2   * AbsSprite.java - An abstract class as the root class of the sprite
3   * inheritance hierarchy.
4   */
5  package pongstru;
6
11 public abstract class AbsSprite {
12
13     private boolean active;
14     private boolean visible;
15     private int priority;
16
17     public boolean isActive() {
18         return active;
19     }
20
21     public void setActive(boolean active) {
22         this.active = active;
23     }
24
25     public int getPriority() {
26         return priority;
27     }
28
29     public void setPriority(int priority) {
30         this.priority = priority;
31     }
32
33     public boolean isVisible() {
34         return visible;
35     }
36
37     public void setVisible(boolean visible) {
38         this.visible = visible;
39     }
40 }
```

```
1  /*
2   * AbsSprite2D.java - An abstract class as a superclass of all sprites of
3   * 2D geometrical shapes.
4   */
5  package pongstru;
6
7  import java.awt.Color;
8  import java.awt.Graphics2D;
9
```

```java
14 public abstract class AbsSprite2D extends AbsSprite {
15
16     private int x;
17     private int y;
18     private int width;
19     private int height;
20     private Color color;
21     private int dx;
22     private int dy;
23
24     public AbsSprite2D() {
25         super();
26     }
27
28     public abstract void initSprite();
29
30     public abstract void updateSprite();
31
32     public abstract void paintSprite(Graphics2D g2d);
33
34     public int getX() {
35         return x;
36     }
37
38     public void setX(int x) {
39         this.x = x;
40     }
41
42 ... remaining getters and setters
89 }
```

```java
 1 /*
 2  * BallSprite.java - A class that implements a ball sprite.
 3  */
 4 package pongstru;
 5
 6 import java.awt.Color;
 7 import java.awt.Graphics2D;
 8 import java.awt.Rectangle;
 9
14 public class BallSprite extends AbsSprite2D {
15
16     private GameCanvas gameCanvas;
17
18     public BallSprite() {
19         super();
20     }
21
22     @Override
23     public void initSprite() {
24         int cvX = (Consts.MAXX - Consts.MINX) / 2;
25         int cvY = (Consts.MAXY - Consts.MINY) / 2;
26         setX(cvX - Consts.BALL_RADIUS);
27         setY(cvY - Consts.BALL_RADIUS);
28         setWidth(2 * Consts.BALL_RADIUS);
```

15.11 Applying the Three-Layer Game Structure: The Project PongStruTwo

```
29            setHeight(2 * Consts.BALL_RADIUS);
30            setColor(Color.RED);
31            setActive(true);
32            setVisible(true);
33            setDx(3);
34            setDy(2);
35        }
36
37        @Override
38        public void updateSprite() {
39            if (isActive()) {
40                setX(getX() + getDx());
41                setY(getY() + getDy());
42                detectCollision();
43            }
44        }
45
46        @Override
47        public void paintSprite(Graphics2D g2d) {
48            if (isVisible()) {
49                g2d.setColor(getColor());
50                g2d.fillOval(getX(), getY(), getWidth(), getHeight());
51            }
52        }
53
54        public void detectCollision() {
55            Rectangle paddleRect;
56            Rectangle ballRect = new Rectangle(getX(), getY(),
57                    getWidth(), getHeight());
58
59            // whether the sprite hits on any unit of the field-wall
60            for (int i = 0; i < 4; i++) {
61                if ((gameCanvas.getTheWall().getaWall()[i]).intersects(ballRect)) {
62                    switch (i) {
63                        case 0: // top
64                        case 1: // bottom
65                            //ballSprite.setDy(-ballSprite.getDy());
66                            setDy(-getDy());
67                            break;
68                        case 2: // left
69                            setDx(-getDx());
70                            break;
71                        case 3: // the ball is lost
72                            if (isActive()) {
73                                setActive(false);
74                            }
75                            if (isVisible()) {
76                                setVisible(false);
77                            }
78                            gameCanvas.resetGame();
79                            break;
80                    }
81                }
82            }
```

```java
            // whether the element collides the paddle
            Paddle aPaddle = gameCanvas.getThePaddle();
            paddleRect = new Rectangle(aPaddle.getX(), aPaddle.getY(),
                    Consts.PADDLE_WIDTH, Consts.PADDLE_HEIGHT);
            if (paddleRect.intersects(ballRect)) {
                gameCanvas.setHitPaddle(gameCanvas.getHitPaddle() + 1);
                setDx(-getDx());
            }
    }

    public GameCanvas getGameCanvas() {
        return gameCanvas;
    }

    public void setGameCanvas(GameCanvas gameCanvas) {
        this.gameCanvas = gameCanvas;
    }
}
```

```java
/*
 * RectSprite.java - A class defines a rectangle sprite.
 */
package pongstru;

import java.awt.Color;
import java.awt.Graphics2D;
import java.awt.Rectangle;

public class RectSprite extends AbsSprite2D {

    private int maxSpeed;
    private int ranSign;
    private GameCanvas gameCanvas;

    public RectSprite() {
        super();
    }

    @Override
    public void initSprite() {
        int cvX = (Consts.MAXX - Consts.MINX) / 2;
        int cvY = (Consts.MAXY - Consts.MINY) / 2;
        setX(cvX - Consts.RECT_W / 2);
        setY(cvY - Consts.RECT_H / 2);
        setWidth(Consts.RECT_W);
        setHeight(Consts.RECT_H);
        setColor(Color.BLUE);
        setActive(true);
        setVisible(true);

        // randomly initializing the speed of the rectangle object
        maxSpeed = 6;
        setDx((int) (Math.random() * maxSpeed) + 1); // [1, 6]
        ranSign = (int) (Math.random() * 2); // [0, 1]
        if (ranSign == 0) {
```

15.11 Applying the Three-Layer Game Structure: The Project PongStruTwo

```
41                 setDx(-getDx());
42             }
43             setDy((int) (Math.random() * maxSpeed) + 1); // [1, 6]
44             ranSign = (int) (Math.random() * 2); // [0, 1]
45             if (ranSign == 0) {
46                 setDy(-getDy());
47             }
48         }
49
50         @Override
51         public void updateSprite() {
52             if (isActive()) {
53                 setX(getX() + getDx());
54                 setY(getY() + getDy());
55                 detectCollision();
56             }
57         }
58
59         @Override
60         public void paintSprite(Graphics2D g2d) {
61             if (isVisible()) {
62                 g2d.setColor(getColor());
63                 g2d.fillRect(getX(), getY(), getWidth(), getHeight());
64             }
65         }
66
67         public void detectCollision() {
68             Rectangle paddleRect;
69             Rectangle rect = new Rectangle(getX(), getY(),
70                     getWidth(), getHeight());
71
72             // whether the sprite hits on any unit of the bouncing wall
73             for (int i = 0; i < 4; i++) {
74                 if ((gameCanvas.getTheWall().getaWall()[i]).intersects(rect)) {
75                     switch (i) {
76                         case 0: // top
77                         case 1: // bottom
78                             //ballSprite.setDy(-ballSprite.getDy());
79                             setDy(-getDy());
80                             break;
81                         case 2: // left
82                             setDx(-getDx());
83                             break;
84                         case 3: // the ball is lost
85                             if (isActive()) {
86                                 setActive(false);
87                             }
88                             if (isVisible()) {
89                                 setVisible(false);
90                             }
91                             gameCanvas.resetGame();
92                             break;
93                     }
94                 }
95             }
```

```java
                // whether the element collides the paddle
                Paddle aPaddle = gameCanvas.getThePaddle();
                paddleRect = new Rectangle(aPaddle.getX(), aPaddle.getY(),
                        Consts.PADDLE_WIDTH, Consts.PADDLE_HEIGHT);
                if (paddleRect.intersects(rect)) {
                    gameCanvas.setHitPaddle(gameCanvas.getHitPaddle() + 1);
                    setDx(-getDx());
                }
        }

    public GameCanvas getGameCanvas() {
        return gameCanvas;
    }

    public void setGameCanvas(GameCanvas gameCanvas) {
        this.gameCanvas = gameCanvas;
    }
}
```

```java
/*
 * Paddle.java - A class that implements a paddle for the game Pong.
 */
package pongstru;

import java.awt.Color;
import java.awt.Graphics2D;

public class Paddle extends AbsSprite2D {

    public Paddle() {
        super();
    }

    @Override
    public void initSprite() {
        setX(Consts.MAXX - Consts.PADDLE_MARGIN);
        setY((Consts.MAXY - Consts.MINY) / 2 - Consts.PADDLE_HEIGHT / 2);
        setColor(Color.ORANGE);
        setActive(true);
        setVisible(true);
    }

    @Override
    public void updateSprite() {
    }

    @Override
    public void paintSprite(Graphics2D g2d) {
        g2d.setColor(getColor());
        g2d.fillRect(getX(), getY(), Consts.PADDLE_WIDTH, Consts.PADDLE_HEIGHT);
    }
}
```

```java
/*
 * FieldWall.java - A class for implementing a bouncing wall that consists
```

15.11 Applying the Three-Layer Game Structure: The Project PongStruTwo

```java
 3   * of four wallUnits.
 4   */
 5  package pongstru;
 6
 7  import java.awt.Color;
 8  import java.awt.Graphics2D;
 9  import java.awt.Rectangle;
10
15  public class FieldWall extends AbsSprite2D {
16
17      private Rectangle[] aWall;
18
19      public FieldWall() {
20          super();
21      }
22
23      @Override
24      public void initSprite() {
25          aWall = new Rectangle[4];
26          // top wall unit
27          aWall[0] = new Rectangle(Consts.MINX, Consts.MINY,
28                  Consts.MAXX - Consts.MINX, Consts.WALL_THICK);
29          // bottom wall unit
30          aWall[1] = new Rectangle(Consts.MINX, Consts.MAXY - Consts.WALL_THICK,
31                  Consts.MAXX - Consts.MINX, Consts.WALL_THICK);
32          // left wall unit
33          aWall[2] = new Rectangle(Consts.MINX, Consts.MINY,
34                  Consts.WALL_THICK, Consts.FIELD_HEIGHT);
35          // right wall unit
36          aWall[3] = new Rectangle(Consts.MAXX - Consts.WALL_THICK, Consts.MINY,
37                  Consts.WALL_THICK, Consts.FIELD_HEIGHT);
38          setActive(false);
39          setVisible(true);
40      }
41
42      @Override
43      public void updateSprite() {
44      }
45
46      @Override
47      public void paintSprite(Graphics2D g2d) {
48          g2d.setColor(Color.decode("#bbaa00"));
49          for (int i = 0; i < 4; i++) {
50              g2d.fillRect(aWall[i].x, aWall[i].y, aWall[i].width, aWall[i].height);
51          }
52      }
53
54      public Rectangle[] getaWall() {
55          return aWall;
56      }
57
58      public void setaWall(Rectangle[] aWall) {
59          this.aWall = aWall;
60      }
61  }
```

All of four sprite classes implement the three abstract methods initSprite(), updateSprite(), and paintSprite(). But, only animated sprites, such as ballSprite and rectSprite, have an implementation of the method updateSprite(), and the static sprites leave an empty body for the method updateSprite(). In addition, they set the attribute active with false. Other parts are very similar in the four sprite classes except the method initSprite() that initializes each own special shapes.

15.11.2 The Canvas Layer Defines All of Controlling Functions

The class AbsGameCanvas.java contains the common features, and the GameCanvas.java class implements specific functions of the game. Both classes are cited in Listing 15.2.

Listing 15.2 The classes AbsGameCanvas.java and GameCanvas.java

```
1  /*
2   * AbsGameCanvas.java - An abstract class that specifies common features in
3   * a game canvas. It is a superclass of the concrete class GameCanvas.java.
4   */
5  package pongstru;
6
7  import java.awt.Graphics;
8  import java.awt.Graphics2D;
9  import java.util.ArrayList;
10 import javax.swing.JPanel;
11
12 public abstract class AbsGameCanvas extends JPanel implements Runnable {
13
14     private ArrayList<AbsSprite2D> spriteAry;
15     private Thread animThread;
16     private boolean playing;
17
18     public AbsGameCanvas() {
19         spriteAry = new ArrayList<>();
20         // wait for startGame() is called
21     }
22
23     private void initAnimation() {
24         if (animThread == null) {
25             animThread = new Thread(this);
26             animThread.start();
27         }
28     }
29
30     @Override
31     public void run() {
32         try {
33             while (isPlaying()) {
34                 updateComponent();
35                 repaint();
36                 Thread.sleep(60);
37             }
38         } catch (InterruptedException ex) {
39         }
40     }
```

```java
41
42      public void updateComponent() {
43          for (AbsSprite2D element : spriteAry) {
44              if (element.isActive()) {
45                  (element).updateSprite();
46              }
47          }
48      }
49
50      @Override
51      public void paintComponent(Graphics g) {
52          super.paintComponent(g);
53          Graphics2D g2d = (Graphics2D) g;
54
55          for (AbsSprite2D element : spriteAry) {
56              if (element.isVisible()) {
57                  (element).paintSprite(g2d);
58              }
59          }
60      }
61
62      public void startGame() { // is called by someone, e.g. splashScreen
63          setPlaying(true);
64          initAnimation();
65      }
66
67      public void pauseGame() {
68          setPlaying(false);
69      }
70
71      public void resumeGame() {
72          setPlaying(true);
73      }
74
75      public void stopGame() { // clean up the thread
76          setPlaying(false);
77          animThread.interrupt();
78          animThread = null;
79      }
80
81      public ArrayList<AbsSprite2D> getSpriteAry() {
82          return spriteAry;
83      }
84
85      public boolean isPlaying() {
86          return playing;
87      }
88
89      public void setPlaying(boolean playing) {
90          this.playing = playing;
91      }
92  }
```

```java
1  /*
2   * GameCanvas.java - A concrete class implements the game canvas. It is the
3   * subclass of the abstract class AbsGameCanvasOri.java.
4   */
5  package pongstru;
6
7  import java.awt.CardLayout;
8  import java.awt.Color;
9  import java.awt.Font;
10 import java.awt.Graphics;
11 import java.awt.Graphics2D;
12 import java.awt.event.KeyAdapter;
13 import java.awt.event.KeyEvent;
14
19 public class GameCanvas extends AbsGameCanvas {
20
21     private ScreenPanel parent;
22     private CardLayout cardLayout;
23
24     private BallSprite ballSprite;
25     private RectSprite rectSprite;
26     private FieldWall theWall;
27     private Paddle thePaddle;
28
29     private int currScore;
30     private int hitPaddle;
31
32     public GameCanvas() {
33         super();
34         addKeyListener(new MyKeyAdapter());
35     }
36
37     public void initComponent() {
38         super.getSpriteAry().clear(); // clear the spriteAry
39         // then instantiate all components for a new game
40         initBallSprite();
41         initRectSprite();
42         initFieldWall();
43         initPaddle();
44         currScore = 0;
45         hitPaddle = 0;
46     }
47
48     public void initBallSprite() {
49         ballSprite = new BallSprite();
50         ballSprite.initSprite();
51         ballSprite.setGameCanvas(this);
52         getSpriteAry().add(ballSprite);
53     }
54
55     public void initRectSprite() {
56         rectSprite = new RectSprite();
57         rectSprite.initSprite();
58         rectSprite.setGameCanvas(this);
59         getSpriteAry().add(rectSprite);
60     }
61
```

15.11 Applying the Three-Layer Game Structure: The Project PongStruTwo

```java
62      public void initFieldWall() {
63          theWall = new FieldWall();
64          theWall.initSprite();
65          getSpriteAry().add(theWall);
66      }
67
68      public void initPaddle() {
69          thePaddle = new Paddle();
70          thePaddle.initSprite();
71          getSpriteAry().add(thePaddle);
72      }
73
74      public void resetGame() {
75          if (!(ballSprite.isActive()) && (!(rectSprite.isActive()))) {
76              stopGame();
77              cardLayout.show(parent, "SplashSheet");
78          }
79      }
80
81      // an inner class for implementing the key event adapter
82      // for catching the up or down keys to move the paddle
83      class MyKeyAdapter extends KeyAdapter {
84
85          @Override
86          public void keyPressed(KeyEvent evt) {
87              switch (evt.getKeyCode()) {
88                  case KeyEvent.VK_DOWN:
89                      if ((thePaddle.getY() + Consts.PADDLE_HEIGHT)
90                              < (Consts.MAXY - Consts.WALL_THICK)) {
91                          thePaddle.setY(thePaddle.getY() + 10);
92                      }
93                      break;
94                  case KeyEvent.VK_UP:
95                      if (thePaddle.getY() > (Consts.MINY + Consts.WALL_THICK)) {
96                          thePaddle.setY(thePaddle.getY() - 10);
97                      }
98                      break;
99                  default:
100             }
101             repaint();
102         }
103     }
104
105     // override the method paintComponent defined in the AbsGameCanvas.java
106     // for painting the current score.
107     @Override
108     public void paintComponent(Graphics g) {
109         super.paintComponent(g);
110         Graphics2D g2d = (Graphics2D)g;
111
112         paintCurrScore(g2d);
113     }
114
115     // this is a special method that is not included in the AbsGameCanvasOri.java
116     // it is repeatedly called in both BallSprite.java and Rectsprite.java
117     // such that only when both lost, the current score is invisible
118     public void paintCurrScore(Graphics2D g2d) {
```

```java
            currScore = Consts.SCORE_UNIT * hitPaddle;
            g2d.setFont(new Font("TimesRoman", Font.BOLD, 20));
            g2d.setColor(Color.red);
            g2d.drawString("Score: " + currScore, 25, 25);
        }

        public BallSprite getBallSprite() {
            return ballSprite;
        }

        public void setBallSprite(BallSprite ballSprite) {
            this.ballSprite = ballSprite;
        }

        public void setParent(ScreenPanel screenPanel) {
            this.parent = screenPanel;
        }

        public RectSprite getRectSprite() {
            return rectSprite;
        }

        public void setRectSprite(RectSprite rectSprite) {
            this.rectSprite = rectSprite;
        }

        public CardLayout getCardLayout() {
            return cardLayout;
        }

        public void setCardLayout(CardLayout cardLayout) {
            this.cardLayout = cardLayout;
        }

        public int getHitPaddle() {
            return hitPaddle;
        }

        public void setHitPaddle(int hitPaddle) {
            this.hitPaddle = hitPaddle;
        }

        public FieldWall getTheWall() {
            return theWall;
        }

        public void setTheWall(FieldWall theWall) {
            this.theWall = theWall;
        }

        public Paddle getThePaddle() {
            return thePaddle;
        }

        public void setThePaddle(Paddle thePaddle) {
            this.thePaddle = thePaddle;
        }
}
```

The common features in the class AbsGameCanvas.java include the global linear data structure spriteAry, the game loop, and the game-level methods, such as updateComponent(), paintComponent(), startGame(), pauseGame(), resumeGame(), and stopGame(), etc.; all of them are needed in all games. The class GameCanvas.java specifies some special functions for the specific game, which mainly are the method initComponent() and event listeners. Here, two methods are worth to be emphasized. (1) The initComponent() instantiates all of sprites and then adds all of them into the spriteAry. This is one of the major jobs of the class GameCanvas.java. The abstract class AbsGameCancas.java will do all remaining works. It is a beauty of the three-layer game structure. (2) The special method paintCurrScore() is a function needed by all games. Logically, it should be placed in the class AbsGameCanvas.java. However, each different game has its special score counting principle. It can only be implemented in the GameCanvas.java class. But, the method can still be accessed by any game because of the "dynamic binding." We know that the game loop is defined in the class AbsGameCanvas.java. As long as the game loop invokes repaint(), it will in turn invokes the method paintComponent(). Even though we override the paintComponent() method in the class GameCanvas.java, the "dynamic binding" can search for a method paintComponent() starting from the bottom of the inheritance hierarchy up to the root. It will find the paintComponent() method in the class GameCanvas.java, which paints all of sprites as well as the current score. This example demonstrates that a specific function can also be reached as a generic method. It illustrates the power of the "dynamic binding" and the "override" again.

15.11.3 The Frame Layer Defines Multiple Screens Structure

Other classes include ScreenDeck.java, SplashScreen.java, and Consts.java. They mainly construct multiple screens structure and constants. The detailed codes have been seen in the previous chapter.

This project PongStruTwo is our first example that is based on the three-layer game structure. We can see that the three-layer game structure provides a clear guideline for constructing a game that is driven by the animation technique. We will apply this structure for more games such that the features and advantages of the software structure will be more appearing.

15.12 Why the Three-Layer Game Structure?

Go through the example project PongStruTwo, we could see that all of the abstract classes won't be modified in the future for different games because they are formal specifications. The modifications will happen in the concrete classes that implement the specific requirements in each individual game. In addition, when we would like to add old kind of sprites or create new kind of sprites, we only need to modify the lower layer of the sprite inheritance hierarchy without the necessity for creating a brand new software structure. This style of implementation makes the three-layer game structure framework satisfying the so-called open-closed principle (OCP) [Meyer, B., 1998][1], which says, "Software entities should be open for extension but closed for modification." Due to the fact that the inheritance hierarchy can be extended with inserting or deleting any subclasses according to the specific game needs, it confronts the requirement of the "open" aspect of the OCP principle. On the other hand, the abstract classes among different levels of the inheritance hierarchy extract common shared features; they themselves not only won't be modified but also keep the entire software structure won't be touched. It confronts the "closed" aspect of the OCP principle, which enhances the reusability and maintainability of the software system.

15.13 Summary

This chapter developed a framework of three-layer game structure for games, and the chapter also applied the structure for developing an example project, which demonstrates the framework satisfying the open-closed principle for software. The three-layer game structure clearly arranges all units into an appropriate position with all possible communication channels; all sprites have a same root class so that they all can be loaded into a linear data structure and can be accessed with a single "for" loop; and all sprites only need one thread to construct one game loop. All together, the structure of the frame layer and the canvas layer is very stable and reusable for any game; and the structure of the third layer is very scalable and maintainable. Therefore, the three-layer game structure allows developers to concentrate on the design and implementation of sprites without worrying about the game software structure and the management of the sprites. On the other hand, the same software architecture can satisfy different requirements in developing different games.

For building up the three-layer game structure, many important OOP techniques such as inheritance, abstract class, abstract method, dynamic binding, polymorphism, and the like are applied. The framework also deals with some significant issues, such as compile time inspection and run time verification. All of them are import technical concepts and knowledge. They are worth to be understood thoroughly.

---

[1][Meyer, B., 1998] Bertrand Meyer, "*Object Oriented software Construction*", Prentice Hall, 1998.

15.14 Exercises

Self-Review Questions

1. How to define an inheritance hierarchy that can accommodate all different kinds of sprites involved in a game?
2. What OOP techniques are required for building up the sprite inheritance hierarchy?
3. How can we use one linear data structure and a single "for" loop to animate all different kinds of sprites? What OOP techniques are employed for that?
4. What are an abstract class and an abstract method? Why do we need them for building up the three-layer game structure?
5. What are the three major methods required for every sprite in using animation?
6. Why do we implement the game loop in the class AbsGameCanvas.java?
7. What the three-layer game structure looks like? Draw its UML class diagram.
8. What are advantages of the three-layer game structure?
9. How to apply the three-layer game structure for implementing a game?
10. What are the stability, scalability, reusability, and maintainability of the three-layer game structure?
11. What are compile time errors? What are run time errors? Make an example to explain them.
12. How to solve compile time errors? How to solve run time errors? Make an example to explore the solution.

Projects

1. Apply the three-layer game structure for re-implementing the project Pong8.
2. Apply the three-layer game structure for re-implementing the project AnalogClock.
3. Apply the three-layer game structure for re-implementing the project ImageSlider.
4. Enhance the project PongStruTwo to add eight new different bouncing objects.
5. Enhance the project PongStruTwo for testing and improving the methods of pauseGame() and resumeGame().

16 Usage of the Three-Layer Structure for Games: A Project SymBall and a Project Tornado

The original intention for developing the three-layer game structure is to find a software structure that may easily handle 10 or 100 sprints in a game. A project SymBall is developed to challenge the ability and power of the software structure. The project approved that the higher layer of the software structure allows adding more levels of threads; the lower layer has a sprite inheritance hierarchy for easily inserting different kinds of sprites and increasing any number of sprites. Another project Tornado that involves more then 10000 sprites further illustrates the stability and flexibility of the framework.

The objectives of this chapter include:
1. The game structure can handle a great number of sprites, even 10,000.
2. The game structure is flexible enough for handling special requirements.
3. Initializing a great amount of sprites as a pattern and then animating them.
4. One thread supports two different animation tasks.
5. The sprite inheritance hierarchy makes adding new type of sprites easy.
6. Adding another level of threads for supporting random colors.
7. A project Tornado handles more than 10,000 sprites.
8. The stability, scalability, reusability, and maintainability of the three-layer structure.

The original intention for developing the three-layer game structure is to find a software structure that may easily handle 10 or 100 sprints in a game. The previous chapter applied the three-layer software structure for developing the extension of the game Pong with two different kinds of sprites in addition to the other sprites of field-wall and paddle. In this chapter we are going to apply the game structure for developing more applications with even 10,000 sprites in order to further challenge the stability, scalability, reusability, and maintainability of the software structure for games. These example projects not only emphasize the importance of the sprite inheritance hierarchy but also stress the significance of the usage of the threads. In the new projects, the multiple screen part is ignored for making the projects simple.

16.1 The Outline of the Project SymBall

One of the special features of the three-layer game structure is that whenever we properly designed and initialized sprites and stored them into the global linear data structure sprite-Ary, other remaining major jobs would be done by the class AbsGameCanvas.java. In other words, developing a game by applying the three-layer game structure is thus simplified as designing and implementing sprites, and all the remaining tasks will be taken care of by the three-layer game structure itself. For further illustrating this significant feature, we are designing a project with a title of SymBall (symbolic ball) that will tell us as long as we arrange all sprites nicely, the project will work fine. The project has only one kind of sprite called SymBall, but it adds a great amount of sprites with increasing dynamic actions for demonstrating the stability for the management of sprites in the framework. The steps that it is going to experience include:

1. Paint a single symbolic ball at the center of the canvas.
2. Add symbolic balls group-by-group to make a pattern and then animate all balls to the right.
3. Divide the pattern into two parts. The left part is moved to the left, and the right part is moved to the right.
4. Change the color of every ball randomly to make a twinkling effect.

Going through these steps, we can see that all of the abstract classes are not modified because they are kind of specifications. The modifications happened in the concrete classes that implement the real requirements. In addition, when we would like to add old kind of sprites or create new kind of sprites, we only need to modify the sprite inheritance hierarchy without creating a brand new software structure. It further approves that three-layer game structure satisfies the open-closed principle (OCP).

16.2 Applying the Three-Layer Game Structure for a New Project: SymBall1Init

The version 1 of the new project is named as SymBall1Init that places a static ball at the center of the canvas. It is an old topic but using the three-layer game structure. All of abstract classes are exactly copied from the project PongStruTwo discussed in the previous chapter without modification. Only the concrete classes of GameCanvas.java and BallSprite.java have a little bit of editing. The codes of the two classes are shown in Listing 16.1.

Listing 16.1 The classes SymBall.java, GameCanvas.java, and BallSprite.java in the project SymBall1Init

```
1  /*
2   * SymBall.java - A main class for the project SymBall in applying the
3   * three-layer game structure.
4   */
5
6  package symball;
7
8  import javax.swing.JFrame;
9
14 public class SymBall extends JFrame {
15
16     public SymBall() {
17         setTitle("Symbolic Ball");
18         setSize(Consts.CV_WIDTH, Consts.CV_HEIGHT);
19         setDefaultCloseOperation(JFrame.EXIT_ON_CLOSE);
20
21         GameCanvas gameCv = new GameCanvas();
22         add(gameCv);
23
24         setVisible(true);
25     }
26
30     public static void main(String[] args) {
31         new SymBall();
32     }
33 }
```

```
1  /*
2   * GameCanvas.java - A concrete class implements the game canvas. It is the
3   * subclass of the abstract class AbsGameCanvas.java.
4   */
5  package pongstru;
6
11 public class GameCanvas extends AbsGameCanvas {
12
13     private BallSprite ballSprite;
14
15     public GameCanvas() {
16         super();
17         initComponent();
18         startGame();
19     }
20
```

```
21     private void initComponent() {
22         initBallSprite();
23     }
24
25     public void initBallSprite() {
26         ballSprite = new BallSprite();
27         ballSprite.initSprite();
28         getSpriteAry().add(ballSprite);
29     }
30 }
```

```
1  /*
2   * BallSprite.java - A class that implements a ball sprite.
3   */
4  package pongstru;
5
6  import java.awt.Color;
7  import java.awt.Graphics2D;
8
13 public class BallSprite extends AbsSprite2D {
14
15     public BallSprite() {
16         super();
17     }
18
19     @Override
20     public void initSprite() {
21         int cvX = (Consts.MAXX - Consts.MINX) / 2;
22         int cvY = (Consts.MAXY - Consts.MINY) / 2;
23         setX(cvX - Consts.BALL_RADIUS);
24         setY(cvY - Consts.BALL_RADIUS);
25         setWidth(2 * Consts.BALL_RADIUS);
26         setHeight(2 * Consts.BALL_RADIUS);
27         setColor(Color.RED);
28         setActive(false);
29         setVisible(true);
30     }
31
32     @Override
33     public void updateSprite() {
34     }
35
36     @Override
37     public void paintSprite(Graphics2D g2d) {
38         g2d.setColor(getColor());
39         g2d.fillOval(getX(), getY(), getWidth(), getHeight());
40     }
41 }
```

16.3 One Thread Supports Two Different Animation Tasks: SymBall2ToRight

When developing a game, usually we won't be able to insert all sprites into the game at once but to initialize some sprites in the game and then add more sprites into the game gradually through several project versions. The sprite inheritance hierarchy in the framework is a perfect structure for that purpose. The project SymBall1Init has only one static sprite. The second version of the project SymBall2ToRight is

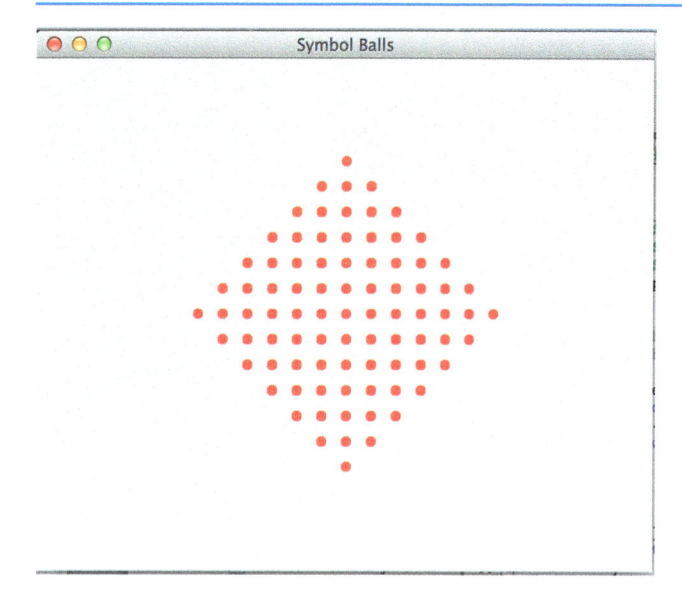

Fig. 16.1 The resulting pattern of sprites

designed to add eight groups of sprites in eight steps to form a pattern as shown in Fig. 16.1. After that, the project animates all of the balls to the right direction.

The pseudo code for making the pattern is as follows.

1. Place a ball at the center of the canvas.
2. For each existing ball, add four balls on its right, left, up, and down directions with a constant distance GAP without duplication (if a position has a ball already, a new ball would not be added on the position).
3. Repeat the step 2 for eight times for adding a great amount of balls.
4. Animate all of the ball sprites to the right direction.

The pseudo code tells that only after finishing the eight steps for setting up the ball pattern and storing all of the ball sprites into the spriteAry, all of the ball sprites start their animations. In other words, the dynamic behaviors of ballSprites have two phases. The first phase is to dynamically add ball sprites group-by-group into the pattern; the second phase is to animate all of the ball sprites.

We have known that the three-layer game structure has the class AbsGameCanvas.java that implements the game loop for animating all of sprites. That is, the second phase can be taken care of by the game loop in the three-layer game structure already. Then, what about the first phase for adding ballSprites to make the pattern? The code of the class GameCanvas.java cited in Listing 16.2 answers this question.

Listing 16.2 The class GameCanvas.java in the project SymBall2ToRoght

```
 1  /*
 2   * GameCanvas.java - A class that implements the game canvas.
 3   */
 4  package symball;
 5
10  public class GameCanvas extends AbsGameCanvas {
11
12      private BallSprite ballSprite;
13      private int midx = (Consts.MAXX - Consts.MINX) / 2;
14      private int midy = (Consts.MAXY - Consts.MINY) / 2;
15      private int step = 0;
16      private final int tSTEPS = 8;
17
18      public GameCanvas() {
19          super();
20          initComponent();
21      }
22
23      private void initComponent() {
24          getSpriteAry().clear();
25          // all ballSprites are initialized by the run() method
26          startGame(); // set playing true and start thread in AbsGameCanvas
27      }
28
29      // This application needs to dynamically add balls in eight steps and
30      // each step should be displayed. It is similar with update-repaint-pause
```

16.3 One Thread Supports Two Different Animation Tasks: SymBall2ToRight

```java
31      // process. Thus, we need the following overridden method run().
32      // Above startGame() call activates the thread in the superclass
33      // AbsGameCanvas.java. Due to the "dynamic binding", the system searches
34      // for a run() method from the bottom of the inheritance hierarchy. It
35      // finds this overridden run() first.
36      // After this run() finishes, it invokes the run() in the superclass.
37      @Override
38      public void run() {
39          try {
40              while (step < tSTEPS) {
41                  // all balls are inactive so that no animation
42                  growBalls();
43                  repaint();
44                  Thread.sleep(Consts.SLEEP_TIME);
45                  step = step + 1;
46              }
47              activateBalls(); // setActive(true) for all of balls
48              super.run();
49          } catch (InterruptedException ex) {
50          }
51      }
52
53      public void growBalls() {
54          int length = getSpriteAry().size();
55          if (length == 0) {
56              addBall(midx, midy);
57          }
58          int idx = 0;
59          while (idx < length) {
60              BallSprite ball = (BallSprite) getSpriteAry().get(idx);
61              int x = ball.getX();
62              int y = ball.getY();
63              if (x == midx) {
64                  addBall(x + Consts.GAP, y);
65                  addBall(x - Consts.GAP, y);
66              } else if (x > midx) {
67                  addBall(x + Consts.GAP, y);
68              } else if (x < midx) {
69                  addBall(x - Consts.GAP, y);
70              }
71
72              if (y == midy) {
73                  addBall(x, y + Consts.GAP);
74                  addBall(x, y - Consts.GAP);
75              } else if (y > midy) {
76                  addBall(x, y + Consts.GAP);
77              } else if (y < midy) {
78                  addBall(x, y - Consts.GAP);
79              }
80              idx++;
81          }
82      }
83
```

```
84      public void addBall(int x, int y) {
85          // don't add a same ball multiple times
86          boolean toAdd = true;
87          for (int i = 0; i < getSpriteAry().size(); i++) {
88              BallSprite ball = (BallSprite) getSpriteAry().get(i);
89              if ((ball.getX() == x) && (ball.getY() == y)) {
90                  toAdd = false; // once find a same ball, don't add it
91                  break;
92              }
93          }
94          if (toAdd) {
95              addBallSprite(x, y); // every ball has different (x, y)
96          }
97      }
98
99      public void addBallSprite(int x, int y) {
100         ballSprite = new BallSprite();
101         ballSprite.initSprite(); // init all attributes
102         ballSprite.setX(x); // set special attributes
103         ballSprite.setY(y);
104         ballSprite.setActive(false);
105         getSpriteAry().add(ballSprite);
106     }
107
108     public void activateBalls() { // allow marching starting
109         for (int i = 0; i < getSpriteAry().size(); i++) {
110             getSpriteAry().get(i).setActive(true);
111         }
112     }
113 }
```

Because the first phase only adds static balls such that we apply setActive(false) but setVisible(true) for every ball. Then the method growBalls() (lines 53–82) is called eight times for adding balls group-by-group. The method growBalls() uses its first statement "int length = getSpriteAry().size()," to get the length of the global spriteAry. At the beginning, the length of the spriteAry should be 0; thus, the method adds the first ball at the center of the canvas. The following call finds the length is 1; the method adds four balls at the top, bottom, left, and right positions around the first ball as shown in Fig. 16.2 (left). And then, the next step is as shown in Fig. 16.2 (right), which depicts that surrounding every ball sprite added by the previous step, four more ball sprites are added on the four positions. Some new balls may be duplicated with some existing balls. In order to avoid the duplications, the method growBalls() first checks whether the position has a ball already. If not, it sets the Boolean variable toAdd as true; and then a new ball is inserted at the position. Otherwise, the addition action is ignored.

All of the added ballSprites are inserted into the global spriteAry as Fig. 16.3 shows. At the step 0, it has only one ball sprite. The step 1 adds four balls around the first ball. And then, step 2 adds four more balls around each one of balls added in the step 1. Due to one of them exists already, it only adds three new balls for each existing ball.

It is clear that the first phase also needs a loop structure to loop eight times for invoking the method growBalls() to update the pattern and also invoking the paint method to display the new growing. Surely, it is another update-repaint-pause process similar with the game loop. Additionally, the first phase should be executed and finished before the second phase starts.

No doubt that the first phase is a special requirement for this specific application. We cannot modify the game loop already defined in the abstract class AbsGameCanvas.java, but can only implement this special requirement in the concrete class GameCanvas.java. How to do it? It is by recalling that the concrete class GameCanvas.java is a subclass of the superclass AbsGameCanvas.java. We can create a run() method in the GameCanvas.java subclass, which overrides the method run() implemented in the AbsGameCanvas.java superclass as follows (lines 37–51).

Fig. 16.2 Adding more sprites to grow the pattern (*left*) surrounding the first ball; (*right*) surrounding every new added balls

```
@Override
    public void run() {
        try {
            while (step < tSTEPS) {
                // all balls are inactive so that
                //no animation
                growBalls();
                repaint();
                Thread.sleep(Consts.SLEEP_TIME);
                step = step + 1;
            }
            activateBalls(); // setActive(true)
                            //for all of balls
            super.run();
        } catch (InterruptedException ex) {
        }
    }
}
```

The overridden run() method has a "while" loop that is controlled by a variable "step" and a constant tSTEPS = 8 will control the while to loop eight times. When the project starts execution, the class GameCanvas.java invokes the method startGame() defined in the superclass AbsGameCanvas.java to invoke the method initAnimation(), which instantiates an object of thread and invokes the method run() that implemented the game loop for the animation. But, the "dynamic binding" searches for a run() method start from the bottom of the inheritance hierarchy. It finds the overridden run() in the subclass GameCanvas.java first. That is, the overridden run() method defined in the subclass GameCanvas.java executes the first phase first for adding all of the ballSprites in eight steps. In every step, the method growBalls() updates the pattern in adding a set of ball sprites, then the method repaint() paints the pattern, and then the thread is paused for a while. Once the "while" loop is terminated, the overridden run() method immediately invokes the method activateBalls() to apply the method setActive(true) for all of the ball sprites and then invokes the method super.run() to activate the run() method defined in the AbsGameCanvas.java superclass to animate all of the ball sprites. In this order, the class GameCanvas.java performs the first phase, and then the class

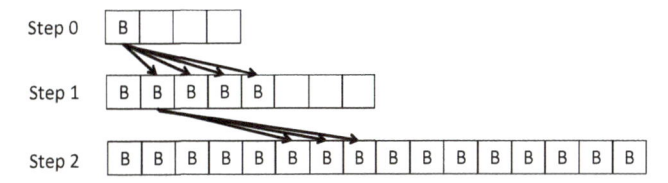

Fig. 16.3 The method growBalls() adds more balls into the spriteAry

AbsGameCanvas.java completes the second phase. By taking the advantages of the inheritance and the dynamic binding, one thread supports two different animation tasks in a sequence.

This version of the project illustrates that the three-layer game structure forms a guideline for implementing a project, and it is flexible enough to allow special features to be added. It also demonstrates that no matter how many sprites are added, the global linear data structure spriteAry can accommodate them, and only a single "for" loop is needed to treat all of the sprites.

16.4 The Sprite Inheritance Hierarchy Eases Adding New Sprites: SymBall3ToRL

The third version is SymBall3ToRL, which separates all ball sprites into three sets. One set is animated to the left direction; the other set is animated to the right direction. The third set is the balls in the central positions that are not moved to either direction. For adding the new sprites, we extend the sprite inheritance hierarchy for adding two new classes corresponding to the two groups as shown in Fig. 16.4. The ToLeftBall.java class implements an updateSprite() method to move the ball to the left, and when the ball reaches the left edge of the canvas, it is wrapped to the right direction. Similarly, the class ToRightBall.java implements an updateSprite() method for moving the ball to the right direction and wrapping it to the left direction when the ball reaches the right boundary. The initComponent() method is still coded in the class GameCanvas.java as shown in Listing 16.3.

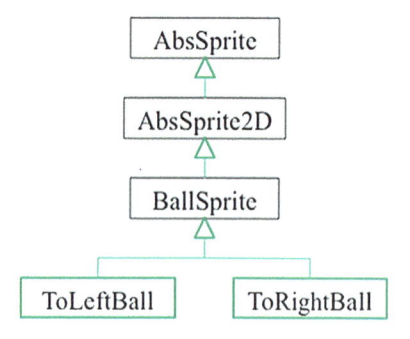

Fig. 16.4 The inheritance hierarchy of sprites in the project SymBall3ToRL

Besides the modification of the sprite inheritance hierarchy, the method growBalls() in the class GameCanvas.java should also be modified to carefully insert three different kinds of balls into proper positions. It inserts balls of the class ToLeftBall.java on the left side of the pattern and inserts balls of the class ToRightBall.java on the right side of the pattern. In addition, all of the balls in the middle column are third kind of balls that won't be animated, which are objects of the class BallSprite.java. However, the controls of the thread are still separated into two phases: the first phase adds all of sprites into the pattern, and the second phase animates all of sprites, that is, the same as in the SymBall2ToRight version.

Listing 16.3 The modified class GameCanvas.java and BallSprite.java as well as the new classes ToRightBall.java and ToLeftBall.java in the project SymBall3ToRL

```
1  /*
2   * GameCanvas.java - A class that implements the game canvas.
3   */
4  package symball;
5
10 public class GameCanvas extends AbsGameCanvas {
11
12     private int midx = (Consts.MAXX - Consts.MINX) / 2;
13     private int midy = (Consts.MAXY - Consts.MINY) / 2;
14     private int step = 0;
15     private final int tSTEPS = 8;
16
17     public GameCanvas() {
18         super();
19         initComponent();
20     }
21
22     private void initComponent() {
23         getSpriteAry().clear();
24         // all ballSprites are initialized by the run() method
25         startGame(); // set playing true and start thread in AbsGameCanvas
26     }
27
28     // This application needs to dynamically add balls in eight steps and
29     // each step should be displayed. It is similar with update-repaint-pause
30     // process. Thus, we need the following overridden method run().
31     // Above startGame() call activates the thread in the superclass
32     // AbsGameCanvas.java. Due to the "dynamic binding", the system searches
33     // for a run() method from the bottom of the inheritance hierarchy. It
34     // finds this overridden run() first.
35     // After this run() finishes, it invokes the run() in the superclass.
36     @Override
37     public void run() {
38         try {
39             while (step < tSTEPS) {
40                 // all balls are inactive so that no animation
41                 growBalls();
```

16.4 The Sprite Inheritance Hierarchy Eases Adding New Sprites: SymBall3ToRL

```
42                  repaint();
43                  Thread.sleep(Consts.SLEEP_TIME);
44                  step = step + 1;
45              }
46              super.run();
47          } catch (InterruptedException ex) {
48          }
49      }
50
51      public void growBalls() {
52          int length = getSpriteAry().size();
53          if (length == 0) {
54              addBall(midx, midy); // the central ball
55          }
56          int idx = 0;
57          while (idx < length) {
58              int x = (getSpriteAry().get(idx)).getX();
59              int y = (getSpriteAry().get(idx)).getY();
60              if (x == midx) {
61                  addRightBall(x + Consts.GAP, y);
62                  addLeftBall(x - Consts.GAP, y);
63                  addBall(x, y - Consts.GAP);
64                  addBall(x, y + Consts.GAP);
65              } else if (x > midx) {
66                  addRightBall(x + Consts.GAP, y);
67                  addRightBall(x - Consts.GAP, y);
68                  addRightBall(x, y - Consts.GAP);
69                  addRightBall(x, y + Consts.GAP);
70              } else if (x < midx) {
71                  addLeftBall(x + Consts.GAP, y);
72                  addLeftBall(x - Consts.GAP, y);
73                  addLeftBall(x, y - Consts.GAP);
74                  addLeftBall(x, y + Consts.GAP);
75              }
76              idx++;
77          }
78      }
79
80      public BallSprite addRightBall(int x, int y) {
81          BallSprite newBall = null;
82          if (allowAdd(x, y)) {
83              newBall = new ToRightBall();
84              insertAry(newBall, x, y);
85          }
86          return newBall;
87      }
88
89      public BallSprite addLeftBall(int x, int y) {
90          BallSprite newBall = null;
91          if (allowAdd(x, y)) {
92              newBall = new ToLeftBall();
93              insertAry(newBall, x, y);
94          }
95          return newBall;
96      }
97
```

```
 98      public BallSprite addBall(int x, int y) {
 99          BallSprite newBall = null;
100          if (allowAdd(x, y)) {
101              newBall = new BallSprite();
102              insertAry(newBall, x, y);
103          }
104          return newBall;
105      }
106
107      public void insertAry(BallSprite newBall, int x, int y) {
108          newBall.setX(x);
109          newBall.setY(y);
110          newBall.setActive(true);
111          getSpriteAry().add(newBall);
112      }
113
114      public boolean allowAdd(int x, int y) {
115          // don't add a same ball multiple times
116          boolean toAdd = true;
117          for (int i = 0; i < getSpriteAry().size(); i++) {
118              BallSprite ball = (BallSprite) getSpriteAry().get(i);
119              if ((ball.getX() == x) && (ball.getY() == y)) {
120                  toAdd = false; // once find a same ball, don't add it
121                  break;
122              }
123          }
124          return toAdd;
125      }
126  }
```

```
 1  /*
 2   * BallSprite.java - A class that implements a ball sprite.
 3   */
 4  package symball;
 5
 6  import java.awt.Color;
 7  import java.awt.Graphics2D;
 8
13  public class BallSprite extends AbsSprite2D {
14
15      @SuppressWarnings("OverridableMethodCallInConstructor")
16      public BallSprite() {
17          super();
18          initSprite();
19      }
20
21      @Override
22      public void initSprite() {
23          int cvX = (Consts.MAXX - Consts.MINX) / 2;
24          int cvY = (Consts.MAXY - Consts.MINY) / 2;
25          setX(cvX - Consts.BALL_RADIUS);
26          setY(cvY - Consts.BALL_RADIUS);
27          setWidth(2 * Consts.BALL_RADIUS);
28          setHeight(2 * Consts.BALL_RADIUS);
29          setDx(0);
30          setDy(0);
31          setColor(Color.RED);
```

```
32            setActive(false);
33            setVisible(true);
34        }
35
36        @Override
37        public void updateSprite() {
38            setX(getX() + getDx());
39        }
40
41        @Override
42        public void paintSprite(Graphics2D g2d) {
43            g2d.setColor(getColor());
44            g2d.fillOval(getX(), getY(), getWidth(), getHeight());
45        }
46  }
```

```
 1  /*
 2   * ToLeftBall.java - A class that extends BallSprite and defines a ball
 3   * animated to the direction of left.
 4   */
 5
 6  package symball;
 7
12  public class ToLeftBall extends BallSprite {
13
14      public void ToLeftBall() {
15          initSprite();
16      }
17
18      @Override
19      public void updateSprite() {
20          setX(getX() - 2);
21          if (getX() <= 0) {
22              setX(Consts.CV_WIDTH);
23          }
24      }
25  }
```

```
 1  /*
 2   * ToRightBall.java - A class that extends BallSprite for defining a
 3   * ball sprite animated to the direction of right.
 4   */
 5  package symball;
 6
11  public class ToRightBall extends BallSprite {
12
13      public void ToRightBall() {
14          initSprite();
15      }
16
17      @Override
18      public void updateSprite() {
19          setX(getX() + 2);
20          if (getX() >= Consts.CV_WIDTH) {
21              setX(0);
22          }
23      }
24  }
```

The project SymBall3ToRL demonstrates that modifying sprites is not difficulty in using the three-layer game structure. It only needs to modify the sprite inheritance hierarchy without touching the entire software structure.

16.5 Every Sprite Has a Thread to Change Its Color Randomly: SymBall4Twinkle

The last version is the project SymBall4Twinkle, which intends to change the color of every ball randomly and quickly for making a twinkling view. The game loop is for animating ball sprites to the right or to the left. Now, we would like to have an additional dynamic behavior for changing the color of every ball sprite with a higher speed than the animation speed.

Clearly, changing the color of every ball sprite requires a continuous update-repaint chain. In addition, the changing sprite color and the sprite animation happen at the same time. That is, this changing color chain and the animation chain are in parallel. Since the color twinkling happens in every ball sprite, the color updating and repainting should be done in every individual ball sprite. It is that the class BallSprite.java itself should implement the Interface Runnable such that its own run() method is able to change its own color randomly. In other words, besides a thread for constructing the "game loop" in order to animate all of the ball sprites, there is the same number of threads as the number of ball sprites work at the same time for changing the color of every ball sprite. For the reality, this project totally has 113 of ball sprites; then, 113 threads besides the thread for the game loop are needed to be added.

Due to the fact that all of the animated ball sprites and the randomly changed color of every ball sprite should be painted at the same GUI, the graphics context should be the same one. Therefore, a variable "Graphics2D gra" is specially declared in the class BallSprite.java. And then, the class GameCanvas.java should set its g2d into the class BallSprite.java through the setter method of setGra() defined in the class BallSprite.java. The implementations of the two classes are shown in Listing 16.4.

Listing 16.4 The BallSprite.java class and the partial code of the GameCanvas.java class in the project SymBall4Twinkle

```
1  /*
2   * BallSprite.java - A class that implements a ball sprite.
3   */
4  package symball;
5
6  import java.awt.Color;
7  import java.awt.Graphics2D;
8
13 public class BallSprite extends AbsSprite2D implements Runnable {
14
15     private Thread twinkling;
16     private Graphics2D gra;
17
18     @SuppressWarnings("OverridableMethodCallInConstructor")
19     public BallSprite() {
20         super();
21         initSprite();
22     }
23
24     @Override
25     public void initSprite() {
26         int cvX = (Consts.MAXX - Consts.MINX) / 2;
27         int cvY = (Consts.MAXY - Consts.MINY) / 2;
28         setX(cvX - Consts.BALL_RADIUS);
29         setY(cvY - Consts.BALL_RADIUS);
30         setWidth(2 * Consts.BALL_RADIUS);
31         setHeight(2 * Consts.BALL_RADIUS);
32         setDx(0);
33         setDy(0);
```

16.5 Every Sprite Has a Thread to Change Its Color Randomly: SymBall4Twinkle

```java
34            setColor(ranColor());
35            setActive(false);
36            setVisible(true);
37        }
38
39        public void ballStart() {
40            if (twinkling == null) {
41                twinkling = new Thread(this);
42                twinkling.start();
43            }
44        }
45
46        @Override
47        @SuppressWarnings("SleepWhileInLoop")
48        public void run() {
49            try {
50                while (true) {
51                    // it changes the color with higher speed than game loop
52                    paintColor(gra);
53                    Thread.sleep(15);
54                }
55            } catch (InterruptedException | NullPointerException ex) {
56            }
57        }
58
59        @Override
60        public void paintSprite(Graphics2D g2d) {
61            g2d.setColor(ranColor());
62            g2d.fillOval(getX(), getY(), getWidth(), getHeight());
63        }
64
65        // This method changes the colors of all balls.
66        // It does not animate any balls that appear in the middle column line.
67        // The classes ToLeftBall.java and ToRightBall.java have their own
68        // updateSprte() methods that animate those balls to left or to right.
69        @Override
70        public void updateSprite() {
71            setColor(ranColor());
72        }
73
74        public Color ranColor() {
75            int redc = (int) (Math.random() * 256);
76            int greenc = (int) (Math.random() * 256);
77            int bluec = (int) (Math.random() * 256);
78            Color ballc = new Color(redc, greenc, bluec);
79            return ballc;
80        }
81
82        public void paintColor(Graphics2D g2d) {
83            g2d.setColor(ranColor());
84            g2d.fillOval(getX(), getY(), getWidth(), getHeight());
85        }
86
87        public Graphics2D getGra() {
88            return gra;
89        }
90
```

```
91      public void setGra(Graphics2D gra) {
92          this.gra = gra;
93      }
94  }
```

```
1   /*
2    * GameCanvas.java - A class that implements the game canvas.
3    */
6   …
15      private Graphics2D g2d;
17
107     public void insertAry(BallSprite newBall, int x, int y) {
108         newBall.setX(x);
109         newBall.setY(y);
110         newBall.setActive(true);
111         // assign each ball a Graphics for painting random color
112         g2d = (Graphics2D) getGraphics();
113         newBall.setGra(g2d);
114         newBall.ballStart();
115         getSpriteAry().add(newBall);
116     }
117 …
144 }
```

The class BallSprite.java thus implements the Interface Runnable to create a method run() (lines 48–57). The while loop invokes the method paintColor(), which invokes the statement "g2d.setColor(ranColor)," for getting a randomly changed color and invokes the g2d.fillOver() for painting the ball sprite. And then, the sleep() method is invoked to allow other threads for sharing the unique CPU. This paintColor() method is called by the independent thread for changing colors. At the same time, the paintSprite() method is invoked by the "game loop" for displaying the animation actions.

These projects raised different special requirements. We can conveniently implement all of the special needs without touching the three-layer game structure. The project SymBall2ToRight uses one thread to control two different dynamic behaviors in two phases in sequence. The project SymBall4Twinkle applies threads for each ball sprite to control the dynamic color changing with a special speed in parallel with the ball's animation. These examples proved that multiple dynamic behaviors could be supported by properly using threads. And the three-layer game structure enables that flexibility. Relying on the thread, override, and dynamic binding, we can insert special needs into the formal defined framework.

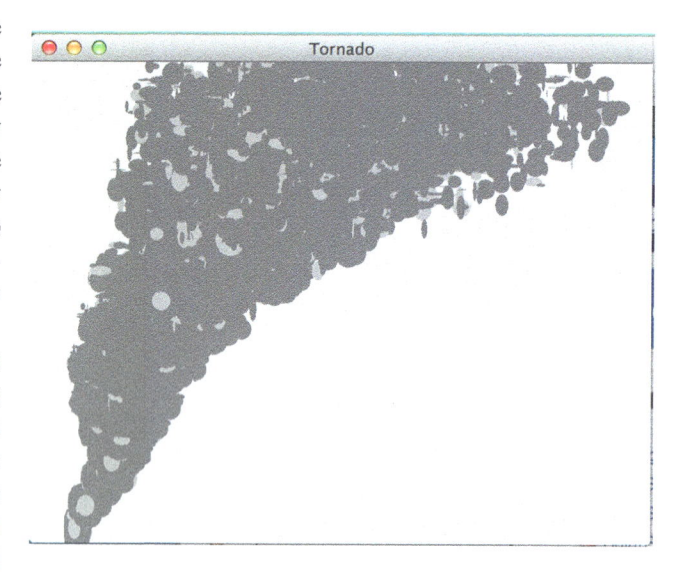

Fig. 16.5 A screen shot of the project Tornado

16.6 A New Project Tornado

Some special scenes can also be made in using the three-layer game structure. Here, a new project Tornado is developed to be an example. A screenshot of a Tornado scene is shown in Fig. 16.5. We imagine that a Tornado consists of thousands of components that circulate along an oval. Thus, it is developed in following steps.

16.6.1 Making a Ball Sprite Circulating Along an Oval: The Project Tornado1

An easy way to think about the components in a Tornado is to use circles and rectangles. Hence, the first version is to make a ball sprite that is circulating along an oval. The three-layer game structure prepared the frame layer and the canvas layer already. We only need to develop a class BallSprite.java for describing attributes and behaviors of a ball sprite. The code of the class BallSprite.java is cited in Listing 16.5.

16.6 A New Project Tornado

Listing 16.5 The code of the class BallSprite.java in the project Tornado1

```java
/*
 * BallSprite.java - A class that implements a ball sprite.
 */
package tornado;

import java.awt.Color;
import java.awt.Graphics2D;

public class BallSprite extends AbsSprite2D {

    private int midx = (Consts.MAXX - Consts.MINX) / 2;
    private int midy;
    private int majorR;
    private int minorR;
    private int currAngle;
    private int moveAngle;

    public BallSprite() {
        super();
    }

    @Override
    public void initSprite() {
        majorR = 150;
        minorR = 50;
        midy = 180;
        setX(midx + getMajorR());
        setY(midy);
        setWidth(Consts.BALL_RADIUS);
        setHeight(Consts.BALL_RADIUS);
        currAngle = 360;
        moveAngle = 10;
        setColor(Color.RED);
        setActive(true);
        setVisible(true);
    }

    @Override
    public void updateSprite() {
        currAngle = currAngle + moveAngle;
        if (currAngle >= 360) {
            currAngle = -360;
        }
        setX((int) (midx + Math.sin(currAngle * Consts.RADIAN) * getMajorR()));
        setY((int) (midy - Math.cos(currAngle * Consts.RADIAN) * getMinorR()));
    }

    @Override
    public void paintSprite(Graphics2D g2d) {
        g2d.setColor(getColor());
        g2d.fillOval(getX(), getY(), getWidth(), getHeight());
    }


...    getter and setter methods
}
```

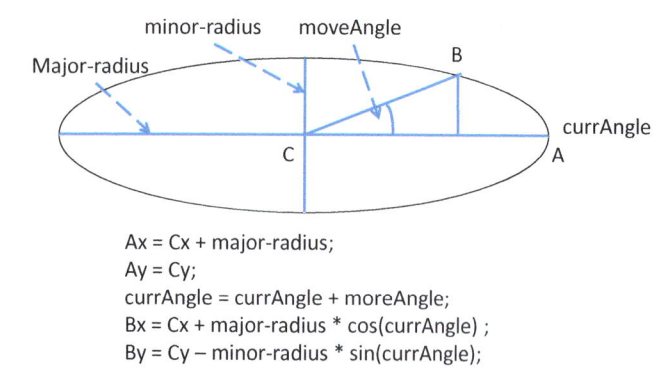

Ax = Cx + major-radius;
Ay = Cy;
currAngle = currAngle + moreAngle;
Bx = Cx + major-radius * cos(currAngle) ;
By = Cy − minor-radius * sin(currAngle);

Fig. 16.6 The computations for circulating along an oval

We know that the class BallSprite.java "is-a" AbsSprite2D. java. The AbsSprite2D.java superclass defines x, y, width, height, and color for a geometrical shape. The BallSprite. java subclass inherits all of these attributes already. In considering that the ball sprite should circulate along an oval, some new attributes should be defined, such as majorR, minorR, currAngle, moveAngle, and so on. Figure 16.6 depicts these attributes. Additionally, the class BallSprite. java needs to override the methods initSprite(), updateSprite(), and paintSprite().

The principle of the circulating computation is as shown in Fig. 16.6. Suppose that the object initially is placed at the point A. The coordinates (Ax, Ay) are defined through the two statements Ax and Ay shown on Fig. 16.6. And then, the currAngle is increased to be (currAngle + moveAngle); the object is moved to the point B with the coordinates of (Bx, By), which are calculated based on the formulae described on the figure. The method updateSprite() in the class BallSprite.java implements these formulae for the computations (lines 42–50).

After the class BallSprite.java is ready, the next step is to ask the method initComponent() in the class GameCanvas. java for instantiating a ballSprite and adds it into the global spriteAry. Then, the game loop in the class AbsGameCanvas. java starts to invoke the updateComponent() method that in turn invokes the updateSprite() method defined in the class BallSprite.java to update the position of the ballSprite, and then the game loop invokes the method paintComponent() that in turn calls the paintSprite() method defined in the class BallSprite.java to paint the ballSprite on its new updated position. All of these functions generate a scene that a ballSprite object circulates along the oval around the center point C of the oval.

16.6.2 Dividing the y-Axis into 13 Sections: The Project Tornado2

Similarly, a class RectSprite.java is developed. It also has the method updateSprite() to implement the behavior for circulating around an oval. After that, the initComponent() method in the class GameCanvas.java adds thousands of object of ballSprites and rectSprites with randomly assigned size, major radius, minor radius, and moving angles and stores them into the global spriteAry.

In order to make the shape along the y-axis looks like a Tornado, we divide the height along the y direction into several sections. Every section sets up its own center point for the oval in that section, defines different ranges of major radius and minor radius, and then generates objects of ballSprite and rectSprite. All of these objects circulate around slightly different ovals with different center points in different sections. The class GameCanvas.java implements all of these ideas as shown in Listing 16.6.

Listing 16.6 The classes GameCanvas.java and BallSprite.java in the project Tornado2

```
1  /*
2   * GameCanvas.java - A class defines the game canvas.
3   */
4  package tornado;
5
6  import java.awt.Color;
7
8  /**
9   *
10  * @author cxu
11  */
12 public class GameCanvas extends AbsGameCanvas {
13
14     private BallSprite ballSprite;
15     private RectSprite rectSprite;
16
```

16.6 A New Project Tornado

```
17      public GameCanvas() {
18          super();
19          initComponent();
20      }
21
22      private void initComponent() {
23          getSpriteAry().clear();
24          initSprite();
25          startGame();
26      }
27
28      public void initSprite() {
29          for (int section = 1; section <= 13; section++) {
30              for (int j = 1; j <= 200; j++) {
31                  ballSprite = new BallSprite();
32                  rectSprite = new RectSprite();
33                  ballSprite.initSprite(section);
34                  rectSprite.initSprite(section);
35                  ballSprite.setColor(Color.LIGHT_GRAY);
36                  rectSprite.setColor(Color.LIGHT_GRAY);
37                  getSpriteAry().add(ballSprite);
38                  getSpriteAry().add(rectSprite);
39              }
40              for (int j = 1; j <= 700; j++) {
41                  ballSprite = new BallSprite();
42                  rectSprite = new RectSprite();
43                  ballSprite.initSprite(section);
44                  rectSprite.initSprite(section);
45                  ballSprite.setColor(Color.GRAY);
46                  rectSprite.setColor(Color.GRAY);
47                  getSpriteAry().add(ballSprite);
48                  getSpriteAry().add(rectSprite);
49              }
50              for (int j = 1; j <= 1; j++) {
51                  ballSprite = new BallSprite();
52                  rectSprite = new RectSprite();
53                  ballSprite.initSprite(section);
54                  rectSprite.initSprite(section);
55                  ballSprite.setColor(Color.LIGHT_GRAY);
56                  rectSprite.setColor(Color.LIGHT_GRAY);
57                  getSpriteAry().add(ballSprite);
58                  getSpriteAry().add(rectSprite);
59              }
60          }
61      }
62 }
```

```
1  /*
2   * BallSprite.java - A class that implements a ball sprite.
3   */
4  package tornado;
5
6  import java.awt.Color;
7  import java.awt.Graphics2D;
8
```

```
 9  /**
10   *
11   * @author cxu
12   */
13  public class BallSprite extends AbsSprite2D {
14
15      private int midx = (Consts.MAXX - Consts.MINX) / 2;
16      private int midy;
17      private int majorR;
18      private int minorR;
19      private int currAngle;
20      private int moveAngle;
21
22      @SuppressWarnings("OverridableMethodCallInConstructor")
23      public BallSprite() {
24          super();
25      }
26
27      @Override
28      public void initSprite() {
29      }
30
31      // a special method that has a parameter "section"
32      public void initSprite(int section) {
33          switch (section) {
34              case 1:
35                  midx = 30;
36                  midy = 360;
37                  majorR = (int) (Math.random() * 3);
38                  minorR = (int) (Math.random() * 10);
39                  break;
40              case 2:
41                  midx = 30 + 10;
42                  midy = 340;
43                  majorR = (int) (Math.random() * 10);
44                  minorR = (int) (Math.random() * 10);
45                  break;
46              case 3:
47                  midx = 30 + 25;
48                  midy = 320;
49                  majorR = (int) (Math.random() * 15);
50                  minorR = (int) (Math.random() * 12);
51                  break;
52              case 4:
53                  midx = 30 + 35;
54                  midy = 300;
55                  majorR = (int) (Math.random() * 20);
56                  minorR = (int) (Math.random() * 15);
57                  break;
58              case 5:
59                  midx = 30 + 38;
60                  midy = 280;
61                  majorR = (int) (Math.random() * 30);
62                  minorR = (int) (Math.random() * 18);
```

```
63                break;
64            case 6:
65                midx = 30 + 40;
66                midy = 260;
67                majorR = (int) (Math.random() * 40);
68                minorR = (int) (Math.random() * 20);
69                break;
70            case 7:
71                midx = 30 + 50;
72                midy = 230;
73                majorR = (int) (Math.random() * 52);
74                minorR = (int) (Math.random() * 24);
75                break;
76            case 8:
77                midx = 30 + 70;
78                midy = 200;
79                majorR = (int) (Math.random() * 65);
80                minorR = (int) (Math.random() * 30);
81                break;
82            case 9:
83                midx = 30 + 100;
84                midy = 160;
85                majorR = (int) (Math.random() * 85);
86                minorR = (int) (Math.random() * 35);
87                break;
88            case 10:
89                midx = 30 + 140;
90                midy = 120;
91                majorR = (int) (Math.random() * 105);
92                minorR = (int) (Math.random() * 45);
93                break;
94            case 11:
95                midx = 30 + 160;
96                midy = 90;
97                majorR = (int) (Math.random() * 130);
98                minorR = (int) (Math.random() * 60);
99                break;
100           case 12:
101               midx = 30 + 200;
102               midy = 50;
103               majorR = (int) (Math.random() * 160);
104               minorR = (int) (Math.random() * 80);
105               break;
106           case 13:
107               midx = 30 + 240;
108               midy = 30;
109               majorR = (int) (Math.random() * 200);
110               minorR = (int) (Math.random() * 100);
111               break;
112           default:
113               break;
114       }
115
```

```java
            setX(midx + getMajorR());
            setY(midy);
            setWidth((int) (2 * Math.random() * Consts.BALL_RADIUS));
            setHeight((int) (2 * Math.random() * Consts.BALL_RADIUS));
            currAngle = (int) (Math.random() * 360);
            moveAngle = (int) (Math.random() * 10);
            setActive(true);
            setVisible(true);
        }

    public Color ranGrayColor() {
        int aColor = (int) (Math.random() * 2);
        Color returnColor = null;
        if (aColor == 0) {
            returnColor = Color.GRAY;
        } else if (aColor == 1) {
            returnColor = Color.LIGHT_GRAY;
        }
        return returnColor;
    }

    @Override
    public void updateSprite() {
        currAngle = currAngle + moveAngle;
        if (currAngle >= 360) {
            currAngle = -360;
        }
        setX((int) (midx + Math.sin(currAngle * Consts.RADIAN) * getMajorR()));
        setY((int) (midy - Math.cos(currAngle * Consts.RADIAN) * getMinorR()));
    }

    @Override
    public void paintSprite(Graphics2D g2d) {
        g2d.setColor(getColor());
        g2d.fillOval(getX(), getY(), getWidth(), getHeight());
    }

    public int getMajorR() {
        return majorR;
    }

    public void setMajorR(int majorR) {
        this.majorR = majorR;
    }

    public int getMinorR() {
        return minorR;
    }

    public void setMinorR(int minorR) {
        this.minorR = minorR;
    }
}
```

The class GameCanvas.java implements the method initComponent(), which has a nested "for" loop. The outer "for" loop divides the height of the canvas into 13 sections, and the inner "for" loop adds objects into the spriteAry. The section number is passed into the method initSprite(int section) defined in the classes BallSprite.java and RectSprite.java. Because the method initSprite(int section) has a parameter, it is a special method other than the abstract method initSprite() defined in the superclass AbsSprite2D.java. Therefore, the classes BallSprite.java and RectSprite.java have to give up the "override" of the abstract method initSprite() but create an "overload" method initSprite(int section). This is another example for treating a special requirement inside the three-layer game structure.

Based on the parameter "section," the "overload" method initSprite(int section) sets different coordinates (midx, midy) for the center point of ovals and defines different range of major radius and minor radius for making a special shape of the Tornado. By adjusting these settings for different attributes, we can change the components' shape and their numbers in a Tornado. The implementations of the classes GameCanvas.java and BallSprite.java are listed in Listing 16.6. The implementation of the class RectSprite.java is very close to the BallSprite.java class.

In the implementations of these classes and methods, we do not care how many sprites are added since the global spriteAry may accommodate any number of sprites with any kinds, shapes, and colors whenever the sprites are in the sprite inheritance hierarchy.

16.6.3 Assigning Different Colors to Sprites

The final step is to assign Color.LIGHT_GRAY to about 1/3 of components and assign Color.GRAY to about 2/3 of components.

16.7 Summary

We applied the framework of three-layer game structure for developing two example projects. Both of them are not video games, but they have hundreds even thousands of objects with some special requirements for making dynamic scenes. The three-layer game structure appears stable and flexible for handling the special requirements. In addition, these two examples also demonstrate multiple OOP concepts and practices, such as the thread, inheritance, override, overload, and the like. We can safely say, the three-layer game structure dramatically reduces our programming burden and allows us to concentrate on designing special treatments to satisfy special needs. In other words, as long as we can design objects with their dynamic behaviors, the framework of the three-layer game structure will take care of the remaining works.

16.8 Exercises

Self-Review Questions

1. What idea does the different versions of the project SymBall demonstrate?
2. What computation is needed for making the pattern in the version SymBall2ToRight?
3. What computation is needed for separating the objects of toRightBall and toLeftBall in the version SymBall3ToRL?
4. How to show the eight steps for adding the balls in order to make the pattern?
5. How to animate objects of balls after finishing the initialization of components?
6. How to twinkling the balls with randomly changed colors?
7. What idea does the project Tornado illustrate?
8. Is there any better algorithm for initializing the objects in order to make the scene of a Tornado?
9. What is the computation principle for making the circulating objects?
10. What are the advantages of the three-layer game structure in making these projects?
11. Draw a UML class diagram for the project SymBall4Twinkle.
12. Draw a UML class diagram for the project Tornado2.

Projects

1. Change the red ball to a blue rectangle for the project SymBall1Init.
2. Replace the drawing red ball by using a ball image for the project SymBall2ToRight.
3. Implement the same actions as the project SymBall3ToRL did, but keep the sprites animated to the right direction as the original red balls, and change the sprites animated to the left direction as blue rectangles.
4. Modify the project SymBall4Twinkle such that the speed of color changes is the same as the animation speed. That is, when the balls are animated one step, the colors of all balls are changed one time with a same color.
5. Modify the project SymBall4Twinkle such that when the balls animated one step, the colors of all balls are changed one time with a different random color.
6. Modify the project SymBall3ToRL to be SymBall3ToUD. That is, change the animation directions from right/left to up/down.
7. Apply the three-layer game structure for creating a new project, which animates a lot of white snowflakes for making a scene looks like a heavy snow.
8. Imagine and implement a scene of wind blowing, a scene of waterfall, a scene of leaves falling, and the like.

17. Image Sprite and UML State Machine: A Game Breakout

It has been proven that the three-layer software structure for games can be a guide for developing video games based on the animation technique. We can simply copy the framework to be the basis of a new video game and then insert the required sprites and implement required special features. The development of the rudimental game Breakout is just based on this strategy. One of the new features of the game is to replace all of sprites with images. Besides that, it also introduces the UML state machine to analyze and synthesize game's dynamic activities.

The objectives of this chapter include:
1. The description of the new game Breakout.
2. The game Breakout actually is an extension of the game Pong.
3. Replacing the graphical drawings with images.
4. A new sprite inheritance hierarchy for image sprites.
5. Converting 1D data structure to 2D arrangement.
6. Checking collisions between a brick and a ball.
7. PropertyChangeListener and its applications.
8. A UML state machine.
9. Dynamically adding or removing an event listener.

We started our first animation-based game Pong from Chap. 13. Over several chapters, we discussed some extensions of the game Pong. However, those extensions have nothing to do with the bouncing ball, which is still bounced around and does nothing. Now, we are going to take the advantage of the bouncing ball sprite as a "weapon" to breakout a group of bricks. This idea extends the game Pong into a new game Breakout.

17.1 The Game Breakout Could Be Understood as an Extension of the Game Pong

Figure 17.1 illustrates a new extension of the game Pong. It shows the basis of the game Pong with an additional set of bricks on the left end of the playing field. The player still controls the paddle on the right end to bounce the ball back in order to prevent the ball being lost. When the ball bounces to the left end and hits on one or more bricks, the brick bounces the ball back, and the brick itself disappears. Gradually, the number of bricks will be reduced until all of them are gone. When a brick is hit, the score of the game is increased. In the process, the ball could be lost, which causes the score of the game to decrease as a penalty. And then, the ball will be placed back to continue the play. Suppose that we design it to allow ball lost for three times at most. Thus, the game would be terminated either when all bricks are gone or when the ball lost more than three times.

Based on the idea above, if we turn the game screen on (Fig. 17.1) 90° clockwise, we get a new GUI as shown in Fig. 17.2. It is the classic video game called Breakout. We have no idea about the implementation of the original version of the game Breakout. However, we can apply the three-layer game structure framework for implementing our own version of the game.

17.2 A New Image Branch in the Sprite Inheritance Hierarchy

Comparing two GUIs shown in Figs. 17.1 and 17.2, we can tell that an important change occurred. In the game Pong, all of the sprites shown on the GUI are made through graphical

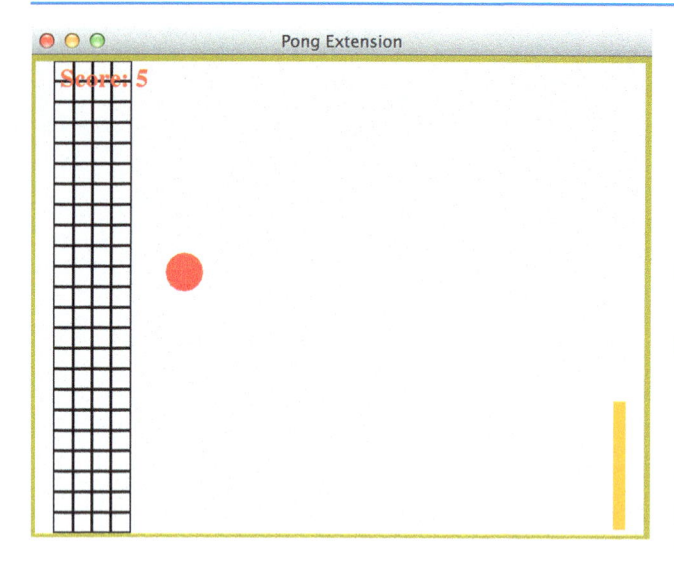

Fig. 17.1 The GUI of the extension of the game Pong

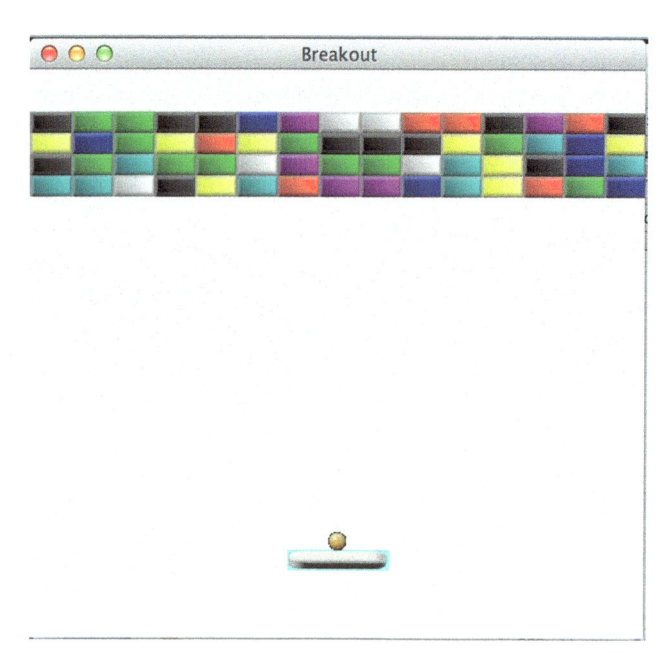

Fig. 17.2 The GUI of the game Breakout at its initial moment

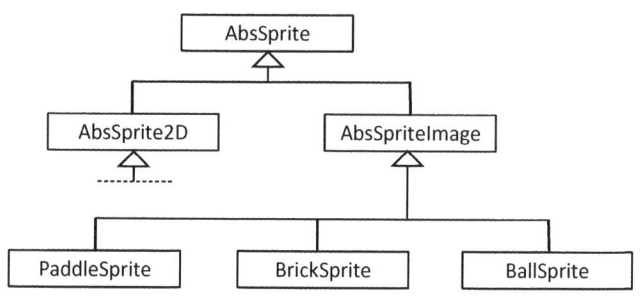

Fig. 17.3 The new sprite inheritance hierarchy for the game Breakout

AbsSprite.java is still the root class of the global sprite inheritance hierarchy. But, we add a new subclass AbsSpriteImage.java into the hierarchy to form a new branch that is for dealing with images. In the new branch, three classes of sprites, BallSprite.java, BrickSprite.java, and PaddleSprite.java, are added for the game Breakout as shown in Fig. 17.3.

Due to the fact that all of the sprites are images, the data type of the global linear data structure spriteAry defined in the abstract class AbsGameCanvas.java should be adjusted as "new ArrayList<AbsSpriteImage>()."

17.3 Imaging in Java

Image has been used in the project PaintXmasCard (Chap. 5). However, it has not been introduced in certain detail. Considering images are used very popular in games and some existing games may involve some "old style" of Java codes, here we very briefly describe the evolution of imaging technique in Java.

Java has changed its image technique in several releases. The changes are caused by the wish of speed. (1) Java image technique starts from AWT imaging model. It was mainly designed for Applets to pull images from Web, which may take time when images crawl along the network. Hence, the method getImage() actually only prepares an empty image object for holding the coming image. The real download is triggered by the method drawImage(). It implies that the method paint(), which invokes the methods getImage() and drawImage(), may not have complete information about the image when it is invoked. This makes difficulty for allocating spaces on the screen for the coming image. (2) In order to satisfy the need in "loading images before drawing them," a new class MediaTracker was developed. The class creates separated threads to download images for speeding up the downloading. But, this improvement increases the length of program writing. (3) Java then developed an ImageIcon class that sets up the object of MediaTracker by itself for reducing the burden of programming. The resulting ImageIcon object can be used in two ways. One is to convert the ImageIcon to

paintings. However, in the game Breakout, all of the sprites are images. No doubt, an image also has a shape. For example, a brick is an image with a shape of a rectangle, and a ball is an image with a shape of an oval. It implies that for updating, such as, bricks arrangement, collisions, ball bouncing, and the like, we should consider their shapes for dealing with computations, but for painting we should take care of their images. Therefore, an image is not a brand new sprite but a geometrical shape plus a pre-drawn picture.

After all, images are different from the geographical drawings. For dealing with images, we need to create a new branch in the global sprite inheritance hierarchy. The class

be the image that is contained in the ImageIcon and then paint the image. The second way is to paint the imageIcon itself directly.

Later, Java 2D was launched. It offers a set of new graphic features and replaces most geometrical shape primitives in AWT. The class Graphics2D is a central class of Java 2D, which is a subclass of the class Graphics defined in AWT. A cast statement "Graphics2D g2d = (Graphics2D) g" must be applied for making the graphics context to be a Graphics2D object as we have learned already.

Java 2D also provides a new built-in class BufferedImage that is a subclass of the original built-in class Image. The class BufferedImage has two advantages in comparison with the class Image. The data required for image manipulation in the class BufferedImage are easily accessible, and objects of the class BufferedImage are automatically converted to so-called managed images by the JVM. A managed image is automatically cached in video memory (VRAM) by the JVM, and a managed image may allow hardware acceleration to be employed when the image is being rendered.

Images are saved as files in the file system. For using an image in a project, first of all we need to get the image from the file system into the project. For getting the image, we need to know the absolute file path plus the image file name or the relative file path plus the image file name. We have discussed about accessing text files in Chap. 2 and about accessing images in Chap. 5; the better approach is to include image files inside the file structure of the project and then go through the relative file path to get the images. In this way the image files are part of the project, which allows the image staying with the entire project being moved or copied to anywhere.

The project Breakout1 adopts this setting, and its file structure is as shown in Fig. 17.4. That is, all of the images are loaded into the subdirectory images under the directory Source Packages.

Under that setting, the class ReadImage.java created in Chap. 5 provides the following statement for reading in one image for the project.

```
BufferedImage im = ImageIO.read(getClass().
    getResource("../images/image.jpg"))
```

where the "../images/" is the "relative path" for reaching the image file. The method read() is defined under the built-in class ImageIO. The method read() has a parameter "getClass().getResource()." The meaning of the parameter has been explained in Chaps. 2 and 5. Here, we repeat it's meaning as a reminder. The file structure of the project Breakout1 is shown in Fig. 17.4. Suppose that the class GameCanvas.java intends to get an image ball.png from the directory "images" by issuing a statement as above. Then the file path should be "../images/ball.png" because the method "getClass()" will return the directory name, in which the class that issues the above statement resides. In our case, the class that issues the above statement is the class GameCanvas.java, which resides in the directory "breakout." Thus, the two dots ".." mean from the current directory "breakout" up one level in the directory structure, which reaches the directory "Source Packages"; the "/images" means from the current directory "Source Packages" down to the directory "images"; one more "/" means entering the directory "images." Thus, "../images/" is the relative path from the GameCanvas.java class to the directory "images." And then, "ball.png" is the image file name. Using the relative path is much more convenient than using an absolute path. Otherwise, as long as the project is moved or copied to other directory, the absolute path must be changed. For fixing the absolute path, the program code should be modified. However, as a user, it is impossible to modify the source code in general.

Java also provides a JAI (Java Advanced Imaging) package, which offers extended image-processing capabilities beyond those found in Java 2D. An intended application domain for JAI is the manipulation of images too large to be loaded into memory in their entirety. However, the extended features are not usually required for programming games. We are simply skipping over it, here.

17.4 Arranging All Bricks in a 2D Format on the GUI: The Project Breakout1

Clearly, the bricks are the new sprites that should be added into the game Breakout. The first version of the game Breakout1 intends to solve this problem. The pseudo code could be as follows:

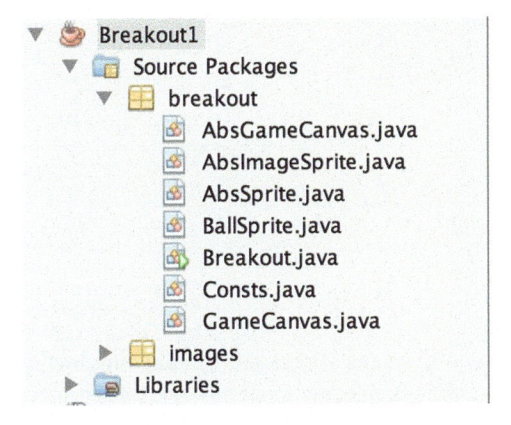

Fig. 17.4 The file structure of the project Breakout1

1. Defining the new classes of AbsSpriteImage.java and BrickSprite.java for building up the new sprite inheritance hierarchy
2. Loading all of images for bricks into an image array
3. Instantiating a brick and randomly assigning one of the images to the brick
4. Arranging all of bricks into a 2D format on the GUI

17.4.1 Defining the Classes AbsSpriteImage.java and BrickSprite.java

As discussed above, the new sprite inheritance hierarchy for the game Breakout shown in Fig. 17.3 needs to create a new image branch with four new classes in order to deal with image sprites. First of all, we need to define the root class AbsImageSprite.java for the new image branch as shown in Listing 17.1.

Listing 17.1 The root class AbsSpriteImage.java in the project Breakout1

```
 1 /*
 2  * AbsSpriteImage.java - An abstract class that specify an image.
 3  */
 4 package breakout;
 5
 6 import java.awt.Graphics2D;
 7 import java.awt.image.BufferedImage;
 8
13 public abstract class AbsSpriteImage extends AbsSprite {
14
15     private BufferedImage anImage;
16     private int x; // top-left corner
17     private int y; // top-left corner
18     private int width;
19     private int height;
20     private int dx;
21     private int dy;
22
23     public AbsSpriteImage() {
24         super();
25     }
26
27     public abstract void initSprite();
28
29     public abstract void updateSprite();
30
31     // The method for painting an image is the same so that
32     // paintSprite() for images can be implemented here
33     public void paintSprite(Graphics2D g2d) {
34         g2d.drawImage(anImage, getX(), getY(), null);
35     }
36
... // all of getter and setter methods
92 }
```

The definition tells that the class AbsSpriteImage.java is very similar with the class AbsSprite2D.java. It defines x, y, width, and height for an image because an image also has a geometrical shape. The coordinates (x, y) are for the placement of the image; the width and height defines the dimension of the image. But, it has a new attribute BufferedImage, which is for loading the image. In addition, the method paintSprite() can be implemented since no matter what image is in the game Breakout, the painting method is the same one drawImage() without any special settings.

Because the first version of the project Breakout1 is only for treating bricks, we define the class BrickSprite.java first. A brick is an image; thus, the class BrickSprite.java extends AbsSpriteImage.java. And the brick is a static sprite at this moment; we leave the method updateSprite() "empty." The class BrickSprite.java is cited in Listing 17.2.

Listing 17.2 The class BrickSprite.java in the project Breakout1

```java
1  /*
2   * BrickSprite.java - A class that defines one brick sprite, which is an
3   * image.
4   */
5  package breakout;
6
11 public class BrickSprite extends AbsSpriteImage {
12
13     @SuppressWarnings("OverridableMethodCallInConstructor")
14     public BrickSprite() {
15         super();
16         initSprite();
17         // some parameters will be assigned by the method
18         // initComponent() defined in the class GameCanvas in order to
19         // arrange all bricks in a 2D array format.
20     }
21
22     @Override
23     public void initSprite() {
24         setX(0); // unknown at this moment
25         setY(0); // unknown at this moment
26         setWidth(Consts.BRICK_W);
27         setHeight(Consts.BRICK_H);
28         setActive(false); // a static sprite
29         setVisible(true);
30     }
31
32     @Override
33     public void updateSprite() {
34         // at this moment, bricks are static.
35     }
36 }
```

17.4.2 The Class GameCanvas.java Initializes All of the bricks

Now, the class GameCanvas.java can instantiate the objects of class BrickSprite.java. However, we need to define the following constants for arranging the set of bricks:

1. Every brick has the same width and height. Therefore, two constants BRICK_W = 30 and BRICK_H = 15 could be defined for matching with the size of the brick images.
2. Usually, the GUI width CV_WIDTH is set up first before arranging sprites. But, this time, we would like to let the total width of one-row bricks fits with the width of the GUI frame. For that, the constant CV_WIDTH is not assigned but calculated as "CV_WIDTH = BRICKS_PER_ROW * BRICK_W." That is, we need to preset the constant BRICKS_PER_ROW = 15, then CV_WIDTH = 15 * 30 = 450.
3. We also define another constant MAX_ROWS = 4. Consequently, the total number of bricks = BRICK_PER_ROW * MAX_ROWS = 15 * 4 = 60.

And then, the class GameCanvas.java loads eight brick images and stores them into an image array brickImages[]. After that, the class instantiates total 60 bricks and randomly assigns one of the images stored in the brickImages[] to each individual brick.

As Fig. 17.2 shows, the set of bricks are arranged as a 2D format on the GUI. A new question is how to arrange the 60 bricks onto the 2D format?

17.4.3 Deriving the Algorithm for Converting a 1D Array to a 2D Array

The class GameCanvas.java needs to instantiate 60 bricks. We may imagine that it uses a "for" loop to do it such that each brick has one of index of [0] to [number of bricks − 1]. They form a 1D array. But, they should be arranged as a 2D format. That is, we need to find a corresponding algorithm for converting a 1D array to a 2D array.

As we know that every element in a 2D array has an index consisting of two numbers [row][col]. For example, an element at row 1 and column 5 has an index of [0][4]. But every element in a 1D array has an index with only one number such as [5]. In other words, mapping a 1D array into a 2D array is the mapping of their indexes. The mapping process is illustrated in Fig. 17.5, which displays a 1D array that holds 15 objects with index [0] to [14]. Suppose that the 2D array has 5 objects in one row with the index of [0] to [4], then the objects in the first row have index of [0][0] to [0][4], where the first [0] is the row index. The objects in the second row have index of [1][0] to [1][4] with the row index of [1]. And the objects in the third row have index of [2][0] to [2][4] with the row index of [2]. Therefore, the first five objects with index of [0] to [4] in the 1D array are naturally mapped to the first row in the 2D array.

Then, the object with the index [5] and up in the 1D array should be mapped to which position in which row in the 2D array? For that mapping, we need to use the "division" and "mod" operations. Taking the index [5] in the 1D array as an example, the "division" operation (the original index in the 1D array/the row length of the 2D array) gives the quotient of (5/5) = 1, and the "mod" operation gives the remainder of (5 % 5) = 0. The quotient of 1 gives the object a row index of [1], which refers to the second row in the 2D array. The remainder of 0 is the index [0] along the second row in the 2D array. That is, the original index of [5] in the 1D array should be mapped to the index of [1][0] in the 2D array, which is the first position at the second row.

Similarly, the object with the original index of [6] in the 1D array will map to (6/5 = 1) and (6 % 5 = 1), which is index of [1][1] that refers to the second position of the second row in the 2D array. Applying this calculation, (10/5 = 2) and (10 % 5 = 0) indicates that the object with the index of [10] in the 1D array is mapped to the index of [2][0] that refers to the first position at the third row in the 2D array. Thus, we can easily map the bricks in the 1D array to be arranged in a 2D format.

Once we find the index [row][col] in the 2D array, the coordinates (x, y) of the up-left corner of each brick can be calculated as follows:

```
x = (index-1D % BRICK_PER_ROW) * BRICK_W
y = (index-1D / BRICK_PER_ROW) * BRICK_H
```

All of the constants are defined in the class Consts.java, and the calculations are coded in the method initBrickSprites() in the class GameCanvas.java.

17.4.4 The Implementation of the Class GameCanvas.java

After we found the mapping algorithm, we can implement the class GameCanvas.java now. The code of the class is shown in Listing 17.3.

Fig. 17.5 Mapping 1D array to 2D arrangement

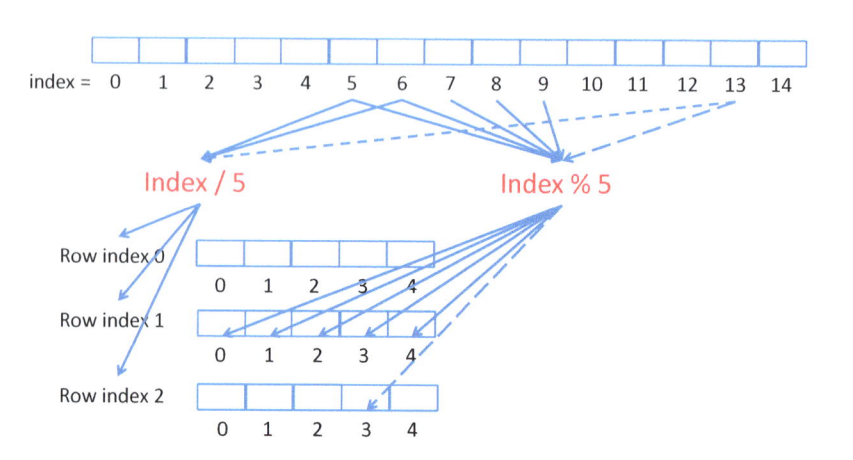

17.4 Arranging All Bricks in a 2D Format on the GUI: The Project Breakout1

Listing 17.3 The class GameCanvas.java in the project Breakout1

```java
1  /*
2   * GameCanvas.java - A class that implements the game canvas.
3   */
4  package breakout;
5
6  import java.awt.image.BufferedImage;
7  import java.io.IOException;
8  import javax.imageio.ImageIO;
9
14 public class GameCanvas extends AbsGameCanvas {
15
16     private BufferedImage[] brickImages; // holds 8 different brick images
17
18     public GameCanvas() {
19         super();
20         initComponent();
21     }
22
23     private void initComponent() {
24         brickImages = new BufferedImage[Consts.NUM_BRICK_IMAGES];
25         initBrickImages();
26         initBrickSprites();
27         startGame();
28     }
29
30     private void initBrickImages() { // get and hold 8 brick imagess
31         try {
32             brickImages[0]
33                     = ImageIO.read(getClass().getResource("../images/aquaTile.gif"));
34             brickImages[1]
35                     = ImageIO.read(getClass().getResource("../images/blackTile.gif"));
36             brickImages[2]
37                     = ImageIO.read(getClass().getResource("../images/blueTile.gif"));
38             brickImages[3]
39                     = ImageIO.read(getClass().getResource("../images/greenTile.gif"));
40             brickImages[4]
41                     = ImageIO.read(getClass().getResource("../images/lightGreyTile.gif"));
42             brickImages[5]
43                     = ImageIO.read(getClass().getResource("../images/purpleTile.gif"));
44             brickImages[6]
45                     = ImageIO.read(getClass().getResource("../images/redTile.gif"));
46             brickImages[7]
47                     = ImageIO.read(getClass().getResource("../images/yellowTile.gif"));
48         } catch (IOException ex) {
49         }
50     }
51
52     private void initBrickSprites() {
53         BrickSprite aBrick;
54         int numBricks = Consts.BRICKS_PER_ROW * Consts.MAX_ROWS;
55         int x = 0;
56         int y = 30; // leave a line for the value of global score
57         int idx;
```

```
58              for (int i = 0; i < numBricks; i++) {
59                  if ((i % Consts.BRICKS_PER_ROW == 0) && (i != 0)) {
60                      x = 0;
61                      y += Consts.BRICK_H; // move to next row
62                  }
63                  aBrick = new BrickSprite();
64                  aBrick.setX(x);
65                  x += Consts.BRICK_W; // move the coor x to the next position
66                  aBrick.setY(y); // stay at the same row
67                  idx = (int) (Math.random() * Consts.NUM_BRICK_IMAGES);
68                  aBrick.setAnImage(brickImages[idx]); // randomly pick up an image
69                  getSpriteAry().add(aBrick);
70              }
71          }
72  }
73
```

The class GameCanvas.java provides the method initComponent() to invoke two methods initBrickImages() and initBrickSprites() for initializing all of the bricks. The method initBrickImages() (lines 30–50) simply reads in eight images from the subdirectory "images" in the file structure of the project as shown in Fig. 17.4 and stores them in an array brickImages[]. And then, the method initBrickSprites() (lines 52–71) instantiates bricks one by one with a randomly selected image from the array brickImages[]. At the same time, it applies the mapping algorithm to determine the index of the 2D array and then calculates the coordinates of (x, y) for every brick in order to fit the brick at the 2D arrangement on the GUI. Finally, it adds every brick into the global spriteAry.

Once the three classes, AbsSpriteImage.java, BrickSprite.java, and GameCanvas.java, are prepared, the three-layer game structure is adopted to build up the project Breakout1. All of the other abstract classes are the same as coded in the game Pong. Only the global data structure spriteAry is modified as

```
ArrayList spriteAry = new
    ArrayList<AbsSpriteImage>()
```

where its type is AbsSpriteImage instead of AbsSprite2D because all sprites in the game Breakout are images.

17.5 Detecting Collisions by Using PropertyChangeEvent: The Project Breakout2

The second step is to add a BallSprite.java class. The object ball is a bouncing ball. The function of the bouncing ball is to hit the bricks for eliminating them. In other words, collisions between the ball and the bricks become the objective of the game. Definitely, the collisions also bounce the ball back. The bouncing direction depends on the collision occurred on which surface of the brick as shown in Fig. 17.6. Due to that, the collision detections become more complicated.

So far, we consider the collision between two sprites as the intersection between the two bounding rectangles of the two objects. This approach is simple, but it cannot be applied for the game Breakout since we need to determine on which surface the ball collides with the brick. We need to design another approach.

The new approach sets up computations to find out the coordinates of the left, right, top, and bottom points of the ball, and then check the bounding rectangle of a brick contains which point of the ball when a collision occurs. For example, if the bounding rectangle of a brick contains the coordinates of the left point of the ball, it implies that a collision happens on the right side of the brick; the ball will be bounced back along the x direction by negating its dx value.

Since the class GameCanvas.java initializes all of the sprites, it is that place for checking possible collisions between two different sprites. In the game Pong, we implemented the method detectCollision() in the class BallSprite.java and passed the object gameCanvas into the class BallSprite.java for providing other objects that possibly collide with the ball Sprite. In the game Breakout, we would like to introduce an "opposite" way for checking collisions. That is, when the ball is animated, its coordinates (x, y) are changed. We are going to pass the dynamically changed coordinates' values to the

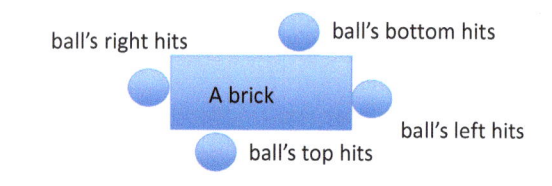

Fig. 17.6 The collisions between the ball and a brick

17.5 Detecting Collisions by Using PropertyChangeEvent: The Project Breakout2

class GameCanvas.java for checking possible collisions with other objects. This new strategy opens a new way for communications among all of the objects.

Surely, a new question followed is how to pass the dynamically changed coordinates of the ball sprite from the class BallSprite.java into the class GameCanvas.java? For a better understanding, we would be better to have a brief review about event handling. Taking a button and the ActionEvent as an example, we learned a piece of code as follows:

```
// a source component
JButton aBtn = new JButton();
// registers a listener
aBtn.addActionListener(
  new MyActionListener());
```

These two statements indicate that a button aBtn registered with an event listener myActionListener. When a mouse clicks on the component aBtn, an action event is generated; when the action event listener myActionListener receives the event, its event handler is invoked to handle the event as a response to the click action. Here, an external human player triggers the action event. For handling the event, we need a special setting: (1) identifying an event source component, (2) implementing an event listener with an event handler, and (3) registering the source component with the event listener. After that setting, when the event source component creates an event due to a corresponding action, the event listener can receive the event that triggers the event handler to handle the event.

Similarly, if we understand the coordinates (x, y) are one of the properties of the ballSprite and define a value changing of the coordinates as an action, then the action will generate an event, and we can also design an event listener to listen the event and handle the event. Fortunately, Java implemented this idea as a PropretyChangeEvent and provides an Interface PropertyChangeListener as the event listener for listening and handling the PropertyChangeEvent. Therefore, the ball-Sprite is the source component that can register with the object (new MyPropertyChangeListener()) as follows:

```
// a source component
BallSprite aBall = new BallSprite();
// registers with a listener
aBall.addPropertyChangeListener(
  new MyPropertyChangeListener())
```

Because the class GameCanvas.java instantiates the object aBall, the first statement should be implemented inside the class GameCanvas.java. Hence, the inner class of the event listener MyPropertyChangeListener in the second statement should also be implemented in the class GameCanvas.java.

However, the class BallSprite.java is a user-defined class. The programmer has to code everything, which is different from the built-in class, such as JButton. For registering with the listener, the BallSprite.java should define a method addPropertyChangeListener() to accept the object of "new MyPropertyChangeListener()." Meanwhile, as long as a new value of (x, y) generated, the class BallSprite.java should issue a fire action internally for sending a property change event out of the class BallSprite.java to the event listener that resides in the class GameCanvas.java. For supporting this action firing, Java provides a special built-in class PropertyChangeSupport. Therefore, for making the class BallSprite.java as the "source component," the programmer should add the following piece of code into the class BallSprite.java:

```
// in the class BallSprite.java
// declare an event source
private PropertyChangeSupport pChange;
// instantiate the event source object
pChange = new PropertyChangeSupport(this);
// provide the following method in the source
// component aBall to allow the event
//source registering with the event listener
public void addPropertyChangeListener(
    PropertyChangeListener pcl) {
    pChange.addPropertyChangeListener(pcl);
}
// when needed, the event source object fires
// an property change event
pChange.firePropertyChange("newP", oldLoc,
    newLoc); // fires an event
```

It seems that the pChange works as a real event source and it registers with the event listener pcl. When the property coordinates are changed, the pChange fires an event with the invocation of the method firePropertyChange() for sending out the event with the name of "newP" and the old value of oldLoc as well as the new value of newLoc, where the name "newP" is the identification of this event; the value carried by the variable oldLoc is the old value of the property, and the value carried by the variable newLoc is the new value of the property. When the MyPropertyChangeListener defined in the class GameCanvas.java receives the new event of the property change, the event handler in the listener performs the coded function for treating the property change. For a better understanding, Fig. 17.7 depicts the interactions among the coded statements inside two classes BallSprite.java and GameCanvas.java. The marks 1–6 on the figure indicate the order of settings and communications.

We would like to explain the meaning of the codes following the marks 1–6. (1) The class BallSprite.java initializes the object pChange for supporting the property changes. Then, the BallSprite.java class adds a method addPropertyChangeListener(pcl) for assigning the parameter pcl to the pChange.addPropertyChangeListener(). (2) The GameCanvas.java class implements an inner class LocChangeListener with an event handler method proper-

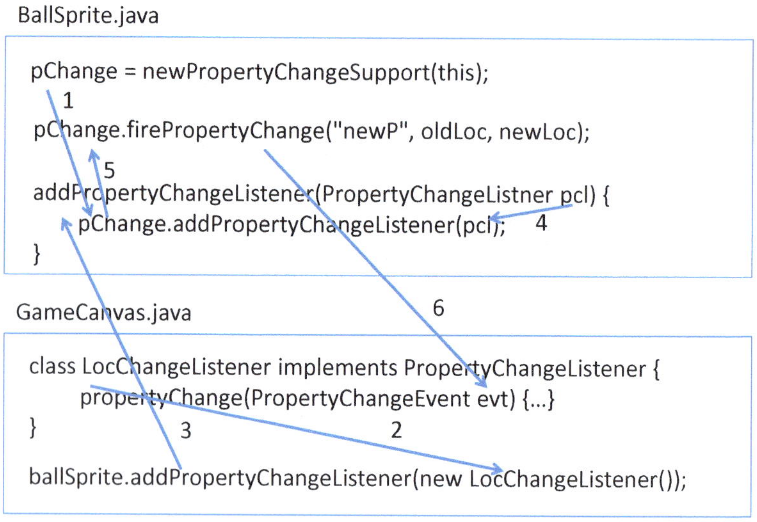

Fig. 17.7 The linkages of methods for making the data communication channel

BallSprite.java

```
pChange = newPropertyChangeSupport(this);
pChange.firePropertyChange("newP", oldLoc, newLoc);
addPropertyChangeListener(PropertyChangeListner pcl) {
    pChange.addPropertyChangeListener(pcl);
}
```

GameCanvas.java

```
class LocChangeListener implements PropertyChangeListener {
    propertyChange(PropertyChangeEvent evt) {...}
}
ballSprite.addPropertyChangeListener(new LocChangeListener());
```

tyChange(), which waits for a property change event and handles the event for a predefined goal. (3) After the GameCancas.java instantiated the ballSprite object, the object registers with the event listener by calling the method addPropertyChangeListener() with the actual parameter "new LocChangeListener()" object. (4) Since the method addPropertyChangeListener() was defined in the class BallSprite.java, the object of the event listener "new LocChangeListener()" is passed into the class BallSprite.java and is assigned to the pChange object. (5) As long as the property coordinates (x, y) of the ball object is changed, the method pChange.firePropertyChange() is immediately issued to carry the oldLoc value and the newLoc value with an identification "newP" and (6) send them to the event listener resides in the GameCanvas.java class to be handled.

Clearly, the class BallSprite.java is the sender for sending the new value of the changed property with the event to the receiver of the event listener. If we would like to perform the collision detection, then when the inner class LocChangeListener inside the class GameCanvas.java receives the event, the event handler propertyChange() performs the following functions.

1. It gets the event identification "newP."
2. It gets the value of the new location newLoc of the ballSprite.
3. It constructs a bounding rectangle of the ball at the new position.
4. It finds the four points of the ball.
5. It goes over every brick stored in the global spriteAry for checking whether one brick contains any of the four points of the ball.
6. If one brick contains the point of ballLeft or ballRight, it assigns the variable hitPosn with "hitX"; if the brick contains the point of ballTop or ballBottom, it assigns the variable hitPosn with "hitY"; and if no containing, it assigns the variable hitPosn with the value of "noHit."
7. It invokes the method ballSprite.hitBrickResetVelocity(hitPosn) to pass the value held by the variable hitPosn to the class BallSprite.java for bouncing the ballSprite according to the direction indicated by the value of "hitX" or "hitY." This is a two-way communication between the classes BallSprite.java and GameCanvas.java.

The detailed implementations of the two classes are cited in Listing 17.4.

Listing 17.4 The new class BallSprite.java and the modified class GameCanvas.java in the project Breakout2

```
1  /*
2   * BallSprite.java - A class that defines an image ball sprite
3   */
4  package breakout;
5  ...
17 public class BallSprite extends AbsSpriteImage {
18
19     private BufferedImage ballImg;
20     private PropertyChangeSupport pChange;
```

```
21
22      public BallSprite() {
23          super();
24          pChange = new PropertyChangeSupport(this);
25      }
26
27      @Override
28      public void initSprite() {
29  ...
42      }
43
44      @Override
45      public void updateSprite() {
46          setX(getX() + getDx());
47          setY(getY() + getDy());
48          checkEnv();
49          // send the new position to its listener for checking whether
50          // it hits bricks or not
51          fireNewLocation(new Point(getX(), getY()));
52      }
53
54      // collides with the four edges to make a bouncing ball
55      public void checkEnv() {
56          if ((getX() <= 0)
57                  || ((getX() + 2 * Consts.BALL_RADIUS) >= Consts.MAXX)) {
58              setDx(-getDx());
59          }
60          if ((getY() <= 0)
61                  || ((getY() + 2 * Consts.BALL_RADIUS) >= Consts.MAXY)) {
62              setDy(-getDy());
63          }
64      }
65
66      public void fireNewLocation(Point p) {
67          Point oldLoc = new Point(0, 0);
68          Point newLoc = p;
69          pChange.firePropertyChange("newP", oldLoc, newLoc);
70      }
71
72      public void hitBrickResetVelocity(String dir) {
73          if (dir.equals("hitX")) {
74              setDx(-getDx());
75          } else if (dir.equals("hitY")) {
76              setDy(-getDy());
77          }
78      }
79
80      public void addPropertyChangeListener(PropertyChangeListener pcl) {
81          pChange.addPropertyChangeListener(pcl);
82      }
83  }

 1  /*
 2   * GameCanvas.java - A class that implements the game canvas.
 3   */
```

```
 4 package breakout;
 5 …
19 public class GameCanvas extends AbsGameCanvas {
20
21     private BufferedImage[] brickImages; // holds 8 different brick images
22     private BallSprite ballSprite;
23
24     public GameCanvas() {
25         super();
26         initComponent();
27         startGame();
28     }
29
30     private void initComponent() {
31         brickImages = new BufferedImage[Consts.NUM_BRICK_IMAGES];
32         initBrickImages();
33         initBrickSprites();
34         initBallSprite();
35     }
36
37     private void initBrickImages() { // get and hold 8 brick imagess
56 …
57     }
58
59     private void initBrickSprites() {
60 …
78     }
79
80     public void initBallSprite() {
81         ballSprite = new BallSprite();
82         ballSprite.initSprite();
83         ballSprite.addPropertyChangeListener(new LocChangeListener());
84         getSpriteAry().add(ballSprite);
85     }
86
87     class LocChangeListener implements PropertyChangeListener {
88
89         @Override
90         public void propertyChange(PropertyChangeEvent evt) {
91             if ((evt.getPropertyName()).equals("newP")) {
92                 Point newL = (Point) evt.getNewValue();
93                 Rectangle ballRect = new Rectangle((int) newL.getX(),
94                         (int) newL.getY(), 2 * Consts.BALL_RADIUS,
95                         2 * Consts.BALL_RADIUS);
96                 Point ballLeft = new Point((int) ballRect.getX(),
97                         (int) (ballRect.getY() + ballRect.getHeight() / 2));
98                 Point ballRight = new Point(
99                         (int) (ballRect.getX() + ballRect.getWidth()),
100                        (int) (ballRect.getY() + ballRect.getHeight() / 2));
101                Point ballTop = new Point(
102                        (int) (ballRect.getX() + ballRect.getWidth() / 2),
103                        (int) (ballRect.getY()));
104                Point ballBottom = new Point(
105                        (int) (ballRect.getX() + ballRect.getWidth() / 2),
106                        (int) (ballRect.getY() + ballRect.getHeight()));
```

```java
107                    // ball hits bricks
108                    BrickSprite aBrick;
109                    ArrayList<AbsSpriteImage> aryList = getSpriteAry();
110                    String hitPosn = "noHit";
111                    for (AbsSpriteImage element : aryList) {
112                        // only it is a brick for the checking
113                        if (element instanceof BrickSprite) {
114                            aBrick = (BrickSprite) element;
115                            if (aBrick.isVisible()) { // it exists
116                                Rectangle brickRect = new Rectangle(aBrick.getX(),
117                                        aBrick.getY(), aBrick.getWidth(),
118                                        aBrick.getHeight());
119                                if (brickRect.contains(ballLeft)) {
120                                    aBrick.setVisible(false);
121                                    hitPosn = "hitX";
122                                } else if (brickRect.contains(ballRight)) {
123                                    aBrick.setVisible(false);
124                                    hitPosn = "hitX";
125                                } else if (brickRect.contains(ballTop)) {
126                                    aBrick.setVisible(false);
127                                    hitPosn = "hitY";
128                                } else if (brickRect.contains(ballBottom)) {
129                                    aBrick.setVisible(false);
130                                    hitPosn = "hitY";
131                                }
132                                if (!(hitPosn.equals("noHit"))) {
133                                    ballSprite.hitBrickResetVelocity(hitPosn);
134                                    break; // ones hit, don't hit other brick
135                                }
136                            } else { // the element is not valid, go to the next
137                            }
138                        }
139                    }
140                }
141            }
142        }
143 }
```

17.6 Using Mouse to Control the Paddle Sprite: The Project Breakout3

The new version Breakout3 adds the paddle sprite, which is controlled by the user to prevent the ball from falling down to the bottom edge of the playing field. Adding a new sprite is not difficult. It could be realized through two steps.

First step is to add the paddle object by adding a new class PaddleSprite.java, which extends AbsSpriteImage.java and implements the method initSprite(). In this game Breakout, the player will use mouse to control the paddleSprite instead of keys. Because paddle is dragged by the player but not animated through the game loop, we can leave the method updateSprite() of the class PaddleSprite.java with an empty body. However, we would still like to add the object paddleSprite into the global spriteAry because this setting allows the paintComponent() method defined in the class AbsGameCanvas.java to paint the paddle and other sprites on the GUI. After finishing this step, the paddle can be seen in the game screen.

Second step, we should check the collisions between the ball sprite and the paddle sprite to allow the paddle bouncing the ball. Due to the fact that the class GameCanvas.java has implemented the inner class LocChangeListener for accepting the new coordinates sent out from the ballSprite for checking the collisions between the ball and the bricks, we can take advantage of the listener and append new codes with the class LocChangeListener for checking whether the ball hits the paddle. The checking principle is the same as checking the collisions between the ballSprite and the bricks. We create a bounding rectangle of the paddle and check whether the bounding rectangle of the paddle contains the point of ballLeft, ballRight, or ballBottom of the ball. The ballTop point is out of consideration because it is impossible to be collided with the paddle here. After finishing the second step, we can see that the ball is bounced by the three edges: top, left, and right of the playing field, by the bricks, and by the paddle.

And then, we start another step to add a mechanism for allowing the player to control the paddle and the ball. We have experienced the control of the paddle in the game Pong by employing the key event listener. Here, we change it to use the mouse device. The reason for making this change is that in the game Breakout the paddle and the ball not only collide with each other but also work together sometimes. Under this situation, the mouse is more convenient than keys. The following list describes the behaviors of both the ball sprite and the paddle sprite.

1. The initial game screen of the game Breakout statically shows the bricks, the ball, and the paddle at their initial positions, where the ball is placed at the middle position on the paddle as Fig. 17.2 shows. That is, the ball statically stays with the paddle initially. To make it, we have to set the ball's "active" attribute as false to disconnect it from the game loop temporarily.
2. When a player would like to play the game, the player has two different controls. He/she may start the game simply clicks the paddle at the initial position. When the clicked mouse is released, the ball immediately starts animation. That is, the ball sprite is changed from static to be dynamic, and the paddle sprite is moved following the mouse. The player may have another control. He/she can click the mouse on the paddle and drag both the ball and the paddle together to any position along the x-axis until he/she releases the mouse for triggering the ball's animation. This feature allows the player to find a proper position for the ball to start its animation in order to more effectively hit the bricks. During the time period of dragging, the ball and the paddle keep the initial relative position together. After releasing the mouse, the ball sprite animated and bounced; only the paddle sprite follows the movement of the mouse. We will implement the second control in the version Breakout3.
3. If the player loses the ball, the game resets both the ball and the paddle back to the initial position but leave the remaining bricks untouched. And then, the game comes back to the initial situation as described in step 1. The three steps circulate until the number of ball lost exceeds a limitation or all of bricks are gone.

17.7 Applying the UML State Machine to Describe Game States [Samek, M., 2008][1]

A UML state machine is an extension of the traditional FSM (finite-state machine). It associates with a visible diagram for describing a program, a device, and the like. A well-defined UML state machine can guide programmers for avoiding deeply involved if-then-else condition checking and increasing the reusability of codes.

In a fundamental UML state machine, a round rectangle with a state name represents a state. An arrow leaves a state and arrives another state represents a state transition. A label on an arrow indicates the event that causes the state transition. Sometimes, a "/" and actions (actions coded in an event handler) follow the event on the label. Every state machine has a solid circle for representing the initial state and an optional solid circle inside a hollow circle represents the final state.

In order to clearly describe the controls of the ball sprite and the paddle sprite listed in the previous section for making the coding easier, we employ a UML state machine to express the game states as depicted in Fig. 17.8. It is an incomplete UML state machine just for graphically illustrating the state transitions and related actions exist in the three requirements above. In our terminology, the "related actions" actually means the event listener and its event handler.

In the UML state machine shown in Fig. 17.8, the state1 represents the initial state that matches with the first requirement, where the ball and the paddle statically stay together at the middle position along the x-axis of the playing field. As long as the player drags the paddle with the mouse, the state1 is transitioned into the state2, where the PaddleDraggedListener is triggered to make the ball and the paddle together following the mouse dragging, which matches with the second requirement. When the player releases the mouse, the state3 starts, where the MouseReleasedListener makes the ball separating from the paddle and to be bounced around and a new PaddleMovedListener is added to allow the paddle to be moved alone by the mouse. The state3 is the regular state of the game, which satisfies the third requirement in keeping the ball bounced by the edges of the playing field, the brick, and the paddle. Therefore, it is a loop as indicated by the looping curve on the top of the state3. The loop will be terminated when the ball is lost. At this moment, the method fireInitPosition() inside the class BallSprite.java sends out the event signal "initP" through the property change event to the inner class LocChangeListener defined in the class

---
[1][Samek, M., 2008] Miro Samek, "A Crash Course in UML State Machines", 2008. http://www.state-machine.com/psicc2.

17.7 Applying the UML State Machine to Describe Game States [Samek, M., 2008]

Fig. 17.8 A UML state machine illustrates the three states for controlling the ball and the paddle sprites

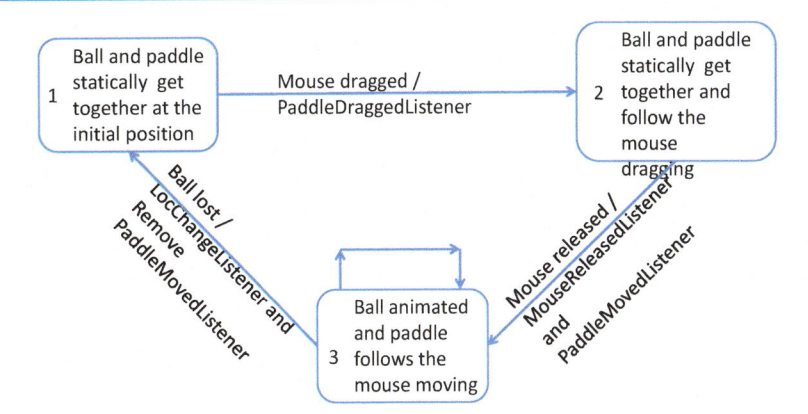

GameCanvas.java, which switches the state from the state3 back to the state1. Meanwhile, the existing listener PaddleMovedListener is removed off in order to enforce the two objects of ball and paddle statically stay together and eliminate the possibility for player to move the paddle alone. The implementations of these states are shown in Listing 17.5.

Listing 17.5 The classes PaddleSprite.java, BallSprite.java, and GameCanvas.java in the project Breakout3

```
 1  /*
 2   * PaddleSprite.java - A class that implements a paddle sprite. Its function
 3   * is to prevent the ball falling down to the bottom edge of the game canvas.
 4   */
 5  package breakout;
 6
 7  import java.awt.image.BufferedImage;
 8  import java.io.IOException;
 9  import javax.imageio.ImageIO;
10
15  public class PaddleSprite extends AbsSpriteImage {
16
17      public PaddleSprite() {
18          super();
19      }
20
21      @Override
22      public void initSprite() {
23          BufferedImage paddleImg = null;
24          try {
25              paddleImg = ImageIO.read(getClass().getResource("../images/paddle.gif"));
26          } catch(IOException ex) {
27
28          }
29          setActive(true);
30          setVisible(true);
31          setX((Consts.MAXX-Consts.MINX)/2 - Consts.PADDLE_W/2);
32          setY(Consts.MAXY - Consts.PADDLE_INIT_Y);
33          setWidth(Consts.PADDLE_W);
34          setHeight(Consts.PADDLE_H);
35          setAnImage(paddleImg);
36      }
37
```

```
38      @Override
39      public void updateSprite() {
40      }
41 }
```

```
1  /*
2   * BallSprite.java - A class that defines an image ball sprite
3   */
4  package breakout;
5
6  …
17 public class BallSprite extends AbsSpriteImage {
18
19      private BufferedImage ballImg;
20      private PropertyChangeSupport pChange;
21
22      public BallSprite() {
23          super();
24          pChange = new PropertyChangeSupport(this);
25      }
26
27      @Override
28      public void initSprite() {
29          try {
30              ballImg = ImageIO.read(getClass().getResource("../images/ball.png"));
31          } catch (IOException ex) {
32          }
33          setAnImage(ballImg);
34          setX((Consts.MAXX - Consts.MINX) / 2 - Consts.BALL_RADIUS);
35          setY(Consts.MAXY - Consts.PADDLE_INIT_Y - 2 * Consts.BALL_RADIUS);
36          setWidth(2 * Consts.BALL_RADIUS);
37          setHeight(2 * Consts.BALL_RADIUS);
38          setDx(1);
39          setDy(2);
40          setActive(false);
41          setVisible(true);
42      }
43
44      @Override
45      public void updateSprite() {
46  …
52      }
53
54      // collides with the four edges to make a bouncing ball
55      public void checkEnv() {
56          if ((getX() <= 0
57                  || ((getX() + 2 * Consts.BALL_RADIUS) >= Consts.MAXX)) {
58              setDx(-getDx());
59          }
60          if (getY() <= 0) {
61              setDy(-getDy());
62          }
63          if ((getY() + 2 * Consts.BALL_RADIUS) >= Consts.MAXY) {
64              setActive(false);
65              setX((Consts.MAXX - Consts.MINX) / 2 - Consts.BALL_RADIUS);
```

17.7 Applying the UML State Machine to Describe Game States [Samek, M., 2008]

```
66                  setY(Consts.MAXY - Consts.PADDLE_INIT_Y - 2 * Consts.BALL_RADIUS);
67                  setActive(false);
68                  setVisible(true);
69                  Point initP = new Point(getX(), getY());
70                  fireInitLocation(initP);
71              }
72          }
73
74          public void fireNewLocation(Point p) {
75              Point oldLoc = new Point(0, 0);
76              Point newLoc = p;
77              pChange.firePropertyChange("newP", oldLoc, newLoc);
78          }
79
80          public void fireInitLocation(Point p) {
81              Point oldLoc = new Point(0, 0);
82              Point newLoc = p;
83              pChange.firePropertyChange("initP", oldLoc, newLoc);
84          }
85
86          public void hitBrickResetVelocity(String dir) {
87              if (dir.equals("hitX")) {
88                  setDx(-getDx());
89              } else if (dir.equals("hitY")) {
90                  setDy(-getDy());
91              }
92          }
93
94          public void addPropertyChangeListener(PropertyChangeListener pcl) {
95              pChange.addPropertyChangeListener(pcl);
96          }
97      }
```

```
 1  /*
 2   * GameCanvas.java - A class that implements the game canvas.
 3   */
 4  package breakout;
 5
 6  ...
22  public class GameCanvas extends AbsGameCanvas {
23
24      private BufferedImage[] brickImages; // holds 8 different brick images
25      private BallSprite ballSprite;
26      private PaddleSprite paddleSprite;
27
28      public GameCanvas() {
29          super();
30          addMouseMotionListener(new PaddleDraggedListener());
31          addMouseListener(new MouseReleasedListener());
32          initComponent();
33          startGame();
34      }
35
36      private void initComponent() {
37          brickImages = new BufferedImage[Consts.NUM_BRICK_IMAGES];
```

```java
38            initBrickImages();
39            initBrickSprites();
40            initBallSprite();
41            initPaddleSprite();
42        }
43
44    private void initBrickImages() { // get and hold 8 brick imagess
45 ...
64    }
65
66    private void initBrickSprites() {
67 ...
85    }
86
87    public void initBallSprite() {
88 ...
92    }
93
94    public void initPaddleSprite() {
95        paddleSprite = new PaddleSprite();
96        paddleSprite.initSprite();
97        getSpriteAry().add(paddleSprite);
98    }
99
100    class LocChangeListener implements PropertyChangeListener {
101
102        @Override
103        public void propertyChange(PropertyChangeEvent evt) {
104            if ((evt.getPropertyName()).equals("newP")) {
105                Point newL = (Point) evt.getNewValue();
106                Rectangle ballRect = new Rectangle((int) newL.getX(),
107                        (int) newL.getY(), 2 * Consts.BALL_RADIUS,
108                        2 * Consts.BALL_RADIUS);
109                Point ballLeft = new Point((int) ballRect.getX(),
110                        (int) (ballRect.getY() + ballRect.getHeight() / 2));
111                Point ballRight = new Point(
112                        (int) (ballRect.getX() + ballRect.getWidth()),
113                        (int) (ballRect.getY() + ballRect.getHeight() / 2));
114                Point ballTop = new Point(
115                        (int) (ballRect.getX() + ballRect.getWidth() / 2),
116                        (int) (ballRect.getY()));
117                Point ballBottom = new Point(
118                        (int) (ballRect.getX() + ballRect.getWidth() / 2),
119                        (int) (ballRect.getY() + ballRect.getHeight()));
120                // ball hits bricks?
121                BrickSprite aBrick;
122                ArrayList<AbsSpriteImage> aryList = getSpriteAry();
123                String hitPosn = "noHit";
124                for (AbsSpriteImage element : aryList) {
125                    // only it is a brick for the checking
126                    if (element instanceof BrickSprite) {
127                        aBrick = (BrickSprite) element;
128                        if (aBrick.isVisible()) { // it exists
129                            Rectangle brickRect = new Rectangle(aBrick.getX(),
130                                    aBrick.getY(), aBrick.getWidth(),
```

17.7 Applying the UML State Machine to Describe Game States [Samek, M., 2008]

```
131                                aBrick.getHeight());
132                        if (brickRect.contains(ballLeft)) {
133                            aBrick.setVisible(false);
134                            hitPosn = "hitX";
135                        } else if (brickRect.contains(ballRight)) {
136                            aBrick.setVisible(false);
137                            hitPosn = "hitX";
138                        } else if (brickRect.contains(ballTop)) {
139                            aBrick.setVisible(false);
140                            hitPosn = "hitY";
141                        } else if (brickRect.contains(ballBottom)) {
142                            aBrick.setVisible(false);
143                            hitPosn = "hitY";
144                        }
145                        if (!(hitPosn.equals("noHit"))) {
146                            ballSprite.hitBrickResetVelocity(hitPosn);
147                            break; // ones hit, don't hit other brick
148                        }
149                    } else { // the element is not valid, go to the next
150                    }
151                }
152            }
153            // ball hits the paddle?
154            hitPosn = "noHit"; // don't forget re-initialize it
155            Rectangle paddleRect = new Rectangle(paddleSprite.getX(),
156                    paddleSprite.getY(), paddleSprite.getWidth(),
157                    paddleSprite.getHeight());
158            if (paddleRect.contains(ballLeft)) {
159                hitPosn = "hitX";
160            } else if (paddleRect.contains(ballRight)) {
161                hitPosn = "hitX";
162            } else if (paddleRect.contains(ballBottom)) {
163                hitPosn = "hitY";
164            }
165            if (!(hitPosn.equals("noHit"))) {
166                ballSprite.hitBrickResetVelocity(hitPosn);
167            }
168        } else if ((evt.getPropertyName()).equals("initP")) {
169            // there are two mouseMotionListeners, remove the
170            // PaddleMovedListener that is in the array[1]
171            removeMouseMotionListener(getMouseMotionListeners()[1]);
172            paddleSprite.setX((Consts.MAXX - Consts.MINX) / 2 - Consts.PADDLE_W / 2);
173            paddleSprite.setY(Consts.MAXY - Consts.PADDLE_INIT_Y);
174        }
175    }
176 }
177
178 class PaddleDraggedListener extends MouseMotionAdapter {
179
180     @Override
181     public void mouseDragged(MouseEvent evt) {
182         paddleSprite.setX(evt.getX() - Consts.PADDLE_W / 2);
183         ballSprite.setX(evt.getX() - Consts.BALL_RADIUS);
184     }
185 }
```

```
186
187     class PaddleMovedListener extends MouseMotionAdapter {
188
189         @Override
190         public void mouseMoved(MouseEvent evt) {
191             paddleSprite.setX(evt.getX() - Consts.PADDLE_W / 2);
192         }
193     }
194
195     // release mouse to make the ball bouncing and to let the paddle
196     // follow the mouse movement
197     class MouseReleasedListener extends MouseAdapter {
198
199         @Override
200         public void mouseReleased(MouseEvent evt) {
201             ballSprite.setActive(true); // ball starts animation
202             // making ball move up
203             ballSprite.setDx(ballSprite.getDx());
204             if (ballSprite.getDy() < 0) {
205                 ballSprite.setDy(ballSprite.getDy());
206             } else {
207                 ballSprite.setDy(-ballSprite.getDy());
208             }
209             // switch from paddle dragged event to paddle moved event
210             addMouseMotionListener(new PaddleMovedListener());
211         }
212     }
213 }
```

The state1 in the UML state machine corresponds to the first requirement that requires the ball and the paddle statically stay together at the initial position as Fig. 17.2 shows before the game starts. This state is made by the initSprite() method defined in the class PaddleSprite.java (lines 31–32) and the initSprite() method defined in the BallSprite.java class (lines 34–35). These statements define the coordinates of (x, y) for placing them at their initial positions, respectively.

When the player drags the mouse, both the ball and the paddle still stay together to follow the mouse dragging as the state2 said. The mouse dragging action is taken care of by the event handler mouseDragged() (lines 181–185) in the inner class PaddleDraggedListener defined in the class GameCanvas.java. The handler mouseDragged() sets the x-coordinate of both the paddleSprite and the ballSprite to follow the x-coordinate of the mouse (the value of evt. getX()) when the user drags the paddle. It makes them dragged together.

Once the user releases the mouse, the state2 is transitioned into the state3, where the third requirement starts. The inner class MouseReleasedListener in the GameCanvas.java class (lines 197–212) realizes the requirement. The event handler mouseReleased() does the following: (1) immediately sets the active attribute of the ballSprite to be true and sets up its dx and dy to make the ball animated up; (2) as long as the ball animates, the initial condition that keeps both the ball and the paddle stay together defined in the method mouseDragged() is terminated, and a new condition is realized, where the ball won't be controlled by the mouse anymore, and only the paddle should be moved following the movement of the mouse. In other words, the paddle switches from the dragging to the moving. For realizing this action, the inner class PaddleMovedListener (lines 187–193) should dynamically replace the function of the inner class PaddleDraggedListener (lines 178–185) at this moment. This is made through the last statement in the inner class PaddleReleasedListener.

```
addMouseMotionListener(
    new PaddleMovedListener()); (line 210)
```

Since then, the game enters the state3 that is the regular state for playing the game. Therefore, there is a loop around the state3 until the ball lost.

Whenever the ball is lost, the condition should be set back to the initial situation, where both the paddle and the ball should be statically stick together. The ball lost is caught by the method checkEnv() in the class BallSprite.java. When the ball is lost, the "active" attribute of the ball is set to be false, its coordinates (x, y) are set as the initial values, and the method fireInitPosition() is invoked to send the "initP" to the class GameCanvas.java, where the LocChangeListener receives the information and resets the paddle back to the initial position. At this moment, the paddle should be relinquished from the player's control, which is made by the following statement:

```
removeMouseMotionListener(
    getMouseMotionListeners()[1])
```

That statement is inside the inner class LocChangeListener (line 171, GameCanvas.java). The meaning of the index [1] in the above statement is worth to be explained.

Due to the fact that two MouseMotionListeners were added through the following two statements, these two MouseMotionListeners form an array.

```
addMouseMotionListener(new
    PaddleDraggedListener);// (line 30)
addMouseMotionListener(new
    PaddleMovedListener); // (line 210)
```

Hence, the method call getMouseMotionListeners() returns the array. The index of [1], thus, refers to the second added PaddleMovedListener and the first element in the array has the index of [0], which refers to the PaddleDraggedListener. Clearly, the method call removeMouseMotionListener() above removes the getMouseMotionListeners()[1], which is the PaddleMovedListener. This removing breaks the linkage between the paddle and the mouse movement. Consequently, even the player still move the mouse, the paddle won't be moved. Only when the user drags the paddle, both the paddle and the ball can be dragged together since the PaddelDraggedListener still exists. Here, we should distinguish the mouse drag action from the mouse move action.

This example further explores the skills for event programming. First, we should very clearly define what actions should be performed, which in turn defines which event handler should be implemented. And then, we should assert which event listener declares the related event handler. Second, event listeners usually are statically added. However, they can also be dynamically added, switched, or removed.

17.8 Summary

This chapter applies the three-layer game structure for developing a new game Breakout. Actually, this game can be understood as an extension of the game Pong. This thinking makes us easier to design and implement the new game. The framework provides us all of the abstract classes. Even though the "extension" only requires one new class BrickSprite.java. But, we introduce two new techniques. One of them is to change objects from 2D graphical drawing to images. It promotes a new sprite inheritance hierarchy that has a new branch with a new root class of AbsSpriteImage.java. The other is to adopt the new type of event listener PropertyChangeListener for passing dynamically changed data among classes. It opens a new door for communications. In addition, we also specially design the new requirements for the actions of the two objects of ball and paddle. For satisfying the new requirements, we adopt the UML state machine and implement more action listeners to work together with dynamically switch and replacement. All these ideas and techniques are important for gaming.

For completing the game Breakout, we need to add more functions with new versions. We are continuing the discussion in the next chapter.

17.9 Exercises

Self-Reviewing Questions

1. What are the different look-and-feels in using images instead of graphical painting?
2. What technique is applied for getting images and using images?
3. What does the new sprite inheritance hierarchy for image sprites look like?
4. What change should be done in the class AbsGameCanvas.java when we replace sprites with images instead of graphical painting?
5. How to map 1D array storage to 2D array arrangement?
6. How to assign the coordinates (x, y) to each brick sprite?
7. How to use the event listener PropertyChangeListener?
8. What are the advantages and disadvantages in using the PropertyChangeListener instead of other listeners, such as the ActionListener?
9. How to check the collision between the ball and the bricks in the game Breakout?
10. Draw a UML state machine for the three states discussed in the chapter for the game Breakout.
11. How to dynamically switch from one listener to the other in the game Breakout?
12. How to remove an added listener in the game Breakout?

Projects

1. Design and implement a project LaughCry in using the ActionListener. The project has a GUI that has two buttons with labels of "Laughing" and "Crying." When the button "Laughing" is clicked, a laughing face is shown

up on the GUI; when the button "Crying" is clicked, a crying face is shown up. And then, create another version that replaces the ActionListener with the PropertyChangeListener and replaces the buttons on the GUI with a textfield for allowing the user to type in an age with an integer type. When the age is less than or equal to 30, a laughing face shows up; when the age is larger than 30, a crying face shows up. That is, when the value of the property age is changed, the new value is fired and is sent to an inner class that implements the property change handler for switching the images between the laughing face and the crying face.

2. Implement a project that checks collisions between the ball and the bricks without using the PropertyChangeListener.

3. Implement a project that has no bricks but only for realizing the three states related with the ball sprite and the paddle sprite according to the UML state machine shown on Fig. 17.8.

18. Sound Effect and Composite Class: Enriching the Game Breakout

The previous chapter designed and implemented a rudimental version of the game Breakout. This chapter enriches the game by adding more functions, such as, the score system, the counter for the ball-lost, some system level methods, and the like. The more important is that the sound effect is also added. In addition, the group of brick sprites in the game is redesigned as a composite class for further exploring the affects of the redesign on the software structure and the setting of communications among classes. All of these additions also further improve the three-layer game structure.

The objectives of this chapter include:
1. The current score counter.
2. The ball lost counter (live).
3. Renewing the game and more game-level methods.
4. Adding sounds for the game.
5. Widely applying the PropertyChangeListener.
6. Constructing a composite sprite.
7. A better control of the bouncing ball.
8. Extensions of the game Breakout.
9. A better improved three-layer game structure.

The previous chapter applied the incremental development strategy to implement three versions of the game Breakout. Every version added a new sprite and some new functions. The incremental developing strategy that progressively builds up a project step-by-step is a natural approach for programming. The stability and scalability of the three-layer game structure perfectly support this approach. We only need to take care of sprites definitions, their insertions, and their dynamic behaviors in different versions without worrying about the software structure. This chapter continues the development for enriching the game Breakout and for improving the three-layer game structure.

18.1 More Steps for Completing the Game Breakout

For completing the game Breakout, the following tasks should be accomplished:

1. The current score counting needs to be added.
2. The number of ball lost counter needs to be added.
3. The announcement of the game termination needs to be added.
4. The sound is an important part of a game, which should be added.
5. The group of 60 bricks together can be considered as a composite sprite, which is a general topic that should be discussed because composite sprites are popular in games.

18.2 Adding the Current Score Counting and the Ball Lost Counting: Breakout4

We have experienced the score counting mechanism in the game Pong, where the score counting sometimes is not only a simple addition or subtraction of scores; it can also be used to trigger other functions, such as changing the speed of the bouncing ball, increasing the number of bouncing balls, terminating the game, and the like.

On the GUI of the game Breakout, we reserved a space above the bricks. The space is used for displaying the current score. Every time when the ball hits a brick, the current score will be increased certain points that defined in Consts.SCORE_UNIT. The "hit" is determined by the method for detecting collisions between the ball sprite and the bricks, which is implemented in the class GameCanvas.java. Consequently, we simply add a variable numBrickHit in the class GameCanvas.java and employ the statement "score = numBrickHit * Consts.SCORE_UNIT" to count the current score. In addition, a paintCurrScore() method is added for painting it. Actually, all of these functions have discussed in the game Pong already. Considering the method is needed by almost every game, we declare an abstract method paintCurrScore() inside the abstract class AbsGameCanvas.java. But it is implemented in the concrete class GameCanvas.java since different games may require different displaying styles.

Meanwhile, the variable numBrickHit also performs another function. That is, when the value of the variable numBrickHit is equal to the total number of bricks, it implies that all of bricks are hit and gone, which is one of the situations for the termination of the game. The treatment of the termination of the game will be discussed in the following section.

Another new function should be considered is the ball lost counting. The game Breakout allows the player to lose the ball sprite three times at most. It means that if the ball lost for more than three times, the game Breakout should be terminated. Therefore, we need to add a counting mechanism for it. Due to it is a special function for the game Breakout, the ball lost counting should be implemented in the concrete class GameCanvas.java. A variable numBallLost is added in the class GameCanvas.java for that purpose. When its value is less than or equal to the constant Consts.MAX_LOST = 3, the game should reset the ball and the paddle on their initial position automatically to allow the player continuing to play the game. Otherwise, whenever the ball lost value is larger than the constant Consts.MAX_LOST, the game should be terminated.

The detection of the ball lose is performed by the method checkEnv() defined in the BallSprite.java class. When the ball loses, the value of numBallLost is increased by one and the method fireInitLocation() is invoked to send out a message "initP" (initializing the ball position) from the class BallSprite.java to the inner class LocChangeListener defined in the class GameCanvas.java. The event handler of the LocChangeListener invokes the method resetBallAndPaddle() to reset the position of the ball to its initial position through the invocation of the method ballSprite.initXY() and also reset the paddle to its initial position by invoking the method paddleSprite.initXY(). In addition, we have to remove the listener PaddleMovedListener for preventing the paddle from moving if the mouse is moved before the game starts. The related methods defined in the classes BallSprite.java and GameCanvas.java are cited in Listing 18.1.

Listing 18.1 The partial codes of the class GameCanvas.java for the implementations of score counting and ball lost counting

```
1  /*
2   * GameCanvas.java - A class that implements the game canvas.
3   */
4  package breakout;
5
6  ...
25 public class GameCanvas extends AbsGameCanvas {
26
27      ...
30      private int numBrickHit;
31      private int numBallLost;
32      private int currScore;
33
34      public GameCanvas() {
35          ...
38      }
39
40      // it is invoked in the class AbsGameCanvas.java
41      @Override
42      public void initComponent() {
43          ...
49          currScore = 0;
50          numBrickHit = 0;
51          numBallLost = 0;
52          ...
53      }
```

18.2 Adding the Current Score Counting and the Ball Lost Counting: Breakout4

```
 54
 55    private void initBrickImages() { // get and hold 8 brick imagess
 56        ...
 75    }
 76
 77    private void initBrickSprites() {
 78        ...
 96    }
 97
 98    public void initBallSprite() {
 99        ...
103    }
104
105    public void initPaddleSprite() {
106        ...
109    }
110
111    @Override
112    public void paintCurrScore(Graphics2D g2d) {
113        currScore = Consts.SCORE_UNIT * numBrickHit
114                - Consts.PENALTY_LOST_BALL * numBallLost;
115        g2d.setFont(new Font("TimesRoman", Font.BOLD, 20));
116        g2d.setColor(Color.red);
117        g2d.drawString("Score: " + currScore, 20, 20);
118    }
119
120    @Override
121    public void announceTermination(Graphics2D g2d) {
122        g2d.setColor(Color.RED);
123        g2d.drawRect(Consts.MAXX / 2 - 110, Consts.MAXY / 2 - 50, 200, 100);
124        g2d.drawString("Game Terminates", 140, Consts.MAXY / 2);
125        g2d.setColor(Color.BLUE);
126        g2d.drawString("Start A New Game By Clicking The Paddle",
127                40, Consts.MAXY / 2 + 30);
128        addMouseListener(new NewGameListener());
129    }
130
131    // click the paddle to re-start a new game.
132    class NewGameListener extends MouseAdapter {
133
134        @Override
135        public void mouseClicked(MouseEvent evt) {
136            if ((evt.getX() > (Consts.MAXX / 2 - paddleSprite.getWidth() / 2))
137                    && (evt.getX() < (Consts.MAXX / 2 + paddleSprite.getWidth() / 2))
138                    && (evt.getY() > (Consts.MAXY - Consts.PADDLE_INIT_Y))
139                    && (evt.getY() < (Consts.MAXY - Consts.PADDLE_INIT_Y
140                    + Consts.PADDLE_H))) {
141                renewGame();
142            }
143        }
144    }
145
146    class LocChangeListener implements PropertyChangeListener {
147
148        @Override
```

```
149        public void propertyChange(PropertyChangeEvent evt) {
150            switch (evt.getPropertyName()) {
151                case "newP":
152                    ...
228                case "initP":
229                    ...
230                    resetBallAndPaddle();
231                    numBallLost++;
232                    if (numBallLost > Consts.MAX_LOST) {
233                        stopGame();
234                    }
235                    break;
236            }
237        }
238    }
239
240    public void resetBallAndPaddle() {
241        // there are two mouseMotionListeners, remove the
242        // PaddleMovedListener that is in the array[1], which is
243        // PaddleMovedListener so that the paddle won't move
244        if (getMouseMotionListeners().length == 2) {
245            removeMouseMotionListener(getMouseMotionListeners()[1]);
246        }
247        paddleSprite.initXY();
248        ballSprite.initXY();
249    }
250
251    class PaddleDraggedListener extends MouseMotionAdapter {
252
253        ...
258    }
259
260    class PaddleMovedListener extends MouseMotionAdapter {
261
262        ...
266    }
267
268    // release mouse to make the ball bouncing and to let the paddle
269    // follow the mouse movement
270    class MouseReleasedListener extends MouseAdapter {
271
272        ...
287    }
288 }
```

18.3 Adding New Abstract Methods in the Class AbsGameCanvas.java: Breakout4

Previous section tells that both the current score counting and the ball lost counting relate with the termination of the game. When numBrickHit = Consts.BRICKS_PER_ROW * Consts.MAX_ROWS or when numBallLost > Consts. MAX_LOST, the game should be terminated. At this moment the method stopGame() that has been implemented in the class AbsGameCanvas.java is invoked.

When the termination of the game happens, the game is better to give the player an announcement or even better to show some additional screens for indicating the new scores or some statistic data about the players' achievement. Here, we simply add a new method announceTermination() for that purpose. It is game-level method for all games. However, different games may have different implementations of that method. Thus, it is declared as an abstract method in the class AbsGameCanvas.java and is coded in the class GameCanvas.java.

After terminating the game, the player may like to play the game again starting from the initial setting. For that, a new method renewGame() is necessary. It is also a game-level function for all of games. We add it in the class AbsGameCanvas.java. The principle for implementing the method renewGame() is "to reset all of variables that initialize the game."

Reaching this point, we have added the following new methods: paintCurrScore(), announceTermination(), and renewGame(). They are activated to perform their functions through the following invocations. The method paintComponent() defined in the class AbsGameCanvas.java invokes the abstract method paintCurrScore() for displaying the current score and when the Boolean variable "gameOver" is true, the paintComponent() invokes the abstract method announceTermination() for displaying the termination statement. For this version, the method announceTermination() only displays the notation "Game Terminates" and shows a message for the player "Start A New Game By Clicking The Paddle."

If the player would like to play a new game again, he/she follows the termination announcement to click the paddle.

A new added inner class NewGameListener inside the class GameCanvas.java accepts the player's mouse click; its event handler invokes the method renewGame() defined in the abstract class AbsGameCanvas.java to renew the game of Breakout for allowing the player to play a new game again.

Besides these new methods, the initComponent() (line 30) method is a game-level method so that we declare it as an abstract method in the AbsGameCanvas.java class and later the class GameCanvas.java overrides it for different games.

Clearly, as long as adding a new method, we need to consider whether it is a game-level method or not. A game-level method means that the method is needed by all of games. Furthermore, we should consider whether the game-level method should be implemented specifically for individual game. If a game-level method, such as the method renewGame(), that is a general method for every individual game, it can be implemented in the abstract class AbsGameCanvas.java. If a game-level method, such as the method paintCurrScore() or the method announceTermination(), is a specific method for an individual game, we need to declare an abstract method in the class AbsGameCanvas.java and override it later in the concrete class GameCanvas.java.

Following this principle, the code of the modified class AbsGameCanvas.java is shown as Listing 18.2.

Listing 18.2 The modified abstract class AbsGameCanvas.java in the project Breakout4

```
1  /*
2   * AbsGameCanvas.java -- A abstract class that specifies a game canvas.
3   */
4  package breakout43;
5
6  import java.awt.Graphics;
7  import java.awt.Graphics2D;
8  import java.util.ArrayList;
9  import javax.swing.JPanel;
10
15 public abstract class AbsGameCanvas extends JPanel implements Runnable {
16
17     private ArrayList<AbsSpriteImage> spriteAry;
18     private Thread animation;
19     private boolean playing;
20     private boolean gameOver;
21
22     @SuppressWarnings("OverridableMethodCallInConstructor")
23     public AbsGameCanvas() {
24         gameOver = false;
25         spriteAry = new ArrayList<>();
26         initComponent();
27         startGame();
28     }
29
```

```java
30      public abstract void initComponent();
31
32      public abstract void paintCurrScore(Graphics2D g2d);
33
34      public abstract void announceTermination(Graphics2D g2d);
35
36      private void initAnimation() {
37          if (animation == null) {
38              animation = new Thread(this);
39              animation.start();
40          }
41      }
42
43      @Override
44      public void run() {
45          try {
46              while (isPlaying()) {
47                  updateComponent();
48                  repaint();
49                  Thread.sleep(8);
50              }
51          } catch (InterruptedException ex) {
52          }
53      }
54
55      public void updateComponent() {
56          for (AbsSprite element : spriteAry) {
57              if (element.isActive()) {
58                  (element).updateSprite();
59              }
60          }
61      }
62
63      @Override
64      public void paintComponent(Graphics g) {
65          super.paintComponent(g);
66          Graphics2D g2d = (Graphics2D) g;
67
68          for (AbsSprite element : spriteAry) {
69              if (element.isVisible()) {
70                  (element).paintSprite(g2d);
71              }
72          }
73          paintCurrScore(g2d);
74          if (gameOver) {
75              announceTermination(g2d);
76          }
77      }
78
79      public void startGame() {
80          setPlaying(true);
81          initAnimation();
82      }
83
```

```
 84      public void pauseGame() {
 85          setPlaying(false);
 86      }
 87
 88      public void resumeGame() {
 89          setPlaying(true);
 90      }
 91
 92      public void stopGame() {
 93          setPlaying(false);
 94          animation = null;
 95          gameOver = true;
 96      }
 97
 98      public void renewGame() {
 99          stopGame();
100          // remove NewGameListener and PaddleMovedListener
101          removeMouseListener(getMouseListeners()[1]);
102          removeMouseMotionListener(getMouseMotionListeners()[1]);
103          gameOver = false;
104          initComponent();
105          startGame();
106      }
107
108      public ArrayList<AbsSpriteImage> getSpriteAry() {
109          return spriteAry;
110      }
111
112      public boolean isPlaying() {
113          return playing;
114      }
115
116      public void setPlaying(boolean playing) {
117          this.playing = playing;
118      }
119 }
```

This step shows that the abstract class AbsGameCanvas.java is a core class in the three-layer game structure. However, its contents can be modified and enriched along the more games will be developed. New games promote the problem-solving, which in turn creates more methods. All of these new methods improve the three-layer game structure toward its completion.

18.4 Adding Sound Effect with the Game Breakout: Breakout4

An important addition for the version Breakout4 is the sound. Definitely, sound is one of key topics in video games. Java supports three different approaches for making sounds: the basic applet play() method, the more sophisticated built-in class AudioClip, and the top sound package Java Sound API, which supports the recording, playback, and synthesis of sampled audio and Musical Instrument Digital Interface (MIDI) sequences.

The applet play() method is simple. It loads a sound and plays the sound once. It has two major drawbacks. One is that during the time period of the audio data retrieved, the applet's drawing and event handling are frozen. The other is that if the audio won't be found, it won't raise an exception.

The AudioClip class separates loading from playing. It allows sound looping via the method loop() and sound termination via the method stop(). In addition, it supports a large number of file formats, and it permits multiple AudioClips playing at the same time. However, it also has some drawbacks. One of them is the suspension while calling getAudioClip() and newAudioClip() methods. One of solutions is to allocate a separate thread to load the audio while allowing the main program to continue. A big problem with AudioClip is the lack of information about the length of a piece of audio and that information usually is useful in games. A third issue is the lack of capability to perform runtime effects like volume changing, panning between speakers, and echoing.

The Java Sound API has more extensive playback capabilities than AudioClip. It offers low-level access to audio data and the underlying machine's audio hardware and software. The API also supports audio capture and synthesis features. The Java Sound API has two major packages, a javax.sound.sampled package for manipulating sampled audio and a javax.sound.midi package for MIDI sequences. We intend to play some existing sounds in our games; we only consider the package javax.sound.sampled for our usages. The package javax.sound.midi supports the creations of a new melody.

The Java Sound API has the class Line that allows digital audio to be moved around the audio system, for example, from a microphone to the mixer and from the mixer to the speakers. The class Mixer may be a hardware audio device or a software interface. A mixer can accept audio streams coming from several source lines and pass them onto target lines. In Java SE, the Direct Audio Device is the default mixer, which supports playback and recording. The class Line has a subclass DataLine, which adds media features to the class Line, including the ability to determine the current read/write position, to start-stop-pause-resume the sound, and to retrieve status details. The classes of SourceDataLine, TargetDataLine, and Clip are subclasses of the class DataLine, as shown in Fig. 18.1. The SourceDataLine is a buffered stream that adds methods for buffering data and permits chunks of audio to be delivered to the mixer in stages over time without requiring the entire thing to be in memory at once. The TargetDataLine is a streaming line for transferring audio data from the mixer to the speakers. A Clip holds sampled audio small enough to be loaded completely into memory during execution. A Clip is preloaded rather than streamed so its duration is known before playback. This permits it to offer methods for adjusting the starting position and looping.

In general, our games only play simple sounds and the Interface Clip is suitable for our needs. Therefore, here we select the Clip without discussing other classes. As mentioned above, the Clip interface defined in the Java Sound API represents a special kind of data line whose audio data can be loaded prior to playback, instead of being streamed in real time. Because the data is preloaded and has a known length, we can set a clip to start playing at any position. We can also create a loop so that when the clip is played it will cycle repeatedly. Loops are specified with a starting and ending sample frame, along with the number of times that the loop should be played. Audio data is loaded into a clip when it is opened. Playback of an audio clip may be started and stopped using the methods of start() and stop(). These methods do not reset the media position. The method start() causes playback to continue from the position where playback was last stopped. To restart playback from the beginning of the clip's audio data, simply follow the invocation of stop with setFramePosition(0), which rewinds the media to the beginning of the clip.

When we found a suitable sound stored in a disk file, say aSound.wav, we can preload the sound stored in the disk file into the memory and play it later. The loading procedure is very similar with opening a file for reading. The procedure for reading a file has been discussed several times in previous chapters. It consists of the following major steps:

1. Allocating the file name, say "word.txt"
2. Copying or moving the file into a subfolder inside the project, say "txt," and finding its file path, say "../txt/word.txt"
3. Allocating the URL corresponding to the file path by using the statement "URL url = getClass().getResource("../txt/word.txt");"
4. Allocating a pipe "BufferedReader reader = new BufferedReader(url.getPath());" for reading
5. Reading a line from the file "String line = reader.readLine();"

Similar with the steps above, for making a sound clip from a sound file are as follows:

1. Allocating a disk file, say "aSound.wav" that stored a sound in a format including "wav," "tiff," and "au"
2. Copying or moving it into a subfolder in the project, say "sounds" and finding its relative file path as 'String filePath = "../sounds/aSound.wav"'
3. Converting the file path to be either a File or a URL:

   ```
   File aSoundF = new File(filePath)
   URL url = getClass().getResource(filePath)
   ```

4. Allocating an reading channel AudioInputStream from the aSoundF or the URL:

   ```
   AudioInputStream audioIn = AudioSystem.
      getAudioInputStream(aSoundF)
   AudioInputStream audioIn = AudioSystem.
      getAudioInputStream(url)
   ```

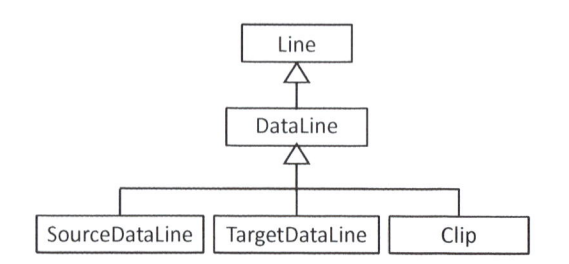

Fig. 18.1 The UML class diagram of class Line and its subclasses

18.4 Adding Sound Effect with the Game Breakout: Breakout4

5. Allocating a sound Clip resource via the static method AudioSystem.getClip():

   ```
   Clip clip = AudioSystem.getClip()
   ```

6. Opening the clip to load sound from the audio input stream:

   ```
   clip.open(audioIn);
   // for small-sized file only
   ```

7. Playing the clip by invoking either the start() or the loop() method:

   ```
   clip.start(); // play once
   clip.loop(0); // repeat none (play once)
   clip.loop(3); // repeat 3 times (play 4 times)
   clip.loop(Clip.LOOP_CONTINOUSLY);
   // repeat forever
   ```

8. Stopping the play with stop(), which may be useful to stop a continuous loop():

   ```
   if (clip.isRunning()) {
       clip.stop();
   }
   ```

Where, the class AudioSystem acts as the entry point to the sampled-audio system resources. This class includes a number of methods for converting audio data between different formats and for translating between audio files and streams. Among them, the method getAudioInputStream() is used to obtain an audio input stream from a File or from a URL, and the method getClip() is used to obtain a clip for playing back an audio or an audio stream. Furthermore, the Interface Clip defines a set of methods. The method clip.open() opens the clip with the format and audio data present in the provided audio input stream. Clearly, the method clip.start() plays back the audio input stream audioIn once, and the method clip.loop() repeatedly plays back the audio input stream audioIn according to the specified number of times.

For supporting the game Breakout, we installed four sound disk files in the subdirectory "sounds" of the project Breakout4. One of the four sounds is for the ball hits with left, right, or top edge; the other is for the ball hits on bricks; the third one is for the ball touches the paddle; the last one is for the ball lost event. We define a MakeClip.java class to implement the steps listed above for loading every individual sound from the corresponding disk file as a clip. The class MakeClip.java also provides two methods play() and stop() for playing back the preloaded clips. Meanwhile, we define another class AllClips.java to instantiate four objects of the class MakeClip.java for loading four sounds from the four source files, respectively, and organize them into an array with the name of "clips." Therefore, a specific sound in the array can be conveniently accessed through an index. In addition, the class AllClips() also provides a specially defined static method getClips(int idx) for the project to get an object of the class LoadSound.java from the array clips through the parameter idx and immediately let the object invoke the method play() for playing the specific sound. The reason for designing the method getClips() as a static method since a static method can be invoked through the class name AllClip without the necessity of instantiating an object. The complete implementation can be found from the codes in Listing 18.3.

Listing 18.3 The sounds related classes MakeClip.java, AllClips.java, BallSprite.java, and GameCanvas.java in the project Breakout4

```
 1 /*
 2  * MakeClip.java - A class that loads all sounds from disk files as clips.
 3  */
 4 package breakout;
 5
 6 import java.io.IOException;
 7 import java.net.URL;
 8 import javax.sound.sampled.AudioInputStream;
 9 import javax.sound.sampled.AudioSystem;
10 import javax.sound.sampled.Clip;
11 import javax.sound.sampled.LineUnavailableException;
12 import javax.sound.sampled.UnsupportedAudioFileException;
13
18 public class MakeClip {
19
```

```java
20      private String filename;
21      private Clip clip = null;
22
23      public MakeClip() {
24      }
25
26      public void loadClip() {
27          try {
28              URL url = getClass().getResource(getFilename());
29              AudioInputStream audioIn = AudioSystem.getAudioInputStream(url);
30              clip = AudioSystem.getClip();
31              clip.open(audioIn);
32          } catch (LineUnavailableException ex) {
33              System.out.println(ex.getMessage());
34          } catch (UnsupportedAudioFileException ex) {
35              System.out.println(ex.getMessage());
36          } catch (IOException ex) {
37              System.out.println(ex.getMessage());
38          }
39      }
40
41      public void play() {
42          if (clip != null) {
43              if (clip.isRunning()) {
44                  clip.stop();   // stop the clip if it is running
45              }
46              clip.setFramePosition(0); // rewind to the beginning
47              clip.start();
48          }
49      }
50
51      public void stop() {
52          if (clip != null) {
53              clip.stop();
54              clip.setFramePosition(0); // start over
55          }
56      }
57
58      public void setFilename(String filename) {
59          this.filename = filename;
60      }
61
62      public String getFilename() {
63          return filename;
64      }
65  }
```

```java
1  /*
2   * AllClips.java - A class that holds all clips and provides a static
3   * getter method for getting a clip so that it can be invoked from anywhere.
4   */
5  package breakout;
6
11 public class AllClips {
12
```

18.4 Adding Sound Effect with the Game Breakout: Breakout4

```
13      private String[] soundFiles;
14      private static MakeClip[] clips;
15
16      public AllClips() {
17          soundFiles = new String[4];
18          soundFiles[0] = "../sounds/TOFF.wav"; // hits wall
19          soundFiles[1] = "../sounds/CRISP.wav"; // hits bricks
20          soundFiles[2] = "../sounds/WBLBEEP.wav"; // hits paddle
21          soundFiles[3] = "../sounds/CRASHBUZ.wav"; // ball lost
22
23          clips = new MakeClip[soundFiles.length];
24          for (int i = 0; i < soundFiles.length; i++) {
25              MakeClip aClip = new MakeClip();
26              aClip.setFilename(soundFiles[i]);
27              aClip.loadClip();
28              clips[i] = aClip;
29          }
30      }
31
32      public static MakeClip getClips(int idx) {
33          return clips[idx];
34      }
35  }
```

```
 1  /*
 2   * BallSprite.java - A class that defines an image ball sprite
 3   */
 4  package breakout;
 5
 6  import java.awt.Point;
 7  import java.awt.image.BufferedImage;
 8  import java.beans.PropertyChangeListener;
 9  import java.beans.PropertyChangeSupport;
10  import java.io.IOException;
11  import javax.imageio.ImageIO;
12
17  public class BallSprite extends AbsSpriteImage {
18
19      private BufferedImage ballImg;
20      private PropertyChangeSupport pChange;
21
22      public BallSprite() {
23          super();
24          pChange = new PropertyChangeSupport(this);
25      }
26
27      @Override
28      public void initSprite() {
29          try {
30              ballImg = ImageIO.read(getClass().getResource("../images/ball.png"));
31          } catch (IOException ex) {
32          }
33          setAnImage(ballImg);
34          initXY();
35          setWidth(2 * Consts.BALL_RADIUS);
```

```
36            setHeight(2 * Consts.BALL_RADIUS);
37            setDx(1);
38            setDy(2);
39            setActive(false);
40            setVisible(true);
41        }
42
43        public void initXY() {
44            setX((Consts.MAXX - Consts.MINX) / 2 - Consts.BALL_RADIUS);
45            setY(Consts.MAXY - Consts.PADDLE_INIT_Y - 2 * Consts.BALL_RADIUS);
46        }
47
48        @Override
49        public void updateSprite() {
50            if (isActive()) {
51                setX(getX() + getDx());
52                setY(getY() + getDy());
53            }
54            checkEnv();
55            // send the new position to its listener for checking whether
56            // it hits bricks or not
57            fireNewLocation(new Point(getX(), getY()));
58        }
59
60        // collides with the four edges to make a bouncing ball
61        public void checkEnv() {
62            if ((getX() <= 0) // hits left and right edges
63                    || ((getX() + 2 * Consts.BALL_RADIUS) >= Consts.MAXX)) {
64                setDx(-getDx());
65                AllClips.getClips(Consts.HIT_EDGE).play();
66            }
67            if (getY() <= 0) { // hits top edge
68                setDy(-getDy());
69                AllClips.getClips(Consts.HIT_EDGE).play();
70            }
71            if ((getY() + 2 * Consts.BALL_RADIUS) >= Consts.MAXY) { // ball lost
72                setActive(false);
73                setVisible(true);
74                initXY();
75                AllClips.getClips(Consts.BALL_LOST).play();
76                Point initP = new Point(getX(), getY());
77                fireInitLocation(initP);
78            }
79        }
80
...
104 }
```

For accessing one clip from the array clips, we can pass in an integer index as the actual parameter, such as AllClips.getClips(0). However, the integer index has no meaning; it is not convenient for us. We would be better to use a mnemonic index. An easy way is to define constants in the class Consts.java, such as HIT_EDGE = 0, HIT_BRICK = 1, HIT_PADDLE = 2, BALL_LOST = 3, and so on. These constants clearly indicate which sound should be played. Both the BallSprite.java and GameCanvas.java classes (for saving spaces, only the class BallSprite.java is cited) insert statements like the following in proper places for making sounds.

```
AllClips.getClips(Consts.HIT_EDGE).play();
```

Another approach is to use the type of enum for defining a variable, say sounds, to include the set of constants as follows:

```
public static enum sounds {HIT_EDGE,
    HIT_BRICK, HIT_PADDLE, …};
```

And then, in the place where we would like to play one of sounds, adding the following statement:

```
AllClips.getClips(AllClips.sounds.HIT_
    EDGE.ordinal()).play();
```

The method ordinal() will return the integer 0, 1, or 2 corresponding to the position of the constants inside the enum variable sounds.

18.5 Constructing a Composite Sprite: Breakout5

The project Breakout4 works fine. However if we look at the codes of the project, we can feel that the class GameCanvas.java is too long in comparing with other classes. This length unbalancing is better to be improved. Just like writing a book, we would like to see every chapter has similar length, but not one chapter is very short and the other is very long. At the same time, we can see that the 60 bricks are treated as individual 60 sprites in the previous versions. It is better to think of them together as one composite sprite, which contains 60 individual items. The benefit of this new thinking is to make an easier understanding because we can look at them as one group; in turn, it is easy for coding because it greatly reduces the number of sprites and many codes can be implemented inside the composite sprite class. Even this new design asks for modifications of the three-layer game structure framework, it is worth to do it because the new improvement will make more sense for later due to the fact that composite sprites are popular. Therefore, we are going to develop a new version of the project Breakout5 for improving coding better.

For realizing the new idea, we add a new class BrickGroup.java for implementing the brick group as one sprite, and then the sprite inheritance hierarchy should be modified as shown in Fig. 18.2. That is, the inheritance hierarchy adds a new concrete class BrickGroup.java and that new concrete class "has" the class BrickSprite.java. The class BrickGroup.java extends the AbsSprite.java class so that it enforces the type of the global spriteAry list to be changed from <AbsSpriteImage> to <AbsSprite> for covering all of required sprites. Meanwhile, this change enforces to move the abstract methods initSprite(), updateSprite(), and paintSprite() from the class AbsSpriteImage.java up to the class AbsSprite.java. Actually, these modifications make the global spriteAry list more generic than before because since then the spriteAry can accommodate any kind of sprite no matter it is a geometrical shape, an image, or something else like the BrickGroup. In other words, the type of the global arrayList won't be changed any more.

The codes of the new class BrickGroup.java are shown in Listing 18.4. The comparison of the codes with the codes in the project Breakout4 reveals that the BrickGroup.java class mainly copies related codes from the original class GameCanvas.java. As a side effect, this copy reduces the length of the original class GameCanvas.java, which improves the length balancing expectation discussed in the previous section. The class BrickGroup.java stores the 60 bricks as a 1D array and still assigns every brick with the coordinates (x, y) for arranging them as a 2D format on the GUI. All of bricks are inside the same class that makes the manipulation of them directly and easily. Meanwhile, the class AbsSprite.java is also modified to add the three abstract methods: initSprite(), updateSprite(), and paintSprite() as mentioned above.

Fig. 18.2 The new sprite inheritance hierarchy for the composite sprite

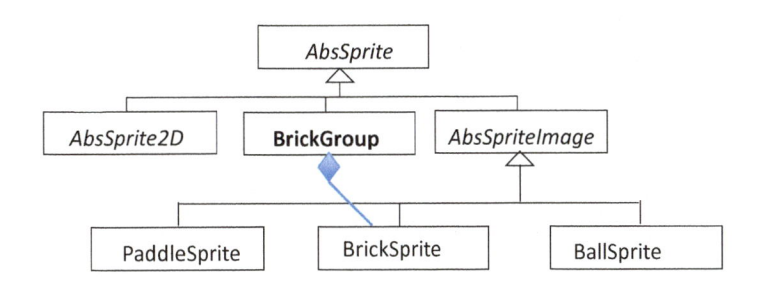

Listing 18.4 The new classes of BrickGroup.java and AbsSprite.java in the project Breakout5

```java
1  /*
2   * BrickGroup.java - A class that groups all brick sprites into
3   * an array so that it is easy to treat all bricks.
4   */
5  package breakout;
6
7  import java.awt.Graphics2D;
8  import java.awt.Rectangle;
9  import java.awt.image.BufferedImage;
10 import javax.imageio.ImageIO;
11
12 public class BrickGroup extends AbsSprite {
13
14     private BufferedImage[] brickImages; // holds 8 different brick images
15     private BrickSprite[] brickAry;
16     private BrickSprite aBrick;
17     private int numBricks;
18
19     public BrickGroup() {
20         numBricks = Consts.BRICKS_PER_ROW * Consts.MAX_ROWS;
21         brickImages = new BufferedImage[Consts.NUM_BRICK_IMAGES];
22         brickAry = new BrickSprite[numBricks];
23         initBrickImages();
24         initBrickSprites();
25     }
26
27     private void initBrickImages() { // get and hold 8 brick imagess
28         try {
29             brickImages[0] =
30                     ImageIO.read(getClass().getResource("../images/aquaTile.gif"));
31             brickImages[1] =
32                     ImageIO.read(getClass().getResource("../images/blackTile.gif"));
33             brickImages[2] =
34                     ImageIO.read(getClass().getResource("../images/blueTile.gif"));
35             brickImages[3] =
36                     ImageIO.read(getClass().getResource("../images/greenTile.gif"));
37             brickImages[4] =
38                     ImageIO.read(getClass().getResource("../images/lightGreyTile.gif"));
39             brickImages[5] =
40                     ImageIO.read(getClass().getResource("../images/purpleTile.gif"));
41             brickImages[6] =
42                     ImageIO.read(getClass().getResource("../images/redTile.gif"));
43             brickImages[7] =
44                     ImageIO.read(getClass().getResource("../images/yellowTile.gif"));
45         } catch (Exception ex) {
46         }
47     }
48
49     private void initBrickSprites() {
50         int x = 0;
51         int y = 30; // leave a line for the value of global score
52         int idx;
53         for (int i = 0; i < numBricks; i++) {
```

18.5 Constructing a Composite Sprite: Breakout5

```
54              if ((i % Consts.BRICKS_PER_ROW == 0) && (i != 0)) {
55                  x = 0;
56                  y += Consts.BRICK_H; // move to next row
57              }
58              aBrick = new BrickSprite();
59              aBrick.setActive(true);
60              aBrick.setVisible(true);
61              aBrick.setLocx(x);
62              x += Consts.BRICK_W; // move the coor x to the next position
63              aBrick.setLocy(y); // stay at the same row
64              aBrick.setWidth(Consts.BRICK_W);
65              aBrick.setHeight(Consts.BRICK_H);
66              idx = (int) (Math.random() * Consts.NUM_BRICK_IMAGES);
67              aBrick.setAnImage(brickImages[idx]); // randomly pick up an image
68              brickAry[i] = aBrick;
69          }
70      }
71
72      @Override
73      public void updateSprite() {
74      }
75
76      @Override
77      public void paintSprite(Graphics2D g2d) {
78          for (int i = 0; i < brickAry.length; i++) {
79              brickAry[i].paintSprite(g2d);
80          }
81      }
82
83      public String hitOneBrick(Rectangle ballRect) {
84          String hitDir = "noHit";
85          for (int i = 0; i < brickAry.length; i++) {
86              // only checking for a brick
87              aBrick = (BrickSprite) brickAry[i];
88              hitDir = aBrick.hitBrick(ballRect);
89              if (!(hitDir.equals("noHit"))) {
90                  break;
91              }
92          }
93          return hitDir;
94      }
95  }
```

```
1  /*
2   * AbsSprite.java - A abstract class that specify the root of the sprite
3   * inheritance hierarchy.
4   */
5  package breakout;
6
7  import java.awt.Graphics2D;
8
13 public abstract class AbsSprite {
14
15     private boolean active;
16     private boolean visible;
```

```
17      private int priority;
18
19      public abstract void initSprite();
20
21      public abstract void updateSprite();
22
23      public abstract void paintSprite(Graphics2D g2d);
24
25      public boolean isActive() {
26          return active;
27      }
28
29      public void setActive(boolean active) {
30          this.active = active;
31      }
32
33      public int getPriority() {
34          return priority;
35      }
36
37      public void setPriority(int priority) {
38          this.priority = priority;
39      }
40
41      public boolean isVisible() {
42          return visible;
43      }
44
45      public void setVisible(boolean visible) {
46          this.visible = visible;
47      }
48  }
```

18.6 Modifying the Communication Path: Breakout5

The original GameCanvas.java class contains all of event listeners. In order to reduce the length of the class GameCanvas.java, we can move some of the event listeners out of the class GameCanvas.java and add them to individual sprite classes. It is such a practice that the new class BrickGroup.java implements a new method hitOneBrick() that plays the role for checking the collisions between the ball and all of bricks. The method has a parameter ballRect that is a bounding rectangle of the ball sprite. When the ball updates its position coordinates and fires a property change event, the class GameCanvas.java receives the new coordinates and forms a bounding rectangle ballRect of the ball and then passes the ballRect into the method hitOneBrick() defined in the BrickGroup.java class. The method uses a "for" loop for accessing bricks one-by-one and passes the ballRect into each individual brick for checking the collision. This new implementation moves the collision detection from the original class GameCanvas.java to the class BrickGroup.java. Consequently, the class GameCanvas.java only organizes the collision detection among sprites but pushes the real codes down to the individual sprite's class. The original communication path is shown as Fig. 18.3; but the new approach enforces the data communication to be changed as shown in Fig. 18.4.

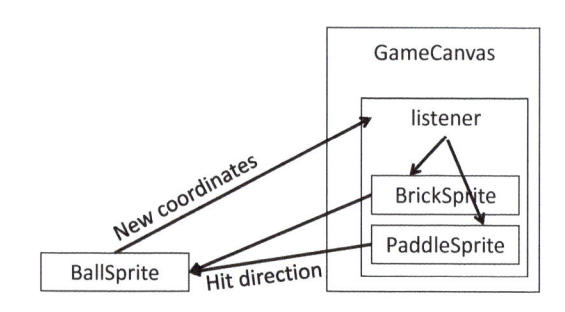

Fig. 18.3 The original communication channel for collision detections in Breakout4

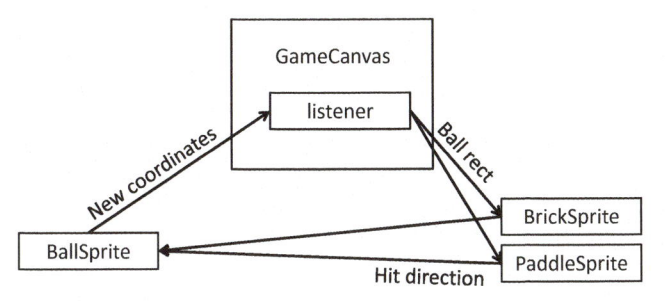

Fig. 18.4 The new communication channel for collision detections in Breakout5

If we would like to further reduce the length of the class GameCanvas.java, we may apply the third alternative approach for implementing event listeners, which we discussed before. For implementing event listener, the first approach is to use inner classes. The second approach is to let the JPanel class itself to implement the interface of event listeners. The third alternative approach is to implement event listeners as independent classes. That is, the third alternative approach moves the event listeners out of the class GameCanvas.java completely. However, the third approach might ask for some extra works. For instance, currently we have the inner class LocChangeListener inside the class GameCanvas.java; it can easily access all of ball sprite, brick sprite, and paddle sprite. In case, if we move the inner class out of the class GameCanvas.java to be an outer class LocChangeListener.java, clearly, all of the sprite objects should be passed into the outer class by using setter methods. Furthermore, the listener also counts for the numBrickHit and the numBallLost. These counter variables are game-level variables, and the purpose of the counting is to eventually invoke some game-level methods, such as stopGame() or so. These invocations cannot be done directly, which require more codes and even more event listeners. Therefore, some event listeners are better kept as inner classes inside the GameCanvas.java class since the class deals with all game-level methods and variables directly. In contrast, if some event listener has nothing to do with the methods and variables in the game level, they can be implemented in some outer ways.

18.7 Improving the Control of the Ball Sprite: Breakout5

The original game only bounces the ball up when the ball hits on the paddle, which cannot control the ball up to left or up to right. In other words, the player has no control on the bouncing to up-left or to up-right such that the player is unable to have a wish which brick is better to be hit upon the ball is bounced up. For providing the player a better control, we divide the paddle into two portions: left portion and right portion. When the ball hits on a position on the left portion of the paddle, the ball is always bounced to up-left; when the ball hits on the right portion of the paddle, the ball is always bounced to up-right. That is, the player can control the bouncing direction of the ball through the control of the paddle position. For performing this function, the class PaddleSprite.java adds a method hitPaddle() as shown in Listing 18.5. The method divides the paddle into left portion and right portion for distinguishing the bouncing direction upon the ball.

Listing 18.5 The modified class PaddleSprite.java in the project Breakout5

```
 1 /*
 2  * PaddleSprite.java - A class that implements a paddle sprite. It function
 3  * is to prevent the ball falling down to the bottom edge of the game canvas.
 4  */
 5 package breakout;
 6
 7 …
16 public class PaddleSprite extends AbsSpriteImage {
17
18     public PaddleSprite() {
19         super();
20     }
21
22     @Override
23     public void initSprite() {
24 …
36     }
37
```

```java
38      public void initXY() {
39  ...
41      }
42
43      @Override
44      public void updateSprite() {
45      }
46
47      public String hitPaddle(Rectangle ballRect) {
48          String hitPosn = "noHit";
49          int paddleMiddle = getX() + getWidth() / 2;
50          int paddleTop = getY();
51          int paddleLeft = getX();
52          int paddleRight = getX() + getWidth();
53          int ballTop = (int) (ballRect.getY());
54          int ballBottom = (int) (ballRect.getY() + ballRect.getHeight());
55          int ballLeft = (int) (ballRect.getX());
56          int ballRight = (int) (ballRect.getX() + ballRect.getWidth());
57          if ((ballBottom >= paddleTop) && (ballTop <= paddleTop)) {
58              if ((ballLeft >= (paddleLeft - ballRect.getWidth() / 2))
59                      && (ballRight <= paddleMiddle)) {
60                  hitPosn = "hitYL";
61              } else if ((ballLeft >= paddleMiddle)
62                      && (ballRight <= (paddleRight + ballRect.getWidth() / 2))) {
63                  hitPosn = "hitYR";
64              } else if ((ballRight >= paddleLeft) && (ballLeft < paddleMiddle)) {
65                  hitPosn = "hitXL";
66              } else if ((ballLeft <= paddleRight) && (ballRight > paddleMiddle)) {
67                  hitPosn = "hitXR";
68              }
69          } else if (ballTop >= paddleTop) {
70              hitPosn = "noHit";
71          }
72          return hitPosn;
73      }
74  }
```

18.8 A GameStruTemplate Model

In the process for developing the game Breakout, more and more functions are required and more and more modifications are implemented. The added functions and the more modifications affect many classes, especially the abstract class AbsGameCanvas.java and the concrete class GameCanvas.java. Actually, all of these push the three-layer game structure becoming more mature gradually along the way for developing more games. However, the three-layer structure and its usage principle are still there.

Reaching this point, we are trying to make a model project as a template for developing more games later. The model project is named GameStruTemplate that is a new version of the three-layer game structure with more additional functionality, such as more game-level methods, the classes for making sound effect, and so on. Whenever a new game would be developed, we are not starting from a "nothing" but starting from the model project GameStruTemplate. We can copy the template project and change its title to fit the new game needs. Definitely, the template can be further improved or modified. The folder of this chapter includes the complete source codes of the template project.

18.9 More Extensions of the Game Breakout5

The version Breakout5 could be further extended. For example, we can set up a threshold value, say 100, based on the score counting. As long as the score reaches the threshold, the current ball will be replaced with a bigger ball with higher speed in order to increase the difficulty level of the control. Another extension could be to bury some flags with some bricks. These flags carry some extra scores or other benefits, for example, adding the max number of ball lost from 3 to 5. When the ball hits these bricks, the flags will fall down and the score will be increased with those extra scores or some settings would be changed.

The original game has all bricks arranged in a 2D rectangle shape. We may change the shape to be oval, stack, or others. Also we can modify the scene when a brick is hit as a random number of broken pieces falling down instead of disappearing.

18.10 Games that Could Be Understood as an Extension of the Game Pong

We understand that the game Breakout is a kind of extension of the game Pong so that we can borrow some ideas and codes from the game Pong in the development of the game Breakout. Extending this approach, if a new game could be considered as an extension of some existing game, it will save us efforts for design it as a brand new game. Following this idea, we can further find out that some other games can also be understood as an extension of the existing game Pong or the game Breakout.

For example, the classic game Alien, which has the following story [Fan et al., 1996].[1] "The year is 2217, and humans have been discovered by hungry aliens from the Andromeda Galaxy who are seeking a tasty, warm, and nutritious meal. These aliens have decided to stage a final assault on the last bastion of humans--New York City--since the large population there will provide a bountiful harvest for years to come. As humanity's last hope, the player's job is to protect the city from these alien marauders. The player commands the last remaining weapon: a mouse-controlled missile launcher. The launcher moves left and right according to the x-coordinate of the mouse. Clicking the mouse fires a single missile. The aliens will try to land on the planet surface. They are defenseless and any contact with the missile launcher will destroy them. But if three aliens land successfully, the banquet begins, with the player as the first appetizer! They can also go on kamikaze attacks, with the purpose of destroying the missile launcher. When an alien is in attack mode, it's invulnerable to missiles if the launcher is hit by an attacking alien, it is destroyed."

Based on the story, the GUI of the game Alien will show a set of flying aliens from the top edge move down to the bottom edge gradually. The player moves the missile launcher left or right and fires a single missile to shoot the aliens. Once an alien is shoot, it disappears, but a new alien will be placed on the top edge and flying down. Imagine that we would make the static bricks in the game Breakout animating from the sky down to the earth and we would treat the paddle as a missile launcher as well as the ball as a missile, then we will have a fundamental idea about the game Alien. And even the implementation of the new game Alien may also have many similar codes as the game Breakout.

We can take the game Space Out as another example [Morrison, M., 2003].[2] The story of the game Space Out says, "You are the driver of a small green car on a trek across the desert. Quite a few UFOs appear in remote desert places. Your traveler in the game can't seem to get away from a constant onslaught of alien visitor from above. Your traveler also shoot them with missiles." It creates a similar scene as the game Alien. And we can treat it as an extension of the game Breakout or the game Alien.

Even the game Snooker, we can also imagine it as an extension of the game Breakout. We can treat the cue ball as the ball sprite; treat all of snooker balls as the brick sprite. The difference is that the collisions among the balls are complicated. However, some similarities may reduce the complexity when we think of the game Snooker.

18.11 Summary

This chapter completes the implementation of the game Breakout by adding some new functions, such as the current score counter, the number of ball lost counter, the game termination announcement, the game renew functions, and the important of sound effects, which is one of the key topics in gaming.

The chapter also discussed a new design for a composite sprites. It is popular that games have a group of same sprites. You can treat them individually or treat them as a group. Generally speaking, treat a set of same sprites as a group is more convenient than treat them individually.

After finishing the discussion about game Breakout, we can see that a game consists of frame level, game level, and sprite level. The frame level organizes a set of screens, such as splash screen, game screen, and the like to allow the player to understand the game, the playing rules, the settings of game-level variables, etc. The game level uses a set of event listeners to catch the players' inputs and actions, to build up data communication channels for connecting classes and synchronizing their functions. The sprite level has an inheritance hierarchy that includes all of sprites that the game required. Every sprite class has a set of common methods,

---

[1] [Fan, J., Ries, E., and Tenitchi, C., 1996] Joel Fan, Eric Ries, and Calin Tenitchi, "Black Art of Java Game Programming", Waite Group Press, 1996.

[2] [Morrison, M., 2003] Michael Morrison, "Game Programming in 24 Hours", Sams, 2003.

such as initSprite(), updateSprite(), paintSprite(), and all required methods for collision detections.

Due to the fact that the class GameCanvas.java initializes all of instances of sprites, it is a convenient place to communicate sprites each other. However, too many communications in one place may cause the class becoming a "cluster." In order to make all of classes loosely coupled, the event listener PropertyChangeListener is mostly welcomed for passing data among classes instead of passing objects among classes. This natural communication approach not only further improves the software structure but also suitable for moving games into network environment, which allows communications becoming data passing. Keeping this picture in mind will make game programming much better.

18.12 Exercises

Self-Reviewing Questions

1. Why do we need to add the current score counting mechanism?
2. Does the current score counter affect other part of codes of the game?
3. Why do we need to add the ball lost counting mechanism?
4. Does the ball lost counter affects other part of codes of the game?
5. Comparing the new design for the composite sprite with the original design, what advantages and disadvantages does the composite sprite have? Why?
6. What ideas can be applied to balance the length among classes?
7. What different communication mechanisms among classes do we have applied?
8. What are the advantages and disadvantages of different communication mechanisms?
9. The project provides mouse for the player to control the paddle. Is it possible to use keys for playing the game? Which control is better? Why?
10. What other games could be considered as an extension of the game Pong?
11. What games could be considered as an extension of games that we have discussed?
12. What are the major steps for adding sounds into a game?

Projects

1. Extending the game Breakout for setting up certain thresholds, when the current score reaches the values of thresholds, increasing the ball speed to increase the difficulty level of the control.
2. Extending the game Breakout by adding a super ball that has a bigger size and a higher speed than the ball used currently. When the current score exceeds a certain value defined by a threshold, the super ball will replace the ball currently used for making it more difficult to control.
3. Extending the game Breakout by hiding some flags that carry bonus scores with some bricks. When those bricks are hit, the flags will fall down dynamically, and the bonus scores will be added.
4. Extending the game Breakout by arranging the bricks with different patterns other than a 2D format, such as a triangular shape, a circular shape, and the like.
5. Adding a splash screen with the current version of the game Breakout.
6. Implement the game Alien as an extension of the game Breakout as described in Sect. 18.8.
7. Implement the game Space Out as an extension of the game Breakout as described in Sect. 18.8.

19
Changing the Structure of Sprites Dynamically: A Game Worm

A game Worm is a single player game. The body of the worm in the game consists of multiple body units. The number of body units and their moving directions are dynamically changed when the game Worm is in execution. It requires a special data structure "circular array" to store the body units of the worm and to synchronize the changing of its moving direction. Furthermore, another auto-animated worm is added to compete with the player-controlled worm, and several extensions are proposed for raising the complexity of the game.

The objectives of this chapter include:
1. The story of the game Worm.
2. Designing the Worm.java as a composite class.
3. Building the GUI of the game Worm.
4. Dynamically growing the body of the worm.
5. Applying a circular array for animating the worm.
6. The player guides the worm to eat a treat.
7. Adding another worm wormAuto for competition.
8. The calculation for automatically changing the moving direction.

As mentioned in the previous chapter, all of the abstract classes plus some concrete classes in the three-layer game structure contribute a model project GameStruTemplate, which forms a template for building all of video games. Since then, we can copy the model project and rename it for starting the construction of a new game project. Definitely, if necessary, we should modify the existing classes, including the abstract classes, for new games. This chapter discusses and implements a new game Worm just follows this approach.

The game Pong has only one animating object, the bouncing ball. The game can be extended to be the game Breakout, which is still based on the bouncing ball. The ball is bounced by colliding with the edges of plying field, with the paddle, and with the bricks randomly. Now, we change the direction to see a classic game Worm, in which a ball becomes a unit of the body of a worm. The body of the worm will be growing such that the number of animating sprites is dynamically added into the game. In addition, the animation direction of the worm is under the control of the game player. These new features make the new game Worm different from the game Pong and the game Breakout that we just developed, in which the number of sprites is fixed. Consequently, the new game Worm will more clearly demonstrate the significance of the three-layer game structure.

19.1 The Story of a Game Worm

The story of the game Worm says a worm is moving automatically. A treat randomly appears somewhere. The player uses up, down, left, and right keys to change the moving directions of the worm for guiding the worm toward the treat for eating. Whenever the worm eats the treat, not only the current game score will increase but also the worm body will grow one body unit long. During the eating, all of actions will pause for a moment for indicating the worm's swallowing and growing. As long as the worm hits on any edge of the playing field, the game is terminated.

Based on the simple story, we need to take care of two sprites: a worm and a treat. Based on the three-layer game structure, the UML class diagram of the game Worm could be as Fig. 19.1.

19.2 Constructing the Class Worm.java as a Composite Class

Clearly, the story of the game Worm indicates that the worm is an animated sprite. It can dynamically move around, and its body can dynamically grow whenever it eats a treat. The ability of changing the moving direction implies that the worm body is not a "stick" but consisting of a set of units. The ability of growing means that its body can be increased with extra units. In our daily life, a worm really consists of "units." Therefore, we design the worm that has a head unit

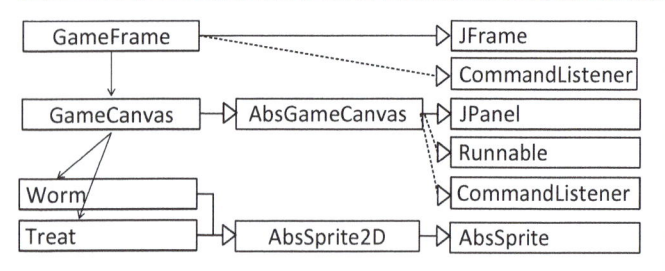

Fig. 19.1 The UML class diagram of the game Worm

with a color of red and a body that initially has four units with a color of black each. Later, its body can grow through appending more units dynamically.

In the game Breakout, we have experienced the design and the implementation of a composite class for the set of bricks. Here, we have a new chance to practice the composite class for the worm sprite by defining a class Worm.java as a composite class. Usually a composite class "has" a set of objects of another class as its components. For example, the class BrickGroup.java in the game Breakout "has" a set of brickSprite of the class BrickSprite.java. For the composite class Worm.java, we also need another class, say WormUnit.java that defines the coordinates of (x, y), width, height, and color as a unit of the worm body. In order to conveniently animate the entire worm and dynamically grow the worm body, we tried to give up the component class WormUnit.java but define every body unit as a circle such that we only need a constant WORM_UNIT_RADIUS for every body unit and create an arrayList to hold the attribute coordinates of (x, y) for every body unit. That is, we define an "ArrayList<Point> wormBody" in the class Worm.java for holding the set of body units as a set of Point that represents the coordinates (x, y) of each worm body unit. This design also simplifies the UML class diagram of the game so that it only has two sprite classes instead of three.

Defining the class Worm.java as a composite class also has its special reason. A composite class like the class BrickGroup.java defined in the game Breakout in the previous chapter can be considered as an option because the total number of bricks is fixed. Without a composite class, all of bricks can be directly stored in the global spriteAry. The effect is the same as stored in the local ArrayList defined in the class BrickGroup.java. However, if we do not define the class Worm.java as a composite class, we have to store the initial five body units directly into the global spriteAry. And then we also add other sprites, such as the treat, into the global spriteAry. It has no problem at the initial stage. But, later when the worm eats some treats, new body units should be gradually appended with the worm body. All of these new added body units have to be added into the global spriteAry such that all of the body units are not consecutively stored in the spriteAry as shown in Fig. 19.2 (Left). It will cause a difficulty in moving the entire worm along the GUI as an entity because the indexes of all of body units are not consecutive. Under that case, grouping all of body units into a single composite class and storing all of body units into a local ArrayList as shown in Fig. 19.2 (Right) becomes necessary. In other words, sometimes a composite class is necessary but not optional.

19.3 Painting a Worm and a Treat Statically on the GUI: The Project Worm1

As usual, the first step is to realize a static GUI for the game Worm. The GUI includes a worm and a treat as shown in Fig. 19.3.

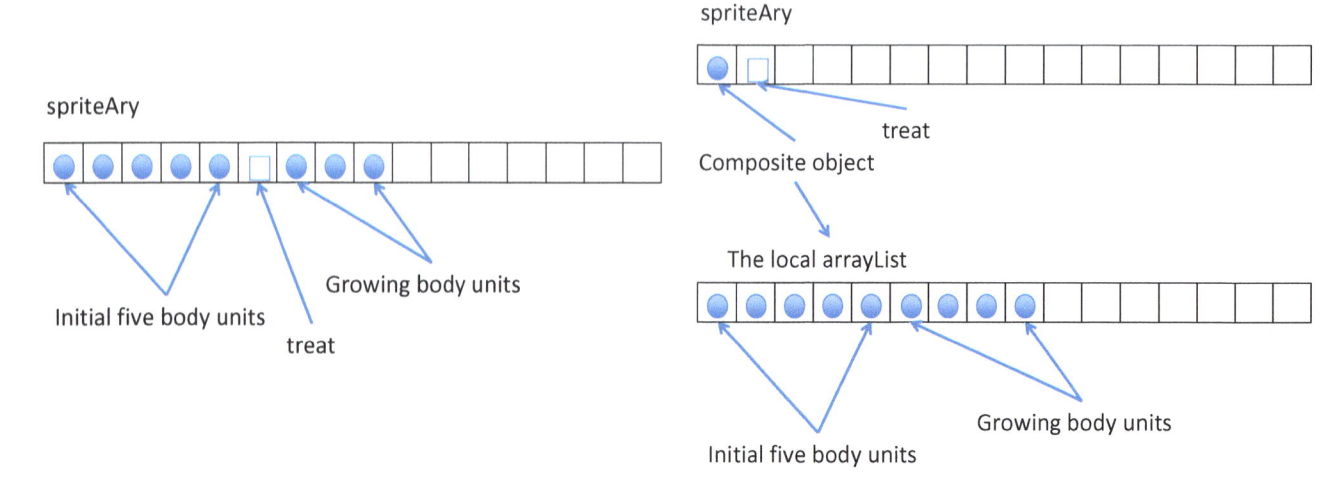

Fig. 19.2 It is necessary to construct the class Worm.java as a composite class. (Left) Without defining a composite class, the body units mix with other sprites in the global spriteAry. (Right) Storing the body units in a local arrayList and only loads the composite sprite in the global spriteAry

19.3 Painting a Worm and a Treat Statically on the GUI: The Project Worm1

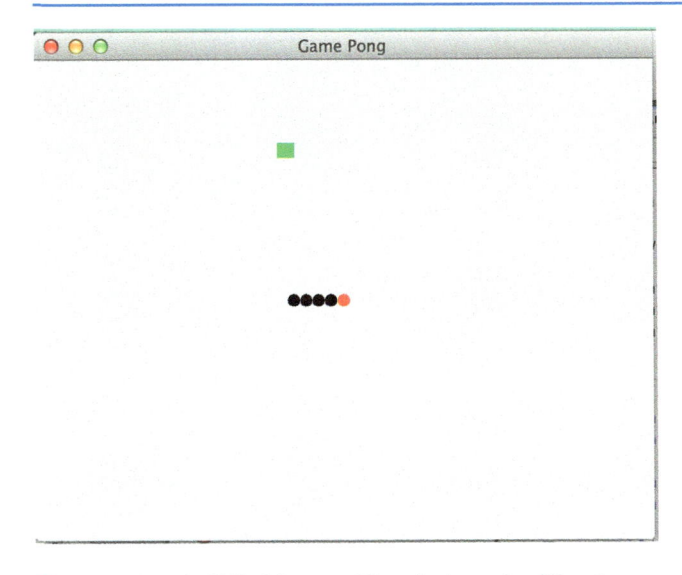

Fig. 19.3 A static GUI of the game Worm in the project Worm1

A pseudo code for the Worm GUI could be as follows.

1. A canvas has a width of 500 pixels and a height of 400 pixels.
2. Place a red head of the worm on the center of the canvas and four black body units on the left of the head.
3. Place a green square as a treat at a randomly selected position on the canvas.
4. Make sure that the body of the worm and the treat won't overlap each other.

For starting the construction, we simply copy the model project GameStruTemplate and rename it as Worm1. Then, add two classes Worm.java and Treat.java into the project and instantiate their objects in the class GameCanvas.java. The codes of the two new classes are shown in Listing 19.1.

Listing 19.1 The classes Worm.java and Treat.java in the project Worm1

```
1  /*
2   * Worm.java - A class that implements an animated worm body
3   */
4  package gamestru;
5
6  import java.awt.Color;
7  import java.awt.Graphics2D;
8  import java.awt.Point;
9  import java.util.ArrayList;
10
15 public class Worm extends AbsSprite2D {
16
17     private ArrayList<Point> wormBody;
18     private int initLen;
19     private Point wHead;
20     private int direction;
21     private int headP, prevP, tailP;
22     private int nUnit; // total number of body units (include head)
23
24     public Worm() {
25         wormBody = new ArrayList();
26         initLen = 5;
27     }
28
29     @Override
30     public void initSprite() {
31         // add the head
32         setX((Consts.MAXX - Consts.MINX) / 2 - Consts.WORM_UNIT_RADIUS);
33         setY((Consts.MAXY - Consts.MINY) / 2 - Consts.WORM_UNIT_RADIUS);
34         wHead = new Point(getX(), getY());
35         wormBody.add(wHead);
36         // add remaining body units (initLen - 1)
37         int i;
```

```java
38          for (i = 1; i < initLen; i++) {
39              wormBody.add(new Point(getX() - i * 2 * Consts.WORM_UNIT_RADIUS, getY()));
40          }
41
42          // set up pointers
43          headP = 0;
44          prevP = 1;
45          tailP = i - 1; //i = initLen; the tail index = i - 1;
46          nUnit = initLen;
47          direction = Consts.EAST;
48          setVisible(true);
49          setActive(false);
50      }
51
52      @Override
53      public void updateSprite() {
54      }
55
56      @Override
57      public void paintSprite(Graphics2D g2d) {
58          g2d.setColor(Color.RED);
59          Point head = wormBody.get(headP);
60          g2d.fillOval(head.x, head.y,
61                  2 * Consts.WORM_UNIT_RADIUS, 2 * Consts.WORM_UNIT_RADIUS);
62          g2d.setColor(Color.BLACK);
63          int ptr = prevP;
64          for (int i = 0; i < nUnit - 1; i++) {
65              g2d.fillOval(wormBody.get(ptr).x, wormBody.get(ptr).y,
66                      2 * Consts.WORM_UNIT_RADIUS, 2 * Consts.WORM_UNIT_RADIUS);
67              ptr = (ptr + 1) % (nUnit);
68          }
69      }
70
71      public int getDirection() {
72          return direction;
73      }
74
75      public void setDirection(int direction) {
76          if ((this.direction == Consts.EAST)
77                  || (this.direction == Consts.WEST)) {
78              if ((direction == Consts.SOUTH) || (direction == Consts.NORTH)) {
79                  this.direction = direction;
80              }
81          } else if ((this.direction == Consts.SOUTH)
82                  || (this.direction == Consts.NORTH)) {
83              if ((direction == Consts.EAST) || (direction == Consts.WEST)) {
84                  this.direction = direction;
85              }
86          }
87      }
88
89      public ArrayList<Point> getWormBody() {
90          return wormBody;
91      }
92  }
```

19.3 Painting a Worm and a Treat Statically on the GUI: The Project Worm1

```java
/*
 * Treat.java - A class that implements a treat.
 */
package gamestru;

import java.awt.Color;
import java.awt.Graphics2D;

public class Treat extends AbsSprite2D {

    public Treat() {
        super();
    }

    @Override
    public void initSprite() {
        boolean regXY = true;
        boolean regTreat = true;
        while (regXY && regTreat) {
            regXY = false;
            regTreat = false;

            int xRan = (int) Math.abs(Math.random() * Consts.MAXX) + 1;
            if ((xRan + Consts.TREAT_WIDTH) > Consts.MAXX) {
                regXY = true;
            } else if (xRan < Consts.MINX_DIS) {
                regXY = true;
            } else {
                setX(xRan);
            }
            int yRan = (int) Math.abs(Math.random() * Consts.MAXY_DIS) + 1;
            if ((yRan + Consts.TREAT_HEIGHT) > Consts.MAXY_DIS) {
                regXY = true;
            } else if (yRan < Consts.MINY_DIS) {
                regXY = true;
            } else {
                setY(yRan);
            }
        }
        setVisible(true);
        setActive(false);
    }

    @Override
    public void updateSprite() {
    }

    @Override
    public void paintSprite(Graphics2D g2d) {
        g2d.setColor(Color.decode("#00dd00")); // light green
        g2d.fillRect(getX(), getY(), Consts.TREAT_WIDTH, Consts.TREAT_HEIGHT);
    }
}
```

Because both worm and treat are geometrical shapes, both the classes Worm.java and Treat.java extend the AbsSprite2D.java class that defines the set of attributes x, y, width, height, and color for all of 2D shapes. And then, both classes implement the abstract method initSprite() for setting up initial values of the set of attributes and the abstract method paintSprite() for painting themselves. The abstract method updateSprite() has an empty body currently since at this step both worm and treat don't have dynamic behaviors yet. They only show their drawing on the canvas. For that, both of them setVisible(true) and setActive(false).

The class Treat.java will be instantiated as a single sprite with a shape of rectangle. But the class Worm.java is a composite class that "has" a set of body units, and each of them is a shape of circle. Therefore, the Worm.java class needs an ArrayList to hold the multiple units of its body. The reason for selecting an ArrayList is that the story said whenever the worm eats a treat, its body increases one body unit. That is, how many body units the worm would have depends on how many treats the worm would eat. In other words, the length of the array is unknown. Thus, an ArrayList is suitable. As discussed in Sect. 19.2, the type of the ArrayList is defined as the built-in type of Point because every body unit has a same shape as a circle with a same size; the only difference lies on its position coordinates (x, y), which can be easily expressed as a Point. The paintSprite() method will paint every body unit as a circle based on the stored coordinates (x, y) and the constant 2*WORM_UNIT_RADIUS as its width and height. Due to the same reason, the position of the entire worm is expressed in using the coordinates (x, y) of its head unit.

As a composite class, it still needs to extend the class AbsSprite2D.java because the object of the composite class still needs to be inserted into the global spriteAry, which has a type of AbsSprite2D.

At the moment when the game starts, the position of the head unit of the worm is set up at the center of the canvas. The position of other body units can be calculated based on the circle size. The position of the treat is randomly determined. However, in order to satisfy the requirement, "the treat cannot be overlapped with the body of the worm"; whenever an object of the treat is instantiated, a special method detectCollision() defined in the class GameCanvas.java must check whether the treat touches any body unit of the worm. If yes, a "while" loop enforces a new instantiation of a new treat until no any body unit of the worm overlaps with the treat.

19.4 Animating the Worm Along the X-Axis: The Project Worm2

The second step is to animate the worm along the direction of EAST but keep the treat as static. For that, the class Worm.java needs to setActive(true) and implement the method updateSprite(), which should animate the worm body toward EAST direction with a distance of one body unit in every step. An intuitive thinking of making the animation is to define the value of dx as the length of a body unit, 2*WORM_UNIT_RADIUS, and then add the value of dx with the x coordinate of every body unit. Theoretically, this thinking works, and the repaint shows the entire worm body moves up dx distance towards the EAST direction. However, a difficulty will be encountered when we extend the moving direction from EAST to others including WEST, NORTH, and SOUTH.

Suppose that the worm changes its moving direction from EAST to SOUTH, the head node should move to the SOUTH direction by adding a value of dy to its y coordinate; the second body unit and all of the remaining body units are still moving to the EAST by adding a dx. And then, at the second step, after the head adds a dy, the second body unit should also add a dy, but the third and all of remaining body units still add a dx. How to remember which body unit should add a dy and which body unit should add a dx? Even worth, if at the third step, the moving direction is changed to be WEST, then the entire worm body needs to be divided into three parts: the body units in the first part are moving to WEST by subtracting a dx, the body units in the second part are moving to SOUTH with adding a dy, and the body units in the third part are still moving to EAST and should add a dx. The implementation becomes almost impossible. In other words, this thinking is unpractical.

A new approach is adopted for overcoming this difficulty as follows. (1) Add a new unit in the front of the body as a new head unit. (2) Delete the last tail unit. (3) Keep the coordinates (x, y) of other body units the same. This approach only has one computation dealing with the new head unit and nothing to do with any other body unit. Any direction change can be applied to the new head unit with an addition of a dx or a dy. The new head unit appears on the new position, and all remaining body units have the same positions excepting the tail body unit which is deleted. The entire body moves toward one step. It is just like in the real world; some worm "shrinks" its body for moving its tail and then "stretches" its body for moving its head. The new computation is depicted in Fig. 19.4 (Left).

However, following the three steps above, we need a data structure that can hold the five body units initially, and then its length would be changed for adding a new head and remove an old tail. When the game executes for a long time, what the length of the data structure would be?

Fortunately, a special type of array called "circular array" is suitable for this computation. As mentioned in the previous section, the body of the worm is stored in the ArrayList wormBody. Initially, the worm has five body units. We can imagine that the arrayList is bent to be a circle such that its head unit immediately follows its tail unit. In order to indicate the tail unit and the head unit, we can set up two point-

Fig. 19.4 (Left) Adding a new head and removing the tail unit for animating the worm; (right) applying the circular array approach for animating the worm

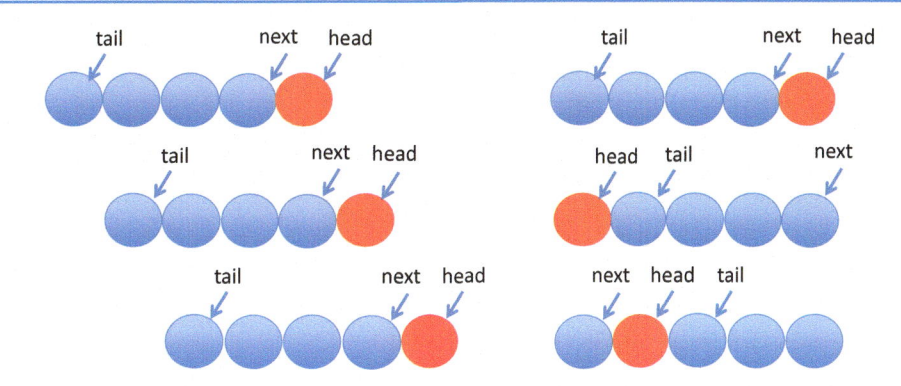

next = head; head = tail;
head.x = next.x + 2*WORM_UNIT_RADIUS;
tail = tail − 1.

ers "tail" pointer and "head" pointer pointing to the related units. In addition, we set up a third pointer "next" pointing to the unit just immediately following the head unit. And then, we can move the three pointers to perform the three step computations above. That is, physically, a circular array is just a regular array with a certain fixed length. However, logically, the three pointers make the three nodes: head, next, and tail are linked together and move along the array.

This approach is illustrated in Fig. 19.4 (Right). Initially, we set up three pointers as on the first row. Assume that the worm is moving toward EAST direction. Then, as the second row shows, we (1) assign the next pointer pointing to the current head position; (2) move the head pointer pointing to the current tail position; (3) assign the value of "next.x + 2*WORM_UNIT_RADIUS" to the head.x; and (4) move the tail pointer pointing to the current (tail − 1) position. This computation is equivalent to add a new head unit with a new x coordinate and store the value into the original tail unit to "delete" the old tail unit. The third row shows the same computation for the following movement. Repeating this computation, the worm is animated toward the EAST direction. The worm.updateSprite() method implements this computation. Whenever the method updateComponent() in the class AbsGameCanvas.java invokes the method worm.updateSprite(), the computation will be executed to move the worm forward one step. The code of the method worm.updateSprite() in the class Worm.java is shown in Listing 19.2.

Listing 19.2 The method updateSprite() of the class Worm.java in the project Worm2

```
1  /*
2   * Worm.java - A class that implements an animated worm body
3   */
4  package gamestru;
5
6  import java.awt.Color;
7  import java.awt.Graphics2D;
8  import java.awt.Point;
9  import java.util.ArrayList;
10
15 public class Worm extends AbsSprite2D {
16
17      private ArrayList<Point> wormBody;
18      private int initLen;
```

```java
19      private Point wHead;
20      private int direction;
21      private int head, next, tail;
22      private int nUnit; // total number of body units (include headP)
23
24      public Worm() {
25          super();
26          wormBody = new ArrayList();
27          initLen = 5;
28      }
29
30      @Override
31      public void initSprite() {
32  ...
50      }
51
52      @Override
53      public void updateSprite() {
54          next = head;
55          head = tail;
56          Point nextP;
57          nextP = wormBody.get(next);
58
59          // set up the direction = EAST
60          switch (direction) {
61              case Consts.EAST:
62                  wormBody.set(this.head, new Point(
63                          nextP.x + 2 * Consts.WORM_UNIT_RADIUS, nextP.y));
64                  break;
65              default:
66          }
67          tail = tail - 1;
68          if (tail == -1) {
69              tail = nUnit - 1;
70          }
71      }
72
73      @Override
74      public void paintSprite(Graphics2D g2d) {
75  ...
86      }
87
88      public ArrayList<Point> getWormBody() {
89          return wormBody;
90      }
91  }
```

A trivial point that is worth to be noticed is the thread sleep time. Depending on the object to be animated, the sleep time should be adjusted. For example, the game Breakout animates a single ball; the sleep time was set as 8 ms. However, this game Worm needs to animate an array of objects. If we still keep the 8 ms, the animation would be very fast so that the animation cannot be shown. We adjust it as 300 ms so that the animation is shown up. It is not caused by any bad coding but caused by the time setting because the computation takes a longer time. Consequently, the class AbsGameCanvas.java adds a new variable sleepTime, and the concrete subclass GameCanvas.java can invoke the method setSleepTime() to adjust the sleep time for different games.

19.5 The Player Controls the Game Through Keys: The Project Worm3

After animating the worm, the following tasks should be completed. (1) The worm is animated to the EAST direction at the beginning. The player needs to use the four keys: up, down, left, and right for changing the moving direction of the worm. Clearly, the KeyListener should be adopted. (2) The purpose for controlling the worm is to guide the worm to eat the treat. The eating appears as that the head of the worm collides with the treat. Thus, a method for checking the collision between the worm head and the treat should be developed. (3) The story of the game says, "Whenever the worm collides with one of four edges, the game is terminated." We need to add a new method for checking the collision between the worm head and the edges of the playing field.

19.5.1 Controlling the Animation Direction of the Worm in Using Keys

For controlling the animation direction of the worm, the pseudo code could be as follows. The implementation of the pseudo code is listed in Listing 19.3:

1. Adding a key listener in the class GameCanvas.java.
2. The key listener implements the event handler keyPressed() to accept the four keys and passing the corresponding direction to the class Worm.java.
3. The method updateSprite() in the class Worm.java changes the animation direction if any.

Listing 19.3 The inner class MyKeyAdapter resides in the class GameCanvas.java and the methods worm.setDirection() and worm.updateSprite() of the class Worm.java in the project Worm3

```
  1 /*
  2  * GameCanvas.java - A class that implements the game canvas.
  3  */
  4 …
 28    public GameCanvas() {
 29        …
 31        addKeyListener(new MyKeyAdapter());
 32        setFocusable(true);
 33    }
 34
 35 …
109
110    // an inner class for implementing the key event adapter
111    // for catching the key control
112    class MyKeyAdapter extends KeyAdapter {
113
114        @Override
115        public void keyPressed(KeyEvent evt) {
116            switch (evt.getKeyCode()) {
117                case KeyEvent.VK_DOWN:
118                    worm.setDirection(Consts.SOUTH);
119                    break;
120                case KeyEvent.VK_UP:
121                    worm.setDirection(Consts.NORTH);
122                    break;
123                case KeyEvent.VK_RIGHT:
124                    worm.setDirection(Consts.EAST);
125                    break;
126                case KeyEvent.VK_LEFT:
127                    worm.setDirection(Consts.WEST);
128                    break;
```

```
129                default:
130            }
131        }
132    }
133 }
```

```
  1 /*
  2  * Worm.java - A class that implements an animated worm body
  3  */
  4 ...
 51
 52     @Override
 53     public void updateSprite() {
 54         next = head;
 55         head = tail;
 56         Point nextP;
 57         nextP = wormBody.get(next);
 58
 59         switch (direction) {
 60             case Consts.EAST:
 61                 wormBody.set(this.head, new Point(
 62                         nextP.x + 2 * Consts.WORM_UNIT_RADIUS, nextP.y));
 63                 break;
 64             case Consts.WEST:
 65                 wormBody.set(this.head, new Point(
 66                         nextP.x - 2 * Consts.WORM_UNIT_RADIUS, nextP.y));
 67                 break;
 68             case Consts.SOUTH:
 69                 wormBody.set(this.head, new Point(
 70                         nextP.x, nextP.y + 2 * Consts.WORM_UNIT_RADIUS));
 71                 break;
 72             case Consts.NORTH:
 73                 wormBody.set(this.head, new Point(
 74                         nextP.x, nextP.y - 2 * Consts.WORM_UNIT_RADIUS));
 75                 break;
 76             default:
 77         }
 78         tail = tail - 1;
 79         if (tail == -1) {
 80             tail = nUnit - 1;
 81         }
 82     }
 83 ...
 98
 99     public int getDirection() {
100         return direction;
101     }
102
103     public void setDirection(int direction) {
104         if ((this.direction == Consts.EAST)
105                 || (this.direction == Consts.WEST)) {
106             if ((direction == Consts.SOUTH) || (direction == Consts.NORTH)) {
107                 this.direction = direction;
108             }
109         } else if ((this.direction == Consts.SOUTH)
```

```
110                 || (this.direction == Consts.NORTH)) {
111             if ((direction == Consts.EAST) || (direction == Consts.WEST)) {
112                 this.direction = direction;
113             }
114         }
115     }
116 …
120 }
```

Clearly, the key listener is the inner class MyKeyAdapter (lines 112–132) added in the class GameCanvas.java. For accepting the function of the key event, the constructor of the class GameCanvas.java adds the following two statements.

```
addKeyListener(new MyKeyAdapter());
setFocusable(true);
```

The event handler keyPressed() checks on the source key component and converts the key value to the corresponding direction value. Further, it passes the direction to the method worm.setDirection() in the class Worm.java.

The function of the method worm.setDirection() (lines 103–115) is not only to receive the value of the direction sent by the key listener but also filter out two unacceptable cases. We consider the following two cases unacceptable: (1) changing the moving direction from EAST directly to WEST or vice versa and (2) changing the moving direction from NORTH directly to SOUTH or vice versa. The method worm.setDirection() simply ignores these cases.

The method worm.updateSprite() (lines 52–82) just moves the worm according to the value stored in the variable "direction."

19.5.2 The Worm Eats the Treat

The process that the worm eats the treat can be described as the following pseudo code, which is implemented as the codes cited in Listing 19.4.

1. The class Worm.java checks whether the worm head collides with the treat. If so, it means the worm eats the treat:
   (a) The thread pauses the game for a short moment to allow the worm swallowing the treat and growing itself.
   (b) The class Treat.java makes a new treat.
   (c) The class Worm.java grows its body by inserting a new unit.

Listing 19.4 The class Worm.java is modified to add these codes for eating a treat in the project Worm3

```
 1 /*
 2  * Worm.java - A class that implements an animated worm body
 3  */
 4 …
16 public class Worm extends AbsSprite2D {
17
18     …
54
55     @Override
56     public void updateSprite() {
57         moveHeadOneStep();
58         // if the worm eats the treat
59         if (eatTreat()) {
60             gameCanvas.setNumOfEat(gameCanvas.getNumOfEat() + 1);
61             treat.initSprite();
62             insertNewHead();
63             // pause it for a half second
64             try {
65                 Thread.sleep(500);
66             } catch (Exception ex) {
67             }
68         }
```

```java
69              if (collideEdge()) {
70                  gameCanvas.stopGame();
71              }
72          }
73
74          public boolean eatTreat() {
75              boolean eat = false;
76              Rectangle treatRect = new Rectangle(treat.getX(), treat.getY(),
77                      Consts.TREAT_WIDTH, Consts.TREAT_HEIGHT);
78              Point wHeadP = wormBody.get(head);
79              Rectangle wUnitRect = new Rectangle(wHeadP.x, wHeadP.y,
80                      2 * Consts.WORM_UNIT_RADIUS, 2 * Consts.WORM_UNIT_RADIUS);
81              if (treatRect.intersects(wUnitRect)) {
82                  eat = true;
83              }
84              return eat;
85          }
86
87          // replace the original tail position with a new head object
88          // it keeps the total number of units but move the head one step
89          public void moveHeadOneStep() {
90              next = head;
91              head = tail;
92              Point nextPoint;
93              nextPoint = wormBody.get(next);
94              Point newHeadP = prepareNewHead(nextPoint);
95
96              wormBody.set(head, newHeadP); // replace the tail with new head
97              tail = tail - 1;
98              if (tail == -1) {
99                  tail = nUnit - 1;
100             }
101         }
102
103         // insert a new head object at the head position and nUnit++
104         public void insertNewHead() {
105             next = head;
106             head = tail;
107             Point nextPoint;
108             nextPoint = wormBody.get(next);
109             Point newHeadP = prepareNewHead(nextPoint);
110
111             wormBody.add(head + 1, newHeadP);
112             head = head + 1;
113             nUnit++;
114         }
115
116         // create a new head object: x = nextP.x + a unit
117         public Point prepareNewHead(Point nextPoint) {
118             Point newHeadP = null;
119             switch (direction) {
120                 case Consts.EAST:
121                     newHeadP = new Point(nextPoint.x + 2 * Consts.WORM_UNIT_RADIUS,
122                             nextPoint.y);
123                     break;
124                 case Consts.WEST:
```

19.5 The Player Controls the Game Through Keys: The Project Worm3

```
125                 newHeadP = new Point(nextPoint.x - 2 * Consts.WORM_UNIT_RADIUS,
126                         nextPoint.y);
127                 break;
128             case Consts.SOUTH:
129                 newHeadP = new Point(nextPoint.x,
130                         nextPoint.y + 2 * Consts.WORM_UNIT_RADIUS);
131                 break;
132             case Consts.NORTH:
133                 newHeadP = new Point(nextPoint.x,
134                         nextPoint.y - 2 * Consts.WORM_UNIT_RADIUS);
135                 break;
136             default:
137         }
138         return newHeadP;
139     }
140
141     public boolean collideEdge() {
142         boolean hitEdge = false;
143         Point headP = wormBody.get(head);
144         if (headP.x <= Consts.MINX) {
145             hitEdge = true;
146         } else if (headP.x >= Consts.MAXX) {
147             hitEdge = true;
148         } else if (headP.y <= Consts.MINY) {
149             hitEdge = true;
150         } else if (headP.y >= Consts.MAXY) {
151             hitEdge = true;
152         }
153         return hitEdge;
154     }
155
156     @Override
157     public void paintSprite(Graphics2D g2d) {
158         ...
169     }
170
171     public int getDirection() {
172         return direction;
173     }
174
175     public void setDirection(int direction) {
176         if ((this.direction == Consts.EAST)
177                 || (this.direction == Consts.WEST)) {
178             if ((direction == Consts.SOUTH) || (direction == Consts.NORTH)) {
179                 this.direction = direction;
180             }
181         } else if ((this.direction == Consts.SOUTH)
182                 || (this.direction == Consts.NORTH)) {
183             if ((direction == Consts.EAST) || (direction == Consts.WEST)) {
184                 this.direction = direction;
185             }
186         }
187     }
188
189 ...
204 }
```

The pseudo code indicates that the major modifications for realizing the task "the worm eats the treat" are in the class Worm.java as cited in Listing 19.4. The eating is a collision detection that should be done after the worm completing a moving step. Thus, when the updateSprite() method invokes the method moveHeadOneStep(), the method eatTreat() is called, which performs the function for checking whether the worm head collides with the treat or not. If the method eatTreat() returns a Boolean value of true, the method gameCanvas.setNumOfEat() is invoked to increase the value of the variable numOfEat declared in the class GameCanvas.java by one for increasing the current score, and then the method treat.initSprite() is invoked for placing a new treat somewhere; in addition, the method insertNewHead() is called to insert a new head unit into the worm for growing the worm body one more unit. Immediately, the statement "Thread.sleep(500)" puts the thread into sleep for a short moment in order to indicate the actions that the worm is swallowing and its body is growing.

As mentioned above, the body growing is done through inserting a new head unit. At beginning, we thought that we could add the new unit at the tail position. But, it encounters a difficulty for determining the coordinates of the new tail unit since we have no idea at that moment which moving direction the tail node should be. However, adding the new unit at the head position won't have the problem because the moving direction of the new inserted head must be the same as the moving direction that the current head unit has.

The implementation of the method insertNewHead() (lines 104–114) is very similar with the implementation of the method moveHeadOneStep() (lines 89–110). Both invokes the method prepareNewHead() to have a new head unit. The difference is that the method moveHeadOneStep() calls the method wormBody.set() to replace the original tail unit in the arrayList wormBody with the new head unit so that the worm will move toward one step; but the method insertNewHead() calls wormBody.add() to insert the new head unit in the front of the current head position without touching the original tail unit so that a new body unit is added into the arrayList wormBody. It is not only growing the body but also moves the body forward one step.

19.5.3 Terminating the Game If the Worm Hits on Any Edge of the Playing Field

The third task is to terminate the game if the worm hits on any one of four edges of the playing field. The action chain starts from the class Worm.java, which has new method collideEdge() for checking whether the head of the worm body hits on any edge. The worm.updateSprite() method adds an "if" statement to invoke the method collideEdge(). If the collideEdge() method returns a value of true, the method gameCanvas.stopGame() is invoked. The implementation of the method stopGame() resides in the class AbsGameCanvas.java. It sets the thread null and turns the Boolean variable gameOver to be true to let the method paintComponent() of the class GameCanvas.java to invoke the announceTermination() method for displaying the message of "Game Terminated" and indicates that "Starting a new game if clicking the mouse." The NewGameListener inner class which resides in the class GameCanvas.java will accept the mouse click and invokes the method renewGame() in the class AbsGameCanvas.java for resetting a new game. Consequently, the entire chain of the method invocation is as follows:

```
worm.updateSprite() -> gameCanvas.stopGame()
-> AbsGameCanvas.setGameOver(true) ->
AbsGameCanvas.paintComponent() -> gameCanvas.
announceTermination()
```

19.6 Adding Another Worm for Extending the Game: The Project Worm4

For making the game more interesting, we would like to add another worm with a name of wormAuto, which is an automatically animated worm, and it can automatically find the direction toward the treat and eat the treat without the player's attention. The purpose of adding this new worm wormAuto is to create a new challenge for the player since the wormAuto will compete with the worm that is under the control of the player for eating the treat.

The pseudo code for adding the new worm wormAuto could be as follows:

1. Copy the class Worm.java and paste it as the new class WormAuto.java.
2. Add method initWormAuto() for initializing the wormAuto in the initComponent() method of the class GameCanvas.java.
3. Add a method collideTreat() in the class WormAuto.java for eating the treat. But, when the wormAuto eats a treat, its body does not grow.
4. The wormAuto won't cause game termination even it touches any edge.
5. Whenever the method treat.initSprite() is invoked for creating a new treat, it invokes wormAuto.setTreat() for passing the new position of the treat to the wormAuto such that the wormAuto can determine its moving direction by itself for eating the treat:
   (a) The wormAuto's moving direction is calculated from the current head position straightforward to the treat without the limitations of the four moving directions, such as EAST, SOUTH, and so on. The detailed calculation is explained below.
   (b) The eating is made by calling the wormAuto.collideTreat().

6. Clearly, the wormAuto can take the advantage of short path toward the treat directly. In order to prevent the wormAuto always faster than the existing worm from reaching the treat, a rule is set up, which says that the wormAuto cannot cross over the body of the existing worm; but the existing worm can cross over the body of the wormAuto. Therefore, the player would like to not only guide the worm toward the treat but also attempt to use the worm body for blocking the movement of the wormAuto. Thus, we add a wormAutoCollideWorm() method into the class GameCanvas.java to check whether the wormAuto hits on the body of the existing worm. If true, the movement of the wormAuto should be blocked until the existing worm moved over as shown in Fig. 19.5. It is realized by the following statement that is added inside the method wormAuto.updateSprite().

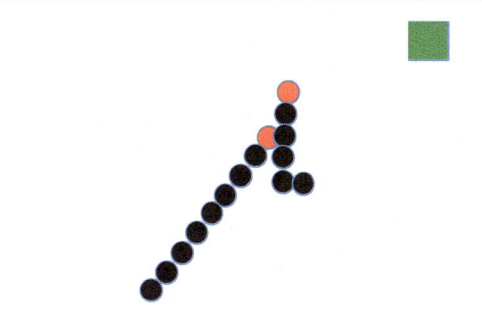

Fig. 19.5 The player controlled worm blocks the movement of the wormAuto

```
if (!gameCanvas.wormAutoCollideWorm()) {
    moveHeadOneStep();
}
```

It means that only when the wormAuto head does not collide with the body of the existing worm, the wormAuto can be animated.

How does the wormAuto automatically trace the treat? The calculation of the moving direction of the object wormAuto is shown in Fig. 19.6. The implementation of these calculations is shown in Listing 19.5.

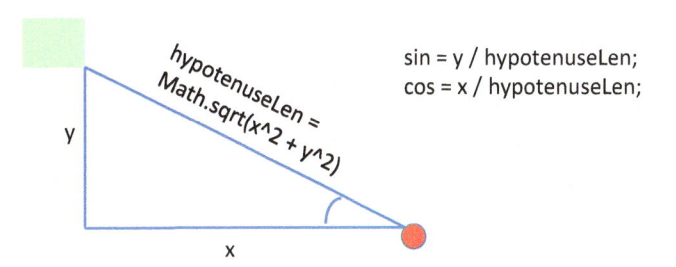

Fig. 19.6 The calculation of the moving direction of the object wormAuto

$\text{sin} = y \,/\, \text{hypotenuseLen};$
$\text{cos} = x \,/\, \text{hypotenuseLen};$

$\text{hypotenuseLen} = \text{Math.sqrt}(x^2 + y^2)$

Listing 19.5 The class WormAuto.java in the project Worm4

```
1  /*
2   * WormAuto.java - A class that implements an automatically animated worm body.
3   * It does not grow when eat a treat. It won't cause game termination.
4   */
5  package gamestru;
6
7
17 public class WormAuto extends AbsSprite2D {
18
19     private ArrayList<Point> wormBody;
20     private int initLen;
21     private Point wHead;
22     private int head, next, tail;
23     private int nUnit; // total number of body units (include headPoint)
24
25     private GameCanvas gameCanvas;
26     private Treat treat;
27
28     private double sin, cos;
29     private Point distanceP;
30
31     public WormAuto() {
32         super();
```

```java
33         wormBody = new ArrayList();
34         initLen = 10;
35     }
36
37     @Override
38     public void initSprite() {
39         // add the headPoint
40         setX((Consts.MAXX - Consts.MINX) / 2 - Consts.WORM_UNIT_RADIUS);
41         setY((Consts.MAXY - Consts.MINY) / 2 + 5 * Consts.WORM_UNIT_RADIUS);
42         wHead = new Point(getX(), getY());
43         wormBody.add(wHead);
44         // add remaining body units (initLen - 1)
45         for (int i = 1; i < initLen; i++) {
46             wormBody.add(new Point(getX() - i * 2 * Consts.WORM_UNIT_RADIUS, getY()));
47         }
48
49         // set up pointers
50         head = 0;
51         next = 1;
52         tail = initLen - 1; // - 1; //i = initLen; the tail index = i - 1;
53         nUnit = initLen;
54         setVisible(true);
55         setActive(true);
56     }
57
58     @Override
59     public void updateSprite() {
60         if (!gameCanvas.wormAutoCollideWorm()) {
61             moveHeadOneStep();
62         }
63         // if the worm eats the treat
64         if (collideTreat()) {
65             treat.initSprite();
66             setTreat(treat);
67             // pause it for a half second
68             try {
69                 Thread.sleep(500);
70             } catch (Exception ex) {
71             }
72         }
73         // wormAuto won't cause the termination of the game
74         //if (collideEdge()) {
75         //    gameCanvas.terminateGame();
76         //}
77     }
78
79     // replace the original tail position with a new head object
80     // it keeps the total number of units but move the head one step
81     public void moveHeadOneStep() {
82         next = head;
83         head = tail;
84         Point nextPoint;
85         nextPoint = wormBody.get(next); // current, next points to the head node
86         Point newHeadP = prepareNewHead(nextPoint);
87
```

19.6 Adding Another Worm for Extending the Game: The Project Worm4

```
88              wormBody.set(head, newHeadP); // replace the tail with new head
89              tail = tail - 1;
90              if (tail == -1) {
91                  tail = nUnit - 1;
92              }
93          }
94
95          // create a new head object: x = nextP.x + a unit
96          public Point prepareNewHead(Point nextPoint) {
97              Point newHeadP = new Point();
98              int moveLen = 2 * Consts.WORM_UNIT_RADIUS;
99              findDir(); // get values of cos and sin
100             int moveX = (int) (moveLen * cos);
101             int moveY = (int) (moveLen * sin);
102
103             if ((distanceP.x <= 0) && (distanceP.y <= 0)) { // NW
104                 newHeadP = new Point(nextPoint.x - moveX, nextPoint.y - moveY);
105             } else if ((distanceP.x <= 0) && (distanceP.y >= 0)) { // SW
106                 newHeadP = new Point(nextPoint.x - moveX, nextPoint.y + moveY);
107             } else if ((distanceP.x >= 0) && (distanceP.y <= 0)) { // NE
108                 newHeadP = new Point(nextPoint.x + moveX, nextPoint.y - moveY);
109             } else if ((distanceP.x >= 0) && (distanceP.y >= 0)) { // SE
110                 newHeadP = new Point(nextPoint.x + moveX, nextPoint.y + moveY);
111             }
112             return newHeadP;
113         }
114
115         public void findDir() {
116             distanceP = findDistance();
117             int hypotenuseLen = (int) (Math.sqrt(distanceP.x * distanceP.x
118                     + distanceP.y * distanceP.y));
119             sin = Math.abs((double) (distanceP.y * 1.0) / hypotenuseLen);
120             cos = Math.abs((double) (distanceP.x * 1.0) / hypotenuseLen);
121         }
122
123         public Point findDistance() {
124             Point treatP = new Point(treat.getX(), treat.getY());
125             Point headP = wormBody.get(next); // current, head is the next
126             int xDistance = treatP.x - headP.x;
127             int yDistance = treatP.y - headP.y;
128             Point disP = new Point(xDistance, yDistance);
129             return disP;
130         }
131
132         public boolean collideTreat() {
133             boolean collide = false;
134             Rectangle treatRect = new Rectangle(treat.getX(), treat.getY(),
135                     Consts.TREAT_WIDTH, Consts.TREAT_HEIGHT);
136             Point wHeadP = wormBody.get(head);
137             Rectangle wUnitRect = new Rectangle(wHeadP.x, wHeadP.y,
138                     2 * Consts.WORM_UNIT_RADIUS, 2 * Consts.WORM_UNIT_RADIUS);
139             if (treatRect.intersects(wUnitRect)) {
140                 collide = true;
141                 gameCanvas.setNumEatWormAuto(gameCanvas.getNumEatWormAuto() + 1);
142             }
```

```
143            return collide;
144       }
145
146       @Override
147       public void paintSprite(Graphics2D g2d) {
148            g2d.setColor(Color.RED);
149            Point headPoint = wormBody.get(head);
150            g2d.fillOval(headPoint.x, headPoint.y,
151                 2 * Consts.WORM_UNIT_RADIUS, 2 * Consts.WORM_UNIT_RADIUS);
152            g2d.setColor(Color.BLACK);
153            int ptr = next;
154            for (int i = 1; i < wormBody.size(); i++) {
155                 g2d.fillOval(wormBody.get(ptr).x, wormBody.get(ptr).y,
156                      2 * Consts.WORM_UNIT_RADIUS, 2 * Consts.WORM_UNIT_RADIUS);
157                 ptr = (ptr + 1) % (nUnit);
158            }
159       }
160
161 … getters and setters
176 }
```

In Fig. 19.6, the square represents a treat; the circle represents the current head node of the wormAuto. The method findDistance() (lines 123–130) returns the value of xDistance = treat.x − head.x and the value of yDistance = treat.y − head.y. The xDistance and yDistance not only carry the values of moving distance but also carry the moving direction of the wormAuto indicated by their signs. Continuously, the method findDir() (lines 115–121) based on the right-angled triangle finds out the length of the hypotenuse with the formula hypotenuseLen = Math.sqrt($x^2 + y^2$). Thus, sin = y/hypotenuseLen and cos = x/hypotenuseLen. And then, the method prepareNewHead() (lines 96–113) intends to forward the head node of the wormAuto one step with the distance of moveLen = 2*Consts.WORM_UNIT_RADIUS. But, the real moving distances on the directions of x and y depend on the current values of sin and cos. That is, "moveX = moveLen * cos" and "moveY = moveLen * sin." Immediately, according to the signs of xDistance and yDistance, the real moving values can be found by adding or subtracting the moveX and moveY (lines 103–111).

19.7 Adding Sound Effects to the Game: The Project Worm4

The project Worm4 also adds the sounds when either one of the worms is eating the treat. In addition, another sound is also added when the game is terminated due to the player-controlled worm hits one edge of the playing field. It is still based on the class MakeClip.java and the class AllClips.java. These two classes are part of the project GameStruTemplate. The only things we should do are (1) modifying the sound file names inside the class AllClips.java; (2) setting up new constants in the class Consts.java for new sounds; and (3) invoking the method AllClips.getClips().play() with the appropriate indexes of the sounds in proper locations for playing proper sounds.

19.8 Some Extensions of the Game Worm

The game ChaseWorm developed in Davison, A. [2005][1] could be seen as an extension of the game Worm. The story of the game ChaseWorm says a worm animates on eight possible directions randomly with a certain angle limitation in order to make the movement looks natural. The game player intends to click on the worm's head unit for catching it. If the player misses the worm's head, then an obstacle (a blue rectangle) is added on the clicking position. The worm cannot move over any obstacle, so the added obstacles may enforce the worm to change its moving directions very often for making the player easier to chase the worm. The worm starts at certain length, say 5, and increases to a maximum length, say 50, and then it keeps maximum length from then on. When the player catches the worm, a score is displayed, which is calculated based on the number of obstacles and the time spent for the chasing. Less obstacles and less time mean a higher score.

We may also add some new features to extend our game Worm. For example, (1) Placing rocks and ponds on the game screen so that the worm and the wormAuto have to go around

---

[1] [Davison, A., 2005] Andrew Davison, "Killer Game Programming", O'Reilly, 2005.

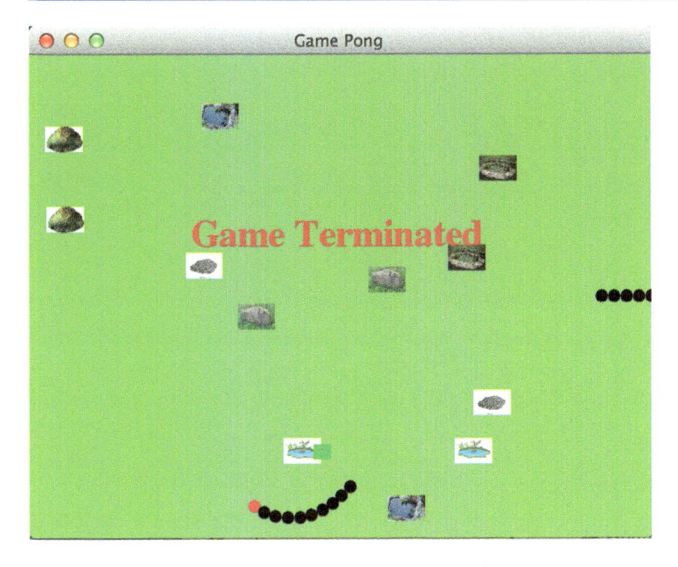

Fig. 19.7 Set up some ponds and rocks on the scene

those rocks and ponds, which increases the difficulties in moving the worms as shown in Fig. 19.7. (2) Applying two threads for animating the two worms separately, which allows the two worms having different animating speeds. (3) Changing the body unit from a circle to an oval or to an image. (4) Adding an eagle that will join the competition for eating the treat. (5) When the worm body grows and reaches a certain threshold value, the moving speed of the worm will be increased.

19.9 Summary

This chapter introduces a new game Worm. The worm's body consists of a set of units. When the worm eats a treat, its body grows one unit. That is, the number of sprites is dynamically increased after initial setting. This feature asks for designing the class Worm.java as a composite class such that the composite class has its own local ArrayList that guarantees all of body units are consecutively stored so that only one index is required to continuously access all of body units for moving the worm. If the class Worm.java is not a composite sprite, then all of the new growing body units will be directly inserted into the global spriteAry. Some other sprites in the spriteAry may interrupt the consecutive arrangement of all body units.

For animating the worm and for inserting new body unit, a circular array is adopted. This data structure is manipulated in using three pointers. It is a nice approach to animate a group of sprites synchronously.

Adding a wormAuto into the game is an extension, which makes the game more fun. It indicates that the competition is an important factor for games. Thinking of developing the game as a networked game, two worms would be controlled by two remote players for a competition.

19.10 Exercises

Self-Reviewing Questions

1. How to create a static worm?
2. How to animate the worm that has a fixed length?
3. How to insert new body unit dynamically into the body of the worm?
4. How to terminate the game Worm?
5. What is a circular array? What is the difference between a circular array and a regular array?
6. Why the game Worm adopts a circular array? Can it be implemented without the circular array?
7. Is the version with two worms interesting? Why?
8. How to determine the moving direction of the worm wormAuto? Are there other approaches that can perform the same function?
9. Is the three-layer game structure powerful for developing a new game, such as the game Worm?
10. Are there new features that can be added to extend the game Worm?

Projects

1. Replace the circle body unit with an oval body unit for the game Worm.
2. Replace the circle body unit with an image body unit for the game Worm.
3. Add a third sprite, say an eagle, into the game Worm for competing the treat.
4. Add rocks and ponds on the GUI for making the movement of the worms more difficult.
5. Add a second thread for animating the new worm wormAuto.
6. Add a splash screen for the game Worm.
7. An iRobot is an industrial product that can automatically move around a room for cleaning the floor of the room. When it touches an obstacle, it will change its moving direction. It has an electrical charge station at a fixed position in the room. Whenever it finishes its job, it will automatically move back to the charge station. Design and implement such an iRobot.

Chess-Like Games: A Game Othello

A chess-like game Othello is introduced to illustrate games played by two players. The game Othello deals with some new techniques, such as, to control the take-turn actions between two players, to make image transparency, to flip the pieces with the frame-animation technique, and the like. The more crucial issue is to physically separate the GUI unit from the logic unit but logically link them together as a complete game. Thereafter, the game Othello is further converted from a two-player game to be a single-player game for introducing the concept of artificial intelligence.

The objectives of this chapter include:
1. A revisiting of the abstract model of games.
2. The story of the game Othello.
3. The UML state machine of the game Othello.
4. Events cause the transitions from one state to the other.
5. A cellBoard for browsing and a pieceBoard for placing pieces.
6. The principle of a game playing rule.
7. The structure of all of playing rules.
8. Applying artificial intelligence for developing a single-player Othello.

This chapter opens a new kind of game for discussion. The game is called Othello, which normally is a chess kind of game and played by two human players. After completing the game, we are also going to develop a new version that is played by a single human player against the computer on the purpose of introducing the concept of artificial intelligence. The game Othello is also a classic game. We are still following the strategy to implement it according to our own thinking and based on the three-layer game structure framework.

20.1 Revisiting the Abstract Model of Games

After we have rather rich experiences on gaming through precious chapters, we would like to revisit the abstract game model as duplicated in Fig. 20.1, which was introduced in Chap. 1. The purpose is to better understand the model and apply it for developing the new game Othello. The model is an abstraction of the common features of games. The abstract model emphasizes the separation of the game GUI from the game logic as well as the synchronization of the two units based on data passing. This model promotes the analysis of a game and the synthesis of the system, which is important for constructing a loosely coupled software structure. In designing and implementing desktop applications, sometimes it is not easy to think about what loosely coupled software structure is. It is helpful if we consider networked games, where the games have to pass data along networks for synchronizing the GUI and the logic. Under that environment, the software structure should be loosely coupled just as the abstract model demonstrated.

The abstract model says that a game has a GUI portion for displaying the scenes of the game for the players and accepting the inputs issued by the players. The GUI consists of sprites, which are components animated independently from each other. Another unit is the game logic portion that internally controls the animations and the entire game according to the game logic and player inputs. Besides the specifically designed controls, the animations may cause collisions among sprites, which further trigger new pieces of logic to change the structure and the properties of the sprites on the GUI. Even though different games may have different stories, different

Fig. 20.1 The abstract model of games

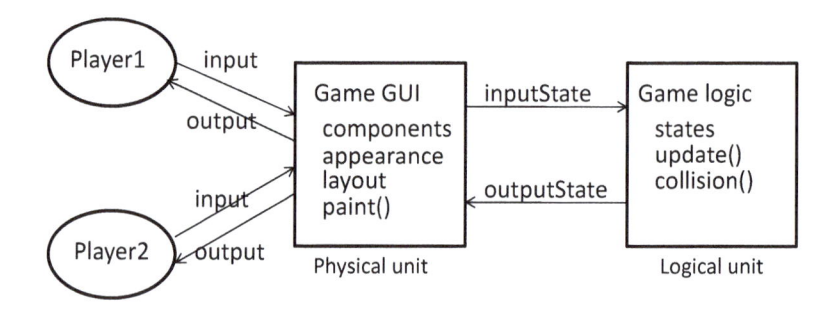

Fig. 20.2 A UML state machine diagram of the game Othello

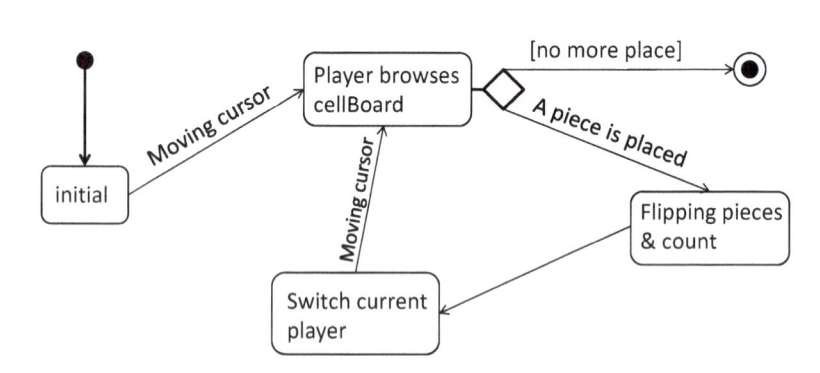

sets of sprites, different control logic, and different numbers of players, the same abstract model can be used to represent the majority of games. This model constructs a game as a loosely coupled software system that increases the scalability, reusability, and maintainability of the system.

The GUI of a game consists of GUI components, which are the sprites. The logic of a game refers to a set of states combined with certain units of artificial intelligence. All sprites should be held by data structures, and the game logic should be defined as a state machine. These two units are synchronized through the communication mechanism via the passing of the input states and the output states. These input states and output states are associated with the players' external actions and game's internal functions. The abstract model also reveals the fact that although games exist in hundreds of thousands of variations, they share some common principles, which include certain specific OOP principles and general software principles. The three-layer game structure framework that we have introduced just follows these principles.

20.2 The Story and Its UML State Machine of the Game Othello

Under the umbrella of the abstract model and the three-layer framework for gaming with the global software structure, designing and implementing a game mainly depends on the game's story. The basic story of the game Othello says that two players, distinguished by playing white or black color pieces, take turn to place their own color pieces on an 8 × 8 board. When the current player places an own color piece on the board, as long as the new piece pairs with another existing own color piece and these two own color pieces appear on the two ends of a sequence of opponent color pieces along a horizontal, vertical, or diagonal direction, the sequence of opponent color pieces between the two own color pieces should be flipped over to be the current player's own color pieces. The two players just apply this principle to compete for making more own color pieces on the board until it is impossible to place any additional piece on the board. The player who gains the more own color pieces on the board wins the game.

According to the story, the logic of the game Othello can be depicted as a UML state machine diagram as shown in Fig. 20.2. Actually, we can understand the UML state machine as a refinement of the logic unit in the abstract model shown in Fig. 20.1.

We have introduced the UML state machine in Chap. 17. A UML state machine illustrates the states and the state transitions caused by related events. In reality, the UML state machine also implies the components that are needed for making the GUI unit and the logic unit. Surely, the UML state machine should be further refined in the iterative development process if necessary.

Fortunately, the UML state machine shown on Fig. 20.2 not only shows the logic of the game but also gives the steps for building up the game. Every state can be designed and implemented independently, and later all of the states are linked together through a set of events. In other words, the UML state machine could act as a blueprint for step-by-step building up sophisticated software. Meanwhile, the three-layer game structure physically supports the step-by-step strategy due to the flexibility and extensibility of its global sprite inheritance hierarchy. These step-by-step design and implementation are described in the following sections.

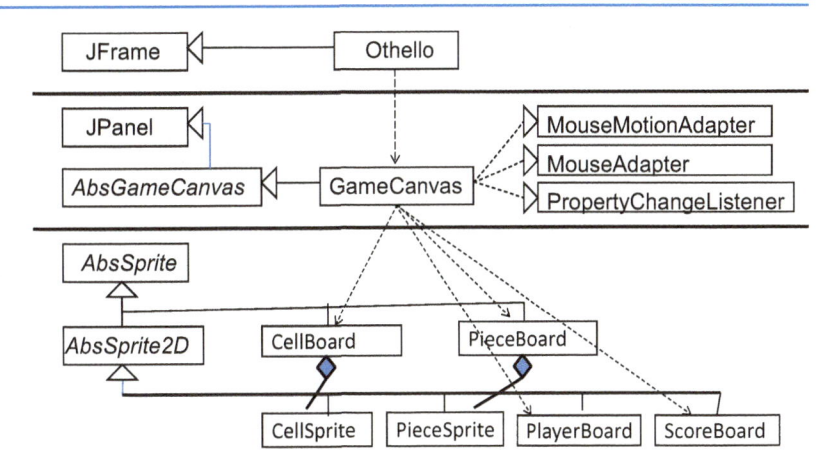

20.3 Initializing the Game with a Board and Four Pieces: The Project Othello1

Fig. 20.3 The UML class diagram of the project Othello1

The initial state, labeled "initial" in Fig. 20.2, can be further divided into sub-state "initBoard" and sub-state "initGame." The sub-state "initBoard" deals with a board made of 8 × 8 cells. The board is named as cellBoard that is an instance of the CellBoard.java class, which is a composite class that "has" 8 × 8 objects cellSprite of the CellSprite.java class. The class CellBoard.java extends the abstract class AbsSprite.java; and the class CellSprite.java extends the abstract class AbsSprite2D.java.

The game allows two players to play the game by placing pieces. Each piece is an object of the class PieceSprite.java. In the initial stage, all pieces are graphical circles with a color of either white or black. Therefore, the class PieceSprite.java should extend the abstract class AbsSprite2D.java. Later, the pieces will be changed to images. A player that places a piece on the board for flipping opponent color pieces is a dynamic action. In order to keep track of these dynamic actions, a special class PieceBoard.java is required. The PieceBoard.java is also a composite sprite. It initially has 8 × 8 null objects prepared for accepting 8 × 8 objects of the class PieceSprite.java. The 8 × 8 board is a 2D data structure; thus, every piece in the pieceBoard has a 2D index [row][col] that has the same values as the corresponding cell in the cellBoard. In other words, the PieceBoard.java class is part of logic used to keep track of the dynamic behaviors of all pieces; while the class CellBoard.java is part of GUI used to display all cells and all pieces.

Following the completion of the cellBoard and the pieceBoard, the sub-state "initGame" pre-initializes two black and two white pieces onto the predefined coordinates in the pieceBoard and displayed on the cellBoard. For the entire game, two more boards are attached to the cellBoard. One of them is called playerBoard, which displays either a white piece or a black piece for the indication of the current player; the other is named as scoreBoard, which displays the current game scores that are the current number of white pieces and black pieces as well as the difference of them. After completing the initial state, all classes of the three-layer game structure and the classes required by the game Othello1 are shown as the UML class diagram in Fig. 20.3, and the resulting game GUI is shown in Fig. 20.4.

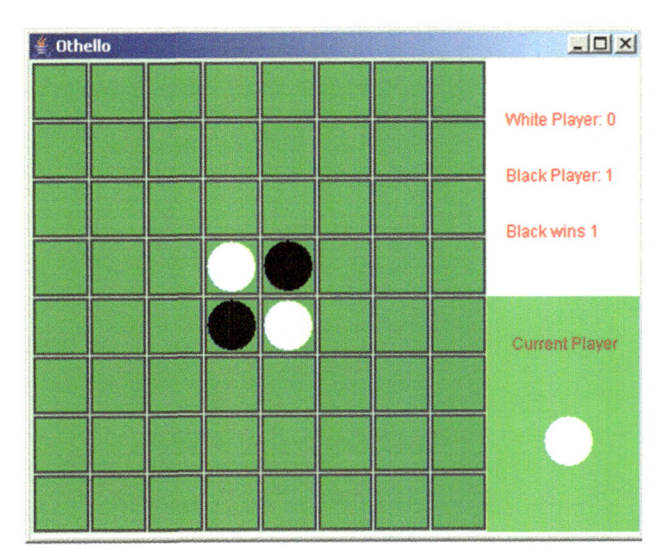

Fig. 20.4 The GUI of the game Othello1 after finishing the state "initial"

The implementation starts from copying the project GameStruTemplate in Chap. 18 and renaming it as Othello1. And then, we gradually add the following new classes CellBoard.java, CellSprite.java, PieceBoard.java, PieceSprite.java, PlayerBoard.java, and ScoreBoard.java into the project. As the UML class diagram shown in Fig. 20.3, the CellBoard.java "has" CellSprite.java; and the PieceBoard.java "has" PieceSprite.java. The codes of these new sprites and the global class GameCanvas.java that initializes these sprites are shown in Listing 20.1, where the classes PieceBoard.java and PieceSprite.java are not shown because they are similar with the two classes of CellBoard.java and CellSprite.java, respectively. The codes of these classes are not very complicated. Readers can understand them without difficulty.

Listing 20.1 The class GameCanvas.java and the new sprites classes CellBoard.java, CellSprite.java, PlayerBoard.java, ScoreBoard.java in the project Othello1

```
 1  /*
 2   * GameCanvas.java - A class that implements the game canvas.
 3   */
 4  package othello;
 5
 6  import java.awt.Color;
 7  import java.awt.Graphics2D;
 8  import java.awt.event.MouseAdapter;
 9  import java.awt.event.MouseEvent;
10
15  public class GameCanvas extends AbsGameCanvas {
16
17      private CellBoard cellBoard;
18      private PieceBoard pieceBoard;
19      private PlayerBoard playerBoard;
20      private ScoreBoard scoreBoard;
21
22      public GameCanvas() {
23          super();
24          setSleepTime(300);
25      }
26
27      @Override
28      public void initComponent() {
29          getSpriteAry().clear();
30          new AllClips();
31
32          initCellBoard();
33          initPieceBoard();
34          initScoreBoard();
35          initPlayerBoard();
36
37          // initialize two white and two black pieces
38          pieceBoard.initPieces();
39          scoreBoard.setNumWhite(scoreBoard.getNumWhite() + 2);
40          scoreBoard.setNumBlack(scoreBoard.getNumBlack() + 2);
41      }
42
43      private void initCellBoard() {
44          cellBoard = new CellBoard();
45          getSpriteAry().add(cellBoard);
46      }
47
48      private void initPieceBoard() {
49          pieceBoard = new PieceBoard();
50          getSpriteAry().add(pieceBoard);
51      }
52
53      private void initScoreBoard() {
54          scoreBoard = new ScoreBoard();
55          getSpriteAry().add(scoreBoard);
56      }
```

20.3 Initializing the Game with a Board and Four Pieces: The Project Othello1

```
57
58     private void initPlayerBoard() {
59         playerBoard = new PlayerBoard();
60         getSpriteAry().add(playerBoard);
61     }
62
63     // Othello is played by two players. It does not have a current score
64     @Override
65     public void paintCurrScore(Graphics2D g2d) {
66     }
67
68     @Override
69     public void announceTermination(Graphics2D g2d) {
70         ...
79     }
80
81     // A listener for re-starting the game.
82     // Assume it is based on a mouse click
83     class NewGameListener extends MouseAdapter {
84
85         @Override
86         public void mouseClicked(MouseEvent evt) {
87             ...
90         }
91     }
92 }
```

```
1  /*
2   * CellBoard.java -- A class that defines the cellBoard of 8x8 cells.
3   */
4  package othello;
5
6  import java.awt.Graphics2D;
7
12 public class CellBoard extends AbsSprite {
13
14     private CellSprite[][] cellBoard;
15
16     @SuppressWarnings("OverridableMethodCallInConstructor")
17     public CellBoard() {
18         super();
19         initSprite();
20     }
21
22     @Override
23     public void initSprite() {
24         int startX = Consts.GAPW;
25         int startY = Consts.GAPW;
26         cellBoard = new CellSprite[Consts.MAXCELL][Consts.MAXCELL];
27         for (int row = 0; row < Consts.MAXCELL; row++) {
28             for (int col = 0; col < Consts.MAXCELL; col++) {
29                 CellSprite aCell = new CellSprite();
30                 aCell.setX(startX);
31                 aCell.setY(startY);
32                 cellBoard[row][col] = aCell;
```

```java
                startX += (Consts.CELLW + Consts.GAPW);
            }
            startX = Consts.GAPW;
            startY += (Consts.CELLH + Consts.GAPW);
        }
        setActive(false);
        setVisible(true);
    }

    @Override
    public void paintSprite(Graphics2D g2d) {
        g2d.setColor(Consts.BGCOLOR);
        g2d.fillRect(0, 0, Consts.BOARDW, Consts.BOARDH);
        for (int row = 0; row < Consts.MAXCELL; row++) {
            for (int col = 0; col < Consts.MAXCELL; col++) {
                cellBoard[row][col].paintSprite(g2d);
            }
        }
    }

    @Override
    public void updateSprite() {
    }
}
```

```java
/*
 * CellSprite.java - A class that defines a cell on the cellBoard.
 */
package othello;

import java.awt.Graphics2D;

public class CellSprite extends AbsSprite2D {

    private boolean fill;

    @SuppressWarnings("OverridableMethodCallInConstructor")
    public CellSprite() {
        initSprite();
    }

    @Override
    public void initSprite() {
        setWidth(Consts.CELLW);
        setHeight(Consts.CELLH);
        setColor(Consts.CELLCOLOR);
        setFill(true);
        setActive(false);
        setVisible(true);
    }

    @Override
    public void paintSprite(Graphics2D g2d) {
        g2d.setColor(Consts.CELLCOLOR);
        g2d.fillRect(getX(), getY(), getWidth(), getHeight());
```

20.3 Initializing the Game with a Board and Four Pieces: The Project Othello1

```java
35            g2d.setColor(Consts.BORDERC);
36            g2d.drawRect(getX(), getY(), getWidth(), getHeight());
37            g2d.drawRect(getX() + 1, getY() + 1, getWidth() - 2, getHeight() - 2);
38        }
39
40        @Override
41        public void updateSprite() {
42        }
43
44        public boolean isFill() {
45            return fill;
46        }
47
48        public void setFill(boolean fill) {
49            this.fill = fill;
50        }
51 }
```

```java
1  /*
2   * PlayerBoard.java - A class that defines a player board, which displays
3   * the current piece for indicating the current player.
4   */
5  package othello;
6
7  import java.awt.Color;
8  import java.awt.Graphics2D;
9
14 public class PlayerBoard extends AbsSprite2D {
15
16     PieceSprite aPiece;
17
18     @SuppressWarnings("OverridableMethodCallInConstructor")
19     public PlayerBoard() {
20         super();
21         aPiece = new PieceSprite();
22         initSprite();
23     }
24
25     @Override
26     public void initSprite() {
27         setX(Consts.PLAYERX);
28         setY(Consts.PLAYERY);
29         setWidth(Consts.PLAYERW);
30         setHeight(Consts.PLAYERH);
31         setActive(false);
32         setVisible(true);
33     }
34
35     @Override
36     public void paintSprite(Graphics2D g2d) {
37         g2d.setColor(Color.GREEN);
38         g2d.fillRect(getX(), getY(),
39                 Consts.PLAYERW, Consts.PLAYERH);
40         g2d.setColor(Color.RED);
41         g2d.drawString("Current Player", getX() + 18, getY() + 40);
```

```
42
43            aPiece.setX(getX() + getWidth() / 2 - Consts.PIECEW / 2);
44            aPiece.setY(getY() + (getHeight() + 40) / 2 - Consts.PIECEH / 2);
45            aPiece.setWidth(Consts.PIECEW);
46            aPiece.setHeight(Consts.PIECEH);
47            aPiece.setColor(Consts.WHITEP);
48            aPiece.paintSprite(g2d);
49        }
50
51        @Override
52        public void updateSprite() {
53        }
54 }
```

```
 1 /*
 2  * ScoreBoard.java - A class that defines a score board, which displays
 3  * the current scores of both while player and black player.
 4  */
 5 package othello;
 6
 7 import java.awt.Color;
 8 import java.awt.Graphics2D;
 9
14 public class ScoreBoard extends AbsSprite2D {
15
16     private int numWhite;
17     private int numBlack;
18
19     @SuppressWarnings("OverridableMethodCallInConstructor")
20     public ScoreBoard() {
21         super();
22         numWhite = 0;
23         numBlack = 0;
24         initSprite();
25     }
26
27     @Override
28     public void initSprite() {
29         setX(Consts.SCOREX);
30         setY(Consts.SCOREY);
31         setWidth(Consts.SCOREW);
32         setHeight(Consts.SCOREH);
33         setColor(Color.WHITE);
34         setActive(false);
35         setVisible(true);
36     }
37
38     @Override
39     public void paintSprite(Graphics2D g2d) {
40         g2d.setColor(getColor());
41         g2d.fillRect(getX(), getY(), getWidth(), getHeight());
42         g2d.setColor(Color.RED);
43         int x = getX() + 14;
44         int y = getY() + 48;
45         g2d.drawString("White Player: " + numWhite, x, y);
```

```
46            y = y + 40;
47            g2d.drawString("Black Player: " + numBlack, x, y);
48            int diff = numWhite - numBlack;
49            if (diff > 0) {
50                y += 40;
51                g2d.drawString("While wins " + diff, x, y);
52            } else if (diff < 0) {
53                y += 40;
54                g2d.drawString("Black wins " + Math.abs(diff), x, y);
55            } else {
56                y += 40;
57                g2d.drawString("Two players tied", x, y);
58            }
59        }
60
61        @Override
62        public void updateSprite() {
63
64        }
65
66   … getters and setters
81   }
```

20.4 Building up a Mouse Control Mechanism for Players: The Project Othello2

After the "initial" state, a player may start playing the game. The player's actions are external inputs, which need a mechanism for receiving the player's input and converting them as inputState to be sent to the logic unit of the game. For this game Othello the mouse is chosen as the input mechanism. If the game is implemented for other devices like a cell phone, the input mechanism could be a key or a "finger."

The first external action is that the player moves the mouse to "Browse the cellBoard" as the state machine indicated in Fig. 20.2. For better displaying the current cell that the player is browsing in, when the player leaves an "old" cell and enters a "new" current cell, the cellBoard displays a special color that differs from the background color for the "new" current cell and replacing the color for the "old" cell with the background color. That is, the cell that the mouse is in always shows a special color. Before changing the color of the current cell, the cell should be verified as "index valid," which means the coordinates (row, column) of the new current cell should be in the valid index range of [0, Consts.MAXCELL-1].

The pseudo code for making this browsing mechanism could be as follows:

1. A MouseListener that implements the method mouseMoved() catches the current position of the mouse in (x, y) with the unit of pixel.
2. Converting the (x, y) to be the coordinates (row, col) on the cellBoard.
3. Assigning the two values (row, col) to the two variables (newRow, newCol). If the pair of (newRow, newCol) that are the indices of the new entered cell is different from the pair of (curRow, curCol) that are the indices of the "old" cell just left, then the "new" cell is assigned the special color and the "old" cell is assigned with the background color. Here, only those cells that have no pieces on them can be browsed.
4. The updateSprite() method in the class CellBoard.java incorporates the validation and the color changes; and then the paintSprite() method paints these color changes on the cellBoard.

Obviously, this is only a mechanism that clearly indicates the current position of the mouse at this moment without any semantics meaning. The purpose of browsing the cellBoard is looking for those cells where a piece is "worth" to be placed, which means that if the player places an own color piece on those cells, it is possible to form a pair with an existing own color piece for flipping the sequence of opponent color pieces between the two own color pieces. We call those cells as "possible (or valid) playing cells." Which cell is a possible playing cell depends on the definition of a set of flipping rules. Consequently, the real browsing algorithm should be finalized after finishing the implementation of flipping rules in the project Othello3.

The second action of the player is to click on a selected possible playing cell. The first action "browsing" is to change the color of the current cell on the cellBoard. This second action "clicking" is to add a new piece to the clicked cell on the pieceBoard. The clicking action transfers the state into a new state "Flipping pieces" as shown in the state machine of Fig. 20.2. Receiving the clicking action requires a MouseMotionListener to implement a method mouseClicked(). Once clicking, a pieceSprite of the current player is placed on the clicked cell on the pieceBoard. After this event completes, the playing authority should be switched to the other player, and the piece color is also switched to the opponent color. The system state is immediately transitioned to the new state "Switching current player" as shown in Fig. 20.2. This switching between the two players should be taken care of by the class GameCanvas.java because whenever the current player is switched, the class GameCanvas.java should be able to announce the next player color to both of the pieceBoard and the playerBoard. Due to the player switching has to be taken place immediately after the click action is done, the class PieceBoard.java should be able to send property change information to the class GameCanvas.java. For that, the class GameCanvas.java needs to add an inner class that implements PropertyChangeListener for receiving the information. Listing 20.2 shows the major part of these two actions.

A minor change also needs to be mentioned. When the mouse browses on the cellBoard, it changes the color of the current cellSprite. Thus, the method paintSprite() in the class CellSprite.java must invoke getColor() to find out the special color and paint the cell with the new color. Similarly, after a player clicks on the board for adding a pieceSprite onto the pieceBaord, the current player's color should be switched. The current player color shown on the playerBoard should also be switched. Thus, the method paintSprite() in the class PlayerBoard.java should invoke getCurPlayerColor() for keeping track of painting the current player's color.

Listing 20.2 The major part of the two actions on the modified classes GameCanvas.java, CellBoard.java, and PieceBoard.java in the project Othello2

```
 1  /*
 2   * GameCanvas.java - A class that implements the game canvas.
 3   */
 4  …
18  public class GameCanvas extends AbsGameCanvas {
19
20      …
24      private Color curPieceColor;
25
26      @SuppressWarnings("OverridableMethodCallInConstructor")
27      public GameCanvas() {
28          …
30          addMouseMotionListener(new BrowseCellBoardListener());
31          addMouseListener(new ClickPieceBoardListener());
32          setCurPieceColor(Consts.WHITEP);
33      }
34
35      …
55
56      private void initPieceBoard() {
57          pieceBoard = new PieceBoard();
58          pieceBoard.addPropertyChangeListener(new ClickChange());
59          // pieceBoard is used inside cellBoard
60          cellBoard.setPieceBoard(pieceBoard.getPieceBoard());
61          getSpriteAry().add(pieceBoard);
62      }
63
64      …
103
```

20.4 Building up a Mouse Control Mechanism for Players: The Project Othello2

```
104     class BrowseCellBoardListener extends MouseMotionAdapter {
105
106         @Override
107         public void mouseMoved(MouseEvent evt) {
108             int x = evt.getX();
109             int y = evt.getY();
110             cellBoard.setMoveXY(x, y);
111         }
112     }
113
114     class ClickPieceBoardListener extends MouseAdapter {
115
116         @Override
117         public void mouseClicked(MouseEvent evt) {
118             int x = evt.getX();
119             int y = evt.getY();
120             pieceBoard.setClickXY(x, y);
121         }
122     }
123
124     class ClickChange implements PropertyChangeListener {
125
126         @Override
127         public void propertyChange(PropertyChangeEvent evt) {
128             String theChange = evt.getPropertyName();
129             if (theChange.equals("clickDone")) {
130                 if (getCurPieceColor().equals(Consts.WHITEP)) {
131                     setCurPieceColor(Consts.BLACKP);
132                 } else if (getCurPieceColor().equals(Consts.BLACKP)) {
133                     setCurPieceColor(Consts.WHITEP);
134                 }
135             }
136         }
137     }
138
139     public Color getCurPieceColor() {
140         return curPieceColor;
141     }
142
143     public void setCurPieceColor(Color curPieceColor) {
144         this.curPieceColor = curPieceColor;
145         pieceBoard.setCurPieceColor(getCurPieceColor());
146         playerBoard.setCurPieceColor(getCurPieceColor());
147     }
148 }
```

```
 1 /*
 2  * CellBoard.java -- A class that defines the cellBoard of 8x8 cells.
 3  */
 4 …
12 public class CellBoard extends AbsSprite {
13
14     private CellSprite[][] cellBoard;
15     private PieceSprite[][] pieceBoard;
16     private int moveX = -1, moveY = -1;
```

```java
17      private int curRow = -1, curCol = -1;
18      private int newRow, newCol;
19
20      ...
56
57      @Override
58      public void updateSprite() {
59          if (isValidMove()) {
60              enterNewCell();
61              exitOldCell();
62          }
63      }
64
65      public void setMoveXY(int x, int y) {
66          this.moveX = x;
67          this.moveY = y;
68      }
69
70      private boolean isValidMove() {
71          boolean validMove = false;
72          if ((moveX >= 0) && (moveX <= Consts.BOARDW)
73                  && (moveY >= 0) && (moveY <= Consts.BOARDH)) {
74              newRow = getRow(moveY);
75              newCol = getCol(moveX);
76              if ((newRow != curRow) || (newCol != curCol)) {
77                  validMove = true;
78              }
79          }
80          return validMove;
81      }
82
83      private void enterNewCell() {
84          // if the pieceBoard does not have a piece
85          if (pieceBoard[newRow][newCol] == null) {
86              cellBoard[newRow][newCol].setColor(Consts.MOUSEENTERC);
87          }
88      }
89
90      private void exitOldCell() {
91          // exit from the previous cell
92          // prevent curRow == -1 and curCol == -1
93          if ((curRow >= 0) && (curRow < Consts.MAXCELL)
94                  && (curCol >= 0) && (curCol < Consts.MAXCELL)) {
95              cellBoard[curRow][curCol].setColor(Consts.CELLCOLOR);
96          }
97          curRow = newRow;
98          curCol = newCol;
99      }
100
101     public void setPieceBoard(PieceSprite[][] pieceBoard) {
102         this.pieceBoard = pieceBoard;
103     }
104
105     public int getRow(int mouseY) {
106         int numRow = 0;
```

20.4 Building up a Mouse Control Mechanism for Players: The Project Othello2

```
107            if (mouseY < Consts.VALIDMAXSIZE) { // won't make index of 8
108                numRow = mouseY / (Consts.CELLH + Consts.GAPW);
109            }
110            return numRow;
111        }
112
113        public int getCol(int mouseX) {
114            int numCol = 0;
115            if (mouseX < Consts.VALIDMAXSIZE) { // verify x value is valid
116                numCol = mouseX / (Consts.CELLW + Consts.GAPW);
117            }
118            return numCol;
119        }
120    }
```

```
 1  /*
 2   * PieceBoard.java - A class defines a pieceBoard for keeping track of
 3   * dynamic behaviors of pieces placed by players.
 4   */
 5  …
16  public class PieceBoard extends AbsSprite {
17
18      PieceSprite[][] pieceBoard;
19      private int clickX = -1, clickY = -1;
20      private Color curPieceColor;
21      private PropertyChangeSupport pChange;
22
23      @SuppressWarnings("OverridableMethodCallInConstructor")
24      public PieceBoard() {
25          …
27          pChange = new PropertyChangeSupport(this);
28      }
29
30      …
57
58      @Override
59      public void paintSprite(Graphics2D g2d) {
60          for (int row = 0; row < Consts.MAXCELL; row++) {
61              for (int col = 0; col < Consts.MAXCELL; col++) {
62                  if (pieceBoard[row][col] != null) {
63                      pieceBoard[row][col].paintSprite(g2d);
64                  }
65              }
66          }
67      }
68
69      @Override
70      public void updateSprite() {
71          if (isValidClick()) {
72              int newRow = getRow(clickY);
73              int newCol = getCol(clickX);
74              addPiece(newRow, newCol, curPieceColor);
75              fireClickDone();
76          }
77          // reset the isValidClick() back to false
```

```
78              // otherwise, the color will continue changing
79              clickX = -1;
80              clickY = -1;
81          }
82
83      public void setClickXY(int x, int y) {
84          this.clickX = x;
85          this.clickY = y;
86      }
87
88      public boolean isValidClick() {
89          boolean validClick = false;
90          if ((clickX >= 0) && (clickX <= Consts.BOARDW)
91                  && (clickY >= 0) && (clickY <= Consts.BOARDH)) {
92              validClick = true;
93          }
94          return validClick;
95      }
96
97      public void fireClickDone() {
98          pChange.firePropertyChange("clickDone", "-1", "1");
99      }
100
101     ...
122
123     public void addPropertyChangeListener(PropertyChangeListener pcl) {
124         pChange.addPropertyChangeListener(pcl);
125     }
126 }
```

The class GameCanvas.java has three important inner classes. One of them is the inner class BrowseCellBoardListener that implements the event handler mouseMoved() for receiving the mouse browsing action and passes the current coordinates (x, y) of the mouse to the method setMoveXY() in the class CellBoard.java for indicating the current browsing cell. It is the listener for the state of "Player browses cellBoard." The another inner class ClickPieceBoardListener implements the method mouseClicked() to receive the coordinates (x, y) of the mouse click point and passes them to the setClickXY() method in the class PieceBoard.java for placing a new piece on the position of clicked. It is the listener of the state "Flipping pieces and count." The third inner class ClickChange is for receiving the property change information sent out by the class PieceBoard.java for switching the current player to the next player with the switching of the corresponding color. It is the listener for the state "Switching current player." These three listeners keep the game regularly running on the three states until the checking condition "Whether more pieces can be placed on the board" returns false, which terminates the game.

When the class CellBoard.java sets the new coordinates (x, y) of the current position of the browsing mouse, its updateSprite() method invokes the method isValidMove() for verifying the validation of the position. If it is a valid move, the method enterNewCell() is invoked to assign the special color to the new cell, and the method exitOldCell() is invoked to assign the background color back to the cell where the mouse just left off.

As long as the class PieceBoard.java sets up the new coordinates (x, y) of the mouse click point, its updateSprite() method invokes the method isValidClick() for asserting the validation of the (x, y) and then coverts the (x, y) to be (newRow, newCol) and invokes the method addPiece() to place a current color piece on the pieceBoard at the clicked cell. After all, it invokes the method fireClickDone() to send the "click-done" information to the listener ClickChange in the class GameCanvas.java for switching the current color to be the opponent color.

20.5 Implementing the Playing Rules: The Project Othello3

Both the states "Player browsing board" and "Flipping pieces and count" on the state machine of Fig. 20.2 are now ready to be completely studied and implemented. As mentioned above, whether a cell could be a possible playing cell or not

20.5 Implementing the Playing Rules: The Project Othello3

and whether a sequence of pieces could be flipped over or not all depend on a set of playing rules. In other words, each of the rules should be able to perform two functions. (1) Once the mouse enters a new cell, the rule searches for a matching piece, which is a piece that belongs to the current player on the opposite end of a sequence of opponent pieces. If the new entered cell is a possible playing cell, its color should be changed to be the current player's color. (2) If the mouse clicks on a possible playing cell for placing a new piece on the cell, the rule flips over the sequence of opponent pieces between the two matched pieces with the current color. Consequently, every rule should implement a method isValid() for performing the first function and a method flipPiece() for performing the second function. For any cell, there are eight directions that should be searched: left, right, up, down, upLeft, upRight, downLeft, and downRight. Therefore, eight rules are needed. They perform same functions but on different searching directions. In other words, when the player moves the cursor on the cellBoard, a possible playing cell could be verified by one rule or by multiple rules. Thus, a mouse click for adding a new piece on the pieceBoard could flip one sequence of opponent pieces or flip multiple sequences of opponent pieces. In contrast, if the mouse clicks on a "not possible playing" cell, nothing will happen.

Based on these considerations, the software structure of the rule unit (logic portion) can be designed similar as the sprite inheritance hierarchy implemented for the GUI portion. That is, an abstract class AbsRule.java is created as the root of an inheritance hierarchy of eight rules. The abstract class AbsRule.java declares two abstract methods isValid() and flipPiece(), and then eight concrete subclasses corresponding to the eight rules implement the two methods. In addition, a concrete class RuleBase.java instantiates eight objects corresponding to the eight rules and defines a linear data structure to hold the objects of all eight rules. It seems like the class GameCanvas.java. Every time a player moves the mouse into a cell or places a new piece on a possible playing cell, the coordinates of the cell are sent to the class RuleBase.java, which involves a "for" loop to check every rule stored in the linear data structure. Whenever a method isValid() in a rule returns "true," the corresponding rule performs the method flipPiece() to flip over the corresponding sequence of opponent pieces.

Once all of the sequences of pieces are flipped over, a counting function counts the number of pieces of the two colors on the pieceBoard and sets a Boolean variable true or false based on the condition associated with whether the game can be continued playing or should be terminated, which is indicated with the diamond symbol in Fig. 20.2. Listing 20.3 shows the two classes AbsRule.java and RuleBase.java, as well as one of eight rules, the class LeftRule.java.

Listing 20.3 The classes AbsRule.java, RuleBase.java, and the LeftRule.java in the project Othello3

```
1  /*
2   * AbsRule.java - An abstract class as the root of the rule inheritance hierarchy.
3   */
4  package rule;
5
6  import java.awt.Color;
7  import othello.PieceSprite;
8
13 public abstract class AbsRule {
14
15     protected Color curPieceColor;
16     protected PieceSprite[][] pieceBoard;
17     private boolean flipFlag = false;
18
19     public AbsRule() {
20     }
21
22     public abstract boolean isValid(int newRow, int newCol);
23
24     public abstract void flipPiece();
25
26  ... getters and setters
49 }
```

```java
/*
 * LeftRule.java - A class that defines the left rule.
 */
package rule;

import java.awt.Color;


public class LeftRule extends AbsRule {

    int startRow, startCol;
    int untilRow, untilCol;

    public LeftRule() {
        super();
    }

    @Override
    public boolean isValid(int newRow, int newCol) {
        boolean valid = false;
        Color theColor = getCurPieceColor();
        if (verify(newRow, newCol, theColor)) {
            valid = true;
        }
        return valid;
    }

    public boolean verify(int newRow, int newCol, Color theColor) {
        boolean flag = false;
        if (((newCol - 1) >= 0)
                && ((getPieceBoard())[newRow][newCol - 1] != null)) {
            if (!(pieceBoard[newRow][newCol - 1].getColor().equals(theColor))) {
                if (getFlipFlag()) {
                    startRow = newRow;
                    startCol = newCol - 1;
                    untilRow = newRow;
                    untilCol = newCol - 1;
                }
                int col = newCol - 2;
                while ((col >= 0) && (pieceBoard[newRow][col] != null)) {
                    if (pieceBoard[newRow][col].getColor().equals(theColor)) {
                        if (getFlipFlag()) {
                            untilRow = newRow;
                            untilCol = col;
                        }
                        flag = true;
                        break;
                    } else {
                        col = col - 1;
                    }
                }
            }
        }
        return flag;
    }
}
```

20.5 Implementing the Playing Rules: The Project Othello3

```
60      @Override
61      public void flipPiece() {
62          if (getFlipFlag()) {
63              Color theColor = getCurPieceColor();
64              int row = startRow;
65              int col = startCol;
66              while (col > untilCol) {
67                  pieceBoard[row][col].setColor(theColor);
68                  col--;
69              }
70          }
71          untilRow = startRow;
72          untilCol = startCol;
73      }
74  }
```

```
 1  /*
 2   * RuleBase.java - A class defines a rule base for instantiating all of
 3   * flipping rules and inserting them into the linear data structure
 4   */
 5  package rule;
 6
 7  import java.awt.Color;
 8  import java.util.ArrayList;
 9  import othello.PieceSprite;
10
15  public class RuleBase {
16
17      private ArrayList<AbsRule> rules;
18      private PieceSprite[][] pieceBoard;
19      private Color curPieceColor;
20      private int newRow, newCol;
21
22      public RuleBase() {
23          rules = new ArrayList<AbsRule>();
24      }
25
26      public void initRules() {
27          UpRule upRule = new UpRule();
28          rules.add(upRule);
29          DownRule downRule = new DownRule();
30          rules.add(downRule);
31          LeftRule leftRule = new LeftRule();
32          rules.add(leftRule);
33          RightRule rightRule = new RightRule();
34          rules.add(rightRule);
35          UpRightRule upRightRule = new UpRightRule();
36          rules.add(upRightRule);
37          UpLeftRule upLeftRule = new UpLeftRule();
38          rules.add(upLeftRule);
39          DownRightRule downRightRule = new DownRightRule();
40          rules.add(downRightRule);
41          DownLeftRule downLeftRule = new DownLeftRule();
42          rules.add(downLeftRule);
43      }
44
```

```java
45      public void setRulesPieceBoard() {
46          for (int i = 0; i < rules.size(); i++) {
47              rules.get(i).setPieceBoard(pieceBoard);
48          }
49      }
50
51      public void setRulesColor() {
52          for (int idx = 0; idx < rules.size(); idx++) {
53              rules.get(idx).setCurPieceColor(getCurPieceColor());
54          }
55      }
56
57      public void flipPiece() {
58          for (int idx = 0; idx < rules.size(); idx++) {
59              AbsRule aRule = rules.get(idx);
60              // set flipFlag true to measure and flip pieces
61              aRule.setFlipFlag(true);
62              aRule.isValid(newRow, newCol); // it meauses startRow-untilRow
63              aRule.flipPiece(); // it flips from startRow to untilRow
64              aRule.setFlipFlag(false);
65          }
66      }
67
68      public boolean isRuleValid() {
69          boolean ruleValid = false;
70          for (int idx = 0; idx < rules.size(); idx++) {
71              if ((rules.get(idx)).isValid(newRow, newCol)) {
72                  ruleValid = true;
73              }
74          }
75          return ruleValid;
76      }
77
78      public void setPieceBoard(PieceSprite[][] pieceBoard) {
79          this.pieceBoard = pieceBoard;
80          setRulesPieceBoard();
81      }
82
83      public PieceSprite[][] getPieceBoard() {
84          return pieceBoard;
85      }
86
87      public void setCurPieceColor(Color curPieceColor) {
88          this.curPieceColor = curPieceColor;
89          setRulesColor();
90      }
91
92  ... remaining getters and setters
103 }
```

Here, we only select one of the eight rules, the LeftRule.java, as an example. Clearly, the class LeftRule.java (and all of rules) implements the major two methods. When the mouse moves into a new cell, it becomes the verifying cell. Every rule should be involved to see whether the verifying cell is a possible playing cell or not. The class LeftRule.java demonstrates that when the method isValid() of the leftRule receives the coordinates (newRow, newCol) of the verifying cell, it invokes another method verify() to check whether the cell is a possible playing cell or not. Clearly, these two methods are invoked by the action of browsing cellBoard. If the current cell is a possible playing cell, then the cellBoard displays the current player's color on the cell. The algorithm for the verification depends on the function of the rule. For the leftRule, it verifies whether a cell is a possible playing cell by looking at the cells that appear on the left direction of the verifying cell. Suppose that the verifying cell has a coordinates (newRow, newCol) and the color of the current player is white, then the left cell of the verifying cell has a coordinates (newRow, newCol-1). If the piece on the left cell is black, the rule needs to look at the piece on the further left side with the coordinates (newRow, newCol-2) until finding a white piece or no more pieces or out of the boundary of the cellBoard. If it found a white piece, the verifying cell is a possible playing cell and isValid() returns true. That is why a "while" loop is used to keep track of the color of the left cells. When the signal of "valid is true" feeds back to the class CellBoard.java, the cell shows the current player's color for the player to indicate the current cell is a possible playing cell.

When the player moves the mouse around, he/she could find multiple possible playing cells. As long as he/she selects one of them and places a white piece on the cell, the class PieceBoard.java accepts a click; it sets the flip flag as true and invokes the method flipPiece() in the concrete rule classes to flip the sequence of black pieces between the pair of white pieces. There are two approaches to flip the sequence of pieces. One approach is to duplicate the same code for verifying a possible playing cell to flip the opponent pieces one-by-one. The other approach is to introduce two pairs of variables startRow-untilRow and startCol-untilCol for measuring the start position and the end position. And the code for the measurement is embedded in the method verify(). Consequently, when the player clicks on a possible playing cell, the RuleBase.java class sets up the flipFlag true and invokes the method isValid() for calling the method verify() to measure the values of startRow, untilRow, startCol, and untilCol and then invokes the method flipPiece() to flip over opponent pieces. The second approach recorded the starting and ending positions so that it provides the information about number of opponent pieces that will be flipped. This information is important for some other algorithms, such as the algorithm for selecting a best possible playing cell in order to flip the maximum number of pieces, where measuring the number of pieces that could be flipped over is required before really flipping them (see the following Chapter.)

In the implementation process, it is better to pick up one of the eight rules and correctly implement it as a code template for other rules because all of rules have the similar codes except the checking directions. One more suggestion is placing all rules inside another package, say "rule," in the project file structure for easy accessing (please see the project Othello3). Otherwise so many different rule classes are mixed with other classes together that may cause confusions.

20.6 Linking the Rules with the Sprites on the GUI: The Project Othello3

Obviously, all of the playing rules are the major contents of the logic part in the abstract model shown on Fig. 20.1. After completely building up all of the playing rules, the next step is to link the logic part with the GUI part. More specific, the linkage that would be set up is to connect any playing rule with the browsing algorithm and the clicking algorithm that have been implemented in the project Othello2. As discussed above, the project Othello2 implemented the browsing algorithm for coloring the current cell with a special color. Now the playing rules will assign a semantics meaning to the mechanism as to only changing the color of those possible playing cells with the current player's color according to the relevant rule so that the player can easily find all of possible playing cells and select one of them to place a piece on it. The semantics meaning assigned to the clicking algorithm is that once the current player places a piece on a possible playing cell by clicking the cell, the playing rule will flip all of the opponent pieces between the two matched current player's pieces.

Intuitively, for the browsing algorithm, the input data sent from the GUI to the logic are the cell coordinates (row, col) touched by the player's mouse; the output data responded from the logic to the GUI is whether the cell is a possible playing cell or not. If a cell is a possible playing cell, the GUI shows the cell with the current player's color; otherwise, simply ignore it. For the clicking algorithm, the input data from the GUI to the logic are the coordinates (row, col) of the cell that the player clicks on; the output data from the logic to the GUI are the flipped pieces. Under the case when the GUI and the logic units are physically separated, such as what we did in this game, knowing what data should be sent from one end to the other end in order to synchronize both sides is the key for implementing, tracing, and debugging the codes.

In more detail, these data should be sent from the cellBoard to all of the playing rules. However, they are separated classes without any communication channel. The better way is to rely on the PropertyChangeListener set up in the class GameCanvas.java. That is, as long as a browsing action occurs on the class CellBoard.java or a clicking happens on the class PieceBoard.java, the two classes fire a property change event with the coordinate data to the class GameCanvas.java, which in turn immediately transfers the data to the playing rules. The methods related to communications are cited in Listing 20.4.

In short, the communication chains are as follows:
  1. Browsing the cellBoard

```
gameCanvas:BrowseCellBoardListener.mouseMoved() -> cellBoard.setMoveXY();
"game loop" -> cellBoare.updateSprite() -> cellBoard.isValidMove() -> cellBoard.fireCheckRules() ->
gameCanvas:CheckRules.propertyChange() -> ruleBase.setNewRow() -> ruleBase.setNewCol() -> rule-
Base.isRuleValid() -> (1) and (2);
(1) cellBoard.setRuleValid(true) -> enterNewCell() -> exitOldCell();
(2) pieceBoard.setRuleValid() // preparing for a click
```

  2. Clicking the pieceBoard

```
gameCanvas:ClickPieceBoardListener.mouseClicked() ->
pieceBoard.setClickXY(); "game loop" -> pieceBoard.updateSprite() ->
pieceBoard.isValidClick() -> pieceBoard.addPiece() -> pieceBoard.fireClickDone() ->
gameCanvas:ClickChange.propertyChange() -> ruleBase.flipPiece() ->
cellBoard.exitOldCell() -> gameCanvas.countPieces() ->
switching color and player.
```

Listing 20.4 The methods relate with communications defined in the GameCanvas.java, CellBoard.java, and PieceBoard.java classes in the project Othello3

```
  1 /*
  2  * GameCanvas.java - A class that implements the game canvas.
  3  */
  4 ...
 20 public class GameCanvas extends AbsGameCanvas {
 21 ...
110
111     public void countPieces() {
112         thePieceBoard = pieceBoard.getPieceBoard();
113         for (int row = 0; row < Consts.MAXCELL; row++) {
114             for (int col = 0; col < Consts.MAXCELL; col++) {
115                 if (thePieceBoard[row][col] != null) {
116                     if (thePieceBoard[row][col].getColor().equals(
117                             Consts.WHITEP)) {
118                         numWhite++;
119                     } else if (thePieceBoard[row][col].getColor().equals(
120                             Consts.BLACKP)) {
121                         numBlack++;
122                     }
123                 }
124             }
125         }
126         scoreBoard.setNumWhite(numWhite);
127         numWhite = 0;
128         scoreBoard.setNumBlack(numBlack);
129         numBlack = 0;
130     }
131 ...
144     class BrowseCellBoardListener extends MouseMotionAdapter {
145
146         @Override
147         public void mouseMoved(MouseEvent evt) {
```

20.6 Linking the Rules with the Sprites on the GUI: The Project Othello3

```
148                int x = evt.getX();
149                int y = evt.getY();
150                cellBoard.setMoveXY(x, y);
151            }
152        }
153
154        class ClickPieceBoardListener extends MouseAdapter {
155
156            @Override
157            public void mouseClicked(MouseEvent evt) {
158                int x = evt.getX();
159                int y = evt.getY();
160                pieceBoard.setClickXY(x, y);
161            }
162        }
163
164        class CheckRules implements PropertyChangeListener {
165
166            @Override
167            public void propertyChange(PropertyChangeEvent evt) {
168                String checkRule = evt.getPropertyName();
169                Point theP = (Point) evt.getNewValue();
170                if (checkRule.equals("checkRules")) {
171                    ruleBase.setNewRow(theP.x);
172                    ruleBase.setNewCol(theP.y);
173                    if (ruleBase.isRuleValid()) {
174                        cellBoard.setRuleValid(true);
175                        pieceBoard.setRuleValid(theP.x, theP.y, true);
176                    }
177                }
178            }
179        }
180
181        class ClickChange implements PropertyChangeListener {
182
183            @Override
184            public void propertyChange(PropertyChangeEvent evt) {
185                String theChange = evt.getPropertyName();
186                if (theChange.equals("clickDone")) {
187                    // add method calls for flip pieces and count pieces
188                    ruleBase.flipPiece(); // flip pieces
189                    cellBoard.exitOldCell(); // make CELLCOLOR
190                    countPieces(); // count number of pieces of both
191                    if (getCurPieceColor().equals(Consts.WHITEP)) {
192                        setCurPieceColor(Consts.BLACKP);
193                    } else if (getCurPieceColor().equals(Consts.BLACKP)) {
194                        setCurPieceColor(Consts.WHITEP);
195                    }
196                }
197            }
198        }
199
200        public Color getCurPieceColor() {
201            return curPieceColor;
202        }
```

```
203
204 …
212 }
```

```java
  1 /*
  2  * CellBoard.java -- A class that defines the cellBoard of 8x8 cells.
  3  */
  4 …
 16 public class CellBoard extends AbsSprite {
 17
 18     …
 64
 65     @Override
 66     public void updateSprite() {
 67         if (isValidMove()) {
 68             fireCheckRules(); // ask GameCanvas for checking rules
 69             if (isRuleValid()) { // GameCanvas setCheckValid(true)
 70                 enterNewCell(); // light on the valid cell
 71                 setRuleValid(false);
 72             }
 73             exitOldCell();
 74         }
 75     }
 76
 77     public void setMoveXY(int x, int y) {
 78         this.moveX = x;
 79         this.moveY = y;
 80     }
 81
 82     private boolean isValidMove() {
 83         boolean validMove = false;
 84         if ((moveX >= 0) && (moveX <= Consts.BOARDW)
 85                 && (moveY >= 0) && (moveY <= Consts.BOARDH)) {
 86             newRow = getRow(moveY);
 87             newCol = getCol(moveX);
 88             if ((newRow != curRow) || (newCol != curCol)) {
 89                 validMove = true;
 90             }
 91         }
 92         return validMove;
 93     }
 94
 95     private void enterNewCell() {
 96         // if the pieceBoard does not have a piece
 97         if (pieceBoard[newRow][newCol] == null) {
 98             cellBoard[newRow][newCol].setColor(getCurPieceColor());
 99         }
100     }
101
102     public void exitOldCell() {
103         // exit from the previous cell
104         // prevent curRow == -1 and curCol == -1
105         if ((curRow >= 0) && (curRow < Consts.MAXCELL)
106                 && (curCol >= 0) && (curCol < Consts.MAXCELL)) {
107             cellBoard[curRow][curCol].setColor(Consts.CELLCOLOR);
```

20.6 Linking the Rules with the Sprites on the GUI: The Project Othello3

```
108            }
109            curRow = newRow;
110            curCol = newCol;
111        }
112
113        ...
132
133        public boolean isRuleValid() {
134            return ruleValid;
135        }
136
137        public void setRuleValid(boolean ruleValid) {
138            this.ruleValid = ruleValid;
139        }
140
141        public void fireCheckRules() {
142            Point oldRowCol = new Point(-1, -1);
143            Point newRowCol = new Point(newRow, newCol);
144            checkRules.firePropertyChange("checkRules", oldRowCol, newRowCol);
145        }
146
147        public void addPropertyChangeListener(PropertyChangeListener pcl) {
148            checkRules.addPropertyChangeListener(pcl);
149        }
150
151        ...
158 }
```

```
 1 /*
 2  * PieceBoard.java - A class defines a pieceBoard for keeping track of
 3  * dynamic behaviors of pieces placed by players.
 4  */
 5 ...
16 public class PieceBoard extends AbsSprite {
17
18     ...
71
72     @Override
73     public void updateSprite() {
74         if (isValidClick()) {
75             int newRow = getRow(clickY);
76             int newCol = getCol(clickX);
77             // only for the possible playing cell; ignore other cells
78             if ((newRow == ruleValidRow) && (newCol == ruleValidCol)) {
79                 addPiece(newRow, newCol, curPieceColor);
80                 setRuleValid(-1, -1, false);
81                 fireClickDone();
82             }
83         }
84         // reset the isValidClick() back to false
85         // otherwise, the color will continue changing
86         clickX = -1;
87         clickY = -1;
88     }
89
```

```java
 90    public void setClickXY(int x, int y) {
 91        this.clickX = x;
 92        this.clickY = y;
 93    }
 94
 95    public boolean isValidClick() {
 96        boolean validClick = false;
 97        if ((clickX >= 0) && (clickX <= Consts.BOARDW)
 98                && (clickY >= 0) && (clickY <= Consts.BOARDH)) {
 99            validClick = true;
100        }
101        return validClick;
102    }
103
104    public void fireClickDone() {
105        pChange.firePropertyChange("clickDone", "-1", "1");
106    }
107 ...
118    public void setRuleValid(int row, int col, boolean b) {
119        ruleValidRow = row;
120        ruleValidCol = col;
121        this.ruleValid = b;
122    }
123
135 ...
136    public void addPropertyChangeListener(PropertyChangeListener pcl) {
137        pChange.addPropertyChangeListener(pcl);
138    }
139 }
```

At this point, it is clear that the design and implementation of the game Othello followed the state machine in Fig. 20.2, based on the guidance of the three-layer game structure framework. With the incremental development strategy, the different versions are gradually inserting sprites into the inheritance hierarchy. The project Othello3 completes the major functions of the game. Its software structure can be summarized as the UML class diagram shown in Fig. 20.5.

multiple states. Player's inputs cause the transition from current state to the other. Thus, the state machine is not only a visible "mind" map but also a blueprint for building up the game.

After finishing all functions, the game needs some polishing, such as replacing the pieces by using images, adding sound effects, completing the method announceTermination(), etc. All of these will be covered in the next chapter.

20.7 Summary

This chapter starts a new game Othello, which is a chess-like game played by two human players. It applies the abstract model of games to separate a game into a GUI unit and a logic unit. They communicate through inputState data and outputState data. This model helps us to analyze the logic flow of the game and to build up a loosely coupled system for increasing its reusability and maintainability. At the same time, the input data and output data form the key for implementing, tracing, and debugging the codes. The logic flow can be further analyzed as a state machine, which divides the entire flow into

20.8 Exercises

Self-Reviewing Questions

1. What is the abstract model of games? Draw the figure for further familiarizing it.
2. Why is the abstract model important?
3. What are the GUI potion and the logic portion in the game Othello?
4. What input data and output data is sending between the two portions?

20.8 Exercises

Fig. 20.5 The UML class diagram of the version Othello3

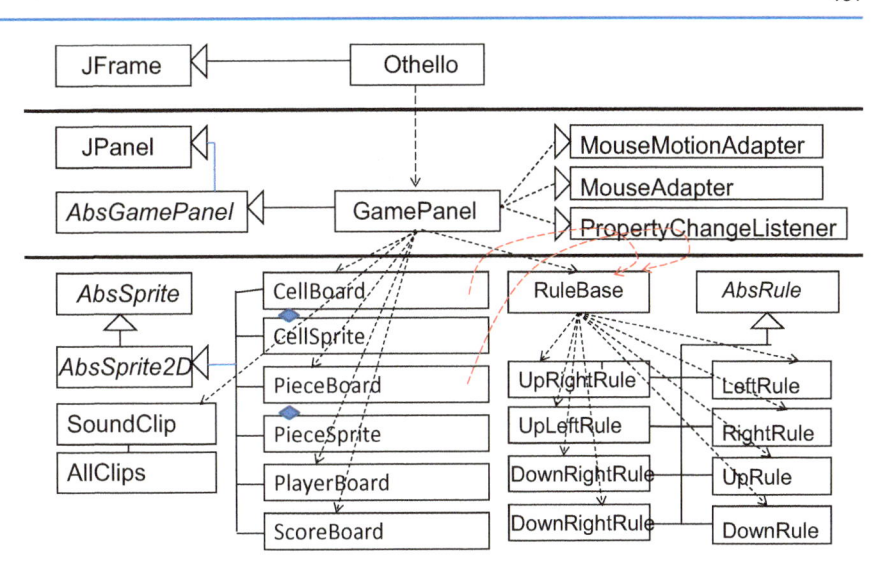

5. What does the UML state machine of the game Othello look like? Is it important?
6. What does the UML class diagram of the Othello1 look like?
7. What does the UML class diagram of the Othello2 look like?
8. What does the UML class diagram of the Othello3 look like?
9. What are the two major dynamic behaviors in the game Othello?
10. What are the communication chains for the two major dynamic behaviors?
11. What event listeners are employed in the game Othello?
12. What classes are the composite classes in the game Othello?
13. Why does the game Othello need the thread and the "game loop"?
14. What does the structure of the playing rules look like?

Projects

1. There are many chess-like games. Select one of them and develop it.
2. Design and implement a game of Max4. It is a game played by two players with pieces in two different colors. The game has a 6 × 6 board of round holes. The players take a turn to drop his/her own pieces along a column of the board. The pieces will flow down along the column and stay at a lowest available hole. If any player will make four same color pieces consecutively along a row, a column, or a dialog, he/she wins the game.

21. An Introduction of Artificial Intelligence: Extensions of the Game Othello

This chapter improves the game Othello with new ideas. The new ideas include replacing the pieces with images, making pixels of images transparency, applying the frame-based animation for flipping the image pieces, adding sound effects, and more. Further, the two players game is constructed as single player against a computer player in order to introduce the artificial intelligence concepts and practices. The new developed artificial intelligence algorithms include "first", "random", "best", and "edge".

The objectives of this chapter include:
1. Enhancing the game Othello.
2. Changing pieces to be images.
3. Frame-based animation: flipping pieces.
4. Constructing a single-player version of Othello.
5. Introducing the concepts of artificial intelligence.
6. Four different algorithms for the computer player.
7. The implementations of the four algorithms.

The previous chapter completed three steps in the development of the game Othello, which made the game working fine. Now, we are going to enhance the game with more functions. The major enhancements include changing the pieces from the drawing circles to the six images that are animated for simulating "real" flipping actions and adding sounds for some major actions, such as moving the mouse and flipping over the sequence of pieces.

A further extension is to develop the chess-like game played by two human players to be one human player against the computer player so that a single player can play the game. This extension provides us a case to introduce the ideas about artificial intelligence, which is one of very important contents of video games.

21.1 Changing Pieces to Be Images: The Project Othello4

The pieces in all versions of Othello so far are drawing circles. They are better to be replaced with images. The piece images are marked with 1–12 and are stored in the folder "images" in the file structure of the game Othello4. The image 1 is a full black piece; the image 7 is a full white piece. All images are read into the game and stored in an array pieces[] with the indexes 0–11. Animating the piece images with the indexes of 0–6 illustrates the color changes from the full black to the full white; animating the piece images with the indexes of 6–12 (0) shows the color changes from the full white to the full black. This kind of animation is based on continuously displaying premade images with a certain speed of frame per second for demonstrating a dynamic behavior. It is named as "frame-based animation," which differs from the "sprite-based animation" that is based on the computer graphics as we used so far. All cartoons or movies adopt this kind of frame animation.

21.2 Making Background Color of Images Transparent: The Project TestFlip1

Before inserting the images with the new animation into the game Othello, we would like to code a small project with the name of TestFlip for introducing and demonstrating the frame animation technique first. We copy the project GameStruTemplate from Chap. 18 and rename it as TestFlip1. The project adds a composite class PieceSpriteTemp.java to load all of the 12 pieces of images into an array oriPieces[] with the type of BufferedImage. And then, the GameCanvas.

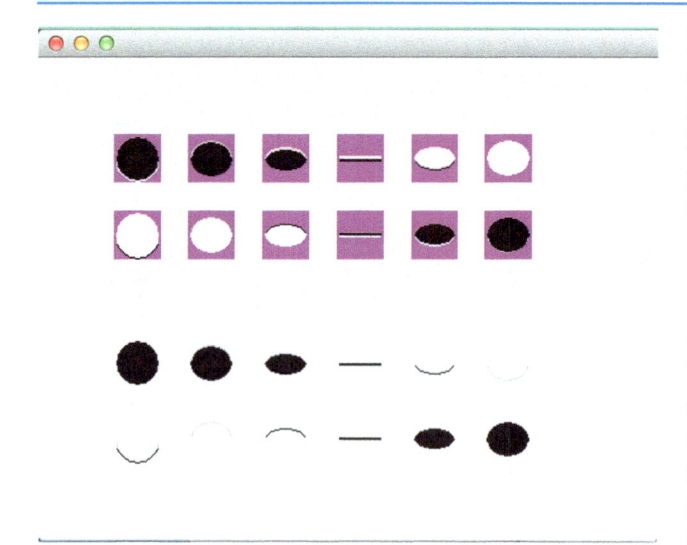

Fig. 21.1 The original piece images and the transparent piece images

java class instantiates an object of the composite class and adds it into the global spriteAry. When the project executes, the paintComponent() method will pick up the object of the composite class from the global spriteAry and invoke the method pieceSpriteTemp.paintSprite() to paint the piece images on the screen.

The class PieceSpriteTemp.java shows the original 12 images on the first 2 rows in Fig. 21.1. It is clear that every image has a shape of square that contains the circle shape of a piece. If we are going to use these original images directly, the pieces that show up on the GUI of the game will be squares. Definitely, it is not what we like. Therefore, we have to cut off the background red color and make each piece have its own shape just like the images shown in the third and fourth rows on Fig. 21.1. In order to cut off the background color, we need to make the background red color transparent. For that, we developed another class PieceSprite.java for loading the original images. And we add a special method makeTransparent() in the class PieceSprite.java. The special method will make the background color transparent for every image. After that, the images just like those that are shown on the third and fourth rows on Fig. 21.1.

The color of a pixel in a PNG image consists of 4 bytes. The Alpha byte represents the transparency of the color. The constant TYPE_INT_ARGB defined in the built-in class BufferedImage represents an image with 8-bit ARGB (Alpha-Red-Green-Blue) color components packed into integer pixels (32 bits). The Alpha value is stored in the bits 24–31 of the 32-bit structure. If we would like to make a pixel complete transparent, we need to make the Alpha value as zero. The following statement can reach this goal:

```
setRGB(x, y, (imageOri.getRGB(x, y) & 0x00FFFFFF));
```

where (x, y) indicates the coordinates of a pixel on the image. The sign "&" represents a bit-wise AND operation. The notation 0x00FFFFFF indicates that it is a hexadecimal number, where one digit represents 4 bits. In other words, it means that in the total of 32 bits (4 bytes), every bit in the leftmost byte (8 bits are represented by two 00) has a value of 0. The remaining 24 bits on the right are all 1s. The entire statement above means that for a pixel at (x, y), we let its RGB original color "bit-wise AND" with the binary value of 0x00FFFFFF. Any value AND with 0 will be 0; any value AND with 1 will keep the original value. Because the leftmost 8 bits are 0s in the value of 0x00FFFFFF, after bit-wise AND, all of bits in the Alpha byte will be 0, that is, the original pixel will be completely transparent.

Therefore, the ideas of the method makeTransparent() are as follows:

1. Load in an original image bTempImage and prepare an empty image bImage that has the exact same size as the original image for holding the processed image.
2. Get the color of the first pixel at the (0, 0) position from the original image bTempImage. The color of the pixel represents the background color of the existing image, and we name it as transparentColor.
3. Get every pixel one-by-one from the original image bTempImage; if the color of the pixel is the same as the transparentColor and if it is required to be transparency, we set the Alpha bits of the pixel as 0 by applying the computation shown above in the processed image bImage.
4. If the color of a pixel is not same as the transparentColor, leave it as is. Consequently, all pixels with the background color will be transparent in the processed image. Finally, the method returns the processed image bImage, which is what we want. The code of the method makeTransparent() is shown in Listing 21.1.

Listing 21.1 The code of the method makeTransparent() in the class PieceSprite.java in the project TestFlip1

```
1  /*
2   * PieceSprite.java - A class that loads original six white images and six
3   * black images. And then, it makes them transparent and displays them.
4   */
5  package testflip;
```

21.2 Making Background Color of Images Transparent: The Project TestFlip1

```java
 6
 7 import java.awt.Graphics2D;
 8 import java.awt.image.BufferedImage;
 9 import javax.imageio.ImageIO;
10
11 public class PieceSprite extends AbsSpriteImage {
12
13     private BufferedImage[] pieces;
14     private final int MAXPIECE = 12;
15     private int transparentColor = -1;
16     private boolean transparent = true;
17     // for flip a piece
18     private int imageIdx = 0;
19     private int numTurns = 0;
20     private boolean flipStop = true;
21     private GameCanvas gameCanvas;
22
23     @SuppressWarnings("OverridableMethodCallInConstructor")
24     public PieceSprite() {
25         pieces = new BufferedImage[MAXPIECE];
26         initSprite();
27     }
28
29     @Override
30     public void initSprite() {
31         loadImages();
32     }
33
34     // To load images with transparent background color into the array pieces.
35     private void loadImages() {
36         for (int i = 0; i < MAXPIECE; i++) {
37             pieces[i] = getBufferedImage(i + 1);
38         }
39         setActive(false);
40         setVisible(true);
41     }
42
43     public BufferedImage getBufferedImage(int i) {
44         BufferedImage bImage = null;
45         try {
46             BufferedImage bTempImage = ImageIO.read(getClass().getResource(
47                     "../images/piece" + i + ".PNG"));
48             bImage = new BufferedImage(bTempImage.getWidth(),
49                     bTempImage.getHeight(), BufferedImage.TYPE_INT_ARGB);
50             bImage = makeTransparent(bImage, bTempImage);
51         } catch (Exception ex) {
52         }
53         return bImage;
54     }
55
56     // Makes background transparent. (1) get the color of the pixel at the
57     // top-left corner (0, 0) from the original image bImageTemp, which is the
58     // background color. Name it as transparentColor. (2) get the color of all
59     // other pixels one-by-one; if the color of the other pixel is the same as
60     // the transparentColor and if it is required to be transparency, set the
```

```
61          // pixel at the same position in the processed image bImage as transparent.
62          // (3) if the color of the other pixel is not same as the transparentColor,
63          // leave it as is. Thus, all pixels with the background color will be
64          // switched to be transparent. Finally, return the processed image bImage.
65          public BufferedImage makeTransparent(BufferedImage bImage,
66                  BufferedImage bImageTemp) {
67              transparentColor = bImageTemp.getRGB(0, 0);
68
69              for (int x = 0; x < bImageTemp.getWidth(); x++) {
70                  for (int y = 0; y < bImageTemp.getHeight(); y++) {
71                      if (bImageTemp.getRGB(x, y) == getTransparentColor()) {
72                          if (isTransparent()) {
73                              bImage.setRGB(x, y, (bImageTemp.getRGB(x, y) & 0x00FFFFFF));
74                          } else {
75                              bImage.setRGB(x, y, bImageTemp.getRGB(x, y));
76                          }
77                      } else {
78                          bImage.setRGB(x, y, bImageTemp.getRGB(x, y));
79                      }
80                  }
81              }
82              return bImage;
83          }
84
85          @Override
86          public void paintSprite(Graphics2D g2d) {
87              int oriX = getX() + 60;
88              setY(getY() + 160);
89              for (int i = 0; i < MAXPIECE; i++) {
90                  if (i % 6 == 0) {
91                      setY(getY() + 60);
92                      setX(oriX);
93                  }
94                  g2d.drawImage(pieces[i], getX(), getY(), null);
95                  setX(getX() + 60);
96              }
97              gameCanvas.stopGame();
98          }
99
100         @Override
101         public void updateSprite() {
102         }
103
...     // getter and setter methods
135     }
```

21.3 Animating Image Pieces: The Project TestFlip2

After 12 processed images are stored in an array, we can animate them to mimic a "real" flip action. We copied the project TestFlip1 to be a new version of TestFlip2. Since the "game loop" updates and repaints a sprite, we need to implement the method updateSprite() and modify the method paintSprite() in the class PieceSprite.java.

The method paintSprite() is simple, which just has one statement for drawing an image. The method updateSprite() needs to continuously switch six images with the indices of 1–6 (the images of 2–7) for dynamically change a piece from black to white or continuously switch six images with the

21.3 Animating Image Pieces: The Project TestFlip2

indices of 7–12 (0) (the images of 8–1) for flipping a piece from white to black.

For that, we initialize two variables imageIdx = 0 and numTurns = 6. Once the game loop invokes the updateSprite(), the following piece of code executes:

```
imageIdx = (imageIdx + 1) % numTurns;
if ((numTurns == 6) && (imageIdx == 0)) {
    // flip black to white
    imageIdx = 6;
    setFlipStop(true);
}
```

The statement "(imageIdx + 1) % numTurns" increases the imageIdx by 1 to make the imageIdx as 1; then the method paintSprite() shows the image with the index 1. The global animation mechanism continuously invokes the method updateSprite(), which continuously invokes the statement "(imageIdx + 1) % numTurns" for changing the index to be 2, 3, ... until imageIdx = 5. Next step, the statement "(imageIdx + 1) % numTurns" makes imageIdx as 0. The two values of numTurn = 6 and imageIdx = 0 makes the "if" statement true. The body of the "if" statement makes the imageIdx = 6; paintSprite() paints the image of the complete white piece on the board and then setFlipStop(true). Hence, the six invocations of updateSprite() continuously change the six image shapes and color that illustrates a flip of a piece.

Similarly, for flipping a while piece to be black one, initialize imageIdx = 6 and numTurns = 12; and another "if ((numTurns == 12) && (imageIdx == 0))" condition will complete a flip of a piece with another color.

Definitely, the initialization of the two variables and starting flip as well as stopping flip signals are all issued from the classes of different playing rules. The code of the method updateSprite() in the class PieceSprite.java shown in Listing 21.2 will continuously flip a piece from black to white and from white to black without stopping because the statement setFlipStop(true) is commented out.

Listing 21.2 The code of the method updateSprite() in the class PieceSprite.java in the project TestFlip2

```
1  /*
2   * PieceSprite.java - A class that loads original six white images and six
3   * black images. And then, it makes them transparent and displays them. When
4   * flip starts, its updateSprite() method animates the images.
5   */
6  package testflip;
7
...
12 public class PieceSprite extends AbsSpriteImage {
13
...
18     // for flip a piece
19     // 0 and 6 will flip black to white
20     // 6 and 12 will flip white to black
21     private int imageIdx = 0;
22     private int numTurns = 6;
...
88
89     @Override
90     public void paintSprite(Graphics2D g2d) {
91         if (isVisible()) {
92             g2d.drawImage(pieces[imageIdx], getX(), getY(), null);
93         }
94     }
95
96     @Override
97     public void updateSprite() { // animate images to mimic flipping a piece
98         if (flipStop == false) { // start flip
99             imageIdx = (imageIdx + 1) % numTurns;
100            if ((numTurns == 6) && (imageIdx == 0)) { // flip black to white
101                imageIdx = 6;
102                numTurns = 12;
```

```
103                    //setFlipStop(true); // stop flip
104                } else if ((numTurns == 12) && (imageIdx == 0)) { // flip white to black
105                    imageIdx = 0;
106                    numTurns = 6;
107                    //setFlipStop(true);
108                }
109            }
110        }
111
... // getter and setter methods
143 }
```

21.4 Inserting the Image Pieces: The Project Othello4

Now we are ready to insert the image pieces with animating flip actions into the project Othello4. The following steps should be done.

21.4.1 Replacing the Graphical Drawing Pieces with the Image Pieces

The class PieceSprite.java that developed in the project TestFlip2, which can animate the image pieces, should replace the original PieceSprite.java that only draws circle pieces. However, actually pieces in the project have two kinds of behaviors. One is static piece such as the piece in the playerBoard that only shows white or black without flipping animation; the other kinds of pieces have dynamic behavior such as all pieces on the pieceBoard. Thus, the method paintSprite() in the class PieceSprite.java needs to take care of these two kinds of painting. Fortunately, the PieceSprite.java class has a Boolean variable flipStop; when it is true, no flipping animation is required, and the paintSprite() sets imageIdx = 6 for painting static black piece and sets imageIdx = 0 for painting static white piece; and when the flipStop is false, flipping animation starts, and the game loop drives the paintSprite() method continuously painting six image pieces. As long as the flipping animation finishes, the value of flipStop will be set up as true. Taking advantage of this variable, the paintSprite() method in the class PieceSprite.java can be implemented as follows:

```
96      @Override
97      public void paintSprite(Graphics2D g2d) {
98          // it takes care of both "no flip" paint (in playerBoard) and "flip" paint
99          // "no flip" paint needs the color. "flip" paint needs changing imageIdx
100         if (flipStop) { // no flip, check the color then set imageIdx
101             if (getColor() == Consts.WHITEP) {
102                 setImageIdx(6); // image with index 6 is a while piece
103             } else if (getColor().equals(Consts.BLACKP)) {
104                 setImageIdx(0); // image with index 0 is a black piece
105             }
106         }
107         // during flip, imageIdx is dynamically changed by updateSprite()
108         g2d.drawImage(pieces[imageIdx], getX(), getY(), null);
109     }
```

21.4.2 Applying Frame-Based Animation for Animating the Image Pieces

For performing the flipping animation, the method updateSprite() in the class PieceSprite.java should be coded. Unfortunately, it cannot be driven directly by the game loop since pieceSprites are components of the composite class PieceBoard.java. Therefore, the method updateSprite() in the class PieceSprite.java should be invoked by the method updateSprite() defined in the class PieceBoard.java. Consequently, an extra piece of code as follows should be added into the method updateSprite() of the class PieceBoard.java:

```
for (int row=0; row<Consts.MAXCELL; row++) {
    for (int col=0; col<Consts.MAXCELL; col++) {
        if (pieceBoard[row][col] != null)
            pieceBoard[row][col].updateSprite();
    }
}
```

21.4.3 Adding the "import rule.RuleBase" into the Class GameCanvas.java

The method initComponent() in the class GameCanvas.java should initialize the rules for finding the possible playing cells and flipping pieces. Because we place all of rules in a separate package "rule," before going to initialize all of rules, we must add the statement "import rule.RuleBase" into the import list of the class GameCanvas.java. Otherwise, the package "rule" won't be able to be accessed. Due to its importance, we emphasize this task by repeating it here.

And then, the method initComponent() adds a new method initRuleBase() for instantiating the object ruleBase of the class rule.RuleBase.java and then invoking ruleBase.initRules() to instantiate all of rules.

21.4.4 Modifying All of Rule Classes from Drawing Pieces to Animating Image Pieces

We need to modify all of rule classes from drawing circle pieces to animating image pieces by setting up the two variables imageIdx and numTurns. Here, the class LeftRule.java is cited in the Listing 21.3 as a rule example for illustrating the variable initialization and the signals for starting and stopping animations in flipping pieces. Since the pieceBoard holds all of pieces, pieceBoard[row][col] refers to the piece positioned at the [row][col]. Based on the current color of the piece at the position, the method setFlipStop() sets the flipStop signal false to start the flipping animation, and then the two methods setImageIdx() and setNumTurns() initialize the variables imageIdx and numTurns in the class PieceSprite.java corresponding to the color of the current flipping pieces. If the rule would like to flip a white piece to be black, the two variables are initialized with a pair of (0 and 6); once the rule would like to flip a black piece to be white, the two variables are initialized with a pair of (6 and 12).

Listing 21.3 The class LeftRule.java in the project Othello4

```
 1  /*
 2   * LeftRule.java - A rule that places a piece on the left position
 3   * to flip the opponent pieces on the right direction.
 4   */
 5  package rule;
 6
 7  import java.awt.Color;
 8  import othello.Consts;
 9
10  public class LeftRule extends AbsRule {
11      int startRow, startCol;
12      int untilRow, untilCol;
13
14      public LeftRule() {
15          super();
16      }
17
...
58      @Override
59      public void flipPiece() {
60          if (getFlipFlag()) {
61              Color theColor = getCurPieceColor();
62              int row = startRow;
63              int col = startCol;
64              while (col > untilCol) {
65                  pieceBoard[row][col].setFlipStop(false);
66                  pieceBoard[row][col].setColor(theColor);
```

```
67
68                    if (theColor.equals(Consts.WHITEP)) {
69                        pieceBoard[row][col].setImageIdx(0);
70                        pieceBoard[row][col].setNumTurns(6);
71                    } else if (theColor.equals(Consts.BLACKP)) {
72                        pieceBoard[row][col].setImageIdx(6);
73                        pieceBoard[row][col].setNumTurns(12);
74                    }
75                    col--;
76                }
77            }
78            untilRow = startRow;
79            untilCol = startCol;
80        }
81    }
```

In addition to add the image pieces, the project Othello4 also adds the sounds for the actions of entering a possible playing cell and flipping a piece. The codes are the same as before: the class SoundClip.java provides a set of methods for loading, playing, and stopping a sound clip. The class AllClips.java employs the methods defined in the class SoundClip.java to load in all sound clips from a folder "sounds" in the file structure of the project into an array and insert the static method playClip() into the codes for making corresponding sounds.

21.5 Constructing a Single-Player Version of Othello

The game Othello is usually played by two human players. It can be converted into a single player game in case a player cannot find a human opponent. Under that case, the single human player is playing the game against a computer player. Consequently, a new class CompPlayerSprite.java is needed. For a human player, all actions are caught by human's eyes and controlled by human's brain. Now, the computer player needs to rely on codes to perform all of its actions. The codes should mimic a human's behaviors for playing the game, which can be achieved by merging so-called artificial intelligence with the logic of the game.

Firstly, we need to synthesize the behaviors of the computer player with the human player. Secondly, we should study what the winning strategy is in playing the game Othello. Regularly, a player needs (1) to wait for a turn, (2) to browse the cellBoard for finding all of possible playing cells, and (3) to click one of possible playing cells for placing a piece on the pieceBoard. Among these mechanical actions, the intelligence lies on the player's strategy for selecting one of the possible playing cells in order to ensure a maximum "earning" and a minimum "losing" for finally winning the game.

Consequently, the computer player should be equipped with these behaviors and intelligence to reach its winning goal. Normally, after the human player finishes his/her turn, the game sends a signal to the object of the computer player through a Boolean property cpTurn (computer-player turn), which is defined in the CompPlayerSprite.java class. When the Boolean property cpTurn is true, the game loop will invoke the method updateSprite() of the class CompPlayerSprite.java, which is going to do two things. (1) It calls the method allPossibleValidMoves() to collect all possible playing cells. (2) It then selects one of the possible playing cells and clicks on it. These actions are mechanically performed by codes. The trickiest part is the intelligence for selecting which one among all of possible playing cells. The possible intelligence algorithms designed for the selection can be classified into three categories as "first," "random," and "best."

21.6 The "First" Algorithm: The Project Othello5First

The "first" algorithm means that the computer player always selects the first possible playing cell when it browses the cellBoard in playing the game. The pseudo code of the algorithm is as follows:

1. To search for a possible playing cell from the first cell with the (row, col) coordinates of (0, 0).
2. Whenever a cell is proved to be the "first" possible playing cell, the algorithm stops its search.
3. And the algorithm "clicks" the first possible playing cell for placing a piece on it.

The computer player mimics a human player to "click" on the "first" possible playing cell by using its method updateSprite() in the class CompPlayerSprite.java. In other words, the computer player always places its piece at the "first" possible playing cell that it found. Therefore, the pseudo code of the method allPossibleValidMoves() is as simple as follows:

21.6 The "First" Algorithm: The Project Othello5First

```
public void allPossibleValidMoves() {
   get the pieceBoard;
   set the findFirst false;
   for every row
      for every column
         if the current cell is null with no piece
            if this cell is a possible playing cell
               add the cell into the ArrayList with the name of validMoves;
               set findFirst true;
         if findFirst is true, break the inner "for" loop;
      if findFirst is true, break the outer "for" loop;
}
```

The codes of the class CompPlayerSprite.java that embeds the code for adding the computer-player sprite into the project are shown in Listing 21.4.

Listing 21.4 The class CompPlayerSprite.java in the project Othello5First

```
1  /*
2   * CompPlayerSprite.java - A class that implements a computer player.
3   */
4  package othello;
5
6  import java.awt.Graphics2D;
7  import java.awt.Point;
8
9  public class CompPlayerSprite extends AbsSprite {
10
11     private boolean cpTurn;
12     private boolean foundFirst;
13     private Point theValidMove;
14     private CellBoard theCellBoard;
15     private PieceBoard thePieceBoard;
16
17     public CompPlayerSprite() {
18     }
19
20     @Override
21     public void updateSprite() {
22         // until all flip finished caused by human player
23         // computerPlayer then can start play
24         if (isCpTurn()) {
25             firstValidMove();
26
27             int newRow = theValidMove.x;
28             int newCol = theValidMove.y;
29             int x = newCol * Consts.CELLW + Consts.CELLW / 2;
30             int y = newRow * Consts.CELLH + Consts.CELLH / 2;
31             // simulate a mouse move and a mouse click
32             // just like a human player does
33             theCellBoard.setMoveXY(x, y);
34             thePieceBoard.setClickXY(x, y);
35         }
36         setCpTurn(false);
37     }
```

```java
        // go through the entire cellBoard and look for
        // all possible valid moves
        public void firstValidMove() {
            foundFirst = false;
            PieceSprite[][] thePieceB =
                    (PieceSprite[][])thePieceBoard.getPieceBoard();
            for (int row = 0; row < Consts.MAXCELL; row++) {
                for (int col = 0; col < Consts.MAXCELL; col++) {
                    // only check null positions -- a final smart idea
                    if (thePieceB[row][col] == null) {
                        theCellBoard.setNewRow(row);
                        theCellBoard.setNewCol(col);
                        // check all rules for valid moves of (row, col)
                        theCellBoard.fireCheckRules();
                        if (theCellBoard.isRuleValid()) {
                            theValidMove = new Point(row, col);
                            theCellBoard.setRuleValid(false);
                            foundFirst = true;
                        }
                    }
                    if (foundFirst) {
                        break;
                    }
                }
                if (foundFirst) {
                    break;
                }
            }
        }

        @Override
        public void paintSprite(Graphics2D g2d) {
        }

        public void setCellBoard(CellBoard cellBoard) {
            this.theCellBoard = cellBoard;
        }

        public void setPieceBoard(PieceBoard pieceBoard) {
            this.thePieceBoard = pieceBoard;
        }

        public boolean isCpTurn() {
            return cpTurn;
        }

        public void setCpTurn(Boolean b) {
            this.cpTurn = b;
        }
}
```

The class CompPlayerSprite.java should be incorporated into the project. As a new sprite, the class GameCanvas.java employs a method initCompPlayer() to instantiate an object compPlayer of the class CompPlayerSprite.java and pass both the cellBoard and the pieceBoard into the compPlayer so that the compPlayer is able to browse the cellBoard for finding the first possible playing cell and to "click" the possible playing cell for placing a piece on the pieceBoard. And then, the object compPlayer will be added into the global linear data structure spriteAry to be accessed by the game loop. The first statement in the method updateSprite() of the class CompPlayerSprite.java is "if (isCpTurn())." If it is true, the computer player will start all of its actions. Whenever it finishes all actions, itself should turn off the cpTurn as false.

Who and when the attribute cpTurn should be set up as true? Definitely, the time should be after the human player finishes all of his/her actions. After the human player clicks a possible playing cell, the action of flipping pieces starts. As we know that the flipping takes six game loops. Fortunately, the pieceSprite will set its attribute flipStop as true when it finishes flipping pieces. Thus, we can check two conditions. One condition is that whether every pieceSprite's attribute flipStop is true, which can be sure through the pieceBoard. Another condition is that whether the current piece color is black if the computer player is playing black pieces. As long as these two conditions are ready, the pieceBoard fires a property change signal to the gameCanvas that transfers the information to the compPlayerSprite for setting its attribute cpTurn as true. Then, in the coming game loop, the computer player will start its actions. Obviously, we should also make sure to set up setActive(true) for the compPlayer to allow the game loop invoking its updateSprite() method.

Clearly, this "first" algorithm saves searching time since it only needs to find the first possible playing cell. But, it is a blind algorithm without intelligence, and it does not mimic the real behaviors of a human player. The biggest drawback is that the computer player always selects the first possible playing cell starting from the coordinates (0, 0) such that the human player can easily estimate which cell the computer player will play. Thus, the human player can easily defeat the computer player. Therefore, the "first" algorithm is an "unfair" algorithm in the sense that the human player may predict the computer player's "thinking."

21.7 The "Random" Algorithm: The Project Othello6Ran

The "random" algorithm allows the compPlayer to browse the entire cellBoard from the first cell until the last cell and collects all possible playing cells into a linear data structure and then generates a random index to pick up one of those cells from the collection. Therefore, this algorithm requires a linear data structure and performs the following functions. Its implementation is shown in Listing 21.5.

1. Whenever the computer player takes a turn, it goes over every cell from the cell (0, 0) until the cell (MAXCELL-1, MAXCELL-1) on the cellBoard for validating whether the cell is a possible playing cell.
2. If it is a possible playing cell, its coordinates are stored in the linear data structure validMoves.
3. After the computer player collects all possible playing cells, it generates a random number as an index for selecting one of the possible playing cells. Then the computer player places a piece on the selected cell.

Listing 21.5 The code of the class CompPlayerSprite.java in the project Othello6Ran

```
 1  /*
 2   * CompPlayerSprite.java - A class that implements a computer player.
 3   */
 4  package othello;
 5
 6  import java.awt.Graphics2D;
 7  import java.awt.Point;
 8  import java.util.ArrayList;
 9
10  public class CompPlayerSprite extends AbsSprite {
11
12      private boolean cpTurn;
13      private boolean foundFirst;
14      private ArrayList<Point> validMoves;
15      private Point theValidMove;
16      private CellBoard theCellBoard;
17      private PieceBoard thePieceBoard;
18
19      public CompPlayerSprite() {
20          validMoves = new ArrayList<Point>();
21      }
22
23      @Override
```

```java
public void updateSprite() {
    // until all flip finished caused by human player
    // computerPlayer then can start play
    if (isCpTurn()) {
        allPossibleValidMoves();
        theValidMove = randomSelect(validMoves);

        int newRow = theValidMove.x;
        int newCol = theValidMove.y;
        int x = newCol * Consts.CELLW + Consts.CELLW / 2;
        int y = newRow * Consts.CELLH + Consts.CELLH / 2;
        // simulate a mouse move and a mouse click
        // just like a human player does
        theCellBoard.setMoveXY(x, y);
        thePieceBoard.setClickXY(x, y);
    }
    setCpTurn(false);
}

// go through the entire cellBoard and look for
// all possible valid moves
public void allPossibleValidMoves() {
    validMoves.clear();
    PieceSprite[][] thePieceB =
            (PieceSprite[][])thePieceBoard.getPieceBoard();
    for (int row = 0; row < Consts.MAXCELL; row++) {
        for (int col = 0; col < Consts.MAXCELL; col++) {
            // only check null positions -- a final smart idea
            if (thePieceB[row][col] == null) {
                theCellBoard.setNewRow(row);
                theCellBoard.setNewCol(col);
                // check all rules for valid moves of (row, col)
                theCellBoard.fireCheckRules();
                if (theCellBoard.isRuleValid()) {
                    validMoves.add(new Point(row, col));
                    theCellBoard.setRuleValid(false);
                }
            }
        }
    }
}

public Point randomSelect(ArrayList<Point> validMoves) {
    int selected = (int) (Math.random() * (validMoves.size()));
    return validMoves.get(selected);
}


@Override
public void paintSprite(Graphics2D g2d) {
}

public void setCellBoard(CellBoard cellBoard) {
    this.theCellBoard = cellBoard;
}

public void setPieceBoard(PieceBoard pieceBoard) {
    this.thePieceBoard = pieceBoard;
```

```
81      }
82
83      public boolean isCpTurn() {
84          return cpTurn;
85      }
86
87      public void setCpTurn(Boolean b) {
88          this.cpTurn = b;
89      }
90
91      public ArrayList<Point> getValidMoves() {
92          return validMoves;
93      }
94
95      public void setValidMoves(ArrayList<Point> validMoves) {
96          this.validMoves = validMoves;
97      }
98  }
```

In comparison with the "first" algorithm, the "random" algorithm takes a longer time to search and collect all possible playing cells. However, the behavior of this algorithm is closer to a real simulation of a human player than the "first" algorithm. In addition, the human player won't be able to predict which possible playing cell would be selected by the computer player, which solves the "unfair" problem embedded in the above "first" algorithm. In other words, the "random" algorithm is a practical algorithm with better performance. However, it still is a mechanism without intelligence.

21.8 The "Best" Algorithm: The Project Othello7Best

The "best" algorithm collects all of the possible playing cells and then selects the one that will give the "best" playing result. There are many kinds of criteria for judging what the "best" result could be. The simple one may be "this play could flip over a maximum number of opponent pieces." For that goal, the algorithm will do the following:

1. Whenever the computer player takes a turn, it collects all possible playing cells into the linear data structure validMoveList. At the same time, the computer player also collects the total number of pieces that world be flipped over by all eight playing rules related with every possible playing cell. These "total number of pieces would be flipped over" are stored into the other linear data structure totalNumFlipList with the same index as the corresponding possible playing cell in the linear data structure of validMoveList.
2. After that, the computer player looks for the maximum value stored in the ArrayList of totalNumFlipList and uses its index to find the corresponding cell coordinates from the validMoveList data structure, which is the selected possible playing cell.
3. The computer player places its piece on the selected cell.

This algorithm has the following pseudo code and implemented in the updateSprite() method defined by the class CompPlayerSprite.java:

```
public void updateSprite() {
   if cpTurn is true
      go over all cells in the cellBoard
         find a possible playing cell
            store its coordinates into the ArrayList validMoveList;
            count the number of pieces that could be flipped over by this cell;
            store the number in the ArrayList totalNumFlipList
      find the largest maximum value from the ArrayList totalNumFlipList;
         get the index of the largest maximum value;
         use the index to find the best playing cell from the validMoveList;
         click the best playing cell on the pieceBoard;
   set the variable cpTurn as false;
}
```

The challenge part in the above pseudo code is the procedure "count the number of pieces that could be flipped over by this cell" because the number of pieces could be flipped over must be collected from multiple rules. Fortunately, the method isRuleValid() in the class RuleBase.java hires a "for" loop to check over every rule whether the rule has a possible playing cell. We can take advantage of this "for" loop and insert a statement "totalNumFlip = totalNumFlip + theRule.getNumFlip()" into the "for" loop as follows:

```
public boolean isRuleValid() {
   boolean ruleValid = false;
   totalNumFlip = 0;
   AbsRule theRule;
   for (int idx = 0; idx < rules.size();idx++) {
      if ((rules.get(idx)).isValid(newRow,
         newCol)) {
         theRule = rules.get(idx);
         totalNumFlip = totalNumFlip+theRule.
            getNumFlip();
         ruleValid = true;
      }
   }
   return ruleValid;
}
```

The variable "theRule" is a reference of the super class AbsRule.java. The AbsRule.java class declares a variable numFlip with its getter method getNumFlip() and setter method setNumFlip(). When every valid rule measures the number of pieces could be flipped and invokes super.setNumFlip(Math.abs(untilRow − startRow)) or (Math.abs(untilCol − startCol)) to assign the number of possible flipping pieces to their super class, the statement theRule.getNumFlip() can get the counting results from each rule and add it with the variable totalNumFlip, which enables the class RuleBase.java to report the total number of pieces that could be flipped over through the method isRuleValid().

When a player browses the cellBoard, the method updateSprite() of the CellBoard.java class always fires a property change event to the class GameCanvas.java for checking whether the cell is a possible playing cell. Whenever a cell is a possible playing cell, the cellBoard can obtain the value of totalNumFlip. Therefore, when the compPlayer browses the cellBoard cell-by-cell, its method allPossibleValidMoves() can go through the following two statements to insert the coordinates of every possible playing cell into the validMoveList and insert totalNumFlip of every possible playing cell into the totalNumFlipList.

```
validMoveList.add(new Point(row, col));
totalNumFlipList.add(
   theCellBoard.getTotalNumFlip());
```

The "best" algorithm in the class CompPlayerSprite.java is cited in Listing 21.6.

Listing 21.6 The "best" algorithm implemented in the class CompPlayerSpring.java of the project Othello7Best

```
 1 /*
 2  * CompPlayerSprite.java - A class that implements a computer player.
 3  */
 4 ...
16 public class CompPlayerSprite extends AbsSprite {
17
18 ...
33    @Override
34    public void initSprite() {
35       validMoveList = new ArrayList<Point>();
36       totalNumFlipList = new ArrayList<Integer>();
37       stopGame = new PropertyChangeSupport(this);
38       setActive(true);
39       setVisible(false);
40    }
41
42    @Override
43    public void updateSprite() {
44       // until all flip finished caused by human player
45       // compPlayer then starts its play
```

21.8 The "Best" Algorithm: The Project Othello7Best

```
46          if (isCpTurn()) {
47              allPossibleValidMoves();
48              theValidMove = findBestMove();
49              if (theValidMove == null) {
50                  System.out.println("No more possible move");
51                  fireTerminate();
52              } else {
53                  int newRow = theValidMove.x;
54                  int newCol = theValidMove.y;
55                  int x = newCol * Consts.CELLW + Consts.CELLW / 2;
56                  int y = newRow * Consts.CELLH + Consts.CELLH / 2;
57                  // simulate a mouse move and a mouse click
58                  // just like a human player does
59                  theCellBoard.setMoveXY(x, y);
60                  thePieceBoard.setClickXY(x, y);
61              }
62          }
63          setCpTurn(false);
64      }
65
66      // go through the entire cellBoard and look for
67      // all possible valid moves
68      public void allPossibleValidMoves() {
69          validMoveList.clear();
70          totalNumFlipList.clear();
71          PieceSprite[][] thePieceB
72              = (PieceSprite[][]) thePieceBoard.getPieceBoard();
73          for (int row = 0; row < Consts.MAXCELL; row++) {
74              for (int col = 0; col < Consts.MAXCELL; col++) {
75                  // only check null positions -- a final smart idea
76                  if (thePieceB[row][col] == null) {
77                      theCellBoard.setNewRow(row);
78                      theCellBoard.setNewCol(col);
79                      // check all rules for valid moves of (row, col)
80                      theCellBoard.fireCheckRules();
81                      if (theCellBoard.isRuleValid()) {
82                          // for the "best" algorithm, get totalNumFlip
83                          validMoveList.add(new Point(row, col));
84                          totalNumFlipList.add(theCellBoard.getTotalNumFlip());
85                          theCellBoard.setRuleValid(false);
86                      }
87                  }
88              }
89          }
90      }
91
92      public Point findBestMove() {
93          int bestIdx = 0;
94          int largestNum = 0;
95          int aNum;
96          Point thePoint = null;
97          if (!(totalNumFlipList.isEmpty())) {
98              for (int i = 0; i < totalNumFlipList.size(); i++) {
99                  aNum = totalNumFlipList.get(i);
100                 if (aNum > largestNum) {
```

```
101                    largestNum = aNum;
102                    bestIdx = i;
103                }
104            }
105            //System.out.println("largestNum = " + largestNum);
106            thePoint = validMoveList.get(bestIdx);
107        }
108        return thePoint;
109    }
110
111    public void fireTerminate() {
112        stopGame.firePropertyChange("terminateGame", "-1", "1");
113    }
114
115    public void addPropertyChangeListener(PropertyChangeListener pcl) {
116        stopGame.addPropertyChangeListener(pcl);
117    }
118
119    @Override
120    public void paintSprite(Graphics2D g2d) {
121    }
122
123    ...
154 }
```

Intuitively, the "best" algorithm will take a longer time and more spaces than both the "first" and the "random" algorithms. However, it gives a hope for getting a "best" result. Actually, the "best" algorithm does not necessarily give the best playing outcome at every step since flipping over the maximum number of opponent pieces at this step could end up with the maximum number of its own pieces to be flipped over by the opponent at the immediate next step. That is, after the compPlayer earned the best playing result, the human player could obtain a best "revenge" result sometimes. However, it is hard for the human player to guarantee a best "revenge" result in every step. Therefore, overall this "best" algorithm is a practical one.

21.9 The "Edge" Algorithm: The Project Othello8Edge

Another "best" strategy is called "edge" algorithm that could be better than the "maximum number" of flips for winning the game. The new strategy is to occupy cells along the four edges of the cell board as early as possible. This is an experience earned by playing the game for a long time. That is, the step 3 in the best algorithm described in the previous subsection could be modified as follows:

3. After the computer player finishes the collection of all possible playing cells and the corresponding number of possible pieces which could be flipped over:
   (a) It goes through the linear data structure validMoveList to find the possible playing cell that is closest to one of the four edges of the cellBoard.
   (b) If only one possible playing cell is the closest, take this cell as the selected one.
   (c) If multiple possible playing cells have the same degree of closeness to either one of four edges of the cellBoard, it goes to the second ArrayList totalNumFlipList to select the cell that may flip over the "maximum" number of pieces so that the selected cell is a closest cell with the maximum possible flipping pieces.

This modified step affects the implementation of the method findBestMove() as follows:

```
public Point findBestMove(ArrayList<Point> validMoveList,
    ArrayList<Integer> totalNumFlipList) {
    // looking for a possible playing cell that is closest to an edge
    for every possible playing cell in the ArrayList validMoveList
        get the coordinates of ith cell;
```

```
        calculate the distances from the ith cell to the four edges;
        compare the distances for finding the closest distance in x-axis direction;
        compare the distances for finding the closest distance in y-axis direction;
        find the closest distance in both the x and y directions to one of four
            edges and getting the index i;
        compare the new closest i with the first element in the ArrayList allClosest
            if the new closest i is closer to an edge than the first element, replace the
                first element and delete all remaining elements;
            else if closer degree is the same, store the new closest i;

    if multiple cells are equally close to one of the edges
        select the one that will flip over maximum number of pieces as the best
            playing cell;
}
```

The ArrayList allClosest stores either single closest or multiple closest cells in a same degree. If it is the latter case, select one of them that will flip the maximum number of pieces. This "edge" algorithm gives a better performance for the computer player. However, if the human player also applies the same "edge" tactic, then both players put forth their best efforts to occupy the cells closest to four edges. This may lead to the game ending in a stalemate. In other words, one player may not have any possible playing cell left due to the fact that the player cannot find a matching piece even though many cells are still available for placing pieces. To solve this problem, the game needs to build up a mechanism to allow any player to give up his/her playing authority to the opponent. Listing 21.7 shows the code for finding the closest cell to either one of four edges.

Listing 21.7 The code of the "Edge" algorithm in the project Othello8Edge

```
 1  /*
 2   * CompPlayerSprite.java - A class that implements a computer player.
 3   */
 4  …
16  public class CompPlayerSprite extends AbsSprite {
17
44  …
45      @Override
46      public void updateSprite() {
47          // until all flip finished caused by human player
48          // compPlayer then starts its play
49          if (isCpTurn()) {
50              allPossibleValidMoves();
51              theValidMove = findBestMove();
52              if (theValidMove == null) {
53                  System.out.println("No more possible move");
54                  fireTerminate();
55              } else {
56                  int newRow = theValidMove.x;
57                  int newCol = theValidMove.y;
58                  int x = newCol * Consts.CELLW + Consts.CELLW / 2;
59                  int y = newRow * Consts.CELLH + Consts.CELLH / 2;
60                  // simulate a mouse move and a mouse click
61                  // just like a human player does
62                  theCellBoard.setMoveXY(x, y);
63                  thePieceBoard.setClickXY(x, y);
64              }
```

```java
65          }
66          setCpTurn(false);
67      }
68
69      // go through the entire cellBoard and look for
70      // all possible valid moves
71      public void allPossibleValidMoves() {
72          validMoveList.clear();
73          totalNumFlipList.clear();
74          PieceSprite[][] thePieceB
75                  = (PieceSprite[][]) thePieceBoard.getPieceBoard();
76          for (int row = 0; row < Consts.MAXCELL; row++) {
77              for (int col = 0; col < Consts.MAXCELL; col++) {
78                  // only check null positions -- a final smart idea
79                  if (thePieceB[row][col] == null) {
80                      theCellBoard.setNewRow(row);
81                      theCellBoard.setNewCol(col);
82                      // check all rules for valid moves of (row, col)
83                      theCellBoard.fireCheckRules();
84                      if (theCellBoard.isRuleValid()) {
85                          // for the "best" algorithm, get totalNumFlip
86                          validMoveList.add(new Point(row, col));
87                          totalNumFlipList.add(theCellBoard.getTotalNumFlip());
88                          theCellBoard.setRuleValid(false);
89                      }
90                  }
91              }
92          }
93      }
94
95      // based on closest to edges and then maximum number of flipping pieces
96      public Point findBestMove() {
97          int bestIdx = 0;
98          int largestNum = 0;
99          int aNum;
100
101         allClosest.clear();
102         findClosest();
103         if (allClosest.size() == 1) {
104             bestIdx = (int) (allClosest.get(0).getY());
105         } else {
106             // if multiple possible playing cells have the same degree of closest,
107             // select the one that makes max number of flipping piece
108             for (int k = 0; k < allClosest.size(); k++) {
109                 int cellIdx = (int) (((Point) (allClosest.get(k))).getY());
110                 aNum = (totalNumFlipList.get(cellIdx));
111                 if (aNum > largestNum) {
112                     largestNum = aNum;
113                     bestIdx = cellIdx;
114                 }
115             }
116         }
117         return validMoveList.get(bestIdx);
118     }
119
```

21.9 The "Edge" Algorithm: The Project Othello8Edge

```
120    public void findClosest() {
121        int toL, toR, toT, toB;
122        int lessX, lessY, lessXY;
123        int closest = -1;
124        int aClosest;
125        Point aPair;
126
127        // looking for a possible playing cell that is closest to an edge
128        for (int i = 0; i < validMoveList.size(); i++) {
129            Point coor = validMoveList.get(i);
130            toL = Math.abs((int) coor.getX() - 0);
131            toR = Math.abs((int) coor.getX() - (Consts.MAXCELL - 1));
132            toT = Math.abs((int) coor.getY() - 0);
133            toB = Math.abs((int) coor.getY() - (Consts.MAXCELL - 1));
134            if (toL < toR) {
135                lessX = toL;
136            } else {
137                lessX = toR;
138            }
139            if (toT < toB) {
140                lessY = toT;
141            } else {
142                lessY = toB;
143            }
144            if (lessX < lessY) {
145                lessXY = lessX;
146            } else {
147                lessXY = lessY;
148            }
149            // the first element of allClosest always keeps the closest.
150            // other elements in allClosest are equal to the first element.
151            // if a new closest comes, update the first element and remove
152            // all remaining elements
153            if (closest == -1) { // the first time
154                closest = lessXY; // to indicate no more first time
155                aPair = new Point(lessXY, i);
156                allClosest.add(aPair);
157            } else { // not the first time
158                // replacing or adding the index of the closest
159                aClosest = (int) (allClosest.get(0).getX()); // return lessXY
160                if (lessXY < aClosest) { // a new closest
161                    aPair = new Point(lessXY, i);
162                    allClosest.add(0, aPair);
163                    if (allClosest.size() > 1) {
164                        for (int j = 1; j < allClosest.size(); j++) {
165                            allClosest.remove(j);
166                        }
167                    }
168                } else if (lessXY == aClosest) { // same degree of closest
169                    aPair = new Point(lessXY, i);
170                    allClosest.add(aPair);
171                }
172            }
173        }
174    }
```

```
175
176     public void fireTerminate() {
177         stopGame.firePropertyChange("terminateGame", "-1", "1");
178     }
179
180     public void addPropertyChangeListener(PropertyChangeListener pcl) {
181         stopGame.addPropertyChangeListener(pcl);
182     }
183
184     @Override
185     public void paintSprite(Graphics2D g2d) {
186     }
187
188     ...
219 }
```

21.10 The Looking Ahead Algorithm: A Discussion

According to the traditional principles of artificial intelligence, the best strategy for playing chess-style games is to build up a tree structure by looking several steps ahead and then applying either a depth-first or breadth-first searching algorithm to find a best playing decision. Figure 21.2 illustrates a tree structure, which assumes that the compPlayer has three possible playing cells for a new play. It would play the three options and record the number of flipping pieces as (1, 2, 1) as shown on the second row. And then, the human player takes a turn. For the three cases, the human player would play all of possible playing cells. Corresponding to every possible playing cell, the human player may "revenge" the number of flipping pieces that are listed on the third row. Based on these data, the "net gain" of the compPlayer would be (0, −1, −2). The best "net gain" is 0. But, the best choice would be the middle case since only this case the compPlayer won't run into the risk of (−1, −2). Thus, the compPlayer would select the middle case to really play this step. This "look ahead" strategy would give the compPlayer a best algorithm. Obviously, if it were possible to look ahead three or four steps, the decision would be safer.

The strategy considers both "gain maximum" and "be revenged minimum." Clearly, this algorithm is both time and memory extensive because every possible playing cell needs to play at least two steps and all of data have to be recorded. In addition, all of cases have to be calculated and compared. Its implementation is not an easy job.

In practice, a set of "safety rules" for reducing the degree of "revenge" could be defined. The safety rules may include "selecting the possible playing cell if it is the last empty cell along either the x or y direction for flipping pieces." This rule means that after the computer player places a piece into the cell, the human player cannot flip over the computer's pieces in the following step, since all pieces are the same color along the direction. This rule implies that the opponent has no possibility to find a matching piece for his/her "revenge." These rules are more heuristic oriented and more suitable for human player to use since they are not easily coded into a program.

21.11 Summary

This chapter completed the game Othello and further developed the two-player Othello to be a single player Othello. The latter allows a human player against a computer player, which introduced the concept of artificial intelligence and discussed different kinds of algorithms as a clue for a further study on this context. In addition, the coding on the computer player demonstrated the ideas for making a mechanism that controls the game's behaviors without human's interactions.

The discussions and implementations exemplify both difficulties and interests in the development of artificial intelligence algorithms. It is worth to be studied and explored.

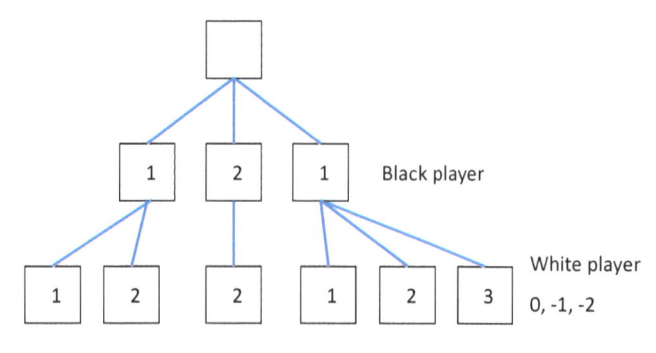

Fig. 21.2 An illustration of the look-ahead algorithm

21.12 Exercises

Self-Reviewing Questions

1. What is the so-called frame-based animation?
2. Is there any difference between the "sprite-based animation" and the "frame-based animation"?
3. Flipping a white piece to a black piece requires an animation of six images. How to realize the animation?
4. The class PieceSprite.java extends AbsSprite2D.java, but it does not extend the class AbsSpriteImage.java. Why? Is there any advantage for making this extension?
5. Why do we convert the two-player game Othello to be a single-player game?
6. In the conversion from the two-human-player version to the single human player version, what mechanical behaviors are required? What intelligent behaviors are needed?
7. What is the meaning of artificial intelligence in the game Othello?
8. There are four algorithms are presented for the computer player. What are the differences among them? What are the advantages and disadvantages among the four algorithms?
9. What does the "look-ahead" algorithm mean? Why is it better than others?
10. Could you design a new algorithm other than these algorithms?

Projects

1. We have discussed four different algorithms for supporting the computer player sprite. Is it possible to construct a unit, such as a class, an interface, a JavaBean, and so on to make the four algorithms separated from the class CompPlayerSprite.java such that the same computer player sprite is possible to switch among the four or more algorithms? That is, make the computer player sprite loosely coupled with the algorithm unit.
2. The current version of the game Othello has an 8 × 8 board. Is it possible to develop a new version that has a 16 × 16 board or other size?
3. Implement the method announceTermination() for displaying the information about the game termination.
4. Implement a mechanism and method that can renew the game Othello so that the players may start over to play a new game.
5. Implement the "look-ahead" algorithm discussed in the section 21.10.
6. Implement a splash screen that provides the game playing instruction and setting options, such as sounds on or off, board size, two players or single player, and so on.

Part IV

Serious Games: Chaps. 22–24

Visualizing Sorting Array Algorithms 22

Video game techniques are welcomed in many different fields. It is that the techniques can be applied to develop so-called "serious games" that have a variety of purposes and usages. This chapter takes the algorithms for sorting data in one-dimensional array as examples to illustrate what "serious games" are and how to dynamically visualize computations with the animation technique. Two sorting algorithms of BubbleSort and QuickSort are simulated. After that, two sorting algorithms are merged in one project for sharing the same GUI. Through the examples, the rich abilities of the three-layer software structure for games are further explored and proved.

The objectives of this chapter include:
1. The three-layer structure is also suitable for developing serious games.
2. A control panel for manipulating an array of integers.
3. An animation displaying panel for visualizing the bubble sorting.
4. An animation under the control of an algorithm.
5. A second thread cooperates with the main thread.
6. Different sorting algorithms share the same animation mechanism.
7. Some special features for implementing the quick sorting.
8. Special features for implementing the project MultiSort.
9. The separation of the GUI from the logic.

The three-layer structure for games is not only applied for developing video games but also is applicable for developing serious games.

22.1 A Definition of Serious Games

"Serious games are simulations of real-world events or processes designed for the purpose of solving a problem. Although serious games can be entertaining, their main purpose is to train or educate users, though it may have other purposes, such as marketing or advertisement. Serious game will sometimes deliberately sacrifice fun and entertainment in order to achieve a desired progress by the player. Serious games are not a game genre but a category of games with different purposes. This category includes some educational games and advergames, political games, or evangelical games. Serious games are primarily focused on an audience outside of primary or secondary education." [Wikipedia, 2015][1]

The following three chapters will develop two teaching tools as serious games. This chapter takes the sorting algorithms as an example to visualize unseen computations. The main thread in the three-layer structure for games animates all of sprites. According to the definition, sprites are animated independently. However, the animated sprites in the sorting should be under the control of sorting algorithms. In order to synchronize the computations of the sorting algorithm with the animated sprites, an extra thread is required. It illustrates one of the differences between serious games and video games. That is, serious games usually require more controls of threads and more communications between the GUI unit and the logic unit.

22.2 A Teaching Tool for Showing Linear Data Structure

The linear data structures mainly include Array and ArrayList that have been introduced and applied in many games already; especially it is one of the major data structures adopted in the three-layer structure for games. When we would like to store a set of data with same data type, a linear data structure is a preferred choice because it is simple and easy to be manipulated. The operations for manipulating a linear data structure include the following: declare a linear data structure with or without a predetermined length; fill in certain number of data (<= length); append a new value at the end of the linear data structure; search for a specified value; delete a value from it; check IsEmpty or isFull; and so on. Especially important is to sort an array into either ascending order or descending order.

___
[1] https://en.wikipedia.org/wiki/Serious_game, 2015.

We dealt some operations listed above in our developed games already and even tried to sort an array of three players in the game WheelVideo in Chap. 11. Sorting is an important topic since it is not only a very popular required operation but also a very good topic for learning how to analyze the performance of algorithms. However, the computations of some sorting algorithms are not easy to trace and follow. Fortunately, many efforts have been applied for developing visible tools to illustrate the sorting process. Here, we would like to apply the three-layer structure for games for developing our own version of visual tool for showing the sorting process. The new idea in our design is that we apply the abstract model of games to separate the GUI part from the logic part such that one GUI part can be reused to link with different sorting algorithms for illustrating different sorting processes. It further shows the significance of the abstract model of games and the benefits for adopting the three-layer structure for games.

In general, a sorting algorithm is used to sort a set of values stored in a linear data structure, an array or an arrayList, into an ascending order or a descending order. The sorting process is based on swapping two selected values into proper positions. In order to visualize the sorting process, a set of bars with different heights is used to represent the set of values. The swaps of two selected values are shown as animated exchanges of two bars. Therefore, the implementation can be divided into two steps. The first step is to build up a "preferred" linear data structure for storing a set of values. The second step is to sort the set of values under the control of corresponding sorting algorithms.

22.3 Preparing the GUI: The Project BubbleSort1

There are many different sorting algorithms. The bubble sorting algorithm is the most fundamental one. We are going to develop a visual tool for illustrating the bubble sorting algorithm first. As the first step, a project BubbleSort1 is used to prepare a linear data structure with fundamental operations. The GUI of the project is shown in Fig. 22.1.

Clearly, the GUI of the project BubbleSort1 consists of two portions. The SOUTH part of the GUI is a control panel for the player to construct a "preferred" arrayList. The control panel possesses four buttons and a textField. The CENTER part of the GUI displays a set of bars that corresponds to the set of values stored in the arrayList and two arrows for indicating the current selected two values to be swapped.

In other words, the project BubbleSort1 is to build up the static part of the application without animation. The UML class diagram of this project is illustrated in Fig. 22.2. From the figure we can tell that we need a class GameCanvas.java that has a BorderLayout manager to arrange an object controlPanel on its SOUTH part and leave its CENTER part for the two sprites: bars and arrows. A composite class BarComposite.java "has" the set of bars of the class BarSprite.java, which are stored in a local arrayList in the class BarComposite.java. The arrow objects correspond to the class ArrowSprite.java.

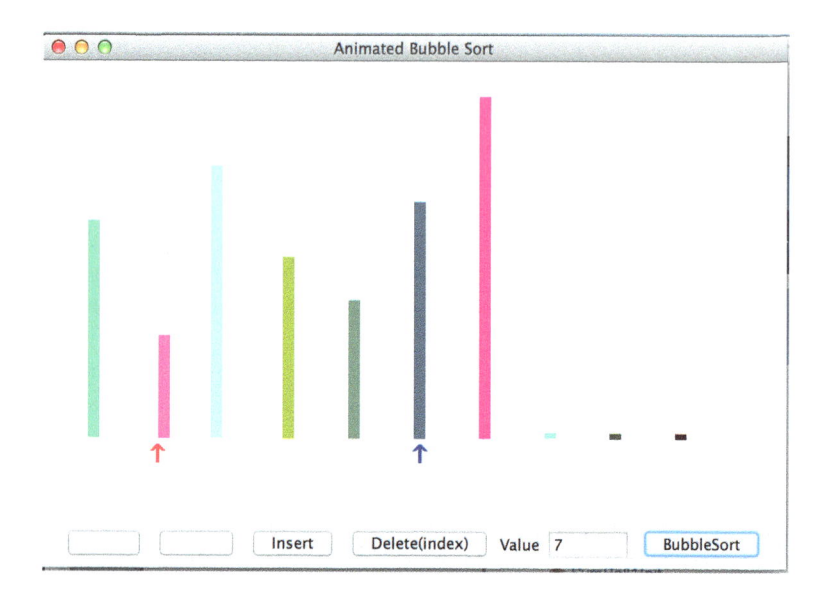

Fig. 22.1 The GUI of the project BubbleSort1

Fig. 22.2 The UML class diagram of the project BubbleSort1

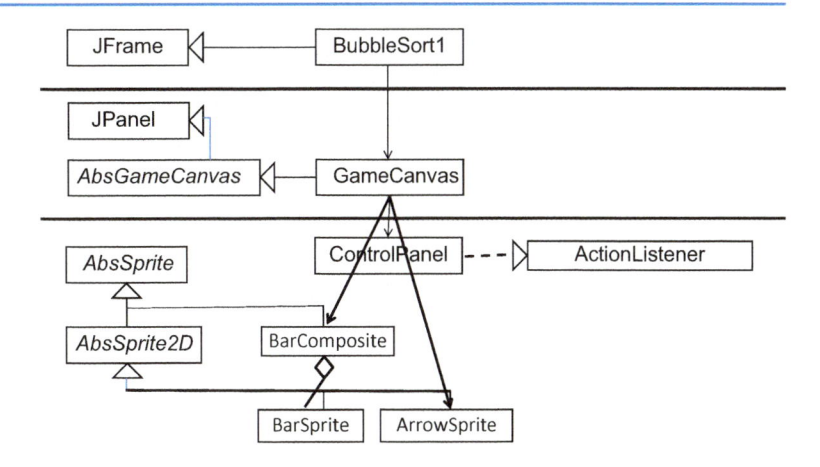

22.3.1 The Class GameCanvas.java Instantiates Three Objects

The UML class diagram shows that the class GameCanvas.java "uses" three objects. They are controlPanel, barComposite, and arrowSprite. Since the class BarComposite "has" the bars that are sprites and the arrows are also sprites, the objects barComposite and arrows should be added into the global spriteAry. The code of the class GameCanvas.java is on Listing 22.1.

Listing 22.1 The class GameCanvas.java in the project BubbleSort1

```
1  /*
2   * GameCanvas.java - A class that defines the game canvas.
3   */
4  package bubblesort;
5
6  import java.awt.BorderLayout;
7  import java.awt.Graphics2D;
8
13 public class GameCanvas extends AbsGameCanvas {
14
15     private ControlPanel controlPanel; // static part
16     private BarComposite barComposite; // sprites
17     private ArrowSprite arrowSprite;
18
19     @SuppressWarnings("OverridableMethodCallInConstructor")
20     public GameCanvas() {
21         super();
22         setLayout(new BorderLayout());
23         initComponent(); // dynamic part: could be re-init
24
25         //startGame(); // before sorting, startGame() cannot be invoked
26     }
27
28     @Override
29     public void initComponent() {
30         initControlPanel(); // static part
31         initBarComposite();
32         initArrowSprite();
33         repaint(); // when game has not been started, repaint() paints sprites
34     }
```

```java
36    public void initControlPanel() {
37        controlPanel = new ControlPanel();
38        controlPanel.setGameCanvas(this); // gameCanvas.repaint() and set arrow
39        add(controlPanel, BorderLayout.SOUTH);
40    }
41
42    public void initBarComposite() {
43        barComposite = new BarComposite();
44        getSpriteAry().add(barComposite); // at position [0]
45        // controlPanel needs to accesses barComponent
46        // after passed gameCanvas and init barComposite
47        // controlPanel finds the barComposite
48        controlPanel.findBarComposite();
49    }
50
51    public void initArrowSprite() {
52        arrowSprite = new ArrowSprite();
53        getSpriteAry().add(arrowSprite); // at position [1]
54    }
55
56    @Override
57    public void announceTermination(Graphics2D g2d) {
58    }
59
60    @Override
61    public void paintCurrScore(Graphics2D g2d) {
62        throw new UnsupportedOperationException("Not supported yet.");
63    }
64
65    public void setCurrentArrow(int curIdx) {
66        BarComposite aBarC = (BarComposite) (getSpriteAry().get(0));
67        BarSprite curBar = aBarC.getBarList().get(curIdx);
68        arrowSprite.setX(curBar.getX() + Consts.BARWIDTH / 2);
69        arrowSprite.setY(Consts.BASEY + Consts.INITBAR);
70    }
71 }
```

Because the project BubbleSort1 only deals with the GUI setting without animation, the method startGame() in the AbsGameCanvas.java class is not invoked so that the game loop keeps silence.

22.3.2 The Class ControlPanel.java Builds Up a "Preferred" arrayList

The class ControlPanel.java provides a set of software components and corresponding action listeners to support the user for making a "preferred" arrayList. As Fig. 22.1 shows, the control panel has four buttons and one textField. The initial default length of the arrayList is ten. Entering a number in the textField as the length of the arrayList and clicking the "New" button, the user can change the default number of cells and instantiate a new arrayList. Entering a number that is less or equal to the length of the arrayList in the textField and clicking the "Fill" button, the application can fill the number of randomly generated data (integers) in the arrayList. Entering a value in the textField as a data and clicking the "Append" button, the entered value can be appended with the arrayList. Entering an index in the textField and clicking the "Delete" button, the item corresponding to the index in the arrayList can be deleted.

We might design an arrayList in the class ControlPanel.java for storing these "preferred" data. Thereafter we might send the "preferred" data to the class BarComposite.java for building up a barList that uses the height of every bar to represent the corresponding data and to be shown on the GUI.

It is an acceptable design. However, it cannot dynamically illustrate the building process of the "preferred" arrayList because the barList is set up after the "preferred" arrayList has been done. We need a design that will visualize every operation such that every data change in the "preferred" arrayList will immediately affect the barList and will be shown on the GUI. For reaching this requirement, we take the following "tricky" to set up a communication path between the two classes ControlPanel.java and BarComposite.java. Its implementation is shown in Listing 22.2.

Listing 22.2 The class ControlPanel.java of the project BubbleSort1

```
 1  /*
 2   * ControlPanel.java - A class that defines the control panel for the project
 3   * BubbleSort. It provides four buttons: New, Fill, Append, Delete for making
 4   * a "preferred" array.
 5   */
 6  package bubblesort;
 7
 8  import java.awt.Color;
 9  import java.awt.GridLayout;
10  import java.awt.event.ActionEvent;
11  import java.awt.event.ActionListener;
12  import javax.swing.JButton;
13  import javax.swing.JLabel;
14  import javax.swing.JPanel;
15  import javax.swing.JTextField;
16
21  public class ControlPanel extends JPanel {
22
23      private int numberCells; // initial size; it can be changed by users
24      private int numberData; // number of data in the array
25      private JPanel controlP;
26      private JButton newButton;
27      private JButton fillButton;
28      private JButton appendButton;
29      private JButton deleteButton;
30      private JLabel valueLabel;
31      private JTextField valueField;
32      private JPanel msgP;
33      private JLabel msgLabel;
34      private JTextField msgText;
35
36      private GameCanvas gameCanvas;
37      private BarComposite barComposite;
38      private ActionListener listener;
39
40      public ControlPanel() {
41          initControlPanel();
42      }
43
44      private void initControlPanel() {
45          setLayout(new GridLayout(2, 1));
```

```java
46              listener = new MyActionListener();
47
48              controlP = new JPanel();
49              add(controlP);
50
51              newButton = new JButton("New");
52              controlP.add(newButton);
53              newButton.addActionListener(listener);
54              fillButton = new JButton("Fill");
55              controlP.add(fillButton);
56              fillButton.addActionListener(listener);
57              appendButton = new JButton("Append");
58              controlP.add(appendButton);
59              appendButton.addActionListener(listener);
60              deleteButton = new JButton("Delete(index)");
61              controlP.add(deleteButton);
62              deleteButton.addActionListener(listener);
63
64              valueLabel = new JLabel("    Value: ");
65              controlP.add(valueLabel);
66              valueField = new JTextField(5);
67              controlP.add(valueField);
68
69              msgP = new JPanel();
70              add(msgP);
71              msgLabel = new JLabel("Message: ");
72              msgText = new JTextField(30);
73              msgText.setForeground(Color.red);
74              msgText.setText(" Enter a value before selecting an operation");
75              msgP.add(msgLabel);
76              msgP.add(msgText);
77          }
78
79          public void findBarComposite() {
80              // so not necessary to pass barComposite, which is in the
81              // global spriteAry as the first element get(0)
82              barComposite = (BarComposite) gameCanvas.getSpriteAry().get(0);
83              numberCells = barComposite.getNumberCells(); // initialize numberCells
84          }
85
86          class MyActionListener implements ActionListener {
87
88              @Override
89              public void actionPerformed(ActionEvent evt) {
90                  if (evt.getActionCommand().equals("New")) {
91                      String inputValue = valueField.getText();
92                      if (!(inputValue.equals(""))) {
93                          numberCells = Integer.parseInt(inputValue);
94                          barComposite.setNumberCells(numberCells);
95                          barComposite.eraseBarList();
96                          barComposite.initSprite(); // re-init a new array
97                          newButton.setEnabled(false);
98                          msgText.setText(" A new array has been created");
99                      } else {
100                         msgText.setText(" Enter the number of cells "
```

22.3 Preparing the GUI: The Project BubbleSort1

```
101                             + "for the new array");
102                     }
103                 } else if (evt.getActionCommand().equals("Fill")) {
104                     String fillNumStr = valueField.getText();
105                     if ((!newButton.isEnabled()) && (fillNumStr.equals(""))) {
106                         msgText.setText(" Enter the number of filling data");
107                     } else {
108                         // using the default value of numberCells
109                         if ((newButton.isEnabled()) && (fillNumStr.equals(""))) {
110                             numberData = numberCells;
111                         } else if (!fillNumStr.equals("")) { // using the specified
112                             numberData = Integer.parseInt(fillNumStr);
113                         }
114                         if (numberData > numberCells) {
115                             msgText.setText(
116                                     " The number of fill in data is larger than "
117                                     + "the number of cells");
118                         } else {
119                             barComposite.setNumberData(numberData);
120                             barComposite.fillBars();
121                             fillButton.setEnabled(false);
122                             newButton.setEnabled(false);
123                             msgText.setText(" The array has been filled");
124                         }
125                     }
126                 } else if (evt.getActionCommand().equals("Append")) {
127                     if (numberData < numberCells) { // possible to insert new data
128                         String appendValueStr = valueField.getText();
129                         if (!appendValueStr.equals("")) {
130                             int appendValue = Integer.parseInt(appendValueStr);
131                             barComposite.setAppendValue(appendValue);
132                             barComposite.appendElement();
133                             numberData++;
134                             barComposite.setNumberData(numberData);
135                             gameCanvas.setCurrentArrow(numberData - 1);
136                             msgText.setText(" The new value has been appended");
137                         } else {
138                             msgText.setText(" Enter the value for appending");
139                         }
140                     } else {
141                         msgText.setText(" No more empty cell for "
142                                 + "appending new data");
143                     }
144                 } else if (evt.getActionCommand().equals("Delete(index)")) {
145                     String deleteValueStr = valueField.getText();
146                     if (deleteValueStr.equals("")) {
147                         msgText.setText(" Enter an index for the deletion");
148                     } else {
149                         int deleteIdx = Integer.parseInt(deleteValueStr);
150                         if ((deleteIdx >= 0) && (deleteIdx < numberData)) {
151                             gameCanvas.setCurrentArrow(deleteIdx);
152                             barComposite.deleteElement(deleteIdx);
153                             numberData--;
154                             barComposite.setNumberData(numberData);
155                             msgText.setText(" The item has been deleted");
```

```
156                } else {
157                    msgText.setText(" The index is out of range");
158                }
159            }
160        }
161        valueField.setText("");
162        gameCanvas.repaint(); // for re-paint the changes
163    }
164 }
165
166 public GameCanvas getGameCanvas() {
167     return gameCanvas;
168 }
169
170 public void setGameCanvas(GameCanvas gameCanvas) {
171     this.gameCanvas = gameCanvas;
172 }
173 }
```

Since every action happened in the class ControlPanel.java will modify the "preferred" data that should be reflected as the bars shown on the GUI and then the new scene of the data needs to be repainted on the GUI by the method gameCanvas.repaint() defined in the class GameCanvas.java. This implies that the object gameCanvas of the class GaemCanvas.java has to be passed into the ControlPanel.java class (Listing 22.1, line 38). Due to the fact that the object barComposite is a sprite that should be assigned to the global spriteAry and the spriteAry belongs to the class GameCanvas.java, therefore, the class ControlPanel.java is able to get the object of barComposite from the passed in object of gameCanvas. We simply define a special method findBarComposite() in the class ControlPanel.java (lines 79–84) for allowing it to get the object barComposite from the global spriteAry. And then, all of the event handlers of operations (lines 86–164) can directly go through the barComposite to assign the "preferred" data into the barList that resides in the class BarComposite.java. The result is that all of data are directly embedded to the barList, which in turn dynamically visualizes the "preferred" data on the GUI. In other words, the barList is nothing else but the "preferred" data arrayList.

A trivial importance is the two values of the two variables numberCells and numberData. The former refers to the length of the arrayList; the latter is the number of data stored in the arrayList, which could be less or equal to the length of the arrayList. Both classes ControlPanel.java and BarComposite.java require knowing the current values of them, and both classes may modify the two values of them. In order to avoid the modification conflict, we let the ControlPanel.java class to take care of the modifications of the two values and then set their new values to BarComposite.java class.

22.3.3 The Composite Class BarComposite.java "Has" a Set of Bars

The composite class BarComposite.java uses a local arrayList barList to hold a number of bars that use their heights to represent the data values. The class supports all of methods to perform the functions associated with the event handlers of the control buttons defined in the class ControlPanel.java. The code of the class BarComposite.java is shown in Listing 22.3.

Listing 22.3 The class BarComposite.java of the project BubbleSort1

```
1  /*
2   * BarComposite.java - A composite class that contains a set of barSprites
3   * for representing the value of the corresponding data in the array. It has
4   * all of methods for manipulating the array.
5   */
6  package bubblesort;
7
8  import java.awt.Graphics2D;
9  import java.util.ArrayList;
10
```

22.3 Preparing the GUI: The Project BubbleSort1

```
15  public class BarComposite extends AbsSprite {
16
17      @SuppressWarnings("FieldMayBeFinal")
18      private ArrayList<BarSprite> barList;
19      private int gap;
20      private int numberCells = 10; // initial size of the array
21      private int numberData; // size of the data in the array
22      private int appendValue;
23
24      @SuppressWarnings("OverridableMethodCallInConstructor")
25      public BarComposite() {
26          barList = new ArrayList<BarSprite>();
27          setVisible(true);
28          setActive(false);
29          initSprite(); // should be invoked by gameCanvas after setNumberCells()
30      }
31
32      @Override
33      public void initSprite() {
34          gap = (int) ((Consts.CV_WIDTH - 2 * Consts.MARGIN - Consts.BARWIDTH)
35                  / (numberCells - 1));
36          BarSprite aBar;
37          for (int i = 0; i < numberCells; i++) {
38              aBar = new BarSprite();
39              aBar.setX(Consts.MARGIN + gap * i);
40              aBar.setY(Consts.BASEY - aBar.getHeight());
41              barList.add(aBar);
42          }
43      }
44
45      @Override
46      public void paintSprite(Graphics2D g2d) {
47          BarSprite aBar;
48          for (int i = 0; i < barList.size(); i++) {
49              aBar = barList.get(i);
50              aBar.paintSprite(g2d);
51          }
52      }
53
54      @Override
55      public void updateSprite() {
56      }
57
58      public void eraseBarList() {
59          barList.clear();
60      }
61
62      public void fillBars() {
63          for (int i = 0; i < numberData; i++) {
64              // multiply 0.9 makes not too height; plus
65              // INITBAR prevents zero
66              int fillValue = (int) (Math.random()
67                      * Consts.BASEY * 0.9) + Consts.INITBAR;
68              BarSprite aBar = barList.get(i);
69              aBar.setHeight(fillValue);
70              aBar.setY(Consts.BASEY - aBar.getHeight());
71          }
```

```java
72      }
73
74      public void appendElement() {
75          int appendIdx = numberData;
76          BarSprite aBarS = getBarList().get(appendIdx);
77          aBarS.setHeight(appendValue);
78          aBarS.setY(Consts.BASEY - aBarS.getHeight());
79          numberData++;
80      }
81
82      public void deleteElement(int idx) {
83          for (int i = idx; i < numberData - 1; i++) {
84              BarSprite nextBar = barList.get(i + 1);
85              int theData = nextBar.getHeight();
86              BarSprite thisBar = barList.get(i);
87              thisBar.setHeight(theData);
88              thisBar.setY(Consts.BASEY - thisBar.getHeight());
89          }
90          BarSprite lastBar = barList.get(numberData - 1);
91          lastBar.setHeight(Consts.INITBAR);
92          lastBar.setY(Consts.BASEY - Consts.INITBAR);
93      }
94
95      public int getNumberCells() {
96          return numberCells;
97      }
98
99      public void setNumberCells(int numberCells) {
100         this.numberCells = numberCells;
101     }
102
103     public void setNumberData(int numberData) {
104         this.numberData = numberData;
105     }
106
107     public void setAppendValue(int appendValue) {
108         this.appendValue = appendValue;
109     }
110
111     public ArrayList<BarSprite> getBarList() {
112         return barList;
113     }
114 }
```

Clearly, the method eraseBarList() supports the button "New" to create a new arrayList. The method fillBar() is for the "Fill" function. The two methods of appendItem() and deleteItem() are corresponding to the "Append" and "Delete" operations. All of these operations are popular functions for manipulating an arrayList.

22.3.4 Both the Classes BarSprite.java and ArrowSprite.java Are Simple Classes

The class BarSprite.java defines a bar object, and the ArrorSprite.java defines an arrow object. In the project BubbleSort1, both the bar and the arrow are static sprites.

22.4 Animating Bubble Sort Algorithm: The Project BubbleSort2

After the local arrayList inside the class BarComposite.java is ready with a set of integer values, the following step is to add the sorting algorithm and add a button "BubbleSort" on the controlPanel to execute the bubble sort.

22.4.1 The Bubble Sorting Algorithm

The bubble sorting algorithm can be expressed as the following code.

```
public void bubbleSortAlgo() {
    for (int out = theAry.size()-1; out > 0; out--) {
        for (int in = 0; in < out; in++) {
            if ((theAry.get(in + 1)) < (theAry.get(in)) {
                swapInt(in, in + 1);
            }
        }
    }
}
```

Assume that a set of integers is stored in an ArrayList<Integer> with the name of theAry. Using an ArrayList instead of an array[] is under the consideration that the length of the ArrayList is unknown, which is defined by the user.

The code shows that the algorithm has two nested "for" loops. The outer loop has an index "out" that starts from the last element backward to the index 1. The inner loop has an index "in" that starts from 0 until the (out − 1). If the value at the index of "in" is larger than the value at the index of (in + 1), these two elements should swap their positions. What is the net effect of this computation? It is not easy to see from the algorithm. When the computation is visualized through animation, then it would be clear to see that the effect is to move the current largest value to the current last position in every outer loop. That is, the largest data is moved to the largest index position in the first step of the outer loop. The second largest data is moved to the second last position in the second step of the outer loop. Therefore, at the end of the outer loop, all data are sorted in the ascending order.

22.4.2 A Crucial and Difficult Issue

The code of the bubble sorting algorithm shown above is for sorting an integer arrayList. In the project BubbleSort2, a new class BubbleSort.java is added for implementing the sorting algorithm. Once the method swapInt() is invoked, it completes the swap of two integers in the arrayList. At the same time, two corresponding bar sprites on the GUI should be animated for exchanging corresponding positions from each other. A method swapBar() defined in the class BarComposite.java sets up related attributes of the two barSprites, and when the game loop invokes the method updateSprite() of the class BarSprite.java, the two bars are animated to exchange their positions on the GUI.

We can say that realizing this idea is not difficult. One swapInt() triggers one swapBar(). Unfortunately, the execution time of the method swapInt() is much shorter than the time required to animate two barSprites to exchange their positions on the GUI. In other words, after invoking the method swapInt(), the bubble sorting algorithm must be paused to wait for the two barSprites to finish their position exchange on the GUI. After that, a signal is needed to be sent to the class BubbleSort.java for resuming the bubble sorting algorithm in order to execute the next swapInt(). How to synchronize the swapInt() action and the swapBar() animation one-by-one correspondingly? This becomes a crucial issue.

22.4.3 Applying a New Thread for Solving the Difficulty

We have learned Thread and applied it for the three-layer structure for games as well as some video games already. A thread can be put into sleep, which does not waste any resource of the system. Meanwhile, the sleeping thread can be awaked when the sleep time is over. Consequently, we can simply design the class BubbleSort.java as a thread such that it can be paused and resumed.

Under this design, the project BubbleSort2 has two threads. In order to emphasize them, the partial UML sequence diagram of the project shown in Fig. 22.3 uses two ovals for representing the two threads. One is the original animThread in the three-layer structure framework. The second thread is the new class BubbleSort.java. The sequence diagram guides us to see the dynamic behaviors of the project as follows.

The label "1. click" indicates that the user clicks the button "BubbleSort" on the GUI. The event handler of the button in the class ControlPanel.java invokes the following three statements.

```
// sets up the data arrayList for sorting
gameCanvas.initBubbleSort();
// instantiates inArrow and outArrow
gameCanvas.initInOutArrow();
// start the second thread
gameCanvas.getBubbleSort().start();
```

Fig. 22.3 The partial UML sequence diagram of the project BubbleSort2

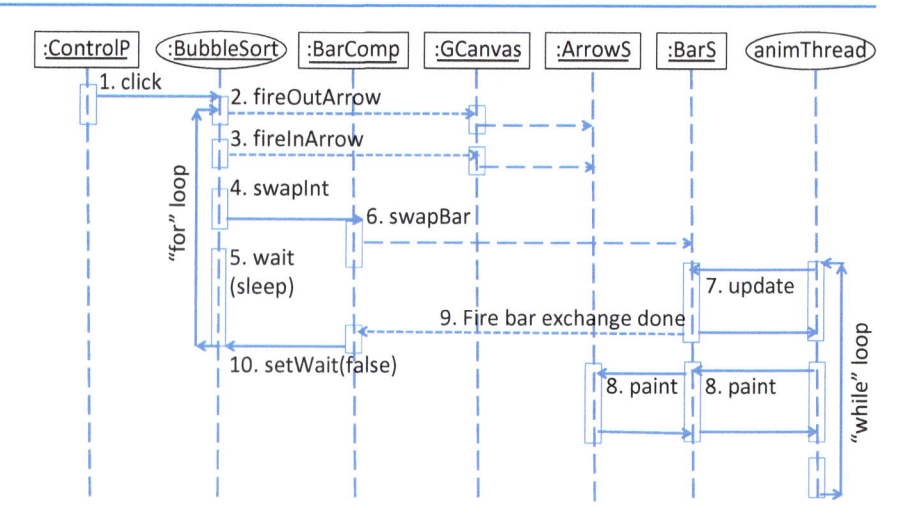

The first statement initBubbleSort() sets up the data arrayList theAry inside the class BubbleSort.java for sorting. The original arrayList barList in the class BarComposite.java is an arrayList of BarSprite.java. The BubbleSort is sorting on an integer data arrayList theAry. Therefore, the data arrayList theAry should copy the data from the "preferred" arrayList barList made by the user. After the sorting starts, the swapInt() swaps two integers in the data arrayList theAry, which triggers the method swapBar() to swap two bars in the original arrayList barList on the GUI, correspondingly.

The second statement initInOutArrow() is for setting up two arrow sprites. The bubble sorting algorithm above shows that the algorithm contains two nested "for" loops. The outArrow sprite follows the iterator "out" of the outer loop for indicating the final position of the current loop. The inArrow sprite follows the iterator "in" of the inner loop for indicating the current positions of the "in" that compares with its neighbor "in + 1" in order to swap them or not.

The third statement getBubbleSort().start() commands the method run() defined in the thread BubbleSort.java to execute the bubble sorting algorithm implemented in the method bubbleSortAlgo().

The label "2. fireOutArrow" and "3. fireInArrow" are involved in every step during the running of the two nested "for" loops to respectively fires a property change event to the class GameCanvas.java for telling the current indexes of the "out" and "in" iterators. The propertyChangeEvent listener GameCanvasListener receives the indexes and updates the position coordinates of the inArrow and outArrow sprites.

The label "4. swapInt" starts the method swapInt(smallerIdx, largerIdx) inside the bubble sorting algorithm to swap the two values in the data arrayList theAry if necessary. And then the method swapInt() immediately follows the label "6. swapBar" to invoke the method swapBar() defined in the class BarComposite.java with the two same parameters smallerIdx and largerIdx for finding the corresponding two bar sprites in the arrayList barList and setting up the attributes necessary for animating the two bar sprites.

The label "5. wait (sleep)" indicates that the method waitForBarExchange() defined in the class BubbleSort.java is invoked to put the thread BubbleSort.java into a sleep, which pauses the execution of the two nested "for" loops in the sorting algorithm.

Now, when the main thread animThread regularly invokes the updateSprite() method defined in the class BarSprite.java, the method follows the new attributes set up in the step "6. swapBar" to update the positions of the two bar sprites as the label "7. update" indicated. And then, the main thread also invokes the paintSprite() methods defined in the class BarSprite.java and ArrowSprite.java to paint the animated bar sprites on the new positions and the inArrow and outArrow on the specified positions as the two labels "8. paint" indicated.

After the two swapping bar sprites animated to the required positions, the updateSprite() method of the class BarSprite.java fires a property change event with the label "9" to the class BarComposite.java, where the inner class UpdateChange as the event listener receives the event and its event handler follows the label "10. setWait(false)" to invoke the method bubbleSort.setWaiting(false) for stopping the wait and resuming the two nested "for" loops of the bubble sorting algorithm, which loops back to the label "2. fireOutArrow" and starts the next cycle.

Thus, we can say that the two nested "for" loops of the bubble sorting algorithm in the class BubbleSort.java is the driving force of the dynamic actions. We design the class as a thread so that the two nested "for" loops can be paused to wait for the two bar sprites to be animated and then the two nested "for" loop will be resumed to continue loop to the next step. The detailed code of the BubbleSort.java class is shown in Listing 22.4.

22.4 Animating Bubble Sort Algorithm: The Project BubbleSort2

Listing 22.4 The class BubbleSort.java in the project BubbleSort2

```
1  /*
2   * BubbleSort.java - A class that implements the bubble sort algorithm.
3   * It is a thread so that it has the run() method and the waitForBarExchange()
4   * method. Due to the swap two integers is faster than the position exchange of
5   * two animated bar sprites, the algorithm needs to be paused and waits for the
6   * finish of the position exchange of two bars.
7   */
8  package bubblesort;
9
10 import java.beans.PropertyChangeListener;
11 import java.beans.PropertyChangeSupport;
12 import java.util.ArrayList;
13
18 public class BubbleSort extends Thread {
19
20     @SuppressWarnings("FieldMayBeFinal")
21     private ArrayList<Integer> theAry;
22     @SuppressWarnings("FieldMayBeFinal")
23     private ArrayList<BarSprite> tempAry;
24     private boolean waiting;
25     private BarComposite barComposite;
26     @SuppressWarnings("FieldMayBeFinal")
27     private PropertyChangeSupport pChange;
28
29     public BubbleSort() {
30         pChange = new PropertyChangeSupport(this);
31     }
32
33     public void initBubbleSort() {
34         // the sorting array theAry could be part of the init array tempAry
35         tempAry = barComposite.getBarList();
36         theAry = new ArrayList<Integer>();
37         for (int i = 0; i < tempAry.size(); i++) {
38             int aValue = tempAry.get(i).getHeight();
39             if (aValue > Consts.INITBAR) {
40                 theAry.add(aValue);
41             }
42         }
43         waiting = true;
44     }
45
46     @Override
47     public void run() {
48         bubbleSortAlgo();
49     }
50
51     private void waitForBarExchange() {
52         try {
53             while (isWaiting()) {
54                 BubbleSort.sleep(100); // "this" is sleep
55             }
56         } catch (Exception ex) {
57         }
```

```java
58            setWaiting(true);
59        }
60
61    public void bubbleSortAlgo() { // ascending sort
62        for (int out = theAry.size() - 1; out > 0; out--) {
63            fireOutArrow(out);
64            for (int in = 0; in < out; in++) {
65                fireInArrow(in);
66                if ((theAry.get(in + 1)) <= (theAry.get(in))) {
67                    swapInt(in, in + 1);
68                    waitForBarExchange();
69                }
70            }
71        }
72    }
73
74    public void swapInt(int smallerIdx, int largerIdx) {
75        Integer temp = theAry.get(smallerIdx);
76        theAry.set(smallerIdx, (int) (theAry.get(largerIdx)));
77        theAry.set(largerIdx, temp);
78        barComposite.swapBar(smallerIdx, largerIdx);
79    }
80
81    // for debugging if needed
82    public void printAry() {
83        for (int i = 0; i < theAry.size(); i++) {
84            System.out.print((theAry.get(i)) + " ");
85        }
86        System.out.println();
87    }
88
89    public boolean isWaiting() {
90        return waiting;
91    }
92
93    public void setWaiting(boolean waiting) {
94        this.waiting = waiting;
95    }
96
97    // asking gameCanvas to assign inArrow
98    public void fireInArrow(int inIdx) {
99        pChange.firePropertyChange("inArrow", "-1", inIdx + "");
100   }
101
102   // asking gameCanvas to assign outArrow
103   public void fireOutArrow(int outIdx) {
104       pChange.firePropertyChange("outArrow", "-1", outIdx + "");
105   }
106
107   public void setBarComposite(BarComposite barComposite) {
108       this.barComposite = barComposite;
109   }
110
111   public void addPropertyChangeListener(PropertyChangeListener pcl) {
112       pChange.addPropertyChangeListener(pcl);
113   }
114 }
```

22.4.4 Setting Attributes for Animating the Bar Sprites

For animating the bar sprites, some attributes should be set up. A bar could be animated to the left or to the right depending on the sorting algorithm. In addition, the distance should be animated depending on the distance between the two swapped bars. Therefore, we add two extra new attributes into the class BarSprite.java. One is the animation direction, moveRight and moveLeft; the other is the distance should be animated, rightLimit and leftLimit. In addition, the class BarComposite.java adds a new method swapBar() for setting these attributes as shown in Listing 22.5.

Listing 22.5 The new methods added in the class BarComposite.java of the project BubbleSort2

```java
1  /*
2   * BarComposite.java - A composite class that contains a set of barSprites
3   * for representing the value of the corresponding data in the array. It has
4   * all of methods for manipulating the array.
5   */
6  package bubblesort;
7
...
17 public class BarComposite extends AbsSprite {
18
...
25     private BubbleSort bubbleSort;
26
...
49
50     @Override
51     public void paintSprite(Graphics2D g2d) {
52         BarSprite aBar;
53         for (int i = 0; i < barList.size(); i++) {
54             aBar = barList.get(i);
55             aBar.paintSprite(g2d);
56         }
57     }
58
59     @Override
60     public void updateSprite() {
61         BarSprite aBar;
62         for (int i = 0; i < barList.size(); i++) {
63             aBar = barList.get(i);
64             if (aBar.isActive()) {
65                 aBar.updateSprite();
66             }
67         }
68     }
69
70     public void swapBar(int smallerIdx, int largerIdx) {
71         BarSprite toRight = (BarSprite) barList.get(smallerIdx);
72         BarSprite toLeft = (BarSprite) barList.get(largerIdx);
73         toRight.setMoveRight(true);
74         toRight.setMoveLeft(false);
75         toRight.setRightLimit(toLeft.getX());
76         toLeft.setMoveRight(false);
77         toLeft.setMoveLeft(true);
```

```
78              toLeft.setLeftLimit(toRight.getX());
79
80              // physically swap the two BarSprite in spriteAry
81              barList.set(smallerIdx, toLeft);
82              barList.set(largerIdx, toRight);
83          }
84
85          class UpdateChange implements PropertyChangeListener {
86
87              @Override
88              public void propertyChange(PropertyChangeEvent evt) {
89                  String theChange = evt.getPropertyName();
90                  if (theChange.equals("updateDone")) {
91                      // stop waiting
92                      bubbleSort.setWaiting(false);
93                  }
94              }
95          }
96
...
153
154         public void setBubbleSort(BubbleSort bubbleSort) {
155             this.bubbleSort = bubbleSort;
156         }
157     }
```

The method swapBar() gets a toRight bar corresponding to the parameter of smallerIdx and a toLeft bar corresponding to the parameter of largerIdx. Then the related attributes are set up as shown in the class BarSprite.java in Listing 22.6.

Listing 22.6 The new additions in the class BarSprite.java of the project BubbleSort2

```
 1 /*
 2  * BarSprite.java - A class that defines a bar sprite.
 3  */
 4 package bubblesort;
 5
...
15 public class BarSprite extends AbsSprite2D {
16
17     private boolean moveRight;
18     private boolean moveLeft;
19     private int rightLimit;
20     private int leftLimit;
21     @SuppressWarnings("FieldMayBeFinal")
22     private PropertyChangeSupport pChange;
23
24     @SuppressWarnings("OverridableMethodCallInConstructor")
25     public BarSprite() {
26         pChange = new PropertyChangeSupport(this);
27         initSprite();
28     }
29
...
42
```

```
43      @Override
44      public void updateSprite() {
45          if (isMoveRight()) {
46              if (getX() < getRightLimit()) {
47                  setX(getX() + 1);
48              } else {
49                  setMoveRight(false);
50                  fireUpdateDone();
51              }
52          } else if (isMoveLeft()) {
53              if (getX() > getLeftLimit()) {
54                  setX(getX() - 1);
55              } else {
56                  setMoveLeft(false);
57              }
58          }
59      }
60
61      public void fireUpdateDone() {
62          pChange.firePropertyChange("updateDone", "-1", "1");
63      }
64
65      @Override
66      public void paintSprite(Graphics2D g2d) {
67          g2d.setColor(getColor());
68          g2d.fillRect(getX(), getY(), getWidth(), getHeight());
69      }
70
...     // getter and setter methods
102
103     public void addPropertyChangeListener(PropertyChangeListener pcl) {
104         pChange.addPropertyChangeListener(pcl);
105     }
106 }
```

The method updateSprite() defined in the class BarSprite.java clearly indicates that it will animate the bar as long as the attributes of the bar sprites have been set up. Whenever the condition (getX() == getRightLimit()) is reached, the method invokes fireUpdateDone() to fire the property change event "updateDone" to the event listener, the inner class UpdateChange defined in the class BarComposite.java. The event handler further invokes the method bubbleSort.setWaiting(false) to resume the thread.

22.4.5 A Trivial Extra Feature of the Project BubbleSort2

After finishing a bubble sorting, if we would like to delete some data from the arrayList and/or append some data into the arrayList, the data appear on the GUI are no longer sorted. We can click the button "BubbleSort" on the controlPanel again to sort the new set of data again.

22.5 Switching the Sorting Algorithm to Be Quick Sort: The Project QuickSort

The project BubbleSort only deals with one sorting algorithm. May we merge multiple sorting algorithms in one project? With multiple sorting algorithms in one project, a more important question would be: "Is it possible to allow multiple sorting algorithms sharing the same GUI with the same animation mechanism?" We are going to answer this question in two steps.

The first step is to develop a new project that animates the quick sorting algorithm only in order to explore the special requirements of the quick sort. And then, the second step is to merge the bubble sort and the quick sort into one project for sharing the same GUI part. Definitely, the new project that merges two sorting algorithms will further demonstrate the significance of the separation of the GUI part from the logic part such that the same GUI can be controlled by different logics.

Actually, in the project BubbleSort2, the class BubbleSort.java was designed to mainly contain two methods only. The method bubbleSortAlgo() is for implementing the bubble sorting computation, and the method waitForBarExchange() is just a mechanism for pausing the thread to wait for the completion of the bar animation. And a Boolean variable "waiting" is for resuming the actions of the algorithm. This design permits us to easily replace the method bubbleSortAlgo() with other new sorting algorithms. Taking advantage of this design, we simply copy the project BubbleSort2 and make a new project QuickSort, in which the new class QuickSort.java has a new quickSortAlgo() method for replacing the original bubbleSortAlgo() method. The new QuickSort.java class is shown in Listing 22.7.

Listing 22.7 The new class QuickSort.java of the project QuickSort

```
 1  /*
 2   * QuickSort.java - A class that implements the quick sorting algorithm.
 3   * It is a thread so that it has the run() method and the waitForBarExchange()
 4   * method. Due to the swap two integers is faster than the position exchange of
 5   * two animated bar sprites, the algorithm needs to be paused and waits for the
 6   * finishing of the position exchange of two bars.
 7   */
 8  package quicksort;
 9
10  import java.beans.PropertyChangeListener;
11  import java.beans.PropertyChangeSupport;
12  import java.util.ArrayList;
13
18  public class QuickSort extends Thread {
19
20      @SuppressWarnings("FieldMayBeFinal")
21      private ArrayList<Integer> theAry;
22      @SuppressWarnings("FieldMayBeFinal")
23      private ArrayList<BarSprite> tempAry;
24      private boolean waiting;
25      private BarComposite barComposite;
26      @SuppressWarnings("FieldMayBeFinal")
27      private PropertyChangeSupport pChange;
28
29      public QuickSort() {
30          pChange = new PropertyChangeSupport(this);
31      }
32
33      public void initQuickSort() {
34          // the sorting array theAry could be part of the init array tempAry
35          tempAry = barComposite.getBarList();
36          theAry = new ArrayList<Integer>();
37          for (int i = 0; i < tempAry.size(); i++) {
38              int aValue = tempAry.get(i).getHeight();
39              if (aValue > Consts.INITBAR) {
40                  theAry.add(aValue);
41              }
42          }
43          waiting = true;
44      }
45
```

22.5 Switching the Sorting Algorithm to Be Quick Sort: The Project QuickSort

```
46      @Override
47      public void run() {
48          quickSortAlgo();
49      }
50
51      private void waitForBarExchange() {
52          try {
53              while (isWaiting()) {
54                  QuickSort.sleep(100); // "this" is sleep
55              }
56          } catch (Exception ex) {
57          }
58          setWaiting(true);
59      }
60
61      public void quickSortAlgo() { // ascending sort
62          recQuickSort(0, theAry.size() - 1);
63      }
64
65      public void recQuickSort(int in, int out) {
66          if ((out - in) >= 1) {
67              Integer pivot = theAry.get(out);
68              firePivotArrow(out);
69
70              int partition = partitionAry(in, out, pivot);
71              recQuickSort(in, partition - 1);
72              recQuickSort(partition + 1, out);
73          }
74      }
75
76      public int partitionAry(int in, int out, int pivot) {
77          int smallerIdx = in - 1;
78          int largerIdx = out;
79          while (true) {
80              while (theAry.get(++smallerIdx) < pivot) {
81                  fireInArrow(smallerIdx);
82              }
83              while ((largerIdx > 0) && (theAry.get(--largerIdx) > pivot)) {
84                  fireOutArrow(largerIdx);
85              }
86              if (smallerIdx >= largerIdx) {
87                  break;
88              } else {
89                  swapInt(smallerIdx, largerIdx);
90              }
91          }
92          // in case when smallerIdx == out, it is impossible
93          // to swap two same bars, then the program cannot
94          // be further executed. To skip this case,
95          // the following checking is necessary.
96          if (smallerIdx < out) {
97              swapInt(smallerIdx, out); // restore pivot
98          }
99          return smallerIdx;
100     }
```

```java
    public void swapInt(int smallerIdx, int largerIdx) {
        // swap integers in theAry
        Integer temp = theAry.get(smallerIdx);
        theAry.set(smallerIdx, theAry.get(largerIdx));
        theAry.set(largerIdx, temp);
        // set arrows and swap bars
        fireInArrow(smallerIdx);
        fireOutArrow(largerIdx);
        barComposite.swapBar(smallerIdx, largerIdx);
        waitForBarExchange();
    }

    // for debugging if needed
    public void printAry() {
        for (int i = 0; i < theAry.size(); i++) {
            System.out.print((theAry.get(i)) + " ");
        }
        System.out.println();
    }

    public boolean isWaiting() {
        return waiting;
    }

    public void setWaiting(boolean waiting) {
        this.waiting = waiting;
    }

    // asking gameCanvas to assign inArrow. In order to
    // display arrows in the "while" loop in sorting algo,
    // pausing the arrow display and let paintSprite() in
    // the ArrowSprite.java to resume it.
    public void fireInArrow(int inIdx) {
        pChange.firePropertyChange("inArrow", "-1", inIdx + "");
        waitForBarExchange();
    }

    // asking gameCanvas to assign outArrow
    public void fireOutArrow(int outIdx) {
        pChange.firePropertyChange("outArrow", "-1", outIdx + "");
        waitForBarExchange();
    }

    public void firePivotArrow(int pivotIdx) {
        pChange.firePropertyChange("pivotArrow", "-1", pivotIdx + "");
    }

    public void setBarComposite(BarComposite barComposite) {
        this.barComposite = barComposite;
    }

    public void addPropertyChangeListener(PropertyChangeListener pcl) {
        pChange.addPropertyChangeListener(pcl);
    }
}
```

The quick sorting is the "fastest" sorting algorithm among all of sorting algorithms. It looks much different from the bubble sorting. The main idea of the algorithm is as follows:

1. Selecting a value in the arrayList as the pivot number, here the pivot number is the last value of the arrayList.
2. And then, it recursively partitions the values in the arrayList into two groups. One group has all values less than the pivot number; the other group has all values larger than the pivot number. For making the two groups, the algorithm looks for a value larger than the pivot number from the leftmost position; at the same time, from the rightmost position, it looks for a value less than the pivot number and then swaps these two values. When the left index meets with the right index, the partition is formed.
3. The algorithm then swaps the pivot number with the first value in the larger value group so that the pivot number becomes the "middle" value and all of values in the less group are on its left side and all values in the larger group are on its right side.
4. At this moment, the recursive call picks up the less value group and selects the last value in the less value group as the pivot number and repeats the computation shown above until all of values are sorted.
5. The recursive call also applies the same computation shown above for the larger value group until all of values are sorted.

In order to control the animation of bars and arrows, the quick sorting algorithm mainly has the following new requirements:

1. It involves the method swapInt() in two places. One is a "regular" swap that swaps a larger value with a less value as described in the second point above. The other is to swap the pivot number with the first value in the larger value group as described in the third point above. We must pay attention to a pitfall in the second swap operation, which may have a chance to swap the pivot number with itself. In the data arrayList theAry, swapping the same value has no problem; however, on the arrayList barList shown on the GUI, swapping the same bar with itself is impossible because it will stop the execution of the program. Therefore, checking the "if (smallerIdx < out)" condition is necessary in order to eliminate the case of swapping the same bar with itself.
2. The algorithm requires three arrows. One indicates the pivot number and the other two for indicating the two swapping bars. Consequently, when the button "QuickSort" is pressed, both the "gameCanvas.initInOutArrow();" and "gameCanvas.initPivotArrow();" should be invoked.
3. The quick sorting involves two "while" loops that is possible to continuously change the values of the two indexes smallerIdx and largerIdx until finding out two satisfied values to be swapped in the data arrayList theAry. For clearly indicating the changes of the two indexes, the corresponding arrows inArrow and outArrow should also be continuously moved on the GUI.
4. Similarly with the bars animation, the changes of the index values are faster than the moving and displaying arrows on the GUI. For synchronizing these two actions, the method waitForBarExchange() should also be invoked to pause the thread for waiting the displaying of the two arrows. Meanwhile, after finishing the painting of the arrows, a signal is needed to resume the thread. For that, a property change event should be added to provide a communication between the classes GameCanvas.java and ArrowSprite.java. When the method fireInArrow() or fireOutArrow() is invoked in the class QuickSort.java, the property change listener InOutArrowListener in the class GameCanvas.java assigns the received coordinates to the inArrow or outArrow for their displaying and at the same time also invokes the method inArrow.setLeftIdx(true) or outArrow.setRightIdx(true) for setting the Boolean variables leftIdx or rightIdx defined in the class ArrowSprite.java as true. Immediately, the two methods fireInArrow() and fireOutArrow() also invoke the method quicksort.waitForBarExchange() to pause the thread quickSort. After the paintSprite() in the class ArrowSprite.java finished the arrow painting, it checks "if ((leftIdx) || (rightIdx))" whenever one of them is true the method quicksort.setWaiting(false) is invoked to resume the thread for the next cycle.

22.6 Supporting Multiple Sorting Algorithms: The Project MultiSort

Based on the successful projects BubbleSort2 and QuickSort, we are going to merge them into one project MultiSort to further verify the sharing of the animation mechanism as well as the separation of the logical controls. Due to the fact that the QuickSort is little bit more complicated than the BubbleSort, we thus copy the project QuickSort as the base of the project MultiSort and then add the necessary part of the project BubbleSort into the project MultiSort. The GUI of the project MultiSort is as shown in Fig. 22.4.

It is clear that the controlPanel now possesses two buttons "BubbleSort" and "QuickSort," which implies that the project contains both classes BubbleSort.java and QuickSort.java. The project must satisfy a fundamental requirement, that is, these two sorting algorithms must be mutual exclusive. It is equivalent to say that during the time period of one

Fig. 22.4 Two sorting algorithms BubbleSort and QuickSort share one GUI

algorithm in execution, any click on either button won't affect the execution. Only after the current sorting finishes, the user is able to select any one of them. For realizing this requirement, we need to add the following controls: (1) The action handlers of the two buttons should be mutually locked such that only one of them is in execution at a time. (2) After the current running algorithm finishes, a signal will be issued to release the mutual lock.

The implementation of the mutual lock is based on a Boolean variable mutualLock defined in the class GameCanvas.java. Initially, the mutualLock has a value of false so that either sorting algorithm can be started. And then, the mutualLock immediately is assigned to a value of true to realize the first control listed above. As long as the current algorithm finished its execution, a property change is fired to release the mutualLock for reaching the second control above. As we know both the classes QuickSort.java and BubbleSort.java have a property change event communication channel with the class GameCanvas.java already for supporting the methods fireOutArrow() and fireInArrow(). Taking advantage of this communication channel, we add a new method fireSortDone() in the classes BubbleSort.java and QuickSort.java. The "SortDone" property change signals the inner class SortAlgoListener defined in the class GameCanvas.java. The event handler simply invokes setMutualLock(false) to release the mutual lock.

Merging multiple sorting algorithms in one project won't affect the static part. That is, the software components and their action handling routines for making a "preferred" arrayList keep the same as before. But, the two sorting action handlers are necessary to be modified. The modifications in the ControlPanel.java class are shown in Listing 22.8.

Listing 22.8 The modifications in the class ControlPanel.java of the project MultiSort

```
 1  /*
 2   * ControlPanel.java - A class that defines the control panel for the project
 3   * QuickSort. It provides four buttons: New, Fill, Append, Delete for making
 4   * a "preferred" array.
 5   */
 6  package multisort;
 7
...
22  public class ControlPanel extends JPanel {
23
...
36
37      private GameCanvas gameCanvas;
38      private BarComposite barComposite;
39      private ActionListener listener;
40
41      private JPanel sortP;
42      private JButton bubbleBtn;
43      private JButton quickBtn;
44
```

22.6 Supporting Multiple Sorting Algorithms: The Project MultiSort

```
45      @SuppressWarnings("OverridableMethodCallInConstructor")
46      public ControlPanel() {
47          setPreferredSize(new Dimension(Consts.CV_WIDTH, Consts.CONT_P_H));
48          initControlPanel();
49      }
50
51      private void initControlPanel() {
52          ...
93      }
94
95      public void findBarComposite() {
96          ...
100     }
101
102     class MyActionListener implements ActionListener {
103
104         @Override
105         public void actionPerformed(ActionEvent evt) {
106             if (evt.getActionCommand().equals("New")) {
107                 ...
119             } else if (evt.getActionCommand().equals("Fill")) {
120                 ...
142             } else if (evt.getActionCommand().equals("Append")) {
143                 ...
160             } else if (evt.getActionCommand().equals("Delete(index)")) {
161                 ...
176             } else if (evt.getActionCommand().equals("BubbleSort")) {
177                 msgText.setText(" Bubble sorting");
178                 // initialize mutual lock as false to allow either one running
179                 if (!gameCanvas.isMutualLock()) {
180                     // when one sort starts, set the mutual lock as true to
181                     // preventing any of them would be started so that only
182                     // one of them running at a time.
183                     gameCanvas.setMutualLock(true);
184                     // until the sorting process finished the mutual lock
185                     // will be released for both algorithms.(see the inner
186                     // class SortAlgoListener in the class GameCanvas.java)
187
188                     // only after "Fill", bubble sort can be initialized
189                     gameCanvas.initBubbleSort();
190                     gameCanvas.initInOutArrow();
191                     gameCanvas.erasePivotArrow();
192                     gameCanvas.getBubbleSort().start();
193                 }
194             } else if (evt.getActionCommand().equals("QuickSort")) {
195                 msgText.setText(" Quick sorting");
196                 // make mutual lock to allow only one of them working at a time
197                 if (!gameCanvas.isMutualLock()) {
198                     // when one sort starts, set the mutual lock as true to
199                     // preventing any of them would be started so that only
200                     // one of them running at a time.
201                     gameCanvas.setMutualLock(true);
202
```

```
203                         // sort should be initialized after "Fill"
204                         gameCanvas.initQuickSort();
205                         gameCanvas.initInOutArrow();
206                         gameCanvas.initPivotArrow(); // quick sort needs pivot arrow
207                         gameCanvas.getQuickSort().start();
208                     }
209                 }
210                 valueField.setText("");
211                 gameCanvas.repaint(); // for re-paint the changes before sorting
212             }
213         }
214         ...
218 }
219
```

22.7 Summary

The project BubbleSort with animated bar sprites is designed for visualizing an unseen computation in the bubble sorting process. The animations of bar sprites are under the control of the main thread embedded in the three-layer structure for games. On the other hand, which bar sprite should be animated is under the control of the sorting algorithm. Once a bar is selected to be animated, the sorting algorithm itself should be paused for waiting the bar animation and should be resumed when the bar animation is finished. An easy way for assigning the pause and resume ability to the sorting algorithm is to design the algorithm as a thread. A communication is needed to make these two threads work together. The sorting thread sets up related attributes for the selected bar sprites, and then it is paused. During the sorting thread paused, the main thread animates the selected bar sprites. When the animations are done, a signal is feedback to the sorting thread for resuming it in order to find next pair of bars to be swapped.

A convenient communication tool is a property change event, which can set up a communication path between any two classes and which also avoids passing objects from one class to the other. Therefore, it is also applied to set and reset the mutualLock for switching different sorting algorithms in the project MultiSort.

The project MultiSort incorporates two different sorting algorithms into one application. The two sorting algorithms share one data array and one GUI. It further demonstrates the significance in separating the GUI from the logic. It also reveals the importance of the loosely coupled architecture of a software system.

22.8 Exercises

Self-Review Questions

1. How does the bubble sorting algorithm sort an integer array?
2. In the project BubbleSort, which part is static? Which part is dynamic?
3. What operations are available in the static part? Why do we need these operations?
4. What functions are performed by the three-layer structure for games in the project BubbleSort?
5. Why is the class BubbleSort.java designed as a thread?
6. What mechanism is used to pause the sorting thread?
7. How to resume the sorting thread?
8. Where and why is the property change event applied?
9. What is the principle built in the quick sorting algorithm for sorting?
10. What are the special requirements that should be implemented in the project QuickSort?
11. How to mutually lock the two different sorting algorithms in the project MultiSort?
12. How can the different sorting algorithms share the same GUI part?
13. Draw a UML sequence diagram for the project QuickSort.
14. Draw a UML class diagram for the project MultiSort.

Projects

1. Add a descending sort function into the project BubbleSort.
2. Add a descending sort function into the project QuickSort.
3. Develop a project that implements the SelectionSort algorithm.
4. Develop a project that implements the MergeSort algorithm.
5. Add both selection sorting and merge sorting algorithms into the project MultiSort.

23. Animating Conversions Between Binary and Decimal

Binary number computations appear as a tough topic in teaching and learning. Students usually repeatedly ask the same questions and teachers often repeatedly illustrate the same computations. Treating numbers as sprites with animation, we can repeatedly demonstrate binary computation processes. It not only reduces teacher's burden but also enhances students' learning. This chapter covers the conversions of binary integers to decimal and decimal integers to binary, as well as floating numbers.

The objectives of this chapter include:
1. Binary computations may be found difficult.
2. Visualizing binary computations dynamically as video games.
   (a) Converting a positive integer in any base to decimal.
   (b) Converting a positive integer in decimal to any base.
   (c) Converting a positive float in decimal to any base.
3. All of computations are step-by-step visualized as on a blackboard.
4. All of projects are based on the three-layer structure for games.

Binary computations are not intuitive for some beginners. They often repeatedly ask for explanations and demonstrations. In doing exercises, they have no confidence on the results of their own. For providing help to these problems, a set of teaching tools about binary computations probably is feasible. The three-layer structure for games is applied for developing the set of tools in order to dynamically illustrate the computational processes just like teachers demonstrate the relevant computations on a blackboard.

The set of tools include "Converting a positive integer in any base to decimal," "Converting a positive integer in decimal to any base," "Converting a positive float number in decimal to any base," "Summation binary integers in signed-magnitude," "Summation binary integers in one's complement," and "Summation binary integers in two's complement." The first three projects are discussed in this chapter. The remaining three projects will be presented in the next chapter.

The purpose of this book is to introduce the programming language Java and skills. Hence we are not going to discuss why and what about the binary computations but only programming serious games for dynamically demonstrating these computations.

23.1 Converting an Integer in Any Base to Decimal: The Project AnyToDecimal

A positive integer could be represented in any base. In daily life, all of computations are based on decimal numbers. The "decimal" indicates that the number has a base of 10. However, the native language of computers is binary, which means that the numbers could be understood by computers have a base of 2. The extensions of base 2 are base 8 (Octal) and base 16 (Hexadecimal). Thus, decimal integers should be converted to be integers in base 2, base 8, or base 16 and vice versa when computers are used for performing numeric computations. Furthermore, integers in any other bases, such as 3, 4, 5, etc., can also be converted in decimal. That is the word "any base" means.

We know that each digit in an integer in base 10 has its position weight. For example, in a decimal integer 234, the digit 4 has its position weight of 10^0, the digit 3 has its position weight of 10^1, and the digit 2 has its position weight of 10^2. Therefore, the value of the decimal integer is calculated as follows.

```
234 = 2 * 10^2 + 3 * 10^1 + 4 * 10^0 = 200 + 30 + 4
```

Following the same concept, the principle for converting an integer in any base to a corresponding decimal integer is simple because each digit of an integer in binary also has its position weight. For example, an integer 1011 in base 2 can be calculated as follows.

```
decimalValue = 1*2^0 + 1*2^1 + 0*2^2 + 1*2^3
= 1 + 2 + 0 + 8 = 11.
```

Follow this principle, an integer 654 in base 8 can be converted to a decimal number as:

```
decimalValue = 4*8^0 + 5*8^1 + 6*8^2 = 4 + 40
+384 = 428.
```

The project AnyToDecimal is such a program that converts an inputted positive integer in any base to the corresponding integer in decimal. In addition, the project also clarifies the entire conversion process step by step dynamically. The GUI of the project is shown in Fig. 23.1.

The GUI consists of a control panel on the top portion for the user to type an input value and to watch the output value, and a rendering panel on the bottom portion for rendering the conversion process. For implementing the project, the three-layer structure for games comes handy because the rendering process is just like a sprite that dynamically updates the computation and paints the entire computation step by step. The three-layer structure brings in the AbsGameCanvas.java, AbsSprite.java, and GameCanvas.java classes. The project only needs two more new classes ControlPanel.java and RenderSprite.java.

The UML class diagram of the project depicts all of classes as shown in Fig. 23.2. The GameCanvas.java class initializes a controlPanel, which "has" software components JLabels, JTextFields, and JButtons. The class GameCanvas.java also instantiates an object of renderSprite and adds it into the global spriteAry such that the methods of updateSprite() and paintSprite() of the renderSprite are under the control of the game loop. Initially both attributes "active" and "visible" of the renderSprite are set to be false. Once the conversion is done, both attributes are set as true such that the renderSprite starts rendering the computational process dynamically.

23.2 Building Up the Control Panel: The Class ControlPanel.java

The class ControlPanel.java consists of two major parts. One of them is to arrange software components for making a control panel, which provides text fields for inputting and outputting data and buttons for the user to perform operations. The other part is inner classes for implementing action listeners to handle the button control actions.

When the user clicks the button "Do Conversion," the event handler of the inner class ConversionListener performs the following functions.

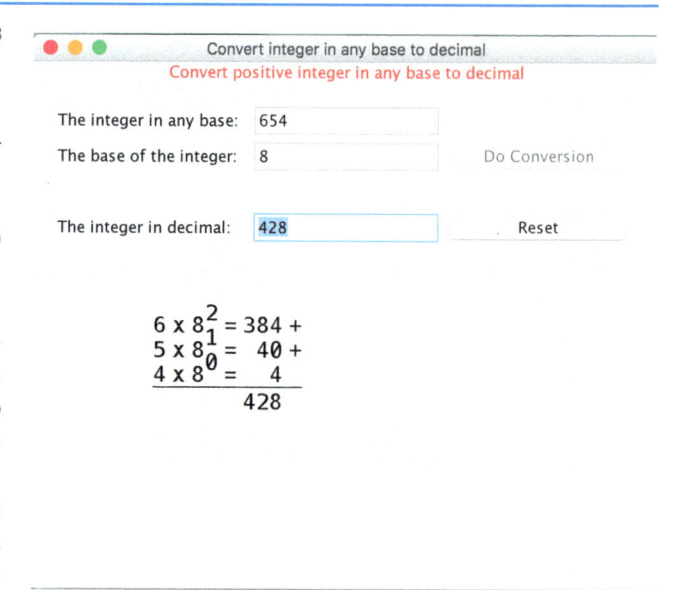

Fig. 23.1 The GUI of the project AnyToDecimal illustrates the computation

1. It accepts the inputted positive integer and its base, and then immediately validates them.
2. If the inputted data are valid, e.g., integer is 1011 and its base is 2,
   (a) It converts and displays the resulting decimal integer, e.g., 11, on the target text field.
3. And then
   (a) It sends the inputted integer and the base to the class RenderSprite.java.
   (b) It sets the attributes "active" and "visible" of the renderSprite as true to activate the methods updateSprite() and paintSprite().
   (c) Under the control of the game loop, the two methods render the computational expressions on the rendering panel of the GUI board step by step.

Once the user clicks the button "Reset," the event handler of the inner class ResetListener starts.

1. It empties the data from the relevant text fields.
2. It invokes both methods gameCanvas.stopGame() and gameCanvas.renewGame() defined in the class AbsGameCanvas.java to reinitialize variables for making a new computation.

The detailed implementations of the class ControlPanel.java are shown in Listing 23.1.

23.2 Building Up the Control Panel: The Class ControlPanel.java

Fig. 23.2 The UML class diagram of the project AnyToDecimal

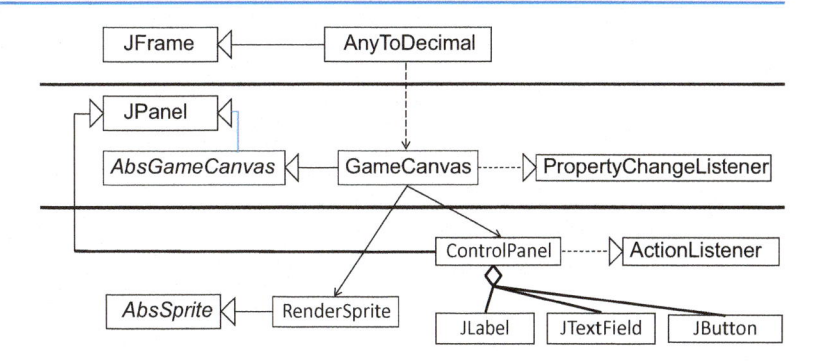

Listing 23.1 The class ControlPanel.java in the project AnyToDecimal

```
1  /*
2   * ControlPanel.java - A class that defines the control panel for the user
3   * to input data and control the conversion.
4   */
5  package anytodecimal;
6
7  import java.awt.BorderLayout;
8  import java.awt.Color;
9  import java.awt.Dimension;
10 import java.awt.GridLayout;
11 import java.awt.event.ActionEvent;
12 import java.awt.event.ActionListener;
13 import javax.swing.JButton;
14 import javax.swing.JLabel;
15 import javax.swing.JPanel;
16 import javax.swing.JTextField;
17
18 public class ControlPanel extends JPanel {
19
20     private JTextField intTxt;
21     private JTextField baseTxt;
22     private JTextField targetTxt;
23     private JLabel statusLbl;
24     private JButton convBtn;
25     private JButton resetBtn;
26     private JPanel inputP;
27
28     private GameCanvas gameCanvas;
29     private RenderSprite renderSprite;
30
31     public ControlPanel() {
32         initControlPanel();
33     }
34
```

```java
35    private void initControlPanel() {
36        setPreferredSize(new Dimension(Consts.CV_WIDTH, 180));
37        setLayout(new BorderLayout());
38        JPanel leftP = new JPanel(); // make a left gap
39        leftP.setPreferredSize(new Dimension(20, Consts.CV_HEIGHT));
40        add(leftP, BorderLayout.WEST);
41        JPanel rightP = new JPanel(); // make a right margin
42        rightP.setPreferredSize(new Dimension(20, Consts.CV_HEIGHT));
43        add(rightP, BorderLayout.EAST);
44        inputP = createInputPanel();
45        add(inputP, BorderLayout.CENTER);
46    }
47
48    private JPanel createInputPanel() {
49        JPanel inP = new JPanel();
50        inP.setLayout(new BorderLayout());
51
52        // the title panel is on NORTH of the input panel
53        JPanel titleP = new JPanel();
54        titleP.setLayout(new GridLayout(2, 1));
55        JLabel titleLbl = new JLabel("Convert positive integer in any base "
56                + "to decimal", 0);
57        titleLbl.setForeground(Color.red);
58        JLabel gapLbl = new JLabel(" ", 0);
59        titleP.add(titleLbl);
60        titleP.add(gapLbl);
61        inP.add(titleP, BorderLayout.NORTH);
62
63        // the data panel is on CENTER of the input panel
64        JPanel dataP = new JPanel();
65        dataP.setLayout(new GridLayout(4, 3));
66        JLabel intLbl = new JLabel("The integer in any base: ");
67        intTxt = new JTextField();
68        JLabel intGap = new JLabel("   ", 0);
69        dataP.add(intLbl);
70        dataP.add(intTxt);
71        dataP.add(intGap);
72
73        JLabel baseLbl = new JLabel("The base of the integer: ");
74        baseTxt = new JTextField();
75        convBtn = new JButton("Do Conversion");
76        convBtn.addActionListener(new ConversionListener());
77        convBtn.setActionCommand(Consts.CONV + ""); // convert int to be String
78        dataP.add(baseLbl);
79        dataP.add(baseTxt);
80        dataP.add(convBtn);
81
82        JLabel empty1Lbl = new JLabel("     ", 0);
83        JLabel empty2Lbl = new JLabel("     ", 0);
84        JLabel empty3Lbl = new JLabel("     ", 0);
85        dataP.add(empty1Lbl);
86        dataP.add(empty2Lbl);
87        dataP.add(empty3Lbl);
88
```

23.2 Building Up the Control Panel: The Class ControlPanel.java

```java
 89            JLabel targetLbl = new JLabel("The integer in decimal: ");
 90            targetTxt = new JTextField();
 91            resetBtn = new JButton("Reset");
 92            resetBtn.setActionCommand(Consts.RESET + "");
 93            resetBtn.addActionListener(new ResetListener());
 94            dataP.add(targetLbl);
 95            dataP.add(targetTxt);
 96            dataP.add(resetBtn);
 97            resetBtn.setEnabled(false);
 98            inP.add(dataP, BorderLayout.CENTER);
 99
100            // the status panel is on SOUTH of the input panel
101            JPanel statusP = new JPanel();
102            statusP.setPreferredSize(new Dimension(Consts.CV_WIDTH, 30));
103            statusLbl = new JLabel("     ", 0);
104            statusP.add(statusLbl);
105            inP.add(statusP, BorderLayout.SOUTH);
106
107            return inP;
108        }
109
110        // inner class ConversionListener -- A listener that converts a positive
111        // integer in any base to an integer in decimal
112        class ConversionListener implements ActionListener {
113
114            int baseInt;
115
116            @Override
117            public void actionPerformed(ActionEvent evt) {
118                if (!(evt.getActionCommand().equals(Consts.CONV + ""))) {
119                    return;
120                }
121                statusLbl.setForeground(Color.red);
122                String inputIntStr = intTxt.getText();
123                String baseStr = baseTxt.getText();
124                if ((inputIntStr.equals("") || (baseStr.equals("")))) {
125                    statusLbl.setText("No input integer or base");
126                    convBtn.setEnabled(false);
127                    resetBtn.setEnabled(true);
128                    return;
129                }
130
131                // verify input data for possible errors
132                int correctValue = verifyInput(inputIntStr, baseStr);
133                switch (correctValue) {
134                    case 0: // no error, start working
135                        statusLbl.setText("");
136                        baseInt = Integer.parseInt(baseStr);
137                        int decimalInt = convertAnyBaseInt(inputIntStr, baseInt);
138                        targetTxt.setText(String.valueOf(decimalInt));
139                        convBtn.setEnabled(false);
140                        resetBtn.setEnabled(true);
141
142                        // start ploting
143                        renderSprite.setInitData(inputIntStr, baseInt);
```

```
144                    renderSprite.setActive(true);
145                    renderSprite.setVisible(true);
146                    break;
147                case 1:
148                    statusLbl.setText("The base should be "
149                            + "in the range of [2, 16]");
150                    convBtn.setEnabled(false);
151                    resetBtn.setEnabled(true);
152                    break;
153                case 2:
154                    statusLbl.setText("Input digits should be "
155                            + "in the range of [0, F]");
156                    convBtn.setEnabled(false);
157                    resetBtn.setEnabled(true);
158                    break;
159                case 3:
160                    statusLbl.setText("Input digits cannot be larger than base. "
161                            + "Enter numbers again");
162                    convBtn.setEnabled(false);
163                    resetBtn.setEnabled(true);
164                    break;
165                default:
166            }
167        }
168
169        private int verifyInput(String sInt, String sBase) {
170            int correctVal = 0;
171            int theBase = Integer.parseInt(sBase);
172            if ((theBase < 2) || (theBase > 16)) {
173                correctVal = 1;
174                return correctVal;
175            }
176            for (int i = 0; i < sInt.length(); i++) {
177                int theV = realValue(sInt.substring(i, i + 1));
178                int theB = realValue(sBase);
179                if (theV > 16) {
180                    correctVal = 2;
181                    break;
182                }
183                if (theB <= theV) {
184                    correctVal = 3;
185                    break;
186                }
187            }
188            return correctVal;
189        }
190
191        public int convertAnyBaseInt(String sAnyBase, int iBase) {
191            int theD = 0;
193            for (int i = sAnyBase.length(); i > 0; i--) {
194                int theValue = realValue(sAnyBase.substring(i - 1, i));
195                theD += (theValue * Math.pow(iBase, sAnyBase.length() - i));
196            }
197            return theD;
198        }
199
```

23.2 Building Up the Control Panel: The Class ControlPanel.java

```
200            private int realValue(String str) {
201                int value;
202                switch (str.charAt(0)) {
203                    case 'A':
204                    case 'a':
205                        value = 10;
206                        break;
207                    case 'B':
208                    case 'b':
209                        value = 11;
210                        break;
211                    case 'C':
212                    case 'c':
213                        value = 12;
214                        break;
215                    case 'D':
216                    case 'd':
217                        value = 13;
218                        break;
219                    case 'E':
220                    case 'e':
221                        value = 14;
222                        break;
223                    case 'F':
224                    case 'f':
225                        value = 15;
226                        break;
227                    default:
228                        value = 20; // an arbitrary value
229                }
230                if (str.charAt(0) < 'A') {
231                    value = Integer.parseInt(str);
232                }
233                return value;
234            }
235        }
236
237    class ResetListener implements ActionListener {
238
239        @Override
240        public void actionPerformed(ActionEvent evt) {
241            if (!(evt.getActionCommand().equals(Consts.RESET + ""))) {
242                return;
243            }
244            if ((JButton) evt.getSource() == resetBtn) {
245                resetBtn.setEnabled(false);
246                convBtn.setEnabled(true);
247                intTxt.requestFocus();
248                intTxt.setText("");
249                baseTxt.setText("");
250                targetTxt.setText("");
251                statusLbl.setText("");
252                gameCanvas.stopGame();
253                gameCanvas.renewGame();
254            }
```

```
255          }
256      }
257
258      public void setGameCanvas(GameCanvas gameCanvas) {
259          this.gameCanvas = gameCanvas;
260      }
261
262      public void setRenderSprite(RenderSprite renderSprite) {
263          this.renderSprite = renderSprite;
264      }
265
266      public JButton getResetBtn() {
267          return resetBtn;
268      }
269 }
```

The code seems lengthy because many error verification procedures are required.

1. When clicking the button "Do Conversion," the input integer and the base should be available.
2. The value of the base must be in the range of [2, 16].
3. Any digit in the input integer must be in the range of [0, F].
4. Any digit in the input integer should be less than the value of base.
5. At any time, only one of the buttons is enabled on the panel so that the user won't be able to click two buttons simultaneously for causing malfunctions.
6. The alternation of the two buttons "Do Conversion" and "Reset" is automatically performed. Once the "Do Conversion" button is clicked, it is disabled so that reclicking the button won't cause any malfunction. The button "Reset" is enabled only when the conversion is finished.

23.3 Rendering the Computation Process: The Class RenderSprite.java

The class RenderSprite.java extends the class AbsSprite.java and implements the methods updateSprite() and paintSprite(). Following the example shown on the GUI in Fig. 23.1, the input integer is "654" and the base is "8", the rendering process needs to paint three expressions on the GUI one by one. An important issue is that after finishing painting the first expression, before going to paint the second expression, the first expression has to be painted again. Similarly, before painting the third expression, the first and the second expressions need to be painted again. After finishing the painting of the third expression, all of the three expressions should be painted again and again until the user clicks the reset button. Otherwise, at any time, only the expression in the painting is shown on the GUI.

In order to realize this painting requirement, the method updateSprite() increases the variable "count" by one in every invocation and stores the corresponding value of position weight in the array values[] for later use. The value of the count is used to control the while loop in the paintSprite() method. The detailed implementation could be as follows.

1. When the method updateSprite() is invoked at the first time, count = 1. And then the method paintSprite() is invoked, which has a local counter localC = 0 and a "while(localC < count)" loop works one time for painting the first expression "6 x 8^2 = 384 + ."
2. Then the updateSprite() method is invoked by the game loop second time, count = 2. When the paintSprite() method is invoked again, the localC = 0 again and the "while(localC < count)" will loop twice for painting both the first and the second expressions, and so on.

The painting of any expression is based on the calculation of the coordinates (x, y) for every character in the expression, and then the method paintSprite() invokes the built-in method drawString() to paint every character. The following piece of code is for painting one expression, such as "6 x 8^2 = 384 + ."

```
92      // paint one expression
93      g2d.drawString(intStr.substring(localC, localC + 1), x, y); // digit
94      g2d.drawString("x", x + digitW + gapW, y); // multiplication sign
95      g2d.drawString("" + base, x + digitW + gapW + digitW + gapW, y); // base
96      g2d.drawString("" + (intStr.length() - localC - 1),
97          x + digitW + gapW + digitW + gapW + baseW, y - powerH); // power
98      g2d.drawString("=", xToEqualSign - digitW, y); // equal sign
99      int valueW = fm.stringWidth("" + values[localC]); // width of max value
100     g2d.drawString("" + values[localC],
101         xToMaxW - digitW - gapW - valueW, y); // the max value
102     if (localC < (intStr.length() - 1)) {
103         g2d.drawString("+", xToMaxW - digitW, y); // "+" sign
104     }
```

Because the inputted integer is "654," the intStr.length() is 3. Once the "if (count == intStr.length())" is true, it means that the count == 3, the paintSprite() just paints three expressions on three lines. Thus, the painting is completed and the method paintSprite() fires a property change event to the class GameCanvas.java for making the button "Reset" enabled such that the user may click the "Reset" button for a new conversion. The code of the class RenderSprite.java is cited on Listing 23.2.

Listing 23.2 The class RenderSprite.java of the project AnyToDecimal

```
1  /*
2   * RenderSprite.java - A class that renders conversion.
3   */
4  package anytodecimal;
5
6  import java.awt.Font;
7  import java.awt.FontMetrics;
8  import java.awt.Graphics2D;
9  import java.beans.PropertyChangeListener;
10 import java.beans.PropertyChangeSupport;
11
16 public class RenderSprite extends AbsSprite {
17
18     private String intStr;
19     private int base, count;
20     private final int lineH = 20, gapH = 2, gapW = 5, powerH = 10;
21     private final int topMargin = 200, leftMargin = 100;
22     private int x, y;
23     private int[] values;
24     private Font theF;
25     private PropertyChangeSupport convDone;
26
27     @SuppressWarnings("OverridableMethodCallInConstructor")
28     public RenderSprite() {
29         initSprite();
30     }
31
32     @Override
33     public void initSprite() {
34         x = leftMargin;
35         y = topMargin;
```

```java
36          count = 0;
37          theF = new Font("Monospaced", Font.PLAIN, 18);
38          values = new int[15];
39          convDone = new PropertyChangeSupport(this);
40      }
41
42      public void setInitData(String inputIntStr, int baseInt) {
43          this.intStr = inputIntStr;
44          this.base = baseInt;
45      }
46
47      // update the count: increased by 1 in every loop
48      @Override
49      public void updateSprite() {
50          if (!(this.isActive())) {
51              return;
52          }
53          if (count < intStr.length()) {
54              // store the max values in the array values[]
55              count += 1;
56              values[count - 1]
57                      = (int) (realValue(intStr.substring(count - 1, count))
58                      * Math.pow(base, intStr.length() - count));
59          }
60      }
61
62      @Override
63      public void paintSprite(Graphics2D g2d) {
64          if (!(this.isVisible())) {
65              return;
66          }
67
68          g2d.setFont(theF);
69
70          FontMetrics fm = g2d.getFontMetrics();
71          int digitW = fm.stringWidth("F");
72          int baseW = fm.stringWidth("" + base);
73          // paint an expression "2 x 8^2 = 128 +"
74          // including equal sign, the length is fixed
75          int xToEqualSign = x + digitW + gapW + digitW + gapW + baseW
76                  + digitW + gapW + digitW;
77          // after equal sign, width depends on the max value
78          int xToMaxW = 0;
79
80          int localC = 0;
81          y = topMargin; // reset the starting y position
82          // depends on the value of count to paint an expression for every digit
83          // count = 1, paint the left most digit calculation expression
84          // count = 2, paint the left first and second digits expressions ...
85          while ((localC < count) && (count <= intStr.length())) {
86              y += lineH;
87              if (localC == 0) { // prepare the width of max value and a "+"
88                  int maxV = values[localC]; // max value were stored in values[]
89                  int maxW = fm.stringWidth("" + maxV);
90                  xToMaxW = xToEqualSign + gapW + maxW + gapW + digitW;
```

23.3 Rendering the Computation Process: The Class RenderSprite.java

```
91              }
92              // paint one expression
93              g2d.drawString(intStr.substring(localC, localC + 1), x, y); // digit
94              g2d.drawString("x", x + digitW + gapW, y); // multiplication sign
95              g2d.drawString("" + base, x + digitW + gapW + digitW + gapW, y); // base
96              g2d.drawString("" + (intStr.length() - localC - 1),
97                      x + digitW + gapW + digitW + gapW + baseW, y - powerH); // power
98              g2d.drawString("=", xToEqualSign - digitW, y); // equal sign
99              int valueW = fm.stringWidth("" + values[localC]); // width of max value
100             g2d.drawString("" + values[localC],
101                     xToMaxW - digitW - gapW - valueW, y); // the max value
102             if (localC < (intStr.length() - 1)) {
103                 g2d.drawString("+", xToMaxW - digitW, y); // "+" sign
104             }
105             localC += 1;
106             if (localC >= intStr.length()) {
107                 // draw a line
108                 g2d.drawLine(x, y + 2 * gapH, xToMaxW, y + 2 * gapH);
109                 // draw the total value under the line
110                 int totalV = 0;
111                 for (int k = 0; k < intStr.length(); k++) { // the total
112                     totalV += values[k];
113                 }
114                 int totalW = fm.stringWidth("" + totalV);
115                 g2d.drawString("" + totalV, xToMaxW - digitW - gapW - totalW,
116                         y + gapH + lineH);
117             }
118             if (count == intStr.length()) { // stop plotting
119                 this.setActive(false); // no update, has paint
120                 convDone.firePropertyChange("convDone", false, true);
121             }
122         }
123     }
124
125     private int realValue(String str) {
126         int value = 0;
127         switch (str.charAt(0)) {
128             case 'A':
129             case 'a':
130                 value = 10;
131                 break;
132             case 'B':
133             case 'b':
134                 value = 11;
135                 break;
136             case 'C':
137             case 'c':
138                 value = 12;
139                 break;
140             case 'D':
141             case 'd':
142                 value = 13;
143                 break;
144             case 'E':
145             case 'e':
```

```
146                 value = 14;
147                 break;
148             case 'F':
149             case 'f':
150                 value = 15;
151                 break;
152         }
153         if (str.charAt(0) < 'A') {
154             value = Integer.parseInt(str);
155         }
156         return value;
157     }
158
159     public void addPropertyChangeListener(PropertyChangeListener pcl) {
160         convDone.addPropertyChangeListener(pcl);
161     }
162
163     // for debugging
164     public void printValues(int idx) {
165         for (int i = 0; i <= idx; i++) {
166             System.out.print(values[i]);
167         }
168         System.out.println();
169     }
170 }
```

23.4 Converting an Integer in Decimal to Any Base: The Project DecimalToAny

An inverse computation for converting an inputted positive decimal integer to any base is implemented as the project DecimalToAny. Given an integer in decimal, say, 123, what is the binary notation of the integer? Its computation involves a sequence of divisions. That is, the integer 123 is divided by the base value 2 to get the remainder 0 or 1; and the quotients are continuously divided by the base 2 until the quotient is 0 or 1. Actually, the continuous divisions give the position weight and the remainders are the digits at the corresponding position. The upside down listing of all remainders is the resulting integer in base 2. The illustration of the computation is as shown in Fig. 23.3.

Apparently, the project DecimalToAny has a very similar UML class diagram as the project AnyToDecimal. Its implementation is also based on the three-layer structure for games. And it also needs two own classes ControlPanel.java and RenderSprite.java. Only one thing is slightly different in the implementation. That is the alternation of the two buttons "Do Conversion" and "Reset." In the previous project AnyToDecimal, both the two buttons are shown on the GUI. We used "Enabled" to alternate them such that one of them is enabled and the other is disabled. The project DecimalToAny used "Visible" to alternate the display of

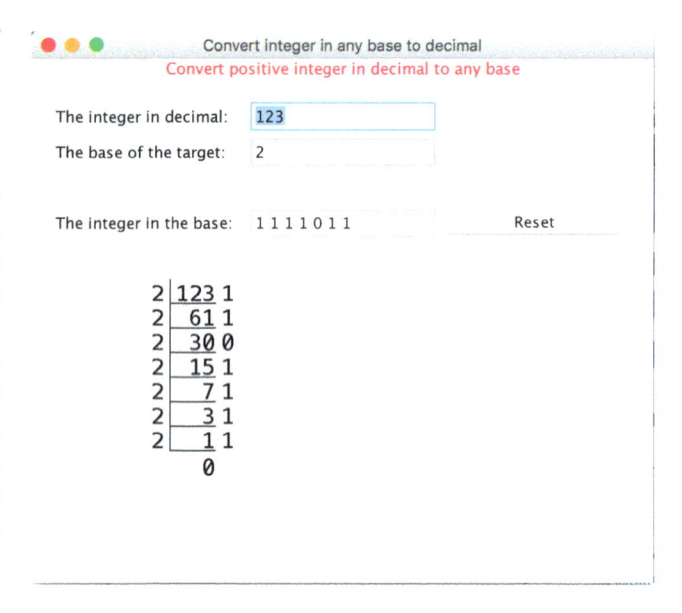

Fig. 23.3 The GUI of the project DecimalToAny that illustrates the computation that convert a given decimal integer to any base

these. When the game starts, only the button "Do Conversion" is shown. After the user enters the input data and clicks on the button "Do Conversion," the button is hidden. Once the rendering completes, the button "Reset" appears. At any time, only one of them is displayed. The functionality of two approaches is equivalent. It depends on the designer's preference. All of the source codes are included in the project

DecimalToAny. We leave it as an exercise for readers to read it and understand it.

23.5 Converting a Float in Decimal to Any Base: The Project DeciToAnyFloat

The two projects shown in previous sections handle the integer conversions. The DeciToAnyFloat project turns to handle float numbers. A float number consists of an integer part and a fractional part. Because the conversion principles are different for these two parts, the project needs to involve two separated pieces of codes that implement different algorithms. Consequently, the class RenderSprite.java has two parts. The computing and plotting of integer part is the same as those in the project DecimalToAny. But a new computing and rendering for the fractional part should be added. A complete output is shown in Fig. 23.4. The left computation is for the integer part of the float; the right side demonstrates the computation of the fractional part in the float number.

Given a float number 1234.56, its binary notation is 10011010010.100011 as shown in the text field of "The float in the base" on Fig. 23.4. The portion before the decimal point is the integer part, which corresponds to the decimal integer 1234 in the inputted float number. The part after the decimal point is the fraction, which comes from the fractional part, 0.56, of the decimal float number.

The conversion of the fractional part is still based on the position weight as follows.

```
0.56 = x1 * 2^(-1) + x2 * 2^(-2) + x3 * 2^(-3) + …
     = x1 * ½ + x2 * ¼ + x3 * 1/8 + …
// multiply 2 on both sides
1.12 = x1 + x2 * ½ + x3 * ¼ + …
```

The value of x1 is either 0 or 1 in binary. Since 1.12 > 0, x1 should be 1. Both sides minus 1 and then multiply 2 on both sides again, the equation becomes.

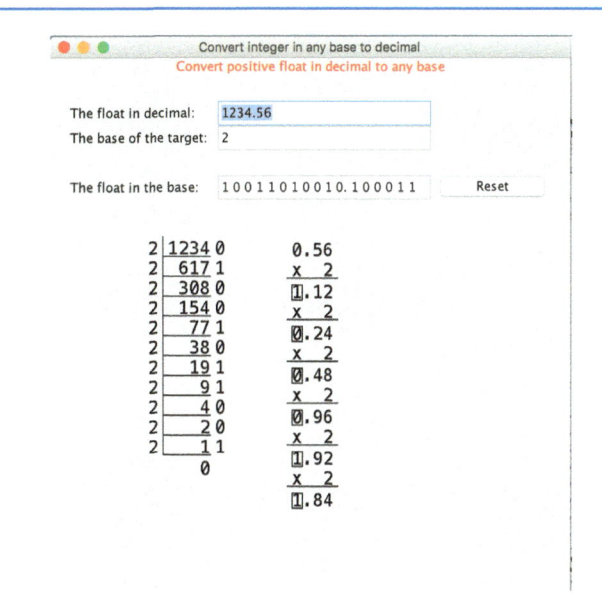

```
0.24 = x2 + x3 * ½ + …
```

Fig. 23.4 The GUI of the project DeciToAnyFloat

where x2 should be 0 because the result is 0.24. Therefore, all of the conversion is just as the rendering format shown on the GUI. The resulting values of x1, x2, and other digits are just as shown inside the small rectangles.

The implementation of the class ControlPanel.java of this project differs from that in the project DecimalToAny in two points. (1) We would like to have a larger width for every text field in this project because a float number consists of two parts that requires a wider text field. Unfortunately, the width of a text field is unable to be controlled in using the layout manager GridLayout. We have to change the layout to the GridBagLayout. Thus, we need to set up parameters of the GridBagConstraints for every component on the control panel. (2) The input float number consists of two parts: the integer part and the fractional part. The conversion of the integer part is the same as that in the project DecimalToAny; but the conversion of the fractional part involves a new algorithm as shown in the previous section. The related partial code that demonstrates the usage of the GridBagLayout and the routines for converting the fractional part are cited on Listing 23.3.

Listing 23.3 The partial code of the class ControlPanel.java that demonstrates the usage of the GridBagLayout and the conversion of the fractional part of a float number in the project DeciToAnyFloat

```
1  /*
2   * ControlPanel.java - A class that defines the control panel for the user
3   *                     to input data for the conversion.
4   */
5  package decimaltoany;
6
…
```

```java
25  public class ControlPanel extends JPanel {
26
...
37
38      public ControlPanel() {
39          initControlPanel();
40      }
41
42      private void initControlPanel() {
43          ...
53      }
54
55      private JPanel createInputPanel() {
56          JPanel inP = new JPanel();
57          inP.setLayout(new BorderLayout());
58
59          ...
69
70          // the data panel is on CENTER of the input panel
71          JPanel dataP = new JPanel();
72          dataP.setLayout(new GridBagLayout());
73          GridBagConstraints c = new GridBagConstraints();
74
75          JLabel floatLbl = new JLabel("The float in decimal: ");
76          floatLbl.setPreferredSize(new Dimension(150, 25));
77          c.gridx = 0;
78          c.gridy = 0;
79          dataP.add(floatLbl, c);
80          floatTxt = new JTextField();
81          floatTxt.setPreferredSize(new Dimension(230, 25));
82          c.gridx = 1;
83          c.gridy = 0;
84          dataP.add(floatTxt, c);
85          JLabel intGap = new JLabel("", 0);
86          intGap.setPreferredSize(new Dimension(120, 25));
87          c.gridx = 2;
88          c.gridy = 0;
89          dataP.add(intGap, c);
90
91          JLabel baseLbl = new JLabel("The base of the target: ");
92          baseLbl.setPreferredSize(new Dimension(150, 25));
93          c.gridx = 0;
94          c.gridy = 1;
95          dataP.add(baseLbl, c);
96          baseTxt = new JTextField();
97          baseTxt.setPreferredSize(new Dimension(230, 25));
98          c.gridx = 1;
99          c.gridy = 1;
100         dataP.add(baseTxt, c);
101         convBtn = new JButton("Do conversion");
102         convBtn.setPreferredSize(new Dimension(120, 25));
103         convBtn.addActionListener(new ConversionListener());
104         convBtn.setActionCommand(Consts.CONV + ""); // convert int to be String
105         c.gridx = 2;
106         c.gridy = 1;
```

23.5 Converting a Float in Decimal to Any Base: The Project DeciToAnyFloat

```
107            dataP.add(convBtn, c);
108
109            c.gridx = 0;
110            c.gridy = 2;
111            dataP.add(intGap, c);
112            c.gridx = 1;
113            c.gridy = 2;
114            dataP.add(intGap, c);
115            c.gridx = 2;
116            c.gridy = 2;
117            dataP.add(intGap, c);
118
119            JLabel targetLbl = new JLabel("The float in the base: ");
120            targetLbl.setPreferredSize(new Dimension(150, 25));
121            c.gridx = 0;
122            c.gridy = 3;
123            dataP.add(targetLbl, c);
124            targetTxt = new JTextField();
125            targetTxt.setPreferredSize(new Dimension(230, 25));
126            c.gridx = 1;
127            c.gridy = 3;
128            dataP.add(targetTxt, c);
129            resetBtn = new JButton("Reset");
130            resetBtn.setPreferredSize(new Dimension(120, 25));
131            resetBtn.setActionCommand(Consts.RESET + "");
132            resetBtn.addActionListener(new ResetListener());
133            c.gridx = 2;
134            c.gridy = 3;
135            dataP.add(resetBtn, c);
136            resetBtn.setVisible(false);
137
138            inP.add(dataP, BorderLayout.CENTER);
139
140            // the status panel is on SOUTH of the input panel
141            JPanel statusP = new JPanel();
142            statusP.setPreferredSize(new Dimension(Consts.CV_WIDTH, 25));
143            statusLbl = new JLabel("      ", 0);
144            statusP.add(statusLbl);
145            inP.add(statusP, BorderLayout.SOUTH);
146
147            return inP;
148        }
149
150        // inner class ConversionListener -- A listener that converts a positive
151        // integer in any base to an integer in decimal
152        class ConversionListener implements ActionListener {
153
154            int baseInt;
155
156            @Override
157            public void actionPerformed(ActionEvent evt) {
158                if (!(evt.getActionCommand().equals(Consts.CONV + ""))) {
159                    return;
160                }
```

```java
                statusLbl.setForeground(Color.red);
                String inputFloatStr = floatTxt.getText();
                String baseStr = baseTxt.getText();
                if ((inputFloatStr.equals("") || (baseStr.equals("")))) {
                    statusLbl.setText("No input integer or base");
                    return;
                }

                // verify input data for possible errors
                int correctValue = verifyInput(inputFloatStr, baseStr);
                switch (correctValue) {
                    case 0: // no error, start working
                        statusLbl.setText("");
                        Float inputFloat = Float.parseFloat(inputFloatStr);
                        baseInt = Integer.parseInt(baseStr);
                        String sOut = deciFloatToAnyBase(inputFloat, baseInt);
                        targetTxt.setText(sOut);

                        // start ploting
                        int dIntPart = getIntPart(inputFloat);
                        float dFracPart = getFracPart(inputFloat);
                        renderSprite.setInitData(dIntPart, dFracPart, baseInt);
                        renderSprite.setActive(true);
                        renderSprite.setVisible(true);
                        break;
                    case 1:
                        …
                    default:
                }
        }

        private int verifyInput(String floatS, String baseS) {
            int correctVal = 0;
            int theBase = Integer.parseInt(baseS);
            if ((theBase < 2) || (theBase > 16)) {
                correctVal = 1;
                return correctVal;
            }
            for (int i = 0; i < floatS.length(); i++) {
                String theS = floatS.substring(i, i + 1);
                if (!(theS.equals("."))) {
                    int theV = realValue(theS);
                    if (theV > 9) {
                        correctVal = 2;
                        break;
                    }
                }
            }
            return correctVal;
        }

        // getIntPart() -- To get the integer part of a float number
        public int getIntPart(float dValue) {
            Float theF = dValue;
            String theFS = theF.toString();
```

23.5 Converting a Float in Decimal to Any Base: The Project DeciToAnyFloat

```
229                int dPoint = theFS.indexOf(".");
230                String intPart = null;
231                if (dPoint != -1) {
232                    intPart = theFS.substring(0, dPoint);
233                }
234                int dIntPart = Integer.parseInt(intPart);
235                return dIntPart;
236            }
237
238            // getFracPart() -- To get the fractional part of a double number.
239            public float getFracPart(float dValue) {
240                Float theF = dValue;
241                String theFS = theF.toString();
242                int dPoint = theFS.indexOf(".");
243                String fracPart = null;
244                if (dPoint != -1) {
245                    fracPart = theFS.substring(dPoint + 1, theFS.length());
246                }
247                int powerN = 0;
248                if (fracPart != null) {
249                    powerN = fracPart.length();
250                }
251                int dFracPart = Integer.parseInt(fracPart);
252                float dFracPartF = (float) (dFracPart * Math.pow(10, -powerN));
253                return dFracPartF;
254            }
255
256            // deciFloatToAnyBase() -- To convert an double in decimal to any base
257            // number system. If base = 2, the method gives binary notation.
258            public String deciFloatToAnyBase(float dValue, int base) {
259                String theResult = null;
260                int dIntPart = getIntPart(dValue);
261                float dFracPart = getFracPart(dValue);
262
263                ArrayList<Integer> intPartV;
264                ArrayList<Integer> fracPartV;
265                if ((dIntPart == 0) && (dFracPart != 0)) {
266                    fracPartV = convertDFrac(dFracPart, base);
267                    theResult = arraylistToString("", fracPartV, 1);
268                } else if ((dIntPart != 0) && (dFracPart == 0)) {
269                    intPartV = convertDInt(dIntPart, base);
270                    theResult = arraylistToString("", intPartV, 0);
271                } else if ((dIntPart != 0) && (dFracPart != 0)) {
272                    String intString;
273                    intPartV = convertDInt(dIntPart, base);
274                    intString = arraylistToString("", intPartV, 0);
275
276                    fracPartV = convertDFrac(dFracPart, base);
277                    theResult = arraylistToString(intString, fracPartV, 1);
278                }
279                return theResult;
280            }
281
282            // convertDFrac() -- To convert a fraction number to any base. The
283            // result stored in the arrayList is in the right order.
```

```java
284        public ArrayList<Integer> convertDFrac(float dFrac, int base) {
285            ArrayList<Integer> bFracPart = new ArrayList<Integer>();
286            float theV = dFrac;
287            while ((theV > 0.0) && (bFracPart.size() < Consts.FRAC_LENGTH)) {
288                theV = theV * base;
289                bFracPart.add(getIntPart(theV));
290                theV = getFracPart(theV);
291            }
292            return bFracPart;
293        }
294
295        // arrayListToString() -- To convert a arrayList to a string.
296        public String arraylistToString(String inS, ArrayList<Integer> aV,
297                int pointStatus) {
298            String theS = inS;
299            switch (pointStatus) {
300                case 0:   // no fractional part
301                    for (int i = aV.size() - 1; i >= 0; i--) {
302                        theS += switchChar(((aV.get(i)))) + " ";
303                    }
304                    break;
305                case 1:   // either only fractional part OR (intPart + fracPart)
306                    if (inS.equals("")) {
307                        theS = theS + "0 ";
308                    }
309                    theS = theS + ". ";
310                    for (int i = 0; i < aV.size(); i++) {
311                        theS += switchChar(((aV.get(i)))) + " ";
312                    }
313                    break;
314            }
315            return theS.trim();
316        }
317
318        // switchChar() -- To switch characters
319        public char switchChar(int value) {
320            char ch;
321
322            switch (value) {
323                case 10:
324                    ch = 'A';
325                    break;
326                case 11:
327                    ...
341                default:
342                    ch = (char) (value + 48);
343                    break;
344            }
345            return ch;
346        }
347
...
487 }
```

23.5 Converting a Float in Decimal to Any Base: The Project DeciToAnyFloat

The method createInputPanel() initializes a JPanel dataP that contains three text fields and two buttons (lines 70–138). The layout manager GridBagLayout requires an object of c from the built-in class GridBagConstraints (line 73). Suppose we would like to place a text field floatTxt at the first row and the second column (lines 80–84), we need to set c.gridx = 1 and c.gridy = 0. The value of c.gridx = 1 means the index of 1 along the x-axis direction, i.e., the second column; the value of c.gridy = 0 means the index of 0 along the y-axis direction, i.e., the first row. By using these two parameters we can place every component on an appropriate position. Under the layout GridBagLayout, we can invoke setPreferredSize() for a component to set up an appropriate size.

The method convertDFrac() (lines 282–293) is the main routine for converting the fractional part of the decimal float number. It has a "while" loop to continuously multiply the base value 2 with the decimal fraction value. The arrayList bFracPart accumulates the integer part of each product as the fractional part of the float number in the target base of 2.

Obviously, the class RenderSprite.java should be able to plot two computations. One is for the conversion of the integer part of the float number; the other is for the conversion of the fractional part. The code looks lengthy and tedious. However, the programming principle is the same. That is, according to the output format to determine the coordinates (x, y) of every character and draw them one by one. The complete code of the class RenderSprite.java is shown in Listing 23.4.

Listing 23.4 The class RenderSprite.java of the project DeciToAnyFloat

```
 1  /*
 2   * RenderSprite.java - A class that renders calculations dynamically.
 3   * it functions like a sprite so that name it as RenderSprite.
 4   */
 5  package decimaltoany;
 6
 7  import java.awt.Font;
 8  import java.awt.FontMetrics;
 9  import java.awt.Graphics2D;
10  import java.beans.PropertyChangeListener;
11  import java.beans.PropertyChangeSupport;
12
17  public class RenderSprite extends AbsSprite {
18
19      private int inInt, inBase, remainder, countInt, countFloat;
20      private final int lineH = 20, gapH = 2, gapW = 5;
21      private final int topMargin = 180, leftMargin = 100, middleGap = 150;
22      private int x, y, xFloat;
23      private boolean intDone = false, fracDone = false;
24      private final int ARYLEN = 15;
25      private int[] quotients = new int[ARYLEN];
26      private int[] remainders = new int[ARYLEN];
27      private float[] wholeFloat = new float[ARYLEN];
28      private float[] fractions = new float[ARYLEN];
29      private Font theF;
30      private PropertyChangeSupport convDone;
31
32      @SuppressWarnings("OverridableMethodCallInConstructor")
33      public RenderSprite() {
34          initSprite();
35      }
36
37      @Override
38      public void initSprite() {
39          x = leftMargin;
40          y = topMargin;
```

```java
41          xFloat = x + middleGap;
42          countInt = 0;
43          countFloat = 0;
44          theF = new Font("Monospaced", Font.PLAIN, 18);
45          convDone = new PropertyChangeSupport(this);
46      }
47
48      public void setInitData(int inInt, float inFrac, int inBase) {
49          this.inInt = inInt;
50          this.inBase = inBase;
51          quotients[0] = inInt;
52          wholeFloat[0] = inFrac;
53          fractions[0] = inFrac;
54      }
55
56      @Override
57      public void paintSprite(Graphics2D g2d) {
58          if (!(this.isVisible())) {
59              return;
60          }
61
62          g2d.setFont(theF);
63
64          FontMetrics fm = g2d.getFontMetrics();
65          int digitW = fm.stringWidth("0");
66          int baseW = fm.stringWidth("" + inBase);
67          int initW = fm.stringWidth("" + quotients[0]);
68          int remW = fm.stringWidth("" + remainders[0]);
69          int x2 = x + baseW + 2 * gapW + initW + gapW + remW;
70          int wholeFloatW = fm.stringWidth("" + wholeFloat[0]);
71          int wholeFloatLen = ("" + wholeFloat[0]).length();
72          int x3 = xFloat + wholeFloatW;
73
74          y = topMargin;
75          int localIntC = 0;
76          int quoLen = 0;
77          // depends on the value of count to paint every digit calculation
78          // count = 1, paint the left most digit calclation expression
79          // count = 2, paint the left first and second digits expresions ...
80          while (localIntC < countInt) {
81              y += lineH;
82              if (quotients[localIntC] > 0) {
83                  g2d.drawString("" + remainders[localIntC], x2 - remW, y - gapH);
84              }
85              quoLen = fm.stringWidth("" + quotients[localIntC]);
86              g2d.drawString("" + quotients[localIntC], x2 - remW - gapW - quoLen,
87                      y - gapH);
88              g2d.drawLine(x2 - remW - gapW, y, x2 - remW - gapW - initW - gapW, y);
89              g2d.drawLine(x2 - remW - gapW - initW - gapW, y,
90                      x2 - remW - gapW - initW - gapW, y - lineH);
91              g2d.drawString("" + inBase, x, y - gapH);
92
93              localIntC += 1;
94          }
95          if (intDone == true) {
```

23.5 Converting a Float in Decimal to Any Base: The Project DeciToAnyFloat

```
 96                 g2d.drawString("0", x2 - remW - gapW - quoLen, y + lineH);
 97             }
 98
 99         String sVal = "0";
100         if ((intDone == true) && wholeFloat[0] > 0.0) {
101             y = topMargin;
102             int localFloatC = 0;
103             while (localFloatC < countFloat) {
104                 renderValue(g2d, sVal, localFloatC, wholeFloatLen, digitW);
105                 if (localFloatC < 8) {
106                     renderMultiSign(g2d, x3, baseW);
107                 }
108                 localFloatC++;
109             }
110             if (fracDone == true) {
111                 // paint last expression
112                 renderValue(g2d, sVal, localFloatC, wholeFloatLen, digitW);
113
114                 this.setActive(false);
115                 convDone.firePropertyChange("convDone", false, true);
116             }
117         }
118     }
119
120     public void renderValue(Graphics2D g2d, String sVal, int localFloatC,
121             int wholeFloatLen, int digitW) {
122         y += lineH;
123         // if missing a "0", append a "0" to the string
124         // e.g., 1.7 needs to be 1.70
125         sVal = "" + wholeFloat[localFloatC];
126         if (sVal.length() < wholeFloatLen) {
127             sVal = sVal + "0";
128         }
129         if (Float.parseFloat(sVal) > 10.0) {
130             g2d.drawString(sVal.substring(0, wholeFloatLen + 1),
131                     xFloat - digitW, y);
132         } else {
133             g2d.drawString(sVal.substring(0, wholeFloatLen),
134                     xFloat, y);
135         }
136         // draw a rectangle for indicating the digit in the result
137         if (localFloatC >= 1) {
138             if (Float.parseFloat(sVal) < 10.0) {
139                 g2d.drawRect(xFloat, y - digitW - gapH, digitW,
140                         digitW + 2 * gapH);
141             } else {
142                 g2d.drawRect(xFloat - digitW, y - digitW - gapH,
143                         2 * digitW, digitW + 2 * gapH);
144             }
145         }
146     }
147
148     public void renderMultiSign(Graphics2D g2d, int x3, int baseW) {
149         y += lineH;
150         g2d.drawString("x", xFloat, y);
```

```java
151            g2d.drawString("" + inBase, x3 - baseW, y);
152            y += gapH;
153            g2d.drawLine(xFloat - gapW, y, x3 + gapW, y);
154        }
155
156        @Override
157        public void updateSprite() {
158            if (!(this.isActive())) {
159                return;
160            }
161            if (intDone == false) {
162                updateInt();
163            } else {
164                updateFrac();
165            }
166        }
167
168        private void updateInt() {
169            countInt += 1;
170            if (inInt > 0) {
171                remainder = inInt % inBase;
172                inInt = inInt / inBase;
173                if (inInt <= 0) {
174                    intDone = true;
175                }
176                quotients[countInt] = inInt;
177                remainders[countInt - 1] = remainder;
178            }
179        }
180
181        public void updateFrac() {
182            countFloat += 1;
183            float theV = fractions[countFloat - 1];
184            if ((theV > 0.0) && (countFloat <= Consts.FRAC_LENGTH)) {
185                theV = theV * inBase;
186                wholeFloat[countFloat] = theV;
187                theV = getFracPart(theV);
188                fractions[countFloat] = theV;
189            } else {
190                countFloat--; // to stop the plot ahead
191                fracDone = true;
192            }
193        }
194
195        public float getFracPart(float dValue) {
196            Float theFloat = dValue;
197            String theFS = theFloat.toString();
198            int dPoint = theFS.indexOf(".");
199            String fracPart = null;
200            if (dPoint != -1) {
201                fracPart = theFS.substring(dPoint + 1, theFS.length());
202            }
203
204            int powerN = 0;
205            if (fracPart != null) {
```

```
206                powerN = fracPart.length();
207            }
208            int dFracPart = Integer.parseInt(fracPart);
209            float dFracPartF = (float) (dFracPart * Math.pow(10, -powerN));
210
211            return dFracPartF;
212        }
213
214        public void addPropertyChangeListener(PropertyChangeListener pcl) {
215            convDone.addPropertyChangeListener(pcl);
216        }
217    }
```

23.6 Summary

For helping in the learning of binary computations, teaching tools are developed based on the three-layer structure for games. The teaching tools visualize the computations through dynamic rendering of the entire computational process step by step just like a teacher demonstrates the computation on a blackboard.

Every project has a control panel and a rendering sprite. The control panel receives the user's inputs including data and button click actions. The action listeners perform required computations according to the given data. The rendering functions are performed through a class RenderSprite.java. The class is a sprite and its updateSprite() and paintSprite() methods are controlled by the game loop for updating and painting the computational process step by step for a clear illustration. Since the project can be repeatedly executed and can accept any valid inputs, it is a feasible tool for helping learners.

This chapter only discussed three tools: "Converting a positive integer in any base to decimal," "Converting a positive integer in decimal to any base," and "Converting a positive float number in decimal to any base." Other three tools will be introduced on the next chapter.

23.7 Exercises

Self-Reviewing Questions

1. What role is played by the three-layer structure for games in the development of the teaching tools?
2. Draw a UML class diagram of the project DeciToAnyFloat and compare it with that of the project AnyToDecimal. Does any difference exist?
3. Write a pseudo code for describing the major functions performed by the event handler of the button "Do Conversion" in the project DeciToAnyFloat.
4. Write a pseudo code for describing the major functions performed by the event handler of the button "Reset" in the project DeciToAnyFloat.
5. The project DeciToAnyFloat has classes ControlPanel.java and RenderSprite.java. What are the communication paths for linking these two classes?
6. How does the class ControlPanel.java separate the integer part from the fractional part after it receives the inputted float number?
7. Why do we name the class RenderSprite.java as a sprite?
8. What is the principle adopted for coding the class RenderSprite.java?
9. How to convert the fractional part of a float number in decimal to be the fractional part of a float number in binary?
10. How does the class RenderSprite.java in the project DeciToAnyFloat render the computations for converting the fractional part?

Projects

1. In a comparison, the project DecimalToAny is simpler than other two projects. But, it could be a base for other projects. That is, it could provide a blueprint and some components for the development of other projects. Therefore, thoroughly understand it would be helpful for understanding other projects. Please analyze the project DecimalToAny and develop it with the following three steps to build up some components for other two projects.

   The first step is to develop a simple project DToAny1, which adopts the three-layer structure for games to create a GUI. And then, the project DToAny1 adds a class ControlPanel.java for making a simple control panel that has: (a) two JTextFields for inputting a positive decimal integer and a base 2, 8, or 16; (b) a button "Get inputs"; and (c) a status label. When the "Get inputs" button is clicked, its action listener accepts the two inputted values (one is a positive decimal integer; the other is a base of 2, 8, or 16) and passes them into a class VerifyBean.java to verify their correctness, respectively. The verifications include: (a) the inputted integer or the base cannot be empty; (b) all of digits in the decimal integer are in [0, F]; (c) the target base is in [2, 16]. Then, echo the returned verification result on the status label.

The second step is to copy the project DToAny1 to be DToAny2. On the control panel, the new project adds a third JTextField with a label of "Result" for displaying the resulting integer in the target base. When the input data are correct, the button "Get Inputs" will be disabled and the button "Do Conversion" will be enabled. When the button "Do Conversion" is clicked, the event handler of the ConversionListener instantiates a new object of a new class ConversionBean.java to convert the inputted integer in decimal to an integer in the target base. When the conversion finishes, the result will be shown on the new added third text field "Result".

The third step is to copy the project DToAny2 to be DToAny3, which adds a new button "Reset" on the control panel and adds a new class RenderSprite.java to render the computational process step-by-step on the GUI dynamically. The rendering is under the control of the game loop defined in the abstract class AbsGameCanvas.java. When the rendering completes, the button "Do Conversion" is hidden and the button "Reset" is appeared. When the user clicks the button "Reset", the entire project will be re-initialized for allowing the user to play a new conversion.

Every project has a class GameCanvas.java that extends the AbsGameCanvas.java class for instantiating all of objects and functions as a communication center for all of necessary communications. Draw a UML class diagram for each step to demonstrate the growing of the projects. And then, follow the steps to implement the three versions of project.

2. Develop a teaching tool that accepts inputted binary float number and converts it to decimal float number.
3. Develop a teaching tool for primary school students in learning mathematical addition, subtraction, multiplication, and division.
4. Develop a tool that reads certain number of questions from a file and arranges them as a quiz sheet with multiple-choice format. When a student finishes answering, the final score will be shown immediately.

Animating Binary Arithmetic Computations

24

Integers have positive or negative. We use "+" or "−" sign for distinguishing them. In order to represent positive or negative integers inside computers, the binary number notation evolved from signed-magnitude notation to one's complement notation and finally to two's complement notation. Such an evolvement lies on the disadvantages of one notation and the advantages of the other. Projects that visualize three notations and corresponding arithmetic summation processes are developed as "serious game" based on the three-layer structure for games.

The objectives of this chapter include:
1. Summation of binary integers in signed-magnitude.
2. Summation of binary integers in one's complement.
3. Summation of binary integers in two's complement.

The previous chapter discussed the development of "serious game" as tools for learning decimal-binary conversions. This chapter continues the effort in developing three more tools for visualizing summation computations with positive and negative binary integers. They are "Summation of binary integers in signed-magnitude," "Summation of binary integers in one's complement," and "Summation of binary integers in two's complement."

A binary integer could be positive or negative. For indicating the positive or negative, a binary integer could be expressed in three different notations: signed-magnitude, 1's complement, or 2's complement. The signed-magnitude notation is intuitive for human reading. But, its drawbacks promoted the 1's complement notation. And further, the 1's complement was improved as 2's complement notation. The three projects discussed in this chapter are not only rendering the summation computations in three different notations but also revealing the pros and cons of the three different notations.

24.1 Summation of Binary Integers in Signed-Magnitude: The Project SumSigned

An integer could be positive or negative, we use a sign of "+" (usually is omitted) or "−" in front of the integer for distinguishing them. Correspondingly, a binary integer requires a specific bit as a sign bit. In other words, if a computer allocates 8 bits for storing binary integers, the leftmost bit (the most significant bit) has to be used as the sign bit: a "1" represents a negative and a "0" represents a positive integer. Only the remaining 7 bits are for the value of the integer. Thus, the 8 bits can store an integer [11111111, 01111111] ([−127, +127], in decimal). This is the so-called signed-magnitude notation. The project SumSigned is just under this assumption. That is, we assume that the computer only allocates 8 bits for a binary integer, which sets up a limitation on the values of the inputted integers with the largest absolute value of 127 in decimal.

The project SumSigned is designed for doing the summation of two binary integers in signed-magnitude notation. It involves two steps. Firstly, it receives two inputted integers in decimal and converts them to be signed-magnitude binary integers with rendering of the conversion process as shown in Fig. 24.1 (Left), where it presents two conversions for the two inputted decimal integers 112 and −45. Secondly, it performs the summation on the two binary integers in signed-magnitude notation and renders the summation process dynamically as shown in Fig. 24.1 (Right), where it presents the binary integer 01110000 (+112 in decimal) − 10101101 (−45 in decimal).

Correspondingly, the GUI shows three buttons. The button "Do Conversion" performs the first step, and the button "Do Summation" performs the second step. The button

© Springer Nature Switzerland AG 2018
C.-w. Xu, *Learning Java with Games*, https://doi.org/10.1007/978-3-319-72886-5_24

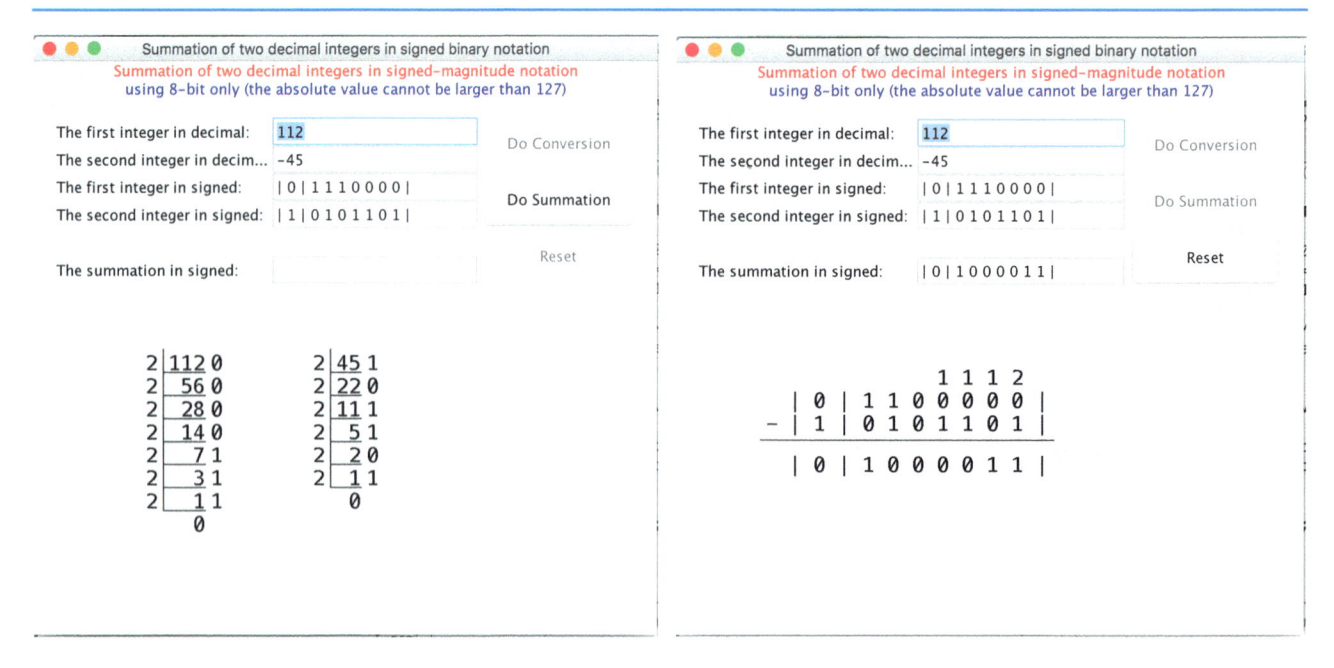

Fig. 24.1 (*Left*) The GUI illustrates the conversion operation of the project SumSigned. (*Right*) The GUI renders the summation computation of the project SumSigned

Fig. 24.2 The UML class diagram of the project SumSigned

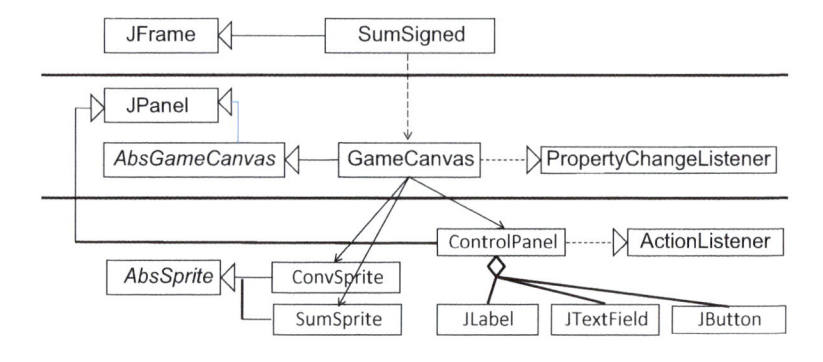

"Reset" just resets all of variables for next usage. Because the conversion from a decimal integer to a binary integer has been completely implemented in the DecimalToAny project on the previous chapter, the new project SumSigned mainly developed the "Do Summation" portion.

Obviously, both the conversion process and the summation process require two major classes respectively. One of them is for the static computation and the other is for the dynamic rendering. For the conversion process, the inner class ConversionListener inside the ControlPanel.java performs the static computation and the class ConvSprite.java is for the dynamic rendering. For the summation process, the SummationListener inner class inside the ControlPanel.java handles the static computation and the class SumSprite.java is for the dynamic rendering. The two sprite classes are under the control of the game loop supplied by the three-layer structure for games. The UML class diagram of the project SumSigned, thus, can be constructed as in Fig. 24.2.

24.1.1 The Inner Class SummationListener Performs Summation Computation

Consequently, the new additions of the project SumSigned are the event handler for the summation computation and the class SumSprite.java for rendering the summation. When the conversions are done, two binary integers in signed-magnitude are displayed on two text fields. As long as the button "Do Summation" is clicked, the corresponding event handler will perform the following functions for summation. The event handler is implemented as the inner class SummationListener in the class ControlPanel.java as shown in Listing 24.1. The pseudo code of the SummationListener could be as follows.

1. Getting the two binary integers in signed-magnitude from the two text fields (lines 396–400).
2. Checking the sign bit of the two binary integers.
3. If the two sign bits are the same (lines 403–410):
   (a) Setting the variable command as ADDB (add-binary) (line 404)

(b) Performing addition and checking overflow (lines 455–485)
4. Else if the two sign bits are different (lines 410–425):
   (a) Setting the variable command as SUBB (sub-binary) (line 411)
   (b) Selecting the larger value minus the smaller value (lines 487–512)
5. Start the execution of SumSprite.java for rendering the summation process (lines 429–438).

Listing 24.1 The inner class SummationListener defined in the class ControlPanel.java of the project SumSigned

```
 1 /*
 2  * ControlPanel.java - A class that defines the control panel for the user
 3  * to input data for the conversion.
 4  */
 5 package sumSigned;
 6
...
23 public class ControlPanel extends JPanel {
24
...
378
379     // SummationListener -- A class that implements the ActionListener.
380     // It performs summation of two signed integers.
381     class SummationListener implements ActionListener {
382
383         final int ARYLEN = 8;
384         int[] binaryIntOne = new int[ARYLEN];
385         int[] binaryIntTwo = new int[ARYLEN];
386         boolean overflowFlag = false;
387
388         @Override
389         public void actionPerformed(ActionEvent evt) {
390             if (!(evt.getSource() == sumBtn)) {
391                 return;
392             }
393             if (overflowFlag == true) {
394                 overflowFlag = false;
395             }
396             String sSignedOne = signedOneTxt.getText();
397             String sSignedTwo = signedTwoTxt.getText();
398             int[] sumResult;
399
400             loadIntToAry(sSignedOne, sSignedTwo);
401             // if both integers have the same sign: do addition
402             // otherwise do subtraction
403             if (binaryIntOne[0] == binaryIntTwo[0]) {
404                 sumSprite.setCommand(Consts.ADDB);
405                 sumResult = addBinary(binaryIntOne, binaryIntTwo);
406                 if (overflowFlag == true) {
407                     statusLbl.setText("Overflow has occurred");
408                     overflowFlag = false;
409                 }
410             } else {
411                 sumSprite.setCommand(Consts.SUBB);
412                 String sOne = "";
413                 String sTwo = "";
414                 // get rid of the"|" character and sign bit
415                 for (int i = 1; i < binaryIntOne.length; i++) {
416                     sOne += binaryIntOne[i];
```

```
417                    sTwo += binaryIntTwo[i];
418                }
419                // determine which one is bigger that minus the smaller one
420                if (Integer.parseInt(sOne) > Integer.parseInt(sTwo)) {
421                    sumResult = subBinary(binaryIntOne, binaryIntTwo);
422                } else {
423                    sumResult = subBinary(binaryIntTwo, binaryIntOne);
424                }
425            }
426            String sSum = sumToStr(sumResult);
427            sumTxt.setText(sSum);
428
429            // start render the operations
430            if (overflowFlag == false) {
431                convSprite.setVisible(false);
432                sumSprite.initSummationData(sSignedOne, sSignedTwo,
433                        binaryIntOne, binaryIntTwo);
434                sumSprite.setActive(true);
435                sumSprite.setVisible(true);
436            } else {
437                System.out.println("Overflow");
438            }
439        }
440
441        private void loadIntToAry(String sSignedOne, String sSignedTwo) {
442            int j = 0;
443            for (int i = 0; i < sSignedOne.length(); i++) {
444                String oneS = sSignedOne.substring(i, i + 1);
445                String twoS = sSignedTwo.substring(i, i + 1);
446
447                if (((!(oneS.equals("|"))) && (!(oneS.equals(" "))))) {
448                    binaryIntOne[j] = Integer.parseInt(oneS);
449                    binaryIntTwo[j] = Integer.parseInt(twoS);
450                    j++;
451                }
452            }
453        }
454
455        private int[] addBinary(int[] binaryIntOne, int[] binaryIntTwo) {
456            int[] tempSum = new int[ARYLEN];
457            int[] carryBit = new int[ARYLEN];
458            int sumBit;
459            for (int i = binaryIntOne.length - 1; i > 0; i--) {
460                sumBit = binaryIntOne[i] + binaryIntTwo[i] + carryBit[i];
461                switch (sumBit) {
462                    case 0:
463                        tempSum[i] = 0;
464                        carryBit[i - 1] = 0;
465                        break;
466                    case 1:
467                        tempSum[i] = 1;
468                        carryBit[i - 1] = 0;
469                        break;
470                    case 2:
471                        tempSum[i] = 0;
472                        carryBit[i - 1] = 1;
473                        break;
474                    case 3:
```

24.1 Summation of Binary Integers in Signed-Magnitude: The Project SumSigned

```
475                    tempSum[i] = 1;
476                    carryBit[i - 1] = 1;
477                    break;
478                }
479            }
480            tempSum[0] = binaryIntOne[0];
481            if (carryBit[0] == 1) {
482                overflowFlag = true;
483            }
484            return tempSum;
485        }
486
487        private int[] subBinary(int[] bOne, int[] bTwo) {
488            // the values of bigger might be changed
489            // here, make a copy to prevent bOne from being changed
490            int[] bigger = new int[ARYLEN];
491            int[] smaller = new int[ARYLEN];
492            for (int i = 0; i < ARYLEN; i++) {
493                bigger[i] = bOne[i];
494                smaller[i] = bTwo[i];
495            }
496            //displayAry(bigger);
497            int[] tempDiff = new int[ARYLEN];
498            int[] borrowBit = new int[ARYLEN];
499            int diffBit;
500            for (int i = bigger.length - 1; i > 0; i--) {
501                if (bigger[i] >= smaller[i]) {
502                    diffBit = bigger[i] - smaller[i];
503                } else {
504                    borrowBit[i] = 2;
505                    bigger[i - 1] -= 1;
506                    diffBit = borrowBit[i] + bigger[i] - smaller[i];
507                }
508                tempDiff[i] = diffBit;
509            }
510            tempDiff[0] = bigger[0];
511            return tempDiff;
512        }
513
514        private String sumToStr(int[] sumAry) {
515            String sumStr = "| " + sumAry[0] + " | ";
516            for (int i = 1; i < sumAry.length; i++) {
517                sumStr += sumAry[i] + " ";
518            }
519            sumStr += "|";
520            return sumStr;
521        }
522
523        private void displayAry(int[] ary) {
524            for (int i = 0; i < ary.length; i++) {
525                System.out.print(ary[i]);
526            }
527            System.out.println();
528        }
529    }
530
...
572 }
```

24.1.2 The Class SumSprite.java Renders the Summation Process

The class SumSprite.java prepared a method initSummationData() for accepting the two binary integers from the inner class SummationListener. It has four parameters. Two of them are strings that correspond to the two binary integers with the "|" and spaces. The format of strings is for the plotting purpose. The other two are int arrays that hold the binary values of the two binary integers. The format of int arrays is for the computation bit-by-bit. In addition, the class SumSprite.java also has a variable command that is used for accepting the ADDB or SUBB command passed from the class SummationListener.

When the event handler SummationListener finishes the computation and displays the summation result on the dedicated text field, it invokes sumSprite.initSummationData() to pass the two binary integers to the class SumSprite.java (SummationListener, lines 429–438). In addition, the event listener also invokes sumSprite.setCommand() method for passing the ADDB (SummationListener, line 404) or SUBB (SummationListener, line 411) to the command defined in the class SumSprite.java. Following the different command, the SumSprite.java class executes different plotting routine for rendering the different summation process.

As usual, the sprite class SumSprite.java mainly implements the methods updateSprite() and paintSprite(). Because the summation could be ADDB or SUBB, the updateSprite() method has to check the variable "command" for making a decision to invoke the method updateAddBinary() or updateSubBinary(). As usual, both updateSprite() and paintSprite() will be invoked one time per game loop. Correspondingly, one invocation paints 1 bit data on the GUI. However, every invocation of paintSprite() should repeatedly paint all of bits that have been painted so far such that all of bits have been painted won't be lost.

Based on this painting principle, we need to use counter for controlling the painting routine. As mentioned, all of the signed binary integers have 8 bits; the rightmost bit has an index of 7. According to the regular addition approach, the addition starts from the rightmost bit and moves to the leftmost bit. The method updateAddBinary() increases the variable "count" by 1 in every invocation and uses the ARYLEN – count = 8 – 1 = 7 as the index to add the eighth bit of the two signed binary integers, and then stores the resulting value in the array tempSum[7] and the carry value in carryBit[6]. As long as the paintSprite() method is invoked, the stored values in tempSum[7] and carryBit[6] are painted on the proper position. When the updateAddBinary() method is invoked second time, the "count" is increased by 1 again, the summation is moved to the index 6, and the results are stored in tempSum[6] and carryBit[5]. The painting will paint both bits in the index 7 and in the index 6 as depicted in Fig. 24.3.

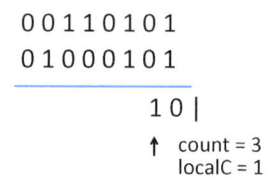

```
  0 0 1 1 0 1 0 1
  0 1 0 0 0 1 0 1
  ─────────────────
              1 0 |
              ↑   count = 3
                  localC = 1
```

Fig. 24.3 The procedure for rendering the summation process

Figure 24.3 indicates that when the method updateSprite() is activated, it invokes the method updateAddBinary() to make the variable "count" as 1. Then, the paintSprite() method is invoked. It initializes a local variable localC as 1, and the painting is started for painting the "|" at the rightmost position. After that, a while loop "while(localC < count)" is reached. At this moment, (localC == count), the condition of the while loop is false, the while loop is terminated, and the method paintSprite() is done. The game loop invokes the updateSprite() for the second time, and the count is updated as 2. When the method paintSprite() is invoked again, it re-initializes localC as 1 and paints the letter '|' again. Immediately, the method reaches the while loop. The condition (localC < count) is true; the code inside the while loop paints the bit tempSum[7] and then increases the localC by 1 that causes the condition (localC < count) becoming false; the while loop is terminated. At the third time, the "count" is updated as 3 and the localC is reset as 1. The method paintSprite() paints the "|," and the while loop paints both the bit tempSum[7] and tempSum[6]. The same procedure is repeatedly executed by the game loop. That is, the game loop paints one more bit than the previous step. In addition, inside one step all of already painted digits are repainted on the GUI repeatedly, which gives an illusion of animation.

After all of 8 bits are painted, the overflow is checked. The rule for checking overflow said that if the two sign bits are the same but the carry bit at the index 1 is set, overflow occurs.

Once the two sign bits are different, the method updateSubBinary() should be invoked to perform a subtraction. The method updateSubBinary() differs from the method updateAddBinary() mainly in three points. (1) Overflow checking is not necessary for subtraction computations. (2) Performing subtraction, the larger value should appear on the top and the smaller value should be on the bottom. Thus, before rendering, the two binary integers should be compared to determine which one minus the other (lines 117–141). (3) A special array borrowBit[] should replace the array carryBit[] used in the addition case. Sometimes, the operations of the array borrowBit[] are more complicated than the carryBit[] when several borrows involved. A special piece of code is dedicated for that case (lines 150–164). The sign bit of the subtraction result is the same as the larger binary integer. Fortunately, the rendering procedure of the subtraction is similar with the addition computations. The implementation of the class SumSprite.java is listed in Listing 24.2.

24.1 Summation of Binary Integers in Signed-Magnitude: The Project SumSigned

Listing 24.2 The class SumSprite.java in the project SumSigned

```java
/*
 * SumSprite.java - A class that performs the summation on two binary
 * integers in signed. It has to look at the sign bit for determining
 * add them or sub them. Then, it renders the summation process
 * dynamically. It looks like a sprite in a game so name it as SumSprite.
 */
package sumSigned;

import java.awt.Font;
import java.awt.FontMetrics;
import java.awt.Graphics2D;
import java.beans.PropertyChangeListener;
import java.beans.PropertyChangeSupport;

/**
 *
 * @author cxu
 */
public class SumSprite extends AbsSprite {

    private int command;
    private final int ADDB = 1, SUBB = 2;
    private int x, y;
    private int topMargin = 280, leftMargin = 100;
    private final int lineH = 20, gapH = 2, gapW = 5;
    private final int FIRSTL = 1, SECONDL = 2; // which one is larger?
    private int whichLarger = FIRSTL;
    private final int ARYLEN = 8;
    private int[] tempSum = new int[ARYLEN];
    private int[] carryBit = new int[ARYLEN];
    private int[] tempDiff = new int[ARYLEN];
    private int[] borrowBit = new int[ARYLEN];
    private int[] bigger = new int[ARYLEN];
    private int[] smaller = new int[ARYLEN];
    private int sumBit;
    private String sSignedOne, sSignedTwo; // string with "|" and space
    private int[] bIntOne, bIntTwo;
    private int count;
    private Font theF;
    private PropertyChangeSupport sumDone;

    @SuppressWarnings("OverridableMethodCallInConstructor")
    public SumSprite() {
        initSprite();
    }

    @Override
    public void initSprite() {
        sumDone = new PropertyChangeSupport(this);
        count = 0;
        theF = new Font("Monospaced", Font.PLAIN, 18);
        for (int i = 0; i < ARYLEN; i++) {
            tempSum[i] = 0;
```

```
54              carryBit[i] = 0;
55              tempDiff[i] = 0;
56              borrowBit[i] = 0;
57          }
58      }
59
60      public void setCoor() {
61          x = leftMargin;
62          y = topMargin;
63      }
64
65      public void initSummationData(String sSignedOne, String sSignedTwo,
66              int[] bIntOne, int[] bIntTwo) {
67          this.sSignedOne = sSignedOne;
68          this.sSignedTwo = sSignedTwo;
69          this.bIntOne = bIntOne;
70          this.bIntTwo = bIntTwo;
71      }
72
73      @Override
74      public void updateSprite() {
75          if (!(this.isActive())) {
76              return;
77          }
78          switch (command) {
79              case ADDB:
80                  updateAddBinary();
81                  break;
82              case SUBB:
83                  updateSubBinary();
84                  break;
85          }
86      }
87
88      private void updateAddBinary() {
89          count += 1;
90          int i = bIntOne.length - count;
91          if (i > 0) {
92              sumBit = bIntOne[i] + bIntTwo[i] + carryBit[i];
93              switch (sumBit) {
94                  case 0:
95                      tempSum[i] = 0;
96                      carryBit[i - 1] = 0;
97                      break;
98                  case 1:
99                      tempSum[i] = 1;
100                     carryBit[i - 1] = 0;
101                     break;
102                 case 2:
103                     tempSum[i] = 0;
104                     carryBit[i - 1] = 1;
105                     break;
106                 case 3:
107                     tempSum[i] = 1;
108                     carryBit[i - 1] = 1;
```

24.1 Summation of Binary Integers in Signed-Magnitude: The Project SumSigned

```
109                    break;
110                }
111            } else {
112                tempSum[0] = bIntOne[0];
113            }
114        }
115
116        private void updateSubBinary() {
117            // the first step (when count == 0) should determine which one is
118            // bigger and place the bigger value on the top
119            if (count == 0) {
120                String sIntOne = "", sIntTwo = "";
121                // ignore the sign bit
122                for (int i = 1; i < bIntOne.length; i++) {
123                    sIntOne += bIntOne[i];
124                    sIntTwo += bIntTwo[i];
125                }
126                // determine which value is larger than the other
127                // and then load the larger one to bigger[]
128                if (Integer.parseInt(sIntOne) > Integer.parseInt(sIntTwo)) {
129                    whichLarger = FIRSTL;
130                    for (int i = 0; i < ARYLEN; i++) {
131                        bigger[i] = bIntOne[i];
132                        smaller[i] = bIntTwo[i];
133                    }
134                } else {
135                    whichLarger = SECONDL;
136                    for (int i = 0; i < ARYLEN; i++) {
137                        bigger[i] = bIntTwo[i];
138                        smaller[i] = bIntOne[i];
139                    }
140                }
141            }
142
143            // Then, computing bit-by-bit
144            count += 1;
145            int i = bIntOne.length - count;
146            int diffBit;
147            if (i > 0) {
148                if ((bigger[i] + borrowBit[i]) >= smaller[i]) {
149                    diffBit = (bigger[i] + borrowBit[i]) - smaller[i];
150                } else {
151                    // the ith position borrows 1 from previous position
152                    // borrowBit[i] += 2 and bigger[i - 1] -= 1
153                    borrowBit[i] += 2;
154                    bigger[i - 1] -= 1;
155                    // if bigger[i - 1] < 0 (== -1), its notation is still 0
156                    // but the borrowBit[i - 1] should be 1 (not 2)
157                    if (bigger[i - 1] < 0) {
158                        bigger[i - 1] = 0;
159                        borrowBit[i - 1] -= 1;
160                    }
161                    diffBit = borrowBit[i] + bigger[i] - smaller[i];
162                    // converting the format of bigger[] to sSignedOne for painting
163                    sSignedOne = aryToPaintStr(bigger);
```

```
164                 }
165                 tempDiff[i] = diffBit;
166             } else {
167                 tempDiff[0] = bigger[0];
168             }
169         }
170
171     public String aryToPaintStr(int[] ary) {
172         String str = "| ";
173
174         str += ary[0] + " " + "| ";
175         for (int i = 1; i < ARYLEN; i++) {
176             str += ary[i] + " ";
177         }
178         str += "|";
179         return str;
180     }
181
182     @Override
183     public void paintSprite(Graphics2D g2d) {
184         if (!(this.isVisible())) {
185             return;
186         }
187         g2d.setFont(theF);
188         switch (command) {
189             case ADDB:
190                 sumAdd(g2d);
191                 break;
192             case SUBB:
193                 sumSub(g2d);
194                 break;
195         }
196     }
197
198     private void sumAdd(Graphics2D g2d) {
199         setCoor();
200         int localC = 1;
201         g2d.setFont(theF);
202         FontMetrics fm = g2d.getFontMetrics();
203         int strLen = fm.stringWidth(sSignedOne);
204         int digitW = fm.stringWidth("F");
205         y += lineH;
206         int yFirstLine = y;
207         g2d.drawString(sSignedOne, x, yFirstLine);
208         y += lineH;
209         g2d.drawString("+", x - 4 * gapW, y);
210         g2d.drawString(sSignedTwo, x, y);
211         g2d.drawLine(x - 5 * gapW, y + 4 * gapH, x + strLen + gapW, y + 4 * gapH);
212         x = x + strLen - digitW;
213         y = y + 4 * gapH + lineH;
214         g2d.drawString("|", x, y);
215
216         int currBit;
217         while (localC < count) {
218             currBit = ARYLEN - localC;
```

24.1 Summation of Binary Integers in Signed-Magnitude: The Project SumSigned

```
219                g2d.drawString("" + tempSum[currBit],
220                        x - 2 * localC * digitW, y);
221                if (carryBit[currBit - 1] != 0) {
222                    g2d.drawString("" + carryBit[currBit - 1],
223                            x - 2 * localC * digitW - 2 * digitW, yFirstLine - lineH);
224                    if (currBit - 1 == 0) {
225                        g2d.drawRect(x - 2 * localC * digitW - 2 * digitW,
226                                yFirstLine - lineH - digitW - gapH, digitW,
227                                digitW + 2 * gapH);
228                    }
229                }
230                localC += 1;
231            }
232            if (count == ARYLEN) {
233                // plot the bit [0]
234                g2d.drawString("| " + tempSum[ARYLEN - count] + " |",
235                        x - strLen + digitW, y);
236
237                this.setActive(false); // keep setVisible(true) for painting
238                // it cannot issue terminate; otherwise the inputPanel will
239                // be erased
240                sumDone.firePropertyChange("sumDone", false, true);
241            }
242        }
243
244        private void sumSub(Graphics2D g2d) {
245            setCoor();
246            int localC = 1;
247            g2d.setFont(theF);
248            FontMetrics fm = g2d.getFontMetrics();
249            int strLen = fm.stringWidth(sSignedOne);
250            int digitW = fm.stringWidth("F");
251            y += lineH;
252            int yFirstLine = y;
253            if (whichLarger == FIRSTL) {
254                g2d.drawString(sSignedOne, x, yFirstLine);
255                y += lineH;
256                g2d.drawString("-", x - 4 * gapW, y);
257                g2d.drawString(sSignedTwo, x, y);
258            } else if (whichLarger == SECONDL) {
259                g2d.drawString(sSignedTwo, x, yFirstLine);
260                y += lineH;
261                g2d.drawString("-", x - 4 * gapW, y);
262                g2d.drawString(sSignedOne, x, y);
263            }
264            y += 4 * gapH;
265            g2d.drawLine(x - 5 * gapW, y, x + strLen + gapW, y);
266            x = x + strLen - digitW;
267            y = y + 4 * gapH + lineH;
268            g2d.drawString("|", x, y);
269
270            while (localC < count) {
271                if (borrowBit[bIntOne.length - localC] > 0) {
272                    g2d.drawString("" + borrowBit[bIntOne.length - localC],
273                            x - 2 * localC * digitW, yFirstLine - lineH);
274                }
```

```
275                 g2d.drawString("" + tempDiff[bIntOne.length - localC],
276                         x - 2 * localC * digitW, y);
277
278                 localC += 1;
279             }
280             if (count == ARYLEN) {
281                 // plot the last item
282                 g2d.drawString("| " + tempDiff[bIntOne.length - count] + " |",
283                         x - strLen + digitW, y);
284
285                 this.setActive(false);
286                 // it cannot terminate the game. Otherwise, the inputPanel will
287                 // be erased
288                 sumDone.firePropertyChange("sumDone", false, true);
289             }
290         }
291
292         // A method for debugging
293         private void displayAry(int[] ary) {
294             for (int i = 0; i < ary.length; i++) {
295                 System.out.print(ary[i]);
296             }
297             System.out.println();
298         }
299
300         public void addPropertyChangeListener(PropertyChangeListener pcl) {
301             sumDone.addPropertyChangeListener(pcl);
302         }
303
304         public int getCommand() {
305             return command;
306         }
307
308         public void setCommand(int command) {
309             this.command = command;
310         }
311 }
```

24.1.3 Drawbacks of the Signed-Magnitude Notation

Clearly, signed-magnitude notation is easy to be understood for human. However, the implementation of the project SumSigned indicates that summation computation in using the signed-magnitude notation is not straight. Once the sign bits of the two inputted integers are different, they have to involve subtraction instead of summation. For implementing the subtraction, the bigger integer of the two inputted integers has to be recognized. In addition, the signed-magnitude notation involves two different representations of zero: the positive zero (00000000) and the negative zero (10000000). These special requirements will increase the complexity of computer hardware if this notation would be adopted for making computers. Surely, we need a better notation.

24.2 Summation of Binary Integers in 1's Complement: The Project SumOnesComp

For overcoming the drawbacks of the signed-magnitude notation, a new notation, so-called 1's complement, is innovated. The concept of the "complement" can be illustrated through a clock. As we know, a clock has 12 h. If we move the hour hand from 6 o'clock back to 2 o'clock, we can express it as 6 − 4 = 2. This expression is equivalent to 6 + (12 − 4) = 6 + 8 = 14 = 2 o'clock, where (12 − 4) is the complement of 4. That is, using a complement value, we can replace the subtraction with an addition.

One binary value is either 0 or 1. The 0 is 1's complement and the 1 is 0's complement. A decimal integer −45 in binary singed-magnitude notation with 8 bits is 10101101.

24.2 Summation of Binary Integers in 1's Complement: The Project SumOnesComp

Its 1's complement is the notation with all of value bits flipped, which is 11010010. When we do the computation 47 − 45, in the binary signed-magnitude notation with 8 bits, it is 00101111 − 10101101 = 00000010 (+2 in decimal). Replacing the two binary integers with their 1's complement notation, the computation becomes 00101111 + 11010010 = 00000001, and the signed bit has a "carry" that should be added with the result and the final result is 00000001 + 1 = 00000010 (+2 in decimal).

24.2.1 The 1's Complement Notation Eliminates Subtraction

The example above shows that the 1's complement notation is better than the signed-magnitude notation because when the minuend and the subtrahend in signed-magnitude notation are substituted with their 1's complement notation, the subtraction can be replaced with an addition. In other words, in using the 1's complement notation, a subtraction operation can be replaced by using an addition such that the subtraction and the distinction of which one is larger and which one is smaller between the two inputted integers become unnecessary. Consequently, the hardware system of computers no longer needs special circuitry for subtraction.

The pseudo code for the project SumOnesComp, thus, could be as follows.

1. The project accepts two inputted decimal integers and validates them.
2. The two validated decimal integers are converted to be binary integers in signed-magnitude notation.
3. The two binary integers in signed-magnitude notation are further converted into 1's complement presentation.
   (a) For a positive binary integer, its 1's complement notation is completely the same as its signed-magnitude notation.
   (b) For a negative binary integer, its 1's complement is to keep the sign bit but flip all of the value bits in its signed-magnitude notation.
4. The summation of the two inputted integers is the summation of the two binary integers in 1's complement notation. The two sign bits of the two binary integers should join the summation. If the summation of the two sign bits creates a carry 1, the carry 1 should be "carry around," which means that the carry 1 should be added with the summation to make a final result. And then, overflow is checked.
5. The result of the summation is still in 1's complement notation, which should be converted back to the signed-magnitude notation and then to the decimal result.

24.2.2 The Project SumOnesComp Renders Three Scenes

Clearly, the project SumOnesComp needs to render three different scenes. The first scene is for converting the two decimal integers to be two binary integers in signed-magnitude. This scene is the same as that in the project SumSigned, which corresponds to step 1 and step 2 in the pseudo code. The second scene is for converting the two binary integers in signed-magnitude to 1's complement as shown in Fig. 24.4 (Left) rendered by the class SToOSprite.java, which corre-

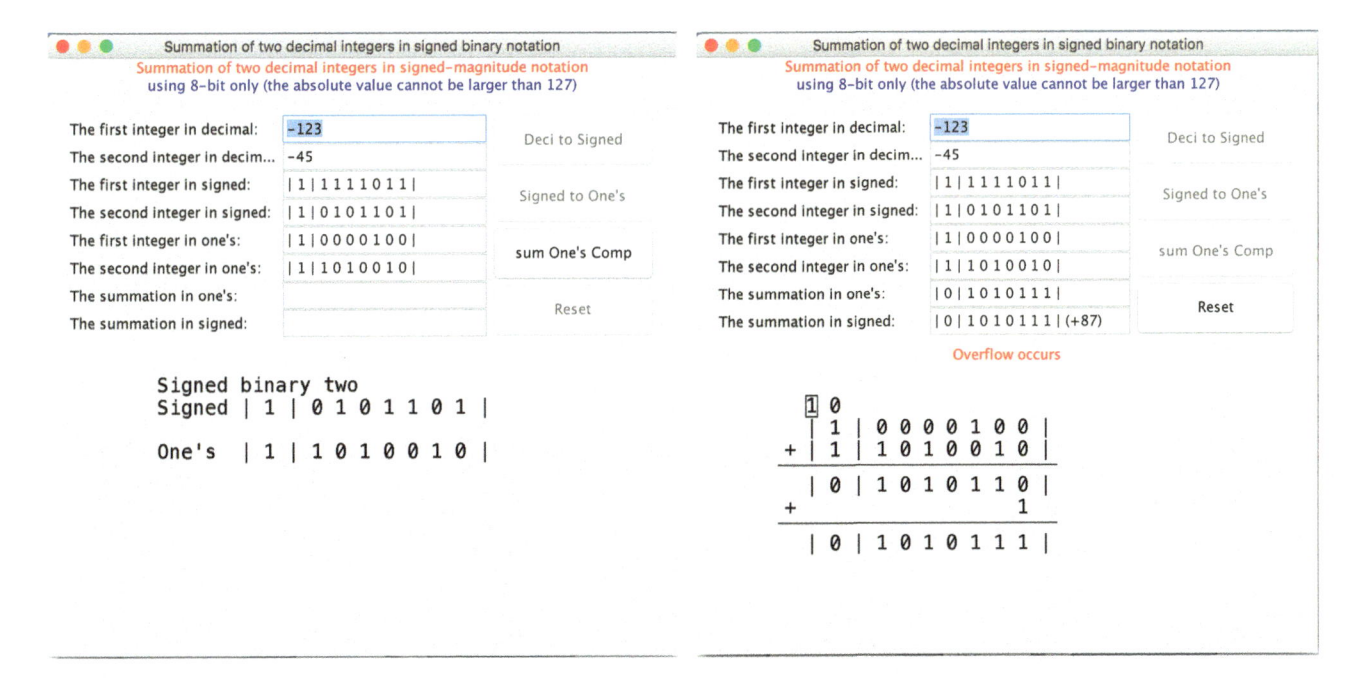

Fig. 24.4 (*Left*) The SToOSprite.java renders the conversion of signed to one's. (*Right*) The SumSprite.java renders the summation of two binary integers in one's complement

sponds to the step 3 of the pseudo code. And the third one is for summing the two binary integers in 1's complement as shown in Fig. 24.4 (Right) rendered by the class SumSprite.java, which corresponds to step 4 of the pseudo code.

This time, the class SumSprite.java needs to render two additions if the "carry around" is necessary. Actually, the rendering of the first addition is similar with the class SumSprite.java implemented in the project SumSigned, which is named as "loop 1" in the class SumSprite.java of this project. And then, "loop 2" appends the second addition for summing the "carry around" bit. The detailed implementation is cited in Listing 24.3.

Listing 24.3 The class SumSprite.java in the project SumOnesComp

```
 1  /*
 2   * SumSprite.java - A class that performs the summation on two binary
 3   * integers in 1's complement. It has to "carry around" the carry bit
 4   * generated by adding the two sign bits if the carry bit is 1.
 5   */
 6  package sumonescomp;
 7
 8  import java.awt.Font;
 9  import java.awt.FontMetrics;
10  import java.awt.Graphics2D;
11  import java.beans.PropertyChangeListener;
12  import java.beans.PropertyChangeSupport;
13
18  public class SumSprite extends AbsSprite {
19
20      private int x, y;
21      private int topMargin = 320, leftMargin = 100;
22      private final int lineH = 20, gapH = 2, gapW = 5;
23      private final int ARYLEN = 8;
24      private int[] tempSum = new int[ARYLEN];
25      private int[] carryBit = new int[ARYLEN];
26      private int[] roundOver = new int[ARYLEN];
27      private int[] roundCarryBit = new int[ARYLEN];
28      private int[] finalSum = new int[ARYLEN];
29      private int sumBit;
30      private String onesCompOneStr, onesCompTwoStr;
31      private int[] onesCompOneAry, onesCompTwoAry;
32      private int countOne, countTwo, loop;
33      private Font theF;
34      private boolean oneDone, twoDone;
35      private int loop2YFirstL;
36      private PropertyChangeSupport sumDone;
37
38      @SuppressWarnings("OverridableMethodCallInConstructor")
39      public SumSprite() {
40          initSprite();
41      }
42
43      @Override
44      public void initSprite() {
45          sumDone = new PropertyChangeSupport(this);
46          countOne = 0;
47          countTwo = 0;
48          loop = 1;
49          oneDone = false;
```

24.2 Summation of Binary Integers in 1's Complement: The Project SumOnesComp

```
50            twoDone = false;
51            theF = new Font("Monospaced", Font.PLAIN, 18);
52            for (int i = 0; i < ARYLEN; i++) {
53                tempSum[i] = 0;
54                carryBit[i] = 0;
55                roundOver[i] = 0;
56                roundCarryBit[i] = 0;
57                finalSum[i] = 0;
58            }
59        }
60
61        public void setCoor() {
62            x = leftMargin;
63            y = topMargin;
64        }
65
66        public void initSummationData(String onesOneStr, String onesTwoStr,
67                int[] onesOneAry, int[] onesTwoAry) {
68            this.onesCompOneStr = onesOneStr;
69            this.onesCompTwoStr = onesTwoStr;
70            this.onesCompOneAry = onesOneAry;
71            this.onesCompTwoAry = onesTwoAry;
72        }
73
74        @Override
75        public void updateSprite() {
76            if (!(this.isActive())) {
77                return;
78            }
79            if (oneDone == false) {
80                updateAddition();
81            } else if (roundOver[7] == 1) {
82                updateRoundOver();
83            } else if (roundOver[7] == 0) { // ignore updateRoundOver()
84                twoDone = true;
85            }
86        }
87
88        private void updateAddition() {
89            countOne += 1;
90            int i = onesCompOneAry.length - countOne;
91            if (i > 0) {
92                sumBit = onesCompOneAry[i] + onesCompTwoAry[i] + carryBit[i];
93                switch (sumBit) {
94                    case 0:
95                        tempSum[i] = 0;
96                        carryBit[i - 1] = 0;
97                        break;
98                    case 1:
99                        tempSum[i] = 1;
100                       carryBit[i - 1] = 0;
101                       break;
102                   case 2:
103                       tempSum[i] = 0;
104                       carryBit[i - 1] = 1;
```

```
105                            break;
106                        case 3:
107                            tempSum[i] = 1;
108                            carryBit[i - 1] = 1;
109                            break;
110                    }
111            } else { // i == 0, the sign bit
112                sumBit = onesCompOneAry[0] + onesCompTwoAry[0] + carryBit[0];
113                switch (sumBit) {
114                    case 0:
115                        tempSum[0] = 0;
116                        break;
117                    case 1:
118                        tempSum[0] = 1;
119                        break;
120                    case 2:
121                        tempSum[0] = 0;
122                        roundOver[7] = 1; // carry round
123                        break;
124                    case 3:
125                        tempSum[0] = 1;
126                        roundOver[7] = 1; // carry round
127                        break;
128                }
129            oneDone = true;
130        }
131    }
132
133    public void updateRoundOver() {
134        countTwo += 1;
135        int i = finalSum.length - countTwo;
136        if (i > 0) {
137            sumBit = tempSum[i] + roundOver[i] + roundCarryBit[i];
138            switch (sumBit) {
139                case 0:
140                    finalSum[i] = 0;
141                    roundCarryBit[i - 1] = 0;
142                    break;
143                case 1:
144                    finalSum[i] = 1;
145                    roundCarryBit[i - 1] = 0;
146                    break;
147                case 2:
148                    finalSum[i] = 0;
149                    roundCarryBit[i - 1] = 1;
150                    break;
151                case 3:
152                    finalSum[i] = 1;
153                    roundCarryBit[i - 1] = 1;
154                    break;
155            }
156        } else { // i == 0, the sign bit
157            sumBit = tempSum[0] + roundOver[0] + roundCarryBit[0];
158            switch (sumBit) {
159                case 0:
```

24.2 Summation of Binary Integers in 1's Complement: The Project SumOnesComp

```
160                    finalSum[0] = 0;
161                    break;
162                case 1:
163                    finalSum[0] = 1;
164                    break;
165                case 2:
166                    finalSum[0] = 0;
167                    break;
168                case 3:
169                    finalSum[0] = 1;
170                    break;
171            }
172            twoDone = true;
173        }
174    }
175
176    @Override
177    public void paintSprite(Graphics2D g2d) {
178        if (!(this.isVisible())) {
179            return;
180        }
181        g2d.setFont(theF);
182        paintAddition(g2d);
183    }
184
185    private void paintAddition(Graphics2D g2d) {
186        if (loop == 1) {
187            renderAddition(g2d, countOne);
188            if (oneDone) {
189                loop += 1;
190            }
191        } else if (loop == 2) {
192            // after finishing the paint for the first summation, the
193            // rendering needs to be kept on the screen and then move to
194            // paint the second summation.
195            renderAddition(g2d, countOne);
196            if (roundOver[7] == 1) {
197                renderRoundCarry(g2d, countTwo);
198            }
199            if (twoDone) {
200                this.setActive(false); // keep setVisible(true) for painting
201                sumDone.firePropertyChange("sumDone", false, true);
202            }
203        }
204    }
205
206    private void renderAddition(Graphics2D g2d, int count) {
207        setCoor();
208        int localC = 1;
209
210        FontMetrics fm = g2d.getFontMetrics();
211        int strLen = fm.stringWidth(onesCompOneStr);
212        int digitW = fm.stringWidth("F");
213        y += lineH;
214        int yFirstLine = y;
```

```
215            g2d.drawString(onesCompOneStr, x, yFirstLine);
216            y += lineH;
217            g2d.drawString("+", x - 4 * gapW, y);
218            g2d.drawString(onesCompTwoStr, x, y);
219            y += 4 * gapH;
220            g2d.drawLine(x - 5 * gapW, y, x + strLen + gapW, y);
221            x += strLen - digitW;
222            y += lineH + 2 * gapH;
223            g2d.drawString("|", x, y);
224            loop2YFirstL = y + lineH; // keep track of y for the loop2
225            // rendering the first summation dynamically
226            while (localC < count) {
227                int currBit = ARYLEN - localC;
228                g2d.drawString("" + tempSum[currBit], x - 2 * localC * digitW, y);
229                if ((currBit - 1 > 0) && (carryBit[currBit - 1] != 0)) {
230                    g2d.drawString("" + carryBit[currBit - 1],
231                            x - 2 * localC * digitW - 2 * digitW, yFirstLine - lineH);
232                }
233                localC += 1;
234            }
235        if (oneDone) { // currBit == 0
236            // plot the sign bit
237            x = x - strLen + digitW;
238            g2d.drawString("| " + tempSum[0] + " |", x, y);
239            // plot the round carry bit with a rectangle
240            x += 2 * digitW;
241            y = yFirstLine - lineH;
242            g2d.drawString("" + carryBit[0], x, y);
243            if (roundOver[7] == 1) {
244                x -= 2 * digitW;
245                g2d.drawString("" + roundOver[7], x, y);
246                g2d.drawRect(x, y - digitW - 2 * gapH, digitW, digitW + 4 * gapH);
247            }
248            // keep the first plotting in running
249        }
250    }
251
252    private void renderRoundCarry(Graphics2D g2d, int count) {
253        setCoor();
254        int localC = 1;
255
256        FontMetrics fm = g2d.getFontMetrics();
257        int strLen = fm.stringWidth(onesCompOneStr);
258        int digitW = fm.stringWidth("F");
259        y = loop2YFirstL; // y continues
260        g2d.drawString("+", x - 4 * gapW, y);
261        g2d.drawString("" + roundOver[7], x + strLen - 3 * digitW, y);
262        y += 4 * gapH;
263        g2d.drawLine(x - 5 * gapW, y, x + strLen + gapW, y);
264        x += strLen - digitW;
265        y += lineH + 2 * gapH;
266        g2d.drawString("|", x, y);
267        // redering finalSum dynamically
268        while (localC < count) {
269            int currBit = ARYLEN - localC;
```

```
270                g2d.drawString("" + finalSum[currBit], x - 2 * localC * digitW, y);
271                localC += 1;
272            }
273            if (twoDone) { // currBit == 0
274                // plot the last item
275                g2d.drawString("| " + finalSum[0] + " |", x - strLen + digitW, y);
276            }
277        }
278
279        // A method for debugging
280        private void displayAry(int[] ary) {
281            for (int i = 0; i < ary.length; i++) {
282                System.out.print(ary[i]);
283            }
284            System.out.println();
285        }
286
287        public void addPropertyChangeListener(PropertyChangeListener pcl) {
288            sumDone.addPropertyChangeListener(pcl);
289        }
290 }
```

Listing 24.3 shows that in using 1's complement notation, the subtraction is no longer needed. However, the method updateAddition() has to have an extra addition:

```
sumBit = onesCompOneAry[0] +
    onesCompTwoAry[0] + carryBit[0];
```

It is for adding the two sign bits plus the carry bit from the leftmost value bit. If the result sumBit is larger or equals to 2, it generates a carry 1, and then a round-over addition needs to be executed, which is performed by the method updateRoundOver() and the method renderRoundCarry().

24.2.3 Drawbacks of the 1's Complement Notation

Unfortunately, the 1's complement notation still has its disadvantages. (a) It still has two different representations for the value of zero: positive zero (00000000) and negative zero (10000000). (b) It requires extra hardware and software to take care of the "end carry around" addition.

24.3 Summation of Binary Integers in 2's Complement: The Project SumTwos

The disadvantages of one's complement notation promoted a further improved notation called two's complement notation. In other words, the two's complement notation was created to eliminate the complexity brought by the one's complement notation.

24.3.1 The 2's Complement Is the Best Notation

A positive binary integer in 2's complement notation is the same as the binary integer in signed-magnitude. A negative binary integer in 2's complement is its 1's complement plus 1. This simple definition completely eliminates the necessity of extra "carry around" addition in the summation of two binary integers in 1's complement notation. Thus, the 2's complement notation is the final adoption in today's computers.

This 2's complement notation allows a computer having only one adder for all of arithmetic calculations because a subtraction can be substituted by an addition; a multiplication can be carried out through multiple additions; and a division can be replaced by multiple subtractions, which are multiple additions in 2's complement notation.

24.3.2 The Three Scenes and Three Special Details

Apparently, the project SumTwos is developed easily by modifying the SumOnesComp project. The class ControlPanel.java is similar with that of the project SumOnesComp but simplified by (a) replacing the 1's complement with 2's complement and (b) totally ignoring the "carry around" computation in the inner class SummationListener which resides in the class ControlPanel.java. Meanwhile, the class SumSprite.java can also be much simplified by eliminating the computing and plotting of the "carry around" summation.

Consequently, the pseudo code for the project SumTwos could be as follows.

1. The project accepts two decimal integers and validates them.
2. The two validated decimal integers are converted to be binary integers in signed-magnitude notation.
3. The two binary integers in signed-magnitude notation are further converted in 2's complement presentation.
   (a) For a positive binary integer, its 2's complement notation is completely the same as its signed-magnitude notation.
   (b) For a negative binary integer, its 2's complement is to keep the sign bit but flip all of the value bits in its signed-magnitude notation, and then plus 1.
4. Sum the two binary integers in 2's complement. And then, check the overflow.
5. The result of the summation is still in 2's complement, which should be converted back to the signed-magnitude notation and then to the decimal result.

In the implementation, three details should be carried out. Firstly, after converting from the signed-magnitude notation to the 1's complement notation, an addition for adding 1 with the 1's complement notation has to be done. That is, an addition method needs to be added to both the conversion listener and the class SToTSprite.java (signed to two's complement). The implementation of the class SToTSprite.java is cited in Listing 24.4. Secondly, the rule for checking the overflow is changed to be "if the carry-in to the sign bit is different from the carry-out from the sign bit, overflow occurs." It means that the sign bit addition is still needed in order to find out the sign bit of the summation result and the carryout value can be used for checking the overflow but not for the "carry around." Thirdly, the notation "10000000" in 2's complement is no longer "−0" but means "−128." The GUIs of the project SumTwos are shown in Fig. 24.5.

Listing 24.4 The class SToTSprite.java in the project SumTwos

```
 1 /*
 2  * SToTsprite.java - A class plays a role of sprite for rendering the
 3  * conversion from signed-magnitude to 2's complement notation.
 4  */
 5 package sumtwos;
 6
 7 import java.awt.Font;
 8 import java.awt.FontMetrics;
 9 import java.awt.Graphics2D;
10 import java.beans.PropertyChangeListener;
11 import java.beans.PropertyChangeSupport;
12
```

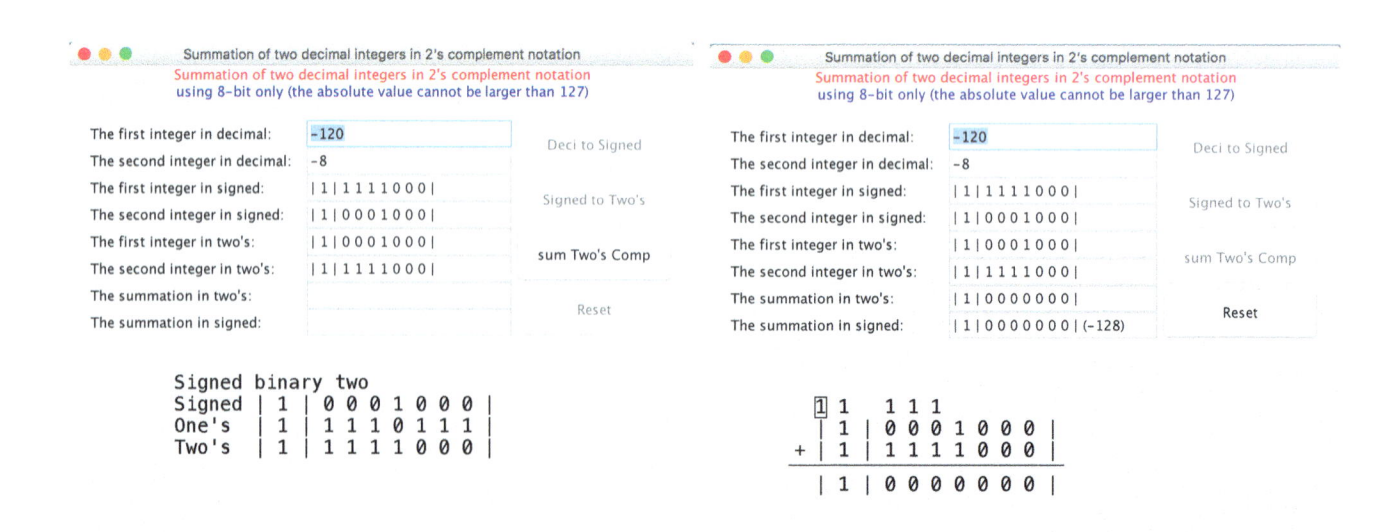

Fig. 24.5 (Left) The SToTSprite.java renders the conversion from signed to 2's. (Right) The SumSprite.java renders the summation of two binary integers in 2's

24.3 Summation of Binary Integers in 2's Complement: The Project SumTwos

```java
17  public class SToTSprite extends AbsSprite {
18
19      private Font theF;
20      private int countOne, countTwo, countThree;
21      private boolean oneDone, twoDone, flipOne, flipTwo;
22      private String signedOne, signedTwo;
23      private String onesCompOne, onesCompTwo;
24      private final int topMargin = 300, leftMargin = 100, lineH = 20;
25      private final int oneMove = 2;
26      private int threeY;
27      private int x, y;
28      private int loop;
29      private final int ARYLEN = 8;
30      private int[] onesAry = new int[ARYLEN];
31      private int[] twosAry = new int[ARYLEN];
32      private int[] carryAry = new int[ARYLEN];
33
34      private PropertyChangeSupport sToTDone;
35      private boolean overflow;
36
37      @SuppressWarnings("OverridableMethodCallInConstructor")
38      public SToTSprite() {
39          initSprite();
40      }
41
42      @Override
43      public void initSprite() {
44          sToTDone = new PropertyChangeSupport(this);
45          theF = new Font("Monospaced", Font.PLAIN, 18);
46          countOne = 4; // value digits in signedOne starts from index of 6
47          countTwo = 4;
48          countThree = 0;
49          oneDone = false;
50          twoDone = false;
51          flipOne = false;
52          flipTwo = false;
53          onesCompOne = "";
54          onesCompTwo = "";
55          loop = 1;
56          overflow = false;
57      }
58
59      public void setCoor() {
60          x = leftMargin;
61          y = topMargin;
62      }
63
64      public void setInitData(String signedOne, String signedTwo) {
65          this.signedOne = signedOne;
66          this.signedTwo = signedTwo;
67          char signChar = this.signedOne.charAt(2);
68          flipOne = signChar == '1';
69          if (!oneDone) {
70              onesCompOne += signedOne.substring(0, 6);
71          }
```

```
72              signChar = this.signedTwo.charAt(2);
73              flipTwo = signChar == '1';
74              if (!twoDone) {
75                  onesCompTwo += signedTwo.substring(0, 6);
76              }
77              setActive(true);
78          }
79
80          @Override
81          public void updateSprite() {
82              if (isActive()) {
83                  if (loop == 1) {
84                      if (!oneDone) {
85                          updateOne();
86                      } else {
87                          updateThree();
88                      }
89                  } else if (loop == 2) {
90                      if (!twoDone) {
91                          updateTwo();
92                      } else {
93                          updateThree();
94                      }
95                  }
96              }
97          }
98
99          public void updateOne() {
100             countOne += oneMove;
101         }
102
103         public void updateTwo() {
104             countTwo += oneMove;
105         }
106
107         public void updateThree() {
108             countThree += 1;
109             int carryOut = 0;
110
111             int sumBit;
112             int currBit = ARYLEN - countThree;
113             if (onesAry[0] == 1) { // negative
114                 if (currBit > 0) {
115                     if (currBit == 7) {
116                         sumBit = onesAry[currBit] + 1;
117                     } else {
118                         sumBit = onesAry[currBit] + carryAry[currBit];
119                     }
120                     switch (sumBit) {
121                         case 0:
122                             twosAry[currBit] = 0;
123                             carryAry[currBit - 1] = 0;
124                             break;
125                         case 1:
126                             twosAry[currBit] = 1;
```

24.3 Summation of Binary Integers in 2's Complement: The Project SumTwos

```
127                        carryAry[currBit - 1] = 0;
128                        break;
129                    case 2:
130                        twosAry[currBit] = 0;
131                        carryAry[currBit - 1] = 1;
132                        break;
133                    case 3:
134                        twosAry[currBit] = 1;
135                        carryAry[currBit - 1] = 1;
136                        break;
137                }
138            } else { // bit 0
139                sumBit = onesAry[0] + carryAry[0];
140                switch (sumBit) {
141                    case 0:
142                        twosAry[0] = 0;
143                        carryOut = 0;
144                        break;
145                    case 1:
146                        twosAry[0] = 1;
147                        carryOut = 0;
148                        break;
149                    case 2:
150                        twosAry[0] = 0;
151                        carryOut = 1;
152                        break;
153                    case 3:
154                        twosAry[0] = 1;
155                        carryOut = 1;
156                        break;
157                }
158            }
159        } else if (onesAry[0] == 0) { // positive
160            twosAry[currBit] = onesAry[currBit];
161        }
162        if (carryAry[0] != carryOut) {
163            overflow = true;
164        }
165    }
166
167    @Override
168    public void paintSprite(Graphics2D g2d) {
169        if (isVisible()) {
170            g2d.setFont(theF);
171            paintSignedOnes(g2d);
172        }
173    }
174
175    public void paintSignedOnes(Graphics2D g2d) { // paint singed and ones comp
176        switch (loop) {
177            case 1:
178                if (!oneDone) {
179                    renderTwosComp(g2d, loop, countOne, signedOne, onesCompOne, flipOne);
180                } else {
181                    renderTwosComp(g2d, 1, countOne, signedOne, onesCompOne, flipOne);
```

```java
                    renderAddOne(g2d);
                }
                break;
            case 2:
                if (!twoDone) {
                    renderTwosComp(g2d, loop, countTwo, signedTwo, onesCompTwo, flipTwo);
                } else {
                    renderTwosComp(g2d, 2, countTwo, signedTwo, onesCompTwo, flipTwo);
                    renderAddOne(g2d);
                }
                break;
            default:
                break;
        }
    }

    // a method shared by two plottings
    public void renderTwosComp(Graphics2D g2d, int loop, int count,
            String signedStr, String onesCompStr, boolean flip) {
        setCoor();
        int localC = 5; // get characters at indexes from 0 to 4
        int localCNext;

        FontMetrics fm = g2d.getFontMetrics();
        int digitW = fm.stringWidth("0");

        // rendering the sign bit
        if (loop == 1) {
            g2d.drawString("Signed binary one", x, y);
        } else if (loop == 2) {
            g2d.drawString("Signed binary two", x, y);
        }
        y += lineH;
        g2d.drawString("Signed ", x, y); // start from the origin
        x += fm.stringWidth("Signed "); // skip the width
        g2d.drawString("" + signedStr.substring(0, localC), x, y);
        x -= fm.stringWidth("Signed "); // move back to the origin
        y += lineH;
        g2d.drawString("One's  ", x, y);
        x += fm.stringWidth("Signed ");
        g2d.drawString("" + signedStr.substring(0, localC), x, y);
        y -= lineH;
        // make onesAry for 2's complement
        onesAry[0] = Integer.parseInt(signedStr.substring(2, 3));

        // rendering the value bits
        int aryIdx = 0;
        while (localC < count) {
            localCNext = localC + oneMove; // get digit at 5 and 6 (" 0")
            g2d.drawString("" + signedStr.substring(localC, localCNext),
                    x + localC * digitW, y);
            y += lineH;
            char origBit = signedStr.charAt(localC + 1);
            char flipBit;
            if (flip) {
```

24.3 Summation of Binary Integers in 2's Complement: The Project SumTwos

```java
237                flipBit = makeFlip(origBit);
238            } else {
239                flipBit = origBit;
240            }
241            g2d.drawString("" + flipBit, x + (localC + 1) * digitW, y);
242
243            if (aryIdx < 7) {
244                aryIdx += 1;
245                // store the 1's comp in an array for making 2's comp
246                onesAry[aryIdx] = Character.getNumericValue(flipBit);
247            }
248            localC += oneMove;
249            y -= lineH;
250        }
251
252        if (loop == 1) {
253            if (count >= 19) { // the total lenght is 21
254                if (!oneDone) {
255                    oneDone = true;
256                }
257            }
258        } else if (loop == 2) {
259            if (count >= 19) {
260                if (!twoDone) {
261                    twoDone = true;
262                }
263            }
264        }
265        threeY = y + lineH;
266    }
267
268    public char makeFlip(char origBit) {
269        char flipBit;
270        switch (origBit) {
271            case '0':
272                flipBit = '1';
273                break;
274            case '1':
275                flipBit = '0';
276                break;
277            default:
278                flipBit = origBit;
279                break;
280        }
281        return flipBit;
282    }
283
284    public void renderAddOne(Graphics2D g2d) {
285        setCoor();
286        int localC = 1;
287        y = threeY + lineH;
288
289        FontMetrics fm = g2d.getFontMetrics();
290        int digitW = fm.stringWidth("0");
291        g2d.drawString("Two's  ", x, y);
```

```
292            x += fm.stringWidth("Signed ");
293            x += 10 * 2 * digitW;
294            g2d.drawString("|", x, y);
295
296            int currBit;
297            while (localC < countThree) { // when countThree is 2 the while starts
298                currBit = ARYLEN - localC;
299                x -= 2 * digitW;
300                g2d.drawString("" + twosAry[currBit], x, y);
301                localC++;
302            }
303            if (countThree == 8) {
304                x -= 6 * digitW;
305                g2d.drawString("| " + twosAry[0] + " | ", x, y);
306                if (loop == 1) {
307                    loop = 2;
308                    countThree = 0;
309                } else if (loop == 2) {
310                    setActive(false); // stop updateSprite but open paint
311                    sToTDone.firePropertyChange("sToTDone", false, true);
312                }
313            }
314        }
315
316        // a method for debugging
317        private void displayAry(int[] ary) {
318            for (int i = 0; i < ary.length; i++) {
319                System.out.print(ary[i]);
320            }
321            System.out.println();
322        }
323
324        public void addPropertyChangeListener(PropertyChangeListener pcl) {
325            sToTDone.addPropertyChangeListener(pcl);
326        }
327    }
```

In short, the 2's complement notation is the best one among the three different binary representations. The only drawback is the asymmetry of the range of values that can be represented by N bits. In 8 bits, "01111111" represents +127; but "10000000" represents −128. It may cause confusion sometimes.

24.4 Reusable Logics and Unshared Differences for the Six Projects

We always pay much attention to code reusability in the implementation of projects. These two chapters covered six projects. No matter which project, all of conversions are based on the position weight principle. Therefore, the principle of position weight and its implementation not only becomes the foundation for understanding all of these conversions but also becomes reusable code.

Starting from the project DecimalToAny, we coded a set of methods for converting a decimal integer to any base including the binary. The set of methods are reusable in all of projects, such as DeciToAnyFloat, SumSigned, and so on, which require the conversion of decimal to binary.

The three projects in this chapter involve summation that requires addition operation. The addition of two binary integers is the sharable routine. The add 1 with a binary integer is another sharable routine for "carry around" addition and for converting from 1's complement to 2's complement notation.

The rendering methods look complicated. But, all of them follow the same logics. The first logic is to determine the coordinates (x, y) of every painted bit. The second logic is to plot bit-by-bit with a "while (localC < count)" loop. Every update method increases the value of count by 1. Every paint method paints the number of (localC < count) bits.

The rules for checking overflow of summations in different notations are different. The overflow may occur only when the two binary integers have the same sign bit. The sign bits of two binary integers in signed-magnitude notation do not join the addition; thus, if the leftmost value bit has a carry of 1, the overflow happened. For the summation of two binary integers in 1's complement notation, the sign bits join the computation. When two sign bits are the same, but the sign bit of the summation result is different, the overflow occurs. In 2's complement summation, if the carry-in of the sign bit (the carry from the leftmost value bit) differs from the carryout of the sign bit, the overflow is true.

24.5 Summary

A computer is so powerful that it can do all kinds of arithmetic calculations. However, its hardware has only one adder. This simplicity is brought by the 2's complement notation. From the three projects SumSigned, SumOnesComp, and SumTwos discussed in this chapter, we can understand the reasons. These projects not only prove the best features of the 2's complement notation but also render the computation processes in details. These three projects also further provide an evidence for evaluating the value of the three-layer structure for games.

The ideas of these projects are not complicated. But, their implementations are rather tedious and lengthy, especially the sprite classes for rendering. One important concept for understanding these sprite classes is that the game loop is a big loop that repeatedly invokes the update and paint methods. Therefore, all of repeated actions should become a single action in the codes and let the game loop invoke it repeatedly.

24.6 Exercises

Self-Review Questions

1. Why do we apply the three-layer structure for games on these projects?
2. What is a signed-magnitude notation for expressing an integer −55?
3. What is the largest value that can be expressed in using the signed-magnitude notation with 8 bit memory? Why do you say so?
4. What is the algorithm for summing two binary integers in signed-magnitude notation?
5. What drawbacks does the signed-magnitude notation have?
6. The action listener SummationListener in the class ControlPanel.java of the project SumSigned performs addition for two binary integers if they have the same sign bits. The method addBinary() has a "for" loop for taking care of addition on every bit in the array. However, the method updateAddBinary() in the class SumSprite.java does not have a loop but only does one bit addition. Why?
7. What is the new notation that can overcome the drawbacks of the signed-magnitude notation?
8. What is the decimal integer 100 in 1's complement binary notation?
9. What are the advantages of the 1's complement notation in comparison with the signed-magnitude notation?
10. What are the drawbacks of the 1's complement notation?
11. How does the 2's complement binary notation overcome the drawbacks of the 1's complement notation?
12. Why do we say the 2's complement notation is the best notation?
13. What is the algorithm for summing two binary integers in 2's complement notation?
14. What is the disadvantage of the 2's complement notation?
15. May we eliminate subtraction operation for summing two decimal integers directly?
16. A computer has only one adder. How does it perform different arithmetic operations?

Projects

1. Write a program with a name of SumDecimal for implementing the summation of two decimal integers (integers could be positive or negative) without rendering function.
2. Add the rendering function with the project SumDecimal above.
3. Extend the functionality of the project SumDecimal with ability of multiplication.
4. Extend the functionality of the project above with ability of division.

Appendix: The Source Codes of the Three-Layer Structure for Games—GameStruTemplate

The three-layer structure for games could be a template for developing video games. The source code of the template version, GameStruTemplate, could be copied into the IDE NetBeans as a basis for developing any new games. The source code of the project is included in Chap. 18.

In order to easier access the source codes, we duplicated the source code in this Appendix. Please find the source code from the project part of the book under the title of "Appendix".